D0186262

BOOK OF BRITISH BIRDS

WARWICK LIBRARY SCHOOL

Reader's Digest

Published by The Reader's Digest Association Limited
London • New York • Sydney • Montreal

Campus Library Services Limited

51104
WARWICK SCHOOL

BOOK OF BRITISH BIRDS

was edited and designed by
The Reader's Digest Association Limited, London.

First edition Copyright © 1969
The Reader's Digest Association Limited,
11 Westferry Circus, Canary Wharf, London E14 4HE.
www.readersdigest.co.uk

We are committed to both the quality of our products and the service we provide
to our customers. We value your comments, so please feel free to contact us on 08705 113366,
or via our web site at www.readersdigest.co.uk
If you have any comments about the content of our books, you can contact us at
gbeditorial@readersdigest.co.uk

Paperback edition 2003

Reprinted 2004

Copyright © 1969 Reader's Digest Association Far East Limited.
Philippines Copyright © 1992 Reader's Digest Association Far East Limited.

All rights reserved. No part of this book may be reproduced,
stored in a retrieval system, or transmitted in any form or by any means,
electronic, electrostatic, magnetic tape, mechanical, photocopying,
recording or otherwise, without permission in writing from the publishers.

® Reader's Digest, The Digest and the Pegasus logo
are registered trademarks of The Reader's Digest Association, Inc,
of Pleasantville, New York, USA.

The typeface used in this book is Caslon.
Printed and bound by Toppan Printing Company, Hong Kong.

ISBN 0 276 42745 9
BOOK CODE 400-161-02

EDITOR Robin S. Hosie   ART EDITOR John Meek

Book of British Birds

The publishers express their gratitude for
major contributions by the following people:

CONSULTANT EDITOR
Richard Fitter, BSC
Formerly Honorary Secretary, Fauna
and Flora Preservation Society

REVISIONS EDITOR
John Parslow

AUTHORS
Phyllis Barclay-Smith, CBE
Jeffery Boswall
Dr Philip J. K. Burton
Dr Bruce Campbell, OBE
Dr John Carthy
Dr C. J. F. Coombs
Dr Peter M. Driver
John Gooders
Dr C. J. O. Harrison
The Rev P. H. T. Hartley, MA, BSC
David Holyoak
Dr R. K. Murton
Dr Ian Newton, FRS
Richard Perry, BA
K. E. L. Simmons, MSC
Robert Spencer, BA
Kenneth Williamson, FRSE

PHOTOGRAPHER
Eric J. Hosking

ARTISTS
Norman G. Barber
Raymond Harris Ching
Kathleen Flack
Eric Fraser
Robert Gillmor
Hermann Heinzel
Rosemary Parslow
Philip North Taylor
Sydney Woods

The full-colour portraits in the section of this
book entitled *The British Birds* were painted
by Raymond Harris Ching. The line drawings
on these pages are the work of Robert Gillmor,
who also painted most of the studies of bird-life
in other sections of the book. Hermann Heinzel
painted the identification keys, the rarer birds
and many other studies.

CARTOGRAPHERS
Map Creation Ltd

The world distribution maps are based on
those in the *Atlas van de Europese Vogels*
(Elsevier, Amsterdam), by Professor Karel
Hendrik Voous of Amsterdam University,
who generously gave permission for his
work to be used in this way. The British Isles
distribution maps are based on information
supplied by John Parslow.

Reader's Digest General Books

EDITORIAL DIRECTOR
Cortina Butler

ART DIRECTOR
Nick Clark

EXECUTIVE EDITOR
Julian Browne

PUBLISHING PROJECTS MANAGER
Alastair Holmes

DEVELOPMENT EDITOR
Ruth Binney

PICTURE RESOURCE MANAGER
Martin Smith

REPRINTS EDITOR
Jill Steed

STYLE EDITOR
Ron Pankhurst

CONTENTS

LAND OF BIRDS
A survey of the past, present and future of bird-life
in the British Isles 6–14

NAMING THE BIRDS

THE BRITISH BIRDS
Illustrated profiles of all the birds commonly seen in Britain,
grouped by the habitats in which they are most likely to be seen,
with a selection of our rarer species

THE CONQUEST OF AIR, LAND AND SEA

BIRD SOCIETY

BIRDS AND MAN

WHERE TO SEE BIRDS

A region-by-region guide, with maps and calendars, to the best
places and times for bird-watching in the British Isles

COUNTING AND LISTING THE BIRDS

LAND

OF

BIRDS

THE PAST, PRESENT AND FUTURE
OF BIRD-LIFE IN THE BRITISH ISLES

IT is only about 7000 years since the Channel swept through what were to become the Straits of Dover, cutting off the British Isles from the Continent of Europe; so the background against which our bird-life must be examined is primarily European.

Measured against the time scale of evolution 7000 years is almost an insignificant span, yet in that period several species of British birds have developed in ways which set them slightly apart from their relatives on the Continent. The individuality of the British Isles is reflected in the differences between the British red grouse and the willow grouse of Scandinavia. Unlike the European bird, the red grouse does not assume a white plumage in winter; this and other points of difference are so marked that until recently the two birds were thought to be separate species. Now, however, they are generally regarded as geographical races of the same bird.

Even within the British Isles, divergent forms of some species have developed. The mantle plumage of English jays is redder than that of jays in central Scotland, but not as red as that of jays in Ireland; there are Irish forms of the dipper and coal tit; and the song thrush and hedge sparrow of the Outer Hebrides are darker than mainland birds.

Such differences suggest that populations have been isolated over many generations, so that the effects of gene-changes, as they have arisen, have been contained within small inter-breeding groups. They also suggest that even within as small an area as the British Isles there are different factors working towards change, ultimately influencing plumage coloration, body-size, habitat selection and behaviour.

One of the most important of these factors is our climate. This has shown small but significant variations over the centuries; but these long-term changes must be seen against the one relatively stable circumstance in the British scene: the dramatic division of the country into highland and lowland zones.

This division is both a structural and a climatic one. The oldest rocks are clustered in the north and west—in Scotland, the Lake District, the Pennines, Wales and Ireland—exposed to the influences of a warm ocean whose temperature oscillates between 12°C (53·6°F) in summer and 8°C (46·4°F) in winter. The newer, more fertile sedimentary deposits to the south and east are exposed to greater extremes of temperature because of the proximity of the continental land-mass beyond the relatively narrow North Sea.

The greatest disparity in seasonal temperatures is in East Anglia and the adjacent counties. Here the land-warmed air of continental anticyclones penetrates in summer; and here also the icy clutch of the Polar and Siberian cold strangles the countryside in mid-winter.

Such weather often initiates vast movements

of lapwings, starlings, skylarks and the wintering thrushes as they flee before frost and snow to the mildness of England's south-west peninsula and southern Ireland.

It is possible that some species, such as the red-legged partridge, hobby, garganey, Kentish plover and wryneck (the last two now lost to us)—judging from their restricted distribution in south-east England—need a climate of Continental type.

Most of our rain is a product of the continual tussle waged in mid-ocean by dry, cold air sweeping south from the Arctic, and moist, tropical air advancing northwards from the latitude of the Azores. The depressions or 'lows' set in train by this mixing of unlike air-masses carry vast amounts of the warm, moist air towards Iceland, brushing past Britain on the way. This makes for cool, cloudy summers in the highland zone; and because of this, the tree-line is at a lower level than anywhere else in Europe.

The greatest rainfall is in the north and west, reaching 200 in. a year in some places among the hills. It is believed that the darker plumage of Irish and Hebridean birds—due to a greater amount of chemicals known as melanins in the feather pigments—is a response to their wetter, cloudier environment.

By the time the air has reached the lowlands it has lost much of its moisture, so that a rainfall of 20-40 in. a year is usual; and although this tarnishes the reputation of the English summer, there is on average one drought a year compared with one every five years in north and west Scotland.

Perhaps the most important climatic factor for small birds dependent largely on insect food and weed-seeds is the length and intensity of the growing-season—that part of the year during which the grassroot temperature rises above 6°C (42.8°F) and is sufficient to maintain active growth of vegetation.

In the maritime climate of the west and south-west, this varies from 300 days to the full year (in the Scillies). But in the more Continental south-east it is reduced to 240-270 days.

**Two major forces have
governed the ebb and flow of bird-life
in the British Isles . . . climate and
man's ability to manipulate
the environment**

DURING the past 5000 or so years man and climate together have juggled with the numbers and distribution of birds in the British Isles; together they have brought about increase or decline, colonisation or extirpation, expansion or limitation of range in the majority of the 200 or so species which have bred here.

We are living on the edge of an Ice Age, the last extreme expression of which was the Würm glaciation, which ended about 18,000 years ago. Much of Britain then must have been as cold and barren as high Arctic Greenland is today. For thousands of years afterwards, Britain remained an inhospitable land for wild-life; the tundra, with its patches of dwarf birch and Arctic willow, can have attracted very few birds beyond the handful which may have survived during the time of the Würm glaciation in the bleak but ice-free south.

Among those which have remained in northern Scotland to the present day are the black-throated and red-throated divers, the ptarmigan, dotterel, red-necked phalarope, golden plover and snow bunting.

About 7500 BC the climate settled into a warm, dry 'boreal phase', with first birch forests and soon afterwards Scots pines becoming dominant over much of the country; and with the pine came an increasing under-storey of hazel.

The greylag goose, osprey, capercaillie and greenshank may have entered Britain at this time—while among the small song-birds (judging by the bird-life in the relatively small areas of Caledonian pine and birch remaining today) were probably the wren, hedge sparrow, coal tit, and redstart—with everywhere the silvery song of the willow warbler.

Two birds which have relict populations in the Cairngorms today, the crested tit and crossbill, doubtless arrived at this time; both have since become special British forms of their species. The Scottish crossbill is the representative of the large-billed, pine-haunting parrot crossbill which spread through Europe from the south. The smaller-billed common crossbill has an eastern origin and is hardly likely to have settled in Britain (since its chief source of food, the spruce, did not manage to reinvade) until the planting of conifers on the Norfolk Brecks and parts of southern England in the late 17th and 18th centuries. Since then, its numbers have been kept up by periodic invasions from abroad.

About 5000 BC, towards the culmination of this warm, dry phase, the weather was a good deal better than it has been since. Indeed, this 'climatic optimum' had a mean annual temperature 2°C (3.6°F) higher than today. The summers were warmer and the winters certainly no colder than now. The tree-line in Scotland would have been near the 3000 ft contour—more than 1000 ft higher than now; and whilst warmth-loving trees like elm, oak and lime grew in the lowlands, birch and hazel spread outwards to Shetland and the Hebrides, reaching their greatest extent in the north-west Highlands and islands around 3000 BC.

It must have been at this time that wrens reached St. Kilda, Fair Isle, Shetland and the Outer Hebrides. The differentiation into well-marked sub-species which is so strikingly evident today is the product of some 5000 years of isolation and adaptation to a gradually changing environment. The song thrush and hedge sparrow went with them to the Outer Isles and these birds have also changed over the centuries.

When the tree-cover finally disappeared from these remote outlying islands, the St. Kilda wren took to a life among the puffins and other seabirds, whose guano nourishes the soil and so ensures a supply of insect food. Its Fair Isle cousin, in the absence of seabird colonies, lived largely by rummaging among tidal debris on small shingle beaches. In-breeding within these closed communities consolidated differences in plumage, body-size, habitat preference and song as these evolved.

By the time the climatic optimum reached its zenith, Britain had become an island. The sea, for long fed by melt-waters from the northern ice, eventually breached the swampy valley which became the Straits of Dover and the southern part of the North Sea.

The 'Atlantic phase' of climate which followed was still warm, but rather wet, and conducive to the development of a vast, billowing green mantle of deciduous forest. Soon this forest was dominated by oak, though alder increased in abundance on the wetter ground—particularly in East Anglia and the maritime west. Peat formed at higher levels, and in the fens and marshes of the south-east.

During the drier 'sub-boreal phase' after 2500 BC, there was some increase in pine, especially in Ireland, but also in East Anglia as the fen peat dried out. In the English lowlands there was a marked increase in beech—especially on the chalk downs, the Chilterns and the Cotswold oolite. Hornbeam increased, too; it appears to have crept into the south-east just before the land connection with Europe disappeared.

With the deciduous forests of the Atlantic phase, the basic pattern of Britain's vegetation, at least in the lowlands, was firmly established. This explains why in this region even today—when woodland cover has been reduced to barely one-tenth of the proportion found in Sweden and Finland, and less than one-third of that of France—about three-quarters of our bird species are of forest origin.

The overall density of bird-life must have been far greater than at any time before or since, if we can judge from the fact that today oakwoods in Surrey, Sussex, Wales and Wester Ross carry more birds to the acre than any other natural habitat in the British Isles.

About 2500 BC, man began to fashion wild-life habitats in Britain, though his contribution was not to be a major one for another 1000 years

SUCH grassland as the men of the New Stone Age and Bronze Age won by felling and clearing the forest on lighter soils, the grazing of their flocks enabled them to retain—though scrub would quickly invade the old plot once the cultivators moved on.

Primitive farming must have had the beneficial effect for bird-life of creating an environment for the spread of grassland and open-country species, and also for those which (like the whinchat and stonechat) are dependent on scattered thorn scrub.

During the latter part of the Bronze Age, a cool, wet 'sub-Atlantic phase' of climate—rather like that of today—brought about some deterioration of the forest, particularly in the north and west. Spreading peat-bogs swallowed up many of the trees. Considerable reaches of highland Britain must have taken on a barren moorland aspect—and the moorland's birds—characteristic of today.

About 100 BC the arrival of the Belgae with their iron axes and wheeled ploughs rang the death-knell of the valley forests, with which, up to then, man had been ill-equipped to deal. The felling and clearing continued throughout Roman and increasingly during Saxon times.

The Celtic field system of long narrow plots bordered by low banks or 'lynchets' thrown up by the plough, on which gorse, broom and bramble provided some sort of cover, afforded a much modified environment for some of the woodland-edge species. Such species may have benefited even further during Norman times, when as a matter of policy a good deal of cultivated land was temporarily laid waste and the continuance of farming within the royal forests was discouraged so that kings and nobles could enjoy their sport.

An important development which must increasingly have affected the numbers and distribution of birds in medieval times was the conversion of much of the high forest to 'coppice with standards', to provide oak-bark for tanning, curved timbers for house- and ship-building, fence-posts, firewood and charcoal for the iron-smelting and glass-making industries.

Trees were felled until about 12 mature oak 'standards' remained to the acre. The increased light encouraged the rapid growth of an under-storey of hazel, or sometimes oak or hornbeam, which was lopped every ten or twelve years on a rotation system, and allowed to grow again from the stumps.

The net change may have been in favour of scrub-living rather than high forest birds, and it probably encouraged the late nesters, since cutting and bark-peeling were spring activities and disturbance must have been very considerable.

This new-look woodland, with its more open canopy, seems likely to have fostered more predators, such as sparrowhawks; and it may well have throbbed to the virtuoso music of the nightingale, no longer heard in many areas where coppicing has died out.

It is possible that the robin, which remains a shy forest bird over much of Europe, adapted well to coppicing, and there established the first friendly links which led to its becoming the constant companion of gardeners and Britain's national bird.

The marsh warbler, another marvellous songster we can ill afford to lose, flourished in Gloucestershire and neighbouring counties where coppicing of osiers provided baskets for the fruit growers. But modern industry offers a wide variety of cheaper containers, and the bird's habitat is becoming overgrown and unsuitable.

Coppicing in its various forms remained virtually the only kind of forest management for centuries, and its importance can be gauged from the 1924 Forestry Commission census, which showed that coppice formed nearly 30 per cent of English woodland.

Conservation did not enter into human activity until the great plantation movement of the early 17th century. Scotland led the way, and by the early 18th century planting in the south of the country was considerable. Early re-afforestation was mainly of native birch and pine, with some introduction of beech from England and sycamore from abroad.

At a later date larch played an increasingly important role. It is recorded that a Duke of Atholl planted 14 million larch, at 2000 trees to the acre. Larch is the only conifer that will permit the growth of a vigorous under-storey, and if this bald statistic is at all symptomatic of the age, such planting must have meant a new lease of life for a number of the old Caledonian forest species, such as the coal tit, goldcrest, siskin and lesser redpoll.

But while landowners in south and central Scotland became more and more tree-conscious, many of the native woods in the north and west were whittled away to fire the furnaces of the iron-smelters, or to make more pasture for sheep. For three centuries afterwards, these voracious animals nibbled away all prospect of regeneration.

Probably the 17th and 18th centuries saw more change and redistribution among Britain's birds than any comparable period before or since.

In addition to the great changes in woodland, there was a surge of fruit-growing and market-gardening in Kent, Somerset and the west midland counties; there was an acceleration of land enclosure with its attendant network of quickset hedgerows, protecting the suckers of English elms so that they could grow into tall trees and spread a new loveliness across the landscape; there was a notable crusade for the amenity planting of ornamental, usually exotic, trees and shrubs.

This movement was initiated by John Evelyn, to whom the greenfinch in particular has good reason to be grateful. Like the swallow and the cliff-nesting house martin at an earlier stage, the scavenger kites of medieval London, and a few other species, it must have been a relatively scarce bird until man afforded it chances of food and shelter.

It was, however, a period when a number of marshland birds must have become scarce, some to vanishing point; for much of the 1300 square miles of East Anglian fen country was drained and brought into cultivation. The resonant boom of the bittern no longer emphasised the loneliness of the marshes; and such striking birds as the spoonbill, avocet, ruff and black-tailed godwit were also casualties.

It is only within recent years that conservation, allied to strict protection, has enabled the Royal Society for the Protection of Birds to bring all of these species, apart from the spoonbill, back to Britain as breeding birds.

There was, as always, the complicating business of climate. Man's vigour must have greatly reduced the overall density of birds as more and more of the forest disappeared; but in theory the diversification of the countryside into a mosaic of coverts, coppices, orchards, fields, hedgerows, parks and so on should have resulted in a wider dissemination of species. However, the greater part of this period has an evil reputation as the 'Little Ice Age'.

The Alpine and Scandinavian glaciers re-advanced further than at any time since the Würm glaciation. May frosts and cool summers brought frequent harvest failures, especially in the north; and a good deal of the sorely oppressed Scottish woodland was either blown down or engulfed by peat-bogs resulting from lack of evaporation in sunless summers. There was enough ice in the North Atlantic to permit polar bears to get to Iceland, and to drift more than one wretched Eskimo in his kayak ('Finnmen', they were called) to Orkney and the Aberdeenshire coast.

When people over 60 recall the 'long, hot summers' of childhood, they are not being misled by nostalgia; for they were born in a period of relative warmth

IN the last decade of the 19th century the world warmed up a little, the most striking gains occurring in the European Arctic sector. In north-west Europe generally this amelioration had profound results for bird-life.

At the peak of the warm-up, in the 1930's, Britain's climate was almost comparable to the 'Little Optimum' of Viking and Norman times (c. AD 900–1200), when vineyards flourished in the vales of Gloucester and Kent.

But while climate alone can be a powerful influence in regulating food supply, the length of breeding season and winter mortality, its impact may be either softened or hardened by human influences. During the first half of the present century the tree-line rose by several hundred feet, and much Forestry Commission planting was near its upper limit; the growing season became a fortnight longer, and root-crops and grain were much more important in Scotland than before.

One unwelcome result of this extension of agriculture has been the rise to pest proportions of the wood-pigeon, whose numbers reach an estimated 4–6 million birds after the breeding season. It has also helped the rook, jackdaw and starling to extend their ranges. Earlier in the period the stock dove, too, spread to Scotland and Wales from a fairly restricted home in south-east England.

The warming-up put an end to the need for Scottish farmers to maintain large dove-cotes for a winter supply of fresh meat (originally, perhaps, a wise provision in the Little Ice Age) and this has contributed to a great expansion in the numbers of feral pigeons now domiciled in the cliffs. The doves are a dynamic group today: the collared dove, a pest in south-east England within a decade of its arrival, has spread with amazing rapidity across Europe from the Balkans in this century; the original cause of its incredible range-expansion remains obscure.

Some of the more successful birds in modern times have been those which invariably suffer heavy losses during prolonged periods of frost and snow; and it is more than likely that many of the gains we have witnessed are in large part a reconquest of ground lost during the worst of the Little Ice Age.

The Common Birds Census, organised by the British Trust for Ornithology, has shown that the recovery of a species after a climatic setback is often a slow, uphill process

FOLLOWING the hard winter of 1962-3 (the worst in parts of England since 1740), wrens were reduced by about 79 per cent and song thrushes by about 59 per cent of their 1962 strength, and not until 1967-8 were the populations on an even keel.

It is evident that in periods when, say, three winters in every ten are severe, recovery will be greatly depressed and the effect on the population disastrous. The wren, among other species, is likely to have been very scarce indeed during the Little Ice Age.

The beautiful grey wagtail of stony streams is another such species. It made great strides all over Europe during the warmer phase, despite the temporary drastic reduction of its numbers in occasional cold winters. The cold of 1962-3 also decimated a thriving population of stonechats which had built up on inland heaths through a succession of mild winters.

The tiny, quarter-ounce goldcrest was a scarce bird for much of the 19th century, but latterly climate and the Forestry Commission have helped it along. The great spotted woodpecker, which had disappeared from Scotland and northern England by 1800, recolonised as far north as Perthshire years later, and has now reached the airy birchwoods and oak-woods of Inverness, Ross and Sutherland. The green woodpecker, even more confined 150 years ago, now has its advance guard on the Moray Firth.

The milder winters were a boon to the Dartford warbler, our only resident warbler, and one which must have come to us from the Mediterranean region in a warm, dry period. It is at the northern limit of its range in the southern English counties, and is so susceptible to hard winters that it is surprising how it managed to survive the Little Ice Age—if indeed it did, for it could have been wiped out in this country during the cold years, and have recolonised later from Brittany.

By the summer of 1961 a very considerable population, estimated at 450 pairs, had grown up in Sussex, Surrey, Hampshire and Dorset; but the sudden onset of snow and frost in the midwinter of 1961-2, followed by the even harsher weather of early 1963, reduced them to a pathetic handful in Dorset. Despoliation of its heathland habitat may be one reason

why its recovery was inclined to be slow; and certainly the species can afford no further losses of habitat.

The song thrush suffers in cold winters much more than the blackbird; its heyday was probably during the 1920s and 1930s, the warmest period of this century so far; for then it outdid the blackbird in the number of nestlings marked each year under the national bird-ringing scheme.

However, since the Second World War the blackbird has far outstripped the song thrush in numbers, and is among the three most abundant song-birds in the British Isles. It has penetrated to the brick-and-mortar 'canyons' of London and other cities, and since the turn of the century has reached the townships and deserted crofts of Shetland. This is one of the dynamic species of the day and after half a century of increase the blackbird population is still expanding.

The tremendous growth of man's technological achievements, and the consequent sprawl of urban and suburban development, has created a variety of artificial situations to which some birds have become adapted, and others may adapt in the future.

A handsome array of waterfowl have made excellent use of reservoirs, ornamental waters and flooded sand- and gravel-pits; indeed one new bird, the little ringed plover, is based almost exclusively on gravel-pits.

The drying-up of many lakes and marshes in south-east Europe and the Russian steppes at the turn of the century triggered off a north-westerly movement of great crested, black-necked and Slavonian grebes, little and black-headed gulls, and ducks such as gadwall, shoveler, pochard and tufted.

The climate of north-west Europe proved congenial to the invaders. The numbers and variety of waterfowl in England, Scotland, Iceland and the Scandinavian countries today are little short of amazing when one considers the impoverished state of half a century ago.

If a water shortage is to be avoided between now and AD 2000, the water supplies for lowland Britain will need to be much increased; and despite their growing use for leisure—sailing and water-skiing especially—there should still be room for further expansion of the duck and grebe populations.

Man cannot make climate, but he can modify it. Destruction of forests and drainage of marshes over the past 3000 years have undoubtedly altered the heat- and moisture-retaining properties of vast areas. Perhaps the Forestry Commission, already the biggest landowners in Britain, will do something to redress the balance if their target of 5 million acres of trees is achieved by the end of the century.

The growth of cities and towns has introduced what climatologists call a 'heat-island effect', in which every town of moderate size is cosseted in a blanket of warmth of its own making. Innumerable domestic and industrial fires, complicated heating and lighting systems, warm effluents discharged into rivers, all tend to raise the temperature. The effect is heightened by dust and smoke carried aloft, since this encourages condensation and creates a cloud-cover which has the greenhouse effect of preventing heat radiation from land to space.

In the greater London area a difference of 7°C (12°F) has been recorded between urban and rural night minimum temperatures in May. This artificial climate must greatly reduce the winter mortality rate among birds which have adapted themselves to town life— house sparrows, blackbirds, pied wagtails, wood-pigeons, black-headed gulls, and a number of park and garden species.

The starling, whose massive roosts bring seething activity to city centres on winter evenings, suffered much during the cold winters of the 18th century, becoming very rare in the north of England and Scotland; but exploitation of the urban environment enabled it to expand spectacularly in the recent warmer period.

An additional factor benefiting birds in towns is the food provided on bird-tables and in city centres. Without these benefits, it is unlikely that London's wood-pigeons could afford a seven month breeding-season; or that many feral pigeons could breed throughout the year; or that the black redstart, one of our post-war gains as a regular nester, could have established itself successfully in England.

The benefit conferred by the 'heat-island' (and 'food-island') on sparrows and small rodents has in turn attracted their predators, among which the tawny owl and the kestrel are prominent.

Our birds of prey, protected though they are, have faced a grave danger: accidental extermination by chemical poisons

IN medieval times protection was assured for such birds of prey as the peregrine, hobby, merlin and goshawk, because of their place in falconry. When sporting fashions changed among the well-to-do in the 19th century, these birds were viciously persecuted because they were considered threats to the rearing of game for shooting.

Now the wheel has turned full circle, and protection has once again come to their aid— though in the 1960s a new menace arose. There would certainly have been very many more eyries of golden eagles if it had not been for the infertility caused by poisonous residues. For eagles take sheep carrion, and deadly dieldrin was used in sheep-dips. The numbers of peregrines and merlins also underwent drastic reduction due to the assimilation of chlorinated hydrocarbons already present in the smaller birds they take as prey; and for the same reason, sparrowhawks became virtually extinct in the 1960s in a dozen English counties where formerly these raptors were common.

The kestrel, though, remained a familiar sight, dancing on the wind; the small mammals on which it pounces are more efficient than small birds at getting chlorinated hydrocarbon poison out of their systems.

Voluntary bans on certain uses of dieldrin and other persistent insecticides have led to a marked recovery in the numbers of eagles, peregrines and sparrowhawks over the last 40 years.

The rapid increase and spread of the buzzard after the First World War, culminating in an estimated 12,000 pairs in Britain by the mid-1950s, was temporarily reversed by an entirely different contaminant—myxomatosis, which proved so dreadfully efficient in killing off its major prey, the rabbit.

New contaminants, industrial as well as agricultural, appear almost annually; and we do not know what their effects, individual and cumulative, are likely to be.

The Forestry Commission's planting of conifers has created new habitats for the buzzard, and also for Montagu's and hen-harriers, and long-eared and short-eared owls. The shelter afforded by the young trees and rough grass attracts large numbers of short-tailed voles, the favourite food of these predators. But Montagu's harriers, after a good period, suffered in the decline affecting most birds of prey, and are now very scarce.

For different reasons, the plantations also provide new haunts for the woodcock and nightjar, capercaillie and blackcock, as well as many small birds such as the whitethroat, grasshopper warbler, yellowhammer and reed bunting, which can enjoy this unusual habitat at least for a time.

Census studies show that in its early stages this strange but exciting 20th-century forest, especially when planted to nurse native hard-woods, has an attractive bird community which, if not traditional, is nevertheless welcome.

The most explosive range-expansion by any seabird in recent times has been that of the fulmar, a master glider which, after the second decade of the 19th century, swept southwards from Iceland and colonised the stark sea-cliffs of the Faeroe and Shetland Islands, infiltrated all the rocky coasts of Britain and moved on in post-war years to Norway and north-west France.

The early part of this sensational spread was long before the warming-up process began, and it has been attributed to the birds' exploitation of the whaling industry, and later to an equally abundant source of food in the offal of the deep-sea fishing fleets. The fulmar has undoubtedly benefited from the activities of man at sea.

A clear link with climate is to be seen in the recent history of the gannet in northern waters. This large, gleaming white bird is dependent upon an abundance of surface-shoaling fish which it catches under water after power-diving from a height, arrowing into the sea and throwing up an impressive fountain of spray.

A warmer marine environment around Newfoundland brought about an enormous expansion of the mackerel fishing industry in the mid-1930s, and with it came a steep rise in the gannet population, with recolonisation of bird-rocks deserted for over 100 years.

An increase in mackerel in the Irish Sea has probably assisted the rapid growth of the Welsh gannetry on Grassholm—a small one before 1914 but now numbering more than 20,000 pairs of breeding birds. Around Shetland the gannet's staple food is the stock of year-old saithe (or coal-fish) which shoals abundantly in inshore waters and has increased in quantity in recent years.

A single pair of gannets nested in the cliffs of Noss in the Shetlands in 1914, and there are now about 6900 pairs there. The Hermaness colony on Shetland's most northerly headland and stacks, begun in 1917, had reached 10,000 pairs in 1991. Other colonies have sprung up in Scotland, Iceland and Ireland; one has been founded in the Channel Islands, and Norway's first colony was established on Rundoy in the 1940s. The British population is probably now around 160,000 pairs, with 50,000 at St. Kilda.

The great skua, or 'bonxie', a powerful buzzard-sized viking of the skies which harries gannets and other large seabirds until they disgorge their catch, has taken advantage of this situation: there are large colonies at Noss and Hermaness and elsewhere in the Shetlands, where bonxies were once so heavily cropped for food that a century ago only a few remained.

As a family, the gulls found the gradual warm-up which started about the end of the 19th century much to their liking

THE herring gull took advantage of the improvement in climate to push northwards, reaching Iceland in 1927, Bear Island in 1932 and Spitsbergen in 1950. The warming of the Arctic may have made colonisation by this and the greater black-backed gull possible; but the spur to expand was probably population pressure from farther south, particularly in the North Sea. A number of other factors, for which man is responsible, have contributed to the birds' expansion— among them intensive ploughing, reservoirs for safe roosting, offal at town and city rubbish dumps, and a never-failing food supply at the sewage outfalls of seaside towns.

The same factors, coupled with milder winters, have made stay-at-homes of many lesser black-backed gulls which used to migrate to the Mediterranean. Common and black-headed gulls have also increased in Britain. The common gull began nesting in the Shetlands and Faeroes in the last decade of the 19th century, and reached Iceland in 1955. It is said that the black-headed gull had become 100 times commoner in Finland and Sweden by 1950 than it was half a century before; and it is likely that the pressure of population, forcing its distribution limits outwards, has made this the most common European visitor to New England and New York. The expansion of this gull has been greatly helped by its ability to adapt to man-made habitats, and it has become a common town bird, feeding on offal and scraps.

The success story of the gulls has its dark side, for their spread has brought about a catastrophic decline in many of our spectacular tern colonies.

It was a memorable experience to wander on Mew Island at the entrance to Belfast Lough in the summer of 1941, in the thick of a blizzard of several thousand terns—common, Arctic, Sandwich and the scarce roseate. There were periodic 'dreads', a little-understood phenomenon of communal behaviour when the great shimmer of sound ceases abruptly as the birds sweep out over the sea.

But by 1959 the 'dread' was permanent, irrevocable—for the island had been completely taken over by gulls. Common, Arctic and Sandwich terns had thriving colonies on the Isle of May in the Firth of Forth as late as 1948, but a decade later 5000 herring gulls had ousted them too; and the same sad story could be told of other sites.

It is not so much brute strength and pugnacity which tell in the gulls' war of attrition against the terns, but the fact that whereas the smaller and daintier terns are long-distance migrants, the herring gulls are not: they have already commandeered the available nesting space, and their breeding-cycle is in full swing, when the terns come back from Africa.

In the middle of the 20th century there was a relapse from warmth; some weather experts even believed that we might be on the edge of yet another long cold spell. The average July-August temperature in central England in the 1950s was 0.5°C (1°F) lower than in the 1930s and 1940s; summer rainfall had risen by nearly 20 per cent; snow lay on the ground for an average of 20 days a year in Shetland compared with eight days previously; and in the 1960s pack-ice around Iceland increased to a density comparable with that in some of the colder winters of the mid-19th century.

It is fascinating to consider some developments among birds in the light of this information. New nestings in Scotland were all of northern birds. The Royal Society for the Protection of Birds triumphed with nine successive broods of snowy owls. Fieldfares have bred in Scotland since 1967, blue-throats have bred occasionally since 1968, and the redwing has now become an established breeding bird in Wester Ross and in parts of Sutherland and Inverness. The purple sandpiper has recently been found nesting in Scotland, while other birds such as the turnstone, long-tailed duck and great northern diver could appear or reappear if the climate gets colder.

The remnant red-necked phalaropes (almost lost to the Hebrides and Ireland, but still present in Shetland), and the snow buntings of the high corries (reduced to a few dozen pairs, where small colonies enlivened the dark crags a century ago) could stage a comeback.

Similarly, the ptarmigan, dotterel and twite could recover some of their lost ground in the southern uplands of Scotland and the Lake District. On the other hand, several small

European birds which were within striking distance of becoming established in Britain before the colder 1960's may have been lost to us, at least for a time. The firecrest has nested in recent years in southern England: the canary-like serin reached the northern shores of France in 1956 and has since nested in the south of England: the non-migratory Cetti's warbler bred in Brittany in 1957, reached these shores as a breeding bird in 1972, and has since gone from strength to strength in the southern half of England.

The great reed warbler and greenish warbler, invaders from the east, have provided a crop of vagrants in recent years, and they too could be on the verge of colonisation.

Differences between one species and another have arisen as birds have adapted to a particular way of life, often in a particular habitat

ANY division of the British Isles into its component habitats is bound to be extremely arbitrary. It must be emphasised, therefore, that the 12 major habitat divisions in this book are for the reader's convenience: one habitat shades into another, and birds do not keep neatly to a single habitat. In a country so packed with variety of scenery as Britain, 'edge habitats' are of immense importance ornithologically.

Of the dozen categories, farmland is by far the most extensive and varied habitat, covering 58 million acres—or 75 per cent of our total land area. Some 31 million of these acres are made up of improved farmland. The proportion of improved to unimproved land is highest in England, with 21 million acres of cultivated ground to 2 million acres of rough pasture; in the highlands of Wales and Scotland, hill pastures cover twice the extent of tilled ground.

Forest now covers nearly 3 million acres: 2 per cent of England, about 6½ per cent of Scotland, 6¾ per cent of Wales and 3½ per cent of Ireland. It seems more than likely that the proportion of forest to open country has been reversed during the last 2000 years.

More than 4 million acres of England and Wales and a further 900,000 acres in Scotland and Ireland are classified as urban—so that more land is under bricks and mortar than is under growing trees.

The farmland of Britain provides a mosaic of habitats perhaps unrivalled for beauty and diversity anywhere in the world. The chequerboard of green and gold, nurturing grass and a variety of root and cereal crops, is crisscrossed by diverse types of field-boundary among which the quickset hedgerow, crocheted with elms and other tall trees, holds pride of place.

Spinneys, shelter-belts, plantations, cottages, orchards, gardens, pools and old marl-pits, meandering rivers and streams, all blend unobtrusively in a landscape which has been modelled by man through 2000 years.

Considering the gradual transformation from forest to field, it is hardly surprising that the birds of this landscape are predominantly woodlanders, now dependent upon scattered shreds of woodland and the scrub alongside streams, ditches, lanes and hedgerows.

Adaptation has been most successful in the case of birds which thrive best in the secondary growth of the clearings and forest margins—species such as the blackbird, hedge sparrow, whitethroat and yellowhammer. But some of the high forest species have done well, too; and where the lines of scrub are tree-studded there are chaffinches, robins, song thrushes and a few others. The quiet moorhen will browse by the smallest pool, and where there are ditches and streams there will usually be wrens.

The 'steppe' birds, such as the skylark, partridge, lapwing and corn bunting, seldom add up to 10 or at most 15 per cent of the community; and frequently the most common of these, the skylark, is outnumbered by the blackbird by three to one.

Upland farms have been invaded by a good selection of typically moorland birds—the curlew, snipe, redshank and lapwing—while in Scotland the coastal oystercatcher has penetrated far up the river valleys in recent years. Hedges are often replaced by stone walls, in which wheatears and redstarts nest. On the ground breed meadow pipits and skylarks, with yellow wagtails in the Pennines; and the willow warbler takes over from the whitethroat as the most common warbler wherever there is scrub or trees.

Suburban gardens have a higher birddensity than any kind of woodland and, despite the danger from cats, this is the preferred habitat of several birds. House sparrows, starlings, blackbirds, song thrushes, hedge sparrows and greenfinches are more abundant in well-grown gardens than anywhere else; robins and chaffinches are about as common as in suitable woodland. Great tits and blue tits are more scarce, but are probably limited as much by lack of nesting places as lack of food.

There are other familiar garden birds, but on the whole this relatively new departure in man's landscaping has benefited a rather restricted group of species.

Broad-leaved woodland is really a whole complex of widely varying habitats, and the structure of the bird community is influenced by a number of different factors. High forest which has been well cared for (as with Forestry Commission holdings) is unpromising for birds compared with untended forest where the 'canopy roof' has been opened and falling trees have damaged their neighbours' boughs, creating natural cavities for hole-nesting birds.

Such untended woods will often have a high proportion of birds, such as jackdaws, starlings and tree sparrows, which take advantage of the holes for nesting but find their food outside the wood.

These may be rare or even absent in well-managed woodlands, and the tit and woodpecker population may also be low, unless artificial nest-boxes are provided for them.

The environment which man shares with the breeding birds of the British Isles has never been, and never can be, stable. Vast changes have been set in motion down the centuries, but in recent years the rate of change has grown alarmingly, and the indications are that it will accelerate as we move into the new century.

By the year 2025 the population of these islands, now about 57 million, is likely to have increased to nearly 60 million with far-reaching consequences for birds

THE population increase will inevitably create a demand for new towns to live and work in, new open spaces for a wide variety of leisure pursuits, and an intricate web of new highways for travel.

The new regimented forests, dominated by introduced conifers, will grow up around us; and—most important of all for birds—the present chemical and mechanical revolution is sure to alter the whole pattern of agriculture. Human pressures on land-use will be enormous and the life-conditions of very many birds will be affected—a few for better, but most for worse. Birds will not have nearly as much time to adapt to new situations as they have enjoyed in the past.

It is in the typically English countryside of the Midlands and South that the changes will be most acute, due partly to expanding conurbations and partly to the progress in agricultural science and the modern trend towards large, commercially viable holdings dedicated to cereal production.

These require bigger fields to make the most economic use of sophisticated farm machinery; and the British Trust for Ornithology's Common Birds Census shows that hedgerows in this part of England are disappearing from farms at the rate of more than one yard per acre per year.

Chemical fertilisers and toxic pesticides have emancipated farming from the crop-rotation system which brought variety to agriculture and ensured a regular food supply for seed-eating birds such as finches and buntings.

Economics will insist that the heavy concentration on growing crops in the lowlands is paralleled by a heavy concentration on conifer growing in the highlands; and this raises similar problems, since exotic trees carry nothing like the fruit and insect food resources of our native broad-leaved trees, such as oak, birch and hawthorn.

The current trend in land-usage puts our existing birds at risk in several ways: through the accumulation in their body-fats of poisonous residues which may prove lethal or impair fertility (and have done so in most of our birds of prey); through the loss of potential food sources; and through the disappearance of hedgerow cover which provides nest-sites, roosting-places and protection from predators. The climate sends conflicting signals concerning its future trends. Poorer summers and slightly colder winters up to the early 1980s suggested that the peak of recent climatic improvements was past, but the past decade has seen some of the warmest years on record.

What is in store for the immediate future? We cannot control the forces which determine our climate, nor can we arrest the forward movement of humans. So we must look to new shapes, new colours, in the unfolding tapestry of British bird-life.

It is impossible to preserve the *status quo* anywhere indefinitely—not even in our 5500 square miles of national parks and nature reserves, since what happens there is bound to be influenced by what happens outside.

Britain moves into the 21st century during a period in which landscape changes will be more rapid and in many ways more extreme than in any comparable period before; and creatures which are more highly specialised and much less adaptable than humans are bound to suffer.

The 'philosophy' of conservation must be that we will not destroy more of the wildlife environment than is consistent with food-production, industry, housing, leisure and other legitimate human needs.

Much is already being done by many societies and other bodies to protect and manage land as refuges and reserves; and in particular waterfowl and a number of rare or threatened species are well catered for. At the same time, much is being done to preserve examples of semi-natural habitats—those which have been little influenced by humans.

This is very desirable, but it is not only the rare, beautiful and interesting that it is important to preserve. It is also important to create new habitats—where this can be done without prejudice to good farming, economic forestry or urban growth—by establishing breeding reserves for common birds.

Artificial areas might be set up, usually of some form of woodland or scrub, where birds could breed at high density and so provide an overspill to pioneer new and marginal habitats. The more our common birds can be induced to do this, the more quickly will they adapt successfully to new situations arising in their environment.

Such scrub already exists (or, where it does not, it could soon be established) along 3000 or more miles of closed branch railway lines, 2500 miles of old canals recently dedicated to leisure boating, numerous old gravel-pits and deserted quarries, and those earlier eyesores, the waste and slag heaps of collieries and other mining industries.

The rehabilitation of this kind of land would not only provide these much-needed power-houses of bird production, but would add considerably to the amenity of devastated areas, and permit the establishment of excellent nature trails for schoolchildren.

The concept of breeding reserves for common birds is important—and urgent—if we are to retain anything like our present-day abundance and diversity of birds, for it will encourage them to adapt quickly to the Britain of the future.

NAMING THE BIRDS

For most people, an interest in birds
begins with identification—with the pleasure
to be had from being able to put the right name to
a bird, whether studied at leisure in a town park or glimpsed
fleetingly on a drive through the country. The following
pages are a comprehensive guide to the species
regularly seen in Britain. Familiarity with them
will make recognition quick and easy.

CONTENTS

THE POINTS TO LOOK FOR

WHAT SIZE IS IT?

The best way to judge a bird's size is by comparing it with one of these nine common birds. Size is measured from the bill-tip to the tip of the tail.

BLUE TIT
4½ in.

HOUSE SPARROW
5¾ in.

STARLING
8½ in.

BLACKBIRD
10 in.

LAPWING
12 in.

ROOK
18 in.

WHAT SHAPE IS ITS BILL?

ROBIN—thin and delicate, for eating insects

HOUSE SPARROW —stout, for cracking seeds

KESTREL—short and hooked, for tearing flesh

SNIPE—a long straight bill, for probing

CURLEW—a long bill which curves downwards

AVOCET—a long bill which curves up at the end

SHOVELER —flattened, for dabbling in mud

HERON—long and dagger-shaped, for killing fish

A bird's bill is designed to suit the way it feeds, and the more specialised the feeding habits, the more distinctive the bird's appearance.

HAS IT ANY FIELD MARKS?

BULLFINCH—a bold white patch on the rump

COLLARED DOVE —a black patch on the neck

BARNACLE GOOSE—a patch on the face

SEDGE WARBLER —a pale stripe over the eye

GOLDFINCH—a bar on the wing and a patch on the face

The ability to spot distinctive patches of colour makes bird identification quick and easy. Key places to look for identification 'flashes' are the face, neck, rump and wings. Has the bird any bars, stripes or patches on any of these places? Or are there any spots or streaks elsewhere on its plumage? There may be a crest on its head; and the colour of its legs and bill are also valuable identification points.

HOW LONG ARE ITS LEGS?

STARLING — medium legs, for general purposes

GREY HERON — long legs, for wading through the water

GREENFINCH — short legs, for perching

The design of a bird's legs reflects its way of life or the sort of habitat in which it lives.

HOW DOES IT STAND AND MOVE?

WREN—hops, with cocked-up tail

BARN OWL —stands upright

WAGTAIL—a more horizontal stance

A bird which lives in the trees moves by hopping; a ground-dwelling bird usually walks. Some birds have an upright stance, others are more horizontal.

Success in identifying birds depends largely on knowing how to look at them; this is not simply a matter of being alert, but is a technique which can easily be learnt.

The most important clues to a bird's identity —the points to which special attention should be paid—are these: size; shape, including the shape and length of the bill and the length of the legs; general colouring of the plumage; any particular field marks; behaviour; song and calls; when and where the bird was seen.

Many birds are programmed to fit into a particular habitat. This makes the task of identification much easier; for birds which are similar in appearance may occupy very different habitats. What looks like a partridge beating low over the moors is much more likely to be a red grouse; and a pipit on a rocky shore is far more likely to be a rock pipit than a tree pipit or a meadow pipit, though birds

WHEN IDENTIFYING BIRDS

MALLARD
23 in.

PHEASANT
33 in. (including 18 in. tail)

MUTE SWAN
60 in.

WHAT SHAPE ARE ITS WINGS?

BARN OWL
—round-winged

ROOK—deeply
slotted wing-tips

KESTREL—long
and pointed

SWIFT—long and
swept back

Even when a bird is flying too high for anything else to show up, its silhouette is often enough at least to place it in a broad group; and practice at 'reading' silhouettes helps more exact identification.

WHAT SHAPE IS ITS TAIL?

PHEASANT—long   SWALLOW—forked   LINNET—cleft

BLACK-BACKED
GULL—square

BUZZARD—blunt
and rounded

The shape of a bird's tail, like the shape of its wings, can be sufficiently distinctive to be a useful recognition feature even when it is flying high.

HOW DOES IT FLY?

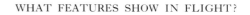
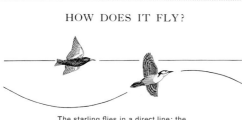

The starling flies in a direct line; the
woodpecker has an undulating flight

Birds glide, soar, flap, hover and perform a multitude of aerobatic tricks; and the way in which they fly can be very distinctive. A kestrel is unmistakable when hovering; so is a spotted flycatcher when it darts from its perch to catch an insect. Some birds rise and fall as they fly, first beating their wings rapidly, then holding them closed.

WHAT FEATURES SHOW IN FLIGHT?

WOOD-PIGEON
—bar on the wings

WATER RAIL
—legs are trailed

Wing-bars and 'flashes' on the tail often show up in flight. Other points to note are how a bird holds its legs and neck, whether it flies in loose flocks or in formation and whether it sings in flight.

can and do move from habitat to habitat. The 217 birds in the section beginning on p. 40 are grouped by the habitats in which they are most likely to be seen.

Since some birds visit Britain only in the summer, others only in the winter and others still mainly in the spring and autumn, the time of year when a bird is seen may be a valuable clue to its identity. The season when it is seen may help, for instance, to distinguish

a hen-harrier, a winter visitor in the south, from a Montagu's harrier, which is unknown in the British Isles in winter. The British Isles maps, in the section beginning on p. 40, give information about the time of year when particular birds are most likely to be seen.

Armed with this information it should be possible, by using the identification keys in the following pages, to recognise any of the birds commonly seen in Britain.

IDENTIFYING BIRDS BY COLOUR

COLOUR is the first feature which strikes most people about a strange bird; but in the British Isles there are too many small brown birds to make instant identification easy. For this reason, the birds in this colour key are separated into manageable groups, with similar-looking birds placed close together so that minor differences show up immediately.

As a first step, the birds are grouped according to where they are most likely to be seen. LAND-BIRDS are those seen mainly on or over land.

WATERSIDE BIRDS are those normally found close to water—either inland or on the coast—but not normally seen swimming.

WATER-BIRDS are those usually seen on water or flying over it.

Birds do not keep rigidly to these categories, but the broad groupings are a good general guide which can save time in identifying an individual bird. Within the three categories,

birds are grouped according to colour; here it is the general effect that counts. A starling, for instance, turns out on close scrutiny to have a spangled plumage, shot with iridescent purples, blues and greens; but from a distance it looks black, so it has been classed as black in this colour key.

When both male and female are illustrated, they are grouped according to the colour of the male's plumage. Hen-harriers and Montagu's harriers, for example, are both given as grey birds because this is the colour of the male, though in both cases the female is brown.

The sizes given are for the length of a bird from the tip of its bill to the end of its tail. A guide to judging sizes is given on pp. 16 and 17. For more information about each bird shown in the identification keys—and to distinguish between two similar birds covered here by a single illustration—refer to the main entry on the page indicated.

Land-birds: BLACK

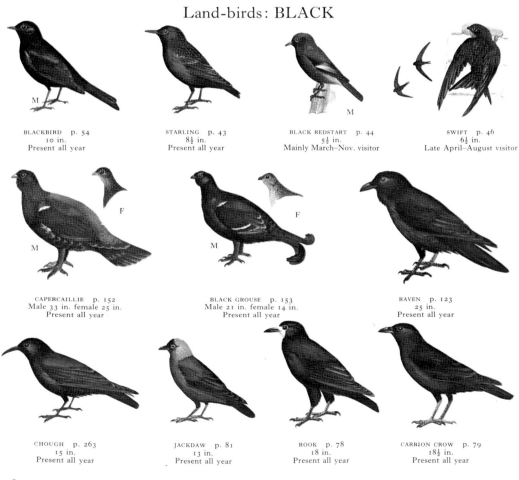

BLACKBIRD p. 54
10 in.
Present all year

STARLING p. 43
8½ in.
Present all year

BLACK REDSTART p. 44
5½ in.
Mainly March–Nov. visitor

SWIFT p. 46
6½ in.
Late April–August visitor

CAPERCAILLIE p. 152
Male 33 in. female 25 in.
Present all year

BLACK GROUSE p. 153
Male 21 in. female 14 in.
Present all year

RAVEN p. 123
25 in.
Present all year

CHOUGH p. 263
15 in.
Present all year

JACKDAW p. 81
13 in.
Present all year

ROOK p. 78
18 in.
Present all year

CARRION CROW p. 79
18½ in.
Present all year

Land-birds: BLACK AND WHITE/GREY

LAPWING p. 68
12 in.
Present all year

MAGPIE p. 80
18 in. (including 8–10 in. tail)
Present all year

HOODED CROW p. 122
18½ in.
Present all year

M in
winter;
or F

M
Summer

LONG-TAILED TIT p. 144
5½ in. (including 3 in. tail)
Present all year

PIED WAGTAIL p. 188
7 in.
Present all year

HOUSE MARTIN p. 47
5 in.
April–Oct. visitor

PIED FLYCATCHER p. 139
5 in.
April–Oct. visitor

RING OUZEL p. 126
9½ in.
March–Oct. visitor

WHEATEAR p. 99
5¾ in.
March–Oct. visitor

LESSER SPOTTED WOODPECKER
p. 134   5¾ in.
Present all year

GREAT SPOTTED WOODPECKER
p. 135   9 in.
Present all year

Land-birds: BROWN

KITE p. 130
Male 22 in. female 24 in.
Present all year

GOLDEN EAGLE p. 112
Male 30 in. female 35 in.
Present all year

BUZZARD p. 131
Male 20 in. female 23 in.
Present all year

KESTREL p. 90
13½ in.
Present all year

PHEASANT p. 69
Male 33 in. (including 18 in. tail) female 23 in.
(including 9 in. tail)   Present all year

RED GROUSE p. 114
Male 15 in. female 13½ in.
Present all year

QUAIL p. 72
7 in.
May–Oct. visitor

Winter

Summer

GOLDEN PLOVER p. 120
11 in.
Present all year

STONE CURLEW p. 94
16 in.
March–Oct. visitor

WOODCOCK p. 128
13½ in.
Present all year

CORNCRAKE p. 73
10½ in.
April–Sept. visitor

Land-birds: BROWN

TAWNY OWL   p. 50
15 in.
Present all year

SHORT-EARED OWL   p. 113
Male 14 in. female 16½ in.
Present all year

LONG-EARED OWL   p. 154
14 in.
Present all year

JAY   p. 149
13½ in.
Present all year

NIGHTJAR   p. 95
10½ in.
May–Oct. visitor

WRYNECK   p. 133
8½ in.
Late March–Sept. visitor

WOODLARK   p. 107
6 in.
Present all year

SKYLARK   p. 85
7 in.
Present all year

MEADOW PIPIT   p. 124
5¾ in.
Present all year

TREE PIPIT   p. 106
6 in.
April–Sept. visitor

SONG THRUSH   p. 52
9 in.
Present all year

REDWING   p. 83
8¼ in.
Mainly Sept.–April visitor

WAXWING   p. 65
7½ in.
Nov.–March visitor

HAWFINCH   p. 150
7 in.
Present all year

GRASSHOPPER WARBLER
p. 105   5 in.
April–Sept. visitor

GARDEN WARBLER   p. 141
5½ in.
April–Oct. visitor

WREN   p. 57
3¾ in.
Present all year

NIGHTINGALE   p. 137
6½ in.
April–August visitor

CRESTED TIT   p. 158
4½ in.
Present all year

CIRL BUNTING   p. 88
6¼ in.
Present all year

CORN BUNTING   p. 89
7 in.
Present all year

TWITE   p. 125
5¼ in.
Present all year

Land-birds: GREY-BROWN OR BROWN AND WHITE

RED-LEGGED PARTRIDGE   p. 70
13½ in.
Present all year

PARTRIDGE   p. 71
12 in.
Present all year

DOTTEREL   p. 121
8½ in.
May–Oct. visitor

BARN OWL   p. 77
13½ in.
Present all year

PTARMIGAN   p. 115
14 in.
Present all year

Winter

Summer

HOOPOE   p. 66
11½ in.
March–Oct. visitor

TURTLE DOVE   p. 136
11 in.
April–Sept. visitor

COLLARED DOVE   p. 51
12½ in.
Present all year

MISTLE THRUSH   p. 53
10½ in.
Present all year

FIELDFARE   p. 82
10 in.
Sept.–April visitor

RED-BACKED SHRIKE   p. 98
6¾ in.
May–Sept. visitor

LITTLE OWL   p. 76
8½ in.
Present all year

SPOTTED FLYCATCHER   p. 64
5½ in.
May–Sept. visitor

TREECREEPER   p. 146
5 in.
Present all year

WHITETHROAT   p. 102
5½ in.
April–Sept. visitor

LESSER WHITETHROAT   p. 103
5¼ in.
April–Sept. visitor

BLACKCAP   p. 140
5½ in.
April–Oct. visitor

DUNNOCK   p. 56
5¾ in.
Present all year

MARSH TIT   p. 145
(willow tit similar)   4½ in.
Present all year

TREE SPARROW   p. 87
5½ in.
Present all year

HOUSE SPARROW   p. 45
5¾ in.
Present all year

Land-birds: GREY

PEREGRINE p. 262
Male 15 in. female 19 in.
Present all year

HOBBY p. 93
13 in.
Late April–Sept. visitor

SPARROWHAWK p. 129
Male 11 in. female 15 in.
Present all year

MERLIN p. 110
Male 10½ in. female 13 in.
Present all year

MONTAGU'S HARRIER p. 92
17 in.
Late April–Sept. visitor

HEN-HARRIER p. 111
Male 17 in. female 20 in.
Present all year

CUCKOO p. 96
13 in.
April–August visitor

WOOD-PIGEON p. 74
16 in.
Present all year

FERAL PIGEON p. 48
13 in.
Present all year

STOCK DOVE p. 75
13 in.
Present all year

COAL TIT p. 159
4¼ in.
Present all year

Land-birds: GREEN, YELLOW OR RED

CHIFFCHAFF p. 142
(willow warbler similar)
4¼ in.   March–Oct. visitor

GREEN WOODPECKER p. 132
12½ in.
Present all year

GOLDCREST p. 160
3½ in.
Present all year

WOOD WARBLER p. 143
5 in.
April–August visitor

SISKIN p. 157
4¾ in.
Present all year

GREENFINCH p. 60
5¾ in.
Present all year

CROSSBILL p. 155
6½ in.
Present all year

YELLOWHAMMER p. 86
6½ in.
Present all year

GREAT TIT p. 58
5½ in.
Present all year

BLUE TIT p. 59
4½ in.
Present all year

Land-birds: RED OR ORANGE ON HEAD OR BREAST

GOLDFINCH   p. 63
4¾ in.
Present all year

CHAFFINCH   p. 61
6 in.
Present all year

REDPOLL   p. 156
5 in.
Present all year

Another form
of the same species

LINNET   p. 108
5¼ in.
Present all year

BRAMBLING   p. 148
5¾ in.
Late Sept.–April visitor

Winter

Summer

WHINCHAT   p. 101
5 in.
April–Sept. visitor

STONECHAT   p. 100
5 in.
Present all year

BULLFINCH   p. 62
5¾ in.
Present all year

DARTFORD WARBLER   p. 104
5 in.
Present all year

ROBIN   p. 55
5½ in.
Present all year

SWALLOW   p. 84
7½ in.
April–Oct. visitor

NUTHATCH   p. 147
5½ in.
Present all year

REDSTART   p. 138
5½ in.
April–Sept. visitor

Waterside birds: BROWN

MARSH HARRIER   p. 167
21 in.
Most common April–Sept.

BITTERN   p. 162
30 in.
Present all year

Males in summer

RUFF   p. 173
Male 11 in. female 9 in.
Present all year

CURLEW   p. 118
22 in.
Present all year

WHIMBREL   p. 223
16 in.
April–Sept. visitor

JACK SNIPE   p. 171
7½ in.
Sept.–April visitor

SNIPE   p. 170
10½ in.
Present all year

REED WARBLER   p. 185
(marsh warbler similar)   5 in.
April–Sept. visitor

SEDGE WARBLER   p. 184
5 in.
April–Sept. visitor

ROCK PIPIT   p. 264
6¼ in.
Present all year

BEARDED TIT   p. 181
6½ in. (including 3 in. tail)
Present all year

Waterside birds: WHITE AND BLACK/BROWN

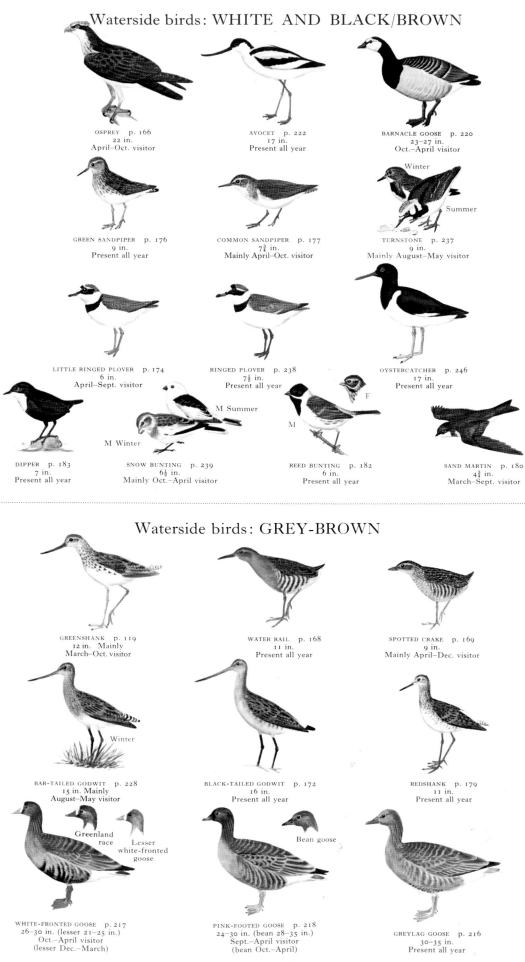

OSPREY p. 166
22 in.
April–Oct. visitor

AVOCET p. 222
17 in.
Present all year

BARNACLE GOOSE p. 220
23–27 in.
Oct.–April visitor

GREEN SANDPIPER p. 176
9 in.
Present all year

COMMON SANDPIPER p. 177
7¾ in.
Mainly April–Oct. visitor

Winter

Summer

TURNSTONE p. 237
9 in.
Mainly August–May visitor

LITTLE RINGED PLOVER p. 174
6 in.
April–Sept. visitor

RINGED PLOVER p. 238
7½ in.
Present all year

OYSTERCATCHER p. 246
17 in.
Present all year

M Summer

M Winter

DIPPER p. 183
7 in.
Present all year

SNOW BUNTING p. 239
6¼ in.
Mainly Oct.–April visitor

M

F

REED BUNTING p. 182
6 in.
Present all year

SAND MARTIN p. 180
4¾ in.
March–Sept. visitor

Waterside birds: GREY-BROWN

GREENSHANK p. 119
12 in. Mainly
March–Oct. visitor

WATER RAIL p. 168
11 in.
Present all year

SPOTTED CRAKE p. 169
9 in.
Mainly April–Dec. visitor

Winter

BAR-TAILED GODWIT p. 228
15 in. Mainly
August–May visitor

BLACK-TAILED GODWIT p. 172
16 in.
Present all year

REDSHANK p. 179
11 in.
Present all year

Greenland
race

Lesser
white-fronted
goose

WHITE-FRONTED GOOSE p. 217
26–30 in. (lesser 21–25 in.)
Oct.–April visitor
(lesser Dec.–March)

Bean goose

PINK-FOOTED GOOSE p. 218
24–30 in. (bean 28–35 in.)
Sept.–April visitor
(bean Oct.–April)

GREYLAG GOOSE p. 216
30–35 in.
Present all year

Waterside birds: GREY AND WHITE

GREY HERON   p. 163
36 in.
Present all year

ROCK DOVE   p. 265
13 in.
Present all year

GREY PLOVER   p. 225
11 in.
Mainly August–May visitor

Summer
Winter

DUNLIN   p. 224
7 in.
Present all year

SANDERLING   p. 236
8 in.
Mainly August–May visitor

KNOT   p. 226
10 in.
Mainly August–May visitor

SANDWICH TERN   p. 245
16 in.
March–Oct. visitor

ROSEATE TERN   p. 243
15 in.
May–Sept. visitor

COMMON TERN   p. 242
14 in. (Arctic tern, 15 in.,
similar)
April–Sept. visitor

LITTLE TERN   p. 244
9 in.
April–Sept. visitor

Waterside birds: BRIGHTLY COLOURED

KINGFISHER   p. 178
6½ in.
Present all year

YELLOW WAGTAIL   p. 187
6½ in.
April–Sept. visitor

GREY WAGTAIL   p. 186
8 in. (including 4 in. tail)
Present all year

Water-birds: BLACK

LEACH'S PETREL   p. 266
8 in.
Mainly April–Dec. visitor

STORM PETREL   p. 266
6 in.
Mainly April–Oct. visitor

BLACK TERN   p. 214
10 in.
May–Sept. visitor

COMMON SCOTER   p. 232
19 in.
Present all year

BLACK GUILLEMOT   p. 261
13½ in.
Present all year

CORMORANT   p. 250
36 in.
Present all year

COOT   p. 213
15 in.
Present all year

MOORHEN   p. 212
13 in.
Present all year

SHAG   p. 251
30 in.
Present all year

25

Water-birds: BLACK AND WHITE

Winter

Summer

GREAT NORTHERN DIVER p. 235
Male 33 in. female 30 in.
Oct.–May visitor

Winter

Summer

BLACK-THROATED DIVER p. 206
27 in.
Present all year

BRENT GOOSE p. 219
22–24 in.
Oct.–May visitor

M

SHELDUCK p. 234
26 in.
Present all year

F

M

EIDER p. 230
24 in.
Present all year

F

M

SCAUP p. 231
19 in.
Oct.–April visitor

F

M

TUFTED DUCK p. 202
17 in.
Present all year

F

M

GOLDENEYE p. 197
18 in.
Mainly Sept.–April visitor

M Summer

F

M Winter

LONG-TAILED DUCK p. 233
23 in.
Oct.–April visitor

F

M

SMEW p. 199
17 in.
Nov.–March visitor

Great black-backed gull

Lesser black-backed gull

LESSER BLACK-BACKED GULL
p. 252 21 in.
Present all year

GREAT BLACK-BACKED GULL
p. 253 27 in.
Present all year

Summer

Winter

GUILLEMOT p. 260
16½ in.
Present all year

Summer

Winter

RAZORBILL p. 258
16 in.
Present all year

Summer

PUFFIN p. 259
12 in.
Present all year

MANX SHEARWATER p. 249
14 in.
Feb.–Oct. visitor

Water-birds: BRIGHTLY COLOURED

F

M

SHOVELER p. 200
20 in.
Present all year

F

M

GOOSANDER p. 204
26 in.
Present all year

F

M

RED-BREASTED MERGANSER
p. 205 23 in.
Present all year

F

M

MALLARD p. 192
23 in.
Present all year

F

M

TEAL p. 195
14 in.
Present all year

Winter

Summer

BLACK-NECKED GREBE p. 210
12 in.
Present all year

Winter

Summer

SLAVONIAN GREBE p. 211
13 in.
Present all year

Water-birds: GREY/BROWN

Light phase

Dark phase

Winter

Summer

GREAT SKUA   p. 257
23 in.
April–Sept. visitor

ARCTIC SKUA   p. 256
18 in.
April–Oct. visitor

DABCHICK   p. 209
9 in.
Present all year

M   F

F   M

F   M

F   M

WIGEON   p. 203
18 in.
Present all year

POCHARD   p. 201
18 in.
Present all year

GARGANEY   p. 194
15 in.
March–Oct. visitor

GADWALL   p. 196
20 in.
Present all year

Winter

Summer

Winter

Summer

CANADA GOOSE   p. 193
38 in.
Present all year

GREAT CRESTED GREBE   p. 208
19 in.
Present all year

RED-THROATED DIVER   p. 207
24 in.
Present all year

Water-birds: WHITE OR GREY AND WHITE

F

M

Winter

F Summer

PINTAIL   p. 198
22 in.
Present all year

FULMAR   p. 255
18½ in.
Present all year

RED-NECKED PHALAROPE p. 175
7 in.
May–Sept. visitor

Winter

Summer

HERRING GULL   p. 241
23 in.
Present all year

COMMON GULL   p. 240
17 in.
Present all year

KITTIWAKE   p. 254
16 in.
Present all year

BLACK-HEADED GULL   p. 42
15 in.
Present all year

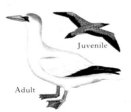

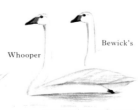

Juvenile

Adult

Summer

Whooper

Bewick's

WHOOPER/BEWICK'S SWAN
p. 190
Whooper 60 in. Bewick's 48 in.
Oct.–April visitors

GANNET   p. 248
36 in.
Present all year

SPOONBILL   p. 221
34 in.
Mainly April–Sept. visitor

MUTE SWAN   p. 191
60 in.
Present all year

IDENTIFYING BIRDS IN FLIGHT

A bird in flight gives many clues to its identification. First, pattern of flight. Is this direct, or meandering? Powerful or fluttering? Does the bird fly in rapid bursts, or is its flight sustained?

Then there is the method of flight. A bird may use its wings almost all the time in flapping flight; or it may glide, coasting along on outstretched wings; it may hover in one place or it may soar, using up-currents of air to gain height. Flight which consists of flapping and gliding in a fairly regular pattern is called undulating. Knowing which bird uses which method often aids identification.

Further points to watch for are the size and shape of the wings, the speed at which the wings move, the depth of the wing-beats and the general appearance of the plumage.

DIVERS AND GREBES

On land they are clumsy, but in the air they come into their own; they fly swiftly on short, pointed wings, with necks stretched out

Summer

RED-THROATED DIVER p. 207
Large, with heavy body and small wings; takes off easily from water and flies fast and direct

Summer

DABCHICK p. 209
Small bird with predominantly brown plumage and small wings; weak, whirring flight

Summer

GREAT CRESTED GREBE p. 208
Heavy-bodied bird with long neck; wings are small and pointed, with prominent white patch

PETRELS AND STORM PETRELS

With their narrow, pointed wings these birds fly far out to sea, skimming over the waves to pick small creatures from the surface

STORM AND LEACH'S PETRELS p. 266
Storm petrel (left) is black with white rump, Leach's larger with forked tail; fluttering flight

MANX SHEARWATER p. 249
Small body; long, pointed wings; black above, white beneath; glides and banks in flight

FULMAR p. 255
Heavy body and 'bull-necked' appearance; grey above, white beneath; gliding, banking flight

GANNETS AND CORMORANTS

These are large birds which live on or near the sea and dive for their fish, either from the surface or from the air; they fly with slow, powerful wing-beats, and carry their long necks well forward

Juvenile

Adult

Juvenile

Summer

GANNET p. 248
Adult white with long, black-tipped wings; young dark, later brown and white

SHAG p. 251
Large bird with long neck; crest in spring and summer; flight is slow and flapping

CORMORANT p. 250
Larger than shag, with slower wing-beats and flapping flight; white thigh-patches in summer

HERONS

Though their long legs seem to adapt them mainly for stalking in deep water, herons are powerful flyers, trailing their legs behind them once in the air

BITTERN p. 162
Broad wings, plumage buff streaked with brown; long, green legs trail in flight

GREY HERON pp. 163–5
Flies with heavy flapping of its long grey and black wings, legs trailing and head drawn back

DUCKS

Superb performers on water, ducks are equally at home in the air; they have stout bodies, long, pointed wings and powerful breast muscles; they fly fast and direct, with long necks stretched out and rapid flapping of the wings, gliding only as they land; they often fly in flocks

GOOSANDER p. 204
Long neck and straight, slender bill; male has grey rump and white wing-patches

RED-BREASTED MERGANSER p. 205
The bird has a long neck and bill; the breast is chestnut, and there is a white wing-patch

SHELDUCK p. 234
Wings beat slowly, showing black tips, white foreparts and lustrous green speculum

EIDER p. 230
The biggest of the British sea ducks, eiders fly powerfully in long lines close to the water

LONG-TAILED DUCK p. 233
Small, with dark wings and dark brown and white body; wings beat mainly below body

SHOVELER p. 200
Heavy bill broadened at the end; pale blue leading edges to the wings in both sexes

WIGEON p. 203
Drake has chestnut head, large white patches on wings and grey back; duck is mainly brown

PINTAIL p. 198
Drake mainly grey, with brown head and neck; light trailing edges on wings in flight

MALLARD p. 192
Both sexes have blue patch on rear of wing; drake has green head and white collar

COMMON SCOTER p. 232
Heavily built; drake black with yellow patch on black bill; duck brown with pale buff cheeks

POCHARD p. 201
Wings grey with indistinct pale stripe; drake has chestnut-red head and black neck

TEAL p. 195
Small and fast-flying; both sexes have green patch bordered with black and white on rear of wings

GOLDENEYE p. 197
Squat shape; large white wing-patches; drake has black head with white patch near eye

TUFTED DUCK p. 202
Black wings with white stripe; drake has black head and neck, with white breast; duck brown

SCAUP p. 231
Dark wings with white stripe; drake has dark green head and black breast; duck is brown

GEESE AND SWANS

Some of the biggest and heaviest birds in Britain come into this group; but thanks to long, broad wings and powerful breast muscles, they are able to fly strongly, with slow wing-beats; they have long necks, and they are often seen in flocks

CANADA GOOSE p. 193
Large, with brown body, black neck, and white face-patch; slow wing-beats; often seen in flocks

BRENT GOOSE p. 219
About the size of a duck; dark wings and swift, flapping flight; often seen in large flocks

MUTE SWAN p. 191
White, with very slow wing-beats and long neck; wings make a whistling noise in flight

GREYLAG GOOSE p. 216
Heavy head, large orange bill, grey-brown with pale grey forewing and rump

WHITE-FRONTED GOOSE p. 217
Grey-brown, with black bars on belly; can rise almost vertically from ground

BARNACLE GOOSE p. 220
Head, neck and breast black, with white face; whitish beneath; black wings, bill and feet

GAME-BIRDS

Their weight, and in some cases lack of stamina in flight, makes these birds tend to keep to the ground, rather than the air; when they do take to the air, flight is fast and direct, and they often rise noisily from cover with whirring wings and loud calls

QUAIL p. 72
Small bird (size of thrush); round wings, streaked brown back, and buff streaks on face

PARTRIDGE p. 71
Small; broad wings, barred flanks, horseshoe mark on breast; creaking call when flushed

RED-LEGGED PARTRIDGE p. 70
Small, with broad wings, brown back and red-brown tail; calls 'chuka-chuka' when flushed

BLACK GROUSE p. 153
Large; male black with white wing-bar and lyre-shaped tail; female brown with forked tail

CAPERCAILLIE p. 152
Very large, with long wings and fan-shaped tail; male has dusky plumage; female smaller, brown

PTARMIGAN pp. 115–17
White in winter with black at sides of tail; in summer, grey with white wings

RED GROUSE p. 114
Male has red-brown plumage; short, rounded wings, and 'go-bak' call; flies close to the ground

PHEASANT p. 69
Short, rounded wings and long tail; rises noisily from cover; male has dark green head

BIRDS OF PREY AND CUCKOO

Superb powers of flight are, for most of the birds of prey, one of the main assets which enable them to catch their victims; their wings are broad and usually long; they can fly slowly when they need to, and they often soar; the cuckoo, though not a bird of prey, has a silhouette similar to that of some birds in this group

GOLDEN EAGLE p. 112
Very large bird with long, broad wings and dark plumage; often soars for long periods

BUZZARD p. 131
Broad wings and wide, rounded tail; soars, hovers and flaps its wings slowly

KITE p. 130
Long wings and long, forked tail; often soars for long periods; rarely seen outside Wales

HEN-HARRIER p. 111
Long wings and tail; flight slow and flapping; male has white rump

MONTAGU'S HARRIER p. 92
Long wings and tail; flight slow and flapping; male has black wing-bars

SPARROWHAWK p. 129
Short, rounded wings, long tail; fast, direct flight; sometimes soars

CUCKOO pp. 96–97
Pointed wings, long tail; direct flight with shallow beats of the wings

MARSH HARRIER p. 167
Large; long wings and long tail; male (left) buff below with grey band and black tips on wings; female (right) rusty-brown

OSPREY p. 166
Very large; dark above, speckled white below; dark mark under 'elbow' of wing

FALCONS

An almost vertical dive to catch their prey in flight is the trade mark of peregrines, and all falcons manoeuvre superbly in chases after small birds. They fly fast, using rapid, shallow beats of their long wings

PEREGRINE p. 262
Long tail, slate-grey back; fast, direct flight; soars and glides at times

HOBBY p. 93
Long, scythe-like wings, slate-grey back, red thigh-patches

KESTREL p. 90
Small and slim; pointed wings and long tail; distinctive hovering flight

MERLIN p. 110
Small; streaked underparts; fast, direct flight with rapid wing-beats

RAILS

Heavy bodies and small, rounded wings limit the rails' powers of flight, and make them more at home on the ground or in water; their flight tends to be weak and whirring, often with legs trailing

COOT p. 213
Black with white wing-bar and white shield-patch on front of head

MOORHEN p. 212
Small; black with white at sides of tail; flight weak, with legs trailing

CORNCRAKE p. 73
Flies weakly on short, rounded wings, with pink legs trailing

WATER RAIL p. 168
Red bill; small, rounded wings; flight weak, with legs trailing

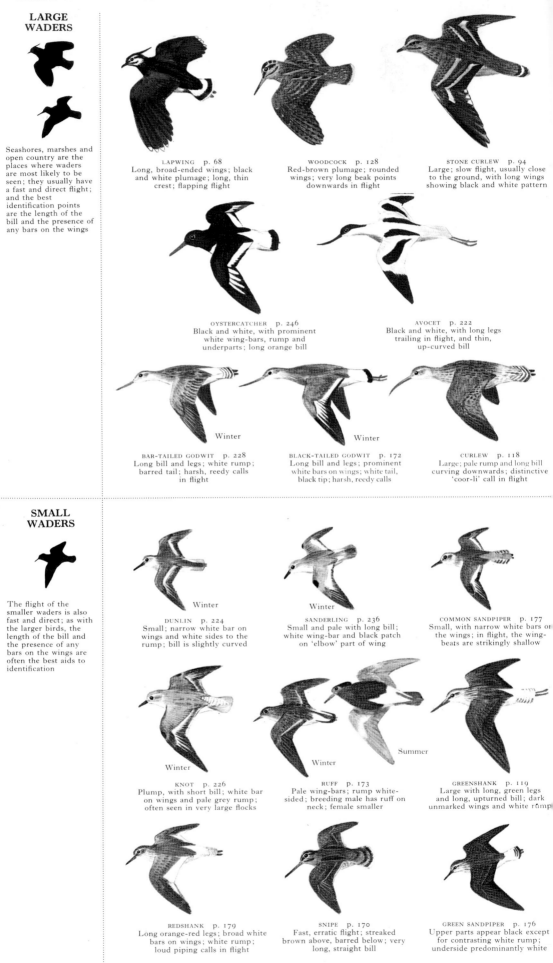

LARGE WADERS

Seashores, marshes and open country are the places where waders are most likely to be seen; they usually have a fast and direct flight; and the best identification points are the length of the bill and the presence of any bars on the wings

LAPWING p. 68
Long, broad-ended wings; black and white plumage; long, thin crest; flapping flight

WOODCOCK p. 128
Red-brown plumage; rounded wings; very long beak points downwards in flight

STONE CURLEW p. 94
Large; slow flight, usually close to the ground, with long wings showing black and white pattern

OYSTERCATCHER p. 246
Black and white, with prominent white wing-bars, rump and underparts; long orange bill

AVOCET p. 222
Black and white, with long legs trailing in flight, and thin, up-curved bill

Winter

Winter

BAR-TAILED GODWIT p. 228
Long bill and legs; white rump; barred tail; harsh, reedy calls in flight

BLACK-TAILED GODWIT p. 172
Long bill and legs; prominent white bars on wings; white tail, black tip; harsh, reedy calls

CURLEW p. 118
Large; pale rump and long bill curving downwards; distinctive 'coor-li' call in flight

SMALL WADERS

The flight of the smaller waders is also fast and direct; as with the larger birds, the length of the bill and the presence of any bars on the wings are often the best aids to identification

Winter

DUNLIN p. 224
Small; narrow white bar on wings and white sides to the rump; bill is slightly curved

Winter

SANDERLING p. 236
Small and pale with long bill; white wing-bar and black patch on 'elbow' part of wing

COMMON SANDPIPER p. 177
Small, with narrow white bars on the wings; in flight, the wing-beats are strikingly shallow

Winter

KNOT p. 226
Plump, with short bill; white bar on wings and pale grey rump; often seen in very large flocks

Winter

Summer

RUFF p. 173
Pale wing-bars; rump white-sided; breeding male has ruff on neck; female smaller

GREENSHANK p. 119
Large with long, green legs and long, upturned bill; dark unmarked wings and white rump

REDSHANK p. 179
Long orange-red legs; broad white bars on wings; white rump; loud piping calls in flight

SNIPE p. 170
Fast, erratic flight; streaked brown above, barred below; very long, straight bill

GREEN SANDPIPER p. 176
Upper parts appear black except for contrasting white rump; underside predominantly white

SMALL AND MEDIUM-SIZED PLOVERS

Winter

GREY PLOVER p. 225
Large; small white patch on tops of wings, black patch beneath

LITTLE RINGED PLOVER p. 174
Small, with plain brown wings; black eye-stripe

RINGED PLOVER p. 238
Small, with white bar on wings; short bill; black stripe across eye

Summer

GOLDEN PLOVER p. 120
Pointed wings, short tail, short bill; belly is black in summer

These are wading birds which fly fast and direct on long wings; all have short bills; the lapwing, shown opposite with similar-looking large waders, is also a plover

SKUAS

Light phase

Dark phase

GREAT SKUA p. 257
Very large and dark, with heavy bill and prominent white wing-flashes; dives to attack intruders

ARCTIC SKUA p. 256
Plumage varies from dark with light underparts to entirely dark brown; short tail-streamers

The broad wings of skuas enable them to fly powerfully, and to remain in the air for long periods; they also manoeuvre well in chases, pursuing other seabirds and robbing them of food

GULLS

Summer

COMMON GULL p. 240
Adult has grey back, yellow-green legs and yellow bill; immatures are brown and white

KITTIWAKE p. 254
Adult has plain black wing-tips, black legs and yellow bill; immatures' wings striped

BLACK-HEADED GULL p. 42
Black tips to white wings; red legs and red bill; immatures are brown and white

In the air, gulls are versatile performers; they fly strongly, with slow wing-beats, often soaring and gliding, and sometimes floating on up-currents of warm air; their wings are long and pointed

HERRING GULL p. 241
Pink legs and yellow bill; adult has grey back; immatures are brown and white

GREAT BLACK-BACKED GULL p. 253
Adult has black back, white body and pink legs; immatures are brown above, pale beneath

LESSER BLACK-BACKED GULL p. 252
Adult has dark grey back and yellow legs; bill less stout than great black-backed

TERNS

Summer

Summer

COMMON TERN p. 242
Pale grey back; white body; black cap; bill is red with black tip; immatures brown and white

SANDWICH TERN p. 245
Large, with slightly forked tail, black legs and small crest; bill black with yellow tip

LITTLE TERN p. 244
Small, with slightly forked tail and white forehead; bill yellow with black tip

Graceful flight marks out the terns from the other birds which haunt our coasts; they have slender bodies and long wings, and the plumage is usually pale grey and white

33

AUKS

The stout bodies of the auks do not prevent them from performing expertly in the air; they have small, pointed wings which give them a fast and direct flight, with rapid, whirring wing-beats

Summer

PUFFIN p. 259
Small; black above and white beneath; heavy triangular bill; very fast, whirring flight

Summer

RAZORBILL p. 258
Black above and light below, with heavy, dark bill crossed by white line; flight fast and direct

Summer

GUILLEMOT p. 260
Dark above and white below, with stout, straight bill; flight is fast; often seen in flocks

DOVES AND PIGEONS

The wings of pigeons and doves are broad, pointed and angled at the wrist, giving them fast, direct flight; they have heavy bodies

STOCK DOVE p. 75
Grey, with two short black bars on each wing, and black tip on tail; often in flocks

FERAL PIGEON p. 48
Plumage variable, often with broad black bars on the wings, and white rump; often in towns

WOOD-PIGEON p. 74
Grey; broad white wing-patches; white neck-patch; fast, direct flight; often seen in flocks

COLLARED DOVE p. 51
Slim, pale grey below; tail long with white and black beneath; fast, direct flight

TURTLE DOVE p. 136
Slim; long tail with white band at the end; flight rapid, with flicking wing-beats

ROCK DOVE p. 265
Grey, with back lighter than head and underparts; two black bars on each wing; rump white

OWLS AND NIGHTJAR

Soft, loose plumage gives the owls the silent flight that is essential if they are to take their prey by surprise; they have rounded wings and fly slowly, with quiet wing-beats; the nightjar has longer wings and tail, and flies more rapidly; most fly at night

LONG-EARED OWL p. 154
Plumage buff with dark streaks under long wings; usually flies at night

SHORT-EARED OWL p. 113
Biscuit-coloured plumage; long wings with dark mark beneath; often hunts by day

TAWNY OWL p. 50
Broad, rounded wings and short tail; large head, round facial disc and very large eyes

NIGHTJAR p. 95
Long wings and tail; twists and zigzags in pursuit of insects; often hovers

LITTLE OWL p. 76
Large head; grey-brown plumage; short wings and bounding flight; often hunts by day

BARN OWL p. 77
Golden buff back and white face and underparts; long wings and slow flight, rather wavering

WOODPECKERS

The wings of these birds are very broad, and when they take to the air, woodpeckers have deeply undulating flight; patterns on the back or face often prove a useful method of identification

GREEN WOODPECKER p. 132
Large; bright green above, with crimson crown and yellow rump; deeply undulating flight

LESSER SPOTTED WOODPECKER p. 134
Small; black and white plumage with barred wings and back; flight undulating

GREAT SPOTTED WOODPECKER p. 135
Broad, barred wings and white patches on back; crimson under-tail feathers; undulating flight

LARKS

Open countryside is the natural home of the larks; they have streaked brown plumage, long wings, and their flight is either bounding or direct

WOODLARK p. 107
Small, with a very short tail and black and white patches on the 'elbow' of each wing

SKYLARK p. 85
Larger, with white at sides of tail and white trailing edges to wings; hovers and soars

SWALLOWS AND SWIFT

Most of the life of these birds is spent in the air; they feed on the wing, catching small insects, and even collect nest materials in mid-air; they have long, pointed wings, and fast, direct flight

SWIFT p. 46
Very long, scythe-like wings; fast flight, rapid wing-beats; often glides

SWALLOW p. 84
Steel-blue upper parts, white beneath; adults have long tail-streamers

HOUSE MARTIN p. 47
Small; blue-black above, white beneath; white rump and forked tail

SAND MARTIN p. 180
Small; white below with brown breast-band; long wings and forked tail

PIPITS AND WAGTAILS

More at home on the ground than in the air, these birds tend to be slim and to have long tails and undulating flight; their calls in flight are often distinctive

MEADOW PIPIT p. 124
Small; olive-brown above, buff below; prominent white tail-sides; 'pheet' flight-call

PIED WAGTAIL p. 188
Black and white, with very long tail; undulating flight; 'tschizzik' call in flight

YELLOW AND GREY WAGTAILS pp. 187 and 186
Both have yellow breasts; male of grey wagtail (right) with longer tail and black throat

THRUSHES AND STARLING

Most birds in this group are plump-looking and spend much of their time on the ground; but they also fly well

RING OUZEL p. 126
Black, with white crescent on breast; pale wing-patch; flight usually fast and direct

BLACKBIRD p. 54
Male is black with yellow bill; female dark brown with lighter throat; flight is direct

STARLING p. 43
Pointed wings and fast, direct flight; sometimes glides; often seen in large flocks

MISTLE THRUSH p. 53
Large; long tail and light under wings; flight is undulating

SONG THRUSH p. 52
Buff under wings; streaked breast; brown back; flight mainly direct

REDWING p. 83
Streaked breast; reddish under wings; white eye-stripe; undulating flight

FIELDFARE p. 82
Large, with long tail; grey rump; chestnut wings and shoulders

35

WHEATEARS, CHATS AND ROBIN

These are plump birds with short wings and tails; their flight is fast and direct

STONECHAT   p. 100
Small and plump, with short tail; male has white rump and wing-patch

WHINCHAT   p. 101
Small and plump, with white wing-bar and white sides to rump

WHEATEAR   p. 99
Plump; pale beneath with prominent white rump; fast, direct flight

ROBIN   p. 55
Rather weak flight, direct or undulating; red upper breast, grey lower down

SHRIKES

Their almost hawk-like bills make these birds efficient hunters of insects and small mammals; they fly fast on rounded wings, but sometimes their flight is bounding; they have long tails

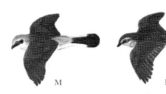

RED-BACKED SHRIKE   p. 98
Male has chestnut back, blue-grey crown and rump, and black eye-stripe; female dull brown

TITS AND NUTHATCH

The flight of tits is weak and undulating; these birds are small, and they have stout bodies and round wings; the head patterns often provide a useful means of identification

GREAT TIT   p. 58
Large; yellow breast; black bib; head black and white

BLUE TIT   p. 59
Short tail; crown is cobalt-blue, side of face white

COAL TIT   p. 159
Small; white nape-patch; pale below; white wing-bars

MARSH/WILLOW TIT   p. 145
Grey-brown above, pale below, black cap

CRESTED TIT   p. 15
Small; grey-brown back; black and white face and cres

LONG-TAILED TIT   p. 144
Small; pink, black and white plumage with very long tail; flight weak and undulating

NUTHATCH   p. 147
Larger than a tit; short tail; grey back and buff underparts; black stripe through the eye

FINCHES, BUNTINGS AND SPARROWS

These small song-birds live mainly on seeds; they have short wings and their flight is either direct or undulating; many species have distinctive wing-patterns or flight-calls

CHAFFINCH   p. 61
Double white wing-bars, white shoulder-patch and white tail-sides

BRAMBLING   p. 148
Double white wing-bars and prominent white rump; often in flocks

Winter

GOLDFINCH   p. 63
Very small with deeply undulating flight; yellow wing-stripes; red on face

BULLFINCH   p. 62
Large, with heavy body; rose-pink breast; white rump and wing-bar

LINNET   p. 108
Small, with deeply undulating flight and twittering calls; white on wings and tail-sides

HAWFINCH   p. 150
Large, with heavy body and heavy bill; white shoulders; short tail with broad white border

GREENFINCH   p. 60
Plump, with olive-green plumage and yellow on wings and tail; flight slightly undulating

CORN BUNTING   p. 89
Dull brown streaked plumage, without white on sides of tail; often trails legs in flight

TREE SPARROW   p. 87
Small, with chestnut crown and deeply undulating flight; makes 'teck-teck' call in flight

HOUSE SPARROW   p. 45
Male has grey rump and narrow white wing-bar; female mainly brown; flight is direct

YELLOWHAMMER   p. 86
Yellow head and underparts, chestnut rump, and white on sides of tail; flight is undulating

CIRL BUNTING   p. 88
Olive rump and white tail-sides; male has black and yellow head-pattern and green band on breast

REED BUNTING   p. 182
Streaked brown upper parts and dark tail with white sides; male has black head and throat

CROWS

These are the largest of the song-birds; strong legs and feet enable them to move swiftly and purposefully on land; in the air, their broad wings fit them for soaring or flying fast and direct; many gather in flocks

MAGPIE   p. 80
Very long, wedge-shaped tail; short black and white wings; white patches on body

JAY   p. 149
Medium-sized; brown-pink body, white rump and black tail; white wing-bars; flight looks laboured

ROOK   p. 78
Adults black with white chin-patch and loose feathers on flanks; often seen in large flocks

JACKDAW   p. 81
Smaller than other crows; faster wing-beats and grey neck-patch; 'tchack-tchack' flight-call

HOODED CROW   p. 122
CARRION CROW   p. 79
Carrion (right) all-black; hooded has grey back and underparts

RAVEN   p. 123
Large, with long wings, long graduated tail and heavy bill; distinctive deep, gruff calls

CHOUGH   p. 263
Very broad wings and acrobatic flight; plumage all-black; bill red and down-curved; red legs

OTHER SMALL BIRDS

For purposes of identification in flight, these birds do not fit conveniently into any of the other groups

PIED FLYCATCHER   p. 139
Breeding male black above, white below; light wing-bar and tail-sides all year; bounding flight

WREN   p. 57
Tiny, with short rounded wings, short tail and rapid, whirring flight; brown above, buff below

DUNNOCK   p. 56
Plump, with brown streaked back; grey throat and breast; slender bill; weak, bounding flight

DIPPER   p. 183
Small, with short tail and round wings; dark brown with white breast; flies fast and low

KINGFISHER   p. 178
Brilliant blue-green above, orange-chestnut below; short tail; flight is fast and direct

THE BRITISH BIRDS

The wildness of birds is revitalising in
a world where nature has so often been tamed
and straitjacketed for the purposes of man. This
quality of wildness is illustrated in the following
pages, which contain profiles of 217 birds,
grouped according to the habitats in
which they are most often seen.

THE WREN. Raymond Harris King. London. 1968.

How to use the maps

Two distribution maps are given on each page, one for the British Isles and one for the world. The Orkneys and Shetlands are shown on the British Isles maps only if the birds concerned can be seen there. The British Isles maps show where birds occur as visitors, as well as their breeding areas. The world maps plot breeding ranges only.

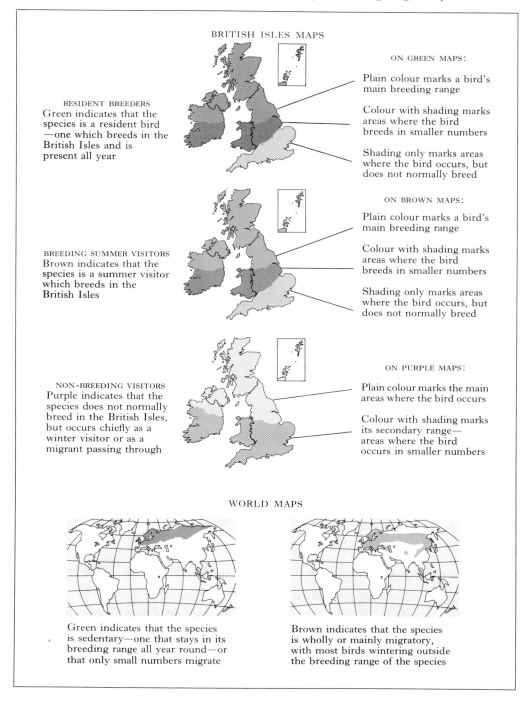

BRITISH ISLES MAPS

ON GREEN MAPS:

Plain colour marks a bird's main breeding range

Colour with shading marks areas where the bird breeds in smaller numbers

Shading only marks areas where the bird occurs, but does not normally breed

RESIDENT BREEDERS
Green indicates that the species is a resident bird —one which breeds in the British Isles and is present all year

ON BROWN MAPS:

Plain colour marks a bird's main breeding range

Colour with shading marks areas where the bird breeds in smaller numbers

Shading only marks areas where the bird occurs, but does not normally breed

BREEDING SUMMER VISITORS
Brown indicates that the species is a summer visitor which breeds in the British Isles

ON PURPLE MAPS:

Plain colour marks the main areas where the bird occurs

Colour with shading marks its secondary range— areas where the bird occurs in smaller numbers

NON-BREEDING VISITORS
Purple indicates that the species does not normally breed in the British Isles, but occurs chiefly as a winter visitor or as a migrant passing through

WORLD MAPS

Green indicates that the species is sedentary—one that stays in its breeding range all year round—or that only small numbers migrate

Brown indicates that the species is wholly or mainly migratory, with most birds wintering outside the breeding range of the species

About the birds

The following section covers 217 species: all those which regularly breed in the British Isles, as well as about a score of regular winter visitors (some of which have bred here on rare occasions) and a few migrants which break their journeys in Britain every year. A label at the side of the illustration indicates the sex of the bird shown, whether it is an adult or a juvenile and whether it is in summer or winter plumage. Unless otherwise labelled, the bird shown is an adult, the male and female of a species are alike and the bird's plumage does not change appreciably from one season to the next. Although the birds are grouped into habitats, it should be remembered that they can move freely from one to another.

TOWNS

Built-up areas, with little vegetation beyond
trees in the streets, weeds on waste ground and the
lawns and borders of small gardens, are the most artificial
of the habitats to which birds have had to adapt themselves. The most
successful species in this environment are those which originally
nested where vegetation was scarce. The bridges, walls
and office blocks of towns and cities provide them
with a substitute for cliffs and ledges.

CONTENTS

Black-headed gull

Larus ridibundus 15 in.

SUMMER

Present all year; birds from eastern and northern Europe come here in winter, outnumbering residents

Northern populations migratory, wintering in western Europe and south to North Africa and Malaysia

In winter the black-headed gull loses its chocolate brown hood

DURING the past 80 years or so, this gull has become a familiar bird in towns, especially in London where it survives as a scavenger. Black-headed gulls moved up from the Thames estuary during hard winters at the end of the 19th century, and found food plentiful around docks, in parks and along embankments where people threw scraps.

The birds are also common in winter along the coast, on estuaries, and on farmland where they follow the plough and eat many harmful insects. They have learnt to live partly by 'piracy' on lapwings. The gull stands by, ready to pounce and snatch as the lapwing patters forward to take a worm or insect; or it will often give chase until the lapwing drops the food.

Thousands of gulls roost on reservoirs in the winter: they stream westwards from London in the late afternoon, sometimes flying in a loose V-formation, sometimes in a wavering stream that may stretch for miles.

Although a few gulls breed on gravel pits near towns, most of them go to coastal sandhills and salt-marshes, or to hills and moors where they nest in colonies in bogs and marshes, some reaching far inland.

Despite the fact that the black-headed gull is so common inland in winter, many people do not realise what it is; for its winter plumage does not include a dark head.

RECOGNITION: *chocolate brown hood (lost in winter); grey back and wings; black wing-tips; rest of plumage white; red feet and bill; young are brown and white, with narrow brown band on tail-tip; sexes alike.*
NESTING: *nests in colonies; both sexes build substantial pile of dried vegetation on tuft of rushes or grass; lays mid-April–July; usually 3 eggs, varying in colour from pale buff to deep brown, sometimes blue-green; incubation about 23 days, by both parents; young, fed by both parents, leave nest in a few days, fly after 5–6 weeks.*
FEEDING: *scraps and offal in towns; elsewhere crabs, sand-eels, moths, snails, earthworms and insects.*

Starling

Sturnus vulgaris 8½ in.

MALE IN SUMMER

STARLINGS, swarming in tens of thousands to their roost-sites just before dusk, have become a spectacular, noisy and inescapable part of life in many cities. Their high-pitched squealing rises above the din of traffic, and their droppings foul masonry and pavements, and spoil the growth of trees.

Many methods to drive them away have been tried. Amplified cries of starlings in distress have been broadcast, but after some initial success, the starlings realised that they were being deceived and stayed put. More successful, on buildings such as the National Gallery in London's Trafalgar Square, has been the painting of ledges with a sticky jelly which makes starlings feel insecure when they land.

In the countryside—for starlings roost there, too—they have been known to snap boughs off trees by sheer weight of numbers. Foresters have tried to drive them off with smoke—a method which cannot be used in cities.

Before going to their roosts, usually along well-defined flight-lines, starlings feed in fields, foraging where the feet of cattle stir up insects. Pests which they take from the soil help to offset damage they do elsewhere.

Their vocabulary includes many clipped notes, and they are good mimics of other birds' voices, and sometimes pick up other sounds, even a human whistle.

RECOGNITION: *iridescent purple, green and blue plumage, handsomely spangled with white or buff in winter; spangling more marked in female than male; jerky walk; swift, direct flight, sometimes varied by gliding.*
NESTING: *usually nests in loose colonies; male builds untidy nest of dried grass and straw in tree hole, on cliff or building; female lines it with feathers or moss; lays April–May; 5–7 eggs, pale blue; incubation about 13 days, by both parents; nestlings, fed by both parents, fly after about 21 days; usually two broods.*
FEEDING: *insects (especially leatherjackets), earthworms, spiders, snails, slugs; fruit, seeds, roots and berries.*

Present all year; many birds from northern and eastern Europe join the British population in winter

Northern populations are migratory, wintering mainly in the breeding range of the southern populations

Hungry young starlings chase their parents, urgently demanding food

43

MALE

Black redstart

Phoenicurus ochruros 5½ in.

March–Nov. visitor (also a few all winter); has bred in several other English counties and the Orkneys

Mainly migratory; northern birds winter chiefly in Mediterranean region and southern Asia

Black redstarts often sing from buildings, perched on a high ledge

UNTIL about 75 years ago the black redstart had been known to nest in the British Isles only once or twice, appearing mainly as a rather uncommon passage migrant and winter visitor, chiefly on southern coasts. Then one pair bred on the south coast in 1923, another in 1924, and two pairs in 1925. Since then, at least one pair has bred in England every year, and now there are 50-100 pairs.

Although originally it nested on sea cliffs, the black redstart is today very much a town bird. It feeds on waste and rubble-strewn ground—the kind of land which was once provided in abundance by bomb sites—and during and immediately after the Second World War it was established in the City of London. As numbers there have dwindled because of rebuilding, the bird has found other nest-sites in docks and other industrial areas in London and its suburbs, and on the east and south coasts, from Norfolk to Sussex—even on the nuclear power station at Dungeness in Kent. Much of its food is caught on the wing, and it is capable of hovering to catch flying insects.

Its call-notes are a short 'tsip' and a 'tucc-tucc' of alarm. The song, a staccato warble, is usually given from a building, often at a considerable height. Migrating birds often sing in April and May, and occasionally in the autumn. They appear to sing as a means of defending territory, even though they may not breed.

RECOGNITION: *male mainly black in summer, grey-black in winter, with white wing-patch; female grey-brown; both sexes have chestnut-red rump and tail.*

NESTING: *female builds nest of grass, moss and roots on ledge or in crevice of building, inside shed or under rafters; lays April–July; usually 4–6 eggs, glossy white; incubation 12 or 13 days, by female only; young, fed by both parents, leave nest after 16–18 days; two broods, often three.*

FEEDING: *mainly insects; also spiders and millipedes; berries at times.*

House sparrow

Passer domesticus   5¾ in.

MALE

FEMALE

Because the house sparrow is so much in evidence, townspeople suppose it to be the most numerous bird in Britain. But in fact it is largely confined to the neighbourhood of human settlements, and is surpassed in numbers by both the chaffinch and the blackbird.

There were probably no house sparrows in Britain before the arrival of man. They are believed to have come with Neolithic men, our first farming ancestors, spreading across Europe from their original home in Africa. Like starlings they have been introduced into North America and have spread widely.

Only in autumn does the house sparrow break its close ties with buildings and move to farmland to feed on ripening corn. Its habit of tearing garden primulas and crocuses—especially the yellow ones—may be connected with its diet, for at least part of the petal is eaten.

The bird utters a wide variety of 'chirps' and 'cheeps' and has a double note, 'chissik', all of which are strung together to form a rudimentary song. The most important element of its courtship display is the 'sparrow party', which usually begins with a single cock displaying to a hen and bowing to her. If he gets too close, she may peck at him. Then other cocks near by are attracted and join in, all chirping loudly until the hen flies off, pursued by the whole flock.

RECOGNITION: *brown upper parts, streaked with black; grey crown and rump, red-brown shoulders and black bib; white wing-bar; more heavily built than tree sparrow; female brown, with streaked back.*
NESTING: *both sexes build untidy nest of dry grass in hole in building or tree, sometimes in open in thick hedgerow, when nest is domed; usually lays April–August; normally 3–5 eggs, white with grey and brown blotches; incubation 12–14 days, chiefly by hen; young, fed by both parents, fly after about 15 days; up to three broods.*
FEEDING: *grain and weed-seeds; insects and their larvae; almost entirely bread and scraps in built-up areas.*

Present all year; generally found only near human habitations; they seldom fly far from their birthplace

Most populations are sedentary; has also been introduced in N. America and other parts of the world

In courtship several cock sparrows surround the hen, chirping loudly

Swift

Apus apus 6½ in.

Late April–August visitor; widespread, except in northern Scotland; absent from Orkney and Shetland

Highly migratory; the entire breeding population winters in Africa, south of the Equator

Swifts fly screeching round houses on late spring and summer evenings

No birds are more aerial in their habits than swifts. Their legs have become so weak, because they are so seldom used, that the birds are helpless and easily caught once on the ground; but swifts never alight on the ground except by accident. They feed on the wing, sometimes mate on the wing, and even sleep on the wing. At dusk, swifts circle higher and higher until they disappear from sight. It used to be thought that they returned after dark to roost at their nests, but it is now known that those which are not incubating eggs or brooding young remain aloft until sunrise, probably cat-napping on currents of rising air between short spells of flapping to gain height.

To countrymen, the swift was once known as the 'devil bird', because of its habit of flying screaming round houses during late spring and early summer evenings. It is one of the latest migrants to arrive and one of the earliest to go. Few can be seen before the last few days of April or after the middle of August.

Swifts appear to pair for life; and they have two courtship displays. On the nest, mating occurs after mutual crooning and preening; in the air there is a spectacular chase before the birds mate on the wing.

If a strange swift intrudes on an occupied nest, fierce fighting may occur. One such battle, watched in a tower in Oxford, lasted 5¾ hours. There are two records of swifts being found alive and interlocked on the ground beneath their nests.

RECOGNITION: *black-brown plumage, except for white chin-patch; long, scythe-shaped wings; forked tail; sexes alike.*
NESTING: *both sexes build nest of straw, grass and feathers, cemented with saliva, under eaves of building or in thatch, occasionally in rock crevice; lays May–June; usually 2 or 3 eggs, white; incubation usually 18–20 days, by both parents; young, fed by both parents, fly after 35 or 36 days.*
FEEDING: *insects taken on the wing, especially flies, small beetles and moths.*

House martin

Delichon urbica   5 in.

A conspicuous white rump makes the house martin the easiest of the swallow family to distinguish in flight. Its nesting habits are distinctive, too, for this is a bird whose mud nests are familiar under the eaves of houses. Surveys suggest that house martins may be slowly decreasing in Britain, but the evidence is conflicting. Certainly there are local fluctuations in their numbers; in 1966 they returned to inner London as a nesting species for the first time since 1889.

A famous colony under the arches of Clifton Hampden bridge, on the Thames near Oxford, reached 513 nests in 1952; but today it is largely deserted, possibly because of increasing vibration from traffic. Another colony—once one of the largest in Britain—is at Atcham bridge, over the Severn, near Shrewsbury. This colony once held more than 400 nests, but here, too, numbers have steadily dwindled. Martins originally nested in cliffs and caves, and there are still colonies in such places in north and west Britain. The birds feed almost entirely on the wing, and rarely go to the ground, except to collect mud for nest-building.

Nesting begins three or four weeks after their arrival in April, and young birds of early broods often continue to roost in the nest until they migrate. Late in the season as many as 13 birds have been counted, crammed into a single nest.

RECOGNITION: *blue-black above, white beneath, with white rump; tail less forked than swallow's; sexes alike.*
NESTING: *both sexes build rounded nest of gobbets of mud, grass and roots, under eaves of house, sometimes under bridge, in caves, or on cliff; nest thickly lined with feathers; lays May–August; usually 4 or 5 eggs, white; incubation 14 or 15 days, by both parents; nestlings, fed by both parents, fly after 19–22 days; two broods, sometimes three.*
FEEDING: *almost entirely insects caught on the wing, especially flies and small beetles.*

April–Oct. visitor; rare in northwest Scotland, and seldom breeds in Shetland

Migratory; winter distribution uncertain, but European birds may go to southern and tropical Africa

House martins build their mud nests under the eaves of houses and barns

47

Feral pigeon

Columba livia 13 in.

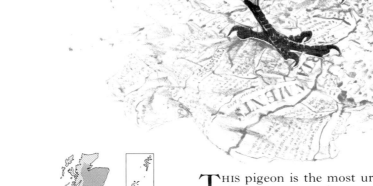

Present all year; common in cities and large towns; also nests on sea cliffs, interbreeding with rock doves

Sedentary; these birds are descended from domestic pigeons which have gone wild

Feral pigeons nest and roost on large buildings in city centres

THIS pigeon is the most urban bird of all; it lives in city squares and town gutters, docks, railway stations and open-air cafés—where it will even snatch scraps from people's plates. Notices at some London stations threaten a heavy fine for feeding the pigeons; but they are unlikely ever to go hungry, for with such sharp wits and alert enterprise they have no trouble finding food for themselves.

The original ancestor of the town pigeon is the wild rock dove of the sea-cliffs, but the forerunners of the city birds were domestic pigeons which escaped from medieval dovecotes. Records show that there were pigeons on Old St. Paul's Cathedral 600 years ago, for the Dean was then complaining that boys broke cathedral windows by throwing stones at the birds.

A study of feral pigeons in Leeds showed that in winter they lived almost entirely on bread, cake and bird-seed offered by the public. In March they went to the country to feed on freshly sown grain and weed-seeds. In summer they ate more weed-seeds and vegetable matter; and in autumn they fed on farmland stubble.

The cooing voice of the feral pigeon is a familiar sound in cities. Familiar too are its courtship display, in which a puffed-out male bows repeatedly to an apparently disinterested female, and its habit of roosting on ledges, hunched up against the cold.

RECOGNITION: *plumage very variable; may be blue-grey, cinnamon-brown, black or white, or any combination of these colours; rock dove ancestry is often shown by double black wing-bars or white rump; sexes alike.*
NESTING: *both sexes build nest of grass and twigs in hollow in building, often under the eaves; lays mainly March–September; usually 2 eggs; white; incubation 17–19 days, by both parents; young, fed by both parents, fly after 35–37 days; usually two to four broods.*
FEEDING: *often bread and other scraps, but includes chocolate, apples and bacon rind; also grain, weed-seeds and small snails.*

PARKS AND GARDENS

Birds and people have nowhere achieved a
happier relationship than in parks and gardens.
All the common garden birds were originally woodland
species, but in living alongside men they have found a security and
a regular food supply which more than compensates them for
leaving their old surroundings. In return, they eat
many harmful garden insects; and they add to the
stock of human pleasure simply by being there.

CONTENTS

Tawny owl

Strix aluco   15 in.

Present all year; never recorded in Ireland, but found in almost all wooded areas elsewhere in Britain

Sedentary; in Europe it lives mainly in broad-leaved woods, but in the Far East it also lives in conifers

In the daytime, a roosting tawny owl is mobbed by small birds

WHEN Shakespeare wrote down the call of the tawny owl as 'tu-whit, tu-who—a merry note' he was, for once, being a poor naturalist. What he heard was not a single owl but two birds—one of them giving out an eerie 'hooo, hooo, hoo-oo-oo-oo' and the other, probably a female, answering with a sharp 'kee-wick'. Both sexes hoot, and both call 'kee-wick', but these two sounds are never uttered together by the same bird.

The tawny owl, a bird of copses and well-wooded parks and gardens, is the most common owl over much of Britain, though absent from Ireland. Like most owls, it hunts by night and roosts by day; but if hard-pressed for food at nesting time, it will hunt in broad daylight. At other times, a roosting owl can often be located by following up the noisy parties of smaller birds, especially jays, blackbirds and chaffinches, which seek out the predator and mob it. The owl may not be dislodged by their clamour, though, and will not be disturbed easily even at the sight of a man. Its astonishingly flexible neck allows it to turn its head almost full-circle, so that its face can be kept towards an observer moving round it.

The nest is usually in a tree hole, but a pair may take over a burrow in the ground, a cliff ledge, a sparrow-hawk's nest or a squirrel's drey. The bird's diet can be studied fairly accurately, for tawny owls bring up pellets of undigested fur, bones and beetles' wings.

RECOGNITION: *mottled brown, with round facial disc and dark brown eyes ; distinctive 'kee-wick' call and hooting song ; sexes alike.*
NESTING: *no nest built ; lays in old tree hole, squirrel's drey, occasionally an old building, rock crevice or on ground ; lays March–May, sometimes earlier ; usually 2–4 eggs, round and white ; incubation 28–30 days, by female only ; young, fed mainly by male, fly after 30–37 days.*
FEEDING: *small mammals, especially mice, voles, young rats and shrews ; some birds ; at times fish, frogs, molluscs, worms and insects.*

Collared dove

Streptopelia decaocto 12½ in.

THE collared dove, easily the most recent arrival among our common breeding birds, has also rapidly become one of the most widespread. Its headlong advance across Europe and Britain reads like the story of a well-planned military campaign.

At the end of the 19th century the bird had only a tenuous bridge-head in Europe, in the Balkans. Seventy years ago the nearest collared dove to our shores was on the far side of the Danube in what was then Yugoslavia. Then, early in the 1930s, came a population explosion among the birds, and collared doves began their advance towards the Atlantic seaboard. By 1947 they were in the Netherlands; by 1948 they had reached Denmark and, a year later, it was the turn of Sweden. They reached Belgium in 1952 and in that same year the first collared dove was seen in Britain – at Manton in Lincolnshire. Three years later the first British nest was discovered, at Cromer in Norfolk; and by 1957 a pair had a nest as far north as Moray, in Scotland. Today, collared doves have reached the remote corners of the British Isles, and they are now to be found in almost every town, suburb and village in the land.

They are chiefly grain-eaters, especially fond of food put out for poultry; their song, a triple 'coo, coo-oo, cuk' with a marked accent on the second syllable, has become a familiar sound, especially in parks and gardens.

RECOGNITION: *grey-brown above, pale grey below; long tail, black and white beneath; black and white half-collar on back of neck; distinctive 'coo, coo-oo, cuk' song; sexes alike.*
NESTING: *both sexes build flat nest of twigs and stems, generally well up in tree, sometimes on ledge of building; lays March–September; 2 eggs, white; incubation about 14 days, by both parents; young, fed by both parents, fly after about 18 days, finally leave the nest a few days later; usually two broods, but up to five may be attempted.*
FEEDING: *mostly grain and weed-seeds; some fruit such as elderberries.*

Present all year; first pair nested in Britain in 1955, in Norfolk; now a widespread breeding bird

Essentially sedentary, but long-distance dispersive movements are made by some birds

In flight the collared dove shows its distinctive white tail-tip

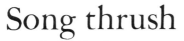

Song thrush

Turdus philomelos 9 in.

Present all year; birds from the Continent occur here on spring and autumn passage and in winter

Resident in western Europe; most other birds migrate, wintering in Mediterranean and south-west Asia

A song thrush uses a stone as an anvil for smashing snail shells

WHEN a song thrush hops across the lawn and cocks its head intently to one side, it is not listening for the stirring of worms in the ground, although it is certainly fond of earthworms; it is looking for food, tilting its head because its eyes are at the sides.

The clutch of sky-blue eggs in a song thrush's cup-nest seems symbolic of spring itself; and Robert Browning, nostalgic for April in England, gave a useful tip for identifying the bird's song: 'That's the wise thrush; he sings each song twice over.' The repetition of each loud, clear phrase—often more than twice—prevents confusion with either the mistle thrush or the blackbird.

The song can be heard in almost any month of the year. The thrush starts singing in January, unless the weather is very severe, and continues steadily until July; late in September it starts up again, and on fine days in October and November it sings almost as strongly as in spring.

Snails, together with earthworms, are the favourite food of the song thrush, and the bird picks a convenient 'anvil' stone which it uses again and again for smashing snail shells. Though the song thrush has a highly successful relationship with man, taking a wide variety of fruit, berries and insects in gardens, its numbers have decreased this century; it is apparently badly hit by hard winters.

RECOGNITION: *brown above; breast buff, heavily streaked with chestnut and shading into white; smaller than mistle thrush, with no white on tail feathers; sexes alike.*
NESTING: *both sexes build bulky cup-nest of dry grass and dead leaves, with lining of mud, in bush or hedge, low in tree or on ledge; lays March–July; 3–6 eggs, light blue with black spots; incubation 13 or 14 days, by female only; young, fed by both parents, fly after 13 or 14 days; usually two or three broods.*
FEEDING: *snails, earthworms; insects and larvae; fruit and seeds.*

Mistle thrush

Turdus viscivorus 10½ in.

THIS largest of our native thrushes is named after its fondness for the sticky berries of the mistletoe. It has another name, too—the storm cock—which pays tribute to the way it will sing from a treetop in all weathers, even in a raging winter gale. The loud ringing song does not have the mellowness of a blackbird's fluting, or the elegantly repeated phrases of a song thrush, but it is often the finest bird music to be heard on a gusty January day.

The mistle thrush is an early breeder, and its bulky nest in an exposed position high in a tree may contain eggs in late February—long before there are any leaves to give it shelter. At this season the mistle thrush, always wary and suspicious, is at its most aggressive; it may attack a man or bird venturing too near the nest, or swoop down to threaten a cat.

After the breeding season, mistle thrushes take to open country, such as downs, moors and marshes. They move about in small family parties, eating mistletoe and other berries, including yew and hawthorn.

They frequently attract attention by the grating 'churr' of their flight-call and alarm note, a sound like a comb being scraped on a piece of wood. At other times, they sing on the wing. In flight their wings close at regular intervals for a perceptible time, and the white under-wing appears to flash on and off.

RECOGNITION: *grey-brown above, very pale beneath, with round chestnut spots; white outer tail feathers; distinguished from song thrush by bolder spots, larger size and often by more upright stance; sexes alike.*
NESTING: *both sexes build bulky cup-nest of grass, twigs, earth and moss, usually high in tree; lays late February–June; usually 4 eggs, pale blue to buff, with red-brown spots and blotches; incubation 13 or 14 days, by female only; young, fed by both parents, fly after 14–16 days; usually two broods.*
FEEDING: *fruit and berries; insects and their larvae, earthworms, snails.*

Present all year; breeds nearly everywhere in British Isles except in the Orkneys and Shetlands

Essentially sedentary; only the most northerly breeding birds migrate in winter, to Mediterranean countries

White patches under the mistle thrush's wings flash as it flies

53

Blackbird

Turdus merula 10 in.

MALE

Present all year; probably our most common resident breeding bird; many continental birds winter here

Mainly sedentary; only the most northerly breeding birds migrate, wintering mainly in western Europe

Young blackbirds are still fed by their parents after leaving the nest

A dynamic expansion into man-made habitats in the past 100 years has made the blackbird the most common resident breeding bird in Britain. Its only rival for that title was the chaffinch, another bird able to live almost anywhere. The blackbird used to be confined to woodland, but it has moved out into gardens, fields, parks, squares, commons, heaths and, in hill districts, to cloughs and combes.

It has taken over the main singing role in the dawn chorus all over the country, and its mellow fluting is one of the most beautiful bird-songs heard in Britain—rated by some people even higher than that of the nightingale. There is also a sweet, muted sub-song, hummed through a closed bill and sounding like a distant echo. Other sounds made by the blackbird are harsher. Its nervous scolding chatter gives notice of a prowling cat, a fox or a human being. At other times its tail-flicking 'chook-chook' shows a mild anxiety, and at dusk it carries on a persistent 'pink-pink'.

The blackbird is the only one of our three common breeding thrushes (the others are the song thrush and the mistle thrush) in which the plumage of the male and female is different; the handsome cock is jet black with a yellow bill; the hen is browner and more thrush-like. There are often a few partly white cocks about, some looking as if they have flakes of snow on their backs; they become well known in their areas.

RECOGNITION: *male jet black with yellow bill; female dark brown, lighter below, slightly mottled, with brown bill.*
NESTING: *female builds neat cup of dry grass, dead leaves and mud in hedge, low tree or on ledge of building; lays late March–July; usually 3–5 eggs, light blue-green with brown spots; incubation about 13 days, by female only; nestlings, fed by both parents, fly after 13 or 14 days; usually two or three broods, occasionally one, four or five.*
FEEDING: *insects and their larvae, earthworms; fruit and seeds.*

Robin

Erithacus rubecula   5½ in.

I^N 1961, the British Section of the International Council for Bird Preservation were set the task of choosing Britain's national bird. After a long correspondence in *The Times* they chose the robin, that chest-puffing individualist whose tameness, according to the late David Lack, the world authority on robins, is a tribute to the British character. On the Continent robins are shy birds, keeping to deep woodland; but in Britain they are bold enough to dog the footsteps of a gardener who might turn over a worm or two for them.

The defence of territory is a robin's life—the main reason for the plaintive warbling song which is heard all year round, except for a brief moulting period in July. Pauses of a few seconds between snatches of the song allow rival cock robins to get in their own songs, and so help to establish a pattern of robin territories. In winter the females sing, too, and hold territories of their own. Only when the cold is so severe that finding food takes precedence over every other activity do robins allow others of their species to intrude on their winter territories.

In late summer, when the young birds have put on adult plumage, there is a great deal of disputing as territories and borders are established. About mid-winter the female goes mate-hunting. She does the choosing; while the cock sings from his tree, she unobtrusively enters the undergrowth, and if she is tolerated for a few weeks, she begins to accompany him.

RECOGNITION: *olive-brown above; orange-red breast, throat and forehead; whitish belly; sexes alike.*
NESTING: *female builds domed nest of grass, dead leaves and moss in hollow in bank, tree hole, wall or ledge in shed; lays March–June; 3–6 eggs, white, usually with red-brown spots and blotches; incubation 13 or 14 days, by female only; young, fed by both parents, leave after 12–14 days; two broods, occasionally three.*
FEEDING: *insects and larvae; fruit and seeds; earthworms.*

Present all year; widespread, except in Shetlands; migrants occur on south and east coasts

Sedentary and migratory; northern birds winter mainly in western Europe and Mediterranean countries

Asserting territorial rights, the robin puffs out its red breast and sings

Dunnock
Prunella modularis 5¾ in.

Present all year; absent from the Shetlands, except as spring and autumn migrant from the Continent

Largely sedentary, but northern populations winter in western, central and southern Europe

The dunnock sings its tuneless ditty almost all the year round

FOR many years this bird was called the hedge sparrow, 'sparrow' being a name given to any small bird in past times. A glance at its bill is sufficient to tell that it is not, in fact, related to the house and tree sparrows, both of them thick-billed seed-crunchers. Sharp and thin, its bill is typical of insect-eaters, although from autumn until spring it does, for the most part, eat small seeds. To end the confusion, the old country word 'dunnock' has been revived as the common name of the species.

The dunnock is probably the cuckoo's most common victim in the south of England. It is not clear why this should be so, since there is rarely any resemblance between the eggs of the cuckoo and the light blue eggs of the dunnock. Cuckoos using meadow pipits' nests have evolved eggs looking like those of the host species, so that they will not be thrown out of the nest, but blue cuckoos' eggs have only been found once or twice in Britain.

The dunnock almost always feeds on the ground, moving in a series of hops. Its high piping song can be heard almost all the year round, although it is generally silent in late summer. Occasional snatches are heard at night, for the bird breaks into song if startled awake. It is an inconspicuous bird, although it is often given away by a shrill, insistent 'tseep' call.

RECOGNITION: *grey eye-stripe, throat and breast; brown back with dark streaks; thin bill; squeaking call; sexes alike.*
NESTING: *both sexes build bulky cup of moss and grass, lined with wool and hair, low in bush, hedgerow or woodpile; lays late March–early July; 3–5 eggs, light blue; incubation usually about 13 days, by female only; nestlings, fed by both parents, fly after about 12 days; usually two broods, sometimes three.*
FEEDING: *mostly insects and larvae in spring and summer; sometimes spiders and small earthworms; chiefly small seeds in winter.*

Wren

Troglodytes troglodytes   3¾ in.

THIS second smallest of our regular breeding birds (it is only ¼ in. larger than the goldcrest) has long been a national favourite; and considering its piercing, trilling song and perky stance with cocked-up tail, it is easy to understand why.

The Jenny Wren—a nickname applied to the male as well as the female—has an absorbing life history. The male often builds several nests and entices its mate to select one. Two broods are normal and the male may take the first brood to roost in one of the 'rejected' nests while the female is incubating the second clutch. In surroundings where the food supply is poor, wrens are monogamous; but in richer habitats, males will set up more than one mate in the nests that they build.

Despite the affection in which they are held, wrens were the victims of a cruel ritual which is still carried on in some parts of the British Isles, although the birds are seldom actually caught these days. In the past, on St. Stephen's Day (December 26th), groups of youths in motley dress would beat the hedgerows, singing and trying to kill any wren they saw. The origin of the wren hunt is obscure, but it has been linked with New Year ceremonies of the Bronze Age megalith builders.

Ten or more wrens have been found huddling inside a single coconut shell; keeping warm is a problem for them and they suffer heavy losses in cold winters.

RECOGNITION: *red-brown, with barring on wings, tail and flanks; small tail, often cocked up; loud shrill song; loud 'churring' alarm call; sexes alike.*

NESTING: *male builds several domed nests of moss, leaves and grass, in bush, creeper, woodstack or hollow in wall; female lines one with feathers; lays late April onwards; eggs, white with fine red-brown spots; incubation about 14 days, by female only; nestlings, fed by both parents, fly after about 15 days; usually two broods.*

FEEDING: *small insects and their larvae; a few spiders and small seeds.*

Present all year; distinctive races occur on St. Kilda, Shetlands, Fair Isle and Outer Hebrides

Essentially sedentary, though some northern European birds are known to move southwards in winter

The wren packs a surprising number of nestlings into its small domed nest

Great tit
Parus major 5½ in.

Present all year; very rarely seen in Orkney and Shetland; colonised the Outer Hebrides (Lewis) in 1966

Mainly sedentary, though individual birds may move hundreds of miles in times of food scarcity

The great tit is one of the most frequent users of garden nest-boxes

THE acrobatics of tits are matched by a mental agility in solving problems and tackling unusual situations. If a great tit, largest of the family, wants to get at a nut dangling from a string it will pull up the string with its beak, and hold down loop after loop with one foot until the nut is reached.

But the liveliness which makes the birds amusing to watch also turns them into clever nuisances at times. Great tits and blue tits are the chief culprits in sporadic outbreaks of milk-stealing. A few birds find they can prise off or peck through the tops of milk bottles to get at the cream, and the rest imitate them. Some years ago 57 out of 300 bottles left at a school in Merstham, Surrey, were opened in a single morning. However, this is more than offset by their value to the gardener. The young are brought up largely on the caterpillars of moths, especially the winter moth, and it has been estimated that in the three weeks of feeding their brood a pair can destroy 7000–8000 caterpillars and other insects; so wise gardeners put up nest-boxes.

The great tit has perhaps the most extensive vocabulary of any British bird. The most frequent spring song, if it can be called one, sounds like, 'tea-cher, tea-cher'; there is a 'pink' call, and another note suggests the sound of a saw being sharpened. When disturbed on the nest, the hen will make a snake-like hiss.

RECOGNITION: *head and neck glossy black; cheeks white; black band on yellow breast; back green; sexes alike.*
NESTING: *often nests in hole in tree or wall, but readily uses nest-box; both sexes carry in nesting material, mostly moss, with hair or down for lining; lays late April–May; 8–12 eggs, white, thickly spotted with red-brown; incubation 13 or 14 days, by hen only; young, fed by both sexes, fly at about 20 days.*
FEEDING: *largely insects, including caterpillars, aphids, scale-insects; some buds, fruit, peas and seeds; occasionally young birds.*

Blue tit

Parus caeruleus 4½ in.

Bᴿɪꜱᴋ, bold and agile, the blue tit is one of Britain's favourite garden birds, whether scrambling for food at the bird table or hanging upside-down to get at a suspended coconut. When it comes to problem-solving, the bird has few rivals. Faced with 'intelligence test' apparatus, blue tits have learnt to pull out a series of pegs or open matchbox drawers to get at food. Some years ago, blue tits solved a less artificial problem; they learnt how to get at the milk left on suburban door-steps, by pecking at the foil of the bottle tops.

Sometimes they take part in an even odder activity. Blue tits, if they get inside a house, may have a mania for tearing paper. Strips are torn from wallpaper and books, newspapers and labels; putty and other objects may be attacked. No one really knows why they do this, but it may be what is known as a 'dissociated' hunting activity, as tits commonly pull bark off trees when they are seeking insects.

Originally, blue tits were woodland birds, and in winter they often join other species of tits, and the occasional nuthatch or treecreeper, in large, loose flocks which move through the woods. An insect stirred up but missed by one bird will be picked up by the next.

The blue tit's trilling song often starts on a sunny day in January. Nest-boxes are used readily, but they should be put up by the end of February, for blue tits start prospecting for nest-holes early in the year.

RECOGNITION: *wings, tail and crown of head blue; cheeks white; back green and underparts yellow; sexes alike.*
NESTING: *nests in tree hole, nest-box or crevice in wall; both sexes collect moss, grass, hair and wool as nesting material; lays late April–May; 8–15 eggs, white with red-brown spots; incubation about 14 days, by female only; young, fed by both sexes, fly after about 19 days.*
FEEDING: *mainly aphids, caterpillars and other insects; some fruit, grain and seeds.*

Present all year; not found in Orkney and Shetland; birds from Europe visit southern counties

Essentially sedentary, though small-scale eruptive movements may occur in some years

The blue tit is the most common of tits taking food hung in gardens

Greenfinch

Carduelis chloris 5¾ in.

MALE

Present all year; widespread except in the Shetlands, where it occurs rarely and does not breed

Mainly sedentary, though the most northerly breeding birds migrate, some as far as the Mediterranean

In flight the greenfinch shows a pale flash on its wings

So completely have greenfinches adapted themselves to life in a man-dominated countryside that they are hardly ever found far from human settlements. In the breeding season, especially, they keep to suburban gardens, shrubberies and bushy places near villages.

In recent years these stout-billed seed-eaters have been well rewarded for their age-old attachment to man. They have greatly increased in numbers because of the quantities of pet food, particularly seeds and peanuts, put out on bird-tables. Greenfinches come to the tables in twittering groups, and they are sociable birds at all times, tending to nest in loose colonies, using adjacent bushes. They usually have two broods in a season, and some even rear a third, so that it is not unusual to find young birds in the nest in August or even early September.

In winter, they may be tempted to leave the shelter of the garden to feed on stubble or waste land with flocks of other finches or buntings. A disturbed feeding group rises with a sudden whirring of wings, and the birds have an up-and-down bounding flight as their wings momentarily close.

As befits a bird so fond of company, the greenfinch has an extensive vocabulary. Its calls include a nasal 'tsweee', a canary-like 'tsooeet' and a 'chi-chi-chi-chi-chit' flight-call; and for its song it strings together a number of calls in a twittering medley.

RECOGNITION: *olive-green with heavy, pale bill; yellow wing-bar and tail-sides; female duller.*
NESTING: *both sexes build untidy cup of grass, moss and roots, with lining of roots, in bush, tree or hedge; lays late April–August; 4–6 eggs, white to pale blue, with red-brown spots and streaks; incubation about 13 days, by female only; young, fed by both parents, fly after 12–16 days; usually two broods, occasionally three.*
FEEDING: *almost entirely seeds, wild fruit and berries.*

Chaffinch

Fringilla coelebs 6 in.

MALE

Most people asked to name the most common bird in Britain would probably choose the house sparrow. In fact the first place for sheer numbers must go to the blackbird, with the chaffinch until recently running it close. Blackbirds have increased, while there seems to have been a decline in chaffinches in some areas through the disappearance of hedgerows.

Chaffinches breed almost wherever there are trees and bushes, but they are less suburban than blackbirds or robins. In winter they join other finches, buntings and sparrows in large flocks to feed on arable land and stubble. Sometimes, though, they form vast chaffinch flocks, all of one sex.

Chaffinches start singing in February, but not all sing in the same way. Striking regional dialects have been recorded, especially among birds which winter here from the Continent. Despite this, the song is easy to identify, for it always ends with an emphatic flourish, 'tissi-cheweeo'. The main flight-note is 'tsup', but the most common call is a loud 'pink-pink'.

The male shares with several other birds the habit of attacking its own reflection in a window, and a female has been seen unsuccessfully trying to imitate great tits pulling up a string of nuts; the bird reached down to peck the string but could not hold on to it, or keep its balance on the branch.

RECOGNITION: *blue-grey head and neck; pink breast and cheeks; chestnut back; white on wings, tail and shoulders; female yellow-brown above, paler below, with white wing-bar and white tail-sides.*
NESTING: *both sexes build neat cup-nest of moss and lichen lined with wool, hair and feathers, in hedge, bush or tree-fork; lays April–early June; usually 3–6 eggs, off-white with red-brown blotches; incubation 12–14 days, by female only; nestlings, fed by both parents, fly after 12–15 days; sometimes two broods.*
FEEDING: *seeds, beech-mast and sometimes grain.*

Present all year; even more common in winter, when large numbers come here from northern Europe

Southern populations are sedentary, but northern birds migrate south and west within the breeding range

In autumn and winter chaffinches flock to feed on stubble-fields

Bullfinch

Pyrrhula pyrrhula 5¾ in.

MALE

Present all year; absent from Isle of Man; visits northern islands as scarce migrant from Scandinavia

Mainly sedentary, but some northern Scandinavian birds migrate as far south as central Europe

Bullfinches are unpopular because of their liking for fruit-tree buds

Handsome though it is, the bullfinch has made enemies in many parts of the country. This is because in late winter and early spring it literally nips fruit trees in the bud. A single bird has been seen to eat the buds on a plum tree at the rate of 30 a minute. During the past 40 years, fruit growers have complained about their depredations, and it seems that the birds' numbers have increased since the mid 1950s. So acute was the problem that in some places bullfinches were deprived of their protection.

Attacks on fruit trees and ornamental shrubs occur mainly when the bird's natural food source is scarce, from January to April. Its short, rounded bill, with especially sharp cutting edges, is an excellent adaptation for this purpose. But even in fruit-growing districts it also takes many weeds and tree-seeds.

Many ornithologists believe, though positive evidence is hard to come by, that bullfinches mate for life. Certainly, once two have formed a bond, they do not seem to split up for the winter, as do most small birds.

Whenever a glimpse is caught of the black-capped, pink-breasted male, its mate will be flitting a little way behind, looking like a toned-down copy with the colours filtered out. They are shy birds and retire quickly from human presence; only a soft, indrawn whistle, usually written down as 'deu', tells where they have gone.

RECOGNITION: *black cap; rose-pink breast; grey back; white rump; female much drabber than male.*
NESTING: *female builds nest of twigs, moss and lichen in thick hedge, bramble, brake or other deep cover; lays late April–July; usually 4 or 5 eggs, green-blue, sparsely streaked and spotted with purple-brown; incubation 12–14 days, mainly by female; nestlings, fed by both parents, fly after about 14 days; two broods, sometimes three.*
FEEDING: *tree-seeds, weeds and berries; buds of fruit trees in late winter and early spring; caterpillars fed to young.*

Goldfinch

Carduelis carduelis 4¾ in.

Towards the end of the 19th century, the number of goldfinches in Britain had been brought dangerously low by intensive trapping for the cage-bird trade. In 1860 it was reported that 132,000 a year were being caught near Worthing in Sussex; a few years later a House of Commons committee was told of a boy who took 480 in a single morning. The Society for the Protection of Birds (later Royal) made the saving of the goldfinch from the trapper and the bird-limer one of its first tasks; and today small flocks and family parties, aptly known as 'charms' of goldfinches, are a familiar sight, feeding on the heads of thistles and other tall weeds in the late summer and early autumn.

The song for which the bird was caged in Victorian times is a tinkling variation of the most frequently heard flight-note, a liquid 'tswitt-witt-witt'. It is given when the male is establishing its territory in large gardens and orchards, and sometimes in thick hedgerows or open woodland. Changes in agriculture have reduced the thistle beds among which it feeds but, at the same time, the reservation of areas for quarries and other development has provided it with new foraging grounds.

In courtship, which always takes place near the nest, the male droops and partly opens its wings, sways from side to side and exhibits its bright yellow wing-flashes.

RECOGNITION: *brown back; black and white tail; wings mainly black, with broad band of yellow; red face, rest of head black and white; sexes alike.*

NESTING: *female builds neat nest of roots, grass, moss and lichen, lined with wool and vegetable down, usually in spreading tree; lays early May–August; usually 5 or 6 eggs, pale blue, lightly spotted with brown; incubation 12 or 13 days, by female only; nestlings, fed by both parents, fly after 13 or 14 days; normally two broods, sometimes three.*

FEEDING: *seeds of thistle, burdock, dandelion, knapweed and other weeds; fruit of birch, alder and other trees; some insects, especially for young.*

Present all year; some of our breeding birds migrate to south-west Europe in winter

Sedentary and migratory; northern populations winter just beyond or in southern half of breeding range

In flight the goldfinch shows its white rump and yellow wing-bars

Spotted flycatcher

Muscicapa striata   5½ in.

May–Sept. visitor; does not breed in Shetland and only recently established in Orkney and Hebrides

Highly migratory, wintering in tropical and southern Africa and in limited numbers in northern India

Spotted flycatcher pounces from its perch to catch a flying insect

So quiet and unobtrusive is the spotted flycatcher that many people do not know when they have one in the garden. There is little point in trying to identify one by looking for spots, for this mouse-grey bird is confusingly named. Only juvenile birds have spots—inconspicuous dark ones on their breasts.

A far better way of recognising a spotted flycatcher is to observe whether it feeds by sitting bolt upright on a fence, spray or branch beside an open space, then darting out at a passing fly. It may have to twist and turn in flight, but it seldom misses; and its bill closes with an audible snap. Usually the bird returns to the same observation-post or one near by. Warblers and other small song-birds sometimes use the same technique, but flycatchers alone have made it a way of life.

The spotted flycatcher is one of our latest summer visitors to arrive, usually reaching Britain in mid- or late May and staying until September. It is a creature of habit, and will return year after year to a favourite nest-site—often a creepered house or a trellis. Its usual call is a shrill, robin-like 'tzee'; and the alarm note, 'whee-tucc-tucc' recalls that of the stonechat. What passes for a song is some half-dozen high-pitched rather squeaky notes, which sound at first as though uttered by several birds in a spasmodic exchange.

RECOGNITION : *mouse-grey ; white below ; adults unspotted, but with dark streaks on head and breast ; juvenile birds have inconspicuous dark spots on breast ; sexes alike.*
NESTING : *both sexes build untidy nest of moss, wool and hair, held together with cobwebs, on ledge, in creeper on wall, in tree, old bird's nest or in cavity ; lays late May–June ; 4 or 5 eggs, shades of green or blue, heavily freckled with red-brown ; incubation about 13 days, mainly by female ; young, fed by both parents, fly after 12 or 13 days ; sometimes two broods.*
FEEDING : *almost entirely flying insects—chiefly flies but also craneflies, butterflies and wasps ; very occasionally earthworms and rowan berries.*

Waxwing

Bombycilla garrulus   7½ in.

EVERY few years, and sometimes for several years in succession, there are mass eruptions of waxwings from their breeding grounds in northern Europe. There may have been a failure in the crop of rowan berries, their favourite food; or there may have been a population explosion among the waxwings after a particularly good rowan year. Britain gets a share of the larger dispersals, and though the invasions are erratic, they have been going on for centuries; a 'waxwing winter' was recorded as long ago as 1679–80.

There were four successive invasions in 1956–60, a series which beat all records. The most massive irruption of all came in 1965–6, with birds arriving in September, and building up to a peak in November, when more than 11,000 were recorded in two weeks.

By the time waxwings arrive, other birds have usually stripped the rowan bushes. The birds may turn up in parks and gardens to gorge on the berries of ornamental trees and shrubs. In Norfolk, in February 1957, in two days a party of seven stripped the berries on 100 sq. ft of a cotoneaster growing on a cottage. One bird ate 390 berries, roughly its own weight, in 2½ hours.

Waxwings are highly sociable and call frequently, usually with a soft trilling 'sirrr'. They were once known as Bohemian chatterers. In courtship, the handsome male displays its colourful wing feathers.

Nov.–March visitor; usually very few, in Scotland and eastern England; occasionally widespread

Eruptive migrant; usually winters just south of range, but occasionally reaches Mediterranean

RECOGNITION: *waxy red, white and yellow markings on wing; bright yellow tip to tail; prominent crest; black throat; chestnut and grey above, pink-brown below; looks like large plump finch at first glance; sexes alike.*
NESTING: *does not nest in Britain; many which 'invade' Britain probably breed in Finland; cup-shaped nest of twigs and moss built in conifer; lays May–July; 4–6 eggs, grey with dark spots; incubation about 2 weeks, chiefly by hen; nestlings, fed by both parents, leave after about 2 weeks.*
FEEDING: *berries, including rowan, cotoneaster, pyracantha, viburnum, juniper, hips and haws.*

Waxwings often eat ornamental berries in surburban gardens

Hoopoe

Upupa epops 11½ in.

March–Oct. visitor, more common in spring than autumn; has nested occasionally in southern England

Only northern birds migrate; European birds winter in Africa, largely south of the Sahara

Hoopoe in flight—like a large black and white moth

WITH its pink-brown plumage, a crest like a Red Indian's head-dress and boldly barred black and white wings, the hoopoe is one of the most exotic birds to be seen in Britain. It has the added fascination of rarity, too; only small numbers arrive regularly each April or May as vagrants from the Continent, though others may turn up at any time of the year. In some years pairs may stay to nest in the south coast counties. Most leave to spend the winter in Africa.

Hoopoes breed regularly across the Channel, and when they do come to Britain, they usually seek places with scattered trees, nesting in a hole in an old willow or a cranny in a farm building. The site may soon become insanitary, for hoopoes do not keep their nests sweet. They are sometimes perceived as filthy birds because of their feeding and breeding habits.

The call-note, a rapid, far-carrying, clipped 'hoo-hoo-hoo', of the same pitch as the cuckoo's, gives the bird its name; it also has a harsh starling-like 'errrr'. Fluttering before its nest, it looks like a gigantic black and white barred moth, but the flight is by no means as feeble as it seems and a hoopoe can out-manoeuvre a falcon.

Courtship leads to much play with the crest as the male, the tip of its bill pressed against a branch, bows to the female. During incubation, the male provides all the food for both birds.

RECOGNITION: *pink-brown plumage; very broad black and white wings and tail in flight; pink crest, black-tipped long curved bill; sexes alike.*
NESTING: *seldom nests in Britain; breeds in southern Europe, in hole in tree or wall, or uses nest-boxes; usually no nesting material but droppings accumulate; lays May–June; 5–8 eggs, light grey to cream; incubation 18 days, by hen only; nestlings, fed by both parents, leave after 3–4 weeks.*
FEEDING: *mainly beetle grubs, locusts, grasshoppers, moths, ants, earwigs, flies, some spiders, centipedes, woodlice, worms.*

FARMLAND

When hedges are destroyed, to open the
way for more efficient farming techniques,
thousands of birds lose their nest-sites. When
pesticides are sprayed on crops, the effect on birds
can be even more disastrous. Farmland, for all its traditional
chequered pattern of fields criss-crossed by winding lanes
and hedges, is the fastest-changing habitat in Britain;
and its birds must change too—or perish.

CONTENTS

Lapwing

Vanellus vanellus 12 in.

In winter some British birds fly to south-west Europe, while many northern European birds come here

Sedentary and migratory; lapwings do not move far in winter, except to avoid frosty weather

Lapwing tumbles earthwards in spring display flight

THIS friend of the farmer, a bird which devours many harmful insects, once had its own Act of Parliament to protect it, but even now the protection is still incomplete, for licences may be issued to allow gourmets to collect lapwings' eggs for eating up to the middle of April. Their argument is that the early clutches are liable to be destroyed during farming operations and that the birds will lay again anyway.

The lapwing, or peewit, derives both of its names from the sounds it makes. In spring it performs a striking aerobatic display, climbing steadily with its wings making a throbbing or 'lapping' sound while it utters its wild song 'p'weet-p'weet, peewit-peewit'. Then it plunges down, over its territory, rolling and twisting apparently out of control. Its call-notes are variations on the 'peewit' theme.

Besides aerial display, the courting male makes scrapes in the ground, rocking forward on to its breast.

Like other plovers, lapwings are highly gregarious, and often flock with golden plovers in winter. At all seasons they feed over farmland, both arable and grass; but when breeding they are also fairly common in damp, rushy fields, coastal marshes and moorland. In winter many join other waders on freshwater margins and sometimes on sands and mud-flats along the coasts.

RECOGNITION: *our only medium-sized black and white bird with rounded wings and short tail, conspicuous in flight; at rest, the only one with crest and long legs; in bright sunshine can look brilliant green above; sexes alike.*
NESTING: *female selects one of several scrapes made by male in ground, often on slight rise, lines it with dried grasses; usually lays late March–May; usually 4 eggs, olive-buff or olive-green, heavily marked with black; incubation about 27 days, mostly by female; chicks, usually tended by female only, leave in a few hours, fly after about 5 weeks.*
FEEDING: *mainly insects, especially wireworms and leatherjackets; also earthworms, sometimes brought up by stamping feet.*

Pheasant

Phasianus colchicus   M 33 in. (including 18 in. tail)
F 23 in. (including 9 in. tail)

FEMALE

MALE

No firm evidence can be found to support the theory that the Romans first brought the pheasant to Britain. It was first definitely recorded a few years before the Norman Conquest, in 1059.

The bird's true home is in Asia, from the Caucasus across to China, and it was birds from the western part of this range, the Caucasus, which were originally introduced to Britain. This form became known as the Old English pheasant, but from the 18th century onwards there were repeated introductions, from eastern Asia, of forms with a white neck-ring. As a result, present-day stocks are an amalgam of forms—those with and those without the white neck-ring in roughly equal proportions.

Every year, gamekeepers release thousands of reared pheasants into woods in preparation for the shooting season, starting on October 1. The bird is also well established as a wild breeding species in copses, heaths and commons, and beds of reeds and sedges. It has increased in almost all areas during the past 20 years.

The pheasant has the typical whirring flight of a game-bird, alternating with gliding on down-turned wings, and it can rocket explosively upwards when disturbed. The cock crows with a loud, hard 'korr-kok', and often responds to a shot or distant explosion by crowing.

RECOGNITION : *cock has mainly copper plumage ; hen is browner and shorter-tailed ; green, grey and black-barred forms of the cock are common.*
NESTING : *hen scrapes hollow in ground, frequently under thick vegetation, lines it scantily with leaves and grass ; occasionally nests in haystack or old nest of other bird in tree ; lays late April–June ; usually 8–15 eggs, pale olive ; incubation 22–27 days, by hen only ; chicks, tended by hen, leave nest when a few hours old, fly after 12–14 days.*
FEEDING : *wide variety of animal and vegetable food, from fruits, seeds, and leaves of wild plants to leatherjackets, wireworms, caterpillars, grass-hoppers and other insects ; occasionally lizards, field voles and small birds.*

Present all year; in some areas numbers are maintained for shooting by artificial rearing

Map shows indigenous population; birds also introduced in Europe, N. America, Japan, New Zealand

Red-legged partridge

Alectoris rufa 13½ in.

Present all year; introduced in 18th century, they now breed wild in many lowland areas

Sedentary; native population restricted to south-west Europe; British stock introduced

Red-legged partridge shows its strongly barred flanks as it flies

THE red-leg, as farmers sometimes call it, is also known as the French partridge because ancestors of the British stock were introduced from France some 200 years ago. For a time, genetically inferior hybrids between this species and the chukar, an Asian relative, were also released, but the practice has now been banned.

Its habitat—heaths, farmland, coastal shingle and chalk downs—is similar to, though often drier than, that of the common partridge, and the red-leg flies and runs with the same action as its relative. But the two birds are distinctive in appearance: the red-leg's black-and-white eye stripes and strongly barred flanks make it easy to identify. Its voice is distinctive, too—a loud, challenging 'chucka-chucka'.

In courtship the cock holds its head up and slightly to one side, erecting the feathers of its white face and throat. The barred feathers on the flanks are also fluffed up and then prominently displayed.

The hen lays a large clutch of up to 15 eggs, in a lined scrape on the ground; she often lays two clutches in separate nests, incubating one herself and leaving the cock to incubate the other. This high rate of egg production is offset by a high rate of loss: for the eggs are never covered when the incubating bird leaves them, and many are destroyed by stoats, rats and other predators.

RECOGNITION: *brown plumage; easily distinguished from smaller common partridge by black and white eye-stripes, rich chestnut barring on grey flanks, and lack of dark horseshoe mark on breast; sexes alike.*
NESTING: *cock makes scrape, sparsely lined with dried grass and other local materials, in ground in thick vegetation, occasionally in haystack; lays late April–May; usually 10–15 eggs, yellow or yellow-brown with thin brown and ash-grey spots; incubation usually 25 days, by either or both parents; chicks, tended by either or both parents, leave nest and run almost as soon as hatched, fly after about 2 weeks; often two broods.*
FEEDING: *predominantly vegetable, like that of native partridge.*

MALE

Partridge

Perdix perdix 12 in.

So many partridges have been imported that it is now difficult to regard the bird as a genuinely native wild species. The main source of imported birds has been central Europe, which accounts for one of the partridge's other names, Hungarian partridge.

At the time when the shooting season opens, on September 1, partridges are gathered in family parties, known as coveys. They break up into breeding pairs in late January and early February, and at this time the cock birds become aggressive in defence of their territories. In courtship, pairs of birds often spring into the air and chase one another; and in one case, a number of birds formed a circle before pairing off.

For nesting and feeding, partridges prefer farmland, either grass or arable, especially with good cover from hedges, bushes, rough grass banks or ditches. They also nest on rough grassland, moorland edges and heaths. A widespread decline throughout the past 40-50 years has been caused by a pesticide-induced reduction in suitable insect food for the chicks.

Partridges have a whirring flight, alternating with gliding on down-curved wings. Their most frequently heard call-note is a loud, high-pitched, creaky 'keev-it', often degenerating into a rapid cackle, 'it-it-it' when flushed.

Present all year; has decreased in recent years, because of pesticide effects on insect supply

Sedentary; it is also found locally in North America where it has been introduced for sport

RECOGNITION: *brown plumage, barred with chestnut on flanks and chestnut tail; neck and underparts grey with dark horseshoe on breast; hen less boldly marked than cock.*
NESTING: *hen makes scrape in ground lined with dried grass and leaves, often approached by runway, and usually in thick vegetation; haystack sometimes used; lays late April–May; usually 12–18 eggs, pale olive; incubation about 24 days, by hen only; chicks, tended by both parents, leave after a few hours, fly after about 2 weeks.*
FEEDING: *mainly grain and buds, flowers, leaves and seeds of low-growing plants; animal matter includes insects, spiders, small snails and slugs.*

Partridges roost together, facing outwards to watch for predators

Quail

Coturnix coturnix   7 in.

MALE

May–Oct. visitor; found annually where shown, but in good years nests more widely

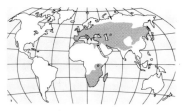

Most populations are migratory; European breeding birds winter in northern tropical Africa

Usually only gun-dogs can force the shy quail into flight

So shy and secretive are quail that they would hardly ever be seen were it not for the dogs of shooting parties, which flush them in the autumn, making them fly low for just a short distance. And the call of the quail, though loud and far-carrying, is hard to pin down to a particular spot among the crops where it hides; sportsmen say that it can 'throw' its voice, with the effect produced by a ventriloquist.

In the breeding season, the cock bird 'advertises' with a persistent 'quic-ic-ic', a call which is sometimes given as 'wet-my-lips'—the hen calling a soft 'bru-bru' until contact is made. Then the cock bird runs up and circles round her, puffing up his neck and breast feathers, stretching his neck and dragging his wings along the ground.

Its normal habitat is farmland, especially light chalk and limestone soils, where the call can be heard in fields of clover, lucerne and young corn, and also in hayfields, fields of root crops and tussocky grassland. A great deal remains to be discovered about its feeding habits, but the seeds of weeds and grasses apparently form the main part of its diet.

Hunters have always taken their toll of quail, but in the early part of the 20th century the birds were netted live, too. London was one of the main exporting centres for this trade, which was halted by law in 1937.

RECOGNITION: *sandy-brown above, paler below; light streaks on flanks; liable to be confused with young partridge, but is distinguished by buff streaks on head and absence of chestnut on tail; cock has long pale stripe over eye; hen drabber than cock, with black spots on breast.*
NESTING: *hen makes scrape in ground among crops or grass, thinly lined with grass or leaves; lays late May–June; usually 7–12 eggs, pale cream, marbled with shades of brown; incubation 18–21 days, by hen only; chicks, tended by hen, leave after a few hours, begin to fly after about 11 days.*
FEEDING: *mainly seeds of grasses and weeds; also snails, caterpillars.*

Corncrake

Crex crex 10½ in.

THE rasping voice of the corncrake, like a piece of wood repeatedly drawn against the teeth of a comb, was once a familiar sound in the English countryside. But during the past 80 years the bird has become virtually extinct as a breeding species over much of Britain. Only in western parts of Ireland and Scotland are any numbers left, and there, too, they are decreasing.

The reason for this decline is not known for certain, but it is probably connected with changes in the method and time of mowing hay. In the 19th century, many hay meadows were either scythed or at least mown later in the year than today, giving corncrakes time to rear their young in the long grass. Modern mechanical haymaking and grass-cutting for silage leads to the destruction of both the nest and the sitting bird.

The corncrake is a relative of the coot and the moorhen and is sometimes called the landrail. Like many of the rails, it is shy and skulking, more often heard than seen. Its insistent, rasping voice—which gave rise to its curious scientific name, *Crex crex*—serves as a song with which to announce its territorial claims. The bird used to winter in small numbers in Britain, but is now reduced to the status of a summer visitor, when it feeds in fields of long grass and sometimes in damp, sedgy meadows or along hedges.

RECOGNITION: *brown, streaked darker above, with chestnut on wings; paler below, with dark bars on flanks; sexes alike.*
NESTING: *nest of dried grasses is always on ground well hidden in thick vegetation, and may sometimes be domed; lays May–June; usually 8–12 eggs, pale cream, heavily spotted with red-brown and grey; incubation about 16 days, mainly by female; chicks, tended by both parents, leave nest a few hours after hatching, fly after about 5 weeks.*
FEEDING: *grasshoppers, earwigs, beetles, crane-flies and other insects; slugs, small snails, earthworms and millipedes; some vegetable food, such as rush seeds.*

April–Sept. visitor; formerly nested widely, now mainly in Ireland and western Scotland

Highly migratory, wintering mainly in the southern half of Africa and southern Asia

In flight, the corncrake trails its legs behind its body

Wood-pigeon

Columba palumbus 16 in.

Present all year; population has greatly increased, even in treeless areas and big cities

Mainly sedentary, but some Scandinavian birds migrate as far south as Mediterranean

In flight, the wood-pigeon shows its handsome wing markings

No bird is a greater enemy of the British farmer than the gentle-looking wood-pigeon, largest of our pigeons and doves. Practically all year round it ravages crops: from January to March it settles on fields of clover and sainfoin, moving in on green crops in hard weather; in early spring it feeds on arable fields, taking newly sown grain, peas, charlock and wild mustard; in summer it takes ripe and ripening grain; and in autumn it stays in the fields, feeding among stubble. By laying its eggs usually in August and September, it is raising its young just when the year's harvest is ripening.

In spite of having so many enemies among farmers, the wood-pigeon's numbers have increased fairly rapidly in recent years. Destruction of nests has proved the most effective method of control.

Although it feeds so widely on farmland, the wood-pigeon has readily adapted itself to town parks and large gardens, where it can become tame enough to feed out of the hand.

The song is the well-known cooing phrase, usually made up of five notes: 'coooo-coo, coo-coo, coo'.

In courtship the male has an up-and-down flight, with wings clapping as it flies up; and displays on the ground include bowing, mutual caressing with the bill, and courtship feeding.

RECOGNITION: *head, neck and tail grey, with black tip on tail and green, purple and white patch at side of adult's neck; back and wings grey-brown, with white wing-patch; breast pale purple-grey; sexes alike.*
NESTING: *female builds flat platform of twigs, usually in tree but sometimes in bush, ivy, on ledge of building or even on ground; may lay in any month, but mainly August–September; usually 2 eggs, white; incubation 17 days, by both sexes; young, fed by both sexes with 'pigeon's milk' from crop, leave after 16–20 days; usually at least two broods.*
FEEDING: *mainly cereals and clover, but also wild fruit and seeds; at times bread and scraps, brassicas and a little animal food.*

Stock dove
Columba oenas 13 in.

A bird as adaptable as the stock dove, which can breed in any kind of country from farmland, woods and parks to rocks, cliffs, old buildings and sand-dunes, might be expected to thrive in modern Britain. Its numbers declined in the 1960s—perhaps the result of poisoning from agricultural chemicals, particularly seed-dressing—but have recovered since.

Whatever its breeding habitat, the stock dove relies heavily on farmland to provide it with food throughout the year. In winter it feeds on stubble-fields, often with flocks of wood-pigeons, concentrating on the seeds of fat-hen, knot-grass and other weeds. In spring it turns to chickweed, charlock and other early flowering weeds, continuing in summer with charlock even in preference to cultivated grains. In autumn it returns to the stubble-fields, and knot-grass.

Its gruff voice, a coughing or double grunting note with the accent on the second syllable, is different from the wood-pigeon's cooing. The stock dove's display flight is also distinctive. Male and female fly round in circles, sometimes gliding on raised wings.

Stock doves are social birds, and tend to breed in loose colonies in suitable places; but territorial disputes still break out between males. They threaten one another on the ground, striking out with their wings.

RECOGNITION: *grey plumage ; distinguished from rock dove by having no white rump ; two short black bars on each wing ; smaller than wood-pigeon and lacks its conspicuous white markings on wings ; sexes alike.*
NESTING: *usually nests in hole in tree, on building, cliff or sand-pit, or in nest-box or rabbit burrow ; no nesting material in holes ; lays late March–September ; usually 2 eggs, white ; incubation about 17 days, by both sexes ; nestlings, fed by both sexes, fly after about 4 weeks ; usually two broods, often three.*
FEEDING: *mainly seeds of weeds and grain ; some animal food, especially cocoons of earthworms.*

Present all year; breeding range includes most of Britain; largely sedentary

Essentially sedentary; northern-most breeding birds migrate a short distance south in winter

In flight, the stock dove shows two black bars on each wing

75

Little owl
Athene noctua 8½ in.

Present all year; introduced to Northamptonshire and Kent in late 19th century and has spread north

Essentially sedentary; lives mainly in lightly wooded country and in semi-desert regions

Little owls often sit on telephone poles or wires in daylight

SOON after it was introduced to Northamptonshire and Kent from the Continent, towards the end of the 19th century, the little owl became one of Britain's most controversial birds. It spread rapidly, and as it spread it fell foul of ever greater numbers of gamekeepers. They accused the little owl of every crime in their calendar, until it seemed as if in their eyes, the bird existed entirely on a diet of pheasant and partridge chicks.

However, one of the earliest investigations launched by the British Trust for Ornithology proved that the charges were unfounded. About half the bird's diet is made up of insects, especially cockchafers and other beetles, earwigs and crane-flies, whose leatherjacket larvae are among the farmer's most serious pests; and the bird is now protected by law, along with native owls. While there is no doubt that game-chicks are taken, they form only a minute part of the diet.

The little owl, our smallest and most common day-flying owl, is a bird of the open countryside. It flies by night, too, and hunts mainly at dusk and dawn. The flight is conspicuously bounding or undulating, with occasional hovering. It can often be seen perched near its nest, on a post, telephone pole, or a haystack, bobbing its body and wagging its tail when anyone approaches it. The commonest call-note of the little owl is a low, plaintive 'kiew-kiew'; there is also an infrequent song, which closely resembles the opening sequence of the curlew's song.

RECOGNITION: *grey-brown plumage, barred and mottled with white; rounded wings, short tail and bounding flight; sexes alike.*
NESTING: *no nest material; nest in hole, usually in tree but also in walls, buildings, cliffs, quarries, sand-pits or burrows in the ground; lays late April–early May; usually 3–5 eggs, white; incubation about 28 days, by female only; nestlings, fed by both parents, fly after about 5 weeks.*
FEEDING: *insects, including beetles, earwigs and crane-flies; voles, mice, young rats and other small mammals; some small birds, frogs and lizards.*

MALE

Barn owl

Tyto alba   13½ in.

THE ghostly form of a barn owl looks white when it is caught in a car's headlights at night; but towards the end of winter when food is so scarce that the bird is forced to hunt by day, its true colour can be seen—a golden buff, with white underparts.

When hunting, it does not rely on sight alone. Experiments have shown that the barn owl can locate its prey in pitch darkness by its sense of hearing; with ears placed asymmetrically on its head, so that there is a fractional interval between the sounds picked up by each ear, it has unusually precise powers of pinpointing the slightest sound made by the small mammals which it hunts. Hardly any noise is made by the bird as it swoops on a victim. But there is nothing muffled about the owl's cry—a prolonged, strangled shriek.

Barn owls were once much more common. Their decline is something of a mystery, for it began long before some other birds of prey were affected by the build-up of pesticides in their bodies. The loss of their main feeding habitat—permanent grassland—has had an effect. Also, as the countryside becomes more efficient, there are fewer abandoned buildings and hollow trees for them to use as nesting sites. They do not build nests but lay their eggs on a heap of pellets made up of the indigestible fur, feathers and bones of their prey.

RECOGNITION: *golden buff with white face and underparts; female slightly greyer.*
NESTING: *no nest material; eggs laid on disgorged pellets; sites include old barns, ruined buildings, church towers, hollow trees, quarry faces, cornricks and nest-boxes; laying recorded in every month except January, but main period is April–early May; 4–6 eggs, white; incubation about 33 days, by female only; nestlings, fed by both parents, fly after 9–12 weeks; often two broods.*
FEEDING: *shrews, mice, field voles, bank voles, water voles, brown rats, moles; small birds; beetles, moths; frogs, sometimes bats and fish.*

Present all year; has much decreased in recent years, particularly in eastern England

Mainly sedentary, but birds from central Europe disperse over considerable distances

In their silent flight, barn owls show white undersides of wings

Rook

Corvus frugilegus 18 in.

Present all year; now nests in all counties, including Shetland—colonised as recently as 1952

Partial migrant; breeding birds from colder areas migrate as far as Mediterranean

Rooks start revisiting their rookeries in late autumn

ROOKS are among the most sociable of birds, with a communal life so well developed that it has given rise to fanciful stories of 'rook parliaments'. Although they nest in colonies and feed in flocks, rooks have a strong sense of territory. Pairs defend a small area around their nests, threatening and driving off intruders. Sometimes they steal sticks from the nests of neighbouring pairs while the rightful owners are away collecting more nesting material. Misinterpretations of aggressive behaviour in the defence of territory have led some observers to claim that they have seen a circle of rooks sitting in judgment on 'criminal' birds.

The treetop rookeries, loud with hoarse cawing, are often near buildings and may even be in cities. They are usually permanent communities; pairs of rooks use the same nest each year, repairing it for each new breeding season. Rookeries vary considerably in size; many contain only a few dozen nests, but one colony in northeast Scotland once held as many as 9000 pairs.

In courtship the male feeds the female—as he does again when she is incubating—and the male bows and caws to the female in the tree tops. The spectacular aerial displays which rooks put on in the autumn, when they tumble, twist and dive headlong through the air, seem to have no connection with courtship.

RECOGNITION: *black with purple gloss; bare, grey-white patches on face and base of bill; thick thigh feathers give 'baggy breeches' effect; young do not have face patch; sexes alike.*
NESTING: *nests in colonies, normally in trees; both sexes build untidy nest of sticks, lined with dry grass, leaves and roots, and often added to each year; lays late March–April; usually 3–6 eggs, pale green to grey or pale blue, heavily flecked with grey and brown; incubation about 18 days, by female only; nestlings, fed by both parents, fly after about 30 days.*
FEEDING: *wireworms, leatherjackets and other insects and larvae; earthworms, snails, grain and weed seeds, fruit; sometimes carrion, shellfish.*

Carrion crow

Corvus corone corone 18½ in.

NOTORIOUS as an egg-thief, the carrion crow has for long been on the black lists of gamekeepers and those responsible for looking after ornamental water-fowl in parks. However, the breathing space allowed by two world wars, when gamekeeping was relaxed to free men for more pressing duties, gave the bird all the opportunity it needed to expand.

Today, its hoarse cry can be heard even above the grinding of London traffic. One of its call-notes sounds oddly like a motor horn; but the chief call is a hoarse 'kaaah', usually uttered three times in succession.

Like some of the gulls, the carrion crow has found a way of smashing open shells, such as those of mussels, crabs and walnuts, by dropping them from a height. This habit suggests that the carrion crow is quicker to learn than most birds—as are all of the crow family.

There are a good many exceptions to the rule that rooks are gregarious birds and crows are solitary or seen only in pairs. Family parties of carrion crows are common in summer, and in autumn and winter they sometimes gather in flocks, to roost in trees.

Courtship consists mainly of bowing by the male, with wings spread and tail fanned; and once the birds are paired, they stay together for life. Their bulky nests of twigs and dry grass are usually high in trees.

RECOGNITION: *black plumage; distinguished from adult rook by fully feathered base of bill (rook has bare face-patch, though young rooks start with faces feathered); sexes alike.*
NESTING: *both sexes build bulky nest of twigs lined with dried grass, dead leaves and sheep's wool, usually in tree or on cliff ledge; lays April–May; usually 3–5 eggs, light blue or green, spotted with dark grey-brown; incubation about 19 days, by female only; nestlings, fed by both parents, fly after 30–35 days.*
FEEDING: *grain, insects and their larvae, worms; eggs and carrion; also wild fruit and seeds, snails, frogs and sometimes small mammals.*

Present all year; gradually spreading north in Scotland; not yet established in Ireland

Partial migrant; map combines distributions of the closely related carrion and hooded crows

Carrion, nestling birds and eggs are eaten by carrion crows

Magpie

Pica pica   18 in. (including 8–10 in. tail)

Present all year; almost unknown outside its breeding range, but expanding in Scotland

Sedentary; the map includes the range of the yellow-billed magpie of California

Short wings and long tail make magpies distinctive in flight

Some of the magpie's feeding habits make it highly unpopular among game preservers, so that it tends to be scarce in areas which are heavily keepered. It was exterminated by keepers in areas of Norfolk before the First World War, but numbers have increased everywhere with the reductions in gamekeeping since then. In the past 50 years, the magpie has moved into many towns and cities, and has successfully colonised even the central parks of London.

The magpie robs other birds' nests, including those of partridge and pheasant, of eggs and young; and this is what has upset gamekeepers. But the greater part of its food consists of insects and grain.

Magpies usually go about alone or in pairs, but late in winter or early in spring as many as 100 or more may be seen in ceremonial gatherings, whose purpose is not understood. They chatter, jump about in branches and chase each other. The hoarding instinct, common to all crows, is highly developed in magpies. They are liable to hide not only surplus food but also any colourful or shiny object which takes their fancy.

The courtship displays of this common but shy bird are complicated and little understood. On some occasions male birds have been seen hovering a foot or so above their mates.

RECOGNITION: *boldly contrasting iridescent black and white plumage; long, wedge-shaped tail; sexes alike.*
NESTING: *both sexes build domed structure of twigs in bush or tree, with lining of mud covered with rootlets; usually lays April–May; usually 4–7 eggs, light green closely speckled with grey-brown; incubation about 21 days, by female only; nestlings, fed by both parents, leave after about 27 days.*
FEEDING: *insects and their larvae, grain, wild fruit and seeds, eggs and young of other birds, small animals and carrion; at times frogs, snails and bread.*

Jackdaw

Corvus monedula 13 in.

M OST crows are robbers, but none is a bigger thief than the jackdaw. It not only steals eggs and chicks when it gets the chance, but it will sometimes pick up useless, inedible objects and hide them away. It will perch on horses or sheep and pluck out tufts of hair to line its nest; and occasionally it even steals a home, making a cranny for itself in the base of the pile of sticks forming a rook's nest.

Jackdaws—once simply called 'daws'—regularly feed alongside rooks or starlings in the fields, though they may also be seen on their own, especially on sea cliffs, around cathedrals and other craggy buildings, and in parkland with old trees. They will eat almost anything that comes their way, but there is a heavy emphasis on animal food and grain in their diet. Often, flocks of them roost in their old nesting-sites, where they set up a clamour with their clipped, metallic calls of 'kow' or 'kyow'. There is also a softer 'tchack'.

Their numbers have greatly increased this century: the reason is unknown, but is perhaps connected with changes in cultivation.

Courtship is elaborate. The male bows, with wings and tail outspread, and sometimes it displays its grey nape by raising the crown feathers while pressing its bill against its breast.

RECOGNITION: *black, with grey nape; flies with fast wing-beats; sexes alike.*
NESTING: *both sexes make untidy pile of sticks, lined with wool or hair, nearly always in hole or crevice in tree, cliff or building and often in a chimney; lays April–May; 3–6 eggs, light blue with black spots and blotches; incubation about 18 days, by female only; nestlings, fed by both parents, fly after 30 days.*
FEEDING: *insects and their larvae, grain, weed seeds, wild and cultivated fruit; sometimes small animals, eggs and young of other birds, potatoes and carrion.*

Present all year; expanding species, now nests in all counties; British birds are mainly sedentary

Partial migrant; some northern birds winter in west and south of the breeding range

Jackdaws sometimes pluck wool from backs of sheep

Fieldfare

Turdus pilaris   10 in.

Sept.–April visitor; a few
now nest each year, mainly
in northern Britain

First colonised Greenland
in 1937; mainly migratory,
but movements are irregular

In winter, flocks of fieldfares are
often seen feeding in the fields

FLOCKS of fieldfares, sometimes hundreds strong, flying overhead in loose formation, can usually be identified by the clamouring, chattering call, 'chack-chack'. This is sometimes varied by a higher-pitched 'week' from a bird which has lost touch with the others and wants to regain contact. They migrate to Britain in the autumn from their breeding grounds in northern Europe, and range over all kinds of rough, open country, including open woodland. They rest or feed on farmland, playing-fields, marshes and, in hard weather, in parks and large gardens.

It was not until 1967 that a pair of fieldfares nested in Britain, in Orkney; since then, up to a dozen pairs have bred annually, mainly in northern Britain. Previous to 1967, 'sightings' were of mistle thrushes, though the two species should not be mistaken for each other. They are about the same size, and both show white flashes under their wings in flight, but the fieldfare is easily identified by its blue-grey head and rump—features which have given rise to one of its country names, 'blue-back'.

This large thrush is unusually aggressive at its breeding grounds; combined attacks by members of the colony can rout animal intruders and this possibly explains the colonial nesting habit, which is unusual in thrushes.

RECOGNITION : *blue-grey head, nape and rump ; chestnut back, dark tail and speckled brown breast ; sexes alike.*
NESTING : *very rarely nests in Britain ; nest of mud, roots and grass built chiefly by hen, usually in tree or bush ; lays April or May–July ; usually 5 or 6 eggs, green or blue-green with red-brown spots ; incubation about 14 days, chiefly by hen ; nestlings, fed by both parents, leave after about 14 days.*
FEEDING : *wild fruit ; garden berries, such as those of pyracantha and cotoneaster ; also insects such as earthworms, snails, beetles, leatherjackets and caterpillars.*

Redwing

Turdus iliacus 8¼ in.

THIS smallest of our thrushes is, like the fieldfare, a winter visitor from northern Europe. But it has come farther than the fieldfare towards establishing itself as a breeding bird as well as a visitor. The redwing was first proved to breed in Britain when a nest was found in Sutherland in 1925; and it has nested here and in other parts of northern Scotland regularly since 1953. The breeding population is now thought to number around 50 pairs.

Redwings often feed alongside fieldfares in farmland, parks, playing-fields and other open grassland. They perish in large numbers during severe winters when the earth is frozen too deep for them to dig up food.

The most frequently heard call-note is a thin, high-pitched 'see-ih', often given by flocks migrating overhead at night. Other notes include a soft 'chup' and a harsher 'chittuck' or 'chittick'. The true song is rarely heard in Britain, but a few stilted, fluting phrases from it sometimes occur in the communal warbling sub-song, with which flocks often greet the approach of spring.

Redwings breeding in Scotland have usually built their nests in birchwoods or areas of scrub; but in Scandinavia they often rest in town parks and gardens, too, and this pattern could be repeated in Britain if their colonisation really gets under way.

RECOGNITION: *rather smaller than song-thrush, from which it can be told by prominent white eye-stripe and red patches on flanks and under wing; sexes alike.*

NESTING: *grass cup, on foundation of twigs and earth, is built in tree, bush or on ground, probably by female only, and sometimes decorated with moss or lichen; lays mid-May–July; usually 4–6 eggs, blue-green with red-brown markings; incubation about 13 days, probably by both parents; nestlings, fed by both parents, leave after about 14 days.*

FEEDING: *earthworms, snails, caterpillars, beetles and their larvae; haws and other wild fruit; occasionally apples.*

Mainly Sept.–April visitor, but has bred regularly in northern Scotland since 1953

Winters south of breeding range in western and southern Europe, N. Africa and south-west Asia

In flight, redwings utter a plaintive, high-pitched call-note

Swallow

Hirundo rustica 7½ in.

MALE

Late March–Oct. visitor; widespread, but absent from city centres; our birds winter in S. Africa

Migratory; wintering in tropical S. America, Africa, and south and south-east Asia

Swallows fly with agile grace in pursuit of flying insects

T HE saying 'One swallow does not make a summer' is based on accurate observation of the birds; when swallows begin to return from their winter quarters in Africa at the end of March or early April, they arrive at first in one's and two's. It is not until mid- or late April that they are here in force, and summer is on the way.

They must have been familiar birds for centuries, to have been drawn on for a folk proverb; but today there is evidence that swallows are decreasing. From more than a dozen counties have come post-war reports of a decline in their numbers, with improved farm hygiene regarded as the most likely cause. Most swallows in Britain nest in farm buildings, and improvements in milking parlours and barns have hit their food supplies by reducing the numbers of insects. Ringing has proved that swallows often return year after year to the same nest. They often nest in loose colonies, and gather with martins on migration or when feeding. Their most common call-note is a twittering 'tswit, tswit, tswit' and the alarm note 'tsink, tsink'. The twittering song is given from a perch or on the wing.

Swallows, martins and swifts look somewhat alike, because what scientists call convergent evolution has made swifts develop a build similar to that of the other two species, with all three adapted to a life spent in catching flying insects. Swallows and martins are closely related but swifts belong to a quite distinct Order of birds.

RECOGNITION : *steel-blue upper parts ; chestnut forehead and breast ; long streamers on forked tail ; female's tail is slightly shorter than male's.*
NESTING : *both sexes build saucer-shaped nest of mud and dried grasses lined with feathers, usually on ledge or rafter in building ; lays May–August ; usually 3–6 eggs, white, heavily speckled with red-brown ; incubation about 15 days, by hen ; nestlings, fed by both parents, leave after 18–21 days.*
FEEDING : *flying insects, sometimes including dragonflies and butterflies.*

Skylark

Alauda arvensis 7 in.

FOR Wordsworth, the skylark was an ethereal minstrel, a pilgrim of the sky; for Shelley it was a blithe spirit, showering the earth with a rain of melody; and lesser poets before and since have added their praises until it has become one of Britain's best-loved birds. Its sustained warbling song, which can last for five minutes without a pause, is usually delivered when the bird is flying high in the air, often nearly out of sight. The skylark is the only British bird which habitually sings while ascending almost vertically, keeps singing while hovering and goes on singing while descending.

A spring day on the downs of southern England or on the moors of the north, when the air is full of the sound of singing skylarks, is an unforgettable experience.

In the breeding season, skylarks nest in any kind of open country, from sand-dunes at sea level to peat bogs and moors on the mountains. Their singing, which has the twin objectives of defending territory and attracting females, is heard regularly from late January to early July, and less often at other times of the year— particularly in August and September, when they are fairly silent. After the breeding season they are often gregarious, gathering in flocks to feed and to migrate. Our home-bred birds are joined by winter visitors and passage migrants from Europe.

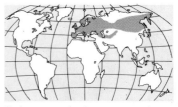

Present all year; many migrants from northern Europe occur here widely on passage and in winter

Sedentary and migratory; northern populations winter in southern parts of the breeding range

RECOGNITION: *streaky brown; white outer tail feathers show in flight; characteristic soaring song-flight; small crest and white line along trailing edge of the wing; sexes alike.*
NESTING: *hen builds cup nest of grass, sometimes lined with hair, on ground; lays April–August; usually 3 or 4 eggs, white, thickly speckled with brown; incubation about 11 days, by hen only; nestlings, fed by both parents, leave nest after 8 days, fly after 16 days; two or three broods.*
FEEDING: *seeds of charlock, chickweed, sow thistle, sorrel and other weeds; leaves of clover and other plants; earthworms, caterpillars, beetles and their larvae, spiders and other small ground animals; some grain.*

Skylark hovers high in the sky in full-throated song

Yellowhammer

Emberiza citrinella 6½ in.

MALE

Present all year; widespread and common, though found only rarely in Outer Hebrides and Shetland

In the eastern part of this range the yellowhammer is replaced by the migratory pine bunting

Yellowhammer perches by the roadside, singing

LIKE most other buntings—all of them seed-eating birds, with short sharp-pointed beaks—the yellowhammer avoids areas of human settlement; it rarely enters a garden, even in the countryside. Yet it is not particularly shy of people; its song, the traditional 'little-bit-of-bread-and-no-cheese' (a Scottish version is 'deil-deil-deil-tak ye') may be heard from almost any roadside hedge from late February until the middle of August, and in some years through to early November. The yellowhammer's song is a familiar sound, too, on bushy heaths and commons, and sometimes on farmland where there are few hedges, but only dykes or field banks. It is often given from a favourite song-post.

Courtship, when a mate has been attracted, includes a chase in which cock pursues hen in twisting flight, at the end of which they may fall to the ground and mate. The cock may also parade around the hen, wings and tail spread and crest erect.

In winter, yellowhammers become gregarious, and often flock with other seed-eaters to feed over stubble-fields and rick-yards. Their call-notes are a sibilant, liquid 'twit-up' and a somewhat grunting 'twink' or 'twit'. Some yellowhammers from Europe come to Britain in winter, but there is no evidence that our native birds leave for warmer countries, or even that within these islands there is much drift southwards.

RECOGNITION: *cock has bright yellow and chestnut plumage; hen duller, more streaked with brown; bright chestnut rump and white sides to tail.*
NESTING: *hen builds nest of dried grasses, lined with finer grass and hair, well hidden, on ground, bank, hedge, ivy or on wall; rarely more than 4 ft up; lays April–August; usually 2–5 eggs, white or pale pink with brown or purple-brown squiggles; incubation about 13 days, by hen only; young, fed by both sexes, fly after 11–13 days; two broods, sometimes three.*
FEEDING: *largely seeds of weeds, with some grain and wild fruit; also insects and small ground animals.*

Tree sparrow

Passer montanus 5½ in.

Dᴜʀɪɴɢ most of this century the tree sparrow has been in retreat, to the point where it almost disappeared from Ireland and many parts of Scotland. But in the 1960s its numbers increased again, with the bird returning to nest in some remote western and northern coastal areas. In the 1990s it was in retreat again, and is now scarce even in former strongholds in eastern England. Its fluctuations may be linked to periodic but increasingly erratic irruptions from the Continent.

Tree sparrows are gregarious birds, breeding in small, loose colonies and often flocking in winter with house sparrows, finches and buntings. In the breeding season they prefer areas with old trees, such as parks, derelict orchards, river banks and even large gardens, especially those with nest-boxes. Less commonly they nest in old buildings, haystacks, quarries and the rocky cliffs of windswept islands. In autumn and winter they feed over stubble-fields and rick-yards.

The tree sparrow chirrups like a house sparrow, but its voice is shriller and its 'chip, chip' and 'teck, teck' notes are distinctive. The simple, chirruping song is delivered from a tree-perch and is sometimes sung in chorus. The male's courtship displays include bowing, spreading the wings and raising the crown feathers.

RECOGNITION: *brown back; grey underparts; can be told from house sparrow by smaller size, and combination of chestnut crown, smaller black bib and black spot on each cheek; sexes alike.*
NESTING: *both sexes build nest of dried grass, straw and similar materials, lined with feathers, usually in hole, but domed when built in open; nest-boxes sometimes used; normally lays late April–July; usually 3–5 eggs, white, often with heavy blotches of brown or chestnut; incubation about 11 days, by both parents; nestlings, fed by both parents, leave after 13–15 days; two broods, sometimes three.*
FEEDING: *mainly seeds of weeds, some grain; also insects and larvae.*

Present all year; declining; now scarce and local in many parts of the breeding range

Mainly sedentary, but birds in central and northern Europe are short-distance migrants

Tree sparrows make their nests in tree holes or sometimes nest-boxes

Cirl bunting

Emberiza cirlus 6¼ in.

MALE

Present all year; breeding formerly extended from Kent to north Wales

Sedentary; lives mainly in sheltered, sunny places

Cirl bunting perches on a bramble—it sometimes feeds in flocks with other seed-eaters

P RIMARILY, the cirl bunting is a Mediterranean species, and its remnant distribution in south-west England suggests that it is not well able to withstand our winter climate. This close relative of the yellowhammer is now one of our rarest breeding birds, its range shrinking from one which once took in much of Wales and southern England, to one restricted to a tiny area of south Devon and Cornwall, where fewer than 400 pairs remain. Here, the climate seems to be just bearable, for cirl buntings do not migrate and depend mainly on the local stubble-fields for their winter food. Hedgerows, usually with trees, are important in their preferred farmland habitat. Unlike other buntings, cirls will visit and even nest in large gardens.

Its normal song, often given from a song-post in the tree tops, is a brief, trilling rattle, quite distinct from the yellowhammer's song. But a rare variant is like the yellowhammer's 'little-bit-of-bread-and-no-cheese' without the terminal 'cheese'. The call-note is a sharp 'zit', with a wren-like 'chur' when the bird is alarmed.

The cirl bunting's courtship display has never been recorded; but this does not mean that it has none, for the bird is extremely secretive and retiring. But it has been recorded luring predators away from its young by fluttering along the ground as if injured.

RECOGNITION: *brown back, yellow underparts; cock distinguished from cock yellowhammer by black throat, grey crown and grey-green band across breast; hen distinguished by olive rump.*
NESTING: *hen builds bulky, untidy nest of grass and roots on foundation of moss, in bush or hedge, sometimes in tree or on ground; lays May–August; usually 3 or 4 eggs, light blue or light green with bold dark streaks and scribbling; incubation about 12 days, by hen only; nestlings, normally fed by hen, fly after 11–13 days; two broods, sometimes three.*
FEEDING: *predominantly weed and grass seeds, with corn or wild fruit; also insects, such as beetles, grasshoppers and caterpillars.*

Corn bunting

Emberiza calandra 7 in.

SOME birds are monogamous and some are polygamous; but the corn bunting may be either. There is a record—not accepted by all ornithologists— of individual buntings running harems of up to seven hens, each with its separate nest, and breeding in the same area as single-mated birds. The cock selects a song-perch, at any height from a clod of earth to 40 ft up a tree, from which it can keep an eye on its nest, or at least on the route used by the incubating female when she leaves the nest to feed. The song it gives from its perch sounds like the jangling of a bunch of keys.

To look at, the corn bunting is one of our more un-distinguished brown birds, and its lack of glamour in the eyes of many bird-watchers may help to explain why it was not until the 1930's that its polygamous habits were suspected.

It is a bird of the open country, ranging over treeless farmland, downland and areas of rough grazing. But though able to live in many different environments, corn buntings are distributed in a curious way. It is possible to travel for miles in country apparently suit-able for the bird, but see and hear no corn buntings; and then, as though crossing some invisible boundary, to find suddenly that they are common.

The bird has declined seriously over the past two dec-ades, possibly due to changes in agricultural practices.

RECOGNITION: *streaked, dull brown plumage; heavy head and pale bill; 'jangling keys' song identifies male in summer; sexes alike.*
NESTING: *hen builds untidy nest of dried grass, well hidden among coarse vegetation on or near ground; lays late May–July; normally 3–5 eggs, pale grey or pale brown with heavy black-brown streaks and lines; incu-bation 12 or 13 days, by hen only; nestlings, usually fed by hen only, start to fly after 9–11 days; usually two broods in south, one in Scotland.*
FEEDING: *weed seeds, leaves and grasses and occasionally a little grain; also insects and small ground animals.*

Present all year; numbers have much decreased in recent years

Sedentary in all parts of its range; occurs mainly on cultivated land

Hour after hour the corn bunting sings its monotonous, jangling song from a bush, post or stem

Kestrel

Falco tinnunculus 13½ in.

MALE

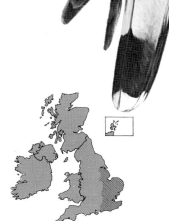

Present all year; widespread on farmland, moorland, sea cliffs, and even in central London

Mainly sedentary, but northern breeding birds migrate as far south as northern Africa

A hovering kestrel watches for movement that might indicate prey

LIKE all birds of prey, the kestrel is protected by law throughout the year; but unlike many of the others, it is not in desperate need of this protection. Farmers recognise the bird as a useful ally against mice, rats, voles and harmful insects; and enlightened game-keepers are prepared to overlook the occasional game-chick it takes, because of its value as a destroyer of pests.

Partly because it does not have to face persecution, and partly because it can adapt to many different kinds of country, the kestrel has become by far the commonest of Britain's day-flying birds of prey. It is equally at home in farmland, moorland and along sea cliffs.

In recent years it has become very much an urban bird, too; in central London, its nesting places have included a tower of the House of Lords. Its hovering flight, with tail fanned out and wings flapping vigorously as it watches the ground for voles and mice, is also a familiar sight along motorway verges.

The main call-note is a shrill 'kee-kee-kee-kee', but it is not often given unless birds are 'playing' together, or the male is chasing the female in courtship. In another courtship ceremony which has been recorded, the male was seen to beat upwind, then fly down fast at the female, which was sitting in a bush. Just when he seemed about to strike her, he shot up in the air. This performance was repeated several times.

RECOGNITION: *pointed wings and long tail; male has blue-grey head, rump and tail, with black band at end of tail; female has barred tail, also with black band; hovering flight is distinctive.*
NESTING: *no nest built; eggs laid on cliff ledge, or high building, tree hole or abandoned nest of other bird; lays mid-April–May; usually 3–5 eggs, white, with heavy red-brown markings; incubation about 28 days, mainly by female; nestlings, fed by both parents, fly after 27–30 days.*
FEEDING: *mainly mice, voles and young rats; also frogs, earthworms and insects; sparrows and other birds in towns.*

HEATHLAND

Heaths and commons, semi-wild places where
for centuries birds were little disturbed by man,
are today a shrinking habitat. Land reclamation, the
military use of 'waste' land, road-building and the advance
of suburbia have all made their encroachments. It is seldom
possible to assign a major decline in bird populations
to a single cause, but there is no doubt that the
heathland birds have suffered heavily from the
whittling away of their breeding grounds.

CONTENTS

Montagu's harrier

Circus pygargus   M 15½ in.   F 17 in.

MALE

Late April–Sept. visitor; among Britain's rarest breeding birds

Migratory; a few winter near the Mediterranean, but the majority fly to tropical Africa

Male Montagu's harrier floats low over heathland and marshes

FLOCKS of Montagu's harriers more than 70 strong have been seen in North Africa, during the long autumn migration flight between their breeding grounds in Europe and winter quarters which are often as far south as the Cape of Good Hope.

The birds usually nest on heaths, in marshland or among farm crops. They are confined to southern England and even there they have declined so seriously that they are now among our rarest breeding birds. There are fewer than 12 nests each year.

Montagu's harrier—named after an early 19th century Devon naturalist, Colonel George Montagu—has the same graceful, buoyant way of flying as our two other breeding harriers, the marsh harrier and the hen-harrier. It is the smallest of the three—the male is not much bigger than a wood-pigeon. The female is like a small female hen-harrier, with less white on the rump.

A safe way of telling them apart in southern England is by the time of year when they are seen. Hen-harriers, which breed farther north, are winter visitors in the south; Montagu's harriers arrive in April and leave in autumn, so that the two birds usually overlap for only a few weeks in spring and autumn. The courtship display consists of spectacular dives, somersaults and loops by the male.

RECOGNITION: *male has grey upper parts, is distinguished from hen-harrier by dark bars on wings and grey, not white, rump; female slimmer than hen-harrier with less white on rump.*
NESTING: *female builds nest of weeds, reeds or grass on ground in rough open country—heaths, downs, sand-dunes, marshes, young plantations, sometimes farmland; lays late May–early June; usually 4 or 5 eggs, white or pale blue; incubation about 30 days, by female only; male does all the hunting during incubation; nestlings, tended by both parents, fly after 4–5 weeks.*
FEEDING: *small mammals, birds and frogs; some insects and earthworms.*

Hobby

Falco subbuteo 13 in.

T HE scythe-shaped wings of the hobby carry it so
rapidly on its hunting flights over downs or heaths
that it can fly down a swift, or even catch a bat in flight.
This handsome falcon is agile enough to twist and turn
after a dragonfly, snatch the insect in its claws and hold
it to its beak to eat, without pausing in flight. Hobbies
sometimes pluck small birds on the wing, though with
bigger prey it is more usual to take the victim to a
branch or to the ground before plucking it.

Hobbies seem to fly for sheer joy, tumbling, gliding
upside-down and looping the loop alone or in family
groups. Their mastery of the air plays an important part
in courtship, when male and female circle together in
long, soaring flights, during which the male 'stoops' at
the female, as if preparing to attack her. After snatching
a small bird, the male climbs high to dive on the female
and pass the prey to her in the air at full speed.

The birds usually breed in open country with scattered
trees in which they may find the old nests of crows and
sometimes sparrowhawks, or even squirrels' dreys. The
hobbies take over, and may remove some lining from
the abandoned nest. Their eggs are laid in June, and the
hatching of the young hobbies a month later coincides
with an abundance of swallows on which they can be
fed. Although thinly dispersed, several hundred pairs
breed in England and Wales.

April–Sept. visitor; recent
increase and northwards
spread to English midlands

Migratory in most parts of range;
in winter it is found mainly in
tropical Africa

RECOGNITION : *slate-grey back ; black 'moustache', white breast and underparts streaked with black ; red thighs ; female similar to male, but slightly
larger ; in flight, scythe-like wings make it look like a large swift.*
NESTING : *takes over abandoned nest high in tree, often a conifer ; lays
June ; usually 3 eggs, white, heavily mottled with red-brown or yellow-
brown ; incubation about 28 days, chiefly by female ; nestlings, fed by both
parents, leave after 28–32 days.*
FEEDING : *grasshoppers, dragonflies and other winged insects ; small birds ;
occasionally bats and larger birds.*

Hobby flies down its prey–often
swallows, martins or swifts

Stone curlew

Burhinus oedicnemus 16 in.

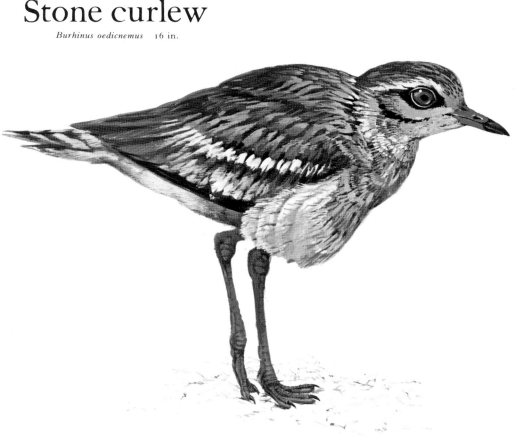

March–Oct. visitor; rarely seen outside breeding areas

Sedentary and migratory; stone curlews from northern Europe winter mainly in N. Africa

In flight, the stone curlew shows the white bars on its wings

To judge by its appearance, the stone curlew could be a wader; its shrill night-time call of 'coo-lee' is like the sound of the curlew. But in fact this rare bird is only distantly related to the curlew; its closest relative could be the oystercatcher. Its favoured habitats in England are the dry sandy heaths of Breckland and east Suffolk, and the chalk downland of the southern counties. Much of this habitat has been converted from grass to crops in the past 50 years, and the survival of the species now largely depends on its ability to fit in its breeding between the farmer's cultivation and harvest.

Stone curlews are believed to mate for life, and they may return year by year to the same nesting territory. Their courtship displays include bowing and touching bills, and the birds have been seen running about excitedly, picking up straws, flints and other small objects and tossing them over their shoulders.

The birds are gregarious, even in the breeding season, calling to one another in the evenings and at night. They form flocks when migration time comes in October. But for all their sociability they are wary, bobbing their heads when suspicious and 'freezing' when taken by surprise; both adults and chicks in the nest crouch low, stretching out their heads and necks and remaining immobile in this pose.

RECOGNITION: *pale buff, streaked with brown; large yellow eyes, pale yellow legs, round head and short bill; sexes alike.*
NESTING: *both sexes make scrapes in ground, near vegetation but not normally among plants; scrape lined with white stones or rabbit droppings; lays late April–July; 2 eggs, buff, usually with heavy brown blotches; incubation about 26 days, by both parents; chicks, tended by both parents, leave soon after hatching, begin to fly after about 40 days; sometimes two broods.*
FEEDING: *snails, slugs, ground insects and their larvae and earthworms; sometimes mice, voles, frogs, and chicks of partridge and pheasant.*

Nightjar

Caprimulgus europaeus   10½ in.

MALE

A<small>T</small> dusk the nightjar leaves its daytime hiding place and takes to the air silently on long, soft-feathered wings, twisting and turning through the twilight as it follows flying insects and traps them in its gaping bill.

It is after sunset, too, that the bird gives its song, the 'churring' sound which gives the nightjar its name. There are abrupt changes of pitch in the 'churr' when the bird turns its head from side to side as it perches along, rarely across, a branch. In flight the nightjar's call is a soft but insistent 'coo-ic', and it makes a sound like a whip-crack with its wings.

During the day, nightjars are almost invisible; they lie motionless on the ground and, at a distance, the delicate marking on their feathers make them look like dead leaves. There are often pieces of wood near the nightjar's nest—an unlined scrape in the ground, to the vicinity of which a pair of birds returns, season after season—and these make the sitting bird even harder to see. Nightjars arrive from Africa in mid-May to breed on heaths, commons and other places with bracken or gorse, as well as on the borders of woodland. Their numbers have been decreasing in Britain for more than 50 years. On its evening flights to catch insects, the nightjar visits pastures where farm animals graze—a habit which has earned the bird its name of 'goatsucker' from a false belief that it milks goats with its huge mouth.

May–Oct. visitor; widely but thinly distributed, and decreasing

Migratory; winters mainly in Africa, from the Sudan south to the Cape of Good Hope

Nightjar feeds mainly at night, catching moths as it flies

RECOGNITION : *night-flying bird with long, hawk-like wings and tail ; grey-brown 'camouflage' plumage ; mouth fringed with bristles ; male has white spots near wing-tips, absent in female ; distinctive 'churring' song.*
NESTING : *nests in unlined scrape in the ground, often near dead wood ; lays late May–July ; 2 eggs, white, marbled with brown or grey ; incubation about 18 days, chiefly by female ; nestlings, fed by both parents, leave nest after about a week but stay nearby, fly after about 17 days ; usually two broods.*
FEEDING : *insects, chiefly those caught in flight.*

Cuckoo

Cuculus canorus   13 in.

April–August visitor; widespread, but the number of breeding birds seems to be decreasing

Mainly migratory, wintering in tropical Africa or southern Asia

Young cuckoo; unguided by adults, the young make their way south to Africa in September

No sound in nature is awaited more eagerly in these islands than the loud, ringing, repeated song of the cuckoo. The male's song, with its promise that summer is not far off, is a national institution, important enough in Britain's country calendar to be dignified by letters to *The Times*. The first cuckoos of the year usually arrive in the second or third week of April from their winter quarters in Africa. March cuckoos are not unknown, but more often than not these early birds turn out to be schoolboys, hoaxing over-eager listeners.

When it is seen on the wing, a cuckoo can easily be mistaken for a male sparrowhawk. But it can be identified by its heavier appearance, pointed wings, and long, graduated tail, spotted and tipped with white.

After their arrival, cuckoos spread out over almost the whole of the British Isles into any kind of country where they can find foster-parents for their young. The double-noted 'cuckoo', heard over woods and thickets, heaths, sand-dunes, moorland and hills, is the male's courtship song. The female has a bubbling trill.

When mating is over, the adult birds leave Britain, flying south in July and early August. Some newly fledged young linger until September after leaving their foster-parents. Then they migrate, finding their way unaided to their winter quarters—a remarkable example of a bird's inborn ability to navigate.

RECOGNITION: *grey head and back, barred underparts; distinguished from sparrowhawk by slender bill, pointed wings and graduated, spotted tail; song distinctive; sexes alike, though a rare variety occurs in which female is chestnut-coloured and barred above and below; juveniles are brown and barred, with white spots on the head.*
NESTING: *see opposite page.*
FEEDING: *insects, chiefly large caterpillars; also spiders, centipedes and earthworms; nestlings share host bird's diet, usually insects but sometimes seeds, as when foster-parents are linnets.*

Risks a bird runs in a cuckoo's territory

The cuckoo is the only British bird which rears its young by fostering them on other birds. This habit—called brood parasitism—means that each female can produce many more offspring than if she had to feed them all herself. But taking the world as a whole, Britain's cuckoo is by no means unique: 77 other species are known to be brood parasites.

Each female cuckoo scouts a large territory for potential foster-parents, watching them as they build their nests. Meadow pipits, dunnocks and reed warblers are the chief victims, followed by robins, pied wagtails and sedge warblers; but cuckoos' eggs have been found in the nests of more than 50 species.

Most of the host birds lay in the early morning, and seeing them lay seems to stimulate the cuckoo so that she is ready to lay her own egg by the afternoon, when the parent birds are usually away from the nest.

The cuckoo removes an egg from the host's nest and lays one of her own in its place. She flies away with the stolen egg, which she either eats or drops. About 48 hours later she lays again, in a different nest, until she has a clutch of 12 or 13 eggs scattered about her territory.

Sometimes, a cuckoo flying down to lay is mobbed by the chosen foster-parents; aggressive pairs of great reed warblers in Hungary are reputed to have forced cuckoos into the water below their nests to drown. But most birds offer no resistance.

The cuckoo's egg hatches in 12 or 13 days—as fast or faster than the foster-parents'. The naked nestling is born with a sensitive hollow in its back, into which it manoeuvres the eggs or nestlings of the host birds before heaving them over the edge. Any left in the nest often starve to death because their parents concentrate on feeding the insistent young cuckoo for about three weeks, until it fledges, and then for another week or two until it becomes independent.

Egg mimicry

CUCKOO   REED WARBLER   CUCKOO   MEADOW PIPIT

CUCKOO   REED WARBLER   CUCKOO   DUNNOCK

If a cuckoo's egg is conspicuously different from the rest, the foster-parents may recognise it as foreign and throw it out of the nest, or even build over it; but cuckoos usually lay in the nests of the species which reared them, and in some cases this has led to the evolution of egg mimicry. Cuckoos which prey on reed warblers and meadow pipits lay eggs closely resembling those of the victimised birds in pattern; and even when there is no egg mimicry, some species accept a cuckoo's egg as their own. A reed warbler will tolerate an egg from a 'meadow pipit' cuckoo, and a dunnock will incubate a cuckoo's egg even though there is no attempt at imitation.

PROSPECTING FLIGHT
The female cuckoo quarters her territory, watching for nest-building work by pairs of birds which could become foster-parents for her young

A VICTIM IS CHOSEN
When the cuckoo lands in the host bird's nest to lay her own egg, she takes one of her victim's eggs in her bill; later she will either eat the egg or destroy it

THE CUCKOO HATCHES
Instinctively it begins to kill its foster-brothers and sisters, holding their eggs in the hollow of its back and thrusting upwards to drop them from the nest

THE CHANGELING GROWS
So rapid is its growth rate that the young cuckoo soon becomes too big for the host's nest, and the foster-parent may have to stand on its back to feed it

Red-backed shrike

Lanius cristatus 6¾ in.

MALE

FEMALE

May–Sept. visitor; formerly nested throughout England and Wales; breeding now sporadic

Migratory, wintering in tropical Africa and southern Asia

A red-backed shrike or 'butcher-bird' impales a bee on a thorn in its 'larder'

A grisly habit of impaling its prey on thorns or barbed wire has earned the red-backed shrike the name of 'butcher-bird'. Its victims are mainly beetles and bees, but they also include young birds: they make up a 'larder' of surplus food, which often remains uneaten. In its hunting technique the shrike is very like a small hawk, sometimes perching on a bush, tree or telephone line, sometimes hovering and sometimes gliding swiftly along a hedgerow, before swooping down on its prey.

Red-backed shrikes used to breed on open heaths and commons with plenty of bushes for hunting posts and nest-sites. They were the only shrikes that bred in Britain, but their numbers decreased rapidly. Before the Second World War, red-backed shrikes nested in almost every English and Welsh county. Today, after decades of steep decline, none are left; the last regular breeding occurred in the Norfolk Breckland in 1988. Now, apart from the odd pair in some years in Scotland, it is extinct as a British breeding bird.

The shrike's calls are usually harsh; the most common is a 'chack-chack' note given when the bird is annoyed or alarmed. It also has a warbling song, containing notes and phrases mimicked from other birds. The male sings in May when the shrikes fly in from winter quarters in Africa. The song is also warbled during short courtship flights.

RECOGNITION: *male has chestnut back, pale blue-grey crown and rump, black stripe through eye; female is duller with brown back and head, lightly barred breast.*
NESTING: *usual nest-site is a thorny bush; nest of grass and moss, lined with hair and roots and sometimes decorated with feathers, is built mainly by male; lays late May–July; usually 4–6 eggs, varying from cream to pink or pale green with dark markings; incubation about 14 days, chiefly by female; nestlings, fed by both sexes, leave after 14 days.*
FEEDING: *insects, especially beetles and bees; small birds and chicks; small mammals, small frogs, worms.*

Wheatear

Oenanthe oenanthe $5\frac{3}{4}$ in.

MALE IN SUMMER

EARLY in March wheatears begin to fly in from their winter quarters in Africa, spreading out mainly to northern and western Britain. When they reach their nesting grounds the birds begin a curious dancing courtship display. A male and a female face one another in a shallow hollow and the male starts leaping into the air with puffed-out feathers, jumping out of the hollow to its banks or from one bank to the other, in rapid rhythm. Then it throws itself down in front of its mate, with wings and tail spread out and head stretched along the ground.

The wheatear sings its squeaky, warbling song, sometimes from a low perch, sometimes in a dancing flight after a display on the ground, and at other times in a hovering flight. When feeding, it chases insects on the ground, bobbing its head and hopping. It has also been observed hovering like a hawk and diving to the ground.

While breeding wheatears are building their nests on bare hillsides, heaths or sand-dunes, and raising their young, bigger and more brightly coloured wheatears pass through Britain, on their way to breed in Iceland and Greenland. Thousands of wheatears used to be trapped each year as they rested on the south coast on migration; they were served up as delicacies on Victorian dinner-tables.

March–Oct. visitor; has decreased in lowland Britain; northern migrants pass through

Migratory, wintering in tropical Africa and southern Asia

RECOGNITION: *both sexes have white rump; male in summer has blue-grey back, black mask and wings, buff underparts; in winter has brown back, mask and wings; female at all seasons similar to male in winter plumage.*
NESTING: *nests on rough open wasteland, in rock crevice, rabbit burrow or even tin can; nest of grass and moss, lined with hair and feathers, built chiefly by female; lays late April–June; usually 6 eggs, pale blue, sometimes with red-brown spots; incubation about 14 days, chiefly by female; nestlings, fed by both parents, leave after about 14 days; sometimes two broods.*
FEEDING: *chiefly insects and larvae; some spiders, centipedes and snails.*

Wheatear in flight—the bird was a favourite delicacy on Victorian dinner-tables

99

Stonechat

Saxicola torquata 5 in.

MALE IN SUMMER

Present all year; once nested in many places where it now occurs only as a visitor

Mainly sedentary, but northern breeding birds migrate to Mediterranean and southern Asia

Female stonechat at its nest, built at foot of a gorse bush

Low over its heathland territory, the handsome male stonechat 'dances' up and down in the air as it gives its squeaky song; or it chases the female in a darting courtship display. The song lasts only a few seconds when the stonechat settles on one of its song-posts on top of a bush or on a telegraph wire. As it sings from a perch, the bird repeatedly flirts its tail, and in the intervals between singing often gives its loud call-note, a harsh, grating 'tsak-tsak' or 'hwee-tsak-tsak'.

Stonechats, which move about in pairs all the year round, often breed in the same kind of habitat as whinchats, though it seems that in districts where one species is numerous, the other is uncommon. Stonechats prefer uncultivated land, usually appearing on farmland only in winter, when they also turn up on building sites and railway embankments.

Once they were common birds throughout Britain, but their distribution is now local, except in the coastal areas of south and west England and Wales; they breed regularly in only three inland counties. Their decline may be due to the steady destruction of their breeding habitat, and to the effects of hard weather; after each bad winter in recent years they have taken a little longer to recover their numbers, and each time some small, isolated population seems to have been wiped out.

RECOGNITION: *plump, round-headed bird; male in summer has black head and back, white patches on neck, wings and rump, chestnut breast; browner and duller in winter; female in summer has streaky brown upper parts, no rump-patch; darker in winter.*
NESTING: *female builds nest on or close to ground, mainly of moss, grass and hair; lays late March–June; usually 5 or 6 eggs, light blue, finely freckled with red-brown; incubation 14 or 15 days, by female only; nestlings, fed by both parents, leave after about 13 days, fly a few days later; usually two broods, sometimes three in south.*
FEEDING: *mainly insects and their larvae, some worms and spiders.*

Whinchat
Saxicola rubetra   5 in.

MALE IN SUMMER

Whinchats are among the earliest of Britain's summer visitors, starting to arrive in one's and two's early in April, after a journey across the Sahara from tropical Africa. The first main wave crosses the south coast towards the end of April; and as more fly in, often accompanied by wheatears and yellow wagtails, the early arrivals are already spreading out and settling to nest and breed in rough grassland on heaths, commons, hillsides and farmland.

They appear on farmland more often than the related stonechats, and are not so closely associated with gorse, though in some districts both birds are known as 'furze-chats'. Whinchats also breed in districts without bushes, provided that there are tall plants such as thistles or bracken where they can perch to sing. The song is a brief warbling which sometimes includes imitations of other birds and the call-note is a sharp 'tic-tic' or 'u-tic'.

In its courtship display the male has been seen singing in front of the female, with wings lowered and quivering, tail fanned out and slightly raised, and head thrown back. The male sings, too, as it keeps watch close to the nest while its mate is sitting on the eggs.

Whinchats fly low and jerkily, with quickly beating wings, from one tall plant to another, where they perch to watch for insects which they catch with a fluttering sally into the air. But they feed chiefly on the ground.

RECOGNITION: *streaky brown upper parts; male has white eye-stripe, female's is duller; both sexes have white patches at sides of tail; male duller in winter, more like female.*
NESTING: *female builds nest of grass and moss, lined with fine grass, on ground in rough vegetation; covered runway may lead to nest; lays May–July; usually 5 or 6 eggs, green-blue with red-brown speckles; incubation 13 days, by female only; nestlings, fed by both parents, leave after 14 days; sometimes two broods.*
FEEDING: *insects and their larvae; some spiders and worms.*

April–Sept. visitor; has decreased in central and south-east England

Highly migratory, wintering exclusively in northern tropical and eastern Africa

Female whinchat at its nest, usually hidden in rough vegetation

Whitethroat

Sylvia communis 5½ in.

MALE IN SUMMER

April–Sept. visitor; widespread in scrub, hedges and heathland

Migratory, wintering in savanna in northern tropical Africa

The whitethroat has a vertical song-flight, so that it seems to dance like a puppet

WHITETHROATS are not such skulking, secretive birds as some of the other warblers; the male will perch in full view on top of a bush to sing its brief but sweet song. The bird may mate with the first female whitethroat to cross the territory it stakes out as soon as it arrives in Britain. The courtship display can be violent, on both sides. The male follows the female closely with a piece of grass in his bill, and then dashes at her with short bursts of singing, as if attacking her. The female responds by spreading her wings and tail and springing at the male as if to drive him away; and at the last moment he turns aside. About the same time of year, the male starts to build 'trial' nests; it may work on as many as three, none of which is usually completed. Call-notes include a harsh 'churr', a hard 'tacc' and a softer 'wheet' or 'whit'.

Whitethroats live in a broad range of habitats—commons, country lanes, wood borders and clearings, and any kind of land with brambles, briers, osiers, bushes and overgrown hedges. Their numbers crashed in the late 1960s, due to drought in their African winter quarters, and have taken many years to recover. After the breeding season, whitethroats will sometimes visit gardens to raid the soft fruit crops. In August and September they fly back to Africa.

RECOGNITION: *male has grey cap in summer, grey-brown cap in winter; white throat; distinguished from lesser whitethroat by absence of dark 'mask' on cheeks; both sexes have chestnut wings; female duller.*
NESTING: *male builds 'trial' nests, female may use one of them or both may build another; deep cup nest, close to ground in cover, is made from grasses, often lined with horse-hair and decorated with down; lays May–July; usually 4 or 5 eggs, often pale green or pale buff with grey markings; incubation about 12 days, by both parents; nestlings, fed by both parents, leave after about 11 days; usually two broods.*
FEEDING: *insects and their larvae; spiders; fruit in autumn.*

Lesser whitethroat

Sylvia curruca 5¼ in.

A tuneless, rattling, repetitive 'chikka-chikka-chikka-chikka' from deep inside an overgrown hedge or some other thick cover is one of the few ways in which the lesser whitethroat gives away its presence. This loud, far-carrying song is often preceded and sometimes followed by a more musical sound, a low-pitched warble. When the male is defending its territory, its song may be given from a song-post near the nest.

It is a much shyer bird than its relative, the whitethroat, and is much less abundant in Britain. It breeds on commons, open woods, shrubberies, large gardens and hedge-lined lanes. Only occasionally has it nested in Scotland, and it has bred in Ireland just once.

Its courtship follows the typical warbler pattern, with the male following the female as she walks or runs through thick vegetation, and posturing before her with breast and crown feathers fluffed out. Occasionally, the male takes off and flutters into a tree, singing. Often the bird gathers grass in its bill; this may be for a 'trial' nest or it may be to give to the female in a ritual presentation of nesting material. A noisy 'tacc-tacc' of alarm is often heard in late summer, when both parents are looking after their fledglings. There is also a well-developed distraction display in which a parent bird runs along the ground, behaving as if injured.

April–Sept. visitor; occasionally nests in Wales and Scotland

Migratory, wintering in N. Africa and, in limited numbers, in India

RECOGNITION: *grey upper parts, dark 'mask' on cheeks; distinguished from whitethroat by absence of chestnut on wings, distinctive song; sexes alike.*
NESTING: *male builds 'trial' nests, female lines chosen one; nest, in bush, hedgerow or evergreen shrub, made from stalks, roots and hair, sometimes decorated with cobwebs; lays May–July; usually 4–6 eggs, pale cream, with a few bold sepia and grey markings; incubation usually 11 days, mainly by female; nestlings, fed by both parents, leave after about 11 days; often two broods.*
FEEDING: *mainly insects and their larvae; some berries in autumn.*

Lesser whitethroat is a shy bird, usually seen only as it flits rapidly from bush to bush

Dartford warbler

Sylvia undata 5 in.

MALE IN SUMMER

Present all year; one of Britain's rarest breeding birds; main strongholds are in Hants and Dorset

Essentially sedentary; northern birds suffer in hard winters

Female Dartford warbler at its nest—its eggs were once much prized by egg-collectors

BECAUSE it remains in Britain all year round, the Dartford warbler has become one of our rarest breeding birds. Other warblers migrate, but this small, red-breasted bird stays on, to face what can sometimes be harsh winters . . . and pays the penalty.

Each spring the survivors set about repopulating their habitat. But the gorsy heathland which Dartford warblers prefer is being swallowed up by farmland and by the advance of suburbia, so that there are now fewer areas which can serve as a refuge.

At the beginning of the 19th century, Dartford warblers bred widely throughout southern England; and they were still found in most counties south of the Thames until just before the Second World War. Then came a succession of hard winters. The worst, 1962-3, cut down the entire British population to a mere ten pairs, but by 1966 this population had doubled. A further series of mild winters enabled the population to increase to about 500 pairs by 1970, to 950 pairs by 1991 and to a massive 1700 pairs by 1994.

All that can usually be seen of the handsome but secretive Dartford warbler is its long tail vanishing rapidly into a gorse bush; but in winter some Dartford warblers become nomadic and may be seen foraging on rough ground. The birds may pair for life.

RECOGNITION: *both sexes have a long tail, often cocked; male in winter has dark brown upper parts and slate-grey head, with dark, wine-coloured underparts; head greyer in summer; female slightly browner than male.*
NESTING: *male builds 'trial' nests; final nest built mainly by female, in gorse or long heather, of grass, roots and stalks decorated with spiders' webs; lays April–June; 3 or 4 eggs, dirty white speckled with grey, sometimes tinged with green; incubation about 12 days, chiefly by female; nestlings, fed by both parents, leave after about 13 days; normally two broods, occasionally three.*
FEEDING: *insects and their larvae; some spiders.*

Grasshopper warbler

Locustella naevia   5 in.

No grasshopper heard in Britain ever made a sound like the song of the grasshopper warbler; but the chirping of some Continental grasshoppers is close enough to justify the bird's name. The song, known as 'reeling', sounds like an angler's reel being wound in, or like a free-wheeling bicycle. After the birds arrive in Britain in April or May, reeling goes on every morning and evening, with occasional bursts during the night.

Grasshopper warblers are shy birds, and spend most of their time feeding in thick bushes or low cover; but sometimes a male perches on an exposed spray to sing with its body quivering and head turning from side to side. The far-carrying song is a poor guide to the bird's whereabouts, for it seems to have the ability to 'throw' its voice.

The spread of dense young plantations in Britain has helped to increase the number of grasshopper warblers breeding here, though more recently they have declined. Their chief winter home is in West Africa, south of the Sahara.

Courtship usually takes the form of a chase through the undergrowth. The female leads the way, pecking as she steps through the grass or through the branches of a bush. The male follows with wings flapping slowly, carrying a piece of grass or a dead leaf in its bill.

RECOGNITION: *brown with streaked back; long tail; buff underparts; distinctive song, longer than song of rare Savi's warbler; sexes alike.*
NESTING: *both sexes build nest on or near ground, hidden in thick vegetation and often reached by covered runway; nest is of grass on foundation of dead leaves; lays May–July; usually 4–6 eggs, pale cream, thickly speckled with red-brown; incubation usually 14 days, by both parents; nestlings, fed by both parents, usually leave after 10–12 days; often two broods in south.*
FEEDING: *mainly insects and their larvae; sometimes spiders.*

April–Sept. visitor; widely but thinly distributed; its range has spread westwards in Ireland

Migratory, wintering in West Africa, Iran and India

Grasshopper warbler at its nest; this species is amongst the shyest of British birds

Tree pipit

Anthus trivialis   6 in.

April–Sept. visitor; found only as a migrant in Ireland and northern islands

Migratory, wintering mainly south of the Sahara and also in southern Asia

Tree pipit descends on uplifted wings during its song flight

A spectacular song-flight makes up for the inconspicuous plumage of this visitor from tropical Africa. The male chooses a high perch and launches into the air, climbing steeply. It begins to sing as it nears the peak of its climb, and continues as it descends, on uplifted wings, to end with a crescendo of 'see-er, see-er, see-er' notes.

Usually the male returns to the same perch or to one near by, and only rarely to the ground. This is one way of telling tree pipits from the closely similar meadow pipits, which normally start their song-flights from the ground and return to it. Another way is by the sounds they make: the meadow pipit has no 'see-er' climax to its song, and the shrill 'pheet' of its call-note is quite different from the tree pipit's loud, high 'teez' call.

Sometimes the tree pipit will deliver a shortened version of its song from a perch. It breeds on commons, heaths or railway embankments—in fact in any rough country near woods or with scattered trees or telegraph poles which the male can use as song-posts, or even in open woodland.

Courtship consists mainly of a sexual chase, with both birds using a jerky flight action. After they have paired, the birds build a well-hidden nest on the ground, sometimes under a tussock of grass and sometimes in a bank, often with a 'mouse-hole' entrance.

RECOGNITION: *upper parts brown; breast buff with heavy stripes; best distinguished from meadow pipit by call and song-flight; sexes alike.*
NESTING: *builds nest on ground with dried grass on foundation of moss, lined with grass and hair; lays May–June; usually 4–6 eggs, variable, often red-brown or grey with darker blotches or marbling; incubation 13 or 14 days, by female only; nestlings, fed by both parents, leave after 12 or 13 days; often two broods.*
FEEDING: *insects and their larvae, including beetles, flies and sometimes grasshoppers; also spiders.*

Woodlark

Lullula arborea 6 in.

T HE fluting song of the woodlark is not as spirited as the skylark's, but it makes up in sweetness for what it lacks in power; and the woodlark's song-flight is just as spectacular as the other lark's. It begins to sing a few feet up in the air, at first repeating one or two notes six times or so; then it pauses, as if to get its breath for a series of liquid phrases. As it sings, the bird some-times spirals high in the air above its territory, circles down until it is about 100 ft from the ground, then drops to earth. The woodlark also sings from the ground or from a song-post overlooking its territory. The song, sometimes given at night, is heard mainly from early March to the middle of June.

Woodlarks will nest in almost any kind of grassy country with a few shrubs and some scattered trees. They prefer sandy heathlands, especially in their East Anglian stronghold, limestone slopes, parkland and the borders of woods; in winter they sometimes join up in wandering flocks to feed.

A series of severe winters since the early 1950's has hit the birds hard. They used to be widespread in southern England, and bred regularly as far north as Yorkshire and North Wales, but now they are almost entirely limited to East Anglia and southern England; the species is seen in Wales, but no longer breeds there.

Present all year; has much decreased; until 1953 it nested in most counties north to Yorkshire

Mainly sedentary, but northern breeding birds migrate south, to winter near the Mediterranean

RECOGNITION: *streaked brown plumage with white eye-stripes meeting across nape; small black and white mark on forewing; distinguished from skylark by smaller size, very short tail without white sides, lower crest and different song; sexes alike.*
NESTING: *both sexes build nest of grass and moss, lined with grass, in depression in the ground; lays late March–July; usually 3 or 4 eggs, pale grey with fine red-brown or olive mottling; incubation 13–15 days, by female only; nestlings, fed by both sexes, leave after 11 or 12 days, fly some days later; usually two broods, sometimes three.*
FEEDING: *mainly insects; some spiders; seeds in autumn.*

Flying round in circles, the woodlark sings its mellow song

Linnet

Acanthis cannabina 5¼ in.

MALE IN SUMMER

Present all year; common and widespread in breeding season, but in winter many birds migrate

Sedentary and migratory; the northern populations winter in southern parts of range

Linnets have the typical dancing flight of the smaller finches

ITS persistent, twittering song helped to make the cock linnet one of the favourite cage-birds of Victorian and Edwardian England. Today the fashion for putting linnets in cages has long passed, and the handsome red-breasted male pours out its medley of notes in the wild. Usually it finds a song-post on a bush or a fence, but sometimes a linnet will sing as it flies, bounding up and down through the air. The usual flight-note is a high-pitched chittering and there is also a 'tsoo-eet' anxiety note. The cock sings again in its courtship ceremony, uttering a series of low, sweet notes as it droops its wings, spreads its tail and rapidly shakes its feathers.

Linnets even sing 'in chorus'; for they are gregarious birds, often nesting in loose colonies. They mix with other finches in winter feeding flocks, sometimes hundreds strong, which roam the countryside on foraging trips to stubble-fields and other farmland, waste ground, and rough country near the coast.

In the breeding season linnets prefer places with plenty of low bushes which provide nest-sites; they frequent gorse-covered commons and heaths and scrub-covered downland, but sometimes move into big gardens. Cuckoos occasionally lay their eggs in linnets' nests, but the young cuckoos usually starve because of the specialised diet—chiefly seeds—on which linnet nestlings are fed.

RECOGNITION: *chestnut back; white wing-bar; forked tail has white sides; male has crimson crown and breast in summer.*
NESTING: *female builds nest of grass and moss, lined with hair and wool, usually close to the ground in bush; lays April–July; usually 4–6 eggs, light blue with sparse purple-red blotches; incubation about 11 days, chiefly by female; young, fed by both parents, fly after about 12 days; two broods, sometimes three.*
FEEDING: *mainly weed-seeds; some insects, especially caterpillars, are fed to the young, and perhaps also eaten by adults.*

MOUNTAIN AND MOORLAND

Life is a constant battle for all birds in
the wild, but to survive on the high tops demands
a special quality of hardiness. Natural selection ensures
that the birds of mountain and moorland have that quality: the
ptarmigan cannot be driven down the slopes by any weather short of
a blizzard; and the red grouse will stand its ground though
it may have to tread for hours to prevent itself
from being buried alive in drifting snow.

CONTENTS

Merlin

Falco columbarius M 10½ in. F 13 in.

FEMALE

MALE

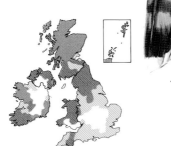

Present all year except in south
where it is a winter visitor

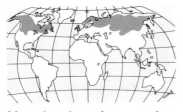

Most winter in southern part of
breeding range or directly south of
it; some reach Tropics

A merlin pursuing its prey follows
every twist or turn the bird makes

THE merlin dashes along close to the heather, following every twist and turn of its quarry's flight as it chases one of the small birds—meadow pipits, twites or ring ouzels—which are its chief prey. The male, or jack, is little bigger than a blackbird, weighing a mere four ounces. Yet it does most of the hunting throughout the breeding season, sometimes flying down birds as big as itself through sheer persistence.

With its prey safely clutched in its talons, the male flies towards its nest, uttering a shrill, chattering 'quik-ik-ik' call. At one of its 'plucking-posts' close to the nest, it often tears off the victim's head, then it brings the body to the female, or occasionally signals to her to take it in mid-air.

Merlins vary their diet with small mammals, lizards and insects during their winter wanderings, which can take them to lowland pastures, marshes or the sand and shingle of the coast. On the upland moors they occasionally kill a few game-chicks, though not enough to justify the persecution they have suffered from game-keepers.

Merlins have declined over most of Britain in the last 60 years or so. The process appears to be continuing, but the reasons for it are unclear; habitat loss, persecution and pesticide contamination may all be involved.

The merlin's name has no connection with the magician of the King Arthur legends; it comes from an old French name for the species, *émerillon.*

RECOGNITION: *slate-blue back and tail ; female larger than male with dark brown back and banded tail ; both have heavily streaked underparts.*
NESTING: *nests on ground or in old crow's nest ; lays May–June ; usually 4 eggs, cream, with heavy red-brown freckles ; incubation about 30 days, by both parents ; nestlings, tended by both parents, leave at 26 days.*
FEEDING: *small birds, usually meadow pipits ; some small mammals and lizards ; a few insects ; occasionally game-chicks.*

Hen-harrier

Circus cyaneus M 17 in.   F 20 in.

FEMALE

THE hen-harrier is one of the few birds of prey to have significantly increased its numbers in Britain since the end of the Second World War. Much of the credit must go to the measures taken to protect all our hawks. Early in the 20th century the hen-harrier was more or less confined to the Orkneys and the Outer Hebrides in its breeding season; but it has gradually recolonised the Scottish mainland and invaded Ireland, Wales and England. There are now well over 500 breeding pairs in the northern and western British Isles. Most of them spend the breeding season on the moors and in moorland valleys, but the birds are beginning to spread into the heaths and sand-dunes; and in winter, hen-harriers regularly visit coastal areas.

In its low-level hunting flight, the hen-harrier is like other harriers; it lazily beats its wings four or five times, glides with them half-raised, and then pounces to seize a mouse, a frog, a lapwing chick or the egg of some other ground-nesting bird. Hen-harriers will also chase small birds through the air; but in spite of their name, they are not much of a threat to hens.

In its spectacular courtship display, the bird flies steeply upwards, turns a somersault at the top of its climb, then plummets down with closed wings. While the female is on the nest, the male will call to her after making a kill and pass the prey to her in mid-air, either directly from foot to foot, or by a drop in the air.

RECOGNITION: *male grey; female brown, with streaked underparts and black bars on wings; male distinguished from Montagu's harrier by white, not grey, rump and absence of black bars on wings.*

NESTING: *female builds nest on ground, often in heather; lays late May–June; usually 4 eggs, white or pale blue; incubation about 28 days, by female only; nestlings, tended by both parents, leave after 6 weeks.*

FEEDING: *small ground-living animals; a few small birds caught on the wing.*

Present all year in Scotland and Ireland; winter visitor elsewhere

Sedentary in southern areas; some northern birds migrate to N. Africa and India

Hen-harrier beats the air lazily in low-level hunting flight

Golden eagle

Aquila chrysaëtos   M 30 in.   F 35 in.

Present all year; has nested in
Lake District since 1969; bred
in N. Ireland 1953–60

Sedentary; survives in Europe in
rugged mountain country

Young eagle in soaring flight
shows black bar at end of tail

Fᴏʀ sheer majesty there is no bird to compare with
the golden eagle. This huge bird of prey soars above
the Highland peaks, the primary feathers splayed at
the tips of wings spanning 7 ft, as it scans the sky and
ground below for its quarry. Then it thrusts towards
the victim at a breathtaking speed of up to 90 mph, and
thumps down to nail a red grouse, ptarmigan or blue
hare to the ground.

Eagles also take lambs occasionally, though these are
usually the weaklings which result from the overstock-
ing of pasture. They also eat carrion—a habit which
recently cut back the bird's range. In regions where
sheep-dips based on dieldrin pesticides were used,
eagles which ate dead sheep were poisoned. But dieldrin
was withdrawn after a Government inquiry, and the
eagle may now spread into new areas.

Eagles pair for life, and usually have two or three
eyries, pitched between 1500 and 2000 ft high, which
they use in rotation. In courtship, the pair soar in
spirals over their territory and plunge earthwards with
half-closed wings, sometimes rolling over in mid-air so
close that their talons appear to link.

The chosen nest, an immense basket of sticks on a
mountain crag, tall pine or sea cliff, is added to year by
year; it is repaired before the breeding season and often
decorated with fresh greenery. As the downy eaglets
grow up, the nest becomes fouled with a litter of bones,
the remains of food brought by their parents.

RECOGNITION: *almost uniformly dark, with golden tinge on head; heavy,
powerful bill; exceptionally long wings; female larger than male.*
NESTING: *both sexes build or repair nests in November or December; lays
March or April; usually 2 eggs, white, often with red-brown markings;
incubation about 40 days, mainly by female; nestlings, fed by both parents,
leave after about 12 weeks.*
FEEDING: *blue hares, grouse, ptarmigan, lambs and carrion.*

Short-eared owl

Asio flammeus M 14 in. F 16½ in.

A good supply of field voles is the main factor controlling the distribution of short-eared owls. Voles are the owl's favourite prey, and it has been calculated that a single bird may eat as many as 2000 of them in four months. Periodically, vole plagues break out in hilly districts—sometimes with devastating effects on grass crops—and then the short-eared owls rapidly move in to breed; if there are enough voles the owls will raise two broods.

The spread of plantations of conifers, an ideal habitat for voles, has helped the short-eared owl to increase in the past 20 or 30 years, extending its breeding range southward to moorland in Yorkshire and North Wales. The owl also breeds regularly in East Anglia, as far south as the Thames estuary. It hunts over open, tree-less country in broad daylight as well as at dusk, quartering the ground in slow-flapping flight.

At sunset and dusk in April and May the short-eared owl patrols high over its territory in a display flight. It circles and hovers, giving its low, booming song, and glides on outspread wings. Then it suddenly twists its wings under its body so that their tips meet behind its tail, and rapidly claps them together a number of times. As it claps its wings, the bird plunges like a stone, dropping several feet before it goes back to its slow flight.

The 'ears' which give the owl its name are, in fact, merely small tufts of feathers, with no function as organs of hearing.

RECOGNITION: *buff-brown plumage with streaked breast; black patches under long, rounded wings; sexes alike.*
NESTING: *nest is a depression in the ground, lined with vegetation; lays April; usually 4–8 eggs, white, almost spherical; incubation about 26 days, by female only; nestlings, fed by female on food brought by male, leave after about 15 days, fly about 11 days later; sometimes two broods.*
FEEDING: *chiefly field voles and other small mammals; small birds; insects.*

Present all year in north; more widespread as a visitor in autumn and winter

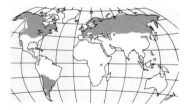

Most populations migrate, spreading deep into the Tropics and temperate areas in winter

The short-eared owl hunts regularly in broad daylight

113

Red grouse

Lagopus lagopus M 15 in. F 13½ in.

MALE

Present all year; rarely strays from moorland breeding areas

Red grouse are confined to Britain and Ireland; rest of range is taken up by the willow grouse

Startled grouse beats low over heather, with whirring flight

ONLY the extreme hardiness of red grouse keeps them alive for the guns which open up on the 'Glorious Twelfth' of August. But it is not the guns that do most damage to their numbers. Recent researches in Scotland have shown that more could be shot without reducing their population in the following year. When grouse stocks fall it is usually because the burning of old heather on the moors has been used too freely or too little.

Red grouse, as native birds, are unique to Britain; but they are closely related to the willow grouse of Norway. They rely for food almost entirely on ling heather, eating different parts of the plant from winter until its seeds fall in autumn. The cock birds mark out their territory in a dramatic display. They leap into the air with spread wings and descend steeply again; extending their necks and feet and fanning their tails; and they challenge rival cocks with their barking call: 'go-bak, go-bak-bak-bak-bak'. Birds which cannot establish a well-heathered territory often fall victim to disease or predators.

In winter on the high, bleak moors, grouse may have to keep treading with their feet for long spells to avoid being buried in drifting snow. Snowstorms are still common in April, when the female is laying; but even if the eggs are badly frosted, grouse chicks rarely fail to hatch—as long as their parents stay on guard against that moorland egg-thief, the hooded crow. The adults sometimes feign injury to distract intruders.

RECOGNITION: *dark wings and tail; male's body dark red-brown; female's browner, more barred.*
NESTING: *female makes scrape in the ground, lines it with grass or heather; usually lays April or May; usually 4–9 eggs, creamy-white, almost obscured by dark chocolate blotches; incubation about 23 days, by female only; chicks, tended by both sexes for about 6 weeks, leave soon after hatching, fly after about 13 days.*
FEEDING: *mostly ling heather; also fruits and shoots of cranberry.*

Ptarmigan

Lagopus mutus 14 in.

MALE IN WINTER

PTARMIGAN are birds of the high barren mountain tops, seldom seen below 2000 ft and for the most part spending their lives at least another 500 ft higher. Early in the morning they move down the mountainsides to feed on the green shoots and fruits of the sparse vegetation above the tree line; but apart from hunger, the only force that can drive these hardy birds down into the sheltered corries is a full-scale blizzard.

The bird's colour change, from mottled brown in summer to nearly all white in winter, helps it in the struggle for survival—a struggle that begins even before the chicks hatch out in a nest that is sometimes scantily lined with grass, and often protected from the upland gales only by a boulder. Hen ptarmigan have been observed using an injury-feigning display, crawling along the ground and thrashing their wings to distract predators from their eggs and chicks.

When ski-lifts were first built in the Cairngorms naturalists feared for the future of the ptarmigan. But the only effect on the birds has been the loss of a few small feeding areas near the ski-lift stations—they have become tamer and pay little attention to the skiers.

Male ptarmigan stake a claim to territory in March, flying up with croaking cries. They chase females in flight and on the ground, fanning their tails and drooping their wings.

RECOGNITION: *white wings and dark body in summer; female tawnier than male; pure white in winter except for black tail; male has black mark through eye.*
NESTING: *female makes scrape near rocks; lays May or June; usually 5–9 eggs, creamy with dark markings; incubation about 25 days, by female only; chicks, tended by both sexes, leave soon after hatching, fly after only 10 days.*
FEEDING: *mainly fruit, shoots and leaves of crowberry, bilberry, heather and other mountain plants; a few insects, mainly crane-flies.*

Present all year in Scottish mountains; once bred in England

Sedentary; one of the few British birds wintering in permanently snow-bound regions

Ptarmigan in summer plumage; only the wings remain white

MALE IN AUTUMN

MALE IN WINTER

The changing plumage of the ptarmigan

What looks like just another dark stone on a rock-strewn mountainside, or a bump that casts a shadow in the snow, can suddenly leap into the air, only to vanish again behind an outcrop of rock after a short burst of rapid, whirring flight. This is the ptarmigan, the only British bird with the Arctic trait of assuming a pure white plumage in winter. Its colour change is gradual, and all the more effective as camouflage for that. In summer, only the wings and underparts are white; the rest of the plumage is brown, mottled with black. In autumn, the upper parts, breast and flanks are grey or grey-brown, mottled with white. In winter the entire bird looks white. Its black or dark brown tail is often covered by other feathers; and the eye markings—a red wattle and, in the male, a dark eye stripe—are not noticeable from more than a few yards away. In this way, with its plumage keeping pace with the seasons, the ptarmigan is able to hide from its enemies by becoming an inconspicuous part of the landscape whatever the time of year.

MALE IN SUMMER

Curlew

Numenius arquata   22 in.

Present all year, with movement to coasts in winter

Essentially migratory, wintering mainly on coasts; some go south, as far as southern Africa

Male curlew planes over breeding grounds in display flight

A loud, melancholy 'coor-li', the cry that gives the curlew its name, is the clearest sign of the bird's presence for most of the year; in spring it is often accompanied by a bubbling song which announces that the breeding season is beginning. The males trill the song as they fly in wide circles and glide down on extended wings to claim territories in the breeding area.

The curlew, Britain's biggest wader, was once confined to moorland, but it extended its breeding range strikingly during the 20th century, until it now nests everywhere in the British Isles except for parts of the Outer Hebrides and a few counties in south-eastern England. Curlews now breed in all kinds of damp, open country: on moors, heaths, sand-dunes, bogs and even river shingle. In winter they often feed in flocks, wading over coastal marshes and mud-flats.

When female curlews arrive at the breeding place, sometimes as early as February, the males follow in a crouching walk, circling them when they stop.

The customary caution of the birds is especially pronounced in the early stages of incubation, when male and female will change places on the nest in wary silence. But later, when the eggs have hatched, the parents become aggressive, running towards intruders and sometimes taking off to sweep down on them.

RECOGNITION: *grey-brown with long legs and downward-curved bill; white rump; larger than whimbrel and without stripes on crown; distinctive 'coor-li' cry; sexes alike.*
NESTING: *nests in hollow, lined with grass or heather, among low vegetation; lays April–May; 4 eggs, buff, brown or olive, spotted with darker brown; incubation about 30 days, by both parents; chicks, tended by both parents, leave a few hours after hatching, fly after 28 days.*
FEEDING: *on coast, small molluscs, crustaceans, worms, small fish and sometimes seaweed; inland, insects and their larvae, worms, molluscs and at times berries and weed seeds; occasionally grain.*

Greenshank

Tringa nebularia   12 in.

SUMMER

THE greenshank was badly harried in the past by egg-collectors, who seemed to find a challenge in the task of tracking down the inconspicuous nest made by the female in a shallow scrape, with often only a boulder or a fallen branch as a landmark. But egg-collecting is illegal now, and the bird is comparatively safe from people who intrude on its desolate expanses of moorland in the Highlands, Skye and the Outer Hebrides.

At dawn and dusk greenshanks leave their breeding grounds and move to the shores of lochs to feed, mainly on water insects. In late summer and autumn, as they move south on migration, they feed in marsh pools, estuaries and reservoirs. In autumn, greenshanks are widespread in the south. Only a few remain in Britain over winter.

Greenshanks have a fast flight with rapid wing-beats. Pairs climb high in display flights, swerving close together and diving steeply to zigzag in a low-level chase. In courtship the male bows to the female on the ground, clicks his bill and sometimes leapfrogs over her.

The song, a repeated 'ru-tu', may be delivered either during a territorial display flight or from a perch. There are excited 'chip-chip-chip' calls when the sexes change places on the eggs, and a loud, ringing 'chu-chu-chu' call when the bird is alarmed.

RECOGNITION: *long green legs; long grey-blue bill, slightly up-turned; rump white, wings unmarked; upper parts ash-grey with dark markings; underparts white, with dark spots and bars in summer; sexes alike.*
NESTING: *female makes scrape in ground, lines it with vegetation and sometimes hare droppings; lays early May–June; usually 4 eggs, buff, with dark blotches and spots; incubation about 24 days, by both parents; nestlings, tended by both parents, leave in a few hours, begin to fly after about 27 days.*
FEEDING: *water insects and their larvae; worms and small fish; occasionally small frogs, more commonly tadpoles.*

Present all year, but only a few winter here, mainly on Irish coasts

Migratory; most go to the Tropics and subtropics, some reaching as far south as Australia

The greenshank—once a tempting target for egg-collectors

Golden plover

Pluvialis apricarius   11 in.

SUMMER

WINTER

Present all year; breeding birds leave moors in winter

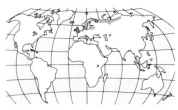

Winters mainly in Britain, south-west Europe and north-west Africa

Feeding flock in Feb.; bird on left is assuming summer plumage

T HE mournful call-note and liquid song of the golden plover are common summer sounds on the open moorland where it breeds. But they are not as common as they once were: the bird's breeding range contracted steadily during the 20th century. Golden plovers no longer breed on any of the Somerset moors, although a few pairs have re-colonised Dartmoor after an absence of more than 100 years.

When the handsome birds arrive at their breeding areas they take part in communal courtship ceremonies. The males skirmish, running at each other with raised wings, and leapfrogging; and several males will chase one female. Later, when the eggs are being incubated, the off-duty parent will keep watch from a hummock near the nest, ready to launch itself at an animal or bird intruder or perhaps to start a distraction display which may at its highest intensity include lying on the ground with thrashing wings.

In autumn and winter the birds form flocks as they move south to farmland and estuaries. There they will feed on insects, worms and small shellfish as well as the grass and weed seeds which form the vegetable part of their diet. They often join feeding flocks of lapwings, but when disturbed the mixed flock splits up in the air into two separate flights, one of each species.

RECOGNITION: *black face and underparts, with spangled black and gold upper parts in summer; in winter black disappears and underparts are white, with golden mottling; sexes alike.*
NESTING: *both sexes make scrapes, then female chooses one to line with twigs, lichen and grass; lays late April–June; usually 4 eggs, creamy, green-tinged or buff, spotted and blotched with dark brown; incubation about 30 days, by both parents; young, tended by both parents, leave after 1 or 2 days, fly after about 30 days.*
FEEDING: *mostly insects and their larvae; snails, worms and small shell-fish; also spiders, weed seeds, algae and moss.*

Dotterel

Eudromias morinellus 8½ in.

FEMALE IN SUMMER

THE tameness of the dotterel, its reputation as a table delicacy and its specialised habitat needs in Britain, make this member of the plover family a rarity. A century ago, dotterels were widespread on the higher hills from Sutherland south to the Pennines. Migrants, flying in small parties known as 'trips', used to visit a few places each spring in eastern and southern England—and often they were promptly shot and eaten. Trips of dotterels still spend a day or two at their traditional resting sites before moving northwards.

Today about 950 pairs are believed to be in Britain. Many of them breed on the Cairngorms and nearby summits, nesting among the rocks on tussocks or mossy ground above 2500 ft.

Dotterels play a curious game of hide-and-seek as part of their courtship. The male hides among the stones of the barren mountain tops and the female, when she finds him, pecks at his neck feathers. In display flights, the female takes the initiative, chasing the male and then leading him to a scrape where the nest will be built.

The duties of hatching the eggs and tending the young are left to the male, which has an elaborate distraction display to protect the chicks. It runs along the ground in a crouch, looking like a small mammal, flies aggressively towards the intruder, then flops back to the ground as though on broken wings.

RECOGNITION: *white eye-stripes, meeting in a V at nape of neck; white breast band; chestnut underparts; faint bar on wing visible in flight; female brighter than male.*
NESTING: *nests on ground in scrape lined with lichen and moss; lays May–June; usually 3 eggs, buff, stone or red-brown, thickly blotched and streaked with dark brown; incubation about 27 days, by male only; chicks, tended by male, leave within 24 hours, fly after about 28 days.*
FEEDING: *mainly insects; also spiders and crowberries; occasionally snails and earthworms.*

April–Oct. visitor; occasionally also nests in north Wales

Winters in North Africa and around the Red Sea and The Gulf

Migrant dotterels have traditional resting sites

121

Hooded crow

Corvus corone cornix 18½ in.

Present all year; Scottish breeding range is retreating as carrion crow spreads north

Mainly sedentary; some northern populations migrate

Grey body distinguishes 'hoodie' from carrion crow

To the gamekeeper on the grouse moor, the hooded crow is a criminal, a menace to the chicks of his precious grouse. In springtime the sharp-eyed 'hoodies' or 'corbies' search the moor, ready to eat the eggs in any nests which the grouse have left unprotected. A combined attack by cock and hen grouse can usually drive away a crow at this stage; but when the chicks have hatched, the hen cannot always keep her brood together, and the crows wait to pick off straying nestlings. Exceptionally, hoodies have been seen to kill birds as big as partridges and fieldfares.

The hooded crow is the northern and western counterpart of the carrion crow. In England it is known as the 'grey' crow or the 'Royston' crow; evidently it was once common in winter on the downs near Royston in Hertfordshire. Most ornithologists now agree that the hoodie, in spite of its distinctive grey body, is simply a different form of the southern bird. In the narrow band across Scotland where the ranges of the two birds overlap, they interbreed, often producing hybrids with intermediate plumage. The hoodie's harsh, rasping call —'kaak', often repeated three or four times—is identical to the carrion crow's.

Hoodies fly strongly, and walk along the ground, occasionally hopping. Courtship includes bowing with outspread wings and tail; eye-witnesses have also seen Scottish birds in a curious display consisting of repeated jumps 12–15 ft into the air.

RECOGNITION: *black, with grey back and underparts; sexes alike.*
NESTING: *both sexes build bulky cup of twigs or heather roots in tree, on cliff ledge or among tall heather; lays April–June; usually 3–5 eggs, pale green-blue with dark brown blotches; incubation about 19 days, by female only; nestlings, fed by both parents, leave after about 33 days.*
FEEDING: *mainly insects and their larvae, grain, other birds' eggs and nestlings, carrion; sometimes root crops, fish or fruit.*

Raven
Corvus corax   25 in.

RAVENS are the vultures of sheep country, patrolling in pairs or family groups in search of carrion—or a sickly sheep or deer, waiting to die. They will eat almost anything, from insects and shellfish to grain and acorns. Once they were common scavengers in the streets of London, but they have gradually been driven northward and westward to the hills and the sea cliffs.

The big black bird, Britain's largest crow, is sometimes ponderous as it flies along giving a deep croaking 'pruk-pruk-pruk' call; but it can also glide and soar freely, and put on a remarkable aerobatic show. In spring particularly, pairs of ravens tumble high in the air, half closing their wings, rolling over sideways, and nose-diving; they also have a trick of flying upside-down for short distances. These antics are perhaps part of the raven's courtship display, though sometimes they seem to be performed from sheer high spirits. Ceremonies on the ground between male and female, who mate for life, include bowing, neck-stretching and ruffling the throat feathers. In the mating display the male spreads its wings and tail and crouches with neck stretched up but bill pointed down; sometimes it jumps into the air or preens the female's face with its bill.

The nest, a substantial cup of sticks and other local materials, lined with sheep's wool or hair, is usually built on an inaccessible ledge; but in some districts ravens nest in trees.

RECOGNITION: *glossy black plumage; massive bill; end of tail wedge-shaped; sexes alike.*
NESTING: *both sexes build nest of sticks cemented with mud and moss, on ledge or in crevice; lays February–April; usually 4–6 eggs, pale green or blue with dark markings; incubation about 19 days, by female only; nestlings, fed by both parents, leave after about 6 weeks.*
FEEDING: *chiefly carrion and small animals; also seeds, fruit, grain, fish; eggs and young of other birds.*

Present all year; rare outside breeding range; formerly nested in eastern England

Sedentary; ravens of Sahara and Arabia may be separate species

Male raven flies upside-down in aerobatic spring display

123

Meadow pipit

Anthus pratensis 5¾ in.

Present all year, though many breeding birds winter in south-west Europe

Essentially migratory, wintering in western Europe and around the Mediterranean

Meadow pipit glides earthwards in territorial song-flight

I<small>F</small> there are such things as born victims among birds, then the meadow pipit is one of them. This small brown bird is the basic prey of the merlin, and a favourite host for the cuckoo. A young cuckoo quickly fills up the pipit's nest among the grass or rush tussocks; and the pipit sometimes stands on the back of its huge foster-child to feed it with insects and spiders which form the diet of both parasite and host.

Ramblers on the northern or western moors often flush meadow pipits, which are easily recognised by their sharp call-note, 'pheet' or a triple 'pheet-pheet-pheet'. But moorland is not the meadow pipit's only habitat; it will breed in most kinds of rough open country, including bogs, lowland heaths, downs and sand-dunes over most of Britain except parts of the extreme south-east. In winter, and when migrating to France or Spain, meadow pipits gather in damp places such as marshes, sewage farms, lake shores and estuaries.

In spring and summer meadow pipits leave the ground in a fluttering territorial song-flight, singing a rather tuneless series of notes as they climb into the air and continuing more musically as they glide down to earth again. Their courtship display consists mainly of a sexual chase. They have the dipping flight characteristic of pipits and their relatives, the wagtails.

RECOGNITION: *upper parts olive-brown with dark brown markings; breast streaked with white; best distinguished from tree pipit by 'pheet-pheet-pheet' call-note; sexes alike.*

NESTING: *grass nest on ground, lined with finer grass or hair; lays late April–June; usually 3–5 eggs, very variable, usually brown or grey, mottled or marbled, but sometimes pale grey with fine streaks or pale blue without markings; incubation about 13 days, by female only; nestlings, tended by both parents, leave after 14 days.*

FEEDING: *chiefly insects—beetles, crane-flies, blowflies, caterpillars and occasionally grasshoppers; spiders; earthworms; seeds.*

MALE IN SUMMER

Twite

Acanthis flavirostris   5¼ in.

THE streaky brown twite, whose name comes from its distinctive nasal 'twa-it' call-note, is the upland counterpart of the linnet. Its twittering song, delivered from a low perch or in flight, is reminiscent of the linnet's, and the bird closely resembles a streaky young linnet. But the male twite, unlike the adult linnet, has no red on its breast and forehead.

Twites breed on heather-covered moorland, high country with bracken or grass, and other rough, open ground in Ireland, the western Highlands, the Pennines, with a few in North Wales. In recent years, their range seems to have contracted in northern England and Scotland. Most twites desert the higher land in winter, and join other seed-eating finches and buntings near the coast, feeding in salt-marshes, and in hard winters on stubble-fields and in rick-yards. Twites eat the seeds of moorland grasses and rushes, weeds and salt-marsh plants, and in spring they may also eat some insects.

Twites have the bounding flight typical of the smaller finches, and hop along the ground. The only courtship display on record is by the male bird, which repeatedly opens and drops its wings to show its pink rump feathers. Nests, often in loose colonies, are usually built close to the ground in long heather, but are sometimes in gorse bushes and crevices in dry-stone walls.

RECOGNITION: *dull buff above, with black and brown streaks; lighter below; male has yellow bill in winter and pink rump feathers, distinctive 'twa-it' call-note.*

NESTING: *small cup of dried grass, lined with wool and built by female on or near ground; lays late May–June; usually 5 or 6 eggs, blue-tinged, with dark red-brown spots and streaks; incubation about 13 days, by female only; nestlings, fed by both parents, leave after 15 days; often two broods.*

FEEDING: *chiefly seeds of rushes, grasses and salt-marsh plants; insects fed to nestlings.*

Present all year; winter flocks on south-east coast may include continental birds

In winter, twites move to coasts within or just south of their breeding range

The twite—its range has contracted in recent years

Ring ouzel

Turdus torquatus · 9½ in.

MALE

March–Oct. visitor; migrants from Continent regularly reach east and south-east coasts

Winters mainly in Atlas Mountains and around Mediterranean

Ring ouzel's favourite song-post is a rock or boulder

Apart from the white crescent on its breast, and the fact that its wings when closed are paler than its body, this summer visitor to Britain looks like a mountain version of the garden blackbird. But though they look alike, the two species are quite different in character. Blackbirds are often tame, but ring ouzels are shy and difficult to approach; they are most often seen perching on distant rocks or flying away. The contact call is a clear, piping 'pee-u', and their alarm call a harsh 'tac-tac-tac'.

There may be special difficulty in distinguishing a ring ouzel from a part-albino blackbird; but there is little danger of confusing them during the breeding season, for nesting ouzels are rare below 1000 ft. The overlap between the two species comes when ouzels arrive in the south to rest and feed on migration. British ring ouzels winter in Africa, and many continental birds pass through Britain on passage.

Like other thrushes, ring ouzels eat animal and vegetable food in roughly equal quantities. In spring and summer they find a plentiful supply of insects, small snails and earthworms; in autumn they turn to wild fruit, especially when on migration.

The nest is built on or close to the ground, often near a moorland stream or track.

RECOGNITION: *male sooty black with broad white crescent on breast; pale wing-patch; female browner, with smaller, duller half-collar.*
NESTING: *both sexes build untidy grass cup nest on ground or on crag, building or bush, often with a base of heather stems; lays mid April–June; usually 4 eggs, pale blue-green with blotches of red-brown; incubation 14 days, mostly by female; nestlings, tended by both parents, leave after 14 days.*
FEEDING: *insects and their larvae; earthworms; occasionally snails and small lizards in summer; wild fruit—bilberries, crowberries, rowan berries, haws, sloes—in autumn.*

BROAD-LEAVED WOODLAND

In spring and summer the broad-leaved woods
offer a host of secret places where birds can
conceal themselves and their nests. It is no coincidence
that many of the woodlanders have distinctive songs; for against
the advantages of concealment must be balanced the need for
advertisement, to attract mates and warn off rivals. The
nightingale, one of the most elusive of birds, has the
sweetest, most compelling song of all.

CONTENTS

Woodcock

Scolopax rusticola 13½ in.

Present all year; wintering population includes birds from northern Europe

Some are sedentary; others migrate, reaching just south of their breeding range

Woodcock beats the bounds of its territory in 'roding' flight

THE woodcock is a wading bird which has taken to the land, especially to the kind of woodland that is opened up by clearings and rides. With eyes set high in its head, and well to the back, it has the all-round vision that enables it to look out for enemies even when it is probing in the ground for earthworms and insects.

At dawn and dusk in spring and summer, male woodcock meander slowly above the treetops in their erratic 'roding' flight—a territorial display in which the bird beats the bounds of its woodland domain. As it flies the woodcock gives two calls: an extraordinary frog-like croak, repeated several times, and a high-pitched, whistling 'twisick'. This leisurely flight is quite different from the woodcock's way of flying when it is flushed from its hiding place in the undergrowth; then it leaps into the air to dodge rapidly through the trees, quickly disappearing into cover again.

Roding occurs mainly between March and early July, when the woodcock are raising their two broods of chicks. If danger threatens before the young have learnt to fly, the female may 'airlift' them to safety, clutching the chicks in its claws or between its thighs.

When the migrant birds which reinforce our breeding stock in winter fly in across the North Sea, they often drop into the first piece of rough cover near the coast, moving inland later. They rest on dry ground by day, and fly at twilight to marshy or boggy ground to feed.

RECOGNITION: *stout; long bill; russet plumage with barred head and underparts; sexes alike.*
NESTING: *nests in a scrape lined with dead leaves; lays mid-March–June; usually 4 eggs, grey-white to brown, thickly marked with chestnut and ash-grey blotches; incubation about 21 days, by female only; chicks, tended by both parents, leave after a few hours; two broods.*
FEEDING: *earthworms, beetles, other insects and their larvae; small molluscs; some seeds and grass.*

Sparrowhawk

Accipiter nisus   M 11 in.   F 15 in.

FEMALE

THE fast-flying sparrowhawk relies on surprise attack as a hunting technique. It will dash quickly along one side of a hedgerow and suddenly dart up and over to burst on an unsuspecting cluster of finches, snatch its victim and dash away again. If its prey escapes, the hawk rarely tries another attack; it flies on until it sees another chance to pounce. In search of prey, it will sometimes glide in a circular, 'prospecting' flight, or it will soar into the sky, to plunge with folded wings.

The male sparrowhawk's main victims are small birds; but the bigger female will occasionally kill birds as big as a pigeon. Sparrowhawks also eat the chicks of game-birds—a 'crime' which led to large-scale persecution of the hawk by gamekeepers until it was given legal protection in 1967.

The sparrowhawk also suffered badly in the 1960s from poisonous agricultural chemicals, becoming extinct in eastern parts of England. The worst of the pesticides were banned and sparrowhawk numbers have made a strong comeback everywhere.

The male hunts single-handedly while the hen is brooding, landing at one of its 'plucking posts' with its prey and calling its mate to feed with a harsh, chattering 'kek-kek-kek-kek'. Later, both parents work hard to feed their young, which will eat two or three sparrow-sized birds a day.

RECOGNITION: *short, rounded wings; long tail; male has slate-grey upper parts and reddish-barred underparts; larger female has browner upper parts, dark brown bars on underparts, white stripe behind eye.*
NESTING: *nest built of twigs in tree, frequently by female alone, lined with thin twigs; usually lays May; usually 4–6 eggs, white tinged with blue with red-brown blotches; incubation about 30 days, by female only; nestlings, tended by both parents, leave after 24–30 days.*
FEEDING: *house sparrows, finches, starlings, other small birds; occasionally mice, voles and young rabbits; insects.*

Present all year; is now on the increase after a setback due to pesticides and gamekeepers

Most populations sedentary, but northern birds winter just south of their breeding range

Hunting sparrowhawk pounces on small finches

Red kite

Milvus milvus   M 22 in.   F 24 in.

MALE

More than 100 pairs nest in Wales;
successfully reintroduced to parts of
England and Scotland in the 1990s

Essentially sedentary, but birds from
northern Europe move to the
Mediterranean in winter

The forked tail identifies this
rare bird of prey

R ED kites were widespread over Britain until the 18th
century; they were common scavengers in the filthy
streets of medieval and Elizabethan London. But for the
past 100 years it has been one of our rarest breeding
birds. Careful protection by the Royal Society for the
Protection of Birds has helped the population to expand
from a handful of breeding pairs at the start of the 20th
century to more than 100 pairs now. They are seen in the
hills of central Wales; also, reintroduction in England
and Scotland has led to successful breeding in the wild
from 1992 onwards.

Kites are magnificent fliers, circling tirelessly for
hours over wooded valleys on their long, slender wings,
usually bent at the 'wrist', and steering with their long,
forked tails as they scan the earth for small mammals
which they kill with a sudden pounce to the ground.
Their effortless flight long ago added a word to the
English language: the kites which children fly get their
name from the bird.

Pairs of kites join in aerobatics in their courtship
ceremony, and there is the diving display flight common
to many birds of prey. Their call is a shrill, mewing
'weeou-weeou-weeou'. Kites build a bulky nest of sticks,
lined with wool, moss, hair and even paper or rags.
Shakespeare acknowledged this when he warned in *The
Winter's Tale*: 'When the kite builds, look to lesser linen.'

RECOGNITION: *rusty brown plumage with streaked, white head; slender
body; narrow wings, sharply bent backwards in flight; deeply forked tail;
female slightly duller.*
NESTING: *both sexes build nest of sticks and earth in tree, often on an old
nest of a crow; lays April or May; usually 2 or 3 eggs, white, with red-
brown speckles; incubation about 30 days, by female only; nestlings,
tended by both parents, leave after 50–55 days.*
FEEDING: *small mammals, rabbits, sheep carrion, fledgling rooks and gulls;
sometimes worms and frogs.*

Buzzard

Buteo buteo   M 20 in.   F 23 in.

SAILING through the sky with slow flaps of its broad wings, and giving its plaintive 'peeiou' call, the buzzard looks almost lazy. But the big bird is anything but aimless: it is quartering the grassland or moor in search of prey which may be as small as a beetle. As soon as its sharp eyes spot a victim it will pounce.

A buzzard will hover with wings angled against a high wind; sometimes it will fold its wings and plunge towards the earth before sailing upwards again; or yet again it will roll and turn in the air as part of its display ceremony. When the bird soars, circling with wing-tips splayed out, it can look like a small eagle.

Buzzards are found in all kinds of country in northern and western Britain: woods, moorlands, mountains, sea cliffs and farmland. Their numbers were increasing steadily, and they were moving eastward, until 1953 when myxomatosis decimated the rabbit population. In spite of losing this important source of food, the buzzard is still the most common of our larger birds or prey; and after the 1950s it began to breed again in Ireland, where gamekeepers had stamped it out.

If a buzzard is mobbed by crows or seagulls it usually flies on, unhurriedly flapping to outdistance its tormentors. But a determined attack will make the buzzard turn over in the air to meet its enemies with its talons.

Present all year; started breeding again in Ireland in 1950s; scarce outside its breeding range

Mostly sedentary, but northern birds migrate; those from northern Europe winter in Africa

RECOGNITION: *dark brown plumage above, pale with darker bars and streaks below; broad wings and wide, rounded tail show in flight; sexes alike.*
NESTING: *both sexes build bulky nest of sticks, usually in trees, sometimes on cliff ledges; nest often decorated with leaves or seaweed; lays late April–early May; usually 2 or 3 eggs, white with chocolate or red-brown markings; incubation about 36 days, by both parents; nestlings, tended by both parents, leave at about 45–50 days.*
FEEDING: *small mammals, especially rabbits; sheep carrion; sometimes birds, earthworms, caterpillars, lizards, beetles; occasionally berries.*

Buzzard in hunting flight soars in slow, wide circles

Green woodpecker

Picus viridis 12½ in.

MALE

Present all year; first bred in Scotland in 1951 and has since spread north

Sedentary; but in winter some birds move into more open country

Green woodpecker scoops up ants with its long sticky tongue

IN country districts, this largest of our woodpeckers is sometimes called the yaffle, because its loud ringing call can sound almost like laughter. Its other country name, rain bird, probably arose through its call being heard more clearly in the atmospheric conditions before rain. The bird also has yelping and squealing cries, but these are most often heard from its young.

The green woodpecker is found in all kinds of well-timbered country, from open woodland, heaths, commons and farmland to parks and large gardens. Its numbers have risen in northern England and southern Scotland in recent years, but the reason for this has not been established. It has been suggested that the widespread planting of conifers has led to an increase in the wood ant, one of its favourite foods; yet the birds usually prefer broad-leaved woods to conifers.

A green woodpecker on the garden lawn is probably performing a useful service by ridding it of ants or other insects; but the birds can be troublesome too, for very occasionally they take fruit, and they have been known to damage beehives, trying to get at the grubs.

Male birds challenging other green woodpeckers for territory will sway their heads from side to side, and usually spread their wings, fan their tails and raise their crown feathers. In courtship they tend to droop their wings and raise the spread tail. Sometimes the male and female chase each other round a tree.

RECOGNITION: *largest and most brightly coloured of British woodpeckers; crimson crown; bright green upper parts; grey-green underparts; yellow rump; stripe under eye is red in male, black in female.*
NESTING: *both sexes bore hole in tree; chips left scattered on ground; lays April–May; 5–7 eggs, white; incubation about 19 days, by both sexes; nestlings, tended by both sexes, fly after 18–21 days.*
FEEDING: *wood-boring larvae of beetles, moths and other insects, mainly ants; occasionally grain, acorns, apples, cherries and other fruit.*

Wryneck

Jynx torquilla 8½ in.

THE wryneck, which was found over the whole of England except the extreme north and west at the beginning of the 20th century, has declined steadily and mysteriously until it has now ceased to breed in this country. Between 1958 and 1978 the breeding population fell catastrophically from some 100-200 pairs to none. Surprisingly, a few wrynecks have been found since 1969, nesting in the Scottish Highlands. These apart, the bird is extinct as a breeding species in Britain, though migrants continue to turn up on the east and south coasts.

The bird's name comes from its habit of twisting its head right round on its neck; and its early arrival in Britain at the end of March has earned it another name among country people: 'cuckoo's mate'. The male announces itself by perching high in a tree and giving a shrill 'quee-quee-quee' song at the top of its voice. In their courtship display male and female wrynecks often perch opposite each other, shaking their heads about, throwing them back on their shoulders and revealing the pink inside to their mouths.

Wrynecks, although they belong to the woodpecker family, do not bore into trees, either to get food or to make nests; instead, they use their long, fast-moving tongues to pick up insects from bark or from the ground. They are fond of orchards and gardens where holes in old fruit trees serve as nests. They will also make use of holes in walls or banks, or nest-boxes.

RECOGNITION: *slim; grey-brown plumage, mottled above and barred below; distinguished from treecreeper by larger size, longer tail and straight bill; sexes alike.*
NESTING: *nests in ready-made hole, without lining material; lays late May; usually 7–10 eggs, dull white; incubation about 12 days, chiefly by female; nestlings, fed by both sexes, leave at about 20 days.*
FEEDING: *chiefly ants and their pupae; also beetles, moths and spiders.*

Late March–Sept. visitor; now down to the odd breeding pair in Scotland

Winters mainly in southern Asia and in tropical Africa

Characteristic pose shows how the wryneck got its name

133

Lesser spotted woodpecker

Dendrocopos minor   5¾ in.

MALE

Present all year; nowhere numerous; absent in Scotland and Ireland

Sedentary; northernmost birds sometimes reach central Europe in winter

Parent bird feeds hungry nestling in tree-hole nest

THE lesser spotted woodpecker, a bird little bigger than a sparrow, is far from easy to pick out as it walks up the small branches high in deciduous trees. It keeps to well-timbered country and avoids conifers. Nowhere in Britain are lesser spotteds really common: they are thinly scattered over the southern part of England and Wales, scarce in Lancashire and Yorkshire and almost unknown farther north. There is something of a challenge in tracking them down, but the crimson-crowned male may sometimes be sighted as it flits from branch to branch, searching for insect larvae, or from tree to tree in a slow courtship display flight; and sometimes a pair can be seen side by side after a court-ship display, perched stock-still on a branch.

The lesser spotted's flight is slow and hesitant, with typical woodpecker 'bounds'. Its calls are a 'tchick' note, weaker and more sibilant than that of the great spotted; and, more often, a 'pee-pee-pee' call like the wryneck's, but lacking its ringing quality. The bird also makes a mechanical drumming sound with its bill, more prolonged than the great spotted's drumming but softer.

The shrill calls of the nestlings often draw attention to the nest-hole, which the parents bore in decaying tree-trunks or branches at almost any height up to 70 ft from the ground. A shaft about 7½–10 in. long leads from the entrance to the nest chamber, which is bare except for a few wood chips.

RECOGNITION: *black and white plumage; wings and lower back barred; male has crimson crown, female's is white.*

NESTING: *both sexes bore nest-hole in decayed wood; lays late April–June; usually 4–6 eggs, glossy white; incubation about 14 days, by both parents; nestlings, tended by both parents, leave after about 21 days.*

FEEDING: *mainly grubs of wood-boring beetles and moths; also grubs of gall-wasps, flies and spiders; some fruit, mainly currants and raspberries.*

Great spotted woodpecker

Dendrocopos major   9 in.

MALE

AFTER becoming extinct in Scotland and northern England in the first half of the 19th century, the great spotted woodpecker has made a come-back during the past 100 years. Today it is the most widespread of the British woodpeckers, breeding in almost every mainland county.

Great spotted woodpeckers nest in all kinds of well-timbered country. Unlike green woodpeckers, they are as much at home in coniferous woods as in broad-leaved woodlands; and they tend to feed rather more in trees and less on the ground. In recent years they have spread even to central London parks, and in some districts regularly visit garden bird tables.

They are unpopular with bee-keepers because they sometimes raid hives in search of grubs; in the same quest they will drill holes in telegraph poles.

Their flight is undulating, with wings folded against the body at the bottom of each bound. The call-note is a sharp 'tchich', and there is also a harsh churring note similar to that of the mistle thrush. But great spotteds have no song; instead, they produce a drumming noise by sharp taps of the bill on a resonant dead bough, making a sound far louder than when they are feeding.

At one time naturalists believed that this sound was created vocally, but this has been disproved.

RECOGNITION: *black, with white patches and blotches; male has crimson on head; young birds have red crown; both sexes and all ages have red under tail; easily distinguished from lesser spotted by larger size.*
NESTING: *both sexes excavate hole in tree, usually at least 10 ft up; no nest material except few chips of wood; often dispossessed by starlings; sometimes uses nest-box; lays May; 4–7 eggs, glossy white; incubation about 16 days, mainly by female; nestlings, fed by both sexes, leave after 19 or 20 days.*
FEEDING: *chiefly larvae of beetles, wood wasps and moths; some spiders; occasionally young birds snatched from nests; small vegetarian element.*

Present all year; a few birds reach Ireland from Scandinavia, but none breed there

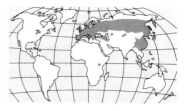

Mainly sedentary, though northernmost birds may move south when food is short

White patches on short wings make this woodpecker unmistakable

Turtle dove

Streptopelia turtur 11 in.

April–Sept. visitor; occurs mainly as rare passage migrant in Scotland and Ireland

Southern birds are sedentary; most others winter in tropical Africa

Distinctive tail pattern shows when turtle dove flies

THE 'voice of the turtle', heard in the Song of Solomon, is a sleepy, romantic song, evocative of a summer's day. But the deep, purring croon becomes more of a wheeze during the turtle dove's energetic territorial display, in which the bird climbs steeply, then it glides down, often circling to perch again on the tree from which it launched itself. In its courtship display the male bows or bobs in front of the female half-a-dozen times in quick succession, with breast slightly puffed out and bill pointing downwards. And in another display, parent birds will flutter 'helplessly' to distract predators from their young.

The turtle dove, the smallest and slimmest of our five breeding pigeons, is a summer visitor to Britain, avoiding the hills and preferring open woods, parkland and large gardens to dense woodland. It breeds commonly in the south and Midlands, and its numbers thin northwards and westwards, having declined dramatically in the past 20 years.

The bird's favourite food is the seed of a weed of arable fields, the common fumitory. The turtle dove's late arrival in Britain—at the end of April or the beginning of May—is probably related to the short supply of the seeds early in the year.

RECOGNITION: *slim with red-tinged upper parts and pink breast; black and white striped patch on neck; long tail with white tip; sexes alike.*
NESTING: *female builds flimsy platform of fine twigs, sometimes lined with roots, in tree or shrub, usually 4–8 ft up; lays May–July; usually 2 eggs, glossy white; incubation about 14 days, by both parents; nestlings, tended by both parents, leave after 18 days, fly a few days later; usually two broods.*
FEEDING: *seeds, mainly from common fumitory, chickweed, charlock and grass; sometimes small molluscs.*

Nightingale

Luscinia megarhynchos 6½ in.

IN spite of their name, and contrary to popular belief, nightingales are as likely to be heard singing by day as by night. But their virtuoso performances are best heard in the stillness of a warm evening in late spring, when the males compete to attract females arriving from the wintering grounds in tropical Africa. The females arrive ten days or so after the males. When the birds sing by day it is partly to warn other males to keep off their territory.

In volume, in variety of notes, and in the vigour with which it is poured out, the song is unforgettable. It consists of a rapid succession of repeated notes—some harsh, some liquid—including a very loud 'chooc-chooc-chooc' and a fluting, pleading 'pioo' building up slowly into a crescendo. Apart from this, there are also call-notes: a soft, chiffchaff-like 'hweet' and a harsh 'tacc-tacc'; and the bird has two alarm notes: a scolding 'krrrr' and a grating 'tchaaaa'.

For every ten people who have heard a nightingale sing there can hardly be one who has actually set eyes on this shy bird. When they do come into the open they are inconspicuous birds, with only their song to draw attention to them. The nightingale hides its nest as carefully as it conceals itself, building close to the ground among thick undergrowth. In its courtship display, the male spreads its tail and moves it up and down, fluttering its wings and bowing to pull its bill down below the level of its perch.

RECOGNITION: *brown plumage; rather like a large warbler, with red-brown tail and grey-brown underparts; whitish throat; sexes alike.*
NESTING: *female builds nest of dead leaves lined with grass and hair, on or close to ground; lays May; usually 5 eggs, olive-green or dark olive; incubation about 14 days, by female only; nestlings, tended by both parents, leave at about 11 or 12 days.*
FEEDING: *mainly ground insects; also earthworms, spiders, some berries.*

April–August visitor; has decreased in recent years; rare outside breeding range

All nightingales winter in tropical Africa, mainly north of the Equator

Nightingale's nest is well hidden in thick undergrowth

Redstart

Phoenicurus phoenicurus 5½ in.

MALE

Visits Britain April–Sept., has bred only rarely in Ireland; continental migrants also occur

Highly migratory; winters in savanna and scrub belt of northern tropical Africa

Redstarts will nest wherever they can find a ready-made hole

THE fiery chestnut tail of the redstart gives the bird its name: *steort* is an Old English word for tail. It helps to make the male, with its white forehead, black throat and grey mantle, one of the most handsome of our smaller birds. It plays an important part in courtship display, too; the male bows, stretches out its neck, droops its wings and splays its tail feathers to show a blaze of flame-red, then chases the female from perch to perch, with both sexes quivering their tails.

Redstarts breed in almost any habitat where they can find holes for nesting: in woodland, parks, gardens and riversides with old trees; and they will breed in treeless districts if stone walls or quarries provide nesting sites. They are most common in old woodland, especially in hill country, but may turn up in open country on their migration flights between Africa and Britain. Over the past 100 years the redstart has declined as a breeding bird in eastern and south-eastern England, and now breeds mainly in the north and west.

Redstarts repeatedly flutter from branch to branch or make hovering sallies into the air to catch flying insects; and they often collect food on the ground. The song begins strongly with a squeaky warble, then peters out in a twitter of feeble notes. Some male redstarts mimic notes from other species. The call is a long 'hooeet' and the alarm note a loud 'twee-tucc-tucc'.

RECOGNITION: *bright chestnut tail and rump; male distinguished from black redstart by chestnut breast and white forehead; female duller, with no white on forehead.*
NESTING: *female builds nest of grass, lined with hair, in natural hole or hollow in ground; may use nest-box; lays mid-May to June; usually 5–8 eggs, pale blue, very occasionally speckled; incubation about 13 days, by female only; nestlings, fed by both sexes, leave after about 16 days.*
FEEDING: *mainly insects and their larvae; also spiders and small worms; some berries.*

Pied flycatcher

Ficedula hypoleuca 5 in.

MALE IN SUMMER

Over the past 50 or 60 years, pied flycatchers have extended their breeding range from Wales into the bordering English counties, and from there into Yorkshire and south Scotland, with outposts in the Pennines, the Highlands and the West Country. This advance seems to have been helped in a few districts by the large-scale provision of nest-boxes; for pied flycatchers have to compete with redstarts and tits for the nesting-holes available in woodland, and suitable holes are often scarce in the hilly districts where they prefer to breed. On autumn migration they often appear on the coast and even in the middle of towns.

Pied flycatchers are retiring birds, usually keeping to the upper branches of trees. They live on insects, usually snapped up on the wing; but they will also feed on the ground and sometimes cling to tree trunks, like tits. In its feeding flight, the bird launches out from a branch to swerve and twist quickly after an insect, then lands again to watch for another victim, flicking its wings and tail as it settles. Unlike the spotted flycatcher, it rarely returns to the same perch.

The song has a rhythm which is echoed in the country-man's version: 'Tree, tree, tree, once more I come to thee'. The call-notes are a swallow-like 'whit' and a short 'tu', sometimes repeated, and they often draw attention to migrants resting on the coast.

RECOGNITION: *male black above, with white forehead; white below, with white bar on wing; female and autumn-plumaged male olive-brown with buff-white bar on wings and sides of tail.*
NESTING: *female builds nest of oak leaves, lined with grass, in a ready-made hole 3–40 ft above ground; lays mid-May; usually 5–8 eggs, pale green-blue; incubation about 13 days, by female only; nestlings, fed by both sexes, leave after about 14 days.*
FEEDING: *flies, flying beetles, sometimes butterflies and moths; occasionally earthworms and grubs.*

Present April–Oct.; migrants from Continent swell coastal population in autumn

Highly migratory; main winter quarters are in savanna belt of tropical Africa

Pied flycatcher—its numbers have increased in past 40 years

Blackcap

Sylvia atricapilla 5½ in.

FEMALE

MALE

April–Oct. visitor; a few winter here, especially in Ireland and southern England

Winter migration takes blackcaps to Mediterranean countries and equatorial Africa

Male blackcap flaps wings vigorously in aggressive display

ITS cap—glossy black in the male and red-brown in the female—makes the blackcap the easiest to identify of Britain's 13 breeding warblers. A further aid to identification is its rich and melodious song, which has won it a reputation as the 'northern nightingale'.

The male, usually singing from a perch in deep cover near the nest-site, pours out a clear, powerful warbling, varied with phrases mimicked from other birds' songs, and ending abruptly. The song is higher-pitched and less sustained than that of the garden warbler. The blackcap's call-notes are a harsh 'churr' and an excited 'tau-tau', rapidly repeated when the bird is alarmed.

Most blackcaps are summer visitors, arriving in April to breed over most of England and Wales, with a sparse population in Scotland and Ireland. They nest in woods, heaths and gardens with a plentiful undergrowth of brambles and rose briers or evergreen shrubs, particularly rhododendrons. In this coarse vegetation they build their frail nests, attached to the surrounding plants with 'basket handles'. They usually keep hidden among the bushes as they feed and their flights from one patch of cover to the next are short and jerky.

The male has a variety of courtship postures. Sometimes it raises its cap feathers and fluffs out its body feathers; sometimes it droops its wings and at other times it flaps them; and it may spread and raise its tail.

RECOGNITION: *grey-brown upper parts; male has glossy black cap; female's cap is red-brown.*
NESTING: *slight nest, built chiefly by hen, of dried grass lined with hair and rootlets, in bushes or other coarse vegetation; lays May–July; usually 4 or 5 eggs, white tinged with green and marbled with brown; incubation about 12 days, by both parents; nestlings, fed by both parents, leave after about 10 days.*
FEEDING: *flies, caterpillars and other insects; fruit and berries in autumn.*

Garden warbler

Sylvia borin 5½ in.

Only a large garden with extensive shrubberies is likely to make a home for garden warblers; the birds prefer deciduous woodland with widely spaced trees and plenty of bushes and briers. Sometimes they breed where there are no trees, in thick brier patches, osier beds and tangled hedges, or in conifer woods with deciduous undergrowth.

Garden warblers are secretive, spending most of their time in the shrubs; and they are not noticeable birds in the open, with their nondescript plain brown plumage. But their song gives them away, even when it comes from a concealed perch deep inside a hawthorn bush. The song is less of a virtuoso performance than the blackcap's, but mellower: a sweet, even warble, low-pitched and well sustained. The calls are typical warbler notes: a 'churr' and a 'tacc-tacc' of alarm.

Garden warblers fly in from central and southern Africa from mid-April to late May, spreading over most of England and Wales to breed. In the extreme west of Cornwall and Wales the birds are rare, and they seldom breed in Scotland outside the Lowlands. The male's courtship display consists of spreading its tail and fluttering its wings in front of its mate; the same behaviour from either sex serves as a distraction display to protect the young. Several 'trial' nests are built by the male before a site is finally chosen.

RECOGNITION: *plump; brown with pale buff underparts; low-pitched warbling song, well sustained; sexes alike.*
NESTING: *both sexes build nest from dry grass, lined with hair and rootlets, in thick cover usually less than 3 ft from ground; lays late May–early June; usually 4 or 5 eggs, white or pale green, with olive freckles; incubation about 12 days, mainly by female; nestlings, fed by both sexes, leave after about 10 days.*
FEEDING: *chiefly insects, with spiders in spring and summer; fruit and berries in autumn.*

April–Oct. visitor; occurs also as a passage migrant from the Continent

Winters exclusively in savannah woodlands of tropical Africa, as far south as KwaZulu-Natal

The nest is built in thick cover, quite close to the ground

Chiffchaff

Phylloscopus collybita 4¼ in.

Willow warbler

Phylloscopus trochilus 4¼ in.

Map shows range of willow warbler, April–Sept. visitor; chiffchaff scarce in Scotland

Range of willow warbler; chiffchaff's extends farther south; both winter mainly in Africa

Willow warbler has a distinctive song, fluent and wistful

THESE two birds are so alike that only an expert can tell them apart by their appearance; but their voices are a clear guide to identification. The chiffchaff's song is a monotonous, high-pitched 'chiff-chaff' or 'zip-zap', sometimes interspersed with a guttural churring note, audible only at close range. The willow warbler has a fluent, wistful song: a gentle series of descending notes, hanging over the woods from April to June; its song may be heard even in suburbs where gardens adjoin woodland. Both willow warbler and chiffchaff have a call-note, 'hoo-eet', but the chiffchaff pronounces it as a single syllable, 'hweet'.

The habitat favoured by both these summer migrants is almost identical: woods and other well-timbered and bushy places such as heaths, commons, shrubberies and large gardens. The chiffchaff, however, shows a preference for trees, for it needs a song-post at least 15 ft high. It is one of the earliest migrants to arrive, appearing from mid-March and often staying into October. The willow warbler usually arrives about a fortnight later and leaves a fortnight or three weeks earlier.

Courtship in both species consists largely of a slow-motion display flight. The willow warbler normally builds a well-hidden nest on the ground, and the chiffchaff nearly always seeks a site in a low bush.

RECOGNITION: *both have green to olive-brown plumage; flesh-coloured legs of some—but not all—willow warblers distinguish them from chiffchaffs; different songs of the two species are best guide to telling them apart.*
NESTING: *hens build domed nest of moss and dried grass, lined with feathers; lay late April–early May; usually 6 or 7 eggs, white with red-brown spots or blotches (willow warbler) or purple-brown spots (chiffchaff); incubation about 13 days, by hen only; nestlings, fed by both sexes (willow warbler) and hen only (chiffchaff), fly after about 13 days; willow warbler often has a second brood.*
FEEDING: *mainly small insects, such as caterpillars, gnats and midges.*

Wood warbler

Phylloscopus sibilatrix   5 in.

SUMMER

WOOD warblers are rarely seen or heard in Britain outside a clearly defined habitat: mature woodland with a closely knit canopy of leaves and sparse undergrowth. Here they find the insect life on which they feed throughout the summer. The birds hover to pick up insects from the underside of leaves, or occasionally sally from their perches to snap up food on the wing.

Because of their preference for a particular type of woodland, they are less common in the south and east than in the north and west; but fair numbers are attracted to the beechwoods of the southern chalk and limestone districts, as well as to the valley oakwoods and birchwoods of Wales and western Scotland. Even outside the breeding season wood warblers keep to the trees. In the autumn, before they migrate back to Africa, they eke out their diet with wild berries.

The 'warbler' part of the bird's name is a tribute to its song, or rather to both of them, for the wood warbler has two distinct songs. The first is a repeated single note, speeding up into a whistling trill; and the second is a mellow, liquid 'dee-ur', also the bird's anxiety note, plaintively repeated seven or more times.

In courtship, the male has two styles of flying: it either quivers its wings rapidly or flaps them slowly.

The nest is built in a hollow in the ground, and the dome shows above ground level.

RECOGNITION: *yellow breast; white belly; yellow-green above; yellow streak above eye; colouring duller in autumn; larger and more brightly coloured than chiffchaff or willow warbler; distinctive song; sexes alike.*
NESTING: *female builds domed nest of grass, leaves and fibres, lined with grass and hair, in natural hollow; lays May–June, usually 5–7 eggs, white, thickly spotted with dark red-brown; incubation about 13 days, by female only; nestlings, fed by both sexes, fly after about 12 days.*
FEEDING: *insects, chiefly small caterpillars, beetles, flies and aphids; some wild berries in autumn.*

April–August visitor; has nested a few times in Ireland; has never been recorded in winter

Highly migratory; winters in forests and savannas of northern tropical Africa

In display flight, the wood warbler quivers its wings like a dragonfly

Long-tailed tit

Aegithalos caudatus 5½ in. (including 3 in. tail)

Present all year; widespread except for Scottish northern islands; generally very sedentary

Essentially non-migratory, though some of the more northern birds wander south in winter

Young tit demands food, from snug protection of domed nest

PAIRS of long-tailed tits start work in late February or early March on the job of building their elaborate nests. In the fork of a tree or bush, at almost any height between 4 ft and 70 ft from the ground, they piece together lichen, cobwebs and animal hair to form the unmistakable oval-shaped domed nest which, with its entrance hole near the top, has earned them the country name of bottle tits. They work from inside the nest, and when the basic structure is finished they add a lining of up to 2000 feathers, and camouflage the outside with cobwebs. The nest is finished in time for egg-laying in late March to early May; and the fit is so snug that the parent birds have to fold their long tails over the back of their heads when they go inside.

In the breeding season, long-tailed tits are found on the outskirts of woods and in woodland clearings; some spread out to hedgerows and thickets but, unlike great tits and blue tits, they rarely visit suburban gardens. When winter comes, they usually keep to the woods; and at night they roost in groups, huddling together on branches.

There are two types of special courtship flight: a fast sexual chase through the leaves and a slower solo flight by the male. There is nothing corresponding to a song, but the bird has a variety of call-notes: a spluttering 'tsirrup', a soft 'tupp', and a thin 'si-si-si'.

RECOGNITION: *distinctive black and white tail, longer than body; pink, black and white plumage; sexes alike.*
NESTING: *intricate domed nest, covered with lichen and cobwebs, built by both sexes in tree or bush; lays late March–early May; usually 8–12 eggs, white with red-brown freckles; incubation about 16 days, mainly by female; nestlings, fed by both sexes, leave after about 14 days; parents often helped to feed young by neighbouring adults whose nesting attempts have failed.*
FEEDING: *mainly insects and spiders; occasionally seeds and buds.*

Marsh tit
Parus palustris   4½ in.
Willow tit
Parus montanus   4½ in

VIRTUALLY the only way of telling these two birds apart is by listening to their calls and songs. In appearance they are almost 'twins', though a long, close scrutiny will reveal that the willow tit has a pale patch on its wing, and that its black cap is sooty rather than glossy like the marsh tit's.

The calls of the marsh tit are a scolding 'chickabee-bee-bee-bee' and a harsh 'tchay', often following a soft 'pitchu' or 'pi', a note which the willow tit never gives. The willow's 'tchay' is more grating, and sometimes follows a 'chick' or 'chickit' call. The difference between their songs is more marked; the marsh tit's is a high-pitched 'schip-schip-schip' or 'schuppi-schuppi-schuppi'. The willow tit has two songs: one is a series of full-throated 'piu-piu' notes, rather like the wood warbler's call; the other consists of liquid notes interspersed with higher-pitched notes in a fluent warble.

The marsh tit is not especially associated with marshes, nor the willow tit with willows, though both live in woodland, often in damp surroundings. They share with other tits a courtship display in which the male parades in front of the female with feathers puffed out, wings drooped and tail held erect. Both nest in holes, but the marsh tit uses natural holes in trees or walls, whereas willow tits excavate holes in rotten wood.

RECOGNITION : *black cap, glossy in marsh tit, sooty in willow ; willow has paler wing-patch ; both have grey-brown upper parts, dull buff-white underparts ; best told from each other by calls and song ; sexes alike.*
NESTING : *marsh tit builds in natural hole with foundation of moss and pad of hair and down ; willow tit digs hole in decaying wood, builds nest mainly of wood chips and fibres with pad of hair ; both lay April or early May ; usually 6–8 eggs, white with red-brown speckles ; incubation about 14 days, by female only ; nestlings, fed by both sexes, leave after about 16 days.*
FEEDING : *insects ; also seeds and wild fruit.*

Present all year; in Scotland, marsh tit keeps to south-east, willow tit to south-west

Map shows range of marsh tit; willow tit's is greater, extending across Eurasia

Marsh tit uses ready-made hole as its nesting site

Treecreeper

Certhia familiaris 5 in.

Present all year, breeds in every county except Orkney and Shetland

Mainly sedentary, but some move south in winter from far north of Canada and Siberia

Treecreeper spirals its way up bark in search of insects

MANY woodland birds are more likely to be heard than seen, and the treecreeper is one of the more elusive of this group. It spends most of its time in trees, well camouflaged as it crawls up the bark like a feathered mouse; and it tucks its nest away behind a tiny entrance hole that is easily overlooked, though tell-tale pieces of nesting material may stick out through cracks. The song, always delivered from a tree, is a high-pitched 'tee-tee-tee-titit-dooee'; and the most frequent call-notes are a high-pitched and rather prolonged 'tseeee' and a tit-like 'tsit'.

In a leafless winter, the treecreeper may sometimes be seen probing tree trunks with its curved needle beak. The bird will work its way up a trunk in short jerks, sometimes spirally, occasionally moving quickly sideways or bracing itself against its stiff tail as it tugs at some stubborn insect. When it moves to another trunk it starts at the foot of the bole again. It is equally agile searching upside-down on the underside of a bough.

Hard winters punish this small bird; but when Wellingtonia trees were introduced from California, treecreepers learned to make crevices in the soft bark to use as snug roosting places.

Courtship displays include chases, a bat-like display flight, wing-shivering and courtship feeding.

RECOGNITION: *brown above, silvery-white beneath ; only small British land-bird with a curved beak ; sexes alike.*
NESTING: *probably both sexes build nest of dried grass and rootlets, lined with feathers, wool and bits of bark, behind loose bark or ivy roots or in other tree cavities, occasionally in nest-boxes, exceptionally in wall crevice or old shed ; lays April–June ; usually 6 eggs, white, with red-brown spots at blunt end ; incubation about 15 days, probably mainly by hen ; nestlings, fed by both parents, leave after about 14 or 15 days ; sometimes two broods.*
FEEDING: *invertebrates such as spiders, woodlice, weevils and other small beetles, earwigs, small caterpillars ; sometimes grain and weed seeds.*

Nuthatch

Sitta europaea $5\frac{1}{2}$ in.

THE nuthatch gets its name from its habit of wedging nuts in the bark of a tree and splitting them open with vigorous blows from its 'hatchet' bill. It often attacks the nut from above, and is in fact the only British bird that regularly climbs down trees head first.

In the past few years, nuthatches have spread north and west. When they disappeared from central London parks in the late 19th century (they returned in 1958) it was suggested that atmospheric pollution, covering the trees with soot, had driven them out. This may be the reason why today nuthatches are not usually seen near industrial centres.

The bird has a remarkable range of call-notes, mostly ringing or piping calls, such as 'chwit-chwit' or more frequently 'chwit-it-it'. Other notes in the range are a tit-like 'tsit'; a sibilant 'tsirrp' reminiscent of the long-tailed tit; and in the breeding season two or three loud repetitions of 'twee', as well as a note that sounds like a boy's whistling. Yet another call-note sounds like the shrill chatter of the kestrel.

In its courtship display the male often flies slowly, or postures with feathers fluffed out and wings and tail spread. The nest is always in a hole, and the birds generally choose a site more than 6 ft up a tree; but nuthatches will use nest-boxes, too, and occasionally they build in a wall or a haystack.

RECOGNITION: *black eye-stripe; white throat; slate-grey upper parts; buff underparts; often climbs down trees head first; sexes alike.*
NESTING: *builds nest of bark flakes (often pine) or dead leaves, usually in tree hole; often reduces entrance with mud to keep out larger birds; lays late April–May; 6–10 eggs, white, spotted with red-brown; incubation about 14 days, by female only; nestlings, fed by both sexes, fly after about 24 days.*
FEEDING: *mainly hazel nuts, beech mast, acorns; also beetles, earwigs and small caterpillars.*

Present all year; a few have been seen in southern Scotland; unknown in Ireland

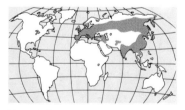

Essentially sedentary, though mass movements west and south from Siberia are on record

Nuthatch wedges nut in tree bark, cracks it open with 'hatchet' bill

147

Brambling
Fringilla montifringilla 5¾ in.

MALE IN SUMMER

Late Sept.–April visitor; also widespread as a passage migrant

Winters south of breeding range, some reaching as far as N. Africa, Iran and Japan

Male in winter plumage has dark mottling on head and upper parts

FROM late September bramblings flock into Britain, travelling across the North Sea from their breeding grounds north of the Baltic. They spread out over the eastern part of the country, often joining other finches to form mixed flocks which feed in beechwoods and on farmland throughout the winter. Beech mast is an important item in the birds' winter diet, but bramblings also visit rick-yards and stubble-fields in search of grain and weeds.

The cock bird's handsome breeding plumage is seen only briefly in Britain before the bramblings return to Scandinavia and Siberia in March and April.

Its spring song—rather like the 'dzwee' of the green-finch—is rarely heard here; and even rarer in Britain is the melodic, fluting song which is given in the breeding season. Until recently there was only one known case— in Sutherland in 1920—of bramblings having nested in Britain. Since 1979 they have bred in Scotland and eastern England on several occasions. In winter the best way of identifying a brambling is by its call-note, a rather grating 'tsweek', or by the 'chucc-chucc-chucc' cry it gives in flight.

Bramblings often turn up in pinewoods before migrating from Britain; and back in their breeding grounds they move into conifers and birchwoods to build their nests.

RECOGNITION: *white rump; orange-buff breast and shoulder patch in male; male's head and upper parts glossy black in summer, mottled brown in winter; female has dull brown upper parts.*
NESTING: *nests in Scandinavia and Siberia; builds deep cup nest in tree; lays mid-May–July; usually 6 or 7 eggs, green-blue to olive-brown with dark spots and streaks, incubation probably about .12 days, by female only; nestlings, fed by both parents, leave after about 14 days.*
FEEDING: *seeds of weeds, beech mast, grain; sometimes berries; insects in spring.*

Jay

Garrulus glandarius 13½ in.

ITS exotically coloured plumage and screeching 'skaak-skaak' cry make the jay a conspicuous bird at most times of the year. But in the nesting season the jay is more silent, and is hard to see as it slips from branch to branch under a thick cover of leaves.

Jays keep to the woods far more than any of the other British crows; they also visit hedgerows, town parks and gardens, but they are seldom far from trees. They prefer open woodland with tall undergrowth in summer; and in winter they seem to depend largely on oak trees to see them through the weeks when food is scarce. In autumn the jays pluck acorns and fly off to bury them in the ground; later, in hard weather, they return to their hidden stores to feed. Any forgotten acorns spring up, so jays are important in spreading oaks to new areas of woodland.

In early spring jays become social birds, gathering for ceremonies in which they chase one another on slowly flapping wings. At other times, outside the breeding season, they move about in pairs or small parties. Courtship consists chiefly of posturing and spreading the wings and tail.

Apart from its characteristic screech, the jay has a wide vocabulary, including a loud, ringing 'kiew' note, and a sound like a chuckle which may be mimicked from the magpie. Like some of our other crows, the jay occasionally gives a low, crooning warble.

RECOGNITION: *brown-pink plumage; blue wing-coverts barred with black; black and white crown feathers; white rump seen in flight; sexes alike.*
NESTING: *both sexes build nest of twigs lined with rootlets and hair in bush or tree, usually 4–20 ft from the ground; lays April–June; usually 3–6 eggs, green-tinged with olive-brown freckles; incubation about 16 days, by female only; nestlings, fed by both parents, leave after 20 days.*
FEEDING: *acorns; eggs and young birds; insects and larvae in spring and summer; occasionally worms, mice and lizards.*

Present all year; immigrants from the Continent sometimes reach south-east England

Essentially sedentary; but northern birds disperse southwards when food is scarce

In autumn, jays fly off with acorns, bury them to eat later

149

Hawfinch

Coccothraustes coccothraustes 7 in.

MALE IN SUMMER

Present all year, but generally scarce; very rare in Ireland

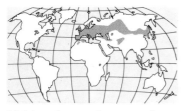

Mainly sedentary, but some of most northerly birds winter in south of breeding range

Outsize bill makes the hawfinch unmistakable even as it flies

THE powerful bill of the hawfinch, operated by highly developed muscles, allows the bird to bring to bear a crushing force of 60–95 lb. to crack open the cherry stones which are one of its favourite foods in autumn and winter. Hawfinches ignore the flesh of cherries; they wait until the ripe fruit has fallen from the tree, then feed on the stones. They crack open the stones of sloes and damsons in the same way. Haws, hips and holly berries also form part of their diet; and their taste for green peas has made them some enemies among farmers and gardeners.

The hawfinch, Britain's largest finch, started nesting here only 150 years ago. It breeds in deciduous woodland, and in orchards, large gardens and bushy places with scattered trees. Hawfinches are shy birds, preferring to perch in the topmost branches of tall trees. In foraging visits to the ground they hop rather heavily. In winter they often move into more open country, forming small feeding flocks.

The song of the hawfinch is feeble, halting and seldom heard; but in flight it has a loud and distinctive clipped 'tick'. The male's courtship display includes puffing out the head and breast feathers, bowing, and drooping the wing-tips; and sometimes the pair touch their bills in what looks like a kiss but is in fact courtship feeding.

RECOGNITION: *upper parts red-brown, underparts peach; black bib and wings with white shoulders; white on wings and tail conspicuous in flight; massive bill is grey-blue in summer, yellow in winter; female duller.*
NESTING: *female builds cup of roots and grass founded on twigs and moss, usually on a high branch; sometimes lined with hair or fibres; lays late April–May; usually 4–6 eggs, pale blue-green or grey-green with dark brown marks; incubation about 12 days, by female only; nestlings, fed by both parents, leave at about 11 days; sometimes two broods.*
FEEDING: *mainly fruit stones and large seeds; sometimes peas, haws and beech mast; occasionally insects.*

CONIFEROUS WOODLAND

Forests of tall conifers, where full daylight rarely
penetrates the dark green roof and the ground is softly
carpeted with needles, once covered large areas of these islands.
As the pinewoods retreated, victims of a changing climate
and of the woodman's axe, life became precarious for those
conifer-dwelling birds which were too specialised to change
their habits. But today new plantations are spreading up
the hillsides, and the birds of this habitat are
reaping the reward of their conservatism.

CONTENTS

MALE

FEMALE

Capercaillie

Tetrao urogallus   M 33 in.   F 25 in.

Present all year in Scottish pinewoods; present population introduced from Sweden in 1830's

Sedentary, keeping to conifer forests or mixed woodland

Capercaillie—unpopular with foresters because it eats the buds and shoots of conifers

TOWARDS the end of the 18th century this, the largest of our game-birds, became extinct in the British Isles—a victim of the disappearance of many natural pine forests and of the guns and snares of huntsmen. But in the late 1830s a collection of 55 birds was brought from Sweden to the Marquis of Breadalbane's estate in Perthshire, and the capercaillie quickly re-established itself in the pine forests there and the surrounding areas. Today it occurs in the greater part of its former range in the Scottish Highlands. For largely unknown reasons, its numbers have declined over the past 20 years. Previous attempts to establish it in other parts of the British Isles have failed.

The cock capercaillie is much the largest bird likely to be seen in a pinewood, and could be mistaken for an escaped and unexpectedly airborne turkey. It can weigh up to 17 lb. In the spring it performs an extraordinary courtship display on a special ground where the ceremonies include mock battles between the males, which leap into the air, and fan their tails. The 'song' of the male is one of the weirdest in the world of birds. It begins with a resonant rattle, continues with a noise like the drawing of a cork and pouring liquid out of a narrow-necked bottle, and ends with a knife-grinding sound.

Some males defend the boundaries of their territories exceptionally boldly, attacking dogs and human beings as well as other birds.

RECOGNITION: *fan tail; plumage grey-black with dark green breast and brown tinge on wings; female smaller, ruddy brown and mottled.*
NESTING: *hen makes scrape in the ground lined with vegetation, often at foot of pine tree; lays late April–May; 5–8 eggs, pale yellow speckled with brown; incubation about 4 weeks, by hen only; young, tended by hen only, can flutter after 2–3 weeks, but are not fully grown until much later.*
FEEDING: *conifer shoots; fruit and berries in summer; occasionally insects.*

Black grouse

Lyrurus tetrix   M 21 in.   F 14 in.

MALE

FEMALE

BLACK grouse are polygamous, with the males, or blackcocks, taking no part in nesting duties. Their remarkable courtship ceremonies take place at communal display grounds known as leks. Blackcocks arrive there in March, about a month before the hens. At the lek, cocks joust with cocks and, to a lesser extent, hens with hens. The fighting is mostly mock, with opponents hopping up and down, their tails fully spread; occasionally the battles become more serious as the birds try to force their way towards the centre of the lek, the best place for securing matings. Sometimes old blackcocks resume their lek displays in the autumn.

Black grouse were once widespread on the heaths and moors of southern England. Recently, the last few pairs on Dartmoor and Exmoor have disappeared and the present most southerly populations—in Wales and the Peak district—are declining alarmingly. In northern Britain, despite local, temporary increases due to new forestry planting, there has also been a general decline over the past 100 years.

The blackcock is easily recognised by its lyre-shaped tail, which is white underneath. The female, confusingly known as the greyhen, is brown, about 7 in. smaller and with a forked tail.

The bird's diet is almost entirely vegetarian, although it will take insects occasionally. Birch buds are its favourite food, and it also has a taste for young conifer shoots, which has made it unpopular with foresters.

RECOGNITION: *male has lyre-shaped tail with white underfeathers; glossy blue-black plumage with white wing-bar; female smaller, with chestnut and buff plumage and forked tail.*
NESTING: *female makes scrape in ground, often among rushes; lays May–June; 6–10 eggs, buff with sparse red-brown spots; incubation about 27 days, by female only; young, tended by female only, fly after 2–3 weeks, but are not fully grown until much later.*
FEEDING: *conifer shoots and birch buds; some beetles and other insects.*

Present all year; formerly bred more widely but now extinct in southern England

Sedentary; most common along edges of wooded country

Blackcocks threaten one another at a lek or courtship arena

Long-eared owl
Asio otus   14 in.

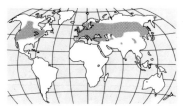

Present all year, but breeding birds are scarce in most parts of England and Wales

Mainly sedentary; some northern birds move south in winter

'Ear tufts' have no connection with the bird's true ears

THE 'ears' of the long-eared owl have nothing to do with hearing: they are simply elongated head feathers, useful in species recognition when they are held erect. The bird breeds in many parts of the British Isles, though it is not common in Wales, the Midlands and the south. Normally it chooses pinewoods, and its low, moaning hoot is one of the most eerie sounds of the woodland night. But it also nests on heathland, dunes and marshes; and sometimes it searches for prey over open country.

The long-eared owl hunts by night and roosts by day, flattening itself against a tree trunk. If the smaller birds which often make up part of its prey find one hiding in a tree they will mob it mercilessly; at other times, its presence may be given away by pellets lying on the ground beneath a favourite roosting tree. A recent study of the food of long-eared owls in Northern Ireland showed that the long-tailed field mouse, or wood mouse, was easily its favourite prey, with the diet made up by house mice, brown rats, pigmy shrews and various small birds.

The male has a special courtship display flight. It claps its wings together, then jumps up in the air. When angry, it threatens with outspread wings, hissing and snapping. As well as hooting, it has a barking call at breeding times, and the young have a hunger cry that sounds like the squeaking of an unoiled hinge.

RECOGNITION: *long ear tufts; plumage buff with pale mottling and dark streaks; yellow eyes; sexes alike.*
NESTING: *usually uses old nest of magpie, raven or other crow, or a squirrel's drey; sometimes builds on ground; lays March–April; 4 or 5 eggs, glossy white; incubation 25–28 days, by female only; young, fed by both sexes, leave after about 25 days.*
FEEDING: *mice, rats, voles, shrews; finches, sparrows, and at times birds as large as jays; some cockchafers and other beetles.*

Crossbill

Loxia curvirostra 6½ in.

Scottish crossbill

Loxia scotica 6¾ in.

FEMALE

MALE

VARIATION in bill shapes to suit a special kind of diet is marked in the finch family; and the crossbill is a specialist among finches. It is the only British bird which has the tips of its bill crossed—an adaptation which enables it to pick seeds out of cones as it moves sideways along the branches, parrot-fashion. Conifer seeds are almost the bird's only food, though occasionally it will take wild fruit and insects.

It is probably their reliance on conifers that causes irregular 'invasions' of crossbills across the North Sea into Britain. Mass irruptions of the birds every few years are believed to be triggered off by a failure in the supply of spruce cones in Scandinavia. They start to arrive on the east coast of Britain in late June or early July, and later spread out to any part of the country where conifers have been planted. Some stay to breed in southern England, but unless they are reinforced by fresh arrivals from the Continent these breeding stocks tend to die out. A distinct breeding population in the Highlands survives independently of fresh arrivals. These birds have larger bills and have specific rank—Scottish crossbill; the only bird species unique to Britain.

The song of the crossbill is rather like that of the greenfinch; but its flight-note, a metallic 'jip-jip', is unmistakable. Its courtship displays include a sexual chase and courtship feeding. The birds nest in conifers, often in loose colonies.

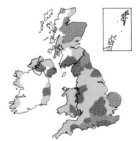

Widespread in years when there are 'invasions' from Europe

Mainly sedentary; irruptions occur in years of food shortage

RECOGNITION: *crossed bill; adult male crimson with orange tint, young male duller; female yellow-green; both have dark brown wings and tail.*
NESTING: *female builds substantial nest of twigs in a conifer, lines it with grasses; usually lays February–March; 3 or 4 eggs, green tinged with purple-red marks at blunt end; incubation about 13 days, by female only; nestlings, fed by both sexes, leave after 18 days.*
FEEDING: *seeds of pine, larch, spruce and other conifers; very occasionally fruit, weed seeds and insects.*

Crossbill extracts seeds from a pine cone

Redpoll

Acanthis flammea   5 in.

MALE IN SUMMER

Present all year; in winter some migrate to France and some northern birds reach Britain

Northern populations are migratory

Black chin distinguishes redpoll from other small brown finches

WITH the spread of conifer plantations, redpoll numbers in Britain increased rapidly to reach a peak in about 1970. Since then, although remaining common locally, the trend has been reversed. The redpoll usually breeds in loose colonies, mainly on heaths and in copses where there are conifers, birch trees and alders, but it will also nest in large gardens and shrubberies. It is slightly smaller and darker than the two forms which normally visit Britain in autumn and winter—the mealy redpoll from the Continent and the Greenland redpoll.

It builds its nest in a bush or tree at any height over about 2 ft. From the outside the nest appears rather untidy, but inside it is neat and compact, with a lining of willow down, and sometimes hair and feathers.

Redpolls are lively, sociable birds, often flocking with siskins in autumn and winter to feed on alder and birch seeds, or sometimes joining other finches and buntings to pick up food as they hop over stubble-fields, rick-yards and salt-marshes. When the birds are feeding, they have a habit of suddenly flying up in a mass, wheeling in the air and returning to their feeding place. Their flight is bounding, and the flight-note, 'chuch-uch-uch-uch-errrr', which also forms the basis of their somewhat primitive song, often enables them to be identified at a distance. The song is a long series of trilling notes, usually given in flight.

RECOGNITION: *plumage brown and streaked; adult has red forehead, black chin; male in summer has pink breast and rump.*
NESTING: *female builds flimsy cup nest lined with down on foundation of thin twigs; lays May–June; 4–6 eggs, blue, spotted and streaked with pale brown; incubation about 11 days, by female only; nestlings, fed by both parents, leave at about 12 days; sometimes two broods.*
FEEDING: *mainly seeds of birch and alder, weed seeds, conifer and willow seeds; young are fed on insects at first.*

Siskin

Carduelis spinus 4¾ in.

MALE

THIS small yellow-green finch, once much admired as a cage-bird under the name of aberdevine, is another species on the advance because of the spread of conifer plantations. It is widespread as a winter visitor, when it often joins feeding flocks of redpolls on birches and alders; but as a breeding species it was almost confined to northern Scotland and the pine plantation areas of Ireland until quite recently. Now it is breeding regularly in newly afforested areas where it was formerly unknown—in East Anglia, Wales, Northumberland, Devon and Hampshire. In the past 30 years it has become a common feeder on peanuts in gardens.

The cock siskin is much yellower than any other British finch except the male greenfinch, and is the only one, apart from the greenfinch, to have yellow patches at the base of its tail.

In the breeding season, siskins live in coniferous woods, but they will also nest in large gardens if there are pine trees present. The males put on a display flight over the nesting territory, and their song, a sweet, twittering succession of notes ending with a creaking sound, is mainly heard from the middle of February to the end of May. In courtship, the male chases the female and postures before her with feathers fluffed out and wings spread. Both sexes build the nest, usually towards the end of a branch and at least 15 ft from the ground.

RECOGNITION: *yellow-green plumage, with dark streaks on back and flanks; bounding flight typical of finches; male has black bib and crown, female is more drab.*

NESTING: *both sexes build neat and compact nest high in conifer, of twigs, lichen, moss and wool, lined with roots, hair, feathers and down; lays April–June; 3–5 eggs, pale blue, spotted and streaked with purple-red; incubation usually 11 or 12 days, by female only; nestlings, fed at first by female only, fly at about 15 days; usually two broods.*

FEEDING: *mainly seeds of trees and weeds; insects during breeding season.*

Present all year in Scotland and Ireland; mainly a winter visitor to England and Wales

Mainly sedentary, though irregular mass movements by northern birds occur when food is scarce

Siskin often mixes with other small birds to feed in woods

Crested tit

Parus cristatus 4½ in.

Present all year; breeds only in east Scottish Highlands and is rarely seen elsewhere

Largely sedentary; found in coniferous forests, and also in deciduous woods in south

Crested tit—its pointed crest distinguishes it from other tits

Extensive felling of woodland in Scotland during the 17th and 18th centuries drove the crested tit into a small area of the Highlands. But now, because of re-afforestation, the species is moving back into areas from which it was once lost. The advance is a slow one. The crested tit, living mainly on insects picked from pines, and sometimes taking the seeds of conifers and juniper berries, has never been recorded as breeding outside Scotland; and even there, its nesting areas are limited to pinewoods in the Highlands, with a spread in recent years to the Grampian region and the eastern part of Sutherland.

The crested tit is the second smallest of our tits, only ¼ in. longer than the coal tit. It is easily identified by its distinctive crest of long black feathers with white tips, and by its white cheeks with a curve of black round the eye. Its vocabulary is mostly restricted to a soft 'tsi-tsi-tsi' contact note and a soft churring sound.

Courtship consists of a special fluttering flight by the male, which goes on to chase the female through the high conifer branches, and feeds her during incubation. There is also a posture in which the male raises its crest and flutters its wings. The female may excavate a nest-hole, usually in a rotten pine stump; but natural holes, in trees and fence-posts, are also used. The male sometimes helps to gather nesting material.

RECOGNITION: *black crest feathers edged with white; black semicircle behind the eye; grey-brown back; sexes alike.*
NESTING: *uses natural hole, or hole excavated by the female, usually in rotten pine stump; male may help to gather deer hair, feathers and wool for nest-building; lays late April–May; usually 5 or 6 eggs, white with red-brown spots; incubation about 14 days, by female only; nestlings, fed by both sexes, fly after about 18 days.*
FEEDING: *aphids, caterpillars and other insects; sometimes conifer seeds and juniper berries.*

Coal tit

Parus ater $4\frac{1}{4}$ in.

THIS smallest of the seven British breeding tits is easily recognised by the white spot on its nape. It is less bold than most other tits and not so brightly coloured; but it constantly draws attention to itself with its clear, high-pitched song. The most characteristic notes of this song, a piping version of the so-called 'saw-sharpening' sound produced by the great tit, are 'teechu-teechu-teechu' and a triple 'tchuee', followed by a trill. Its calls include a plaintive 'tsui-tsui' and a thin, high-pitched 'tsee'.

Coal tits are often seen in town parks and gardens, but their shyness makes them less frequent visitors to bird tables than great tits or blue tits. Their favourite haunts are woods and any place where there are scattered trees, particularly pines, firs, spruce and other conifers. They nest in any convenient hole in a tree, bank or wall, and will often make use of nest-boxes. The male feeds the female during incubation, and if a potential enemy approaches she sits tight on the eggs until the last possible moment, when she starts hissing angrily.

In winter, coal tits often join other tits, treecreepers and goldcrests in foraging parties through the woods. Two different courtship displays have been observed. In one the male parades up and down with tail erect, wings drooping and feathers puffed out; in the other it leans forward with tail outspread and wings fluttering.

RECOGNITION: *glossy blue-black head and white 'flash' on nape; drab olive-buff back, pale underparts apart from black bib; sexes alike.*
NESTING: *nest, in tree hole, bank or wall, built by both sexes with thick pad of animal hair and feathers on moss foundation; usually lays April–early May; usually 6–10 eggs, white with red-brown speckles; incubation about 14 days, usually by female; nestlings, fed by both sexes, fly after about 16 days.*
FEEDING: *insects, including beetles, flies and their grubs, and caterpillars; spiders; seeds of thistles and other weeds; sometimes wild nuts.*

Present all year; in some years immigrants from continental countries reach southern England

Mainly sedentary, but food shortage may cause short-distance movements

Coal tit on cedar cone shows distinctive white patch on nape

Goldcrest

Regulus regulus $3\frac{1}{2}$ in.

MALE

Present all year; more common in broad-leaved woodland after the breeding season

Mainly sedentary, though northernmost breeding birds fly south in winter

Goldcrest's nest is usually slung under the branch of a conifer

LIVELY and fearless, the goldcrest is Britain's smallest bird; and it makes up in pugnacity for what it lacks in size. Cock birds have been known to fight to the death over a hen in the breeding season; and the hen will defend its nest by flying out to peck at any animal intruder, or keep a watchful guard from a few feet away against a human.

The nest is often built in a conifer, even in areas of mixed woodland. Goldcrests look for sites from which they sling an intricate structure of moss, spiders' webs and feathers, suspending it by 'basket handles' at any height up to 50 ft or more. After the breeding season is over they are likely to be seen on heaths, commons and other open places as well as in conifers and deciduous woods.

In courtship, the cock spreads and raises the black-bordered orange crest which gives the bird its name. Its call-note is a thin 'zi-zi', higher pitched than the cries of a coal tit or treecreeper, and its high-pitched song is distinctive: 'cedar-cedar-cedar-cedar-sissa-pee'.

Goldcrests have benefited as a species from the planting of conifer trees, but their numbers are always severely reduced by a cold winter. In some exceptionally hard winters they have almost been wiped out. After a few years, however, they always manage to re-establish their numbers.

RECOGNITION: *yellow-green plumage with double wing-bar; male's crest is orange, female's more yellow; both have black border at base.*
NESTING: *nests usually in conifer, but sometimes in deciduous tree, bush or creepers, 3–50 ft high, sometimes more; both sexes build elaborate nest of spiders' webs, moss and feathers, suspended by 'basket handles'; lays April–June; usually 7–10 eggs, white or pale yellow, freckled with brown; incubation about 15 days, by hen only; young, fed by both sexes, fly after about 20 days; usually two broods.*
FEEDING: *flies and other insects; spiders.*

FRESHWATER MARGINS AND MARSHES

The intensive reclamation of marshland
for agricultural use had a punishing effect on
bird life, wiping out entire breeding communities in
some areas. But the public attitude towards birds changed,
bringing new hope for the birds which remained and bringing
back some species which had once seemed lost to Britain.
The osprey's return after an absence of almost
50 years is the most spectacular triumph of
the bird protection movement.

CONTENTS

Bittern

Botaurus stellaris   30 in.

Present all year; rare outside
East Anglia, although a few
nest in Lancashire

Birds from western Europe and
South Africa are sedentary;
others migrate south to the Tropics

Bittern, pointing its bill to the sky,
merges into the reeds

THE boom of the bittern, resembling something
between a lowing cow and a distant foghorn, is a
sound that has returned to the Norfolk Broads this
century, and now and then is to be heard in other parts
of the country. Two hundred years ago, nesting bitterns
were not uncommon, but with the draining of marshes
they were gradually pressed back into the fens; and
even there they were extinct by 1850. Fifty years later,
the foghorn 'song' of bitterns was heard again on the
Broads, with increasing frequency; but not until 1911
was breeding actually proved, at Sutton Broad. After
this they spread elsewhere in East Anglia and eastern
England, and also to Lancashire and North Wales. However, a renewed decline began in the 1950s and 1960s. Its
causes are not fully understood, but by 1991 the bittern's
British population had fallen to about 16 pairs.

When unaware of being seen, the bittern may look
rather like a large domestic hen, hunched up with its
long neck drawn in. But if the bird suspects danger it
may 'freeze', with neck and beak stretched vertically,
and the streaked plumage provides excellent camouflage
among the dried reeds.

Bitterns are almost entirely confined to extensive
swamps, fens and reed-beds. In the breeding season
they perform collective aerial displays. Booming is not
their only sound. At dusk they produce a harsh flight-
call, 'kow' or 'kwah'.

RECOGNITION: *buff plumage is mottled, streaked and barred with dark
brown and black; green feet and legs; sexes alike.*
NESTING: *female builds untidy pile of sedges and other material, usually in
water or on thick water vegetation; lays April–May; 4–6 eggs, olive;
incubation about 25 days, by female; nestlings, fed by female, leave in
2–3 weeks, fly after about 8 weeks.*
FEEDING: *frogs and small fish; water-voles, water-beetles, water-boatmen,
dragonfly nymphs; some small birds and nestlings; water-weed at times.*

Grey heron

Ardea cinerea 36 in.

L IKE a tall grey sentinel, the heron stands in the shallows, poised to wade forward and strike with its pick-axe bill at a fish, frog or water-vole. Small fish are swallowed whole, head first, and larger ones are stabbed repeatedly, then taken to the bank to have the flesh picked from their bones.

Grey herons will range more than 12 miles for food. Sometimes they raid garden ponds for goldfish; at others they may visit rick-yards and cornfields, searching for small rodents; and occasionally they nest in parks. A small heronry has become established in Regent's Park, London, since 1968.

Besides the bittern, only one species of heron breeds in the British Isles; it is called the grey heron, to distinguish it from the purple heron, which breeds in Holland and sometimes visits Britain on migration. The breeding population is fairly stable at 14,000 pairs, with a temporary drop after severe weather.

Once a heronry has been established, birds will return to the same site, year after year. They have a wide and raucous vocabulary, with the common call a loud, harsh 'krornk'. Courtship is preceded by a 'dance' ceremony in which the male stretches its neck up and then lowers it over its back, with the bill pointing upwards. When there are eggs or nestlings to care for, one parent stays on guard against predators while the other is away feeding.

RECOGNITION: *grey upper parts; dark grey flight feathers; black crest; bushy breastplate and stout yellow bill; usually flies with legs trailing and neck drawn in; sexes alike.*
NESTING: *nests in colonies, usually in trees, but also locally in reed beds or on sea cliffs; female arranges platform of sticks or reeds brought by male; lays February–May; 3–5 eggs, light blue; incubation about 25 days, by both parents; young, fed by both parents, leave after 7–8 weeks.*
FEEDING: *fish, water-voles, beetles, frogs, moles and rats.*

Present all year; in winter some birds move to coasts and migrants arrive from northern Europe

Most are sedentary, but some of the most northerly birds winter as far south as tropical Africa

Grey heron flies with head drawn back and legs trailing behind

163

The heron—patient killer of the marshes

At rest, standing on one leg with eyes half closed and head hunched between its shoulders, the heron seems hardly to be interested in the world around it. But it takes only the rippling of an eel in the shallows or the rustling of a mouse moving through the grass to summon the lightning reflexes which have made the bird one of the most efficient killers of the marshes. The heron's hunting technique is to stalk through the shallows, ready to strike at prey with its pick-axe of a bill. So successful is this method that anglers used to rub fat from the bird on to their bait, in the belief that the heron's feet and legs put out a special oil which had the power of attracting fish. In fact, the bird has no need of mysterious oils, for it has something just as effective . . . endless patience.

Osprey

Pandion haliaetus 22 in.

Rare April–Oct. visitor; more than
100 pairs nest in Scotland, recently
a few in England

Birds from Europe and Asia
winter mainly in tropical Africa
and southern Asia

Osprey plunges towards the water
to snatch a fish near the surface

IN the mid-1950s a pair of large, brown-and-white birds
set up their nest in a tree near Loch Garten on
Speyside; ospreys were back in Britain after an absence
of almost 50 years. Their return captured the public's
imagination, and more than a million people have
visited the Loch Garten site to see the birds—through a
telescope at a discreet distance. The nesting area, now
a bird reserve, is guarded by the Royal Society for the
Protection of Birds. The need for a close guard was
underlined in 1958, when the nest was robbed. Numbers
in Scotland have increased to more than 100 pairs and
recently a few pairs started nesting in England.

The osprey, also known as the fish hawk, is normally
seen near lakes, broads and estuaries outside the
breeding season. It lives almost entirely on fish, and one
reason that it was harried out of the country is that it
competes with fishermen for trout. Fish remains found
at Loch Garten have all proved to be pike or trout. A
hunting osprey has a rather slow, flapping flight, but it
also soars, hovers and drops from a height on its prey,
feet first. Its shrill, cheeping cry is like the call of a
young game-bird.

In early spring, before the female arrives at the eyrie,
the male performs spectacular flights, climbing as high
as 1000 ft, hovering briefly with tail outspread and then
plunging earthwards.

RECOGNITION: *upper parts dark brown, contrasting with white underparts
speckled with brown; dark brown band on side of head; long wings
distinctly angled in flight; sexes alike.*
NESTING: *both sexes build bulky pile of sticks, in tree or on ground near
loch; lays late April–early May; usually 3 eggs, white, heavily blotched
with red-brown; incubation about 35 days, mainly by female; young, fed
by female, fly in 7–8 weeks.*
FEEDING: *almost entirely fish, mainly pike and trout.*

Marsh harrier

Circus aeruginosus   21 in.

FEMALE

THIS long-winged hawk quarters its hunting grounds from just a few feet above the reeds, looking for the ripple that will betray a water-vole below, or sending a party of coots scuttling for cover. But for all the panic it causes, the marsh harrier is highly sensitive to disturbances at its nesting sites. The bird sanctuary at Minsmere in Suffolk is the only place it has nested throughout the past 30 years. Most of the birds there are summer visitors. As a breeder, the marsh harrier is one of our rarest species.

Though once widespread in Britain, marsh harriers stopped nesting here regularly a century ago, mainly because of the draining of the fens. They returned to Norfolk in the late 1920s, and slowly spread and increased, until by 1958 there were 15 nests. After that there was a serious decline, due perhaps to the side-effects of pesticides, to a low point of only one pair in 1971. A resurgence followed, and the number of nests had reached more than 100 by the 1990s.

In courtship the male performs a spectacular soaring flight, diving and somersaulting in descent for as much as 200 ft. Their call is a shrill 'kwee-a'. The female may call loudly for food when she is incubating, and sometimes flies up to take it from the male in a spectacular aerial pass.

RECOGNITION: *mainly dark brown; male has tawny, brown-streaked breast, large blue-grey wing-patches and grey tail; female has pale crown and throat; male in flight shows broad grey band on wings.*
NESTING: *female builds substantial pile of aquatic vegetation, lined with grass, always on the ground among thick growth of marsh plants; lays late April–June; 4 or 5 eggs, very pale blue; incubation about 38 days, mainly by female; young, fed mainly by female, leave nest in 35–40 days, fly a week or two later.*
FEEDING: *water-voles; moorhens, coots, starlings and other birds; eggs and young; frogs and grass snakes.*

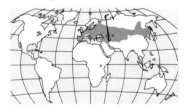

Present all year, but most common April–Sept., nesting mainly in East Anglia

Southern birds are mainly sedentary; northern ones winter mainly in the Tropics

Marsh harrier searching for prey beats low over the ground

MALE

Water rail
Rallus aquaticus 11 in.

Present all year; patchy breeding distribution reflects shortage of suitable marshes

Mainly sedentary, but some northern birds winter in Britain, S. Europe and India

Startled water rail flies off weakly, with trailing legs

THE discordant voice of the water rail often betrays this secretive bird as it moves through the cover of reeds and sedges. The call most often heard starts as a grunt and ends as a piercing squeal, like a pig's. The water rail's other notes are a variety of grunts, groans, whistles, squeaks, hisses and a sharp 'kik-kik-kik' call.

In the marshes, fens and swamps where it breeds the water rail darts from one piece of cover to another in the thick reeds, with its long red bill lowered. It is small and slender enough to move unnoticed through the vegetation, using a high-stepping walk. As it walks it sometimes jerks up its tail, showing the white feathers underneath. Its flights often last for only a few seconds; the bird flutters feebly with its long legs dangling. In hard weather water rails move into the open to feed in unfrozen spots, and if alarmed will stand motionless, allowing time for a close look at them.

Courtship includes the feeding of the female by the male; and the female has been seen to get up from her nest and eggs to walk round the male, rubbing her bill against his and crooning softly.

Water rails are in Britain throughout the year, breeding in wet districts, particularly in East Anglia and Ireland. The population grows in September, when birds fly in from the Continent and Iceland.

RECOGNITION: *long red bill; slate-grey breast, face and throat; flanks barred, upper parts dark brown with black streaks; white under tail; distinctive voice; female duller than male.*
NESTING: *both sexes build nest of dead reeds near lake or river or in marshy ground; nest raised above water level and hidden from above; lays April–July; usually 6–11 eggs, buff with grey or brown blotches; incubation about 20 days, by both parents; nestlings, tended by both parents, leave soon after hatching, fly after about 7 weeks; two broods.*
FEEDING: *insects, spiders, freshwater shrimps, earthworms; perhaps small fish; roots of grasses and watercress, seeds and berries.*

Spotted crake

Porzana porzana   9 in.

MALE

A GREAT deal remains to be found out about the spotted crake, a shy, secretive bird which skulks among water plants in swampy places, and creeps deeper into cover far more readily than it flies out. Naturalists are not certain whether it raises two broods in Britain, as it does on the Continent; for that matter, it has not even been established whether the spotted crake is a regular breeding species here. A total of 10-20 pairs probably nest annually in England, Scotland and Wales, but proof of breeding is difficult to obtain, and the birds are best left to their own devices.

Its nesting sites, in fens, bogs and mosses, are almost inaccessible to man because of the spongy nature of the ground. If it were not for the bird's distinctive call-notes, one of them a loud 'hwit-hwit-hwit', like the crack of a whip, and another a rhythmic 'tic-toc', its presence would hardly be noticed at all. On migration it may turn up in reed beds and ditches, the margins of lakes and other damp places with a thick cover.

When the spotted crake takes to the air it flies weakly, with legs dangling. But for all its unobtrusiveness, the bird has its moment of self-parade; the displaying male struts in front of the female with long, rather exaggerated steps, and later in the courtship may pursue her on land, on water or in the air.

RECOGNITION: *streaked and speckled olive-brown above ; dark brown wings ; grey breast with white spots ; barred flanks and buff under tail ; green legs ; red at base of bill ; female duller than male.*
NESTING: *both sexes build nest of sedges and grasses, usually in tussock ; 8–12 eggs, olive-buff, well speckled with purple-grey and ash-grey ; lays May–June ; incubation 18–21 days, apparently shared by both parents ; young, tended by both parents, leave soon after hatching, fly after about 7½ weeks.*
FEEDING: *beetles, dragonfly nymphs, caddis larvae, caterpillars, slugs, small water-snails ; seeds of water plants.*

Mostly non-breeding April–Oct. visitor, but a few nest in scattered parts of Britain

Mainly migratory, wintering from southern Europe to southern Africa, and also in Asia

In flight, the spotted crake trails its legs like the water rail

Snipe
Gallinago gallinago   10½ in.

Present all year, but most common in winter, when migrants arrive from northern Europe

Most northern birds winter further south, from the British Isles and southern Europe to tropical Africa

Snipe nests in hollow on ground, often near water

THE 'song' of the snipe—a resonant, quavering humming which has earned it the country name of 'heather bleater'—has nothing to do with its voice. As the male plunges through the air at an angle of 45°, with tail outspread, the two outer tail feathers vibrate in the wind to produce the sound mechanically. Almost exactly the same sound has been reproduced by fixing tail-feathers from a snipe on either side of a cork and whirling them round on a string.

The sound may be produced at any time of year, but is usually part of the bird's courtship behaviour, and heard regularly from late March to the middle of June. There is also a courtship display on the ground. The snipe's long straight bill with a flexible tip, used for probing in the mud for worms, makes up a quarter of the bird's total length.

Sometimes it may be spotted feeding quietly at the edge of a pool; but often the bird is not seen until it has been flushed and dashes up zigzagging with a loud harsh 'creech'.

Our resident population is swollen by visitors in autumn and winter, and in hard winters they sometimes move from their damp inland haunts to feed along the shore. Parties of snipe, called 'wisps', carry out manoeuvres in the air; and parent birds have been seen carrying their young, but this is rare.

RECOGNITION: *brown streaked and patterned plumage; long straight bill; boldly striped head; zigzag flight; sexes alike.*
NESTING: *nests in hollow lined with grasses, in tussock of rushes, grass or sedge, usually near water; lays April–August; 4 eggs, pear-shaped, olive-grey or olive-brown, heavily marked with dark sepia; incubation about 20 days, by female only; chicks, tended by both parents, leave the nest in a few hours, fly after about 21 days.*
FEEDING: *chiefly worms, also water-beetles, beetles, caddis larvae, grubs of flies, snails, woodlice; some seeds of marsh plants.*

Jack snipe

Lymnocryptes minimus 7½ in.

E XCEPT in the breeding season, when it performs a
low-key version of the common snipe's display-
flight, the jack snipe is a self-effacing bird. It crouches
when alarmed, and may not fly up until almost trodden
on. Shooting men have reported that it will even allow
a dog to pick it up.

Jack snipe may, at a distance, be confused with
common snipe; but their flight is less erratic, and they
rise from the ground silently or with a low weak call,
move a little slower and alight again sooner. They are
also smaller—which is why they have been given the
diminutive name 'Jack'—and have much shorter bills.
A close look will reveal a distinctive head pattern with
two narrow pale streaks in the centre of the crown
instead of the common snipe's one broad streak.

Both birds prefer damp districts but the jack snipe,
which is exclusively a winter visitor to Britain, may also
be found on drier ground. It is sometimes seen in
'wisps' or small flocks.

The display, to be seen on its continental breeding
grounds and not in Britain, is less spectacular than the
common snipe's. The bird descends at a shallower
angle, and the wings make a whirring rather than a
humming sound. Then it checks, glides silently for a
few yards, and finally hangs suspended and flies up and
down as if jerked by an unseen puppet-master.

RECOGNITION: *streaked brown plumage; stripes on crown; two bold
stripes down back; flight slower than common snipe's; sexes alike.*
NESTING: *nests in Scandinavia, north Russia, Siberia; makes scrape,
lined with dried grasses, in ground, hummock of grass or moss in swamps;
usually 4 eggs, olive-buff or olive-brown, with darker markings; incubation about 24 days, apparently by hen only; chicks leave in a few
hours.*
FEEDING: *earthworms, small land and freshwater snails, beetles, grubs of
flies; also seeds of grasses, rushes and other waterside plants.*

Sept.–April visitor, widespread,
but usually only in small numbers;
unknown in Britain in summer

Small numbers winter in western
Europe, but most fly south to the
Tropics and subtropics

Jack snipe probes the mud for
earthworms and molluscs

171

Black-tailed godwit

Limosa limosa   16 in.

SUMMER

Present all year, mostly as migrant or winter visitor, but a few breed, mainly in East Anglia

Migratory, wintering on coasts or by lakes south to Africa, Tasmania and New Zealand

Black-tailed godwit in flight shows broad white bars on wings

EARLY in the 19th century, the black-tailed godwit was 'lost' to Britain as a breeding bird. Large numbers were netted to be served up as table delicacies, and the remaining birds were driven away by the draining of the fens, so that by the 1830s they had ceased to nest here. But today, because of protection, the black-tail's prospects are promising. It has become a frequent passage migrant and winter visitor, and an increasing, if still rare, breeding species.

Since 1952 black-tails have become established at protected sites on the Ouse and Nene Washes, East Anglia; and pairs have nested in recent years in several other parts of Britain, including Orkney and Shetland.

They nest in damp, grassy and marshy districts and at other times appear on estuaries, mud-flats and sandy shores, and to a lesser extent near fresh water. The flight call is a loud 'wicka-wicka-wicka', but over the breeding grounds two other calls may be heard, 'pee-oo-ee' and a greenshank-like 'wik-ik-ik'. The song, which sounds like a repeated 'crweetuu', is most often heard as part of the display performance over the breeding grounds. The male first rises steeply with rapid wing-beats, then flies in slow motion with tail spread out, calling loudly, before gliding silently downwards and finally side-slipping to the ground.

RECOGNITION: *in winter, brown-grey above, light below; in summer, head and breast red or chestnut; broad black band on end of pure white tail; long legs; straight bill; broad white wing-bar shows in flight; sexes alike.*
NESTING: *both sexes make scrape in ground, usually well hidden in thick grass, padded with dead grass and lined with leaves; lays May; 4 eggs, light green to brown, blotched and spotted with brown; incubation 24 days, by both parents; chicks, tended by both parents, leave nest after a few hours, fly after about 4 weeks.*
FEEDING: *insects, including beetles, grasshoppers, dragonflies, mayflies; shellfish, snails, slugs and earthworms.*

Ruff

Philomachus pugnax M 11 in. F 9 in.

MALE IN SUMMER

Present all year, but mainly autumn migrant; small numbers breed in East Anglia

Winters mainly from Mediterranean to S. Africa; also winters in southern Asia and a few in Britain

THE courtship displays of the ruff are violent and colourful; males rush at one another with ruffs fluffed out, threatening and sometimes coming to blows as they compete for mating territories. After a fight, they crouch with bills on the ground, ruffs spread out and ear-tufts raised, waiting for the females, or reeves, to arrive. The reeves pick their way between the crouched ruffs and select one for mating by preening its ruffs. Mating may take place on the display ground or the paired birds may fly off together. Both sexes are promiscuous, and males take no part in raising the young.

Certain ruffs, known as 'satellite' males, do not fight over territory but often secure matings while the established males are threatening one another. They are tolerated probably because, in their conspicuous white plumage, they attract more reeves to the display ground. In breeding plumage, the exotic ruff feathers and ear-tufts may be shades of purple-brown, black, chestnut, yellow or white.

Ruffs were once quite common as breeding birds; but their popularity as table delicacies and the draining of the marshlands had almost entirely stopped their breeding in Britain before the middle of the 19th century. They come to Britain now mainly as passage migrants in autumn and spring, but since 1963 small numbers have bred in East Anglia and occasionally elsewhere.

RECOGNITION: *male in summer has huge ruff around neck, and ear-tufts; smaller reeve is generally grey with boldly patterned back; in winter sexes are similar, with oval white patches on each side of dark tail.*
NESTING: *reeve alone builds nest, usually hidden in a hollow, and lines it with dried grass; lays May; usually 4 eggs, variable in colour from pale brown to pale blue with dark blotches; incubation about 21 days, by reeve only; chicks, tended by reeve only, leave soon after hatching, become independent in a few days.*
FEEDING: *chiefly insects, with some worms, molluscs and plant seeds.*

Two males in breeding plumage display to female

Little ringed plover

Charadrius dubius 6 in.

Mar.–Oct. visitor; first bred here in 1938; reached southern Scotland for the first time in 1968

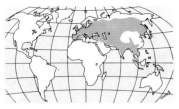

Tropical birds are sedentary; northern and European ones winter south as far as Equator

Little ringed plover lacks pale wing-bars of ringed plover

THE still rare little ringed plover is one of the half-a-dozen birds which have colonised the British Isles in the past 50 to 60 years. It first nested in the Tring reservoirs in Hertfordshire in 1938, and later spread through the Thames Valley. There are now thought to be up to 1000 pairs breeding regularly in England. Wales has recently been colonised and pairs have occasionally bred in southern Scotland.

Gravel pits, before the banks are overgrown, provide the bird's favourite nesting sites, and its distribution therefore tends to follow river valleys where deposits of gravel are being exploited. Lately, it has also been nesting in shingle banks along rivers. In spring and autumn migrating birds may turn up at the edges of lakes or any other stretch of fresh water.

On the ground it looks like a smaller version of its relative, the ringed plover; but in flight, the little ringed plover has no white wing-bar. It also has distinctive call-notes, mainly 'pee-oo' and a continuous 'pip-pip-pip'. The courtship song, a trilling of the call-notes, is usually delivered during a bat-like flight in the air. The showpiece of the display is a performance in which the male flies round erratically with slow wing-beats. Like many other ground-nesters, the little ringed plover uses a show of injury-feigning to distract intruders from its nest or brood.

RECOGNITION: *brown back; white below, with thick black neck-band; black band behind eye and on white forehead; no white wing-bar; sexes alike.*
NESTING: *female selects one of several scrapes, usually in gravel or shingle, sometimes lines it with a few pebbles or stalks; lays late April–June; 4 eggs, pear-shaped, pale buff with black spots; incubation about 25 days, by both parents; chicks, tended by both parents, leave nest almost at once, fly after about 3½ weeks.*
FEEDING: *mainly insects; also spiders, small molluscs and worms.*

Red-necked phalarope

Phalaropus lobatus 7 in.

FEMALE IN SUMMER

ALMOST every rule about the roles of male and female birds in the breeding season is reversed in the case of the red-necked phalarope. It is the female which moves first into the breeding area and establishes a territory, the female which displays to attract the male, the female which takes the initiative in courtship and mating, and the male which, once it has been led to the nesting site, sits on the eggs to incubate them and looks after the chicks until they are able to fly. Not surprisingly, the female is the brighter coloured of the two.

With its slightly webbed feet, the bird is a buoyant swimmer. It constantly bobs its head as it swims, and often spins in circles, stirring up water insects which it picks off the surface. The phalarope is much the smallest bird likely to be seen swimming.

Red-necked phalaropes fly to the open sea in winter, moving well offshore; but after storms they may be blown inland and turn up on almost any small pond.

This rare species has suffered more than any other from egg-collectors determined that, if it should become extinct, they would have the last clutch of eggs in their cabinet. Its numbers fell rapidly in the 19th century; but the Royal Society for the Protection of Birds has helped it to build up a stronghold in the Shetlands, where a few pairs nest on Mainland and Fetlar.

Rare May–Sept. visitor; breeds in very small numbers, mainly in Shetland

Winters at sea off coasts of W. Africa, Arabia, S.E. Asia and western S. America

RECOGNITION: *head and upper parts slate-grey with buff streaks; white throat; white underparts; orange patch on sides of neck in summer; female more strongly marked; in winter plumage is white and grey, with head lighter; delicate, with needle-like bill.*
NESTING: *both sexes make scrapes, lined with grass, in coastal or lochside areas; lays late May–early June; 4 eggs, pear-shaped, buff, heavily blotched with brown; incubation about 20 days, by male only; chicks, tended by male, leave within a few hours, fly after 17 days.*
FEEDING: *almost entirely insects found on the water or on waterside vegetation.*

Phalarope in winter spins round on water to stir up insects

Green sandpiper

Tringa ochropus   9 in.

Most common in spring or autumn; small numbers winter here, mainly in southern England

Winters mainly inland, from western Europe south to central Africa and southern Asia

Green sandpiper in flight shows distinctive white rump

IT is something of a misnomer to call this bird 'green': only the legs are green, and it is usually seen as a dark bird which rises from the water's edge with shrill cries, its conspicuous white rump making it look like a large house martin as it flies away. The green sandpiper almost always rises to a great height on being flushed, uttering a shrill 'weet-a-weet' or a variation on this call. Though it flies off high and fast, it will return to a favourite feeding spot.

Compared with most other waders, the green sandpiper is not a sociable bird. It usually probes the river margins alone; flocks are met with only on migration and even then are seldom large.

In courtship, green sandpipers have been observed 'leapfrogging' one another on the ground, with a flutter of wings; but their displays are unlikely to be seen in Britain, for they have been proved to have nested here only twice—the last time in Inverness-shire in 1959—though it is likely that there have been other nestings.

Green sandpipers appear most often in spring and autumn as birds of passage, in marshes and near fresh water, even around small pools and flood puddles; they may investigate salt-marsh runnels but rarely go to the open shore, and keep more to rivers than most waders. A few birds may stay the winter.

RECOGNITION: *dark brown-grey above, white below; breast slightly mottled; white rump and upper tail with black bars on tip of tail; wings black underneath; sexes alike.*
NESTING: *very rarely nest in Britain; nesting sites are in northern Europe and Asia, in old trees near water; lays often in old nests of other birds; lays mid-April–June, later in north; usually 4 eggs, buff with deep brown and lighter markings; incubation about 21 days, chiefly by hen; young, tended by both sexes, spend brief time in nest.*
FEEDING: *mainly insects, small worms and molluscs; some vegetable matter.*

Common sandpiper

Tringa hypoleucos 7¾ in.

THE head-bobbing sandpiper, about the same size as a starling, breeds in Europe and Asia, and winters in Africa, or even in Australia. (The similar spotted sandpiper replaces it in North America.) It comes to Britain in the summer to nest beside the streams and lochs of the north and west. The first few make their landfall in the last days of March and the main stream pours in at the end of April and early May. They are easily identified by their flight and call. A shrill 'twee-wee-wee' is uttered as the sandpipers fly in a half-circle low over the water, alternately flickering their wings and momentarily gliding.

The trilling song, given from the air, ground or perch, is mainly an elaboration of the call-note; it plays a prominent part in the male's circular courtship flight. Although they are birds of the north and west, odd pairs occasionally nest by rivers or flooded gravel-pits in the south. On their spring and autumn migrations they may be seen by almost any stretch of water where the edge is shallow enough for wading. Exceptionally, individuals may winter in the south.

Common sandpipers are among the many birds which lure intruders away from their nests and eggs by the trick of trailing a 'broken' wing. When flushed they skim low over the water, then land on a convenient perch and start bobbing their heads.

RECOGNITION: *dark brown above, pure white below, with a light buff-grey area on sides of neck ; white wing-bar shows in flight ; sexes alike.*
NESTING: *lines scrape or depression in ground with grass and dead leaves, often close to water ; lays May–June ; usually 4 eggs, pear-shaped, buff, sometimes grey with red-brown blotches ; incubation about 22 days, by both parents ; chicks, tended by both parents, leave nest within few hours, fly after about 4 weeks.*
FEEDING: *mainly insects, such as water-beetles, flies, mayflies, water-bugs, caddis flies ; snails, worms, a few tadpoles ; a little vegetable matter.*

Mainly April–Oct. visitor, but a few may stay the winter, especially in southern England

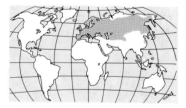

Most winter well south of breeding range, some reaching as far as S. Africa or Australia

Common sandpiper flies low over water with wings deeply bowed

Kingfisher

Alcedo atthis 6½ in.

Present all year; some birds move to coasts in winter; now scarce in Scotland

Mainly sedentary, but frozen waters may force some birds to make limited southward movements

Kingfisher excavates its nest-hole in river bank or sand- or gravel-pit

A FLASH of sapphire is all that is needed to identify the kingfisher as it streaks downstream or bellyflops to snatch a minnow. This most brilliantly coloured of British birds is largely confined to the banks of rivers and streams because of its diet; but it also feeds on lakes and large ponds and—especially in hard weather —on the seashore. Its bright colouring is a defence adaptation: predators have learned to leave the bird alone, because its flesh is foul-tasting.

Kingfishers are liable to starve to death in hard winters, when their food supply is cut off by frozen waters. After the winter of 1962-3, their numbers fell drastically throughout the British Isles. Along upper reaches of the Thames in 1961 there was one pair of breeding kingfishers to every 1¾ miles, but in 1964 only one pair to every 20 miles. In Scotland, partly as a result of mild winters, but also in some areas because of improvements in water quality, kingfishers have recently increased and spread northwards.

The bird fishes with a shallow dive from a perch or from a hovering position, and beats its catch on a branch before bolting it down, head first. A fish swallowed tail first would choke the bird as its fins and scales opened; so the kingfisher carries a fish by its tail only when the fish is going to be presented to another bird.

RECOGNITION: *brilliant blue-green above, orange-chestnut below, with white throat and patch on each side of the neck; sexes alike.*
NESTING: *both sexes fly at bank, often along canal, to dig out hole 2–3 ft long; lined thinly with fishbones; entrance often betrayed by 'whitewash' slime of disgorged fishbones running out after young have hatched; lays April–August; 6 or 7 eggs, glossy white, almost round; incubation 19–21 days, by both sexes; nestlings, fed by both sexes, fly after 23–27 days; two broods.*
FEEDING: *mainly minnows, sticklebacks and gudgeon; also water-beetles, dragonfly nymphs and other water life.*

Redshank

Tringa totanus 11 in.

SUMMER

For most of the year, redshanks are sociable birds, mingling with other waders on muddy, open shores and often collecting in substantial flocks. But when the time comes to raise a brood, pairs prefer to nest on their own, in some damp grassy corner or marsh.

A ringing 'tu-tu-tu' is the redshank's cry. It sets up a clamour when startled, and has a range of loud, yelping, but fairly musical calls, including a scolding 'teuk-teuk-teuk' and a 'chip-chip-chip' of alarm. A yodelling 'tu-udle' song, based on the more musical of its call-notes, is given in the breeding season. The displaying male chases the female with his tail fanned out and head stretched forward; when she stops, he raises his wings above his back and advances slowly, fluttering his wings.

The white on the wings identifies the redshank as it flies or stretches itself while at rest; no other wader of similar size has such a broad white wing-bar. The bird makes a bobbing movement when suspicious, and has a rather erratic flight.

For much of the past 100 years the redshank was rapidly increasing its numbers and range, but this increase has fallen off slightly since about 1940, especially inland in the south, probably because many wet pastures have been drained and cultivated.

Present all year; in winter most move to coast and visitors arrive from Iceland

Most continental birds migrate, some reaching S. Africa and India in winter

RECOGNITION: *grey-brown with darker markings, light below; long orange-red legs; white rump and white patch on back of wings show in flight; appears darker in summer than in winter; sexes alike.*
NESTING: *both sexes make scrapes in marshy ground, usually well hidden by tuft of grass; female lines one with dried grass; lays mid-April–June; usually 4 eggs, pear-shaped, buff with dark brown spots and blotches; incubation about 23 days, by both parents; chicks, tended by both parents, leave as soon as hatched, fly after about 4 weeks.*
FEEDING: *mainly insects, small shellfish, worms and lugworms; some vegetable matter.*

Startled redshank flies off swiftly, often with noisy yelps

Sand martin

Riparia riparia   4¾ in.

March–Sept. visitor, uncommon in north of Scotland; does not breed in northern islands

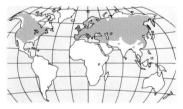

Winters in tropical America, southern Asia and as far south as the Cape in South Africa

Young sand martins in a nest-hole take insects from a parent

THIS is the smallest of our three swallows, and the earliest to arrive. Interweaving flocks fly in at the end of March, gathering over lakes, rivers and reservoirs to feed on gnats. Later they seek the nesting sites of previous years in steep river banks, cliffs, railway cuttings and old sand-pits.

Comings and goings at the colony are abrupt. At one moment the spot seems almost deserted, with perhaps only a young bird, showing its white chin, peering from a hole. The next moment the air is clamorous with wings and chattering as birds dip and swing up to their nest entrances. Birds clinging on to the steep bank side or cliff face keep up a chatter at those flying up. Then suddenly the main body takes off and disperses.

Both sexes drive a tunnel 2 or 3 ft long in the sandy soil at their nesting sites, scooping out a small chamber at the end to be lined untidily with grass and feathers.

There should be little danger of confusing the bird with a swallow or a house martin. The sand martin's brown breast band is distinctive; its tail is the least forked of the three; and it lacks the house martin's white rump. It hardly ever comes to the ground, except to roost in reed-beds and osiers, where large flocks roost outside the nesting season. Communal roosting in Britain does not last long: in September most sand martins leave to winter in Africa.

RECOGNITION : *smallest swallow ; plain brown above, white below ; brown band across the breast ; tail short and slightly forked ; sexes alike.*
NESTING : *both sexes bore tunnel, 2 or 3 ft long, in sandy banks, cliffs, sand- or gravel-pits ; grass and feathers gathered in flight for lining nest chamber ; lays May–August ; 4 or 5 eggs, white ; incubation about 14 days, by both parents ; young, fed by both parents, fly after about 19 days ; normally two broods.*
FEEDING : *mosquitoes, other small flies, beetles, mayflies and other insects, usually caught over water.*

Bearded tit

Panurus biarmicus 6½ in. (including 3 in. tail)

MALE

ON cold days in the fens bearded tits snuggle together on the same reed stem, the cock sheltering the hen under one wing so that they form a single ball of feathers. Several observers have recorded this, though the birds are often difficult to spot, deep in the reed-beds.

Hard weather takes a heavy toll among these small birds. In the winter of 1947 their numbers on the Norfolk Broads were reduced almost to extinction point; and long before this their future looked precarious, because of the reclamation of marshlands, coupled with the demands of collectors who offered high prices for their eggs. But they have recovered from all these misfortunes, helped by protection. In the bird sanctuary at Minsmere in Suffolk, their population has built up to the point where there is a substantial emigration almost every autumn.

The bearded tit is, in fact, misnamed: its 'beard' is a facial stripe that looks more like a moustache, and scientists have decided that the bird is not related to the tits, but to the thrushes. In courtship the male lifts its crown feathers, puffs out its 'beard', and fans out its tail. The hen responds with a kind of dance, also spreading its tail, and sometimes the pair rise in a slow flight together. They breed only in extensive reed and sedge beds, and during winter they wander in small parties.

RECOGNITION: *tawny back, long tail; male's black 'beard' is more like a flowing moustache; female has no black on head or tail coverts.*
NESTING: *both sexes build nest of sedge or reed blades, just above water in beds of reeds or sedge; nest lined with reed flowers by male; lays April–July; 5–7 eggs, creamy-white, speckled and finely lined with brown; incubation about 13 days, by both parents; nestlings, fed by both parents, fly after 9–12 days; two or more broods.*
FEEDING: *almost entirely insects, their larvae and reed seeds in winter; freshwater molluscs and other small animals at times.*

Present all year; formerly bred only in East Anglia, but spread recently to south coast and Lancashire

Essentially sedentary; northern populations suffer heavy losses in severe winters

Bearded tit flies with whirring wings, usually low over reeds

Reed bunting

Emberiza schoeniclus 6 in.

MALE IN SUMMER

Present all year; in autumn and winter immigrants arrive on east coast from Continent

Limited southward movement occurs among northern populations in winter; other birds are sedentary

Female reed bunting in nest built close to ground

BOTH the cock bird, conspicuous with its white collar against a black head, and the drably coloured female, use a bluff that is uncommon among small perching birds. If surprised, they may divert attention from the nest by shuffling along the ground with wings half spread as if broken.

The reed bunting is often seen bounding along in short jerky flight or flicking its tail on a perch as it delivers its rather indifferent song, a succession of squeaky 'tweek-tweek-tweek-tititick' notes. Courtship consists mainly of fast pursuits, often ending in squabbling rough-and-tumbles. The male also puffs out its white collar for its mate's benefit. Not all form simple pairs; a few males run a string of nests, each with its own female and brood.

Many reed buntings stay in Britain all the year, though they move south in the autumn; others visit Britain in the summer, and numbers from northern Europe fly in for the winter, in the same way as some of our nesting birds go south. Marshy places and riversides are their favourite nesting areas, but in recent years there has been an unexpected expansion into drier places, such as chalk downs; and reed buntings have even been seen feeding with chaffinches and sparrows at some suburban bird-tables.

RECOGNITION: *male in breeding season has black head, black throat and white collar, dark brown streaked back, greyish rump, grey-white below; head pattern obscured in winter; female is streaked brown, lighter below with black and white moustache stripe.*
NESTING: *female builds nest of dry grass, lined with hair and finer grass, usually in tussock or on ground among vegetation; lays April–June; 3–5 eggs, olive-buff or pale green, marked with black; incubation about 14 days, mainly by hen; nestlings, fed by both sexes, fly after about 12 days.*
FEEDING: *mainly seeds of marsh plants; some animal food, including freshwater snails, beetles, caterpillars and other insects.*

Dipper

Cinclus cinclus   7 in.

THE idea that the dipper can defy the laws of specific gravity and walk along the river bottom was once ridiculed by some respected naturalists. But those who had seen it happen stuck to the evidence of their eyes, and they have been proved right. Experiments have demonstrated that when the bird walks upstream with its head down looking for food, the force of a fast current against its slanting back keeps it on the bottom. However, a bird-watcher is far more likely to see its plump form simply entering the water either by wading or diving, or swimming buoyantly on the surface. Often it will perch for some time on a rock or stone in mid-stream, dipping its head and curtseying, as if hinged on its legs, its wren-like lyric of a song mingling with the splash of tumbling water.

The dipper is usually confined to fast-running streams in hilly districts in the north and west, but can sometimes be seen on shores of lakes in the hills, and in winter, when some immigrants arrive from the Continent, also by sea lochs. It is rarely seen far from water.

Its most common call-note is 'zit-zit-zit', and there is also a metallic 'clink-clink'. Courtship display includes posturing to show off the white breast, bowing and wing-quivering. Its flight is rapid and direct with short wings whirring.

RECOGNITION : *dark brown plumage with white breast ; highly characteristic bobbing or dipping action ; sexes alike.*
NESTING : *both sexes build substantial domed nest, mainly of moss, lined with dead leaves ; nest nearly always on ledge or in cavity close to water ; frequently on bridges, sometimes under a waterfall ; lays March–early May ; 4 or 5 eggs, white ; incubation about 17 days, by female only ; nestlings, fed by both sexes, fly after about 23 days ; two broods.*
FEEDING : *water-beetles, water-boatmen, caddis larvae and nymphs of dragonflies and mayflies ; worms and tadpoles ; minnows and other small fish.*

Present all year; the few seen in eastern England in winter are from the Continent

Some northern and high altitude breeding birds move a short way south in winter to escape ice

Dipper stands in the middle of a stream, watching for food

Sedge warbler

Acrocephalus schoenobaenus 5 in.

April–Sept. visitor; nests in all British Isles except Shetland; unknown here in winter

Winters exclusively in marshy regions of tropical Africa, as far south as KwaZulu-Natal

Sedge warbler's song is heard most frequently from April to July

THE rule that small, drab brown birds advertise themselves with the most melodious songs has to be stretched a little for the sedge warbler. Its song is a vigorous jumble of mixed-up notes, some sweet, but most of them harsh and grating. The few clear sweet notes, though, are well up to the standard expected of dull-coloured birds: when heard at night they have been mistaken for the notes of a nightingale.

The sedge warbler is a good mimic, and often introduces snatches of other birds' songs in its hurried medley. All this may issue from deep inside a tangle of bushes, from an exposed perch, or during flight. In the excitement of courtship the cock birds sometimes sing while performing an up-and-down flight with quivering wings and outspread tail. The bird also has a harsh churring and a scolding 'tuc' call.

The sedge warbler shows no special preference for sedge, but creeps in and out of any thick cover. It may be found wherever coarse vegetation grows up over bushes and hedgerows fairly near water, and more rarely in bushy places away from water.

Several nests may be located near one another, usually low among nettles or waterside plants, and seldom more than 4 ft from the ground. The female cuckoo finds the sedge warbler one of the more accessible of victims on which to impose its offspring.

RECOGNITION: *dark brown above, distinctly streaked; tawny rump; pale stripe over eye; pale buff below; sexes alike.*
NESTING: *female builds shallow nest of dead grass and stalks, lined with hair, grass heads and sometimes feathers, hidden in waterside vegetation; lays May–July; 5 or 6 eggs, pale green or olive, well speckled with light grey-brown; incubation about 13 days, chiefly by female; nestlings, fed by both sexes, leave after about 14 days; sometimes two broods.*
FEEDING: *mostly insects, including gnats, crane-flies and other flies, beetles, aphids, spiders, caterpillars, small dragonflies.*

Reed warbler

Acrocephalus scirpaceus   5 in.

Marsh warbler

Acrocephalus palustris   5 in.

WITHOUT hearing their songs, the most expert ornithologist might hesitate before distinguishing a reed warbler from a marsh warbler. They are among the most difficult of British birds to tell apart by sight. The reed warbler's song, with a flow of 'churr-churr-churr . . . chirruc-chirruc-chirruc' notes, sounds rather like two pebbles being chinked together, and sometimes is varied with mimicry of other birds. The marsh warbler, an even better mimic, has a much louder, more musical song, with liquid canary-like notes which the reed warbler rarely approaches.

The marsh warbler today is rare, having almost disappeared from its former strongholds in Worcestershire; a few remain in south-east England. It is at home in most waterside habitats, with a strong preference for osier beds. The more widespread reed warbler keeps almost entirely to reed beds; it has a way of sidling restlessly up and down the stems and hopping from one to another.

Both are summer visitors, the first of the reed warblers beginning to arrive at the end of April, and the marsh warblers arriving nearly a month later. The reed warbler, often victimised by cuckoos, attaches a deep cup nest to the reeds; the marsh warbler makes a shallower structure, sometimes in a bed of nettles.

Both are summer visitors; rare marsh warbler breeds in only a few places in England

Reed warbler's range; marsh warbler does not nest in south-west Europe or east of Caspian Sea

Reed warbler weaves its nest around stiff reed stems

RECOGNITION: *both brown above, light buff below, with whitish throat; brown of marsh warbler slightly less 'warm'; reed warbler's legs usually dark, marsh's flesh pink; sexes alike in both cases.*
NESTING: *female does most building in both cases; marsh warbler attaches shallow cup nest of grass, lined with finer grass and hair, to plant stems by 'basket handles'; reed warbler's deep cup nest of dried grasses is usually in reed bed; lays May–July (reed) and June (marsh); usually 4 or 5 eggs, green-white with grey marks; incubation about 12 days, by both parents; young, fed by both parents, fly in about 11 or 12 days.*
FEEDING: *marsh insects—flies, moths and larvae; berries in autumn.*

Grey wagtail

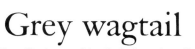

Motacilla cinerea   8 in. (including 4 in. tail)

MALE IN SUMMER

Present all year; southward
movement occurs in autumn

European birds are mostly
sedentary; Asian birds migrate

Grey wagtail—an expert at
snatching insects from the air

IN spite of its name, this is one of the most colourful of
the wagtails; its bright yellow underparts contrast
boldly with its blue-grey back and long black tail whatever the time of year. The bird has a marked preference
for being near water—especially rushing water. It flits
along mountain streams, pausing now and again to
perch on a boulder or overhead branch and flicking
a tail as long as its body as it waits to dart out at an
insect. In hilly country it is often seen in company with
dippers.

In winter, the grey wagtail moves to lowland streams
and may be found around cress beds, sewage farms and
even small pools, but again seldom far from a weir or
some other tumbling water.

The usual call is very like the pied wagtail's double-
noted 'tschizzik', but is more metallic and staccato, and
sometimes only a single 'tit'. The song, a shrill 'tsee-tee-
tee', is not often heard. The male has a variety of courtship displays. In one, a slow-motion flight, the tail is
fanned; and in another the bird runs towards the female
on the ground and takes up a posture presenting its
black throat.

While still most common in the hilly areas of the
north and west, the grey wagtail has for many years
been increasing in eastern and southern England.

RECOGNITION: *blue-grey above, yellow below, including tail feathers; long
black tail with white sides; male's throat is black in summer, white in
winter; female's slightly more buff.*
NESTING: *female builds nest of moss and grass, lined with hair, usually in
hole close to water; sometimes uses the old nest of dipper or other bird;
lays April–June; usually 5 eggs, buff, faintly speckled with grey-brown;
incubation 12 or 13 days, chiefly by female; nestlings, fed by both parents,
fly after 12 days; sometimes two broods.*
FEEDING: *mostly insects, including flies, small beetles, dragonfly nymphs;
on coast, sandhoppers and small molluscs.*

Yellow wagtail

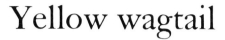

Motacilla flava 6½ in.

MALE IN SUMMER

Any 'yellow wagtail' reported in Britain in winter is almost certain to be a grey wagtail, another small bird with yellow underparts. For the yellow wagtail is a summer visitor, arriving in April and leaving in September and October to winter in West Africa.

Yellow wagtails breed in two distinct types of country —in damp river valleys, water meadows, sewage farms and fresh and salt-marshes, and also on dry heaths and commons, moorland and arable land under crops. They often feed among cattle and horses, snatching at insects stirred up by the animals' hoofs.

In recent years the numbers of yellow wagtails have fallen drastically and they have disappeared entirely from some localities. No convincing explanation appears to have been found for this decrease, for there has been no obvious environmental change in the districts which the birds have forsaken.

The male is one of our most gaily coloured birds; the deep yellow of its plumage is approached only by the colouring of the cock yellow-hammer. Its brief, warbling song, punctuated with 'tsweep' call-notes, is heard mainly in May and is given either from a perch or in bouncing song-flight.

In one of its courtship ceremonies the male runs round the female with feathers fluffed out and wings quivering.

RECOGNITION: *predominantly yellow bird, with long tail; green-brown upper parts; distinctive 'tsweep' call-note; female duller than male, with olive back and paler yellow underparts.*
NESTING: *female builds nest of dried grass and roots, lined with hair, always in hollow in ground, concealed in vegetation; lays May–July; usually 5 or 6 eggs, pale grey, heavily sprinkled with yellow-buff; incubation about 13 days, mainly by female; nestlings, fed by both parents, fly after about 13 days; two broods normal in south.*
FEEDING: *flies, and other small insects and larvae; at times beetles and even caterpillars.*

April–Oct. visitor; has rarely been recorded in winter

Winters mainly in Africa south of the Sahara; also in southern Asia

Yellow wagtail perches readily on fences, hedges and bushes

Pied wagtail

Motacilla alba   7 in.

MALE

Present all year, but some British birds migrate to south-west Europe in winter

Birds from northern half of range winter in southern half and beyond, as far as the Tropics

Pied wagtail springs into the air to catch a passing insect

IN many parts of the country, modern agricultural techniques have robbed this bird of one of its most reliable sources of food. It is a specialist in catching winged insects, and until recently found a plentiful supply in farmyards. But the traditional farmyard is on the way out: hygienic cowsheds, the greatly increased use of piped water and efficient methods of insect control bring bleak prospects for the bird.

The pied wagtail's roosting habits have long drawn the attention of naturalists—or even of casual passers-by. Up to 1000 wagtails at a time roost in trees in a busy Dublin street, and there was another mass roost on the glass roof of a post office in Leicester. Recently, roosts in commercial greenhouses have been reported at more than 20 places, from Kent to Lancashire: the birds may be seeking warmth, shelter and protection from predators.

Nesting is usually in a cavity or ledge on a building, bank, cliff or pile of stones. A pair once built on a mudguard of a car regularly parked outside an Isle of Man school; they waited for its arrival each day to resume building.

The pied wagtail's flight is markedly undulating, and it often gives a high-pitched 'tschizzik' flight-call as it takes to the air. The same call is given in courtship, during which the male chases the female then postures in front of her, its head lowered, wings drooping and tail spread.

RECOGNITION: *black and white plumage, long tail, often wagged up and down; female's back greyer than male's.*
NESTING: *female lines hole in wall, shed, bank or thatch, with hair, feathers and wool; sometimes re-lines old nest of another bird; lays April–June; 5 or 6 eggs, grey-white, marked with grey or brown; incubation about 14 days, chiefly by female; young, fed by both parents, fly after about 2 weeks; normally two broods, sometimes three.*
FEEDING: *flies, beetles, small moths and other small insects.*

LAKES, RIVERS
AND RESERVOIRS

Britain's open inland waters are a haven
for swimming and diving birds retreating before
the onset of the bitter winters of northern Europe and Siberia.
Attracted by the prospect of waters which are not regularly
frozen over, they join our resident populations in the
day-long pursuit of up-ending or diving for food.

CONTENTS

Whooper swan

Cygnus cygnus   60 in.

Bewick's swan

Cygnus columbianus   48 in.

Whooper (on map) is Oct.–April visitor; has nested in Scotland; Bewick's winters further south

Whooper's breeding range; Bewick's nests further north; both migrate south in winter

Family of whooper swans grazes on pasture close to water

BOTH these swans are winter visitors to Britain, flying in from northern Europe and Russia. The larger whooper was once a British breeding bird, but became extinct in Orkney in the 18th century and has so far failed to re-establish itself, although pairs have bred occasionally in Scotland. Bewick's swan is now nearly as common; it visits southern England, particularly the fens, and a large wild flock winters each year at Slimbridge in Gloucestershire.

The two swans carry their necks stiffly erect instead of in the mute swan's gentle curve, and both are noisier. The voice of the whooper is a powerful, trumpeting 'ahng-ha'. Bewick's Swan—named in honour of Thomas Bewick (1753–1828), a famous illustrator of birds—has a softer, higher pitched voice. It usually gives a 'hoo' or 'ho' note, or makes a honking sound.

The whooper's courtship display consists of a sinuous up-and-down movement of the head and neck with the wings outspread. This display may also be the preliminary to an attack on another male; just before it attacks, the bird partly spreads its wings and lowers its head—sometimes to the point where the head is below water. After mating, the female starts to call and the male joins in, spreading its wings as the two birds rise breast-to-breast in the water.

RECOGNITION: *both white; larger whooper has long bill, black at tip with triangular yellow patch at base; Bewick's has shorter bill, with smaller, more rounded, yellow patch; sexes alike in both cases.*
NESTING: *both build on islets, making large mound of moss and lichen or dried plants, with depression in middle for eggs. Bewick's lays June; 3–5 eggs, creamy-white; no reliable data on incubation; cygnets, tended by both parents, fly at about 6 weeks. Whooper lays late May–early June; usually 5 or 6 eggs, creamy-white; incubation 35–42 days, by female only; cygnets, tended by both parents, fly after about 8 weeks.*
FEEDING: *seeds, water plants; whooper may eat insects and molluscs.*

Mute swan

Cygnus olor   60 in.

MALE

LEGEND says that Richard the Lionheart brought the first mute swans home from Cyprus after the Third Crusade; but they were probably breeding wild in England long before this, and gradually becoming semi-domesticated because of their value as ornamental birds and as a luxury food. For centuries the Crown controlled the ownership of swans through royal swanherds and courts called 'swanmotes'. Privately owned swans were pinioned to prevent them from flying away, and branded or nicked in the skin of the upper bill as a mark of ownership. In the reign of Elizabeth I, 900 distinct swan marks were recognised.

Until recently the custom of marking was preserved in the swan-upping ceremony on the Thames every summer, when cygnets' bills were nicked by the bargemaster of the Dyers' Company or the swanmarker of the Vintners' Company. One nick meant that a bird was owned by the Dyers and two that it was a Vintners' swan. An unmarked bird on the Thames belongs to the Queen, as seigneur of the swans. There was a similar ceremony on the rivers Yare and Wensum near Norwich.

In the past 100 years the birds have been allowed to escape from bondage and are now common wild breeding birds. They are not as silent as their name suggests: mute swans snort and hiss when annoyed, and some produce a weak trumpeting. But the legendary 'swan song'—the music said to be made by a dying swan—is a myth, with no foundation in fact.

RECOGNITION: *white plumage ; orange bill with black base and knob (less prominent in female) ; long neck, usually carried in a curve ; sexes alike.*
NESTING: *on ground near water ; male brings sticks and reeds which female arranges in a huge pile ; lays March–May ; usually 5–7 eggs, grey-green ; incubation about 36 days, by both parents ; cygnets, tended by both parents, leave after 1 or 2 days, fly after about 4 months.*
FEEDING: *chiefly water vegetation ; some small frogs, fish and insects.*

Present all year; nests throughout Britain except Shetland and parts of north-west Scotland

Essentially sedentary, but hard winters may drive northern birds farther south or west

Pair of mute swans perform pre-mating ceremony

Mallard

Anas platyrhynchos　23 in.

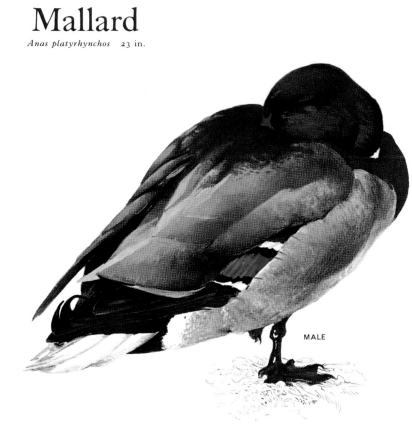

MALE

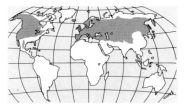

Present all year; large numbers of immigrants from western Europe come to Britain in winter

Mainly sedentary, though some birds move within or just beyond breeding range in winter

Duck (front) dabbles for food while drake up-ends

PROBABLY the best-known of our ducks are the green-headed drake mallard and its dark brown mate; they have learnt to live alongside man in the ponds of town and city parks, and their courtship displays have become so familiar that they are sometimes overlooked. When several drakes chase a duck through the air in the autumn, this is an important part of mate selection. As the display develops, the drakes swim round the duck, sometimes with their necks stretched out along the surface of the water.

Late in the breeding season bands of drakes chase ducks again, and try to mate with them by force, without going through the proper courtship routine. These mallard 'rapes' are especially common in areas where nests are crowded together. Early in the year, pairs of mallard fly off to their breeding grounds, near stretches of water or sea lochs. They usually nest close to the ground, but sometimes they use a hollow tree or the abandoned nest of another bird. The duck makes a loud quacking sound like a farmyard duck; the drake mallard has a softer, higher-pitched call-note, 'quork' or 'quek'.

At dusk, regular flights of mallard take off for farmland —often well away from any stretch of water—to feed on grain and weeds. Some of those which live in towns are reputed to drown and swallow sparrows.

RECOGNITION: *drake has glossy green head, white collar and purple-brown breast; duck is brown; both have purple wing-patch; in eclipse plumage (July–September) drake is almost identical to duck, but slightly darker; hybrids with domestic ducks are often black or white.*
NESTING: *builds well-hidden nest, usually on ground, from leaves and grass, lined with down; lays February–May; usually 7–16 eggs, pale grey-green or olive-buff; incubation about 28 days, by duck only; ducklings, usually tended by female only, leave soon after hatching, fly at about 6½ weeks.*
FEEDING: *mainly seeds, buds and stems of water plants; some animal food.*

Canada goose

Branta canadensis   38 in.

THE handsome appearance of the Canada goose, with its striking black head and neck and white chin patch, led to its introduction as an ornamental bird from North America more than 250 years ago. A number of geese escaped from the lakes of Victorian collectors and established themselves as wild birds, particularly beside lakes, broads and meres in Norfolk, Cheshire, Shropshire and the Thames Valley. The Canada goose population in Britain has increased enormously of late, from about 3000 birds in 1953 to as many as 60,000 today.

Canada geese are sociable birds. They form flocks of up to 2000 outside the breeding season, and often whole colonies make their nests together near lowland lakes —close to marshes and pastures where they graze during the day. Courtship ceremonies include neck-stretching, with the head and neck held out parallel to the ground. When they are pairing in springtime, the birds are particularly noisy, trumpeting out their loud 'ker-honk' calls.

In winter some Canada geese leave the inland water-ways and move out to the coast, feeding in estuaries and salt-marshes. They are heavy fliers, but fast and direct; for long journeys they travel in 'V' formations in the air, trailing each other in a head-to-tail file or spreading out across the sky in an oblique line.

Present all year; was introduced to Britain more than 250 years ago; often semi-domesticated

Range of native populations only; species has been introduced to Europe and New Zealand

RECOGNITION: *grey-brown plumage; black head and neck with white chin-patch extending upwards behind the eye; sexes alike.*
NESTING: *female lines ground depression, on lake islands or marshlands, with dead leaves, grass and down; nest usually well hidden in vegetation; lays April–May; usually 5 or 6 eggs, dirty white; incubation about 28 days, by female only; nestlings, tended by female, leave soon after they hatch, fly after about 6 weeks.*
FEEDING: *almost completely vegetable, chiefly grass; some insects in summer.*

Canada goose flies heavily with slow, regular wing-beats

Garganey
Anas querquedula 15 in.

FEMALE

MALE

March–Oct. visitor; numbers
fluctuate greatly from year to year;
very rare breeding bird

Most winter far south of range;
some may reach southern Africa,
New Guinea and Australia

Drake garganey throws back its
head in courtship display

ON their migration flights of 3000 miles and more
from Equatorial Africa to their breeding grounds
in Europe, garganey have to run the gauntlet of guns,
especially in Latin countries; their fast flight makes
them an attractive challenge to sportsmen. Some
making for Scandinavia pass through Britain—where
they are known as 'summer teal' in some areas—and
small numbers stay to breed here.

They are less gregarious than teal, and are rarely seen
in large parties; but breeding birds share with teal a
preference for thick cover, and nest near fresh water,
particularly on marshes, fenland and damp meadows.
They nest regularly only where they can find this kind
of country—in Yorkshire, Somerset and south-eastern
England, from Norfolk to Sussex—and are among the
rarest of our breeding birds. It is believed that no more
than 50-100 pairs breed here in a normal season, the first
arriving towards the end of March and the last stragglers
flying south again at the end of October.

Another country name for the garganey is the 'cricket
teal' because of the drake's croaking courtship call,
which sounds like a cricket's chirping. Drakes give this
call as a number of them fly after a single duck, which
will pair with the last one to keep up the pursuit. There
is a wide range of courtship displays on the water.

RECOGNITION: *drake has white streak from eye to nape of neck, mottled
brown breast, and grey flanks; duck mainly speckled brown, both sexes
distinguished from teal by obscure wing-patch and pale grey forewing; in
eclipse plumage (July–October) drake is much like duck.*
NESTING: *duck lines space in rushes or long grass near water with grass and
down; lays late April–May; usually 10 or 11 eggs, creamy-buff; incubation about 22 days, by duck only; ducklings, tended by duck, leave soon
after hatching, fly after 30 days.*
FEEDING: *buds and leaves of pond-weeds; some water-beetles, shellfish,
young fish.*

Teal

Anas crecca 14 in.

MALE

COMPACT flocks of teal perform rapid aerial manoeuvres outside the breeding season, wheeling together rather like waders. Their reactions to danger are rapid, too; they catapult themselves almost vertically into the air and dash away in twisting, swerving flight. This quick response to any threat is a vital survival factor; for teal often live in well-wooded areas where the cover is thick and there is little warning of a predator's approach.

Secluded rushy moorland, freshwater marshes, peat mosses and the edges of lakes are their favourite nesting sites, and they will often go some distance from water to find cover for their nests among gorse or bracken. In winter, teal leave their moorland breeding sites and fly to estuaries and mud-flats on the coasts, or to sewage farms and flooded districts.

The handsome drake has a whistling 'crrick, crrick' call-note, and the duck has a short, high-pitched quack. In the courtship display, the drake dips its bill in the water, rises from the surface, then arches its neck to draw the bill in again.

The teal, our smallest native duck, is widely distributed in Scotland and Ireland, and breeds in most of the counties of north and east England, thinning out southwards and westwards.

RECOGNITION: *drake has grey upper parts and chestnut head with metallic green stripe around eye, running to nape of neck, and white stripe above wing; both sexes have green and black wing-patch; in eclipse plumage (July–October) drake is much like female, with browner upper parts.*
NESTING: *duck lines hollow in ground, among thick undergrowth, with dead leaves, bracken and down; lays April–May; usually 8–10 eggs, pale buff, often with green tinge; incubation about 21 days, by duck only; ducklings, tended mainly by duck, leave soon after hatching, fly after about 23 days.*
FEEDING: *water-weeds and their seeds; some insects, worms and molluscs.*

Present all year; in winter large numbers of immigrants come from Continent and Iceland

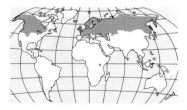

Most of northern part of range is abandoned in winter, when birds migrate west and south

Teal often nest on moors or bogs, well away from open water

195

Gadwall

Anas strepera   20 in.

MALE

Present all year; birds from Iceland and the Continent join the breeding population each winter

Winters mainly near southern limits of breeding range, although a few reach the Tropics

Feeding gadwall dabbles in the water for roots and plants

THE history of the gadwall as a British breeding species goes back little more than about a century-and-a-half. In 1850 a pair of migrant birds caught in a decoy were introduced on the Breckland meres in East Anglia. It seems likely that some of the English breeding colonies are descended from these two birds; their advance was slow but has gathered pace since 1970, so that it is believed that around 1000 pairs now nest regularly in the British Isles.

From their main stronghold in East Anglia, they have spread to many other parts of England. There are other gadwall concentrations in and around Lough Neagh in Northern Ireland, and Loch Leven in Kinross, and the ducks breed sporadically elsewhere in Scotland and Ireland. These Scottish and Irish birds probably represent a natural spread from the main breeding areas in eastern Europe, southern Scandinavia and Iceland. Migrating birds, which visit Britain in small numbers in winter, appear on the coasts and rest on estuaries and coastal waters during their journeys; but gadwall generally prefer quiet inland lakes and reservoirs, and slow-moving streams thickly surrounded by vegetation.

The drake has a deep nasal croak, 'whek', and the duck's quack is soft. Courtship displays include mock preening.

RECOGNITION: *both sexes grey-brown at distance; white patches on back of wings; drake has brown crescents on breast, duck duller; in eclipse plumage (June–late August) drake duller without crescent markings.*
NESTING: *duck lines hollow, in thick cover near water, with dead leaves, sedges and down; lays May; usually 8–12 eggs, yellow-buff; incubation about 28 days, by duck only; ducklings, tended by duck only, leave soon after hatching, fly in about 7 weeks.*
FEEDING: *leaves and roots of sedges and other water plants; some small snails and worms.*

Goldeneye

Bucephala clangula   18 in.

MALE

FEMALE

IN the region of 30,000 goldeneye are believed to visit the British Isles in winter; but it is only since 1970 that breeding has been recorded. In each year since then, increasing numbers have nested in tree-holes or in nesting boxes specially provided for them in the Scottish Highlands.

The winter visitors, arriving about the middle of September, settle to feed on estuaries and sheltered coastal waters, as well as inland lakes, reservoirs and rivers. They are tireless divers, often travelling under water in preference to paddling along the surface. Their rapidly beating wings make a loud, whistling noise as the ducks take off, rising directly into the air instead of pattering along the water like other diving ducks. They usually form small parties, but flocks of 1000 or more of the yellow-eyed birds can be seen regularly in some places, such as the Firth of Forth.

Goldeneye may turn up on the Scottish lochs in summer, performing their complicated courtship ceremonies in which a drake swims round a duck, lifting his head and tail and occasionally kicking up water.

They are quiet birds, though the duck makes a gutteral grunting noise. When they are excited, they stretch up their necks and puff out the feathers on their triangular heads, making them look swollen.

RECOGNITION: *drake has black and white body, black head with green sheen and a white circle in front of the eye; duck is grey with brown head, white collar and wing-patches; in eclipse plumage (August–October or December) drake is like duck, but keeps some dark green head-feathers.*
NESTING: *only twice recorded nesting in Britain; duck lines hole in tree with wood chips, feathers and down; lays mid-April; usually 6–15 eggs, pale blue-green; incubation 26–30 days, by duck only; ducklings, tended by duck, leave after a day, scrambling out of nest and tumbling to ground, fly after 55 days.*
FEEDING: *small water animals, mostly shellfish and insects.*

Sept.–April visitor; a few remain in Scotland in summer and increasing numbers breed

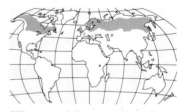

Winters mainly on coasts and large inland waters directly south of breeding range

Displaying drake goldeneye lays its head back and raises its bill

Pintail
Anas acuta   22 in.

MALE

Present all year; few nest, but in winter many birds arrive from Iceland and the Continent

Most Eurasian birds migrate south, some as far as central Africa, Sri Lanka and Borneo

Pintail duck is greyer and more delicate than mallard duck

THE long, sharply pointed tail from which this bird gets its name is only one of the features which make the male unmistakable. Its chocolate-coloured head, pale grey back and white bib help to make it one of the most elegant of British ducks. The female is dowdy by comparison; as with many ducks, this helps to make her inconspicuous to predators during the nesting season. She too has an extended tail, but it is not as long as the male's, which can grow to more than 8 in. long

Pintails walk easily, even gracefully, considering they are ducks, and fly rapidly, particularly when disturbed. In Britain their breeding tends to be sporadic and they rarely keep to the same sites for more than a few years. At present there appear to be three places for them in England and three in Scotland; and all have been established fairly recently. Fifty years ago they bred regularly in three places in Britain, all in Scotland, and none of them in places where pintails nest today. This habit of deserting a site makes their numbers difficult to assess, but a general trend for the breeding population to rise has come to a halt in recent years.

The male guards the nest during incubation, and a distraction display has been recorded in which the bird flies just above the ground, with legs dangling, as though in difficulties.

RECOGNITION: *male has long pointed tail, grey body with brown head and neck, white breast and bronze-green wing-patch; female is speckled brown with grey bill and shorter pointed tail; in eclipse plumage (July–October) male looks like female, but with darker upper parts.*
NESTING: *female lines hollow in ground, often in the open, with grass, leaves and down; lays May; usually 7–9 eggs, pale olive-green, sometimes pale blue; incubation about 23 days, by female only; ducklings, tended by female, leave soon after hatching, fly after about 28 days.*
FEEDING: *feeds on surface, eating mainly water plants; some freshwater insects, molluscs and worms; grain.*

Smew

Mergus albellus 17 in.

MALE

Because of its black and white plumage the old wildfowlers gave this duck the name of 'white nun'; but the description fits the drake only. The female is smaller and greyer, and it has a chestnut-brown patch on the top of its head and nape. At rest, the drake smew looks mostly white, with just a few black markings; but when airborne it appears more black.

The smew is the smallest of our three saw-billed ducks, so called because their bills have serrated edges for keeping a grip on slippery fish. It is a winter visitor and has never bred in Britain; the nearest nesting sites are in northern Scandinavia where the bird chooses a hole in a tree, usually near water, and lines it with down. In an average winter, the number of visitors is unlikely to be more than a hundred or so, and these are mostly confined to large reservoirs in Somerset, Essex and the London area, and to flooded gravel pits in Kent.

Smews constantly dive after fish; they have a rather laboured take-off, like the diving ducks, and walk with an ungainly waddle; but they fly strongly. They are silent birds on the water, though an occasional harsh 'karr' may be uttered. In flight they are silent too: their wings do not make the whistling sound associated with the other saw-bills.

The smews' courtship ceremonies, which may be seen late in winter just before they migrate, include various crest-raising and head-bobbing movements.

RECOGNITION: *male white with black markings, looks more black than white in flight; female grey-white and black with chestnut-brown top of head and nape; short bill.*
NESTING: *does not breed in Britain; nest, in tree hole and usually near water, is lined with down; lays May; usually 6–9 eggs, creamy-buff; incubation, by female only, believed to be 4 weeks; ducklings, tended by female, fly after 5–6 weeks.*
FEEDING: *large variety of small fish, shrimps, snails and water-beetles.*

Nov.–March visitor, mainly on reservoirs around London; unknown here in summer

Migratory; winters on fresh water from the southern limit of ice south to the Mediterranean

Duck's white throat and cheeks contrast with its darker head

Shoveler

Spatula clypeata   20 in.

MALE

Present all year; in winter large numbers of immigrants arrive from northern Europe

Winters mainly just south of breeding range, but some reach S. Africa and Central America

Shoveler collects food with its highly specialised bill

THE enormous heavy bill which gives the shoveler its name is specially adapted for feeding on the surface of ponds and lakes. The duck paddles quickly through the shallows, holding its head low and thrusting the spoon-like bill forward so that it dabbles all the time in water or thin mud, picking up tiny plants and animals and sieving out the water. Unlike most surface-feeding ducks, shovelers rarely 'up-end' to pick up food under the water, but they may dive if alarmed.

They are clumsy on land, and their bills give them a top-heavy look; but they are active fliers, particularly in spring, when duck and drake circle their territory in a courtship flight. The drake chases its mate with a throaty 'took-took' call-note. The duck has a double quack, but shovelers outside the breeding season are usually rather silent birds.

Shovelers are found in varying numbers over most of Britain, most frequently in East Anglia, but their distribution is local. The main reason for this is probably a shortage of suitable breeding sites. For breeding, they prefer marshes, damp meadows and sewage farms with plenty of cover, though they breed sometimes beside more open lakes, provided that there is shallow muddy water where they can feed. In winter they spread to almost any kind of inland shallow water.

RECOGNITION: *both sexes have huge bill and pale blue patch on forewings; drake has dark green head, white breast and chestnut sides; duck has speckled brown underparts; in eclipse plumage (May–December) drake is much like duck, but darker.*

NESTING: *duck lines deep hollow in dry ground with grass and down; surrounding grass stems sometimes form a 'tent'; lays April–May; usually 8–12 eggs, buff or green; incubation about 24 days, by duck only; ducklings, tended by duck, leave soon after hatching, fly after 40 days.*

FEEDING: *animal and vegetable food in equal amounts—freshwater insects and shellfish mixed with seeds, buds and leaves of water plants.*

Pochard
Aythya ferina   18 in.

FEMALE   MALE

Present all year; in winter many immigrants arrive from northern Europe and Siberia

Winters mainly on inland fresh water in western Europe and south of breeding range

Pochard often nests in thick vegetation very close to water

Many town parks have a small party of pochards swimming and diving in their lakes in autumn and winter, when the chestnut-headed birds are among Britain's most common freshwater ducks. But by the time the breeding season comes round, most pochards have vanished; they fly off to breed in eastern Europe and only about 400 pairs stay to nest in Britain, most of them in the south-east.

Pochards breed around inland lakes and slow-moving streams with beds of iris or reeds where they can dive for food, although they sometimes 'up-end' like surface-feeding ducks. Their nests are close to the water, or even above it, in a thick clump of vegetation. They rarely go to land, because the position of their legs, set well back for diving and underwater swimming, makes them 'front heavy' and clumsy when they walk. They are reluctant fliers, too, preferring to swim away from danger. To take off, pochards have to patter across the surface of the water in the typical diving-duck manner. Once launched, they fly fast, often in tight formation. They form flocks, sometimes hundreds strong.

Pochards are quiet except when courting; then the drakes hold up their heads, puff out their necks and give a soft, wheezing whistle. The ducks reply with a harsh, growling 'kurr' sound.

RECOGNITION: *drake has chestnut-red head, black breast, grey body; distinguished from drake wigeon by absence of cream crown and white forewing; duck is brown with pale mark around bill, distinguished from tufted duck by absence of white wing-bar in flight; in eclipse plumage (July–September) drake looks like duck with greyer back.*
NESTING: *nests in cover over or near water on a pile of vegetation, lined with down by duck; lays late April–early May; usually 6–11 eggs, green-grey; incubation about 28 days, by duck only; ducklings, tended by duck, swim a few hours after hatching, fly after 7½ weeks.*
FEEDING: *roots, leaves and buds of water-weeds; small water animals.*

Tufted duck

Aythya fuligula   17 in.

FEMALE

MALE

Present all year; in winter birds from Iceland and north-east Europe swell native population

Most birds winter south of breeding range, some reaching as far as N. Africa and India

Tufted duck dives for food in water usually 2–6 ft deep

U NKNOWN as a breeding species in Britain at the beginning of the 19th century, the tufted duck is now the most common of our diving ducks. About 10,000 pairs breed in Britain and Ireland, and in winter visitors flock in from northern Europe and Iceland, spreading out to reservoirs and other stretches of inland fresh water. In the breeding season, tufted ducks usually keep to lakes and ponds fringed with rushes and other plants to provide cover. They nest in colonies, generally close to the water and often on islands. They are gregarious birds, usually seen in parties of a few dozen, though sometimes in big flocks, and they mix freely with pochards and coots.

Though they are wary in the wild, they become quite tame wherever they are protected, and often set up their colonies in city park lakes—in St James's Park, London, for example.

When they dive, tufted ducks pick up both animal and vegetable food before bobbing back to the surface. But they seem to prefer weeds and grasses to the small freshwater shellfish and insects which form the animal part of their diet. Courtship is simple: the drake tilts back his handsome head and whistles very softly to the duck; she dips her bill repeatedly into the water and gives a raucous, growling call.

RECOGNITION: *drake has long drooping crest; white flanks contrast boldly with rest of plumage, which is dark; duck is browner with smaller crest; both have white wing-bar in flight; in eclipse plumage (July–October) drake looks like duck, but is darker.*
NESTING: *duck lays foundation of grass and reeds on ground near water-side, lines it with down; lays late May–June; usually 6–14 eggs, pale grey-green; incubation about 24 days, by duck only; ducklings, tended by duck, swim and dive in a few hours, fly after about 6 weeks.*
FEEDING: *dives for water plants; also water animals, including insects, frogs, spawn and small fish.*

Wigeon

Anas penelope   18 in.

MALE

A PIPING 'whee-oo' call gives the drake wigeon away even in fog or at a distance. A number of them often chorus the call as they crowd around a duck, raising the crest feathers of their chestnut and cream heads. The duck's answering call is a purring sound. Later in courtship the paired drake and duck raise the tips of their wings and cross them almost vertically over their backs.

About 50 years ago wigeon were in an expanding phase as a British breeding species, but this advance has now come to a halt, and as far as is known there is no regular breeding south of Yorkshire. Lochs, rivers and marshes, especially in wooded country, are their favourite breeding habitat, though they occasionally nest on coastal marshes. The nest is always built on the ground, and several pairs may breed in the same area, the drakes standing guard over the ducks during incubation. Outside the breeding season, they gather mainly on the coasts, flocking inland at dusk to crop the grass in fields and meadows; but some winter inland, in flooded districts and on large lakes and reservoirs.

Wigeon are highly gregarious; flocks hundreds strong rest by day on estuaries and mud-flats, rising straight out of the water together when disturbed and keeping in tight formation during their rapid flights.

RECOGNITION: *drake has chestnut head with creamy-buff forehead and crown, white forewing, grey upper parts, green wing-patch; duck has grey-green wing-patch, is slimmer and has more pointed tail than mallard duck; in eclipse plumage (June–October or November) male looks like dark female, but with white forewing.*
NESTING: *duck makes nest on ground among heather or bracken, lined with grass and down; lays May; usually 7 or 8 eggs, creamy-buff; incubation about 25 days, by duck only; ducklings, tended by duck, leave soon after hatching, fly after about 40 days.*
FEEDING: *mainly grasses; grain; also eel-grass from mud-flats.*

Present all year; in winter many immigrants arrive from Iceland and Siberia

Winters directly south of breeding range, in North Sea area and on the east coast of the U.S.A.

Duck (front) and two drake wigeon rest on the water

Goosander
Mergus merganser 26 in.

MALE

Present all year; spreading south as a breeding bird; winter visitors come from the Continent

Winters just south of breeding range, northern limits determined by ice conditions

Goosander—one of the few ducks which nest in tree holes

THIS largest of the British saw-billed ducks has been rather too efficient for its own good at the task of catching fish. Like the red-breasted merganser, it is unpopular with anglers: when the goosander began to colonise the Tweed Valley in the course of its steady upward spread, water bailiffs succeeded in temporarily exterminating it there. In fact, although the bird lives largely on fish, it takes relatively few salmon or trout. Despite this persecution, goosanders have spread to other parts of Scotland and northern England in the past 100 years, and they have recently spread to Wales, the Peak district and south Devon. They are now protected by law.

They become more widespread in the winter and numbers may reach 100 or more on large English reservoirs, for example, those close to London. On land they look ungainly, but on water they come into their own; they are highly efficient underwater swimmers, able to stay down for longer than a minute. Often they are mistaken for divers or large grebes, but no grebe or diver has the drake's pattern of dark green head and neck and white or pinkish body plumage, or the duck's chestnut head and white chin. In courtship, the male 'stands up' in the water, stretches its neck and raises its crest feathers. The courtship display also includes a sexual chase. The cry of both sexes is restricted to a harsh 'karr' or 'kraah'.

RECOGNITION: *straight, slender bill; male has dark green glossy head and neck and grey rump, with salmon-pink underparts; duck smaller, with chestnut head and grey back.*
NESTING: *nests in a tree hole, or cavity in a bank; duck lines cavity with rotten wood, leaves and feathers; lays April–June; 7–13 eggs, creamy-white; incubation about 5 weeks, by duck only; ducklings, tended by duck, leave after a few days, fly after about 5 weeks.*
FEEDING: *small fish, shrimps and frogs; some caterpillars and other insects.*

Red-breasted merganser

Mergus serrator   23 in.

MALE

Aˡᵗʰᵒᵘᵍʰ this handsome duck is now a protected species throughout Britain, thanks to the Wildlife and Countryside Act 1981, licences to kill it are issued freely in Scotland under the same act, despite the fact that salmon and trout—the two fish that matter most to anglers in Scotland—do not form a large part of its diet.

Before 1981 mergansers were unprotected in Scotland; but even so it became widespread there. Breeding birds are found on many rivers and lochs and in low-lying coastal areas. They are also common in Ireland and in the past 30 years have colonised north-west England and north and central Wales. Given a chance, they may well spread farther south as breeders.

In winter red-breasted mergansers prefer salt water to fresh water, and visit estuaries all round the coasts of the British Isles. Flocks several hundred strong occur regularly on some estuaries in Scotland.

The red-breasted merganser is a saw-billed duck, equipped with serrations on its bill, so that wriggling fish cannot slip away. The drake is easily recognised by the untidy double crest on a head that is dark green but looks almost black from a distance.

Its courtship displays include much bowing and gesturing with the head and bill, raising the crest, arching the wings and pattering along the water in a cloud of spray.

RECOGNITION: *drake has dark green head with double crest; chestnut breast, grey and white back; duck brown and grey, with white bar on wings.*
NESTING: *duck makes lining of leaves and down in hollow in ground, well screened by thick vegetation; lays May–early July; 7–12 eggs, olive-buff, sometimes with blue tinge; eggs covered with down when duck leaves nest; incubation about 28 days, by duck only; ducklings, tended by duck, leave shortly after hatching, fly after about 5 weeks.*
FEEDING: *small fish, eels, crabs, shrimps; worms and insects.*

Present all year; winter population includes birds from Iceland and northern Europe

Mainly migratory; most winter on tidal estuaries directly south of breeding range

Red-breasted merganser's nest is screened by vegetation

Black-throated diver

Gavia arctica 27 in.

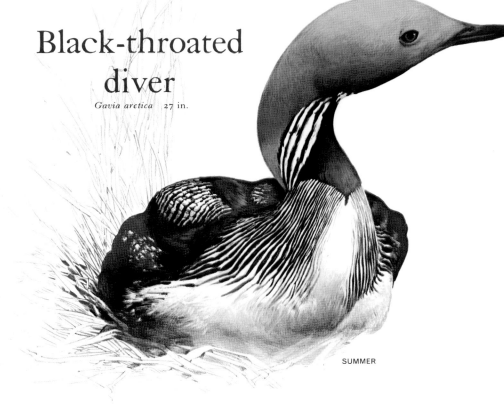

SUMMER

Present all year; in winter found mainly around coasts, only accidentally on inland waters

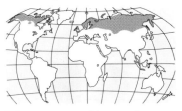

Winters at sea and in coastal waters south of breeding range

Black-throated diver in winter is dark grey above and white below

A black-throated diver has been known to swim for a quarter of a mile under water before coming up for air. Part of the price they pay for being such good swimmers is that on land they are clumsy birds. In fact, they rarely visit land except to nest, and even then the nest is only a few feet away from the waterside. Divers have a superficial resemblance to cormorants and shags, but they can be identified by their manner of swimming: a diver holds its head straight out, instead of pointing it upwards at an angle of 45 degrees.

There are probably not more than 150 breeding pairs of black-throated divers in Britain, and most of them are confined to the larger freshwater lochs of the Highlands and Scottish islands although, since the 1950s, they have also nested on Arran and occasionally elsewhere in south-western Scotland. In winter they are much more widespread, although still not common. At this time of year, many appear on the east coast of England.

In their flight, which is direct and fast, black-throated divers give a barking 'kwuk-kwuk-kwuk' flight-note in the breeding season. Their other calls at this time include a loud hoot, a mournful-sounding wail, and a special cry given during courtship when paired birds fly off. Before pairing up there is a good deal of chasing about on the water, and the female may turn somersaults as she leads the male in this sexual chase.

RECOGNITION: *black throat and striped neck in summer; these become white in winter; distinguished from winter red-throated diver by heavier, straight bill and darker back; sexes alike.*
NESTING: *no proper nest; eggs laid on the ground, very close to water, and exceptionally on a heap of water-weed; lays May–June; 2 eggs, pale green or brown, sparsely marked with black; incubation about 28 days, by one or both parents; chicks, tended by both parents, leave shortly after hatching, fly in about 9 weeks.*
FEEDING: *trout, perch, roach, herrings, sprats; crabs, prawns, mussels.*

Red-throated diver

Gavia stellata   24 in.

SUMMER

THE courtship ceremonies of ducks, bizarre though many of them are, have nothing to equal the displays of the red-throated diver. Up to four divers race across the water, with bodies half-submerged and heads and necks pointed forwards and upwards, looking like the long-extinct plesiosaur. As well as swimming, they sometimes patter along the surface, beating the water with their wings; and during these courtship displays they utter metallic-sounding cries, sometimes starting with a long, loud, mewing wail.

This wail, which is also the bird's cry at other times, apart from a 'kwuk-kwuk-kwuk' given in flight, earned it the old country nickname of 'rain goose'. People believed that when they heard the cry, rain was on the way. Another country name, 'sprat loon', comes from its feeding habits, though the red-throated diver eats many kinds of fish other than sprats.

Red-throated divers nest in the Highlands and Scottish islands, and have also established an outpost in Co. Donegal in north-western Ireland, where a few pairs breed regularly. Attempts to colonise the mainland of south-west Scotland during the 1950s were not successful; but as visitors, the birds are widespread in British coastal waters. Those found inland in winter are either storm-driven or sick.

Present all year; uncommon inland except on breeding grounds; widespread on coasts in winter

Migratory; winters from edge of breeding range to subtropics

RECOGNITION: *red patch on the throat in summer; rest of neck grey; back and wings brown with paler underparts; female smaller, but similar in plumage; both lose red patch in autumn; distinguished in winter from black-throated diver by slightly up-tilted bill and pale grey back.*
NESTING: *eggs laid on the ground or on a heap of water-weed; lays May, 2 eggs, olive-green, spotted with brown; incubation about 28 days, by both parents; chicks, tended by both parents, leave shortly after hatching, fly in about 8 weeks.*
FEEDING: *char, dace, perch, gudgeon, herring, flounders, sprats, shrimps, mussels; some insects.*

The shape of a red-throated diver in flight, this one in winter

Great crested grebe

Podiceps cristatus 19 in.

SUMMER

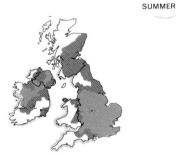

Present all year; in winter, most birds desert small inland waters for large reservoirs and the coast

Mainly sedentary; some northern birds migrate when their breeding lakes freeze over

The wing pattern of a great crested grebe in winter

DURING the 19th century, great crested grebes were all but exterminated in Britain, because they were unfortunate enough to supply a demand of fashion. Grebe feathers—sometimes the entire plumage—were used to decorate women's hats; and around 1860 there were believed to be no more than 42 pairs left in the whole of England.

Their relative abundance nowadays—more than 12,000 adults are present in Britain and Ireland in the breeding season—is one of the triumphs of the bird protection movement. The increase in flooded gravel-pits and other man-made water habitats in the south, in the past 40 to 50 years, helped their recovery, for grebes nest exclusively on inland stretches of fresh water, including slow-flowing rivers. In winter they may also be seen on estuaries and coastal waters.

The great crested grebe's courtship ceremonies, famous for elaborate postures and gestures, were studied intensively by Sir Julian Huxley as long ago as 1914, and his writings on the subject are among the classics of bird-watching literature.

The parents change places on the nest every three hours or so, and after the chicks have hatched they are often carried on the back of one parent while the other brings food.

RECOGNITION: *double-horned crest and chestnut 'frills' about the head in breeding season; long white neck, but this may not show when bird is hunched up and resting; sexes alike.*
NESTING: *both sexes build pile of weeds in water, either floating or grounded; floating nest is anchored to nearby plants; lays April–July; 3–5 eggs, white, but soon discoloured by water-weeds; incubation about 28 days, by both parents; chicks, tended by both parents, leave soon after hatching, begin to dive at 6 weeks and are independent at 9–10 weeks; sometimes two broods.*
FEEDING: *small fish; molluscs; algae, weed and other vegetable matter.*

FEMALE IN SUMMER

Dabchick

Tachybaptus ruficollis 9 in.

THE courtship of the dabchick centres round a strange 'love song'—or rather, a love duet, for the male and female face one another on the water and both go into a trilling song. There is also some scuffling and chasing, and sometimes the male will give the female a symbolic present of weeds.

The dabchick, sometimes called the 'little grebe', is the smallest of the British grebes, and is widespread on inland waters. It breeds on ponds, lakes, slow-moving rivers, and sometimes in town parks. In summer the pale patch on the bird's face is a good guide to identification. The male has black on its chin, and chestnut on its cheeks, neck and breast. In winter, the chin becomes white and the chestnut areas brown.

Like other grebes the dabchick has a weak, direct flight, with its neck stretched out and held rather below the level of the body, and its legs trailing behind. It has a pattering take-off and swims and dives freely. The bird is ungainly on land, and goes there as little as it can. The chicks, which are able to swim almost at hatching, will climb on their parents' backs and hide there in response to the 'whit-whit' alarm note.

Their size does not allow them to swallow large fish, and their favourite food is often sticklebacks, though they also eat shrimps and water insects.

RECOGNITION: *in summer, back dark brown, with chestnut breast, neck and cheeks and small pale patch on face; paler in winter; female duller than male.*
NESTING: *both sexes build nest on a floating tangle of water-weeds, either grounded on or anchored by vegetation; lays April–July; 4–6 eggs, white, soon stained by damp weed; incubation about 24 days, by both parents; chicks, tended by both parents, able to swim almost at birth; two broods, sometimes three.*
FEEDING: *small fish, especially sticklebacks; shrimps; dragonfly nymphs, water-beetles and other water insects, and water molluscs.*

Present all year, mainly on fresh water; some winter visitors may come from Continent

Sedentary in most parts of breeding range; related birds replace it in Australia and N. America

Male dabchick in winter—its plumage is paler than in summer

Black-necked grebe

Podiceps nigricollis 12 in.

SUMMER

Present all year; very rare breeding bird, but visitors arrive from Continent in winter

Mainly sedentary; some birds move to avoid winter ice or dried-out breeding waters

Black-necked grebe in winter has dusky cheeks and neck

BLACK-NECKED grebes provide a perfect illustration of the way in which birds cope with a major change in their environment. In the 19th century there were none breeding in Britain; they were primarily birds of the steppe lakes in southern Russia. Then, in 1904, the first British breeding pair was recorded in Anglesey. The explanation was that the steppe lakes were gradually drying up because of climatic changes; and the grebes reacted to the change by moving westwards. In the early 1930's there was a colony of up to 250 breeding pairs on a lake in Co. Roscommon, Ireland; but breeding in Britain is now confined to a few sites in central Scotland, and occasionally elsewhere.

Shallow lochs with horsetail or some other vegetation growing in the water are the birds' favourite breeding sites. On migration and during hard winters they appear on inland stretches of fresh water, and regularly on estuaries and shallow coastal waters.

The bird is easily identified in breeding plumage by its black neck and face, and the golden-chestnut tuft of feathers fanning out behind its eyes. In winter the head adornments are lost, but at all times the black-necked grebe can be told by its slightly up-tilted blue-grey bill.

The bird's most frequent call is a soft 'pee-eep'. Courtship ceremonies include head wagging and a 'penguin dance' like the great crested grebe's.

RECOGNITION: *black neck; golden fan-shaped ear-tufts behind eyes; up-tilted blue-grey bill; sexes alike.*
NESTING: *frequently colonial; nest, built by both sexes, is a pile of water-weed in water, grounded on or anchored by vegetation; lays May–July; 3 or 4 eggs, white but soon stained because parents cover them with weeds before leaving nest; incubation about 21 days, by both parents; chicks, tended by both parents, leave soon after hatching but are occasionally carried on backs of adults for about 4 weeks.*
FEEDING: *fish; freshwater insects.*

Slavonian grebe

Podiceps auritus   13 in.

SUMMER

IN North America this bird is known as the horned grebe; and the name is appropriate, for the most conspicuous feature of its breeding plumage is its set of 'horns'—golden ear-tufts, pointing upwards. The tufts vanish in winter and the grebe's neck, breast and cheeks turn white; at this time of year the easiest way to tell it from the black-necked grebe is by its bill, which is straight as opposed to being tilted upwards, and by its clean white cheeks.

Like black-necks, Slavonian grebes began nesting in Britain only in the present century, and they are still rare as breeders. About 50 pairs breed regularly on lochs in the Inverness district and there are a few in neighbouring areas. The nest is a pile of weeds, usually anchored in shallow water, and the parent birds pull weeds over the eggs when they leave them untended.

In winter Slavonian grebes are more widespread than in the breeding season. They usually go down to estuaries, but in hard weather they will move to inland waters. Their breeding-season calls include a low rippling trill, and their courtship ceremonies are similar to those of the great crested grebe; they have their own version of that bird's famous 'penguin dance', in which male and female rise up in the water, breast to breast.

Slavonian grebes fly more readily than other grebes, but when suspicious they sometimes sink low in the water, almost disappearing from sight.

RECOGNITION: *golden ear-tufts and chestnut neck in summer ; tufts vanish in winter and neck, breast and cheeks are white ; straight bill ; sexes alike.*
NESTING: *both sexes build floating platform of weeds at loch side ; lays late May–July ; 3–5 eggs, white but soon stained by weeds ; incubation about 24 days, by both parents ; chicks, tended by both parents, leave in a few days, but are fed for over 4 weeks and often carried on adults' backs.*
FEEDING: *small fish ; water-snails and other water insects ; some vegetable matter.*

Present all year; nowhere common, but in winter immigrants join small resident population

Mainly migratory; winters chiefly in coastal waters just south of breeding range

Slavonian grebe in winter has black cap and white cheeks

Moorhen

Gallinula chloropus 13 in.

Present all year; winter population includes immigrants from Europe

Mainly sedentary; some northern breeding birds migrate south and west in winter

Conspicuous white flash shows as a moorhen flirts its tail

THE moorhen has no connection with moors: its name is a form of 'merehen', or bird of the lakes. This bird, possibly the most common of our waterfowl, can sink when alarmed and leave only its bill protruding, like a periscope. It probably stays down by forcing air out of its plumage and air sacs and by treading water.

Moorhens defend their territory jealously. Males fight fiercely in the water, sometimes ending up with broken toes or dislocated thighs. There is even a record of a moorhen trying to drown a homing pigeon by holding it under water.

The birds breed near fresh water among thick cover, and their favourite nesting-sites are by the side of a pond, lake or river. They are often seen in town parks, and feed freely in marshes, sewage farms and meadows.

The moorhen's flight is weak, like that of many swimming birds, and its take-off from water is usually laboured and pattering. It swims with a jerky movement, constantly flicking the white 'flashes' on the sides of its tail. The most frequent call-notes are two loud but rather liquid croaks, 'kurruk' and 'kittic', and a harsh 'kaak'. The male has a special courtship posture in which it tilts its body upwards, points its wing-tips almost vertically, spreads its tail to display the white undertail coverts and points its head downwards.

RECOGNITION: *red on forehead, extending into bill ; white undertail coverts ; tail constantly flicked while swimming ; sexes alike.*
NESTING: *both sexes build platform of dried water plants, usually near water, but sometimes some distance away or in a tree or bush ; lays late March–July ; 5–11 eggs, buff, speckled with red-brown ; incubation 19–22 days, by both parents ; chicks, fed by both parents and sometimes by young of earlier brood, leave in 2 or 3 days, and can swim and dive at once ; normally two broods, sometimes three.*
FEEDING: *wild fruit and seeds, grain, water-weed ; worms, slugs, snails, insects and larvae ; sometimes eggs and chicks of other birds.*

Coot

Fulica atra   15 in.

Coots, so the story goes, will fight off enemies by kicking up spray in their faces; and the story is not far from the truth. If a marsh harrier or some other bird of prey swoops down on a crowd of coots they will paddle furiously towards the nearest reeds, and raise a cloud of spray as they crash-dive to safety.

They are aggressive birds, with a highly developed territorial sense, and much given to quarrelsome pursuits of one another. They prefer large, open stretches of water and often nest in loose colonies. Coots usually breed only where there is good cover for their nests, and are particularly common on flooded gravel-pits in southern England. They are easily recognisable by a white flash on the forehead, contrasting with the black of their plumage. In winter they take to large reservoirs and lakes without much cover; they occur on estuaries too, and will feed along other stretches of the coast when inland waters are frozen.

The bird's name echoes its loud, high-pitched cry. It is completely at home on water and, like the moorhen, can submerge its body until only its bill shows above the surface. On land, it has a rather inelegant walk; and its flight, usually low over the water, is heavy and laboured. The main courtship display consists of stretching out the neck until it almost touches the water.

Present all year; winter flocks often include visitors from Europe

Mainly sedentary; some northern birds may winter as far south as northern tropical Africa

Coot threatens with lowered head and raised wings

RECOGNITION: *all black except for white on forehead and bill, and narrow white wing-bar seen in flight; sexes alike.*
NESTING: *both sexes build substantial nest of reeds in shallow water; nest may be floating or stranded on a half-submerged bough; lays March–May; usually 6–9 eggs, buff with black spots; incubation 21–24 days, by both parents; nestlings, tended by both parents, leave after 3 or 4 days, are independent after about 8 weeks; two broods, sometimes three.*
FEEDING: *shoots of reeds, roots of water plants; corn and seeds; some small fish, newts, tadpoles; dragonfly nymphs and other water insects; sometimes eggs and chicks of other birds.*

Black tern

Chlidonias niger 10 in.

SPRING

May–Sept. visitor; has bred occasionally in East Anglia, and in Ireland since 1967

Winters mainly along coasts of tropical Africa and S. America

The grey and white plumage of a black tern in winter

THE draining of the fens and other marshes wiped out the black tern as a British breeding species, and it is now among the small group of birds which are seen in these islands only during their spring and autumn migrations; for its wintering grounds are also outside Britain—in Africa.

Once the birds bred in large numbers in eastern England. In recent years odd pairs of black terns have nested in East Anglia and Ireland—the first time they have done so in Britain since the middle of the last century. Unfortunately, permanent recolonisation is not yet in sight.

In the spring the black tern is easy to recognise because there is no other bird with its markings—a black head and underparts, and dark grey upper parts —which has the habit of hovering over the water. In autumn its plumage is grey and white, like that of most other terns, but its dipping flight is still distinctive as it plunges to pick up a small fish or water insect.

The black tern is a rather silent bird, though it has an occasional 'kik-kik' call, and flocks sometimes produce a reedy whistling. They often join feeding flocks of sea terns on estuaries, though they are most common over inland waters. On the Continent they usually breed in marshes and swamps, sometimes in huge colonies, choosing nesting sites where reeds grow out of shallow water.

RECOGNITION: *black beak; plumage black and dark grey in spring and summer, paler grey and white in autumn and winter; sexes alike.*
NESTING: *no longer nests regularly in Britain; both sexes build floating platform of weeds; nest is made of grass and rushes; lays May–June; 2–4 eggs, buff to brown, with darker markings; incubation about 14 days, by both parents; nestlings, tended by both parents, leave after about 14 days, fly after about 3 weeks.*
FEEDING: *dragonflies and their nymphs, caddis flies and water-boatmen; occasionally minnows, small frogs and tadpoles.*

SALT-MARSH
AND ESTUARY

Expanses of mud-flats uncovered by the tide,
and salt-marshes intersected by water channels,
have a magnetic appeal for many birds. They are open,
comparatively safe feeding grounds where geese, ducks and waders
can dabble and probe for marine organisms; and for
birds migrating from the far north they are hospitable
winter quarters on the margins of ice-free waters.

CONTENTS

Greylag goose

Anser anser 30–35 in.

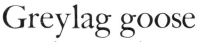

Mainly Oct.–April visitor, but present all year in N.W. Scotland (native birds) and other parts of Britain (introduced stock)

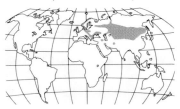

Essentially migratory; winters in and beyond southern parts of breeding range

Wings of greylag in flight have pale leading edge

BRITAIN has only one native breeding goose, the greylag. It has a reputation for intelligence, devotion and lifelong marital fidelity. Year by year a pair cement and renew their bond with a 'triumph ceremony'—triumphant because, during the performance, the gander produces a resonant note like the one it uses after it has driven off an intruder and hastens back to reassure its mate.

The greylag is the ancestor of the farmyard goose, which it closely resembles: the alertness and nervous cackling from the farmyard's sharpest 'watchdog' comes from the wild bird.

Its nest, usually on loch-studded moorland or near lakes and reservoirs, is nearly always in a hollow in deep heather; and the goose pulls the feather-and-down lining over the eggs on leaving. Left to itself, the greylag's breeding grounds would now be confined to the extreme north of Scotland and the Outer Hebrides. But it has become familiar again in places where it once bred: wildfowlers and landowners have introduced wild breeding stock in many parts of the British Isles, where they have become established and thrive. Winter-visiting greylags from Iceland are more widespread than the native breeders, again chiefly in Scotland. The flocks, when they arrive, are not always popular with farmers whose grazing land and crops are invaded.

RECOGNITION: *barred grey-brown back, pale grey forewing; orange bill, pink legs; sexes alike.*
NESTING: *builds nest of heather, grass, moss and other local materials, on ground near water; female lines nest with down; lays late April–May; 4–7 eggs, white, often stained; incubation 27 or 28 days, by female only, male on watch at distance; goslings, tended by both parents, leave in a few hours, begin to fly after about 8 weeks.*
FEEDING: *grass, crops and water-weed.*

White-fronted goose

Anser albifrons   26–30 in.

Lesser white-fronted goose

Anser erythropus   21–25 in.

W HITE-FRONTED geese, often in flocks of hundreds and mixed with pink-feet, are masters of air manoeuvre. Their flight is less heavy than the greylag's, and frequently in the grey goose V-formation. Sportsmen say they can 'reverse engines' and come to a dead stop when alarmed—or can rise almost vertically from the ground. Like greylags, they will swoop from a height towards their feeding grounds in a 'whiffling' spiral dive, with wings half folded.

In winter the white-front is the most common grey goose in the west of Britain. It moves with the tide on estuaries and retreats to marshes and fields at high tide. The rarer lesser white-front occasionally turns up in white-front flocks—especially among those at the Wildfowl Trust, at Slimbridge on the Severn Estuary. Both feed on flooded fields and similar wetland

A characteristic gabble of 'kow-yow' or 'kow-lyow' sounds, harsher and louder than the pink-foot's call, has earned the white-front the name 'laughing goose' in some districts; the lesser white-front's 'ku-ku' or 'ku-yu-yu' is shriller-sounding. White-fronts are the easiest of the grey geese to recognise. The white forehead and black-barred plumage underneath show up both at rest and in flight; and the combination of pink or orange bill with orange legs is distinctive.

White-front (on map) is Oct.–April visitor; rarer lesser occurs on Severn, Dec.–March

Migratory; map shows range of white-front; lesser white-front is not found in N. America

RECOGNITION : *grey-brown ; black bars on belly ; pink or orange bill ; orange legs ; white forehead ; white extends higher in lesser white-front, which also has yellow eye-ring but is otherwise a smaller version of white-front ; immatures have no white on forehead ; sexes alike.*
NESTING: *both nest in Arctic, from Greenland to Siberia, building nest of heather, grasses or lichen, lined with down, in hollow in ground ; both lay late May–June ; 4–7 eggs, creamy-white, often stained ; incubation 27 or 28 days, by female only ; goslings, tended by both parents, leave nest soon after hatching, fly after several months.*
FEEDING: *grass, clover and plant shoots ; grain, sometimes potatoes.*

Adult (top) and immature white-fronts feed in winter pasture

217

Pink-footed goose

Anser brachyrhynchus   24–30 in.

Bean goose

Anser fabalis   28–35 in.

Pink-foot arrives Sept., leaves April. Much rarer bean, mainly Nov.–March, in Norfolk

Pink-foot is confined to Greenland, Iceland and Spitsbergen; both winter south of breeding range

A formation of pink-footed geese in flight

THESE two grey geese look much alike, and ornithologists still cannot agree as to whether they are separate species or races of the same species. The pink-foot is the most common grey goose on the east coast in winter, although there are plenty on the west coast, too. It is noisy and often assembles in large flocks. The much rarer bean goose occurs regularly only in the Yare valley, Norfolk, and just south of Falkirk in Scotland. Its calls are tenor versions of the pink-foot's shrill medley of 'wink-wink' and 'ung-ung' sounds.

At any distance, the dark head and neck distinguish both from other grey geese. The pink-foot has a less conspicuous pale grey forewing than the heavier greylag; no other grey goose has both legs and bill pink. The bean's bill is orange and black.

Pink-feet roost in marshes and estuaries, and move inland to feed on cultivated fields, taking grain, potatoes and other crops, as well as grass and wild shoots and roots. Both share the flight habits of other grey geese, including the 'whiffling' spiral descent from a height; but the pink-foot is more buoyant in flight than the bean goose. Their courtship, too, follows the general pattern of the greys, which suggests that these displays, with their characteristic 'triumph' calls, may have developed early in the evolutionary time scale.

RECOGNITION: *pink-foot has pale blue-grey forewings, upper parts grey-brown ; dark head and neck, pink and black bill and pink legs ; bean goose has dark head and neck, long black and orange-yellow bill ; sexes alike in both cases.*

NESTING: *pink-foot nests in Greenland, Iceland, Spitsbergen, on ground or cliff ledge, lines nest with down ; bean goose nests in northern Europe and Siberia, lines scrape in ground with leaves, moss and down ; both lay late May–June ; 4 or 5 eggs, creamy-white ; incubation about 28 days, by female only in both species ; goslings, tended by both parents, leave nest soon after hatching, fly at about 8 weeks.*

FEEDING: *grass, crops and roots.*

Brent goose

DARK-BREASTED RACE

Branta bernicla 22–24 in.

LONG, irregular lines of small, dark Brent geese, feeding along east coast tide lines in winter, are a much more common sight, except in Scotland, than they were a few decades ago. For winter diet, the Brent relies almost exclusively on eel-grass, one of the few flowering plants which grow submerged in salt water; wherever the weed is abundant, the Brent geese gather. They have a habit of up-ending, like ducks, to get at the plant.

The decline of the large flocks in the 1930s was probably caused by a disease which devastated the eel-grass beds on both sides of the North Sea. Now, thanks to its protection and to its adaptation to feeding on farmland behind sea walls, the numbers of Brents have increased enormously. About half the population of 200,000 dark-breasted Brents wintering in Europe are to be found on the east and south coasts of England. They nest in Arctic Russia and Siberia.

Another race, the pale-breasted Brent, comes from Greenland and winters mainly in Ireland: small numbers, wintering in Northumberland, come from Spitsbergen.

The Brent is very much a sea goose and has only recently taken to feeding on farmland. Huge flocks rest on the sea at high tide and roost there at night. The occasional straggler seen inland is likely to have escaped from a collection of ornamental fowl.

RECOGNITION: *black head, neck and upper breast; small white patch on neck; dark grey back and wings; white above and below the black tail. Two geographical races: dark-breasted (slate-grey underparts) and pale-breasted (whitish underparts); sexes alike.*

NESTING: *nests in hollows between rocks, filled with moss and lined with down; lays June; 3–5 eggs, creamy-white; incubation about 28 days, by female only, male standing guard; goslings, tended by both parents, leave nest soon after hatching, fly after several months.*

FEEDING: *eel-grass (Zostera) in winter; shoots of Arctic plants, seaweed and mussels in summer.*

Oct.–May visitor, dark-breasted from Siberia, pale-breasted from Greenland and Spitsbergen

Winters on Atlantic or Pacific shores, south to British Isles and southern United States

Brent geese fly swiftly in loose but well co-ordinated flocks

Barnacle goose

Branta leucopsis 23–27 in.

Oct.–April visitor; small numbers occur on other coasts, especially in severe winters

Migratory; entire population winters on coasts of British Isles and north-west Europe

Barnacle geese graze together on pasture close to shore

THE barnacle goose owes its name to a medieval myth. Its breeding grounds in the Arctic were unknown to our ancestors, and they believed that it did not come from an egg, like other birds, but was generated from the curiously shaped goose barnacles, which are still washed ashore in clusters, attached to driftwood. To a fanciful eye, there is even today a likeness to a goose in some of these barnacles.

So persistent was the myth that less than 60 years ago barnacle geese were eaten during Lent in parts of Ireland, in the belief that they were more fish than fowl. The barnacle is one of our three 'black' geese, as distinct from the greys, and comes between the other two—the Brent and the Canada goose—in size. The smaller Brent has an all-black head and no wing-bars; and the larger Canada goose is browner than the barnacle, with less white on its face. The striking black and white head of the barnacle make it stand out, too, from white-fronts and other grey geese.

In winter, barnacles visit the western isles of Scotland, the marshes of the Solway Firth, and parts of Ireland. The island birds graze on improved grassland and machair, the short turf found behind sand-dunes in the Hebrides. Together with the Irish birds, numbering about 25,000 in all, they breed in Greenland; the Solway's 10,000 plus breed in Spitsbergen.

RECOGNITION: *white face and black head; neck and upper breast black; lower breast and flanks whitish; back lavender-grey; wings strongly barred; black tail, bill and legs; sexes alike.*
NESTING: *nests in colonies on rock ledges, and sometimes islands, in Spitsbergen, Novaya Zemlya and Greenland; nest depression is lined with down and lichen; lays late May–June; usually 3–5 eggs, grey-white and soon stained; incubation about 28 days, by female only; goslings, tended by both parents, leave nest after a few days, fly after several months.*
FEEDING: *almost entirely grass.*

Spoonbill

Platalea leucorodia 34 in.

SUMMER

SPOONBILLS nested in East Anglia until the 17th century; and in the 16th century they bred in Sussex and Middlesex. Some had a colony only a few miles from the centre of London; for in 1523 the Bishop of London, who had leased a part of his park at Fulham, brought an action to prevent herons and spoonbills— known then as 'shovelars'—being taken from their nests there. Nowadays the nearest colonies to Britain are in Holland. But spoonbills still turn up, singly or in small parties, with fair regularity on some east coast marshes; one of their favourite spots is Breydon Water, near Great Yarmouth. They are usually silent birds, only occasionally raising a grunt or rattling their bills in excitement. But their courtship routine is spectacular—a mixture of dancing, bill-clapping and fanning the crest.

The spoon that makes this white, heron-like bird remarkable is not just a decorative oddity. The bird wades through the shallow waters of lagoons and marshes, or along the shore, sweeping its bill from side to side to scoop up and filter a varied diet of water plants, small fish and water insects.

The bill is distinctive enough on a reasonably close view, but at a distance a flying spoonbill can be told from a heron by the way its neck is extended.

RECOGNITION: *all white, apart from buff patch at base of neck in summer; long bill with yellow tip, widening into 'spoon' shape; adults crested in summer; sexes alike.*
NESTING: *does not now breed in Britain; nearest colonies are in Holland; both sexes build substantial nest, among reeds or in bushes; lays late April–May; usually 4 eggs, white with sparse red-brown markings; incubation about 21 days, by both parents; nestlings, tended by both parents, leave at about 4 weeks, fly after 6 weeks.*
FEEDING: *water plants; small fish, tadpoles, frog-spawn, water-snails, worms and insect larvae.*

Occurs in small numbers, usually April–Sept.; may be seen at other times of year

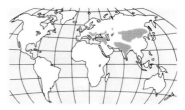

Some are sedentary, but birds in the northern part of the range move south in winter

Spoonbill sifts through mud and salt water for food

Avocet

Recurvirostra avosetta 17 in.

Present all year; breeds mainly in
East Anglia; winters there and
in south-west England

Migratory; winters mainly from
Brittany southwards, large
numbers reaching East Africa

The striking black-and-white
pattern of an avocet in flight

THE return of avocets to nest in Britain is one of the
success stories of bird protection. Two hundred
years ago they were plentiful, but fen drainage reduced
their numbers and the birds that were left could not
survive the treatment they were given by men: they were
shot for feathers to make fishing flies and their eggs
were stolen to make puddings. The last breeding colony,
at Salthouse in Norfolk, was wiped out by 1825.

Then, after the Second World War, a few pairs, probably
dislodged from their Dutch breeding grounds
by wartime flooding of the polders, began to nest on
Minsmere and Havergate Island in Suffolk. The Royal
Society for the Protection of Birds secured both sites as
reserves. The colonies flourished and avocets began to
spread elsewhere. Now more than 500 pairs breed at
several colonies in East Anglia and south-east England,
including even the odd pair inland.

The avocet is mainly a summer visitor to East Anglia;
it winters at the Tamar and Exe estuaries in Devon, at
Poole harbour (Dorset) and at Pagham harbour
(Sussex). Like the spoonbill, it uses its curved, upturned
beak in a side-to-side action to sweep the shallows for
small sea creatures. One of its old names, 'yelper', seems
inappropriate for so elegant a bird, but is understandable
because the bird yelps loudly if an intruder approaches
its nest or young. In calmer moments it calls 'klooit' and
has a soft, grunting note in flight.

RECOGNITION: *bold black and white plumage; long, slender, upcurved
bill; long, leaden-blue legs project behind tail in flight; sexes alike.*
NESTING: *nests in colonies near water, on tussocks or sandbanks; nest is
often a substantial pile of dead vegetation; lays late April–May; usually
4 eggs, pale buff, spotted with grey and dark brown; incubation about 23
days, by both parents; chicks, tended by both parents, leave in few hours,
fly after about 6 weeks.*
FEEDING: *shrimps; water insects and their larvae.*

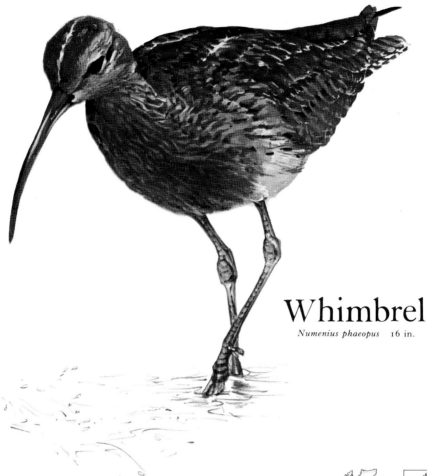

Whimbrel

Numenius phaeopus 16 in.

IT is no use looking for whimbrels in winter, but at migration times small passing flocks may turn up anywhere on the coast, often among the larger curlews, which they resemble. The whimbrel can be told from the curlew by its quicker wing-beats, shorter bill and entirely different call; and at close range by the bold striping on its head—a pale streak sandwiched between two streaks of dark brown.

Another difference is that it is not shy. Long after a curlew has put others on the alert to some fancied danger, the whimbrels, unconcerned, will continue probing for small shellfish or crabs among the shore pools, or catching sandhoppers. Most distinctive of all is the cry, a whinnying, rippling, tittering peal unlike any of the curlew's usual calls. Its song, on the other hand, which is given in courtship flight over its remote nesting grounds, is much like the curlew's bubbling. The whimbrel rises energetically to a great height, then planes in descending circles or tumbles aerobatically, nearly to the ground.

The whimbrel now holds its status as a British nesting species only in the Shetlands, with odd pairs regularly or occasionally on the Orkneys, Lewis and St. Kilda in the Hebrides and the north Scottish mainland. The total population numbers about 500 pairs.

April–Sept. visitor, mainly as coastal migrant, but some nest in Shetland, Orkney and Hebrides

Migratory; winters mainly on coasts of Africa, also south to Australia and S. America

RECOGNITION: *streaky buff-brown; a smaller version of the curlew, distinguished by head markings—two dark stripes separated by pale streak; down-curving bill shorter than curlew's; female slightly larger than male.*
NESTING: *scantily lined scrape in heather or rough grass on moorland; lays late May–June; usually 4 eggs, olive-green to buff-brown, heavily blotched; incubation 27 or 28 days, by both parents; chicks, tended by both parents, leave nest in few hours, fly after 5–6 weeks.*
FEEDING: *inland—insects and larvae; spiders, earthworms, snails; bilberries, crowberries; coasts—small crustacea, molluscs, marine worms.*

Whimbrels searching the shore for molluscs and worms

Dunlin

Calidris alpina 7 in.

SUMMER

Present all year, breeding mainly on upland moors and wintering on coasts

British birds move to coasts, but others migrate and winter on temperate coasts

Dunlin in winter lose their black belly-markings

Great flocks of dunlin, like wisps of smoke blown by the wind, make one of the most charming sights of the shore. They skim low over the water, sweep upwards in a bunch, spill out in a long wavering line, change course, dive and shower down again with a rushing of wings.

Dunlin, among the smallest of our shore birds, were known to the old wildfowlers by a variety of names —ox-bird, ploverspage, sea snipe or stint. Some stay around the estuaries all the year. A small proportion nest in Britain, but sizable flocks come for the winter, and spectacular numbers build up with passage birds at migration times. They mingle with other small waders, probing the tidal runnels for animal life. In spring and summer they are easy to identify, for the dunlin is the only small shore bird with a black belly.

The dunlin's flight-note is a rather weak 'tweep' or 'teerp', and over its breeding grounds the main theme of display is a lark-like ascent with hovering and trilling; and there are fast twisting pursuit flights. Nesting pairs are not abundant in Britain, and may be declining; but they are widely spread over northern and western moorlands down to Derbyshire, mid-Wales and north-western Ireland, and a few breed as far south as Dartmoor.

RECOGNITION: *streaked brown-grey above, white below with grey breast in winter; chestnut, streaked with black above and black belly in summer; white wing-bar and sides of tail show in flight; slightly down-curved bill; sexes alike.*
NESTING: *nest, on ground in scrape or tussock, is lined with grass or leaves; lays May; usually 4 eggs, buff to blue-green, well sprinkled with dark brown blotches; incubation 21 or 22 days, by both parents; chicks, tended by both parents, leave in few days, fly after about 3 weeks.*
FEEDING: *insects and larvae, small molluscs, small crustacea, earthworms, marine worms; occasionally grass or seed.*

Grey plover

Pluvialis squatarola 11 in.

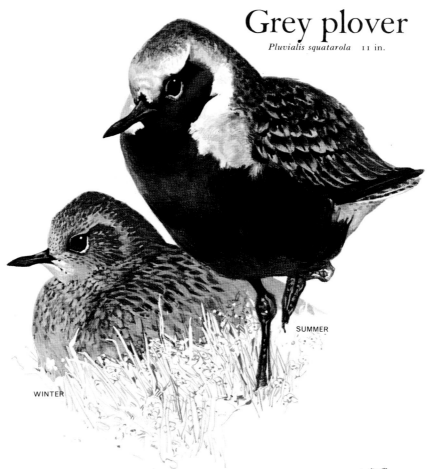

SUMMER

WINTER

THE grey plover, drab in its grey-brown winter plumage and sometimes looking the picture of dejection as it waits on the mud-banks for the tide to turn, is a vastly different bird on its breeding grounds in northern Russia and Siberia. There, in its handsome summer plumage—grey-spangled, white-edged and black-breasted—it plunges and tumbles acrobatically in the air and will boldly attack marauding skuas that come too near its nest.

Its striking summer plumage sometimes lasts until autumn, and from then until spring there are fair numbers of the birds around our coasts, especially in the east. They form loose parties, rather than close flocks, and keep their distance from other waders. Almost all of them return to the Arctic when winter is over, but a few non-breeding birds sometimes stay over summer.

The only bird with which it might be confused is the golden plover, but the grey can always be told by the black mark under each wing, and by white 'flashes' on its rump and on top of the wings. When feeding, it has the regular plover habit of making a short run, then pausing to look around. Its three-note call, 'tee-oo-ee', with the middle syllable the low one, is quite distinct from the golden plover's more musical double call, and sounds rather like a boy's whistling.

RECOGNITION: *brown-grey upper parts, lighter underparts in winter; spangled grey upper parts, black underparts in summer; black patch under wings; white on rump and top of wings; sexes alike.*
NESTING: *breeds on Siberian tundra; nests in depression in peat, lined with moss and lichen; lays June–early July; 4 eggs, buff to green, sometimes with pink tinge, marked with chestnut blotches; incubation 23 days, by both parents; chicks, tended by both parents, fly after about 4 weeks.*
FEEDING: *worms, molluscs, small crabs and other crustacea in winter; worms, slugs, insects and spiders in summer.*

Winter visitor and passage migrant to coasts; a few non-breeders stay through summer

Migratory; outside breeding season occur on coasts as far south as Australia and S. America

Grey plover flying in winter shows black patch under wing

Knot

Calidris canutus 10 in.

'Canutes' from the far North

Winter visitor to coasts and
estuaries; some non-breeders
remain here in summer

Winters around North Sea and on
coasts of Africa, Asia, Australia
and New Zealand

EARLY naturalists were baffled by the knot: its tightly
packed thousands, rippling over the mud-banks like
a grey carpet, came from and returned to no one knew
where. Even its name is ancient and obscure. In the
middle of the 18th century, when the Swedish naturalist
Linnaeus was classifying all the living creatures then
known, it was thought that the knot was a little Canute
at the edge of the waves; and this idea was picked up in
the Latin name, *canutus*. But the derivation is more
fanciful than probable: the name may come from the
birds' hoarse chorus of 'knut, knut'.

We now know that migrating knot sometimes make
vast journeys, quitting their bare breeding grounds far
north of the Arctic Circle to stream south in their
hordes as far as southern Africa, Patagonia, New
Zealand and Australia. They begin to arrive in Britain,
chiefly on eastern and north-western coasts and along
the coasts of northern and eastern Ireland, in late

WINTER

summer and continue into October, the young coming first. Though some non-breeders will remain, the main groups start to return the following April and May, by which time many birds will be in full breeding plumage.

Then follows a brief energetic summer without night —in the Taimyr peninsula of northern Siberia or islands still further north—where the male performs a circling song-flight and engages in courtship chases. On migration the flocks keep up a collective chatter.

RECOGNITION: *grey above, paler below in winter; mottled black and chestnut above, russet below in summer; grey tail; light rump and wing-bar show in flight; dumpy, short neck; sexes alike.*
NESTING: *nests in stony Arctic tundra, in hollow lined with lichen; lays June–July; usually 4 eggs, grey-green to olive-buff, with dark markings; incubation probably 3 weeks, by both parents; chicks, tended chiefly by male, leave nest when dry, fly after about 4 weeks.*
FEEDING: *in winter—crustacea, such as small crabs; worms, small molluscs, insects; in summer—insects, spiders, molluscs, plant buds and other vegetable matter.*

In winter huge numbers of knot feed together on mud-banks and estuaries around the shores of Britain. They keep together as they fly, too. Dense clouds of birds wheel in perfect unison over the water, looking white at first, then darker as the birds tilt over and show their grey upper parts and pale rumps and tails

Bar-tailed godwit

Limosa lapponica   15 in.

WINTER

SUMMER

Chiefly passage migrant; a few non-breeders sometimes stay the summer on coasts

Winters mainly around the North Sea; also on tropical and sub-tropical coasts south to Australia

Distinctive tail markings of bar-tailed godwit in flight

FLOCKS of bar-tailed godwits visit Britain from Scandinavia and northern Russia in winter, but large numbers, making for destinations much farther south, use Britain as a staging post on their spring and autumn migrations. They gather with knots and oystercatchers at the edge of the sea, crowding on the rocks as the tide comes in. New arrivals drop into the thick of the crush, making others leap into the air to find fresh spots. They are constantly moving. Then, when the tide once more uncovers their feeding banks, the birds take wing and often go through aerobatics together before settling down. They are rarely seen inland.

Godwits—nobody knows for certain how they got that name—look rather like small curlews during winter, except that their bills are straight or curved upwards. In summer the chestnut breeding plumage is distinctive; the bar-tail can be told in flight from the larger black-tailed godwit by its lack of a white wing-stripe.

The bar-tail, which has never bred in Britain, is common on passage migration from late April in East Anglia, south-east England and Lancashire. By June, most of them have left, to nest in the Arctic; they return again in the autumn, some young birds arriving first.

Usually they are quiet birds, but the parent birds set up a clamour when a potential enemy approaches their nesting marsh. They also have a 'kirruc-kirruc' flight-note and a more anxious 'wik-wik-wik-wik' call.

RECOGNITION: *mottled grey-brown, whitish below in winter; chestnut breast, neck and face in summer; white rump; straight or slightly upcurved bill; barred tail; sexes alike.*
NESTING: *nests in Arctic, making a scrape in wet bog, lined with birch leaves and lichen; lays late May–June; 4 eggs, olive-green or brown, with darker blotches; incubation about 21 days, by both parents.*
FEEDING: *in winter—sandhoppers, shrimps, lugworms, snails, small shellfish; in summer—insects and small ground animals.*

SEASHORE

The tide is a dominant fact of life for shore
birds, washing in a regular supply of food from the
inexhaustible storehouse of the sea. Oystercatchers are expert
at prising open stranded shellfish; gulls are scavengers
and beachcombers; terns scoop up fish near the surface;
and long-tailed ducks dive deep to mussel beds at the
bottom of the sea. In this way, birds exploit
the shore habitat to the full.

CONTENTS

FEMALE

Eider

Somateria mollissima   24 in.

MALE

Present all year in north; occurs more widely around coasts in winter

Mainly sedentary; winter ice may drive some northern birds south in winter

Duck incubates alone, sitting for days without moving

IF a large black and white duck is seen paired with a brown one, they are almost certainly eiders; and if they slide off the rocks into the sea in the middle of a storm, bobbing up among the waves that look big enough to crush them, there can be no doubt. Their whole life centres around the sea, in all its moods; they will even fall asleep on rocks that are wet with spray.

The female plucks down from her breast to line the nest she and her mate build close to the high tide line. She incubates alone and will sit for days without moving. When at last she leaves, she rearranges the down to cover the eggs. In parts of the Arctic and sub-Arctic, though not in Britain, this down forms the basis of an important industry: the eider's nesting colonies are 'farmed', and the nests are robbed of their fine dark lining, to make into quilts.

Eiders breed on flat rocky and sandy shores, from the Arctic to the British Isles. Their breeding range in Britain reaches Coquet Island off Northumberland on the east coast, Walney Island off Cumbria on the west coast, and parts of Ireland.

Large flocks of non-breeding birds, believed to come from Holland, are seen off the coasts of southern England at all seasons. Their calls, a crooning 'ah-oo' from the male and a harsher note from the female, may be heard on a calm day. Sometimes the birds fly in lines, low over the water.

RECOGNITION: *drake is white above, black below; duck is brown, except for white on wing; forehead has no bulge, joins bill almost in a straight line.*
NESTING: *both sexes build nest of grass and seaweed, always on the ground; female lines nest with feathers and down; lays May–June; 4–6 eggs, light green; incubation about 30 days, by female only; ducklings, tended by female, leave immediately, fly after about 2 months.*
FEEDING: *molluscs, including mussels, whelks, cockles; crustacea, including small crabs; very little vegetable matter.*

Scaup
Aythya marila 19 in.

FEMALE

MALE

A hard winter by British standards is fair weather for scaup. They flock down from the Arctic and sub-Arctic to gather off the coasts of Scotland and in bays and estuaries along the English coast, mainly on the east side, south to the Thames. Large flocks once concentrated in the Firth of Forth, attracted by waste grain discharged by breweries and distilleries.

Scaup are primarily diving birds, though their flight is fast and powerful. Webbed feet, on legs well set to the rear of the bodies, drive them down to mussel beds on the sea floor; but on land their centre of gravity is too far back, and they can only waddle clumsily. In fact, few of them ever come to land, except in the breeding season. Small numbers feed in freshwater lakes close to the shore, but scaup rarely appear farther inland unless they have been driven there by storms.

By early May, most scaup have returned to their breeding grounds in Iceland, northern Europe and Siberia, though odd pairs sometimes breed in the north of Scotland, particularly in Orkney, Wester Ross and the Outer Hebrides. They are silent birds outside the breeding season, apart from the occasional harsh 'karr-karr-karr' call by the duck. During courtship, the drake swims towards her with head and neck stretched fully upright, then suddenly jerks them backwards. Sometimes the duck swims round, dipping its bill into the water and calling gently.

RECOGNITION: *drake has dark green on head, black breast and light grey back; duck is dark brown with large white face-patch; male's eclipse plumage (July–November) is duller.*
NESTING: *rarely nests in Britain; uses down and local materials to line hollow in ground, sometimes sheltered by tussock; lays late May–June; 7–11 eggs, green or olive-green; incubation about 28 days, by female only; ducklings, tended by female, swim almost immediately, fly after 5–6 weeks.*
FEEDING: *mussels and other molluscs; small crabs; eel-grass.*

Oct.–April visitor, mainly to coasts; sometimes breeds in Scotland; bred in Suffolk in 1967

Winters on coasts to south of breeding range, as far as Mediterranean and Gulf of Mexico

Scaup diving for food usually stay down for 25–30 seconds

Common scoter

Melanitta nigra 19 in.

Velvet scoter

Melanitta fusca 22 in.

MALE

Present all year; mainly a winter visitor, but a few stay the summer to breed in Scotland and Ireland

Migratory; winters on coasts of Atlantic and Pacific south of breeding range

Velvet scoters—sometimes seen with flocks of common scoters

THE common scoter is common in Britain only as a visitor, not as a breeding bird. Between September and April, there is an influx of migrants from their breeding grounds in the Arctic and northern Europe. The all-black drakes and brown ducks can be seen diving for crabs or mussels in coastal waters all round the British Isles. They avoid rough water and stay close to the shore, but they rarely come to land unless gale-blown or fouled by oil. The drakes often sit on the water with their short tails cocked up; when disturbed they rise heavily and fly off in line astern, a few feet above the waves. When the breeding season comes round again, some non-breeders stay behind, especially along the east coast of England, and small numbers nest in Scotland and Ireland.

During courtship the drake raises itself high out of the water with tail again cocked up, and sometimes calls with a high piping note.

Sometimes among the large flocks of common scoters one or two birds may appear larger than the rest. If the drakes have a white spot near the eye, and the ducks two white face-patches, then they are a related species, velvet scoters.

These birds are seen around the coasts mainly in winter; a few occasionally summer in Scottish waters, but they have never definitely bred there.

RECOGNITION: *drake is all black, apart from distinctive orange mark on bill; duck is dark brown, with pale buff cheeks.*
NESTING: *nests in hollow in ground, usually well sheltered and close to water; female lines nest with moss, feathers and down; lays late May–June; usually 5–7 eggs, cream on buff; incubation about 28 days, by female only; ducklings, tended by female, leave soon after hatching, usually fly after 6–7 weeks.*
FEEDING: *mussels, shrimps and crabs; sandhoppers; worms, insects and vegetable matter in breeding season.*

Long-tailed duck
Clangula hyemalis   23 in.

FEMALE IN WINTER

MALE IN WINTER

IN Scotland, this bird is sometimes known as 'Coal and Candlelight', a name supposed to echo the cry it makes. But the pitfalls of 'translating' a bird's call into human speech are nowhere better illustrated than in the case of the long-tailed duck. Its loud, ringing 'coal and candlelight' has also been written down as 'ow-ow-owdl-ow', 'cah-cah-coralwee', a simple 'calloo' and, probably nearest of all to the actual sound, 'ardelow-ar-ardelow'.

Flocks of these sea-going ducks start arriving around our coasts in September or October. Most are to be seen around Scotland, with the largest flocks—each numbering more than a thousand birds—in the Moray Firth and Orkney. They keep well out to sea, diving 90 ft deep and more and staying down for more than a minute at a time. Because of its tail (which is not full-sized until the third year) the bird was once known to wildfowlers as the sea pheasant; it shared this name with the pintail, the only other long-tailed duck seen in British waters.

By May, most long-tailed ducks have left Britain for their breeding grounds, mainly on the lake islands of northern Scandinavia. Sometimes a few non-breeding birds will stay in the north of Scotland, and nesting there is not entirely unknown.

RECOGNITION: *drake has long pointed tail, dark brown upper parts and breast, white flanks and belly; head and neck, mainly white in winter, are brown in summer except for white on side of face; duck has short tail, sides of head white, brown upper parts and white underparts; both have short bill and dark wings without bars; moulting male loses tail feathers.*
NESTING: *very rarely nests in Britain; nests always in hollow in ground, near water; lays late May; 6–9 eggs, olive or buff; incubation about 3½ weeks, by duck only; ducklings, tended by duck only, leave nest immediately, fly after about 5 weeks.*
FEEDING: *small molluscs; crabs and shrimps; some vegetable matter.*

Sept.–April visitor; has bred occasionally in Scotland, but not in recent years

Winters at sea south of breeding range, from southern limit of ice to British Isles

Long-tailed ducks in summer have white on sides of face

233

Shelduck
Tadorna tadorna 26 in.

MALE

Present all year; nests mainly on coasts, although it has recently spread inland in England

Mainly sedentary, but may fly several hundred miles to its traditional moulting grounds

Female shelducks attend young from several broods

EVERY July almost the entire population of British shelducks makes for the Heligoland Bight, off north-west Germany, to moult. Only the juveniles stay behind with a few adult 'nurses'. Smaller flocks of moulting shelducks remain in Bridgwater Bay, Somerset, and in large estuaries such as the Wash.

Shelducks are the largest British ducks and are an exception to the rule that the ducks are far more drably coloured and less conspicuous than the drakes. In this species, both have a boldly contrasting plumage pattern of black, white and chestnut. The duck would be an easy target for predators if it nested without cover. But normally it nests in a rabbit burrow, or under the shelter of boulders or bushes; sometimes it finds the kind of cover it needs for its nest in a hollow tree. Sand-dunes are an ideal habitat for breeding shelducks, but they also nest on other rough ground by the sea, and occasionally even in woods and on farmland. They breed in almost every coastal county in the British Isles and increasingly in many inland ones in England.

A shelduck's life follows the ebb and flow of the tide. At high tide the bird rests on the sea or the shore; and when the tide retreats, it hurries down to search the tidal pools for mussels and crabs. It looks like a goose as it waddles along the shore; it flies like a goose, too, with slow wing-beats, often in lines or in wedge formation.

RECOGNITION: *both sexes have black, white and chestnut plumage; adults have red bill, drake's has a knob at base.*
NESTING: *duck lines well-concealed nest with grass and down; lays May-June; 8–14 eggs, creamy-white; incubation about 30 days, by duck only; ducklings, tended by duck, usually leave nest immediately, fly at about 9 weeks; broods often join together.*
FEEDING: *molluscs; small crabs and shrimps; insects; small quantities of vegetable matter.*

Great northern diver

Gavia immer M 33 in. F 30 in.

SUMMER

T HE full courtship display of this largest of our divers is not often seen in the British Isles, for the first British breeding record was not until 1970. But a curious 'speed-boating' display, in which the male and female birds plane through the water with their bodies half submerged, has been recorded off the Irish coast.

Great northern divers, as the name suggests, are strong underwater swimmers; they have been known to stay down for minutes on end. Nothing that swims in the sea and is small enough to be swallowed is safe from them: haddock, herring, sprats, sand-eels, gurnard, whiting, trout, prawns, shrimps and crabs have all been identified in the crops of the birds. With such a variety of food in the sea they seldom need to go to land except to breed.

As winter visitors to Britain, they are most common off the coasts of Scotland and western England, and are seen inland infrequently, usually oiled birds or after coastal gales. Non-breeding birds often spend the summer off northern Scotland.

Its large size, black head with green gloss, back covered in white spots and neck with a band of black and white stripes make this diver fairly easy to distinguish in summer; but in winter it might be confused with the black-throated diver, a smaller bird. The most frequently heard call is a loud mournful wail.

RECOGNITION : *black head and neck, with green gloss and bands of white on neck, and white spots on black back in summer ; dark above, white below in winter ; black bill, heavier than bill of other two divers ; sexes alike.*
NESTING : *breeds in Iceland, Greenland and North America ; nests on flattened tussock, by lake-sides ; lays June ; usually 2 eggs, dark brown to olive, with a few dark spots ; incubation about 30 days, by both parents ; young, tended by both parents, probably fly after 6–10 weeks.*
FEEDING : *many kinds of fish ; prawns and crabs ; some seaweed.*

Oct.–May visitor; a few remain in Scotland during the summer; has bred on the north Highland coast

Winters south of breeding range, mainly on coastal waters of North Atlantic and Pacific

Great northern diver in winter is dark above and white below

235

Sanderling

Calidris alba   8 in.

SUMMER

WINTER

Passage migrant and winter visitor found mainly on sandy coasts, occasionally inland on migration

Outside the breeding season may be found on sandy beaches over almost the whole world

Sanderling scurries along the tide-line looking for food

GROUPS of sanderlings, mingling with other waders along the tide-line, can be picked out at a distance by their restless manner of feeding. They hurry along with heads down, darting after shrimps and sandhoppers uncovered by the waves, and stopping now and then to dab at the remains of a stranded fish or jellyfish. They are so tame—or so intent on feeding—that a man can approach within a few feet before they run off; and even then they will not go far.

They seem reluctant to fly; but when they do they rise with a hubbub of shrill 'twick-twick' calls, and their flight is swift, direct and generally low over the water. The white wing-bar which shows as they fly is more conspicuous than that of dunlin, and the tail is dark at the centre and white at the sides.

Sanderlings are rare in summer, when most fly to the Arctic to breed. A few non-breeding birds may stay all year, but they have never been recorded as breeding in the British Isles. In its display flight at the breeding grounds, the male rises in the air then descends steeply, giving a loud, rather harsh churring 'song'.

Sandy shores are the sanderling's usual winter habitat, but it occasionally feeds on mud-banks too, and sometimes turns up on freshwater margins inland, especially on migration.

RECOGNITION: *winter plumage is pale grey and white, with black shoulder spot; in summer, upper parts are brown with darker streaks; straight bill; can be told from ringed plover by longer bill, and from dunlin by more conspicuous white wing-bar; sexes alike.*
NESTING: *always makes nest in scrape in ground, usually unlined; lays late June; 4 eggs, pear-shaped, olive-green with dark brown spots and blotches; incubation about 24 days, by female only; chicks, tended by both parents, leave nest after a few hours.*
FEEDING: *small crustacea, including shrimps; marine molluscs and worms; remains of fish or jellyfish.*

WINTER

Turnstone

Arenaria interpres 9 in.　　SUMMER

STONES are not the only objects moved about by turnstones as they search the shore for food; seaweed, pebbles, shells, driftwood, dead fish, anything which might conceal insects or small shellfish, may be turned over or levered aside by their probing bills.

Turnstones are common winter visitors to all our coasts, and also appear in Britain as passage migrants in spring and autumn, when a few birds may turn up on fresh water inland. The greatest numbers gather on rocky and stony beaches, where the seaweed covers a rich supply of food. They search along the tideline in small feeding parties, often in the company of other waders—dunlin, ringed plovers and purple sandpipers. They are noisy birds for their size, twittering 'kit-kit-kit' when disturbed, or crying a clear 'kecoo-kecoo'.

In summer almost all of the turnstones return north to breed in the Arctic. They nest on rocky islands, often close to bigger birds, such as gulls and skuas, which would take their eggs if the turnstones did not keep a constant watch. A few non-breeders stay in Britain, especially on the north and west coasts.

The first sight of a flock of turnstones may be as they fly up showing the black and white pattern of their wings. For on the shore their mottled backs conceal them against the stones, pebbles and seaweed.

RECOGNITION: *in winter upper parts are black-brown, underparts white except for broad dark breast-band; in summer upper parts appear tortoiseshell, head is more white; bill short and black; legs orange; sexes alike.*

NESTING: *does not nest in Britain; nest, either on bare rock or in tussock, is sometimes scantily lined with vegetation; lays May–June; 4 eggs, green with brown markings; incubation about 21 days, mainly by female; chicks, tended by both sexes, leave nest within a few hours.*

FEEDING: *sandhoppers, shellfish, insects; young fish and remains of fish; bread and carrion have been recorded.*

Mainly a winter visitor, but a few non-breeders are present on coasts throughout the year

Winters south to southernmost Africa, S. America, Australia, Tasmania and New Zealand

The bold wing pattern of an adult turnstone in summer

Ringed plover

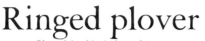

Charadrius hiaticula   7½ in.

Present all year on coasts;
increasing and spreading
inland as a breeder

Mainly sedentary in Britain;
migratory elsewhere, wintering on
southernmost coasts of Africa

Ringed plover distracts enemy by
feigning a broken wing

RINGED plovers, though still among the most common of our shore birds, are fighting a losing battle against disturbance by man in many areas. Bungalows and beach huts have gone up in seaside localities where they used to breed; and once-remote beaches which supported large numbers of the birds are now within the reach of cars and caravans. One area where they have been reduced almost to extinction is the Breckland of East Anglia. At the beginning of this century some 400 pairs bred each year on this wild heathland. But as the area has been increasingly cultivated and afforested, the number of breeding pairs has been reduced to barely ten. But there is another side to the balance: in sanctuaries their numbers have risen in recent years.

Ringed plovers still breed all round our coasts. Some nest in arable fields near the sea; and in Scotland they go miles inland to nest by lochs and rivers. In winter they are widespread on shores and estuaries; and at migration times they are common on freshwater margins inland.

Feeding parties of ringed plovers scatter over the shore, running about energetically and stopping every now and again to bob their heads or pick food from the sand. When disturbed, they fly off in compact flocks which twist and turn low over the water.

RECOGNITION: *black collar; black and white head pattern; yellow legs; short bill; distinguished from little ringed plover by larger size and, in flight, by prominent wing-bar; sexes alike.*
NESTING: *male makes scrape in bare ground or short turf; female adds lining of pebbles, shells or grass; lays May–July; 4 eggs, pear-shaped, stone-buff, spotted and blotched with brown-black and ash grey; incubation about 24 days, by both parents; chicks, tended by both parents, leave nest within a few hours, fly after about 25 days; two broods normal.*
FEEDING: *molluscs, crustacea and insects of many types; also worms and some vegetable matter.*

Snow bunting
Plectrophenax nivalis 6½ in.

MALE IN WINTER

THE flash of white wings when snow buntings are flushed in winter can come as a surprise to anybody who has been watching them feed; for their white markings are much obscured by brown when they are on the ground.

Flocks of snow buntings are widespread along the east coast from autumn until spring, eating the seeds of coarse grass on sand-dunes and other rough open country near the coast. On the mainland they usually feed in small parties, but a flock some 2000 strong has been recorded on Fair Isle. In their northern breeding grounds during summer they often feed on insects carried on air currents and trapped in the snowfields.

A few snow buntings nest in Britain, but they are among the rarest of our breeding species, confined to mist-shrouded peaks in the Highlands. Fifty years ago they were more widespread there, but in recent years it is probable that there have not been more than 25 breeding pairs in Britain at any one time, nearly all of them in the Cairngorms.

During the breeding season the male has a display flight in which it hovers almost like a skylark, singing vigorously.

RECOGNITION : *in winter, both sexes are buff-brown above, white beneath ; more white shows on male ; in summer, male has black on back and centre of tail, rest of plumage pure white, bill orange.*
NESTING : *female builds nest of dry grasses and moss, lined with hair and feathers ; lays late May–June ; 4–6 eggs, yellow-white, sometimes with green or blue tinge, with red-brown spots and blotches ; incubation about 13 days, by female only ; nestlings, tended by both parents, leave after about 11 days ; sometimes two broods.*
FEEDING : *seeds of grass, rushes and weeds ; crane-flies and other flying insects in summer ; occasionally grain, sandhoppers and beetles.*

Mainly a winter visitor to coasts and hills, but a few pairs breed in the Scottish Highlands

Icelandic birds are sedentary; others move south in winter, to more temperate regions

The flash of white wings as snow buntings fly in winter

239

Common gull

Larus canus 17 in.

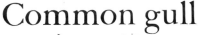

JUVENILE

ADULT

Present all year; immigrants from northern Europe swell the resident population in winter

Some are resident; others winter on Atlantic coasts and south to Mediterranean

Common gulls in winter often feed on fields far inland

DESPITE its name, this bird is not the commonest of our gulls: there are far more herring gulls and black-headed gulls, both inland and round the coasts. But the common gull is by no means rare and it is thought to be slowly increasing. Like the herring gull, it is a scavenger, eating almost anything that comes its way; it also shares the herring gull's habit of dropping shellfish from the air, to burst them open upon the shore. A feeding habit of its own is that it will wait until a bolder, black-headed gull has taken food from a human's hand, then dart in to rob the other bird.

Common gulls are widespread in winter, following herring and black-headed gulls to their feeding places round the coast and in towns. But as breeding birds their range is more limited. They nest on moors, bogs, loch islands, coastal marshes and shingle beaches, usually in small colonies, but sometimes in pairs, apart from other birds. They breed in many parts of Scotland and Ireland; but in England the only long-standing colony is a small one at Dungeness, in Kent.

The characteristic calls of the common gull are a mewing 'kak-kak-kak' and a screaming 'keeee-ya'—both like herring gull calls, but not so piercing. It looks like the herring gull, too, except that it is smaller, its legs are yellow-green and its bill has no red spot.

RECOGNITION: *grey back; white underparts; black wing-tips with white spots; yellow bill and yellow-green legs; young are dark brown above, with white underparts and broad dark band on end of tail; sexes alike.*
NESTING: *usually nests in small colonies, on ground; nest built by both sexes, of local materials; lays late May–early June; usually 3 eggs, olive with dark markings; incubation about 26 days, by both parents; chicks, tended by both parents, leave in first week, fly after 4–5 weeks.*
FEEDING: *any edible refuse; shellfish; earthworms and insects; seeds; small mammals, small birds and their eggs.*

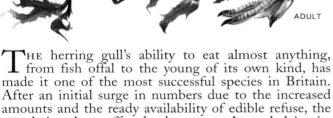

JUVENILE

ADULT

Herring gull

Larus argentatus 23 in.

Yellow-legged gull

Larus cachinnans 24 in.

Present all year; widespread inland in winter, when many come here from the Continent

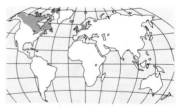

Mainly sedentary; some birds move south along coasts, a few reaching as far as subtropics

The yelping wail of a herring gull is a common sound on the coast

THE herring gull's ability to eat almost anything, from fish offal to the young of its own kind, has made it one of the most successful species in Britain. After an initial surge in numbers due to the increased amounts and the ready availability of edible refuse, the population then suffered a downturn, almost halving its numbers in the past 30 years. Its extended breeding range, however, still includes buildings in coastal towns, inland bogs and lakes, as well as its traditional seacliffs and islands.

In winter it is abundant in fishing ports and harbours. It scavenges along the coastline and has developed a habit of cracking open shellfish by dropping them from the air. Inland, herring gulls feed over farmland and rubbish dumps, and roost at night on large reservoirs; some birds feed in these districts all year round.

At breeding colonies, loud with wailing and yelping 'keeow' calls, one of the parent birds must stand guard against the depredations of neighbouring gulls from the moment the eggs are laid; otherwise few of their chicks would get the chance to begin their four-year growth to full maturity.

The darker-backed, yellow-legged gull, previously regarded as a herring gull sub-species, is now known to visit southern Britain regularly. A few pairs have even begun to nest here.

RECOGNITION: *grey back; white underparts; yellow bill with red spot; pink legs; young are brown-backed with dark tail band; sexes alike.*
NESTING: *nests in colonies; both sexes build fairly bulky nest of local materials, on ground, cliff ledge or building; lays late April–June; usually 3 eggs, olive-brown with darker marks; incubation about 26 days, by both parents; chicks, tended by both parents, stay in or near nest for a week or two, then remain near by, often hidden, until they can fly—after about 6 weeks.*
FEEDING: *edible offal; shellfish; eggs and chicks; fish.*

Common tern

Sterna hirundo 14 in.

Arctic tern

Sterna paradisaea 15 in.

SUMMER

April–Sept. visitors; map shows common's distribution; Arctic tern nests mainly in Scotland

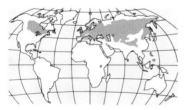

Map shows range of common; Arctic tern nests in high Arctic, winters in Antarctic

Arctic tern: graceful flight makes terns the swallows of the sea

BOTH of these birds are intensely aggressive at their breeding colonies. They dive-bomb intruders, screaming their anger with harsh cries of 'keeyah', and have been known to draw blood from a man's head.

They are alike in other ways, too: both have shrill 'kik-kik-kik' and 'keerree' calls; both have the habit in courtship of presenting a fish to the female; and their plumages are so similar that even experienced bird-watchers have to take special care to sort one from the other. But their legs distinguish them; the Arctic tern's are shorter than the common tern's.

Another guide is their distribution in the breeding season; the common tern is more likely to be seen in the south of Britain than the Arctic tern, a slightly larger bird. Both nest on sand or shingle beaches, rocky islands and salt-marshes but the Arctic tern does not regularly breed south of a diagonal line from Northumberland to Anglesey, and never breeds away from the coast; the common tern's breeding range extends further south, and the bird has increasingly taken to nesting inland in recent years.

Twice yearly the Arctic tern sets out on an amazing journey which carries it from one end of the globe to the other. It nests from Britain northwards to the Arctic, and winters 10,000 miles away in Antarctic seas.

RECOGNITION: *both white, with black crown and nape; common tern has red bill usually with black tip, Arctic's bill is all red; Arctic has shorter legs; young and winter adults have a white forehead; sexes alike.*
NESTING: *both species have same nesting pattern: nest is scrape in ground, tuft of grass or rushes, often lined with shells, grass or bits of wood by female; lays mid-May–June; 2 or 3 eggs, buff, green or blue-white, usually with heavy brown markings; incubation about 23 days, by both parents; nestlings, tended by both parents, leave after a few days, fly after 3–4 weeks.*
FEEDING: *small fish, especially sand-eels; sometimes insects.*

Roseate tern

Sterna dougallii 15 in.

SUMMER

IN most years, the roseate tern—named from the pink flush on its breast in summer—is the rarest of the British terns. Although it reached a peak in population of about 3500 pairs in the early 1960s, the roseate's numbers have since decreased, and there are now fewer than 1000 breeding pairs distributed in a dozen colonies round the British Isles.

Most of them are found in colonies on the east coast of Ireland, and there are other long-standing colonies in the Firth of Forth, on the Farne Islands and on Anglesey. But there is no guarantee that the birds will be there in any particular year: roseates are notorious for their habit of deserting a breeding site suddenly and for no apparent reason, and setting up a new colony elsewhere. In a less intense form of this mass desertion, pairs of roseates often set up their nests in the terneries of other species. They give away their presence by their cries, a long drawn-out 'aach-aach' and a softer 'tchu-ick' and 'chik-ik' note. They breed on sandy beaches or shingle, and their nests are scrapes in the ground, usually unlined.

When the bird is seen at a distance, its pink breast does not show up, and it closely resembles the common and Arctic terns; but it can be told from them by its black bill, which goes red at the base for a few weeks in mid-summer, and by its longer tail streamers.

RECOGNITION: *white, with black crown and nape, and pink flush on breast in summer; black bill, red at the base in midsummer; red legs, long white tail streamers; sexes alike.*
NESTING: *nests in colonies; both sexes make scrapes in sand or shingle; final nest is only rarely lined, with vegetation or rabbit droppings; lays June–July; 1 or 2 eggs, creamy or buff, blotched and spotted with chestnut; incubation about 24 days, by both parents; chicks, tended by both parents, leave in a few days, fly after about 4 weeks.*
FEEDING: *mainly small fish.*

May–Sept. visitor; a few birds have recently nested in Hampshire and Dorset

European birds winter off coasts of southern Africa, tropical breeding birds are mainly sedentary

Roseate tern hovers over water before diving for a fish

243

Little tern

Sterna albifrons 9 in.

April–Sept. visitor; several colonies are decreasing owing to human disturbance

Northern and all inland breeding birds winter chiefly in tropical coastal waters

Male presents female with a sand-eel—a courtship gift

THIS is the smallest of our breeding terns, and, after the roseate tern, the rarest; its numbers have fallen seriously in recent years because its breeding sites on sandy coasts, shingle beaches and islands have been disturbed by holidaymakers. There are still about 100 colonies round the British Isles but most are very small, and it has been estimated that there are not many more than 2800 breeding pairs left.

The largest remaining colonies of little terns are at Blakeney Point, Holkham and Great Yarmouth in Norfolk and at Langstone Harbour in Hampshire.

The nests in a colony of little terns are not as close together as in other terneries; they may be 30 ft or more apart. But the birds are like most other terns in their way of dealing with intruders; they dive-bomb animals or gulls that approach their nests, and warn off interlopers with angry screams. Their chief call-notes are 'kik-kik' and 'pee-e-eer'.

The little tern is the only adult tern with a white patch on its forehead at all seasons. When its head is pointed away, it can be told from another small tern, the black tern, by its more deeply forked tail and less sharply defined shoulder patch. It is unusual to see little terns inland; even on migration, they hug the coastline. Their courtship ceremonies follow the usual tern pattern, with a special display flight and the presentation of fish to the female.

RECOGNITION: *white forehead all the year; yellow bill with black tip; bright orange feet; sexes alike.*

NESTING: *breeds in small colonies on beaches; both sexes make scrape in ground and female sometimes lines chosen site with pebbles; lays May; 2 or 3 eggs, buff with dark spots; incubation about 22 days, by both parents; chicks, tended by both parents, leave after a few hours, fly after about 4 weeks.*

FEEDING: *sand-eels and other small fish.*

Sandwich tern

Sterna sandvicensis   16 in.

SUMMER

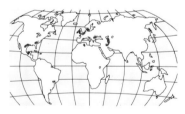

March–Oct. visitor; essentially a coastal bird, but small numbers nest inland in Ireland

Migratory; north-west European birds winter mainly along tropical coasts of W. Africa

Male displays with wings held out and neck stretched up

SANDWICH terns often set up their colonies on the same sites as more aggressive birds, relying on them to drive off intruders. But there is a price to pay for this protection: whenever they leave their nests unattended their chicks are at risk from the other species, which may inflict heavy losses.

An estimated 18,000 breeding pairs of the terns are scattered in about 40 colonies round the British Isles, from Orkney to the south coast of England. The bulk of them nest in a comparatively few colonies from the Firth of Forth, and down the east coast of England to East Anglia. Sometimes they switch their colonies' sites from year to year; but in most years there is a large colony on the Farne Islands, off Northumberland.

The bird is the largest of our terns, and one of our earliest summer visitors; the first arrivals are often in Britain by the end of March. Sandwich terns prefer shingle beaches, sandy coasts and off-shore islands for breeding, but in Ireland they occasionally nest on lake islands; elsewhere they are rarely seen inland, even at migration times. In courtship there is a special gliding flight; and the male will feed fish to the female and lead her to a scrape in the ground. Once the birds have settled in they make the air over their colonies loud with harsh 'kirrick' and 'kirwhit' calls.

The sandwich tern is named after the seaside town in Kent, but it has long since ceased breeding there.

RECOGNITION: *black crest; black bill with yellow tip; wings and back pearly-grey; forked tail; young brown and white; sexes alike.*
NESTING: *nests in colonies; both sexes make scrapes in ground; chosen scrape sometimes lined with grass; lays May–June; usually 1 or 2 eggs, any colour from white to deep brown, usually spotted, blotched or smeared with darker brown; incubation about 23 days, by both sexes; chicks, tended by both sexes, leave within a few hours, fly after about 5 weeks.*
FEEDING: *small fish—often sand-eels.*

Oystercatcher

Haematopus ostralegus   17 in.

Present all year; mainly a coastal bird, though nests widely inland in the north

Essentially sedentary, but some movement may occur among most northerly and southerly birds

Oystercatchers in flight utter a loud, shrill 'kleep-kleep'.

A shrill, penetrating 'kleep' often draws attention to two or three waders flying low over the sea or shore. These are oystercatchers, easily the most conspicuous of our shore birds with their bold black and white plumage and long orange bills. They settle to feed along the edge of the sea, looking for shellfish which they rap with their bills, then prise open.

During the past 40 or 50 years there has been a marked rise in the population of oystercatchers, until there are now perhaps 45,000 pairs breeding annually in the British Isles. The key to this increase is that they have expanded into new breeding habitats. Once they were confined to shores and cliff tops; but a habit of nesting inland began in the Scottish Highlands, and spread from there to the Lowlands and northern England, where now they breed on moorland, arable fields and on riverside shingle beds.

In spring and summer oystercatchers put on what is called a 'piping performance' at their breeding grounds. Groups of birds form circles and run up and down, pointing their bills to the ground and piping out their shrill call. All through the nesting period the off-duty parent stands guard, ready to give its 'klee-ee' alarm call at the first sign of an intruder. Oystercatchers from other nests in the area respond to the call by mobbing the outsider, and the young birds freeze motionless, camouflaged by their down.

RECOGNITION: *black and white; long orange bill, pink legs; sexes alike.*
NESTING: *both sexes make scrape in the ground; female selects final scrape, lines it with shells, pebbles and sometimes vegetation; lays April–May; 2 or 3 eggs, pale buff with black spots and blotches; incubation about 27 days, by both parents; chicks, tended by both parents, leave within a few hours, fly at about 4 weeks.*
FEEDING: *mussels, cockles, periwinkles and other molluscs; crustacea, including crabs and shrimps; inland, worms and insects.*

SEA-CLIFFS AND ROCKY ISLANDS

Nearly all the birds of the open sea are suspicious
of land; and at breeding times, when they have no choice but
to go there, they crowd into colonies, often in vast numbers,
on rocks, ledges and clifftops. Cliff-nesters often make
for sites which, because they are safe, have become
traditional to a species: gannets have massed on the
slopes of the Bass Rock for centuries, making the
air ring with their noisy cries.

CONTENTS

Gannet
Morus bassanus 36 in.

Present all year; breeds in huge
colonies and occurs off all coasts on
passage; most common in the west

Adults disperse offshore; immature
birds migrate, the British ones to
the coasts of West Africa

Adult gannet glides over the sea—
its wings may span 6 ft

Fᴌʏɪɴɢ far across the North Atlantic, the gannets
wheel against the wind on barely moving wings,
resting in the waves when they must, and seldom going
to any shore except when instinct calls them to the
lonely fortresses which are their breeding grounds.
Two-thirds of the world's gannets are hatched on the
cliff ledges of 19 gannetries in the British Isles. The most
famous, though not the largest, of these colonies is the
Bass Rock in the Firth of Forth. A visitor noted in 1518:
'Near to Gleghornie, in the ocean, at a distance of two
leagues, is the Bass Rock, wherein is an impregnable
stronghold. Round about it is seen a multitude of
great ducks that live on fish.' Now, more than 480 years
later, the 'great ducks' are still there, 20,000 pairs of
them, packed close together. So many huge webbed feet
might seem a threat to the eggs; in fact, gannets
incubate with their feet, placing one over the other, and
both over a single egg.

For most of the year, gannets are silent birds, but they
make up for this in the breeding season. The screeching
roar of a gannet colony—the biggest in the world is on
St. Kilda, most remote of the the Outer Hebrides—has
few equals in nature.

The gannets' fishing technique is spectacular. They
dive-bomb their catch from as high up as 100 ft, with
their wings—which can span 6 ft—folded back to form
a living arrowhead.

RECOGNITION: *white plumage with black wing-tips; 6 ft wing-span; pale
blue bill; immatures, dark brown with white cheeks, resemble adults by
fourth year; sexes alike.*
NESTING: *both sexes gather pile of seaweed and flotsam, build on cliff ledge
or flat ground; lays March–June; 1 egg, white; incubation about 44 days,
by both parents; nestling, fed by both parents, flies and makes own way to
sea after 90 days.*
FEEDING: *fish, edible offal.*

Manx shearwater

Puffinus puffinus 14 in.

Balearic shearwater

Puffinus mauretanicus 15 in.

A Manx shearwater, taken from its breeding site on the Welsh island of Skokholm and released in Massachusetts, well away from its normal range, found its way back to its mate and chick in 12 days. The experiment helped to prove what ornithologists already suspected: that the birds have a phenomenal homing ability. Many of those seen round the coast of Britain in summer go halfway across the world in winter, to the South Atlantic. They cover vast distances in an almost effortless gliding flight, sometimes swooping so low that the tips of their long, narrow wings actually shear the waves. On land, by contrast, they are awkward birds, able to move only with an ungainly shuffle; but they never go ashore, except to breed.

Manx shearwaters breed on turfy islands along our western seaboard, with some 95,000 pairs in the Skomer colony. At sea the birds are normally silent, but at night on their breeding grounds they set up an extraordinary noise. They nest in burrows, often taking over rabbit warrens; and in the hour before midnight, particularly when there is no moon, the shearwaters produce an unearthly chorus as their mates fly in from fishing expeditions. The burrows, honeycombing the ground, throb with an eerie range of strangled cooing noises.

Balearic shearwaters, from the Mediterranean, are larger and browner than the Manx and regularly visit British and Irish seas in the autumn.

RECOGNITION: *upper parts, crown and nape black; chin, throat and underparts white; sexes alike.*
NESTING: *both sexes excavate burrow in turf, usually at least 3 ft deep; often takes over rabbit burrow; lays April–May; 1 egg, white; incubation 47–55 days, by both parents; nestling, tended by both parents, fledges in 62–76 days.*
FEEDING: *small fish, such as herring, sprats and pilchards.*

Feb.–Oct. visitor; breeds mainly on west coast islands; visits colonies at night

Migratory; British birds make for the coasts of eastern S. America; a few may reach Australia

Shearwaters gliding over the sea almost touch the waves

Cormorant

Phalacrocorax carbo   36 in.

SUMMER

Present all year; essentially coastal,
but huge increase inland,
including new breeding

Mainly sedentary; limited
migration may occur, and some
British birds reach northern Spain

Cormorant stands with spread
wings, to dry out its feathers

CONTRARY to what its detractors may like to believe, the cormorant eats only a normal amount—about one-sixth of its body weight—of fish in a day. It is a strong underwater swimmer, pressing its wings to its body and driving forward with powerful movements of its webbed feet. Back on the surface, the bird rises heavily from the sea and flaps low over the waves on the way back to its nest and young. The nestlings peck impatiently at the parent bird's bill until it regurgitates its catch; then they jostle to get into position for poking their bills down its gullet.

In between diving after fish and feeding their young, cormorants often perch on posts and buoys, with their wings stretched out. They are the only web-footed birds which do not put out a waterproofing oil for their feathers, and must therefore dry themselves every time they come to land.

Cormorants are among our most widespread breeding seabirds. In recent years their numbers have increased enormously, spreading inland to form new colonies in the English midlands and south-east. During the breeding season cormorants are most often seen on cliffs and marine islands, but at other times of year they can be found on sandy and muddy shores as well, and non-breeding birds are increasingly numerous on island reservoirs and lakes.

RECOGNITION: *black with green gloss and white face-patch ; hooked beak ; white patch on thighs in summer ; upright stance when settled ; sexes alike.*
NESTING: *nests in colonies on cliff ledges, flat rocks, or grassy headlands, occasionally in trees inland ; both sexes make mound of dried seaweed and sticks ; lays April–June ; usually 3 or 4 eggs, pale blue ; incubation about 29 days, by both parents ; nestlings, fed by both parents, leave after about 4 weeks, fly after about 8 weeks.*
FEEDING: *chiefly flat-fish ; also wrasse, sand-eels, sticklebacks, and occasionally crabs.*

Shag

Phalacrocorax aristotelis   30 in.

SUMMER

WITH a show of instinctive courage, the parent shag sticks to its seaweed nest against all intruders, defying them by hissing, croaking and pecking menacingly at the air. It can also grunt, startlingly like a pig. The normally nervous shag maintains this vigil on rocks and cliff ledges throughout the months of its breeding season.

The shag is one of Britain's most rapidly increasing seabirds, and is now breeding widely round our coasts, except between Flamborough Head and the Isle of Wight. The present phase of expansion began some 80 years ago, around the end of the First World War, when the bird established itself on the Isle of May in the Firth of Forth—a colony which has grown to more than 800 pairs. Shags moved into the Farne Islands off Northumberland around 1930 and have built up to more than 350 pairs there; and at the end of the 1940s they began breeding at Flamborough Head, where there is now a thriving colony.

Unlike the cormorant, to which it is closely related, the shag is confined to cliffs, rocky coasts and offshore islands and is rarely seen on muddy or sandy shores or estuaries. It never goes far inland, unless driven by storms. The shag has a fast, direct flight, rather more rapid and graceful than that of the cormorant. It shares with the cormorant a habit of perching on rocks, sometimes with wings outspread.

RECOGNITION: *plumage black, with satin-green tinge ; no white patches on face or thighs ; distinct crest in spring and summer ; sexes alike.*
NESTING: *nests in colonies on rocks, cliff ledges or in a cavity among boulders ; both sexes build nest of sticks and seaweed, lined with grass ; usually lays March–May ; usually 3 eggs, pale blue ; incubation about 31 days, by both parents ; nestlings, fed by both parents, fly after 48–58 days.*
FEEDING: *fish, especially wrasse, blenny, goby, dragonet, garfish and sand-eels.*

Present all year; numbers are on the increase; occurs only accidentally on inland waters

Predominantly sedentary; only rarely strays any distance beyond the limits of its breeding range

Shag flies faster than cormorant, and has no white face-patch

Lesser black-backed gull

Larus fuscus 21 in.

JUVENILE

ADULT

Most common as a summer visitor, though increasing numbers now winter in Britain

Mainly migratory; winters south to coasts of tropical Africa and The Gulf

Lesser black-back's nest is often concealed in vegetation

LIKE its close relative the herring gull, the lesser black-back is a scavenger; it sometimes follows ships for offal thrown into the sea, and it often searches inland rubbish tips, on the look-out for anything that is edible. Its powerful, deliberate flight, with frequent soaring and gliding, is like the herring-gull's too; in fact the two birds have so much in common that it is arguable whether they are not extreme forms of the same species. Their nests, eggs and young are rather alike; their vocabulary, with its wide range of keening, wailing, chuckling and yelping notes, is similar; both have a taste for carrion and are ruthless thieves of other birds' eggs and chicks; and occasionally they interbreed.

The lesser black-back has a few inland breeding colonies, and is primarily a summer visitor. But even this last difference from the herring-gull has been blurred in recent years: the lesser black-back has shown an increasing tendency to spend the winter in Britain, especially in those urban and industrial areas where it finds edible refuse on rubbish dumps.

Lesser black-backs breed round the Irish coasts, along the west side of Britain and down the east side to Yorkshire, and occasionally on parts of the south coast. There are also some inland breeding colonies in moorland bogs.

RECOGNITION: *back usually more grey than great black-back's; bill much less stout; legs yellow (after third or fourth year); immatures have brown backs, pale underparts, broad band on end of tail; sexes alike.*
NESTING: *nests in colonies, on ground or on cliff ledges, sometimes in deep cover, such as bracken or heather; both sexes build nest of grass, seaweed and feathers; lays May–June; usually 3 eggs, olive-brown or light green with brown marks; incubation about 27 days, by both parents; young, fed chiefly by female, fly after about 5 weeks.*
FEEDING: *carrion and garbage; fish, shellfish, worms, insects, mice, voles, birds and eggs; also seaweed and grain.*

Great black-backed gull

Larus marinus   27 in.

WITH its great weight and formidable beak, this largest of Britain's gulls is the likely victor in any fight for offal with other gulls. And it can be a ferocious killer in seabird colonies, tearing its victims inside out. Eider ducklings which stray from their parents are among its favourite prey; it can gulp them down in a single mouthful. In defence of its own eggs and young it swoops low over intruders.

Partly because it will eat almost any animal food, alive or dead, partly because it is no longer a target for marksmen, as it was at the end of the last century, and partly because there has been an increase in the amount of edible offal left unburnt at fish docks and other places, the great black-back is a species on the advance. It breeds widely all round the British Isles, except on the east coast of England and the south-east coasts of both England and Scotland. But unlike most of its close relations, the great black-back does not breed far inland anywhere in the British Isles, and even outside the breeding season is less common inland than most other gulls.

Its voice is basically like the herring gull's 'kyow-kyow-kyow', but deeper and more raucous. The great black-back also has a chuckling 'uk-uk-uk' call, which it utters especially when its breeding territory is being invaded by a human intruder.

RECOGNITION : *black back, white underparts ; dark markings on head in winter ; immatures brown above, pale below ; sexes alike.*
NESTING : *nests in small groups, on ground, rocky stack or cliff ledge ; both sexes build substantial nest of heather, seaweed and other local materials ; lays April–May ; usually 3 eggs, olive or light brown with dark spots ; incubation about 27 days, by both parents ; young, fed by both parents, leave after 2–3 weeks, fly after 7–8 weeks.*
FEEDING : *almost any kind of animal food, including dead fish, offal, carrion and other birds ; small vegetable element.*

Present all year, but most common in winter when visitors arrive from northern Europe

Mainly sedentary, but birds from the far north may disperse south as far as the Mediterranean in winter

Great black-backs keep watch from nest on top of cliff

JUVENILE

Kittiwake

Rissa tridactyla 16 in.

ADULT IN SUMMER

Present all year; number of breeding birds has increased; a few sometimes blown inland

Can be seen near its breeding colonies in winter, though most birds disperse into N. Atlantic

Kittiwakes nest in close-packed colonies on cliff ledges

ALONE among the gulls breeding in Britain, the kittiwake is faithful to the sea. Other gulls have taken advantage of man-made food supplies, flocking to rubbish dumps, sewage outfalls and food markets; but the kittiwake roams the sea for much of the year, following the movements of fish and ships, and rarely goes to land except to breed.

The kittiwake also differs from other British gulls in building a fairly elaborate cup-shaped nest; it uses mud to anchor the nest to narrow ledges, projections on cliff faces, the ledges of piers or even the window sills of seaside boarding houses. A number of special adaptations are connected with its nesting habits. The kittiwake's claws are longer and sharper than those of other gulls, giving it a more secure footing on its ledge; and its young, secure in their cup, stay in their nest for more than six weeks after hatching until they can fly — to leave earlier would mean a fall to death.

At its breeding colonies the air is filled with deafening cries of 'kitt-ee-wayke', from which the bird takes its name. This note features largely in the mutual bowing and bill-rubbing courtship ceremonies.

The kittiwake population increased substantially during the 20th century, perhaps because of the increase in trawling and, therefore, the presence of more food for the birds which follow the ships.

RECOGNITION: *white with black wing-tips; uniform grey head and nape in winter; black legs and yellow bill; immatures have dark stripes on wings; dark markings on head in winter; sexes alike.*
NESTING: *nests in colonies, usually on narrow cliff ledges or inside sea caves; both sexes build cup-shaped nest of seaweed and other local materials; lays May–June; 1–3 eggs, pale blue-grey to buff-brown with dark blotches and spots; incubation 26–28 days, by both parents; young, fed by both parents, leave after 40–45 days.*
FEEDING: *almost entirely fish and fish offal.*

Fulmar

Fulmarus glacialis 18½ in.

ONE hundred years ago, fulmars barely had a toehold in Britain. They bred only on the most westerly of the Outer Hebrides, St. Kilda. Then, at the beginning of the 20th century, they colonised Foula in the Shetlands, and so began a spectacular advance that has been restricted only by the coastline.

There are at least 500 colonies of them, with a total perhaps of more than 600,000 pairs of breeding birds, all round the coastline at places where there are suitable cliffs. There is some argument about the reason for this population explosion, but most ornithologists link it with an increase in the amount of offal being discarded by trawlers.

Like shearwaters and petrels, the fulmar is a bird of the open sea. It has the effortless gliding flight typical of shearwaters, but occasionally flaps its wings like a gull and rises higher than most of the shearwaters.

Colonies are occupied throughout the year except in September and October, although the attendance of individual pairs is rather sporadic outside the breeding season. The female lays a single egg in a hollow in turf or on a bare rock, in May. Fulmars will look over a possible site for several years running before settling there. Any intruders at their colonies risk being hit by a foul-smelling fluid ejected from the mouths of the birds.

Fulmars have an exceptionally long period of immaturity, and on average do not start breeding until they are nine years of age.

RECOGNITION: *dark grey back, wings and tail ; white head and underparts ; tubular nostrils show at close range ; sexes alike.*
NESTING: *nests on cliffs; scrape in turf or depression in rock ; nest sometimes lined with a few pebbles ; lays May ; 1 egg, white ; incubation about 52 or 53 days, by both parents ; nestling, fed by both parents, leaves after about 53 days.*
FEEDING: *fish, whale or seal offal ; also fish and crustacea.*

Present all year; practically the whole of this breeding range has been occupied in the last 100 years

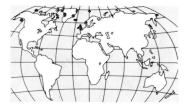

In winter, many birds disperse widely over northern oceans; some adults visit their nesting cliffs

Fulmar holds its wings stiffly as it wheels over the sea

Arctic skua

Stercorarius parasiticus 18 in.

April–Oct. visitor; rare as a breeding bird, but occurs frequently off coasts in autumn

Spends the winter at sea, mainly in the southern oceans

Arctic skua in pursuit of tern—it gives up only when the tern drops its fish

WHEN a seabird is attacked it will often vomit up its last meal, so lightening itself for a quick escape. The skuas, 'pirate' birds of the coasts, take advantage of this behaviour, hurtling down on gulls, terns and kittiwakes and bullying them until they disgorge their meal. Apart from this way of extorting food, Arctic skuas are also experienced nest robbers. Normally they hunt singly, and they can terrorise birds far larger than themselves. But occasionally male and female go hunting together. They make an efficient team, with one bird matching itself against, say, a pair of common gulls while its mate robs their nest.

The Arctic skua is predominantly brown; but there are two main colour variants—a dark form and a light form—and intermediates between them are often seen. But all adult Arctic skuas are easily recognisable because of their two central tail feathers, which stick out in short, straight spikes beyond the rest of the tail.

Its British breeding grounds are confined to Scotland and the western and northern isles, but it is an increasing species. Like other skuas, it nests on moorlands often some distance inland, and not on sea cliffs. It is boldly aggressive towards intruders at its colonies, where its wailing 'ka-aaow' and gruff 'tuk-tuk' are associated with a spectacular display flight.

RECOGNITION: *dark brown upper parts, underparts vary from light brown to dark brown, with intermediate forms; all mature birds have two central tail feathers which stick out in a distinctive point; sexes alike.*
NESTING: *usually nests in colonies on moors and other rough land; both sexes make scrape, sparsely lined with dry grass or other local material; lays June; usually 2 eggs, olive-green to brown with dark markings; incubation 25–28 days, by both parents; chicks, tended by both parents, leave shortly after hatching, fly after about 5 weeks.*
FEEDING: *fish disgorged by other birds; small mammals; eggs and chicks; insects and their larvae; carrion; berries.*

Great skua

Catharacta skua 23 in.

IN common with other skuas, the great skua is a pirate; it harries gulls and other seabirds until its victims choke up their last meal. Slow and heavy in normal flight, the great skua turns into a skilful flier when it hunts, twisting from side to side as it chases a gull as big as itself. A great skua will even tackle a gannet, sometimes hanging onto its tail or a wing-tip until it gives up the fish it has just swallowed.

In their journeys over the Atlantic, great skuas will follow fishing-boats to pick up offal flung overboard. They are also capable of catching their own food, by fishing, killing young birds or scavenging on the carcases of stranded sea animals such as whales and seals.

Great skuas spend most of the year on the ocean, only coming to land to breed. Until 100 years ago, they were found in Britain on only two of the Shetland Islands, Unst and Foula. Today there are large colonies in the Shetlands, and the birds breed in smaller numbers in the Orkneys, Fair Isle, the Outer Hebrides and several places in Caithness and Sutherland.

In courtship, pairs soar in circles over the nesting site. On the ground they have a bowing ceremony. They are aggressive birds, fearlessly driving away people or animals from their colonies. They have been seen to cling to the head of an intruding sheep and batter it with their wings until the bruised animal is driven away.

April–Sept. visitor; breeds chiefly in Orkney and Shetland; seen on passage on other coasts

Some N. Atlantic breeding birds probably reach the S. Atlantic in winter

RECOGNITION: *brown, heavily built, gull-like bird with short tail; white wing-patch; sexes alike.*
NESTING: *both sexes make scrape in ground on heath or rough grass, sparsely lined with lichen and other plants; lays late May–June; usually 2 eggs, olive to green, with dark brown blotches; incubation 29 or 30 days, by both parents; nestlings, tended by both parents, leave nest after a few days and fly after 40–50 days.*
FEEDING: *mainly fish stolen by forcing other birds to disgorge; some young birds, carrion and offal.*

Great skua in flight shows bold white patch on wing

Razorbill

Alca torda 16 in.

SUMMER

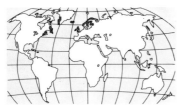

Present all year; less common than guillemot; most birds move out to sea in winter

Mainly sedentary, though some birds disperse as far south as the Mediterranean in winter

Razorbill's throat and sides of neck are white in winter

LIKE all members of the auk family, razorbills are expert divers and underwater swimmers. They use their wings as paddles, forcing their buoyant bodies down below the surface. The greatest depth recorded for a razorbill's dive is 24 ft, and one has been timed as staying down for as long as 52 seconds.

For much of the year razorbills keep well out to sea, but about the middle of winter they move to waters near the cliffs and rock-strewn shores where they will breed. Colonies of nesting razorbills are usually established close to the breeding grounds of the related guillemot, often on another part of the same cliff face. They lay a single egg in a cavity towards the top of a cliff or under boulders on the shore.

Pairs of courting birds often pose in what is known as the 'ecstatic' posture; one bird points its bill upwards, with the jaws slightly parted and vibrating with a castanet-like rattle, while its mate nibbles at its throat. Mated razorbills may also touch, rub and cross their bills—whose similarity to a 'cut-throat' razor gives the birds their name.

At sea, where flocks of razorbills form 'rafts' on the waves, they take part in a communal display. Birds shake their heads from side to side and swim rapidly around within the group; sometimes they make sudden dives, reappearing in the 'ecstatic' pose.

RECOGNITION: *heavy bill; black upper parts; white wing-stripe; in summer, head and neck are black, with white line from bill to eye; in winter, throat and sides of neck are white; sexes alike.*
NESTING: *nests in crevice of cliff or under boulder; no nesting material; lays May–June; 1 egg, with wide colour variation including brown, cream, white and blue-green, with brown or black blotches; incubation about 35 days, by both parents; nestling, fed by both parents, flutters down to sea after 16–21 days.*
FEEDING: *fish, shellfish, worms*

Puffin

Fratercula arctica   12 in.

SUMMER

ITS huge, brightly coloured bill—comical in the eyes of some observers—is for the puffin a weapon, a digging tool and an advertising medium. Puffins thrust their bills at neighbours as a threat which may be the prelude to a fight. They toss their heads, hiding their bills, when they want to make peace; and pairs of birds put their bills together in courtship. On the turf-covered sea-cliffs which are their main breeding sites, puffins hack into the soil—or even into soft rock—with their bills to make nesting-burrows, shovelling away the loose earth with their webbed feet.

The puffin sometimes collects grass and feathers to line its nest, plucking pieces of vegetation until it has a heap of materials clasped in its bill. Then it shuffles back to its nest-hole with the collection.

The bill is at its brightest in summer, when puffins go ashore to breed; in winter, when they live on the sea, the bill changes, losing its horny sheath and exposing the duller colours below. Puffins usually winter in sea areas a little south of their breeding grounds, but they are sometimes seen on deeper water.

Puffins have declined in Britain, particularly in the south. Between the Scillies and the Isle of Wight they once had colonies of thousands, but no more than a few dozen birds remain there.

RECOGNITION: *huge bill, blue, yellow and red in summer; mainly yellow and horn-coloured in winter; black upper parts and white underparts; sexes alike.*
NESTING: *both sexes dig burrow in turf or under boulders, or occupy old shearwater or rabbit burrow; nest may be lined with vegetation and feathers; lays May; 1 egg, white with faint brown markings; incubation about 6 weeks, mainly by female; nestling is fed by parents in burrow for about 6 weeks, then deserted and left hungry; after several days' fast, it crawls out and flutters down to the sea by night.*
FEEDING: *marine organisms, including molluscs and small fish.*

Present all year; only small numbers now breed in the colonies in southern England

Most birds disperse into the N. Atlantic in winter and are only rarely seen close to land

Puffin in winter—its triangular bill is always distinctive

Guillemot
Uria aalge 16½ in.

SUMMER

Present all year; nests in colonies, often large and on same cliffs as other seabirds

Winters at sea; some birds disperse southwards; occasionally driven inland by storms

Guillemot in winter has black streak behind its eye

LATE in January, after months spent at sea, guillemots gather near the cliffs where they will nest. As more birds flock in they begin complex ceremonies, in which groups 'dance' over the water. Weaving and dodging, the birds patter over the waves; suddenly the whole flock may dive at once and the 'dance' may go on under water.

Guillemots also take part in communal display flights, in flocks hundreds strong, wheeling, soaring and diving as if controlled by one mind.

When they begin to move onto their cliff ledges in spring, the guillemots at first leave plenty of space between one bird and the next. But the ledges quickly fill up with jostling birds, their 'arrr' cries combining into a growling chorus as they struggle for breeding sites.

Guillemots make no nest. The female lays her single egg on a bare rock, but the egg is pear-shaped so that if it is jostled or caught by the wind, it is less likely to roll off the cliff. By the time the guillemots have laid their eggs, the ledges are filled with rows of birds packed almost shoulder to shoulder, facing inwards, with their eggs clutched between their legs. Usually, by February, most of their number have arrived off the cliffs and they normally leave in July, spending the rest of the year out at sea.

RECOGNITION: *pointed bill; upper parts dark brown in summer, greyer in winter, though birds in northern Britain are darker; in less common 'bridled' variety, birds have white ring around eye with a white line running back from it over sides of head; sexes alike.*
NESTING: *breeds on rock ledges, without nesting material; lays May–June; 1 egg, pear-shaped, very variable in colour—blue-green, brown, buff, yellow or white, usually with yellow, brown or black blotches; incubation 32–36 days, by both parents; chick, fed by both parents, flutters down to sea after about 16 days, accompanied by a parent.*
FEEDING: *fish, shellfish, worms; some seaweed.*

Black guillemot

Cepphus grylle 13½ in.

SUMMER

WHATEVER the time of year, the black guillemot is unlikely to be mistaken for any other seabird; for no other bird around our coasts is anything like it in plumage. In summer the bird is all black apart from a broad white patch on its wings; and in winter its back is barred black and white, with the head and under-parts mainly white.

In courtship, too, the black guillemot is in a class of its own: it has such a wide variety of displays, most of which involve several pairs of birds. In one, a bird swims around its mate, opening its bill to show its brilliant red gape and giving its squeaky cry; the other bird squeaks and nods its head in reply.

Parties of birds often swim in formation, though this is not a courtship display and is probably connected with feeding. They move with almost military precision over the water in a file, a rank or a staggered line.

Black guillemots are more sedentary than Britain's other breeding members of the auk family. Instead of making for the open sea they spend the winter close to the rocky, cliff-lined coasts where they breed. Their main British breeding grounds are in Shetland, the far north-east of the Scottish mainland, and the islands and mainland of western Scotland. Small numbers breed in Ireland, the Isle of Man, Anglesey and Cumbria.

RECOGNITION: *summer—plumage black, with conspicuous white wing-patch; winter—upper parts barred black and white, head and underparts white, wing-patch as in summer; sexes alike.*
NESTING: *builds no nest; eggs laid in crevices in cliffs or among boulders, in holes in walls, or sometimes in shallow burrows; lays May–June; usually 2 eggs, buff or blue-green with black, red-brown or grey blotches; incubation about 28 days, by both parents; nestlings, fed by both parents, leave and fly after about 35 days.*
FEEDING: *small fish, small crabs, shrimps, prawns and shellfish; some seaweed and drowned insects.*

Present all year; even in winter rarely seen far from the coasts where it breeds

Essentially sedentary; but some birds from northern part of range move south in winter

In winter, black guillemot's back is barred black and white

261

Peregrine

Falco peregrinus   M 15 in.   F 19 in.

MALE

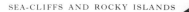

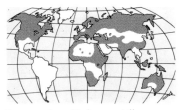

Present all year; its numbers have
recovered from a fall in the 1950s,
to reach an all-time high

Some northern birds, especially
young ones, reach as far south
as the Tropics in winter

Peregrine, stooping headlong from
above, prepares to strike

Soaring high above its hunting territory, the peregrine
looks too remote to be menacing. But once it has
singled out its prey—a gull, perhaps, or an unsuspecting
feral pigeon—it arches through the sky in a breathtaking
'stoop', which gives its quarry little chance of escape.
Speeds of up to 90 mph have been measured for the
diving peregrine, and the bird's talons strike the victim
with such shattering force that they may break off its
head. If the victim somehow manages to dodge the
attack, the peregrine often stoops again and again.

Falconers have always prized these spectacular, efficient
killers, but their reputation as hunters led to large numbers of peregrines being shot during the Second World
War, because it was thought that they were a threat to
carrier pigeons, used when radio silence was imposed on
submarine-spotting planes. As the peregrine population
began to recover from this setback, it was hit by a worse
one: the birds were either poisoned or made infertile by
pesticides used on crops and eaten by their prey.

In 1956 there were more than 650 pairs of peregrines in
the British Isles. Six years later, only 68 breeding pairs
were left; but the peregrine has staged a remarkable
recovery, and there are now nearly 1500 pairs breeding.

Peregrines (the male bird is called a tiercel and the
larger female is the peregrine falcon) mate for life, often
returning year after year to the same eyrie.

RECOGNITION: *long pointed wings and long tail; male has slate-coloured
back, barred underparts, heavy black moustaches; female larger and
browner; distinctive flight, alternating rapid flapping and long glides.*
NESTING: *nests in bare scrape on rock ledge or in abandoned nest of other
species; usually lays April; usually 3 or 4 eggs, red-brown; incubation
about 30 days, chiefly by female; nestlings, fed by both sexes, leave after
35–40 days.*
FEEDING: *birds on the wing; some rabbits and other mammals.*

Chough

Pyrrhocorax pyrrhocorax   15 in.

NOWADAYS the red-billed chough is a rare bird in the
British Isles, breeding mainly on sea-cliffs in Wales
and in Ireland. But it was once much more widespread. The pioneering 18th-century naturalist, Gilbert
White of Selborne, saw choughs on the Sussex cliffs.
In Cornwall it was once so common that it was called
the Cornish chough, but now it no longer breeds there.
Jackdaws have been blamed for invading the choughs'
territory and driving them out, but it seems more likely
that the jackdaws moved in after the choughs disappeared.

Choughs are sociable birds outside the breeding
season, gathering in flocks of as many as 100 to roost on
ledges, crevices and caves along the cliffs. They are
often seen on coastal fields. A communal courtship
ceremony, in which members of the flock strut and flap
their wings together, has been recorded. In other courtship ceremonies, the male 'caresses' the female's bill
and preens her head feathers, often feeding her. The
couple also have a display in the air.

In flight, choughs are spectacular performers, soaring
in the updraught at the edge of cliffs and swooping from
ledge to ledge. They are acrobatic, too, often diving
with wings almost closed, or turning over on their backs
in the air. Their call-notes include the 'k'chuf' note
which gives the birds their name.

RECOGNITION: *black plumage with green and blue gloss; curved red bill;
red legs; sexes alike.*
NESTING: *both sexes build nest of sticks, lined with wool and hair, in
crevice or hole in cliff-face—often in sea cave, sometimes inland in
building or abandoned mine-shaft; usually lays April–May; usually
3–6 eggs, white with green or cream tint and grey-brown blotches;
incubation about 18 days, by female only; nestlings, fed by both sexes,
leave after about 45 days.*
FEEDING: *chiefly insects and larvae; worms, spiders and sometimes lizards.*

Present all year; formerly more
widespread; no longer found in
Cornwall, once a stronghold

Essentially sedentary, but
mountain populations move to
lower ground in winter

Choughs often give spectacular and
acrobatic aerial displays

Rock pipit

Anthus spinoletta 6¼ in.

Present all year; breeds on rocky coasts, but is found around the entire coastline in winter

Northern birds move a short way southwards in winter; mountain birds move to lower ground

Rock pipit—this small song-bird stays by the sea all year round

THIS is the easiest of our three breeding pipits to identify, not only because of its appearance but also because of its distinctive habitat. The rock pipit, somewhat larger and greyer than the tree pipit or the meadow pipit, never breeds anywhere but on coasts, and usually on wild, rocky shores. In winter it is still mainly a bird of the coasts, moving on to flat and muddy shores and salt-marshes; only occasionally does it fly inland, to feed beside reservoirs and other stretches of fresh water.

Another clue to recognition is the rock pipit's call-note, given in dipping flight; its single 'pheet' cannot be confused with the meadow pipit's triple 'pheet-pheet-pheet'. Its fluttering song-flight, though, is similar to the other bird's. The male rock pipit takes off from a rock or cliff ledge and launches into a song which gathers speed as the bird rises, culminating in a trill as it glides down.

In many parts of its range the rock pipit has adapted itself to a diet consisting mainly of very small sea snails; but on coasts with a good supply of seaweed it is chiefly an insect eater. A careful study of its diet on a stretch of coast in Cornwall showed that the most important item was kelp flies, breeding on rotting seaweed; sand-hoppers and shorehoppers were also taken. In other parts of the country, rock pipits have eaten winged ants, beetles, slugs and even small fish.

RECOGNITION: *upper parts grey-brown; larger and greyer than meadow or tree pipit; tail has grey outer feathers; dark brown legs; sexes alike.*
NESTING: *builds nest of dried grass in hole or crevice in cliff, often sheltered by vegetation, sometimes in a bank or wall; lays late April–June; usually 4 or 5 eggs, off-white with grey and brown speckles; incubation about 14 days, by female only; nestlings, fed by both sexes, leave after 16 days; usually two broods.*
FEEDING: *chiefly small molluscs; also sandhoppers and other insects, many picked from rotting seaweed; some small fish, slugs and seeds.*

Rock dove

Columba livia 13 in.

HOMING pigeons, and those which strut about our town and city pavements, are all descended from rock doves. In the days when an all-year-round supply of fresh meat was a rarity, rock doves were kept and eaten in some districts; they were provided with dove-cotes as nesting-places. When tame birds escaped, they interbred with birds from the ancestral stock, and hybrids have now replaced pure rock doves in many of their old breeding haunts. Most of the birds seen on cliffs, no matter how similar in appearance to the rock dove, are really descendants of pigeons that went wild.

The true rock dove is now largely confined to a few colonies in Scotland and Ireland, mainly on the north and west coasts. In other parts of the world, particularly in North Africa, rock doves live away from the sea on inland cliffs and in caves. But doves in these habitats in Britain are either domestic pigeons gone wild, stock doves or wood-pigeons.

The rock dove's cooing voice is like that of the street pigeon. Its bowing courtship display is the same, too, but the bird is difficult to watch at breeding time because it builds in colonies inside dark sea-caves, slippery with spray, or in deep crevices in the cliffs. In flight, the bird climbs for a short distance and then glides down on raised wings. It occasionally perches on trees, though it prefers to land on rocks, on the ground or on buildings.

RECOGNITION: *two black wing-bars, iridescent neck-patch of green and purple; distinguished from stock dove by white rump; sexes alike.*
NESTING: *nests in colonies; builds untidy nest of twigs, roots, stems or seaweed in cliff hole or on ledge in cave; lays throughout the year, but mainly in spring and summer; usually 2 eggs, white; incubation 18 days, by both parents; nestlings, tended by both parents, leave after about 18 days; two broods, often three.*
FEEDING: *mostly seeds and grain; peas, potatoes, shellfish and seaweed.*

Present all year; truly wild birds largely restricted to the north and west coasts of Scotland and Ireland

Sedentary; records in some parts of the world may refer to the feral pigeon—a descendant

Rock dove in flight shows black wing-bars and white rump

Leach's petrel

Oceanodroma leucorrhoa   8 in.

Storm petrel

Hydrobates pelagicus   6 in.

Both arrive April; storm (on map) leaves Oct., Leach's (breeds off N.W. Scotland) may stay to Dec.

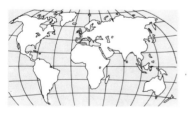

Map shows storm petrel's range; both species move southwards in winter; some reach southern oceans

Storm petrel nests in crevices in rocks on marine islands

THE oceans of the world are home to the petrels; they go ashore only to breed or when driven there by storms. But it takes a storm of more than ordinary fury to get the better of these birds. They shelter from the Atlantic gales by keeping to the troughs of waves and avoiding the crests. On calm days they often patter over the surface of the water as if walking—the very name 'petrel' is said to have been derived from the biblical episode in which St. Peter walked on the water.

The storm petrel, once known to sailors as 'Mother Carey's Chicken', is a follower of ships. It feeds on plankton, offal and oil churned up by the ship's passage. Leach's petrel does not normally follow ships.

When on land for the breeding season, petrels keep to their burrows on rocky islands; only their nocturnal crooning or purring 'songs' show where they are.

The storm petrel is the more widespread of the two as a British breeding species, though less widely distributed on a world scale. It has colonies in the Scillies, on Skokholm and Skomer off the Pembroke coast, and on many islands off the west and north coasts of Scotland and the west and south-west coasts of Ireland. Leach's petrel breeds mainly in four colonies on the most oceanic of the Scottish islands—the Flannans, North Rona, St. Kilda and Sula Sgeir.

RECOGNITION: *storm petrel has sooty plumage, white rump, long wings, square tail; weaving flight near water; follows ships; Leach's petrel, larger and browner with forked tail, has buoyant, erratic flight; sexes alike in both cases.*
NESTING: *both dig burrow, or nest in abandoned rabbit burrow or crevice among stones; lays May or June (Leach's) or usually June (storm); 1 egg, white with faint brown spots; incubation about 50 days (Leach's) or 44 days (storm), by both parents; nestlings, fed by both parents, leave after 7–8½ weeks.*
FEEDING: *chiefly plankton, fish and floating oil; also seaweed.*

A GUIDE
TO RARER BIRDS

IN spring and autumn, when great numbers of migrant birds are entering or leaving Britain, an unfamiliar silhouette flying along the shoreline or a strange bird feeding inland may defy quick identification. This could be one of the birds illustrated in the following pages—perhaps a rare passage migrant, resting in Britain before continuing its journey, or a storm-driven vagrant, hundreds of miles from its proper route. The 'problem' bird may turn out to be a visitor which has come here only because food was short elsewhere; or it could be one of the newcomers—birds which have only recently begun to breed in Britain. Yet again, it could be one of the birds introduced to Britain by man, for sport or decoration, now living and breeding in the wild.

CONTENTS

Newcomers

CHANGES in a bird's distribution are only rarely as sudden and dramatic as that of the collared dove (p. 51). A single pair nested in Britain for the first time in 1955: by 1968 great numbers were breeding over most of the country. But during the present century, several other species have nested in Britain for the first time, including the black-necked grebe, Slavonian grebe, redwing, firecrest, snowy owl, wood sandpiper, black redstart, little ringed plover, serin, fieldfare, bluethroat, bee-eater, gull-billed tern, black-winged stilt, Mediterranean gull, great northern diver, goldeneye, purple sandpiper and Cetti's warbler. In addition, six species have returned to nest in Britain after being driven out in the 19th century by persecution or land reclamation. They are the osprey, avocet, ruff, black-tailed godwit, bittern and Savi's warbler. These species are the newcomers, and are marked from the rest by their rarity or novelty.

SAVI'S WARBLER
Locustella luscinioides 5½ in.
Small breeding population established in southern England since 1960; otherwise almost unknown in this country, though it nested in East Anglia until mid-19th century; skulking; trilling song like that of the grasshopper warbler.

FIRECREST
Regulus ignicapillus 3½ in.
Small numbers have bred in England since 1961; also occurs as passage migrant in southern counties, and a few winter in south-west England; like a goldcrest, with black stripe through eye, white stripe above it.

SERIN
Serinus serinus 4½ in.
First bred 'in southern England' in 1967 and has bred occasionally since. Has spread north-west across Europe in present century; stumpy bill, bright yellow rump; male has yellow on head and breast.

HONEY BUZZARD
Pernis apivorus 21½ in.
A few pairs breed in England and Scotland, but most localities are secret; also scarce passage migrant, most often on east coast; feeds on wasps' nests; barred tail.

WOOD SANDPIPER
Tringa glareola 8 in.
Has bred annually in northern Scotland since 1959; occurs mainly as autumn passage migrant in south-east England; breeds in northern Europe; winters in Africa.

SNOWY OWL
Nyctea scandiaca 24 in.
Bred in Shetland 1967–75; also occasional winter visitor, mostly to far north, and vagrant elsewhere; breeds in northern Europe; buzzard-like flight and white plumage.

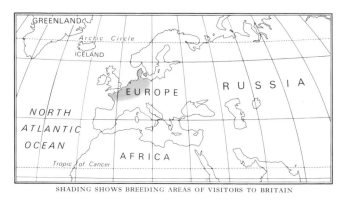

SHADING SHOWS BREEDING AREAS OF VISITORS TO BRITAIN

Visitors from western Europe

IT would seem unlikely that the English Channel or the North Sea would prove much of a barrier to birds; but many which breed on the western shores of the Continent do not breed in the British Isles; and a few, such as the pygmy owl and the middle spotted woodpecker, have never even been recorded here. The tawny pipit and great reed warbler, both of which breed in the Netherlands, are remarkably rare in Britain.

A few of the visitors from western Europe once nested regularly in Britain. The Kentish plover has been lost since the Second World War; Britain was always on the fringe of its range and probably some small change in climate or increase in human disturbance near its breeding quarters caused it to disappear. The goshawk was lost as a regular breeder long before the present century, though it now nests in various parts of England, Wales and Scotland, due mainly to falconers' introductions. It is probably for climatic reasons that the golden oriole has never been firmly established, although it has bred in small numbers for the past three decades.

Several more species have nested in Britain from time to time, often only once or twice. These include the white stork (which nested once on St. Giles' Cathedral in Edinburgh as long ago as 1416), the red-crested pochard, little gull and Baillon's crake. The black woodpecker, woodchat shrike and tawny pipit were formerly believed to have bred here, but their breeding records are now generally discredited. In 1968 the bluethroat nested here for the very first time.

In autumn, regular passage migrants include the ortolan bunting and icterine warbler, which pass over eastern Britain almost every year. In winter, the great grey shrike and red-crested pochard are regular visitors to some parts of Britain.

Another group seems to visit these islands not as regular passage migrants on their way to winter quarters, but during their post-breeding dispersal before migration gets under way. These include the purple heron, which also occurs in spring, the ferruginous duck, which also occurs in winter, and the melodious warbler.

WOODCHAT SHRIKE
Lanius senator 6¾ in.
Irregular visitor, mainly in spring and autumn, to south and east England; may have bred in the Isle of Wight; breeds from North Sea to east of Mediterranean; winters in tropical Africa.

LESSER GREY SHRIKE
Lanius minor 8 in.
Infrequent spring and autumn visitor, chiefly to south and east; breeds from mid-France to Asia; normally winters in tropical and southern Africa; like a small great grey shrike, with broader black band across forehead.

GREAT GREY SHRIKE
Lanius excubitor 9¼ in.
Regular winter visitor in small numbers, especially to Scotland and eastern side of England; breeds across Europe north from central France; winters in southern Europe; grey and white body; black and white wings.

BLUETHROAT
Luscinia svecica 5½ in.
Scarce spring and autumn migrant, mostly on east coast; has bred in Scotland; often skulks on ground, among vegetation.

TAWNY PIPIT
Anthus campestris 6½ in.
Irregular visitor, mainly to coasts of southern England in autumn; breeds in Europe, Asia, north-west Africa; winters in Africa.

GOLDEN ORIOLE
Oriolus oriolus 9½ in.
Breeds in small numbers in East Anglia; otherwise rare, mainly spring visitor; winters mainly in tropical Africa.

ORTOLAN BUNTING
Emberiza hortulana 6½ in.
Scarce spring and autumn passage migrant, especially on Fair Isle and along east coast, probably from Scandinavia.

GOSHAWK
Accipiter gentilis 21 in.
Rare resident, breeding in several parts of Britain, some of these birds being introduced or falconers' escapes; resident in much of Europe; looks like a huge sparrowhawk.

LITTLE BUSTARD
Otis tetrax 17 in.
Irregular visitor to a variety of British counties, mainly in spring and autumn; breeds in Europe and north-west Africa; round-winged; shows much white when it flies.

WHITE STORK
Ciconia ciconia 40 in.
Rare vagrant, chiefly to East Anglia in spring and summer; bred once in Britain; decreasing as a breeding species in parts of Europe; also breeds in north-west Africa, Asia.

NIGHT HERON
Nycticorax nycticorax 24 in.
Irregular visitor from Netherlands and southern Europe, mainly to south and east coasts in spring and autumn; feral colony in Edinburgh; breeds in Europe, Asia, Africa.

LITTLE BITTERN
Ixobrychus minutus 14 in
Irregular spring, early summer and autumn visitor, especially to southern England; has nested at least once in Britain; breeds in Europe, Asia, North Africa.

PURPLE HERON
Ardea purpurea 31 in.
Scarce visitor from Netherlands, mainly to south and east coasts in spring and autumn; breeds in Europe, Asia, Africa; grey-brown appearance, with black and chestnut striped neck.

BAILLON'S CRAKE
Porzana pusilla 7 in.
Rare spring and autumn vagrant to coastal counties; bred here occasionally until 1889; breeds in Europe, north to France, Holland and Germany; winters in North Africa; weak flight; heavily barred flanks.

FERRUGINOUS DUCK
Aythya nyroca 16 in.
Irregular visitor, mainly in autumn to East Anglia, from scattered breeding colonies in France, but chiefly in south and central Europe; breeds here in waterfowl collections; also breeds in north-west Africa, Asia.

RED-CRESTED POCHARD
Netta rufina 22 in.
Rare winter visitor to eastern England from Netherlands and central Europe; however, most are escapes from waterfowl collections, some now nesting in the wild; drake has crimson-chestnut head, duck has pale cheeks.

KENTISH PLOVER
Charadrius alexandrinus
6¼ in.
Now uncommon passage migrant on south and south-east coasts; nested in south-east England until 1950s; winters in Africa.

GULL-BILLED TERN
Gelochelidon nilotica 15 in.
Rare passage migrant, mainly spring, on Channel and south-east coasts; nested in Essex 1949-50; winter range includes Red Sea and The Gulf.

LITTLE GULL
Larus minutus 11 in.
Regular passage migrant and winter visitor in small numbers, chiefly on east coast and in Scotland; odd pairs have nested in eastern England since 1975.

BLACK WOODPECKER
Dryocopus martius 18 in.
Probably rare vagrant, but not yet included on official 'British list'; none seen north of Yorkshire; breeds in Europe west to Netherlands and Belgium.

ICTERINE WARBLER
Hippolais icterina 5 in.
Scarce passage migrant found mainly in autumn on south and east coasts; winters in southern tropical Africa.

MELODIOUS WARBLER
Hippolais polyglotta 5 in.
Scarce passage migrant, mostly in the south in autumn; breeds mainly in south-west Europe; winters in Africa.

AQUATIC WARBLER
Acrocephalus paludicola
5 in.
Annual autumn visitor, but in very small numbers, especially to coastal counties of southern England.

GREAT REED WARBLER
Acrocephalus arundinaceus
7½ in.
Rare visitor, mainly to the south coast in spring and autumn; winters in Africa; bold white eye-stripe.

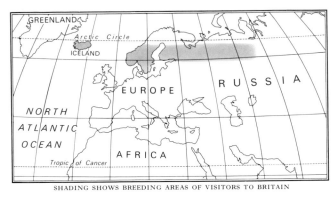

SHADING SHOWS BREEDING AREAS OF VISITORS TO BRITAIN

Visitors from northern Europe

A belt of territory which stretches from Scandinavia eastwards across Russia to the Ural Mountains is the home of a substantial group of Britain's rarer visitors. They come here when hard weather drives them farther south than their usual winter range, or when they are blown off course on migration. Some of those which breed in Russia are often completely off any normal migration course when they come here. Others, and especially the spotted redshank, are on their normal route and occur here in substantial numbers each year.

The other more frequently recorded of these visitors from northern Europe are the shore lark, rough-legged buzzard and Lapland bunting—all regular on parts of the east coast of Britain—and the little bunting.

Most of the north European visitors are land birds, but a few—the crane, great snipe, broad-billed sandpiper and Caspian tern—are marsh or water birds. The crane, a local

British breeding species, performs one of the most remarkable known migrations: normally it flies non-stop from its breeding grounds in Norway and Sweden to southern Spain. Occasionally, birds fail to make the journey in a single flight, perhaps because the wind and weather are against them, and they may then come down somewhere in the British Isles, usually in the eastern half of England.

The land birds fall into two groups. One group breeds all the way from Scandinavia eastwards through Siberia; it includes the rough-legged buzzard, the sea eagle, which has just begun to breed again in north-west Scotland following a lengthy re-introduction programme, Tengmalm's owl, the shore lark, Lapland bunting, pine grosbeak, nutcracker and Arctic reedpoll. The other group has a more easterly breeding range, normally within Russia, and includes the Arctic warbler, the rustic and little buntings, and the two-barred crossbill.

ARCTIC WARBLER
Phylloscopus borealis 4¾ in.
Rare passage migrant from northern Russia; completely off-course, for migration is usually to south-east Asia; narrow pale wing-bar; prominent straight eye-stripes.

SHORELARK
Eremophila alpestris 6½ in.
Scarce winter visitor to coasts of eastern England; breeds in the Scandinavian uplands; has been known to breed occasionally in Scotland in recent years; black and yellow markings on head and breast.

NUTCRACKER
Nucifraga caryocatactes 12½ in.
Rare winter vagrant, chiefly in south and east England, from southern Scandinavia and Siberia; large influx of birds in 1968 came from Siberia; dark brown, flecked with white.

RUSTIC BUNTING
Emberiza rustica 5¾ in.
Rare passage migrant, chiefly in autumn; recorded mainly in northern isles of Scotland; breeds in northern Russia and winters in Asia; like reed bunting, with white underparts.

LITTLE BUNTING
Emberiza pusilla 5¼ in.
Scarce passage migrant, usually in autumn, mainly to Fair Isle, other Scottish islands, and east coast of England; breeds in northern Russia and normally migrates south-east.

LAPLAND BUNTING
Calcarius lapponicus 6 in.
Scarce autumn and winter visitor, mainly in northern and western islands and on south-east coast; has bred in Scotland; breeds from Arctic America to Siberia.

ARCTIC REDPOLL
Acanthis hornemanni 5 in.
Very rare winter vagrant, mainly to Fair Isle and north-east England; breeds in northern Scandinavia and Russia; spreads south in winter; white rump and underparts.

TWO-BARRED CROSSBILL
Loxia leucoptera 5¾ in.
Winter vagrant, mostly to east of Britain; breeds in northern Russia; winters around Baltic and in central Europe; double white wing-bars; same size as chaffinch.

PINE GROSBEAK
Pinicola enucleator 8 in.
Very rare winter vagrant to south-east England; breeds in northern Scandinavia and Russia, spreads south in winter; heavy bill, long tail and double white wing-bar.

GREAT SNIPE
Gallinago media 11 in.
Irregular winter visitor and autumn passage migrant from Scandinavia, most often in Scotland and on south and east coasts of England; normally migrates to southern Africa; larger than snipe with much more white on sides of tail.

BROAD-BILLED SANDPIPER
Limicola falcinellus 6½ in.
Rare autumn and occasional spring passage migrant from Scandinavia, most sightings recorded in south-east England; usual migration to eastern Mediterranean and southern Asia; like dunlin in autumn plumage, with prominent pale eye-stripes.

SPOTTED REDSHANK
Tringa erythropus 12 in.
Regular spring and autumn passage migrant from northern Scandinavia, mainly in small numbers on coast of south-east England; winters in Africa; a few winter in Britain; longer-billed than common redshank, without wing-bars; loud 'tu-ip' call.

TENGMALM'S OWL
Aegolius funereus 10 in.
Irregular winter visitor from Scandinavia, chiefly to Orkney and north-east England; moves south in winter if food is scarce; plumage warmer brown than little owl's.

CASPIAN TERN
Sterna caspia 21 in.
Irregular summer visitor mainly to southern Britain; in northern Europe breeds only on coasts of the Baltic sea; black crown and heavy, orange-red bill.

SEA EAGLE
Haliaetus albicilla 32 in.
Rare winter visitor from Scandinavia or north Germany to eastern Britain; now breeds west Scotland following recent re-introduction programme on Rhúm; adult tail white, young dark brown.

CRANE
Grus grus 45 in.
Rare passage migrant from Scandinavia, with a small resident population breeding in Norfolk since 1981; red patch on head.

ROUGH-LEGGED BUZZARD
Buteo lagopus 22 in.
Annual winter visitor from Scandinavia to northern Scotland and eastern counties south to Kent; most winter in central Europe; tail white, with broad black band at end.

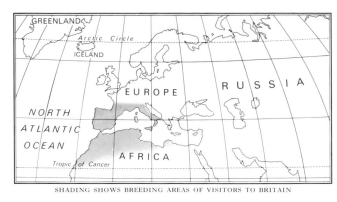

SHADING SHOWS BREEDING AREAS OF VISITORS TO BRITAIN

Visitors from south-west Europe and Africa

FEWER birds are likely to visit the British Isles from south-west Europe than from western or northern Europe, for Britain is not on the main migration routes from this region, as it is on those from north and west Europe. In winter, most of the south-west European birds travel south or south-west from their breeding areas, towards or into Africa.

Many of the south-west European birds are very infrequent and irregular visitors—wanderers which have reached Britain by overshooting their normal breeding grounds when returning from their winter quarters; others are young birds, scattering in the short interval between the end of the breeding season and the beginning of the southward migration.

Most of the birds shown here, including the collared pratincole, scops owl and subalpine warbler are Mediterranean species. The Alpine accentor is, as its name suggests, a bird of the mountains. Its nearest breeding areas are the Alps and the Pyrenees. The Alpine swift breeds throughout much of southern Europe, north to Switzerland.

Until recently, of all the south-west European visitors, only the black-winged stilt, which has nested three times, and the bee-eater, which has nested twice, had ever been known to breed within the British Isles. Now, however, following a remarkable surge in numbers in the 1990s, little egrets have begun to breed in Dorset and look set to spread.

If few birds from south-west Europe can wander to Britain, fewer still are likely to come from Africa. Indeed, of the birds shown here, only the cream-coloured courser and ruddy shelduck may have done so. Equally, the few which have reached the British Isles may have come from south-west Asia since both species inhabit that region too.

SHORT-TOED LARK
Calandrella brachydactyla 5½ in.
Vagrant, most often to Fair Isle but now annual in southern and eastern England in spring and autumn; short straight beak; underparts almost white, unstreaked.

BEE-EATER
Merops apiaster 11 in.
Vagrant, mainly to south-east in summer, but also recorded in spring and autumn; bred Sussex 1955; brilliantly coloured with chestnut, yellow, blue-green and black.

ROLLER
Coracias garrulus 12 in.
Vagrant, mainly to southern England on spring and autumn migration; used to breed as far north as southern Sweden; blue-green plumage, with chestnut back.

SUBALPINE WARBLER
Sylvia cantillans 4¾ in.
Vagrant, mainly on coasts in spring and autumn; in spring has blue-grey back, pink breast and narrow white 'moustache' stripe; paler than Dartford warbler.

ALPINE ACCENTOR
Prunella collaris 7 in.
Rare vagrant, mainly to southern England in autumn; like a large, pale hedge sparrow, with black spots on whitish chin and throat; streaked red-brown back.

BLACK-EARED WHEATEAR
Oenanthe hispanica 5¾ in.
Very rare spring and autumn vagrant to widely scattered counties; largely black and white, with prominent black face-patch; sandy coloured back, with white rump.

CREAM-COLOURED COURSER
Cursorius cursor 9 in.
Rare vagrant from African or Asian deserts, most often to southern England in autumn; pale sandy plover-like bird with black wing-tips; runs rapidly on open ground.

COLLARED PRATINCOLE
Glareola pratincola 10 in.
Vagrant, mainly to south and east England; mostly in May; long forked black tail, short bill; chin and throat light buff; back is grey-brown in spring.

BLACK-WINGED STILT
Himantopus himantopus 15 in.
Rare vagrant, mainly to south-east England in spring and autumn; bred Notts 1945, Cambs 1983, Norfolk 1987; thin straight bill; black and white plumage, pink legs 8 or 9 in long.

ALPINE SWIFT
Apus melba 8¼ in.
Vagrant, mainly to southern England in summer; large pale brown swift with white underparts except for a brown band across the breast; in flight looks like a small, pale hobby.

RUDDY SHELDUCK
Tadorna ferruginea 25 in.
Rare vagrant to many coastal counties, possibly from North Africa; birds seen singly could have escaped from waterfowl collections; goose-like, with deep buff plumage and pale head.

winter

summer

SCOPS OWL
Otus scops 7½ in.
Rare vagrant to scattered parts of Britain, mainly during April-June; probably on spring migration; smallest owl with ear-tufts likely to be seen in Britain.

WHISKERED TERN
Chlidonias hybrida 9¾ in.
Rare vagrant, mainly to south-east England on spring and autumn migration; black cap, white cheeks; resembles a dark Arctic tern; bill, legs and feet dark red.

LITTLE EGRET
Egretta garzetta 22 in.
Remarkable increase; many now throughout the year, especially on southern coasts, with some breeding in Dorset; all-white plumage, black legs; long head-plumes.

GREATER FLAMINGO
Phoenicopterus ruber 50 in.
Perhaps a vagrant, chiefly in autumn and winter to England; most British occurrences are probably escaped birds; pink and white plumage, with very long legs and neck.

SQUACCO HERON
Ardeola ralloides 18 in.
Rare vagrant, mainly to southern England in early summer; breeds in many parts of southern Europe, Asia, Africa; buff back and conspicuous white wings in flight.

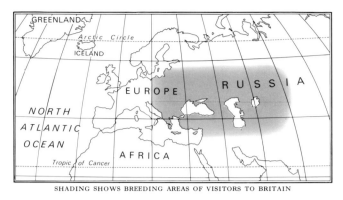

SHADING SHOWS BREEDING AREAS OF VISITORS TO BRITAIN

Visitors from eastern Europe and Asia

UNTIL 1832, the huge and bulky great bustard, a turkey-sized bird quite unlike any other in Europe, used to breed in Britain. But this strong and wary bird was driven out, probably by human interference. It is almost certainly lost to us for ever as a breeding bird, and today it occurs only as a very rare vagrant from eastern Europe, usually in winter.

The breeding range of many of Britain's eastern European visitors has its western limit on the North Sea in Denmark or northern Germany; these include the red-necked grebe, little crake, barred warbler and red-breasted flycatcher. For others, including the black stork, great bustard, greenish warbler, red-footed falcon, scarlet rosefinch and white-winged black tern, the limit is not so far west, although both the great bustard and black stork have separate breeding populations in Spain and Portugal.

The eastern European visitors seen most frequently in the British Isles, usually on the east coast, are the red-necked grebe, a winter visitor, the barred warbler, usually an autumn passage migrant, and the Mediterranean gull. This gull is a bird of remote origin in the Black and Aegean Seas, but in recent years an increasing number of them have taken to spending the winter on the south and east coasts, and a few pairs now breed.

Every year small numbers of yellow-browed warblers and Richard's pipits make a surprising journey from beyond the Ural Mountains to the east and south coasts of Britain. Normally they migrate to their winter quarters on a course that takes them nowhere near Britain. The red-breasted goose occurs much more rarely but is liable to get caught up in migrating flocks of other geese, such as white-fronts, which carry it off its proper course. When the flock of white-fronts reaches its wintering area, the stray may attach itself to a particular pair or family. But it is hard to see why the other two birds should wander so often and so far from their normal southward route. Richard's pipit has now been recorded in Britain over 2000 times; more than 100 occurred in Britain during exceptional influxes in several autumns since 1967.

The rose-coloured starling can also be classed as an Asian bird. Its main breeding area extends far into Asia, and though it also breeds as far west as the plains of the Danube, it is more likely to come to Britain from its more regular locations in Asia.

GLOSSY IBIS
Plegadis falcinellus 22 in.
Vagrant, mainly in autumn and winter on coasts of southern England and Ireland; plumage has bronze gloss; very round-winged in flight; long downward curving bill.

BLACK STORK
Ciconia nigra 38 in.
Rare vagrant, chiefly to southern England in May-June, but many other months except winter; breeds from eastern France eastwards, also Iberia; black plumage, white breast.

GREAT BUSTARD
Otis tarda 40 in.
Exceptionally rare vagrant to widely scattered counties, mainly in winter; bred in England until 1832; wings of both sexes show black and white markings when they fly.

SCARLET ROSEFINCH
Carpodacus erythrinus 5¾ in.
Scarce autumn visitor in a variety of English counties, but most numerous in northern Scottish islands; plump, with heavy bill and distinctive sharp 'chup' call. Bred Scotland 1982 and 1990.

ROSE-COLOURED STARLING
Sturnus roseus 8½ in.
Very irregular visitor, recorded especially in north-east Scotland, eastern England, mainly in June-August, also autumn; pink with black head, wings and tail.

RED-FOOTED FALCON
Falco vespertinus 12 in.
Irregular visitor, especially in late spring, chiefly to eastern and southern England, but has occurred elsewhere; legs and patch round each eye are bright red.

RED-BREASTED FLYCATCHER
Ficedula parva 4½ in.
Regular but scarce autumn passage migrant on east and south coasts; breeds eastward from Denmark, winters in India and Near East; white patches at the base of the tail.

BARRED WARBLER
Sylvia nisoria 6 in.
Fairly frequent autumn passage migrant found on the east coast of Britain; winters in North Africa and Arabia; a large warbler with grey back and long tail.

GREENISH WARBLER
Phylloscopus trochiloides 4¼ in.
Increasing but still rare autumn visitor to coastal counties; breeds on south side of Baltic; best distinguished from chiffchaff by voice and single pale wing-bar.

1 YELLOW-BROWED WARBLER
Phylloscopus inornatus 4 in.
Regular but scarce autumn passage migrant, especially in northern islands and on east coast.

2 RICHARD'S PIPIT
Anthus novaeseelandiae 7 in.
More than 2000 recorded, mostly in autumn in various coastal counties of Britain and on Fair Isle.

WHITE'S THRUSH
Turdus dauma 10¾ in.
Rare vagrant, mainly in winter to southern England, but also recorded in Scotland and Ireland; breeds in Siberia; black crescents on upper parts and underparts; black and white band under wing is distinctive when it flies; similar to mistle thrush, but larger and more boldly patterned.

RED-BREASTED GOOSE
Branta ruficollis 21½ in.
Rare vagrant in winter from west Siberian tundra, usually after being caught up in flocks of other geese and carried off its proper migration route; about 40 recorded in last two centuries; black and white, with red-brown throat and breast; white patch between eye and delicate black bill.

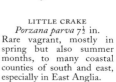

RED-NECKED GREBE
Podiceps grisegena 17 in.
Scarce but regular winter visitor, chiefly to eastern counties; has bred 2-3 times; neck is darker than great crested grebe's.

WHITE-WINGED BLACK TERN
Chlidonias leucopterus 9¼ in.
Rare vagrant, mainly in spring and autumn to south and east coasts; white wings in summer.

MEDITERRANEAN GULL
Larus melanocephalus 15 in.
Increasing visitor east and south coasts; bred southern England occasionally since 1968; like black-headed gull, but no black on wings.

LITTLE CRAKE
Porzana parva 7½ in.
Rare vagrant, mostly in spring but also summer months, to many coastal counties of south and east, especially in East Anglia.

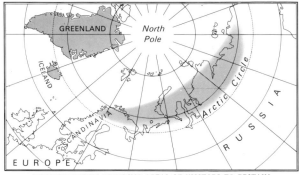

SHADING SHOWS BREEDING AREAS OF VISITORS TO BRITAIN

Visitors from the Arctic

A number of birds take advantage of the brief Arctic summer to breed within the region stretching from Greenland through Iceland, Spitsbergen and Lapland, and across Arctic Siberia. Most are marsh and water birds; few strictly land birds breed in the Arctic because of the lack of food.

A few birds not only breed but also spend the winter in the far north, on the fringe of the ice-pack; the king eider and ivory gull are among these. The rest usually fly south to warmer latitudes or spend the winter at sea.

The Orkneys and Shetlands are the first landfall for many of these northern birds. Even the colourful king eider drakes are recorded there quite frequently, especially in years when the Arctic winter is particularly severe and the polar ice-cap extends farther south than usual.

Other visitors, such as the glaucous gull and Greenland and Iceland forms of the gyr falcon, are most likely to be seen in the northern islands; but sometimes they also penetrate farther south into Scotland, England and Ireland as they move away from their breeding grounds. The weather, and the availability of food, determine when and how far into Britain these birds come.

The Arctic-breeding waders are more common, for their migrations take many of them far south of Britain, to parts of Europe and Africa. The purple sandpiper is a regular visitor to rocky shores around the entire coastline and has bred in Scotland; and the little stint and curlew sandpiper can be seen in autumn, resting or feeding on the coast before continuing on their long journey to Africa.

The pomarine and long-tailed skuas, grey phalarope, Sabine's gull and little auk normally winter at sea. The little auk regularly comes south into the North Sea, and is occasionally driven ashore in numbers by storms.

The others migrate to warmer waters, usually following routes which keep them over the sea. But gales may drive them to land. Some Sabine's gulls—many of which breed also in the North American Arctic—are regularly blown on to our western coasts in the autumn, and sometimes remain here all winter.

The navigational ability of birds is so remarkable that it seems unthinkable that it should ever go wrong; yet apparently this happens from time to time. Some of our rare visitors are so far off course that either they have only a rudimentary navigational sense or something has seriously dislocated its functioning. The Pechora pipit, for example, breeds in Arctic Russia and normally migrates in the autumn to south-east Asia, on a journey which takes it through China. Yet occasionally at migration time, Pechora pipits turn up in Britain thousands of miles off course, almost always on Fair Isle.

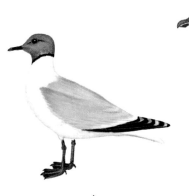

SABINE'S GULL
Larus sabini 13 in.
Scarce but regular visitor, mainly in autumn to Atlantic and Channel coasts; breeds Greenland, Spitsbergen, Arctic Russia; winters in South Atlantic; forked tail.

GLAUCOUS GULL
Larus hyperboreus 27 in.
Scarce winter visitor in north and east England, but sometimes abundant in Shetlands and on Scottish mainland; breeds Iceland, Arctic Russia; pale grey wings and mantle.

IVORY GULL
Pagophila eburnea 17½ in.
Rare winter vagrant in many counties but chiefly in Shetlands and Orkneys, from Spitsbergen and elsewhere in Arctic; normally winters on Arctic coasts; pure white plumage.

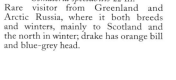

LONG-TAILED SKUA
Stercorarius longicaudus 21 in.
Regular but scarce passage migrant in autumn, mostly off east coast of England, migrating from Lapland to unknown, probably oceanic, winter quarters; very long tail feathers.

POMARINE SKUA
Stercorarius pomarinus 20 in.
Rather uncommon but regular passage migrant along both eastern and western coasts; breeds in Arctic Russia and Spitsbergen; winters off west coast of Africa.

KING EIDER
Somateria spectabilis 22 in.
Rare visitor from Greenland and Arctic Russia, where it both breeds and winters, mainly to Scotland and the north in winter; drake has orange bill and blue-grey head.

LITTLE STINT
Calidris minuta 5¼ in.
Mainly autumn passage migrant on eastern seaboard, moving from Arctic to winter quarters in Africa; occasionally seen on return passage; whitish breast and short bill; cream streaks on back.

TEMMINCK'S STINT
Calidris temminckii 5¼ in.
Scarce passage migrant from Lapland, seen in both spring and autumn, mostly in southern and eastern counties; has nested on a few occasions in northern Scotland; also Yorkshire; uniform grey plumage.

CURLEW SANDPIPER
Calidris ferruginea 7½ in.
Regular passage migrant, mainly in autumn down east coast, moving from breeding grounds in Siberia probably to Africa; also seen irregularly and in smaller numbers on return passage; like dunlin, with white rump.

RED-THROATED PIPIT
Anthus cervinus 5¾ in.
More than 200 recorded, mostly in May or autumn in Scottish islands; from Lapland or farther east; winters mainly in East Africa and southern Asia.

PECHORA PIPIT
Anthus gustavi 5¾ in.
Rare vagrant from Siberia, most often seen on Fair Isle in autumn; usual autumn migration through China to south-east Asia; like tree pipit, with two pale streaks down back.

PURPLE SANDPIPER
Calidris maritima 8¼ in.
Winter and autumn visitor from Iceland and Arctic to rocky coasts, especially in north and west; has bred in Scotland; slate-grey back, yellow legs and bill.

winter

summer

summer

winter

LITTLE AUK
Alle alle 8 in.
Winter visitor from Spitsbergen, to North Sea coast south to Norfolk but is irregular round other coasts; outside breeding season usually remains at sea near pack-ice; very short bill.

GREY PHALAROPE
Phalaropus fulicarius 8 in.
Regular passage migrant from Iceland, in autumn and rarely in spring, on coasts of Ireland, Wales, south-west and south England; normally winters in South Atlantic.

GYR FALCON
Falco rusticolus 21 in.
Three geographical forms occur—Iceland, Greenland and gyr, from Scandinavia and Arctic Europe; white form of Greenland form is the most frequent visitor.

SHADING SHOWS BREEDING AREAS OF VISITORS TO BRITAIN

Visitors from North America and the Oceans

EVERY year numbers of North American birds are carried across the Atlantic by cross-winds while they are making their autumn migration—in most cases southward down the east coast of Canada and the United States. The majority of these birds are waders, such as the long-billed dowitcher, the lesser yellowlegs, and the buff-breasted sandpiper, pectoral sandpiper and white-rumped sandpiper. These are the most numerous of the score or so of American waders which have been recorded on our shores. The next most numerous group is water birds such as the American bittern, Iceland gull (which comes from Greenland, despite its name), snow goose, blue-winged teal, American wigeon and surf scoter.

But land birds make the journey, too. The yellow-billed cuckoo is among those most frequently recorded; and in recent years there have been sightings of the American robin, Baltimore oriole, red-eyed vireo and white-throated sparrow (see p. 462). Since 1951, as many as 50 species of American land birds have been recorded here for the first time. Only since about 1952 have the majority of British ornithologists come to accept that these birds can fly completely across the Atlantic helped only by the wind. Before this it was always assumed that they must have travelled at least part of the way on board ship. Possibly a few of them do make part of the Atlantic crossing on ships, but this no longer debars them from a place on the official list of British birds. Species brought here deliberately by man, on the other hand, are not credited with a place on the list unless they escape from captivity and breed successfully in the wild.

The regular appearance in waters off the British Isles in late summer or autumn of small numbers of sooty and great shearwaters is one of the highlights of the year for British bird-watchers. The sooty shearwater breeds only on remote islands in the southern oceans, around New Zealand and south of South America; its nearest breeding places to Britain are around the Falkland Islands. The great shearwater breeds only on the Tristan da Cunha group in the South Atlantic. Both species migrate in large loops round the Atlantic each year, and the fringes of their migrations just touch the British Isles.

The appearance of Cory's shearwater is less remarkable because it breeds as near to us as the Berlenga Islands off the coast of Portugal, as well as in Madeira, the Canaries and the Azores. What is remarkable is that it is the least frequent visitor of the three rare shearwaters, appearing as a late summer wanderer in the Western Approaches.

SNOW GOOSE
Anser caerulescens 28 in.
Winter vagrant mainly in Ireland; breeds across Arctic America and usually winters in western states; two forms, one white with black wing-tips, other dark with white head.

AMERICAN BITTERN
Botaurus lentiginosus 30 in.
An infrequent vagrant from North America; occurs in Britain usually in autumn; breeds from Arctic to California, winters in southern states and Central America.

GREAT SHEARWATER
Puffinus gravis 18 in.
Regular late summer and autumn visitor off Outer Hebrides, south-west Ireland and south-west England; breeds in islands of Tristan da Cunha group; dark cap and white patch on upper part of tail.

CORY'S SHEARWATER
Calonectris diomedea 18 in.
Late summer wanderer, mostly off south-west England on post-breeding dispersal from Madeira and other Atlantic islands right across Atlantic; lacks great shearwater's black cap; pale bill.

SOOTY SHEARWATER
Puffinus griseus 16 in.
Regular late summer and autumn visitor in small numbers round all coasts; breeds around New Zealand and south of South America; sooty brown plumage with paler tract under long, narrow wings.

ICELAND GULL
Larus glaucoides 22 in.
Scarce winter visitor, mainly to northern isles; breeds in Greenland, and winters south to New York and in Iceland; smaller than glaucous gull, with more black on young bird's bill.

LESSER YELLOWLEGS
Tringa flavipes 10 in.
Irregular but increasing autumn vagrant, now recorded in many counties; breeds widely in Canada and winters from southern U.S.A. to Argentina; bright yellow legs.

LONG-BILLED DOWITCHER
Limnodromus scolopaceus 11½ in.
Scarce but increasing autumn vagrant to various counties; breeds in eastern U.S.A. and winters in southern U.S.A. and northern South America; grey with white rump and lower back.

PECTORAL SANDPIPER
Calidris melanotos 9 in.
North American sandpiper most frequently reported on this side of Atlantic; mainly autumn vagrant from Canada, chiefly to eastern counties of England and Scillies; normally winters in South America.

BUFF-BREASTED SANDPIPER
Tryngites subruficollis 8 in.
Rare but increasing vagrant, mainly in autumn, usually to eastern and western coastal counties; breeds in Arctic tundra and winters on South American pampas; buff plumage; usually seen on dry ground.

YELLOW-BILLED CUCKOO
Coccyzus americanus 12 in.
One of the North American land birds seen most frequently in Britain, usually on west side in autumn; breeds in North America; winters in South America; chestnut on wings, white marks on tail.

SURF SCOTER
Melanitta perspicillata 20 in.
Scarce winter vagrant from north-west Canada, mainly to northern isles of Scotland; usually winters on Atlantic and Pacific coasts of U.S.A. and on Great Lakes.

BLUE-WINGED TEAL
Anas discors 15½ in.
Over 100 winter vagrants recorded in all parts of British Isles; breeds in east and central North America; winters in Bahamas, West Indies, South America.

AMERICAN WIGEON
Anas americana 20 in.
Rare winter vagrant, mainly in western areas; normally breeds in North America; winters in Central America; head pattern distinguishes it from European wigeon.

Birds introduced to Britain

THE birds which man has introduced to the British Isles are mostly game birds or ornamental waterfowl. Some have escaped or have been released deliberately and now breed in such large numbers in the wild that they are considered officially to be native British birds. This category includes the pheasant (p. 69), the golden pheasant, Lady Amherst's pheasant, the red-legged partridge (p. 70) and the capercaillie (p. 152). Two other introduced game-bird species— Reeves's pheasant and the bobwhite quail—

still breed in only small numbers in the wild.

The introduced waterfowl that have become natives—mandarin duck, Egyptian goose, mute swan (p. 191), Canada goose (p. 193) and gadwall—were brought in like the non-native ruddy duck to embellish landowners' estates or as part of a waterfowl collection, such as that of the Wildfowl Trust at Slimbridge. The latest to have become established, as the result of cage-birds escaping, is the ring-necked parakeet, a native of Africa and southern Asia.

LADY AMHERST'S PHEASANT
Chrysolophus amherstiae 23 in.
Ornamental pheasant from East Asia, breeds around Woburn, Beds.; introduced for ornament; dark green and white cock; hen brown, with yellow eyes and grey legs.

REEVES'S PHEASANT
Syrmaticus reevesi 36 in.
Ornamental pheasant from Asia; bred near Inverness during last century but died out; recently re-introduced to Scottish Highlands; largest pheasant in Britain, tail over 6ft long.

RING-NECKED PARAKEET
Psittacula krameri 16 in.
Since about 1970, this long-tailed, small green parrot has been breeding in parks and gardens in Kent and South London. It shows signs of becoming established.

BOBWHITE QUAIL
Colinus virginianus 9½ in.
North American game-bird, released in large numbers for shooting on estates in Suffolk, the Cotswolds and Isles of Scilly; but few have survived; white markings on face; perches in trees.

GOLDEN PHEASANT
Chrysolophus pictus 23 in.
Ornamental pheasant from East Asia; small numbers, probably released for shooting, nest in Breckland and elsewhere; brilliant red and yellow cock; hen paler brown than hen of common pheasant.

BARBARY DOVE
Streptopelia risoria 9½ in.
Escaped cage-birds may be establishing themselves in Lancashire and elsewhere, alongside the closely related collared dove; not known as a wild bird abroad; pale fawn plumage, with black half-collar.

MANDARIN DUCK
Aix galericulata 17 in.
Ornamental duck from China; breeds wild in south-east England—mainly Surrey and east Berkshire—Perth and elsewhere; drake has orange-chestnut wing-fans; duck grey-brown.

RUDDY DUCK
Oxyura jamaicensis 15½ in.
North American duck, escaped from waterfowl collections, increasingly common in central and southern England, where it now nests regularly. Has now spread to Scotland

EGYPTIAN GOOSE
Alopochen aegyptiacus 25 in.
Ornamental waterfowl from Africa; wild breeding populations are established in north Norfolk and elsewhere; dark brown patches on face and breast, brown ring at base of neck.

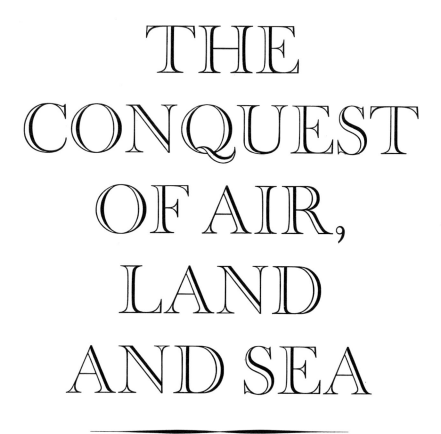

THE CONQUEST OF AIR, LAND AND SEA

Birds have been on earth for at least
150 million years, have diversified into thousands
of different species and in terms of sheer numbers have
probably surpassed mankind's present total of more than
3000 million. Their ability to fly is the main reason for this
spectacular success, but not the only one. Birds are well
adapted to live on land, too; and some species are
at home in the sea, where all life began.

CONTENTS

The ancestors of birds

EVOLUTION: THE RECORD IN THE ROCKS

O N a day unimaginably distant, when the continents had not yet begun to drift apart, a creature with the jaws of a reptile and the feathers of a bird was drowned in the warm, shallow waters of a chain of mud-flats. Its body, fossilised and silted over, lay undisturbed for 147 million years, until it was unearthed by a workman quarrying slate for lithographic printing. The place was the Solnhofen district of Bavaria; the year was 1860, just one year after the publication of Darwin's *Origin of Species*; and the workman had discovered *Archaeopteryx lithographica*, the most famous missing link in history.

Darwin's difficulty had been to convince people that his theory of evolution was true, even though the fossil evidence was incomplete. He had predicted that great discoveries might well be made, but he could hardly have hoped for confirmation of his ideas so soon. For the message clearly written by *Archaeopteryx*, the 'ancient winged creature', in the Bavarian slate was that birds have descended from reptiles.

Archaeopteryx, about the size of a magpie, had a brain that was much more reptilian than bird-like. Its jaws had sockets to hold teeth, and it had a long, bony tail—both characteristics of reptiles. There were three separate fingers on each hand (modern birds have two), each with a claw; and there was little, if any, tendency for the hand and wrist bone to fuse together, as in modern birds. Above all, *Archaeopteryx* had no keel on its breastbone for the attachment of flight muscles. It probably relied mostly on gliding flight, but is thought to have been capable of weak flapping flight.

The first bird

Yet *Archaeopteryx* is rightly regarded as the first bird. Mainly this is because it had feathers, and was therefore warm-blooded. Its feathers were indistinguishable in structure from those of modern birds. Its legs and feet, too, were almost completely like those of modern birds. One digit on the foot was opposable to the others, in the way that a human thumb is opposable to the fingers; this meant that it was able to grasp with its feet, and therefore probably lived in trees. Its bones were honeycombed with air spaces—a common weight-saving adaptation in birds.

This fossil, which represents one stage between reptiles and modern birds, is now in the Natural History Museum in London. A

Birds in the vastness of time

Life on this globe began more than 3500 million years ago. If this immensity of time could be compressed into 24 hours, birds would have been on earth for just over 61 minutes; and modern man, *Homo sapiens*, would have made his first appearance about 12½ seconds ago.

Geologists divide time into eras—the Proterozoic ('Former Life'), Palaeozoic ('Ancient Life'), Mesozoic ('Middle Life') and Cainozoic ('Recent Life')—with each era sub-divided into periods.

Modern techniques, based on the rate of disintegration of radio-active elements in fossil-bearing rocks, allow an ever greater accuracy in determining the time span of different periods; and as more recent ages are approached, knowledge of the past becomes so much more precise that further subdivisions, called epochs, can be accurately dated.

On this chart the eras are divided into periods, except for the last era, the Cainozoic, which is broken down into its epochs.

ERA	PROTEROZOIC	PALAEOZOIC		
PERIOD/ EPOCH	Pre-Cambrian More than 3500 to 570 million years ago	Cambrian From 570 to 510 million years ago	Ordovician From 510 to 440 million years ago	Silurian From 440 to 408 millio[n] years ago
CRUST OF THE EARTH	Britain lies on a 'supercontinent'—the land-mass of Pangaea	Most of British Isles covered by water	Warm, shallow seas over much of Britain Volcanic activity in Wales forms present-day Snowdon, an eroded pile of lava and ashes	Sea over much of the British Isles is silted u[p] towards end of period
CLIMATE AND VEGETATION	Earth's atmosphere cools, forming seas and rivers; life begins—as primitive organisms in the sea	All life still in the sea		Coral grows in warm, shallow Midlands Sea; first simple land plants
ANIMAL LIFE				First backboned anima[ls] appear, in the sea

Left margin, reading vertically: FROM MORE THAN 3500 MILLION TO 195 MILLION YEARS AGO

second *Archaeopteryx* fossil, discovered in 1877, is in Berlin; since then a further five specimens have been discovered. All seven seem to have died on estuarine mud-flats, about 147 million years ago.

Generally, tree-living creatures are very uncommon as fossils; when they die, they fall to the ground and are soon eaten. For this reason, the record of bird fossils after *Archaeopteryx* is on the whole a poor one. During the 80-odd million years of the Cretaceous period, which began about 145 million years ago, only about a dozen different groups of birds are known to have left fossil remains. Most were seabirds—the most likely to be fossilised—and many are known only from a few bones. The most famous are both from Kansas—the huge flightless diver-like *Hesperornis* which was 6 ft long, and the tern-like *Ichthyornis* which had a well-developed keel on its breastbone, and was therefore presumably a good flyer. Other bones of the time have been described as like those of cormorants, flamingoes and geese, but the evidence is poor.

A 'species explosion'
There are better remains from the Eocene epoch (56–35 million years ago). Bones from herons, a vulture, and perhaps a form of kingfisher have been found in the London Clay; and remains assigned to flamingoes, rails, game-birds and New World vultures were deposited in the Paris basin and in North America. Other groups have been identified from the Oligocene epoch (35–23 million years ago) and the Miocene (23–25 million years ago). It seems certain that once flight was achieved there was a great 'species explosion' among birds as the possibilities of new modes of life were rapidly exploited. But the fossil record is extremely incomplete.

Land-birds and the smaller species are extremely poorly represented. Perhaps over-represented are a number of species which became big enough to resist or escape swiftly from predators, and reverted to flightlessness. Gigantic birds 7 ft high, and with skulls 18 in. long, are known from the Eocene epoch in North America (*Diatryma*) and the Oligocene and Miocene epochs in South America (*Phorusrhacus*).

Flightlessness was also often developed on oceanic islands where there were no predators. In New Zealand there were giant moas and flightless geese; Madagascar had *Aepyornis,* said to be the original of Sinbad the Sailor's fabled Roc; dodos lived on Mauritius; and two other islands in the Indian Ocean, Reunion and Rodriguez, had solitaires. All of these species are now extinct—victims of their inability to evade human predators.

Some early seabirds had clearly lost the power to fly: their wings had either been converted into paddles, as with the penguins (some Miocene penguins were 5 ft high), or they had been reduced until they were non-functional, as with *Hesperornis.*

The search for an ancestor
It is now widely accepted that birds are the direct descendants of small carnivorous dinosaurs. *Archaeopteryx* shares many skeletal novelties with them: indeed, one of the seven known *Archaeopteryx* specimens was wrongly identified for several years as a skeleton of *Compsognathus*, a small coelurosaur (hollow-boned lizard) which occurs in the same 147 million year-old rocks in Bavaria. The co-

HYLONOMUS A primitive early reptile which lived about 300 million years ago, and cannot have been far removed from the common ancestor of all later reptiles.

EUPARKERIA An example of the group of reptiles which was ancestral to birds and dinosaurs; lived about 241 million years ago.

			MESOZOIC		ERA
Devonian From 408 to 362 million years ago	**Carboniferous** From 362 to 290 million years ago	**Permian** From 290 to 245 million years ago	**Triassic** From 245 to 208 million years ago		PERIOD/ EPOCH
Sandstone rocks cover much of Britain; Scotland, Lake District, Wales and Ireland uplifted, but southern England under Devonian Sea	Volcanoes active in Scotland and Derbyshire	Volcanoes in southern England, north under sea	Britain covered by deserts, dotted with warm salt lakes and with a network of rivers		CRUST OF THE EARTH
Britain warm and semi-arid	Equatorial climate in Britain; lush swamp vegetation decays into coal-forming peat	Violent climatic change; Britain hot and arid, only 200–300 miles north of Equator	Most of British Isles hot and semi-arid		CLIMATE AND VEGETATION
Age of fishes First amphibians crawl out of lakes and rivers First air-breathing insects	Age of amphibians, creatures able to live on land or in water First primitive reptiles	Primitive reptiles spread over land	*Euparkeria* and other pseudosuchians; first small mammals; first dinosaurs		ANIMAL LIFE

elurosaurian dinosaurs which are closest to the ancestry of birds are the dromaeosaurs (running lizards), a group of lightly built, agile reptiles which included *Deinonynchus*. They and *Archaeopteryx* showed the same specialised wrist bones, which increased hand mobility; evidence of a close relationship.

It is likely that feathers first evolved in small carnivorous dinosaurs as a means of insulation. Down or body feathers and reptilian scales are connected—a feather is effectively a frayed scale. Birds probably arose from small, agile, feathered, tree-climbing dinosaurs which developed the ability to glide from tree to tree, thus avoiding ground-based predators. The hand claws of *Archaeopteryx* are remarkably similar to those of modern tree-climbing birds such as woodpeckers.

Going farther back in time, dinosaurs arose from a group of early Triassic reptiles called thecodonts (socket-toothed), some of which developed the ability to run on their hind legs. Among them was *Euparkeria*, which lived about 241 million years ago. The earliest reptiles known—small, superficially lizard-like animals such as *Hylonomus*—date back more than 300 million years to the Carboniferous Period.

Pterosaurs evolved flight independently from birds and had membranes connecting their hind and fore legs like present-day bats. They flourished for more than 150 million years and then, quite suddenly in geological terms, became extinct about 75 million years ago. Along with the dinosaurs on land, and the ichthyosaurs and plesiosaurs of the sea, they were the victims of a major extinction probably linked to the combined effects of a meteorite impact and volcanic activity.

The theory of natural selection, expounded by Darwin and confirmed by other scientists, explains how a creature like *Hylonomus* could have become one like *Euparkeria*; how something like *Euparkeria* could have led to *Archaeopteryx*; and how *Archaeopteryx* in turn could have led to modern birds.

Darwin's starting point was that living things vary. It was a matter of observation that every species produced more individuals than survived, and a logical deduction that this implied a struggle for existence. He argued that, in the struggle for existence, any inheritable variation giving its possessor a better chance than others of surviving to produce offspring will, by natural selection, spread in the population.

Secret in the cells

He knew little about the causes of variation, but today this subject is better understood. The secret of variation lies in the genes, 'information centres' carried in the body and sex cells, which control development. Genes are made up of complex molecules of deoxyribonucleic acid, or DNA, which are capable of duplicating themselves, and so duplicating the information they carry.

Basically, genetic variation arises by mutation—a random change in the genes. In the body cells the genes are present in pairs; but in the formation of the sex cells the pairs divide haphazardly to produce single sets. Sexual reproduction brings together two sets, one from each parent, to create a new individual.

Many variations are harmful, and are 'selected out' by other genes or do not persist in a population because the bird possessing

BIRDS IN THE VASTNESS OF TIME (CONTINUED)

ARCHAEOPTERYX The first fossil which can be described as a bird; it still had many reptilian features, including teeth and a long, bony tail; lived about 147 million years ago.

PTERANODON An example of the pterosaurs, a very successful group of reptiles which became extinct about 65 million years ago; it had a wing-span of up to 25 ft, but probably did little more than glide.

ERA	MESOZOIC		CAINOZOIC	
PERIOD/ EPOCH	**Jurassic** From 208 to 145 million years ago	**Cretaceous** From 145 to 65 million years ago	**Palaeocene and Eocene** From 65 to 35 million years ago	**Oligocene** From 35 to 23 million years ago
CRUST OF THE EARTH	Warm seas over much of Europe	A great rift in the earth's crust starts the continents drifting apart; microscopic plants form chalk deposits in southern England building up 1 ft every 30,000 years	Rocky Mountains formed in America Chalk Sea recedes from Britain in Palaeocene	Sea retreats from parts of Britain, but still covers much of Europe volcanoes in north and west of British Isles become extinct
CLIMATE AND VEGETATION	Seas retreat towards end of period; southern England becomes an area of freshwater swamps	Lush vegetation in swamplands covering southern England First flowering plants	Marshy, low-lying plains over most of British Isles; vegetation sub-tropical	Britain's climate turns colder; conifers replace sub-tropical vegetation
ANIMAL LIFE	Age of giant reptiles Dinosaurs dominate the land, pterosaurs the air and huge marine reptiles the sea *Archaeopteryx*, the first bird, in Bavaria	Age of giant reptiles continues, but change at end of period wipes out dinosaurs *Enaliornis* (possible early diver) found in England; *Apatornis* and *Hesperornis* found in Kansas	Most modern orders of insects found Birds diversify further: 15 different orders including herons, kingfishers and vultures in London Clay; flamingoes in Paris Basin	Many new bird species including first known kites and plovers; flightless *Phorusrhacus* in South America Ancestors of modern cats, bears and dogs evolve

them does not survive and breed. But any variation which gives even a slight advantage in the struggle for survival will, through natural selection, be reinforced.

Originally random variations making a bird better able to escape its enemies, find food or attract its mate will become part of the 'gene-pool' of a breeding population.

New species are formed as breeding populations, isolated from one another by barriers of land, sea, climate or behaviour, have their variations 'screened' by natural selection to the point where they can no longer breed with other populations. In the process known as 'adaptive radiation', each species has evolved its own special features according to its way of life. The hawfinch, for instance, has a short, tremendously powerful bill with which it cracks fruit stones; and the crossbill, another finch, has a specialist tool for extracting the seeds from pine cones—its cross-tipped bill.

Natural selection has also produced similarities between species which are not closely related, but which have been subjected to similar selective forces. This process, known as 'convergent evolution', has resulted, for instance, in owls and hawks—unlike in many other ways—all having strong, curved talons for gripping their prey and hooked bills for tearing flesh.

Evolution in modern times

Because of the Ice Age, few if any species can have been in Britain for longer than about 10,500 years. Yet in that time, differences have built up between some British birds and their European counterparts. Some of our resident birds—examples are the jay, coal tit and dipper—even have a British and an Irish

form; and in the outlying islands several local races have been differentiated. There are separate Hebridean races of the song thrush, stonechat, dunnock and wren; and in the wren, even the Shetland and St. Kilda populations are distinct.

Nearly all the distinct British forms tend to be duller in colour and often somewhat larger than the corresponding continental birds.

The two most striking variations in British birds are seen in the grouse and crows. The British red grouse does not assume a white plumage in winter as does the willow grouse, its counterpart on the Continent; and because of this it was once considered a separate species—the only one confined to Britain. The hooded crow has a grey body, and the carrion crow is all black; but where their ranges meet, a remarkable and stable hybrid zone is formed, with birds of every degree of intermediate plumage. The explanation seems to be that the carrion and hooded crows were separated from each other in different refuges during the Ice Age, and on meeting since have not proved so different that they are prevented from hybridising.

Evolution is not something which happened in the past and was then switched off, though thousands of species have become extinct because they have not evolved fast enough to keep pace with new challenges. At present there are some 8600 species of birds in the world, and the processes of variation and natural selection are still going on.

But man's understanding of how evolution works has introduced a new factor: the free play of natural selection can now be checked, either to save a species from extinction or to create a new species in captivity.

COMMON TERN A modern bird. Its reptilian ancestry can be traced in several features—including the scales on its legs and the structure of its palate and jaw. A major difference from reptiles is that birds have a four-chambered heart, which is much more efficient than the usual reptilian three-chambered heart.

Miocene	Pliocene	Pleistocene	Holocene	ERA
From 23 to 5 million years ago	From 5 to 1.64 million years ago	From 1.64 million to 10,500 years ago	From 10,500 years ago to present day	PERIOD/ EPOCH
Underground pressures buckle earth's crust, throwing up great mountain ranges—Alps, Andes and Himalayas Most of British Isles becomes dry land	British Isles begin to take roughly their present shape; present day mountains raised, but sea still covers parts of east and south England	Ice Age; glaciers cover much of Europe and North America in a series of invasions; ice sheet at its greatest extent reaches a line from the Severn to the Thames	Much as today Channel cuts off Britain from Europe about 7000 years ago	CRUST OF THE EARTH
Climate all over Europe damp and warm	Britain's climate similar to that of modern Tropics except at end of period	Forests flourish in warm inter-glacial periods	Much as today	CLIMATE AND VEGETATION
Most modern families of birds in existence; elephants spread from Africa into Europe	Mastodons roam as far north as Suffolk and Norfolk; Hominids (the family of man) appear	Man appears (first modern man, *Homo sapiens*, not until 400,000 years ago); woolly mammoths in Britain; ice invasions wipe out many species of birds; lions in Yorkshire in inter-glacial periods	All modern animals and birds evolved	ANIMAL LIFE

FINGERS A bird's hand has two fingers and a thumb; the fingers carry some of the primary flight feathers, which drive the bird through the air.

FOREARM Consists of two bones, the radius (front) and the ulna, which carries the secondary flight feathers.

UPPER ARM (humerus) In many birds this bone more than any other is honeycombed with air spaces, as a weight-saving adaptation. It is moved by the flight muscles, anchored to the breast.

SHOULDER BLADE (scapula)

BACKBONE Supports the rest of the skeleton and protects the spinal cord. Some of its bones, or vertebrae, are fused together, giving rigidity, and others are free, allowing movement.

RIBS Overlapping projections near the backbone—known as uncinate processes—add strength to the rib cage.

THIGH (femur) Anchorage point for some of the powerful leg muscles.

KNEE This joint is usually concealed by feathers.

HIP GIRDLE A firm, fused plate of bone, strong enough to stand the shock of landing; it also provides a broad surface for the attachment of leg muscles.

PLOUGHSHARE BONE (pygostyle) Consists of fused vertebrae; supports the tail and acts as an anchor point for its muscles.

WISHBONE Formed by fusion of the collarbones at their base; helps to brace wings from the body in flight.

CORACOID A strong strut which braces the wings away from the body in flight.

BREASTBONE (sternum) Deep keel provides anchorage for the powerful flight muscles.

SHIN It is lengthened by fusion with some of the ankle bones.

FALSE 'KNEE' What looks like a knee is in fact a mid-ankle joint.

FALSE 'SHIN' What looks like the bird's shin is formed by the fusion of bones from the lower ankle and upper foot.

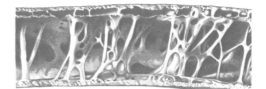

HONEYCOMBED BONE

The upper arm bone of most birds is hollow—a cavity criss-crossed with struts to give both strength and lightness. This adaptation is most pronounced in large gliding and soaring birds.

Designed for flight

THE ANATOMY OF BIRDS

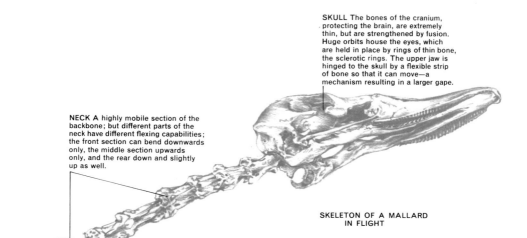

SKULL The bones of the cranium, protecting the brain, are extremely thin, but are strengthened by fusion. Huge orbits house the eyes, which are held in place by rings of thin bone, the sclerotic rings. The upper jaw is hinged to the skull by a flexible strip of bone so that it can move—a mechanism resulting in a larger gape.

NECK A highly mobile section of the backbone; but different parts of the neck have different flexing capabilities; the front section can bend downwards only, the middle section upwards only, and the rear down and slightly up as well.

SKELETON OF A MALLARD IN FLIGHT

THE demands of flight impose strict limitations on the size and shape of birds. Their bodies must combine extreme lightness with compact, robust construction, to an extent unparalleled in creatures which live on the ground.

A cross-section through the upper arm bone of most birds will reveal a remarkable weight-saving adaptation. The bone is hollow—honeycombed with air spaces. It is strengthened by criss-crossing struts, arranged like the struts on an aeroplane's framework. This honeycombing, or pneumatisation, is found in many other bones, especially in those of large gliding and soaring birds.

Fusion for strength

In those parts of its skeleton where strength is the paramount consideration, bones which were separate in the reptilian ancestors of birds have fused together, forming rigid girders and platforms. Such fusion strengthens bones in the skull, chest region, pelvis, wings and sections of the backbone but it is absent in the neck; a bird's neck must be able to twist and bend freely in feeding and preening, and as an aid to all-round vision. Flexibility is increased by the large number of neck vertebrae, ranging from 13 in some cuckoos and song-birds to 25 in swans; this compares with only seven for nearly all mammals—including giraffes.

The most striking feature of a bird's skeleton is its breastbone, a plate of bone with a keel jutting down to anchor the massive flight muscles. Generally, the deeper the keel, the more powerful the flight; in the course of evolution, it has vanished entirely in the case of some flightless birds. Another plate of bone, the hip girdle, needs to be firm, strong and rigid because it takes the entire weight of a bird on the ground; it must withstand the shocks and stresses of landing, hopping and running, as well as providing anchorage for the leg muscles.

A bird's knee lies close to its body, and is usually hidden by the feathers. What looks like a knee, bending the opposite way to a man's, is a joint in the mid-ankle position; some ankle bones are fused to the shin bone above, and the rest have knitted with some of the foot bones below, forming a longer lower leg.

The wing bones have been drastically modified from the original reptilian forelimbs, to meet the stresses of flight. The upper arm, or humerus, is moved by the flight muscles, anchored at their other end to the breastbone. One of the forearm bones, the ulna, bears the secondary flight feathers, which give a bird 'lift'. The primary feathers, which drive the bird through the air, are attached to the hand and to one of the bird's two fingers. What corresponds to a thumb bone forms an attachment point for the alula, a group of small feathers used to stabilise flight, especially at slow speeds.

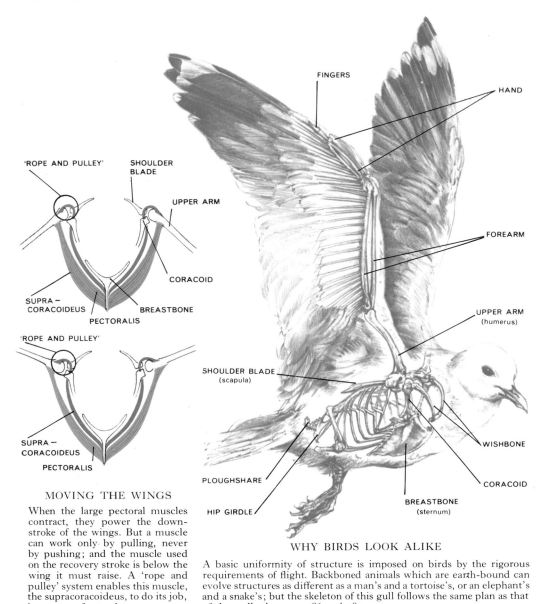

'ROPE AND PULLEY'   SHOULDER BLADE

UPPER ARM

CORACOID

SUPRA – CORACOIDEUS   BREASTBONE

PECTORALIS

'ROPE AND PULLEY'

SUPRA – CORACOIDEUS

PECTORALIS

FINGERS

HAND

FOREARM

UPPER ARM (humerus)

SHOULDER BLADE (scapula)

WISHBONE

PLOUGHSHARE

CORACOID

HIP GIRDLE

BREASTBONE (sternum)

MOVING THE WINGS

When the large pectoral muscles contract, they power the down-stroke of the wings. But a muscle can work only by pulling, never by pushing; and the muscle used on the recovery stroke is below the wing it must raise. A 'rope and pulley' system enables this muscle, the supracoracoideus, to do its job, by means of a tendon.

WHY BIRDS LOOK ALIKE

A basic uniformity of structure is imposed on birds by the rigorous requirements of flight. Backboned animals which are earth-bound can evolve structures as different as a man's and a tortoise's, or an elephant's and a snake's; but the skeleton of this gull follows the same plan as that of the mallard on pp. 286 and 287.

Muscles for energy and stamina

A bird has some 175 different muscles, controlling the movements of its wings, legs, feet, jaws, tongue, eyes, ears, neck, lungs, sound-producing organs, body wall and skin.

Largest of all are the pectorals, breast muscles, which contract to produce a down-beat, the wing's power stroke. In most birds they average about 15 per cent of body weight; and in pigeons, fast flyers with great stamina, the entire group of breast muscles accounts for more than a third of the body weight.

Apart from the massive breast muscles many others act in flight. The involuntary dermal (skin) muscles, for instance, which are at-tached to almost every feather follicle, can raise, lower, or move feathers sideways to assist flight manoeuvres.

The muscles of the neck are highly intricate. Some extend from only one vertebra to the next, while others link the movement of long series of vertebrae. The jaw muscles, too, are more complex than those of mammals.

Colour differences between muscles (seen in the familiar 'white meat' of a chicken's breast and the 'red meat' of its legs) are due to the relative proportions of three types of muscle fibres. Broad, white fibres are fuelled by glycogen, a carbohydrate, to provide the instant energy needed for explosive take-off and short bursts of rapid flight; the waste products of this process quickly accumulate and induce fatigue. Narrow, red fibres have greater stamina because they use blood-carried oxygen to burn fat, which leaves less waste. Intermediate fibres produce energy by a combination of both processes. White fibres predominate in the breast muscles of chickens, intermediate fibres in those of soaring birds such as kites.

The heart is a specialised muscle, pumping blood to other muscles and organs of the body. A human heart beats about 70 times a minute when the body is at rest; but birds live to a time scale of their own, much faster

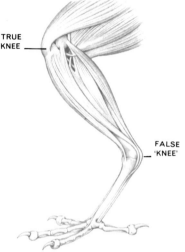

BICEPS FOREARM

POWER IN THE AIR

Bulky muscles, such as the massive pectorals (which in many birds account for about 15 per cent of body weight) are concentrated near a bird's centre of gravity, an arrangement which gives stability in flight. They transmit their power through long tendons, some of which move the limbs through a 'rope and pulley' mechanism.

PECTORAL   TRICEPS   ELBOW

TRUE KNEE

FALSE 'KNEE'

AIR SAC   LUNGS

GIZZARD (partly obscured by other organs)

CROP, Storage bag for food.

HEART

STOMACH

CLOACA   LIVER

POWER ON THE GROUND

A bird needs powerful leg muscles both for walking and for maintaining posture. The heaviest of the muscles are in the thigh, near to the bird's centre of gravity. Tendons stretch over the false 'knee' to operate the toes.

FUEL FOR THE MUSCLES

Muscles work by burning fuel, with the help of oxygen carried in the bloodstream. Food, also used for growth and the repair of body cells, is converted into fuel after being broken down by the bird's digestive processes. In the case of the pigeon, above, this includes a period in the gizzard, where rough or hard food is crushed. The liver hoards energy-giving sugar in the form of glycogen; and waste products are eliminated by the kidneys and excreted through the cloaca.

than ours. The heart of a North American humming-bird keeps up a fantastic patter of 1000 beats a minute; other examples, nearer home, are 570 beats a minute for a robin, 460 for a sparrow and 342 for a crow.

Like mammals, but unlike most reptiles, birds have evolved a four-chambered heart, consisting of two pumping chambers (the ventricles) and two receiving chambers (the auricles). In this, the most efficient circulation system known, 'used' blood is pumped by the right ventricle to the lungs, where it picks up a supply of oxygen. It returns to the left auricle and, still rich in oxygen, is pumped round the body by the left ventricle, returning to the heart through the right auricle. A human heart works in a similar way. Birds need this efficient two-pump heart because of the rate at which they use energy.

In general, the smaller the bird the larger its heart size relative to the rest of its body. Within a species the heart tends to be larger in those birds which live at high altitudes or in cold climates. A larger heart is also neces-

sary for long flights; a racing pigeon may have a heart up to 1·29 per cent of its body weight, while the similar-sized South American tinamous, which make only short flights, often have hearts making up only 0·19 per cent of their body weight.

A bird breathes with virtually the whole of its body, not just with its lungs, which are relatively small and capable of only slight expansion. The lungs are connected to the air sacs within the body, and these in turn are linked with many of the cavities within the bones, providing a more efficient use of inhaled air than in any other creature.

There is good evidence that breathing in flight is synchronised with wing-beats. A sparrow at rest breathes in and out 50 times a minute (the figure for a man is 9–14 times) and this rate can rise after flight to a flurry of panting which produces 212 breaths every minute. At the other extreme, when nestling swifts are left without food for long periods, they become torpid and their breathing rate may fall to as low as eight times a minute.

A world of sight and sound

HOW BIRDS GATHER INFORMATION ABOUT THEIR SURROUNDINGS

THE five senses in birds are adapted and attuned to their needs as flying creatures. Sight, the sense which provides the greatest possible amount of information at the fastest possible speed, has reached in birds a degree of perfection found in no other animal. Hearing, too, is acute within its limits. But the senses of smell, taste and touch are poorly developed compared with the stage they have reached in many mammals.

The keen eyesight of a bird

In almost every facet of its existence, a bird depends on sharp, wide-ranging vision. Predators need keen sight for spotting and catching their prey; victims need it for spotting and evading their enemies; birds which live in the open need to be able to change focus rapidly; and birds which live in thick cover need a rapid and reliable warning of the obstacles ahead as they dart through branches and bushes.

Every bird has eyes which are relatively huge; for the larger the eye, the greater number of light-sensitive cells it can hold, and the better the vision. All that shows from the outside is the protective cornea, but this is only a small part of the eye. If a human eye were as big in ratio to the rest of the head as, say, a starling's, men would have eyes the size of cricket balls; a starling's eye is proportionately about 15 times heavier than a man's.

Some large birds of prey, such as the golden eagle, have eyes which are actually bigger than a man's. They are, in fact, as large as they could be without becoming so heavy as to impair flight; and the ostrich, which has lost the power of flight, has the largest eyes of any creature living on land—five times as massive as human eyes.

Two other adaptations in the eyes of a bird are the pecten and the nictitating membrane. The pecten, a comb-shaped structure near the base of the eye, supplies it with blood and may also increase its ability to pick up faint images. The nictitating membrane is a transparent 'third eyelid', absent from most mammals, which cleans and protects the eye. In diving birds it often acts as a kind of contact lens, correcting the refraction of light which occurs under water.

A bird blinks by drawing this membrane sideways across its eye; because it is transparent, vision is never completely lost, even for a split second, except in sleep.

Birds have a reputation for high visual acuity —the ability to discern detail—but it is not in all cases fully deserved. The eyesight of many

HOW THE RADIUS OF VISION VARIES

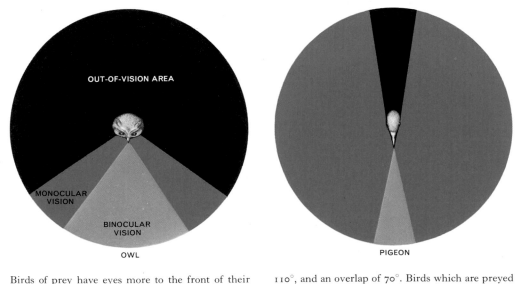

OWL

PIGEON

Birds of prey have eyes more to the front of their heads than most other birds—the best position for keeping an intended victim in view. This also allows them to judge distance accurately, for the visual fields of the two eyes overlap, giving an area of binocular, three-dimensional vision. The forward-facing eyes of the owl give a total visual field of 110°, and an overlap of 70°. Birds which are preyed upon have a different problem: danger can come from any direction, so their eyes are positioned at the sides of their heads, giving a greater total field of vision but limiting the angle of binocular sight. The pigeon has a total visual field of 340°, but its binocular vision extends over only 24°.

birds is no keener than man's, and in some small song-birds it is up to three times worse than man's. This is because, no matter how efficient its design, a very small eye can accommodate fewer light-sensitive cells than a human eye. With larger birds the reputation for keen eyesight is fully justified. The buzzard's eyes may be as much as eight times better than human eyes at picking out details.

Birds' eyes can also take a wide-angle 'snapshot' over a visual field which a man could cover only by slow scanning. They need this ability because of the speed with which danger can appear or a victim vanish; it is important, too, in migration, for birds probably navigate by assessing the rate at which the sun or stars move across the sky.

The angle of vision, controlling the amount of a bird's horizon which it can take in at a single glance, depends on the position of its eyes in its head and on the structure of the eye. Birds of prey have their eyes towards the front—the best position for keeping an intended victim in view. Grain- and seed-eaters, species which are preyed upon, need as wide a field of vision as possible, and have eyes at the sides.

Judging distance

The frontal position increases the angle of binocular vision, formed by the overlap of the visual fields of both eyes. Each eye relays to the brain a slightly different image of the same object, and these combine to make a three-dimensional picture which is essential for judging distance.

Binocular vision seems to be best developed in owls, whose forward-facing eyes have a total visual field of only 110°, but an overlap of 70°. Another predator, the kestrel, has a total field of 150° and an overlap of 50°.

The pigeon, basically a grain-eater, has a visual field of 340°, but its angle of binocular vision is only 24°; and the woodcock's total field, allowing for eye movement, actually spans a full circle, in effect giving the bird eyes in the back of its head.

Birds with only a small area of binocular vision establish distance by moving their heads to obtain different views of an object. This probably explains the bobbing head action of pigeons, chickens and moorhens, or the raising and lowering of the head seen in many waders.

Detection of moving objects, though, is easiest when the head is still; and many birds have a remarkable ability to hold the head in a fixed position despite body movement.

Focusing

The eyes themselves usually have little mobility within their orbits; and in the case of owls, none at all. Highly flexible necks compensate for this lack of mobility. An owl, turning its head almost in a full circle, or a robin, cocking its head as if to listen for worms on the lawn, are both keeping an object in focus by the only means available.

The ability to change focus rapidly is important to many birds, both for avoiding obstacles and for catching food in flight. A camera is focused by moving the lens towards or away from the film at the back; but birds focus by compressing the lens between two muscles to make it more convex. In hawks and owls the curvature of the cornea at the front of the eye can also be altered.

The range within which an eye can bring objects into sharp focus is measured in diopters. In humans, children have the widest range, with about 13·5 diopters, and this falls to 6 diopters at about 40 years old. Among birds, owls have the lowest range, with 2–4 diopters; pigeons range from 8–12 diopters;

TO MATCH A BIRD'S WAY OF LIFE

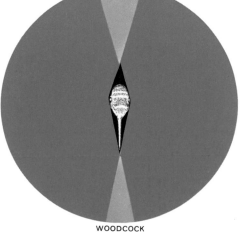

FRONT VIEW

BACK VIEW

SIDE VIEW

WOODCOCK

The woodcock is a bird which can literally see out of the back of its head. In the course of evolution its eyes have moved to a position high in its head, and well to the sides, allowing a full 360° visual field, but cutting the overlap between the fields of the two eyes; in fact the woodcock has a slightly larger field of binocular vision at the back than at the front. When the bird is probing for food, its bill up to the hilt in soft earth, it can still keep an alert look-out for an enemy approaching from any angle. In addition, the woodcock has ears which are slightly to the front—below the eyes. They occupy this unusual position because there is no room for them anywhere else.

EYESIGHT EIGHT TIMES KEENER THAN MAN'S

SCLEROTIC RING Bony ring which protects the eye and maintains its shape.

CORNEA Transparent protective cover which refracts light into rough focus on the lens.

IRIS Muscular sheet which expands or contracts to alter the size of the pupil.

LENS Throws an image in sharp focus on to the retina.

PUPIL Controls the amount of light entering the eye behind it.

LENS MUSCLES Alter the shape of the lens by squeezing or relaxing, and so control focusing.

Enlargement of retina, showing:
RODS ONLY

RODS AND CONES

CONES ONLY

RETINA Screen, containing light-sensitive rods and cones, and the nerve fibres and cells serving them.

OPTIC NERVE Transmits images from the retina to the brain.

PECTEN Structure full of blood vessels, which probably nourishes the eye, and probably cuts down dazzle.

The globose, or rounded, eye of the buzzard: the cells of the retina consist of rods (with great light-gathering power), and cones (necessary for keen vision and colour perception). Sight is sharpest on that part of the retina called the fovea. It also has most cells: the buzzard has 1 million per square millimetre (an area the size of a pin-head) compared with man's 200,000.

BIRD'S EYE VIEW

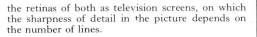

MAN'S EYE VIEW

The ability to discern detail sharply may be as much as eight times keener in a buzzard than in a man. The difference may be illustrated by imagining the retinas of both as television screens, on which the sharpness of detail in the picture depends on the number of lines.

and cormorants, by squeezing the cornea, can produce a range of 40–50 diopters.

Birds see colours essentially in the same way as humans do. This is suggested by their use of colours in display, and as an aid to identifying food. But there is one significant difference. Many birds have droplets of oil in their eyes: red, orange, yellow, transparent and, rarely, green. These probably act as filters, improving vision in hazy conditions and sharpening the contrast between their prey and the background vegetation.

Human eyes are spherical, but the eyes of most birds are flattened at the front—a shape which increases the area of retina on which an image can fall. This shape also makes for a weaker structure, but the deficiency is overcome by a ring of small bones, the sclerotic ring, which supports the eye at the front.

But there are exceptions to the rule that birds' eyes are flat. The globose, or rounded, shape of the eyes of day-hunters enables hawks and falcons to isolate their prey at great distances, because it helps to increase the size of the image falling on the retina, and so to stimulate more light-sensitive cells. In the tubular eyes of owls, the pupil and lens are greatly enlarged, increasing the light-gathering power of the eye; and the large, almost spherical lens throws a small, bright image on to the retina.

The retina of an owl also contains a high proportion of cells with poor visual acuity and no colour perception, but great sensitivity to light. The result is a gain in light-gathering efficiency so great that long-eared owls and barn owls can see in light up to 100 times poorer than the minimum needed by a human.

The sense of hearing

Birds depend on sound for communication of many kinds; their flight-notes help to keep flocks together, and alarm calls and songs play an important part in mating and in guarding territory. Sound also plays a part in food-hunting. There is experimental evidence to show that golden plovers and lapwings, at least, actually listen for earthworms burrowing underground; and experiments have shown that barn owls can find their prey in pitch darkness, by sound alone.

Some song-birds have a hearing range similar to that of a normal human ear: 20–20,000 cycles, or vibrations, per second. But for most birds the range is narrower. The crow and mallard are limited to a range of 300–8000

cycles; the pigeon to 50–11,500 cycles; and the long-eared owl to 100–18,000 cycles. None of these birds would be able to hear the lowest note on a piano, which registers 27 cycles, though the 4000 cycles of a piano's top note would be well within their range.

Birds are receptive mainly to sounds pitched at the same level as their own voices; and it has been claimed that sparrows and canaries may not be able to hear a normal low-toned human conversation.

Birds hear sound faster than humans, picking out details of song which are too rapid for the human ear to distinguish. This was graphically demonstrated when a scientist tape-recorded the American whip-poor-will's song, played it back eight times slower than it was recorded, and found that the bird's distinctive 'whip-poor-will' call was actually 'whip-pup-poor-will'.

To find out what other birds heard, the voice of a mocking bird was recorded while it was mimicking the whip-poor-will; and when the tape was again slowed down, the mocking bird was heard calling 'whip-pup-poor-will', putting in the note that was too fast for the human ear.

Locating sound

Like mammals, birds pinpoint the source of a sound by instinctively assessing the time lag between its arrival at either side of the head. Because of the time factor, it is easier to locate a series of brief sounds rather than one continuous note. This probably explains why the alarm call given by many birds when a hawk is near is a pure tone, with a gradual beginning and end, and not a position-betraying series of rapid notes.

Most mammals have external ears to help in locating sounds, but birds have no 'outside' ears. The nearest equivalent is a flap of skin, fringed by feathers, cupping the front edge of the ear-opening in owls.

The 'ears' of long-eared and short-eared owls are simply tufts of feathers, which have no connection with hearing but are used in courtship or aggressive display. The actual ears of many owls are placed asymmetrically on the sides of their wide heads, exaggerating the time-lag between the reception of sound by each ear.

As in other mammals, including man, a bird's ears also control its equilibrium. It is likely that the ear originally evolved in back-boned animals not as an instrument of hearing, but as an organ of balance.

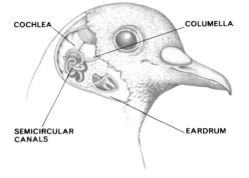

INSIDE A PIGEON'S EAR

Pressure of fluid on microscopic hairs in the semi-circular canals maintains balance. Sound produces vibrations in the eardrum which are transmitted by the columella bone, and translated to nervous impulses by the cochlea, a fluid-filled tube.

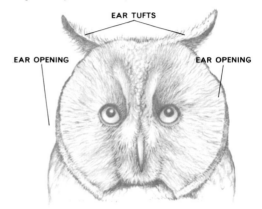

PINPOINTING SOUND

The long-eared owl's ears are placed asymmetrically on its head, increasing the time-lag between the arrival at each ear of the same sound wave, so allowing the bird to pinpoint the source of the sound. The 'ear' tufts have no hearing function.

Touch, taste and smell

Since most birds find their food by sight, the sense of smell is of little value to them. Experiments suggest that even vultures, feeding on decaying carrion, are guided to it by their eyes, not their sense of smell.

The nasal chambers are directly connected to the mouth as well as the nostrils, and it is thought that this ability to smell food while it is in the mouth allows birds such as falcons and owls to spit out tainted meat from their beaks.

In seabirds, the nasal glands are highly developed; they produce a secretion which traps dust particles and removes excess salt. The nasal chambers of petrels and some other gliders have another function, divorced from smell. On either side of the nasal partition these birds have a pocket-like flap which can be distended and may act as an air-pressure indicator, helping to regulate their skilful gliding flight.

All birds possess senses of taste and touch, but they are poorly developed—probably because birds in general have to snatch their food quickly and rely on vision to discern good from bad.

The taste buds are mainly at the base of the tongue and on the palate, and are similar to those of mammals, though far fewer in number. Bullfinches and pigeons have 50–60, starlings 200, and parrots 300–400, compared with 3000 in man and 17,000 on the tongue of a rabbit.

What the bird's taste buds actually taste is in doubt; chickens can apparently distinguish several sugars and the bitter taste of quinine, while pigeons seem to prefer salty foods. No thorough experiments have been carried out on any wild birds.

Touch, which includes the sensations of heat, cold and pain, is perceived in essentially the same way as by man, through nerve endings in the skin.

But birds have a more rudimentary system than ours, and their nerve endings tend to be concentrated in easily exposed areas of skin. Birds, though, do have specialised touch receptors, called Herbst's corpuscles, which occur in other parts of the body and are probably especially sensitive to vibrations and pressure changes. Stories were told during the First World War of birds reacting to the vibrations of naval battles taking place up to 120 miles distant.

The versatility of feathers

AN ADAPTATION THAT MAKES BIRDS UNIQUE

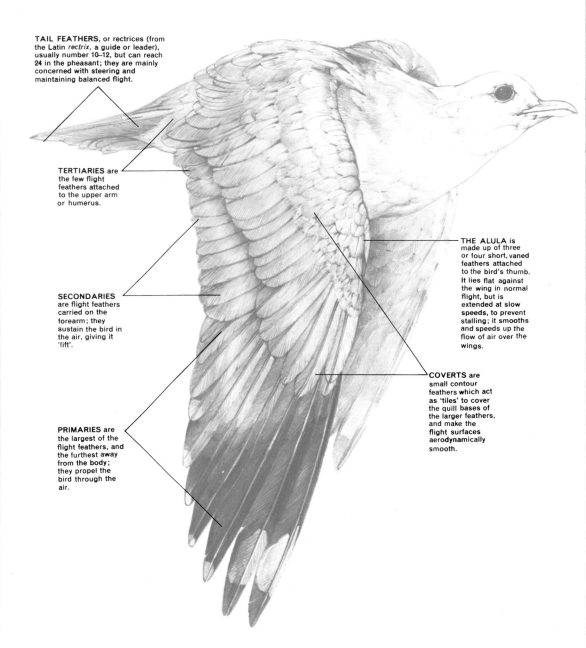

TAIL FEATHERS, or rectrices (from the Latin *rectrix*, a guide or leader), usually number 10–12, but can reach 24 in the pheasant; they are mainly concerned with steering and maintaining balanced flight.

TERTIARIES are the few flight feathers attached to the upper arm or humerus.

SECONDARIES are flight feathers carried on the forearm; they sustain the bird in the air, giving it 'lift'.

PRIMARIES are the largest of the flight feathers, and the furthest away from the body; they propel the bird through the air.

THE ALULA is made up of three or four short, vaned feathers attached to the bird's thumb. It lies flat against the wing in normal flight, but is extended at slow speeds, to prevent stalling; it smooths and speeds up the flow of air over the wings.

COVERTS are small contour feathers which act as 'tiles' to cover the quill bases of the larger feathers, and make the flight surfaces aerodynamically smooth.

IT is not the power of flight that sets birds in a class of their own; for bats and insects can fly, and some birds cannot. What distinguishes them from all other animals, present or past, is that they have feathers.

The main functions of feathers—flight, heat conservation, waterproofing, camouflage and display—are all crucial to the existence of birds. Yet their origin is a mystery; there is no clue as to how feathers evolved from the scales of reptiles. So far as can be told, they were fully developed in the earliest bird of which fossils have been found, *Archaeopteryx*, which lived 150 million years ago. Scientists can only deduce that feathers evolved from scales as a primitive, fluffy insulation, and later developed into the highly complex structure which seems complete in *Archaeopteryx*. But until the fossilised 'missing link' is found, the intermediate stage will remain an enigma.

Types of feathers
Feathers, whatever their origins, are of two main kinds: outer flight and contour feathers (pennae), which give the bird its shape and provide insulation, and inner down feathers (plumulae), which provide an extra insulating coat. Other types are either intermediate

between these two basic kinds or seem to be derived from them.

Filoplume feathers (the 'hairs' on a plucked fowl) grow around the base of contour and down feathers; they seem to be degenerate feathers with no known function, except in the case of some foreign species in which they have been developed as display plumes.

Powder-down feathers, which are found in herons, bitterns and hawks, are the only feathers which grow continuously and are never moulted; instead, their tips continually disintegrate into a fine, water-resistant powder, used in preening to waterproof and preserve the other feathers. In the fish-eaters, this process is particularly important, for the powder helps to eliminate fish slime.

In addition to these types of feathers, a few birds, such as the nightjar, have bristles around their mouths to increase the area with which to catch insects during flight; and cuckoos have bristles which seem to act as eyelashes.

The structure of a flight feather

The typical flight or contour feather is made up of a central shaft, hollow at its base for conveying nourishment, and becoming solid for strength further up, in a part called the rachis, where the two webs of the vane are supported.

These webs are marvellously intricate structures which can only be appreciated in full under a microscope. They consist of hundreds of parallel filaments or barbs, each virtually a complete feather in itself. For every barb in turn carries several hundred tiny barbules, equipped with minute hooks. The hooks catch on the barbules from the next barb above them—a fastening system so efficient that if two barbs are separated and the web is split, the bird has only to draw the feather through its beak a few times to restore the entire web. A ruffled feather can be restored to shape even by running it between a human finger and thumb.

Feathers as insulators

Often, the vaned feather grows a secondary after-feather from a tiny opening at the point where the base and rachis meet. This after-feather is usually small and downy, and was probably developed as an extra layer of insulation against heat loss.

Down feathers are fluffy because their barbules have no hooks. Their main function is heat preservation—the same purpose as the semi-plume feathers which lie under the covering of contour feathers.

When a bird fluffs itself out in cold weather, it is giving itself a thicker blanket of warm air between its inner and outer covering of feathers. Conversely, in warm weather the bird often disarranges its outer feathers to speed up the process of heat loss.

Birds need effective insulation, especially against cold, because they live at what for a human would be fever heat: they must maintain a body temperature of about 41 °C (106 °F). In very severe winters, when food is scarce, even feathers cannot always prevent

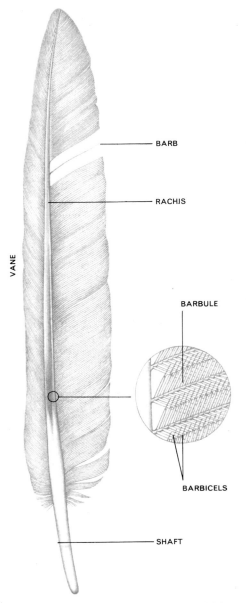

BARB

RACHIS

VANE

BARBULE

BARBICELS

SHAFT

A FEATHER UNDER THE MICROSCOPE

The amazingly complex mesh of a vaned feather, as only a microscope can reveal it. The magnification shows how each barb of the vane is in effect a miniature feather. The top row of barbules, carried on the barbs, in turn carry minute hooks—the barbicels; and each hooked barbule interlocks with its unhooked neighbour on the next barb.

birds from freezing to death. Millions of birds in Britain, weakened by starvation, died in this way in the winter of 1962–3.

Body size is the main factor affecting the number of feathers on a bird. A large bird, such as a swan, can carry more than 25,000, while most small song-birds have 1500–3000. These smaller birds, though, have more feathers weight-for-weight—which is to be expected, since they have relatively more heat-losing surface.

The number of feathers can vary considerably, even between two birds of the same sex and species. But all birds carry more feathers in winter. This was spectacularly illustrated when an American ornithologist counted the feathers on two female white-throated sparrows (more closely related to British finches than to our sparrows). One count, taken in

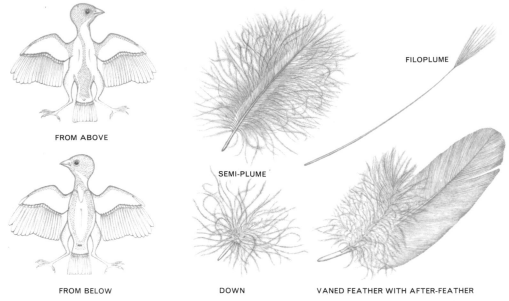

FROM ABOVE

FROM BELOW

FILOPLUME

SEMI-PLUME

DOWN

VANED FEATHER WITH AFTER-FEATHER

FEATHER DISTRIBUTION

Shaded areas show the main tracts, or pterylae, from which feathers grow. The example shows a pigeon, but the way in which the tracts are distributed is typical of most other species.

FOUR KINDS OF FEATHER

Down feathers and vaned outer feathers are the basic types from which the others seem to be derived. The down feather has a minute central shaft and fluffy barbs; the vaned feather has a long shaft with interlocked barbs, and may have a small, downy after-feather at its base; the semi-plume has elements of both in its distinct shaft and fluffy barbs; and the filoplume is a hair-like feather with a vestige of barbs.

February, added up to 2710 vaned feathers; the other, in October, totalled only 1508.

Because of the tremendous density of its plumage, a bird's feathers can weigh a good deal more than its skeleton—in some cases more than twice as much. The best known example of this is the American bald eagle (the equivalent of the sea eagle, a rare winter visitor to Britain). One specimen of a bald eagle had vaned feathers weighing 1 lb 4½ oz. and down feathers adding another 3⅕ oz., while its entire skeleton weighed only 9½ oz. The proportional weight of feathers to bones in British birds of prey is likely to be similar.

Variations in the quantity of down at hatching range from the thick covering of grouse, pheasants, ducks and owls, through the scanty coats of sparrows, warblers and thrushes, to the almost complete absence of any natal covering at all in woodpeckers and kingfishers.

Feather growth

Apart from powder-down feathers, which never stop growing, all fully formed feathers are dead structures, receiving nothing from the body but physical support. But at first each feather grows from a tiny papilla, or 'goose pimple', and is built up largely of the horny, lightweight substance keratin—the material which also makes up the leg scales and beak covering in birds, and the hooves, horns and hair of mammals. For the whole of the time that it is growing, the feather receives nourishment through its open-ended base.

Despite the 'fully-clothed' appearance of most birds, feathers do not grow all over the body—except in rare cases such as the penguins—but in clearly defined patches called pterylae, or feather tracts. The naked regions in between are called the apteria; among birds with dense plumage, such as ducks, the apteria are reduced in size and often covered with down.

Apart from these featherless regions, many birds have developed brood spots—areas on the breast and belly from which feathers moult when the bird is incubating an egg. For feathers are such efficient insulators that they would keep much of the bird's body heat from the egg.

When the feathers from them have moulted, the naked skin of the brood spots becomes warmer than normal, as swollen vessels carry more blood to them.

The number of brood spots varies, but most song-birds, pigeons, grebes and predators have only one. Gulls and waders have three. If the male helps in the work of incubating, it too develops these spots.

The many colours of feathers

Birds as a class are the most vividly coloured of all backboned animals, though bright coloration is far from universal. The general rule is that the warmer and dryer the climate, the brighter the bird. British birds, in line with this rule, tend to be more drably coloured than those which live in the Tropics; the outstanding exception is the kingfisher, whose brilliant plumage probably serves as a warning to predators that its flesh is foul-tasting.

Two of the main functions of plumage colours seem to be contradictory, for one is self-advertisement and the other is self-concealment. In many species a balance is struck between these two needs; the male is brightly coloured, especially in the breeding season, and the female is camouflaged by drab coloration. This sex-based difference is especially marked among ducks, in which the brown or grey females of different species tend to resemble one another more closely than they resemble their own males.

Brilliant plumage, such as the cock pheasant's, does more than simply attract the opposite sex; it serves, too, as a kind of flag or battle standard to warn off rivals when the bird is defending territory.

A third function of colour is to reduce wear and tear on feathers. Black feathers, for instance, contain wear-resistant pigments; the white wings of many seabirds are tipped with black, because the wing-tip feathers are those most likely to be scuffed and worn.

How feathers get their colours

The different hues in the feathers of a bird are built up in two ways: by pigments and by the surface structure of the feathers themselves. Pigments known as melanins, produced in the body of the bird, give rise to colours ranging from blacks and browns to light tans. Those known as carotenoids, taken in with food and usually deposited directly on the

feathers with little or no chemical change, produce bright yellows, oranges and reds.

Blue is not a pigment in feathers; it is caused by the structure of the barbs, which reflect blue light and filter the rest of the spectrum through to be absorbed by the dark melanin layer beneath. Green—except in a few cases— is produced in the same way, though the reflective part of the barb may be pigmented with melanin for olive-greens, or with carotenoids for brighter greens. White is produced by barbs which reflect almost all light.

The iridescent effect on the heads of mallard drakes and on the necks of pigeons is a further refinement. Laminations under the structure of the barbules modify the wavelength of reflected light in much the same way as tiny soap bubbles show rainbow colours.

The overall appearance of a bird's plumage —whether it is shiny or dull—depends on the surface of the feathers and the way they lie. Shiny plumage usually consists of feathers which lie with their flat surfaces exposed; short feathers growing at right angles to the bird's body, on the other hand, produce a velvet-like sheen; and the dullness of many plumages is produced by a fine powder which covers the surface of the feathers.

BRIGHT FEATHERS FROM BRITISH BIRDS

JAY

GREEN WOODPECKER

COCK PHEASANT

PARTRIDGE

KINGFISHER

DRAKE MALLARD

A few of the colourful exceptions to the rule that the feathers of British birds tend to be duller and drabber than those of birds which live all year round in warmer climates.

Care of the plumage

HOW BIRDS KEEP THEIR FEATHERS IN PEAK CONDITION

FEATHERS are not everlasting or indestructible; and though they are replaced periodically in moulting, an efficient all-the-year-round system of feather maintenance is vital to the bird's well-being and survival.

Two groups of feathers need special attention—the flight feathers of the wings and the 'steering' feathers of the tail. If the primaries and secondaries of the wing become damaged or excessively worn their aerodynamic efficiency is reduced. This, in turn, imposes strain on the bird's energy and resources, so that its general ability to cope with the challenges of life is reduced; it becomes less efficient in feeding and in escaping from predators—and therefore less likely to survive.

Preening

It is not surprising, then, that birds have an elaborate system of feather-care, and spend as much time as possible on it each day—not only in special sessions, but at any odd moment they have to spare from other activities.

The most important form of feather-care is preening, a habit shared by all birds. This is essentially the treatment of the feathers by the bird's bill, using two main actions. With the body feathers fluffed up, a bird 'nibbles' individual feathers between the tips of its bill, working from the base of the quill outwards, with a series of tiny and precise pecking movements. The bird also draws feathers one at a time through its bill, with a single, quick pull of the head—particularly the wing and tail feathers, which are rather awkward to reach and require special attention.

By such preening movements, the bird cleans itself; it removes foreign matter from the plumage and skin, works in fresh oil from the preen gland just above its tail, puts any disarranged feathers back in place and repairs feather vanes and webs by 'zipping up' any barbs and barbules which have come apart.

Preening also removes feather parasites, especially feather lice and feather mites—a vital operation; birds which are ill or have malformed or damaged bills, preventing adequate preening, often have an abnormally large number of parasites which eat away the feathers and affect general health.

Birds are liable to be victimised by several groups of body parasites—blood-sucking flies and louse flies, feather-eating feather lice, and ticks and feather mites which live on either feathers or blood. None of these parasites, as far as is known, is harmful to humans handling the birds; and some birds are at times free at least from feather lice.

A recent study of 249 chaffinches showed that 51 per cent carried no feather lice; other figures were 49 per cent for robins (172 examined), 59 per cent for blackbirds (out of 54), 55 per cent for great tits (out of 172) and as many as 90 per cent for blue tits (out of 704).

Infestation varies according to the time of year, and is at its height just before the breeding season. One bird may carry more than 200 feather mites alone.

Scratching

A bird cannot, of course, preen its own head Instead, it must scratch with one foot while it balances on the other. This rather crude method seems to serve most species in keeping the head feathers in good order.

Birds have two different ways of head-scratching. In 'direct' scratching, the foot is simply lifted up to the head, along the outside of the body. In 'indirect' scratching, a wing is drooped and the foot on the same side is brought up over the shoulder to the head. As

PREENING

A male blackbird (left) 'zips up' its wing feather barbs; its mate nibbles her under-tail feathers.

DIRECT SCRATCHING

With wings closed, a lesser black-backed gull reaches a leg forward to scratch its head feathers.

a general rule, the method of head-scratching is characteristic of each species and family of birds. The majority of British song-birds and related groups, such as swifts, nightjars and kingfishers (but not woodpeckers) scratch indirectly; most others do so directly, except for the plovers (but not turnstones), oyster-catchers, stilts and avocets.

A few birds, such as the cormorant, gannet and heron, are equipped with what is known as a pectinated claw—a special 'comb' on the inside edge of the third toe, which they use to scratch the head and neck.

In a few groups, including some crows, bearded tits, martins and pigeons, mated birds preen one another's heads. This behaviour, termed allopreening, is often an important part of courtship. There is no reason to doubt that, in some species at least, it is also extremely useful in helping to keep the head plumage in good order.

Bathing

A bird may preen some of its feathers at any time of day, often because of some temporary irritation; but birds also preen more completely as part of an elaborate toilet sequence, which begins with bathing.

Apart from cleansing, the main object of bathing for many birds seems to be to dampen the plumage so that preen oil may be spread over it more effectively

Land-birds bathe in shallow water, such as puddles or the edges of streams or ponds, where they can stand safely. A bird-bath put out in a garden is an excellent place to watch bathing song-birds, such as blackbirds or song thrushes. The bird gets into the water with its body feathers fluffed up and first dips forward with head, breast and wing-joints in the water, at the same time shaking its bill violently from side to side and flicking its wings forward. Then it squats back, with tail and belly in the water, and flicks its wings upwards to send the water splashing and showering.

A bathing bird alternates between these two sets of movements several times—but does not spend very long over its dip because of the risk from predators. At the end, it shakes its feathers vigorously, to throw off the water, then moves quickly away. Water-birds, such as ducks, grebes and various seabirds, spend more time over bathing because they are usually safe on open water and can dive to escape from predators if necessary.

Ordinary surface bathing in these species consists of repeated head-ducking, scooping water up on to the back, then rubbing the head against the flanks. They also beat their wings vigorously in the water, raising sheets of spray.

More elaborately still, ducks, swans and geese will also roll over, somersault and dive while bathing. Grebes kick vigorously under the surface, and gannets roll over sideways with one wing lifted.

After bathing, water-birds start to dry themselves by shaking their feathers, in the same way as land-birds, and also by flapping their wings. Cormorants and, to a lesser extent, shags, perch on rocks and 'hang out' their wings to dry after bathing.

Swallows, swifts, various terns and other birds which are most in their element when flying, bathe from the air by repeatedly plopping to the surface for a brief moment, without actually alighting. Kingfishers, too, launch from a perch over the water, dip momentarily under the surface, and fly up again.

As well as bathing in standing water—in which they often wallow, unlike other land-birds—pigeons will bathe in the rain, lying with one wing lifted. Many song-birds, such as tits, will bathe clumsily against dew- or rain-soaked vegetation. Skylarks never bathe in standing water, but lie down in the rain with both wings extended.

Oiling

After its bath, the bird oils its plumage, applying a feather dressing in the form of a secretion from its own preen gland. Oiling waterproofs the plumage and maintains its heat-insulating properties, and so is particularly important to water-birds and very small land-birds.

The preen gland—the well-known 'parson's nose' of birds—is situated just above the tail. Nipple-like in shape, with the orifice facing upwards, it is surrounded in some species by a ring of special feathers which act as a wick in dispensing the oil.

A blackbird, song thrush or almost any other song-bird oils its feathers in the same way.

INDIRECT SCRATCHING
A chaffinch scratches its head by drooping a wing, then bringing its foot up over its shoulder.

BATHING
Fluffing up its body feathers, a song thrush bathes by splashing in shallow water.

OILING

A great crested grebe rubs its head on its preen gland (the parson's nose), stimulating the gland to produce oil.

SUNNING

A blackbird spreads its wings and tail in the sunshine—possibly as an aid to keeping down the numbers of feather parasites.

The bird twists its tail sideways, reaches back and nibbles at its preen gland, stimulating the flow of oil. Usually it oils its head first. After getting the oil on the bill, it scratches its bill with its foot, transferring oil to the foot, then quickly and carefully spreads the oil over the feathers on its head.

It also gives careful attention to the wings, quivering its oily bill, and to a lesser extent its oily head, under the wings, and paying particular attention to the primary flight feathers. Oil is spread over the rest of the plumage during the thorough preening which follows.

Many long-necked water-birds, such as grebes and geese, use their heads as an oily 'mop', spreading oil over the rest of the plumage, rubbing the head on the preen gland and then over the flanks and back.

Powdering

The full sequence of feather-care in many birds is bathing followed by preening and oiling. But there are exceptions. Some birds, for example game-birds, never voluntarily bathe in water; and others, including some pigeons, do not oil themselves. Pigeons have a functional alternative to preen oil; they powder themselves instead, using their powder-down. This consists of specially modified body feathers which grow continuously and disintegrate into a fine 'talc' of minute, dusty particles which permeate the plumage, especially when the birds preen.

Many other species probably possess a little powder-down; it reaches its highest develop-

ment in birds of the heron family, which have the down distributed in well-defined patches on the body. There is a set of three such 'powder puffs' in the heron, and two in the bittern.

These birds powder themselves carefully after getting their heads and necks soiled by slime from fish and eels. Bitterns are especially fond of eels, which wriggle and lash when caught, spreading their slime on the bird. The bittern first rubs its head on its powder puffs, then dusts its befouled feathers with powder and particles of down. It combs itself, scratching off the powder and slime with its pectinated claw, then oils and preens, perhaps repeating the whole process more than once.

Sunning

There remain three activities which are very probably concerned in feather-care, but over which there is much controversy. Firstly, most species sun themselves, lying out in the sun with tail and one or both wings spread. This behaviour can readily be seen in blackbirds, song thrushes, robins, starlings and other garden birds.

Sunning could be regarded simply as a cooling device, helping the bird to lose heat through exposing sparsely feathered areas to the air and breeze. Certainly, sunning may have this function in, for example, incubating birds unavoidably caught in strong sunlight (such behaviour has been reported in the reed warbler). But the majority of birds which sun themselves deliberately seek the sun.

It has been argued that they derive great

POWDERING

A bittern rubs its head on its breast, gathering powder-down to clear fish slime off its feathers.

DUSTING

House sparrows make scrapes in the ground, then work dust into their feathers.

pleasure from sunning, but this cannot be the biological purpose of the behaviour because the instincts of birds have been selected for survival value, and birds when sunning are vulnerable to predators.

Sunning, which is associated with preening and scratching, may help to de-louse the bird by making its feather parasites move about the plumage so that they are more accessible when the bird preens; and ultra-violet light from the sun may affect the properties of the preen oil on the bird's feathers in some beneficial way.

Dusting

A minority of bird groups, notably game-birds such as pheasants and grouse, dust themselves in dry, fine earth, grit or sand. They scrape hollows in the ground and work the dust up among the feathers, shaking it all out before preening.

Dusting has also been reported among owls, hoopoes, certain hawks and nightjars and among a few song-birds, including wrens, skylarks and—as every gardener with a seed-bed or newly sown lawn knows—house sparrows. Several at a time may pit the earth with their dusting scrapes.

The value of dusting as a method of feather-care is not fully understood. Certainly, it does not seem to serve the same main purpose as bathing in water—that is, to facilitate oiling. As with sunning, together with the associated preening and scratching, it probably helps to combat feather parasites.

Anting

Finally, the most bizarre and controversial feather-care habit of all—anting. This seems to be confined to song-birds and has been reported in at least 22 British native species and well over 200 species in all.

A great deal has been written at second-hand about anting, and much of this information is unreliable. First-hand observation has shown firstly that when birds ant they always use worker ants of formic-acid producing species—in Britain mainly the common garden ant *(Lasius niger)*, the yellow hill ant *(Lasius flavus)* and, probably, the wood ant *(Formica rufa)*.

The ants are used in two main ways. In the first, the 'active' or 'direct' method, the bird picks up one or more ants in its bill, lifts one wing, presses its tail sideways to steady the wing and rapidly applies ants to the under-side of its primary feathers, near their tips. It rubs them on its feathers, spreading formic acid and any other body fluids of the ants, together with its own saliva.

Chaffinches and meadow pipits use a single ant at a time; but starlings and magpies collect a billful before starting. Magpies appear to be the only 'direct' anters among British birds which apply ants to the tail as well as to the primary feathers.

In the second form of anting, the 'passive' or 'indirect' method, the bird allows live ants to run over its plumage, deliberately arousing them so that they aggressively squirt out their formic acid. The jay leans back on its tail, with wings spread out in front of it; the blackbird, song thrush and mistle thrush half squat among the ants with wings out; and the carrion crow and rook lie down, spread-eagled, to wallow among the ants.

Among garden birds, especially starlings and blackbirds, anting may best be seen in late summer, when ants are swarming for their mating flights.

The purpose of anting is highly controversial. Some ornithologists believe that birds ant purely for the sensuous pleasure of having their skins stimulated by formic acid; but there is no doubt that formic acid is an insecticide.

This was proved when a Russian scientist counted the feather mites on four meadow pipits which had been anting with wood ants and, for control purposes, on four others which had not. He found dead mites only on the birds which had been anting. The surviving mites on the anting birds were crawling at random over the birds' plumage, whereas those on the controls remained undisturbed among the barbs of the feathers. Out of 642 live mites taken from the anting birds, 163 died within 12 hours; but of 758 taken from the controls, only five died within the same period.

Anting seems to kill some of the mites sooner or later, and to make the survivors more accessible for preening. It may have other effects, not yet fully understood, especially as a dressing for the all-important primary feathers—the main target for anting.

DIRECT ANTING

The starling's technique is to gather a billful of ants and rub them on its flight feathers.

INDIRECT ANTING

A jay allows worker ants to run over its plumage, aggressively squirting out formic acid.

How birds fly

AERODYNAMICS IN ACTION

THE splendour and freedom of a bird in flight have been a source of wonder and envy to men since Icarus, in the Greek myth, put on feathers and flew too near the sun. Today, man's ability to build flying machines of his own has taken the edge off that envy; and modern techniques of observation and analysis have unlocked many of the secrets of bird flight. But the wonder remains: a bird, whether it be an eagle or a sparrow, is still the most efficient flying machine the world has ever seen or is likely to see.

The simplest form of flight, the one which makes the least demands on a bird's muscle power and probably the form used by the ancestors of birds more than 150 million years ago, is gliding. The earliest gliders may simply have spread their wings and parachuted down from a height; but many present-day birds have so mastered the exploitation of air currents that they can maintain or even increase height without flapping their wings.

Over land, eagles, buzzards and other soaring birds are carried to great heights in huge bubbles of warm, rising air. Over the sea, master gliders such as the fulmar wheel and swing for hours at a stretch on wings which move only in response to the wind.

Overcoming the force of gravity

STAYING IN THE AIR The wings of a bird are rounded above and hollowed beneath. When they cut through an airstream, air moving over the top travels faster than the air moving below, because it has further to go. This creates pressure beneath the wings and a partial vacuum above them, resulting in the upward force known as 'lift'.

As a bird moves through the air, three forces are acting against it: the 'drag' caused by the resistance of the air, the downward pull of gravity and the turbulence caused by its own movement. The aerodynamic design of its body and wings enables it to overcome all three. Bones make the leading edge of a bird's wing blunt, stiff and rounded; feathers make the trailing edge taper almost to a point. This streamlined shape reduces drag to a minimum. A bird's wings are curved so that when they cut through the air they produce lift—an upward force counteracting the force of gravity. Turbulence is controlled by an arrangement of slots. The alula, a tuft of feathers carried on the thumb, can be projected to form a slot in front of the wing; and some birds have deeply slotted wing-tips, reducing turbulence even further. Each feather becomes a separate aerofoil, and large eddies are broken down into manageable small ones.

GAINING HEIGHT To climb higher a bird tilts up the leading edge of its wings, so increasing what is known as the angle of attack' between the wings and the airstream. But the greater the angle, the greater the turbulence. If the angle became too steep, this turbulence would break up the flow of air over the wings, and make the bird stall.

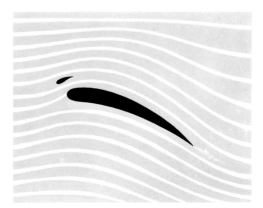

PREVENTING STALLING At the critical point, when the bird is about to stall, it brings into play its alula —a tuft of feathers which can be spread forward to form a slot on the leading edge of its wing. Air rushes through this slot, keeping the airstream over the whole wing fast and turbulence-free. In normal flight, the alula is folded back against the wing.

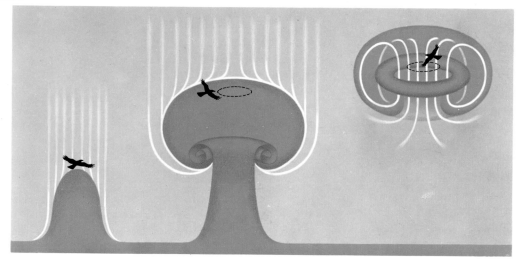

SOARING ON THERMALS

The surface of a land-mass heats up unevenly, producing thermals—rising columns of warm air which expand at the top into huge bubbles. In-rushing cold air cuts off the bubble, which continues to rise, and air currents within the bubble set up a central ring of revolving warm air, with a constant updraught of cold air through the middle. An eagle or any other soaring bird is able to circle on this updraught and rise with the bubble.

(Illustration based on diagram from *The Soaring Flight of Birds* by Clarence D. Cone, Jr. Copyright © April 1962 by Scientific American, Inc. All rights reserved.)

SOARING AT CLIFFS

Black backed gulls and other seabirds can gain height by riding the updraughts caused when a wind hits cliffs or some other obstacle. Even when the wind is off-shore they can still gain height effortlessly by riding the eddies which curl upwards as the wind spills over the edge of the cliff.

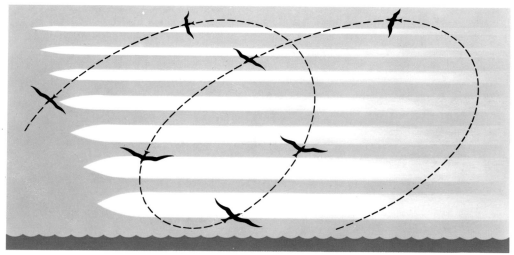

DYNAMIC SOARING

Winds over the sea are slowed down near the surface by friction with the waves. A gradient of velocities is set up, with the wind at its maximum speed 50–100 ft above the waves. Birds such as the fulmar instinctively exploit this variation in wind speeds. They pick up momentum on a high, fast windstream, then wheel down to a lower level, using their momentum to rise again, this time against the wind. Fast-gliding seabirds need to be big enough not to be buffeted off course by minor eddies of swirling air; and they need long wings—the best shape for maximum speed and stability.

305

Taking off

A bird cannot become airborne unless it is moving against an airstream. This means that it must either take off into the wind or make an airstream of its own. Most birds get their initial impetus by jumping into the air, flapping their wings backwards and forwards rather than up and down, to create an airstream; or they take a short run, and push off strongly from the ground.

Take-off is a special problem for some of the best flyers; for specialisation in one direction often leads to under-development in another. Swifts and swallows have poorly developed legs because they spend so much of their life in the air. A grounded swift is fairly helpless, but normally swifts do not get into this predicament. Instead, they alight on ledges and take off by dropping into the air.

SWIFT

STARLING

TAKE-OFF FROM A LEDGE OR THE GROUND The swift, which has poorly developed legs, falls forward from a high ledge; the stronger-legged starling jumps up, flapping to create an airstream.

TAKE-OFF FROM WATER The object of any bird on take-off is to get air moving over its wings at a speed fast enough to produce lift. Tufted ducks and many other water-birds work up speed by pattering along the surface of a lake, river or stretch of sea, flapping their wings until they gain sufficient momentum to fly into the on-coming airstream, or are thrown upwards by a collision with a wave.

Powered flight: what happens

Flapping flight is much more complex than gliding flight, and all its subtleties are not yet understood. But the basic facts have been established.

The most important is that a bird does not 'swim' through the air, as was once thought, pushing against the air with its wings as a swimmer pushes against water; instead, it is propelled by the large primary feathers controlled by its hand.

The function of the secondary feathers and of the inner part of the wing is to maintain lift. The down-stroke is the power stroke, and it is made with the feathers closed flat against one another, so as to encounter the maximum amount of air resistance. The wing moves downwards and forwards, and as it does so the primaries are bent back at their ends, shaping the wing into a propeller which pulls the bird forward.

The up-stroke is mainly a recovery stroke, during which the primary feathers twist open, with an action like that of Venetian blinds, allowing air to pass through the gaps between them. On this stroke, the bird rotates its wing at the shoulder, increasing its angle of attack to maintain lift. The primary feathers are again bent back on this stroke; each individual

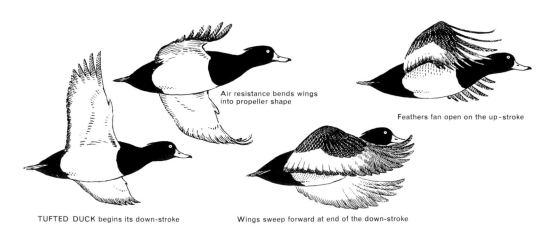

Air resistance bends wings into propeller shape

Feathers fan open on the up-stroke

TUFTED DUCK begins its down-stroke

Wings sweep forward at end of the down-stroke

Steering

A bird turns in the air by tilting its body, adjusting its wings, and using its tail (and sometimes its feet, too) as a rudder. Manoeuvrability depends on two factors: the total area of control surfaces which a bird can bring into play, and the speed at which it is flying. At high speeds, a slight 'touch on the rudder' can produce as abrupt a turn as a heavier touch at slow speeds.

Pheasants can twist skilfully through the branches of their woodland habitats because of their long tails. Partridges and woodcock, both short-tailed, turn readily because their broad wings give them sufficient control surfaces. Some short-tailed birds, such as swifts, are highly manoeuvrable because they are such fast flyers. Swallows fly fast, too, yet they have long, forked tails. In fast flight, they keep their tails closed; but when flying slowly, control is improved by spreading the tail.

REDSTART

NIGHTJAR IN HOVERING FLIGHT

Hovering

This form of flight, used by some birds as a substitute for spying for food from a perch, is expensive on energy. In true hovering, the wings are flapped backwards and forwards, to produce lift without propulsion. Birds such as the nightjar hover in this way for only a few seconds at a time. Larger birds, such as buzzards and kestrels, also use a different, less energetic form of hovering. They fly into the wind at the same speed as it is blowing them back, and so remain stationary in relation to the ground. The kestrel, once known as the 'windhover', has carried this technique to the highest degree of perfection.

when a bird flaps its wings

feather becomes a separate small propeller. The driving force of the primaries during this stroke, though less powerful than on the down-stroke, is especially important for large, heavy birds. They cannot afford a 'wasted' stroke, especially on take-off or when climbing, so their feathers do not open to the same extent as those of smaller birds.

In the complete cycle of a flapping stroke, the wing-tips, which move faster and further than the rest of the wings, go through a figure-of-eight pattern, with a wide loop at the top. They complete the up-stroke with a rapid snap, which helps to drive the bird forward.

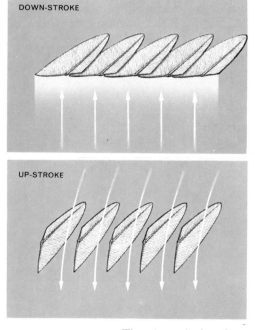

DOWN-STROKE

UP-STROKE

ACTION OF THE FEATHERS The primary feathers form an unbroken, airtight surface on the down-stroke, but open on the up-stroke with a Venetian blind action, allowing air to pass through them easily. In many species the front vanes are narrower than the rear ones, and hold them in place on the down-stroke. On the recovery stroke the bird twists open its feathers, helped initially by air resistance, which tips the flexible rear vanes downwards.

Primaries snap back, ready for a new down-stroke

Each primary becomes a small propeller

307

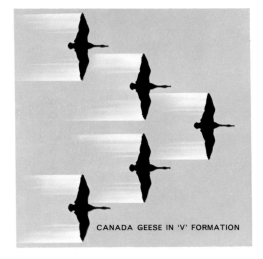

CANADA GEESE IN 'V' FORMATION

Formation flying

The eddies of air caused by a bird in flight represent much wasted energy; but geese, ducks, cranes and gulls are among the species which conserve some of this energy by flying in 'V' formations on long journeys. Each bird gets extra lift from the slip-stream of the bird in front. From time to time, the leader may drop back and let another bird take over the hard work of making the pace up front.

Many other birds fly in flocks, mainly as a defence adaptation against predators; but small birds probably do not produce large enough eddies to make formation flying worth while.

Birds are careful to choose the easiest conditions for flight. When there are strong head winds over the sea, they fly low; where the winds are slowed down by friction with the waves, and when there are following winds, they move higher. The extra lift given by a head-wind is invaluable to a bird taking off from the ground, and whenever possible it makes use of such winds.

Landing

A bird coming in to land must, like an aircraft, reduce speed if it is to avoid damaging itself. There are various ways of doing this; but perhaps the simplest is that used by wood-peckers, and often by pigeons, when landing on a perch above the ground. The bird dips down as it approaches the landing place, and takes the momentum out of its flight with an upward glide.

A bird landing on the ground or on a perch from above brakes by spreading its wings and tail. The bird moves its body into a vertical position to assist braking, and if its speed is still too high, flaps its wings against the direction of flight. As its speed falls to near stalling-point, the bird spreads its alula feathers and finally stretches out its legs to absorb the shock of landing.

Water-birds do not need to be so efficient at landing: the water cushions them against the effects of any mistakes. Those with webbed feet generally throw them forward to assist the braking action of their back-beating wings. A water-bird such as the black-throated diver can make a clumsy landing if forced to alight on land, and may even crash forward on to its face. Divers have never evolved the skills and structural modifications necessary for efficient landing on the ground, for they have never needed to.

That considerable learnt skill is involved in landing is evident in the first attempts made by many young birds. They often misjudge their landing, overshooting the perch or crashing forward when landing on the ground. Large, heavy birds land into the wind if there is one, but this is not essential for small birds.

Some birds—the nightjar is one—can land vertically like a helicopter; but to do so they must have the ability to hover, and this demands the expenditure of much energy.

LANDING ON A PERCH A robin's approach to its landing perch is in three stages. Stage 1: the bird spreads its wings and tail and brings its body into a near-vertical position—all ways of reducing speed.

Stage 2: with its body even closer to the vertical, the bird beats its wings against the direction of flight, spreading its alula to prevent stalling. Stage 3: legs of the bird absorb the final shock.

LANDING ON WATER A tufted duck coming in to land on water can brake by skidding to a halt on its webbed feet, at the same time 'back-pedalling' with its wings to reduce momentum. Water-birds often have difficulty in making an efficient landing on the ground, and they try to avoid this kind of landing.

Special shapes for special jobs

Natural selection, in an experiment lasting millions of years, has produced a multiplicity of different wing designs, each fitting a bird for a particular way of life. But taking broad differences only, wing shapes can be reduced to a few basic types. Similarly, the design factors controlling the job a wing can do may be narrowed down to a few basic points: whether the wing is slotted or not; how pronounced is its degree of curving; its 'aspect ratio'—the proportion between wing length and breadth; and the 'wing loading'—the total area of wing surface compared with the weight of the bird.

BUZZARD

WINGS FOR SOARING Soaring birds need long, broad wings, deeply cambered to provide maximum lift. Deeply slotted wing-tips and well-developed alula feathers smooth out turbulence. The full tail adds manoeuvrability, stability and extra lift.

FULMAR

WINGS FOR GLIDING Long, narrow wings are the most efficient for sustained fast gliding. Flapping flight with wings of this design is demanding on muscular energy, and the design is typical of birds which glide over the sea.

SWIFT

WINGS FOR HIGH-SPEED FLIGHT Fast flying calls for swept-back wings, long and narrow to minimise turbulence. Such wings lack slots, for slots are a positive disadvantage in high-speed flight. Control surfaces can be kept to a minimum—hence the very small tail.

PHEASANT

WINGS FOR RAPID TAKE-OFF Short, broad wings, strongly arched for maximum lift, allow the pheasant to rise explosively, its deeply slotted primaries aiding propulsion as each one is twisted into a propeller shape. The bird's long tail helps it to twist through the branches as it rises.

The highest and the fastest

Fairly accurate information about the heights at which birds fly can be gained from radar echoes and from sightings by airline pilots. But information about speeds is less reliable. Apart from the difficulty of clocking a bird in flight, the speed and direction of the wind must be taken into account.

Peregrines, which are among the fastest birds of all, can chase their prey at 50 mph in level flight, and speeds of 180 mph have been claimed for a peregrine in a diving 'stoop' on its intended victim. Buzzards and other large birds of prey can glide at 70–80 mph.

Swifts have been timed at around 60 mph in their courtship display flights, and top speeds of more than 100 mph have been claimed for swallows, though these seemingly fast flyers rarely go above 30 mph, except on migration flights. A house martin, taken 10 miles from its nest, flew back at 50 mph. This is the usual speed for homing pigeons, too, though they have reached 90 mph with wind assistance.

Top speeds are used only when the situation demands it. A flushed pheasant can power to safety at 60 mph, but it cannot keep this speed up for long. Woodpeckers, thrushes, finches and other small birds rarely go over 20 mph in day-to-day flight, but reach 30 mph on migration. Migrating ducks keep up speeds in the region of 40–50 mph, and starlings have crossed the North Sea at 70 mph with following winds.

HOW HIGH THEY FLY

HEIGHT IN FEET	
23,000	Radar echoes from small birds—possibly dunlin or knot—migrating into Britain from Scandinavia
20,000	Godwits and curlews seen migrating south from Everest
16,000	Autumn migrants from Scandinavia occasionally recorded
10,000	Thrushes moving from Scandinavia in autumn recorded fairly frequently
7000	Kestrel seen by airman over Birmingham. Pink-footed geese seen by airman over Carlisle
6000	Swifts may rise to this height to spend the night roosting on the wing. Migrating lapwings recorded crossing the North Sea at 3000–6000 ft
5000	Most song-birds migrate below this level
4000	Small song-birds flying from Holland to Britain by night
3000	Day migrants such as starlings or chaffinches moving from Holland to Britain
500	Birds spend most of their lives below this height

The air temperature falls by about 1.7°C (3°F) for every 1000 ft of ascent

Patterns of bird migration

A RESPONSE TO THE EVER-CHANGING SEASONS

OF all aspects of bird-life, migration has always held the most fascination for mankind. More than 2500 years ago, Homer wrote in the Iliad of 'a clamour of cranes, which flee before the onset of winter'; and the author of the Old Testament's Song of Solomon rejoiced because 'The flowers appear on the earth; the time of the singing of birds is come, and the voice of the turtle is heard in our land.'

Early theories
But this fascination did not always lead to accurate observation. The formidable, inquiring mind of Aristotle did not prevent him from believing that when redstarts vanished in winter it was because they had changed into robins. In western Europe, the belief was widespread for centuries that swallows curl up together and sink into the mud at the bottom of ponds and marshes for the winter.

Some early theories were not entirely ridiculous, considered as attempts to explain one of Nature's great mysteries on the basis of inadequate knowledge. Later research has established that there is, in fact, such a thing as hibernation among birds. The North American poor-will hibernates through spells of severe cold, its heart slowed down to the point where no sign of life can be detected.

Almost all birds, however, remain active throughout the year. Like men, they are warm-blooded and need to keep their body temperature from falling below the danger level. By migrating, birds seek to avoid this risk in winter; and in summer they take advantage of a temporary abundance of food in their breeding grounds.

In northern latitudes the rising temperatures of spring, by melting the snow and thawing the frozen ground, set in motion a vast surge of insect life. At the same time the retreating snow lays bare seeds, fruit and berries which have lain buried in a natural deep-freeze since the previous autumn. Here, for birds, is an abundance of food, at a time when they are raising their ever-hungry young—and long hours of daylight in which to seek it.

Striking a balance
The hazards of migration range from storms to starvation, but they are outweighed by the advantages to be found in the temporary superabundance of food in the summer home. The process of evolution ensures that a species migrates only if it pays it to do so.

Birds of the same species may be migratory in one area, but sedentary elsewhere. Most song thrushes migrate from northern Scotland; but in the south of England, the balance of advan-

tage against disadvantage is so delicately poised that while some migrate to Spain and Portugal the majority normally stay in England over winter. These patterns are not immutable: Britain's winters have been getting warmer since the late 1980's and if the trend continues it is likely that our song thrushes will become increasingly sedentary.

There is no hard evidence to say how or when migration began; but one intriguing theory links much present-day migration with the end of the last Ice Age. The speculation runs that as the ice slowly retreated, birds from the Tropics extended their breeding range northwards, returning every winter to the warm south.

There is, in fact, much still to be explored about present-day patterns of migration. Even with modern techniques of bird-ringing, radar-scanning and the meticulous checking that goes on at bird observatories, the destinations of many migratory birds have not yet been plotted.

Bird-ringing as we know it today began in Denmark at the end of the last century, and started in Britain in 1909. Each year some 750,000 birds are ringed here, and information is subsequently recovered on about 14,000 of them.

The ring, a strip of aluminium alloy, is closed round the bird's leg. A serial number is stamped on the ring, with the message: 'Inform British Museum, London SW7' (the address of the Natural History Museum). If there is no room, the word 'Inform' is omitted. Since 1937, ringing in Britain has been organised by the British Trust for Ornithology.

The recovery rate is highest for large birds, such as swans (top of the list with 40 per cent recovered), geese and birds of prey; and it is lowest for small song-birds, many of which winter in primitive, remote areas of Africa.

The timing of migration
There are four great events each year in the life of a migratory bird: the spring and autumn migrations, and breeding and moulting—the process of growing a new set of feathers. Each lasts a minimum of several weeks, and makes great demands on the physique of the bird.

The timing of the spring migration is of paramount importance. If a bird arrives at the breeding ground too early, it may starve or freeze to death; if it arrives too late, the time available for breeding and moulting may be dangerously reduced.

The urge to breed and to migrate and the process of moult are all triggered off by chemical changes in the body. Chemicals released by the glands lead a bird to do the appropriate thing at the appropriate season. In some species which have been placed in aviaries for observation, it has been shown that this biological clock can be advanced or retarded if the length of 'day' is altered by means of electric lights.

Before migrating, birds feed more actively than usual, following an instinctive pattern which is set in motion by the biological clock. There is evidence that the amount of fat deposited is directly related to the number of hours the bird is likely to have to fly without rest.

In extreme cases, a bird may double its weight; a sedge warbler, for instance, can go from 11 to 22 grams (⅖ to ¼ oz.) in the few weeks before its departure to winter quarters south of the Sahara.

It has been calculated that a small bird in this state is carrying enough fuel to fly without rest for between 60 and 90 hours.

Within the broad migratory time-table of most species there are often differences based on age, sex or destination. As a general rule, males arrive at the breeding grounds a few days ahead of females. This enables them to stake out a territory, without which they would have little chance of attracting a mate. In the autumn the young from first broods may depart while the adults are still occupied with raising another; but adult cuckoos leave before their young.

Flying by night or day

Individuals whose 'home' lies in the northern part of the total range of their species leave their winter quarters later than those which breed in southern parts of the range. Wheatears breeding in southern England, for example, may already be incubating eggs by the time wheatears heading for Greenland pass through. With the exception of aerial feeders, such as swallows, most insect-eating migrants start their journeys at dusk and, except on long stages, alight at dawn. This allows them the daylight hours for feeding and offers them greater security from birds of prey.

Most seed-eating species migrate by day, taking off at dawn and flying for only a few hours at a stretch. This routine is possible because their migratory journeys, with rare exceptions, are carried out within Europe and do not involve long flights over water.

Other mass movements

A generally accepted definition of migration is that it is a seasonal shift, in a regular direction, of the 'centre of gravity' of a bird population.

But not all mass movements of birds can be regarded as migration. Several species of gulls move seasonally, but in random directions. Individual black-headed gulls may winter well to the north of where they bred, while others wander just as far to the south, east or west. Such movements, termed dispersal, occur to some extent in many of our resident species.

A curious and imperfectly understood type of movement is eruption, which again does not fit the definition of true migration. Some northern species, notably the crossbill and the waxwing, periodically break out of their homes in the conifer woods of northern Europe and head south and west. These eruptions tend to occur at intervals of three or four years and are considered to be caused by abnormally high population levels, poor food crops or a combination of both.

The scale varies considerably from invasion to invasion, but in some years the visiting species may be reported in 30 or 40 counties in the British Isles. In the case of the crossbill, some pairs may remain to breed with us. It has never been established whether more than a few of the birds taking part in these eruptions eventually succeed in returning to their northern homelands.

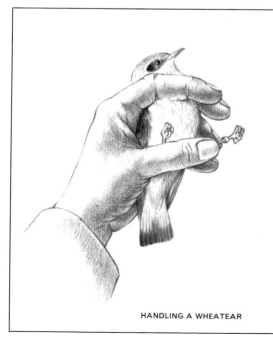

HANDLING A WHEATEAR

HOW TO HANDLE A RINGED BIRD
Birds on migration sometimes fly into buildings by mistake, or become exhausted and are easily caught. If you find a ringed bird, send its serial number, with details of when and where the bird was found and whether it was alive or dead, to:

Bird Ringing
British Museum (Natural History)
London SW7 5BD

Do not attempt to take the ring off a live bird; you may injure the bird and will certainly spoil any chance of further recoveries.

Large birds are fairly robust, but small birds need great care in handling. Do not grab at any particular part of the bird but use the fingers of one hand as a cage. Secure the bird so that it cannot flap, but do not apply any pressure against its fragile ribs. Let the bird's head stick out from the 'cage' between your index and middle fingers, and with your other hand, gently draw out the leg which is ringed. Before you release the bird to go on its way, you may be able to coax it to eat by tempting it with currants or milk-soaked bread; and remember that drinking water is as important as food.

Summer visitors

AFRICA is the great, dramatic heartland into which most of our summer visitors disappear; though a few winter in Mediterranean countries. From the point of view of detailed plotting on maps, the word 'disappear' is all too appropriate, for there are species—the house martin is one of them—whose winter quarters are not really known.

There is a further problem, even more difficult to resolve: when a species breeds over much of Europe and winters over a large part of Africa, do individuals from eastern and western Europe mingle in Africa, or do the different populations take up different but possibly overlapping winter quarters? The evidence is conflicting, which probably means

that both situations occur. It is known from the results of marking birds with identity rings that swallows from the British Isles and from Russia winter together in the extreme south-east of Africa, whereas those from Germany winter mainly in Central Africa.

It is also known that in some species there is a 'migratory divide'—a kind of invisible watershed. In the case of the blackcap, for example, this divide is roughly on a line between Scandinavia and the Adriatic Sea. Birds from the west side of the divide migrate south-westwards through Spain into Africa, while populations living to the east of the divide travel south-east to reach Africa via the Near East. It is not known to what extent

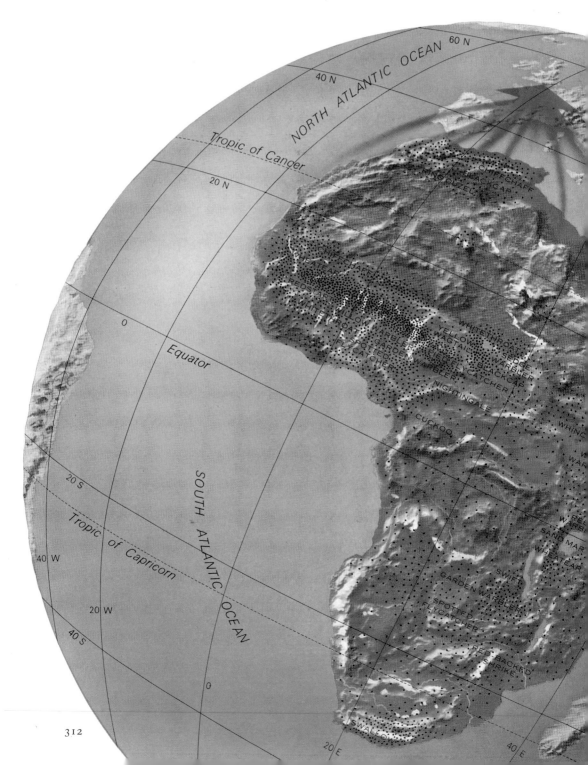

the two populations in such cases meet in Africa. On the other hand, yellow wagtails from Britain, Finland, France, Italy, Spain and the Balkans may be seen feeding together in flocks at their winter quarters in Africa. They can be distinguished from one another because males from different breeding populations have evolved different head colours, ranging from yellow through lavender-blue to grey and even black.

Not all migrants penetrate far into Africa. The great barrier of the inhospitable Sahara, in few places less than 1000 miles wide and spanning the entire continent from east to west, imposes so great a physical strain on birds that there must be considerable advantages for a species if it retains the habit of making the crossing.

South of the Sahara, the vast evergreen equatorial forests of the Congo are shunned by nearly all our northern species. One theory put forward to explain this surprising fact suggests that because there is little seasonal variation in the climate of the forests, the resident birds exploit a stable food supply all year round, leaving no surplus for newcomers. It is not known whether those species which winter immediately south of the forests reach their destination by flying over the Congo (though swallows probably do) or around it.

The majority of our small song-birds which migrate to Africa winter in the savanna and scrub country stretching in a great horseshoe round the Congo forests.

Plotting the routes

In recent years, with information gained by expeditions, radar scanning and bird-ringing, much has been learnt about the routes taken by migrants through southern Europe and Africa north of the Sahara. As might be expected, it has been discovered that the majority of birds from the British Isles and western Europe follow a south-westerly course via Morocco; but some, such as the wood warbler and the cuckoo, are recorded much more frequently passing through Italy and Tunisia; and a few—notably the lesser white-throat and the red-backed shrike—apparently travel south-eastwards in autumn to the eastern Mediterranean and then move south down the Nile valley.

Evidence is also accumulating that routes may differ in autumn and spring. Both the swallow and the sand martin, for example, are believed mostly to cross the Mediterranean near to the Straits of Gibraltar in autumn but to return in spring by a course which may be as far east as Malta. The process of discovery is an accelerating one, and it may one day be possible to show routes with precision.

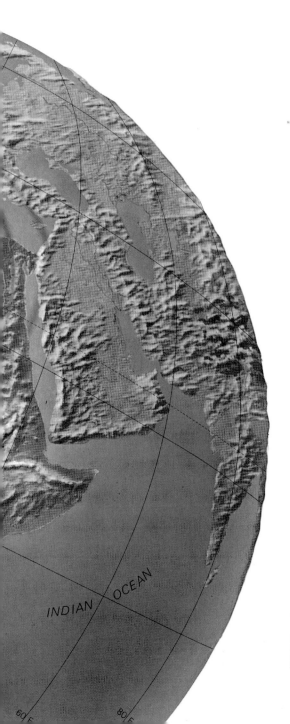

Paths shown are a guide only—not meant to suggest narrow, precise routes; density of dots indicates relative density of birds.

KEY TO VEGETATION BELTS

SAVANNA AND SCRUB

EQUATORIAL RAIN FOREST

MOUNTAINS

DESERT

Winter visitors

BECAUSE of their position on the edge of the Atlantic, lapped by the warm waters of the Gulf Stream, the British Isles enjoy a mild winter climate. In the extreme south-west of England and Ireland, snow lies for an average of only three days in the year. Further east and north in Europe, this figure increases rapidly, with 82 days of snow in Moscow and 184 days at the head of the Gulf of Bothnia.

So it comes about that as our summer visitors are leaving Britain for the Mediterranean lands and Africa, millions of birds from vast tracts of the Arctic, northern Europe and even western and mid-Siberia are quitting their summer homes and coming to winter in the milder, relatively snow-free British Isles.

The islanders
It is convenient to divide our winter visitors into two broad categories, according to their area of origin: the island birds and the continentals.

The islanders come from such places as the Faeroes (250 miles distant), Iceland (600 miles), Greenland (1200 miles), Spitsbergen (1400 miles), Novaya Zemlya (2100 miles) and Bear Island (1300 miles). Their journeys take them across some of the stormiest waters in the world, and they must all be robust, powerful flyers.

For the most part they are geese, ducks and seabirds—all birds which can at least rest on the sea if necessary; but there are also numerous wading birds and a very few species of song-birds—Iceland redwings, meadow pipits, Lapland buntings, snow buntings and redpolls—from the nearer islands.

As a general rule, winter visitors tend to be larger than those migrants which leave us in summer: for the smaller the bird, the greater the amount of heat it loses in ratio to its weight, and the less able it is to withstand cold.

The continentals
The continentals come to us from over almost the whole of Europe north of about latitude 51° N and from up to 2000 miles east of the Urals—that great mountain divide between Europe and Asia. This vast area, with a diversity of habitats ranging from the rich pastures of the Netherlands to the forests of Finland and the tundra of Siberia, produces a far wider range of species than the northern islands. There is also a greater representation of song-birds, including song thrushes, black-birds, fieldfares, redwings, robins, skylarks, chaffinches, bramblings, siskins and redpolls.

Most numerous of all are the starlings, which arrive in stupendous numbers and form night-time roosts which may total a million or more birds. Sometimes the roosts are in trees, sometimes on industrial buildings. Birds from half-a-dozen different countries may roost together each night.

The 'winter' visitors start to arrive early. The first lapwings and green sandpipers may join us before the end of June, at a time when some birds in the north have only just started their breeding rituals. These early arrivals are possibly birds which have been unsuccessful in breeding and have no further reason to stay on in their summer home. Many other wading birds arrive during July and August, often congregating in such lonely places as the Wash and the Solway Firth.

The main influx of song-birds does not begin until September, building up to a peak in October and early November, then falling away to a trickle in December.

Arrivals from the Continent are plotted at bird observatories around the coasts of the British Isles, with the northernmost at Fair Isle in the Shetlands. On any fine morning in October, thousands of birds may be watched coming in across the North Sea. For most of them, this is the only obligatory water crossing and even it can be minimised by taking a southerly route into East Anglia or Kent. Some species—chaffinches and starlings, for example—may fly south from Scandinavia to the Netherlands before heading west, to use the shortest sea crossing.

The one major gap in the chain of observatories is along the western coast of Scotland; and migrants from the north-west tend to arrive unnoticed, filtering in through western Scotland.

Across the Irish Sea
Once they have arrived in Britain, many continental species continue to make their way westwards across England, to spend the winter in the milder western counties; and there is a massive passage westwards again across the Irish Sea and into the west of Ireland. If January or February brings a severe cold spell, there may be a further huge influx of birds from western Europe, while many of those which were already wintering in England move on to the extreme west of Ireland, to Cornwall and Devon, or even to Brittany, Spain and Portugal.

For a few species, such as the continental redwing and fieldfare, the British Isles are only one of several winter homes. These birds are, in a sense, winter nomads rather than migrants; an individual bird which winters in England one year may wander to Spain, Italy, Cyprus or even near the Caucasus the next.

Other species, however, are remarkably faithful to their winter homes. It is known from ringing recoveries that many of the black-headed gulls and tufted ducks which come so readily for food in the London parks in winter breed in the countries surrounding the Baltic and in the far north of Russia, and come back year after year to the same few acres of water.

The departure of our winter visitors is a gradual but accelerating process. In a mild winter, the first birds may start working their way back towards the east coast before the end of February; but the main departures occur in March. Birds from the most northerly regions will linger on through April and often well into May, until their homelands are ready for their return.

Breeding ranges plotted are not
meant to be complete for each
species, but only a guide; density
of dots indicates relative numbers.

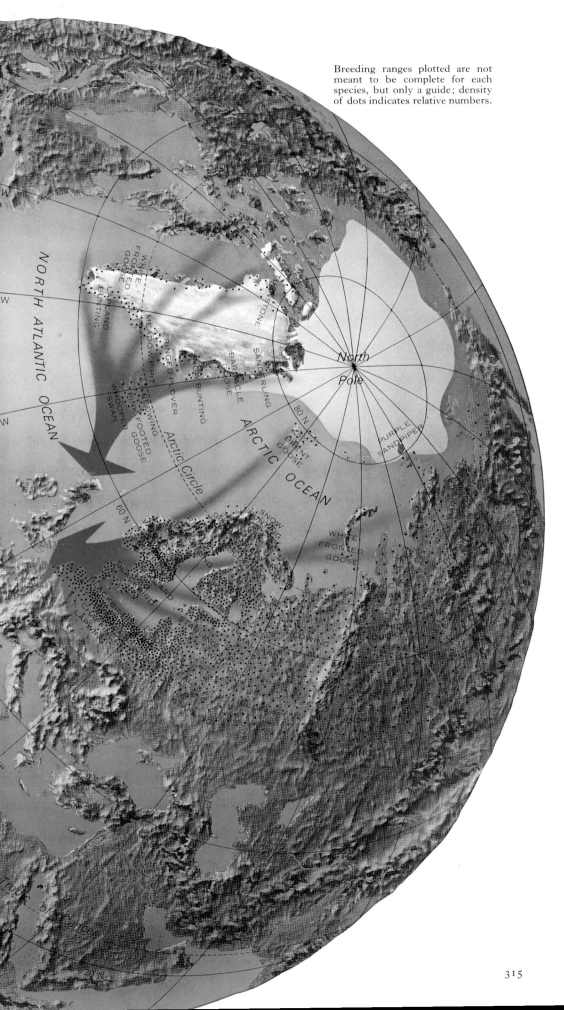

Winter wanderers of the Atlantic

PERHAPS the 'champion' traveller in the entire world of birds is one of the seabirds breeding on the coasts of Britain—the Arctic tern. It has been said of this bird that it enjoys more hours of daylight than any other living creature. The northern limit of its breeding range is high inside the Arctic Circle, within 700 miles of the North Pole; but some Arctic terns winter off the coast of South Africa, and many rove the Antarctic Ocean, right to the edge of the pack-ice.

Ornithologists divide seabirds into three groups, according to their way of life: oceanic birds, which winter far out at sea; off-shore birds, which normally stay within 200 miles of the coast; and inshore birds, which seldom move out of sight of land.

The main oceanic species are kittiwakes, petrels and skuas. In winter, kittiwakes and fulmars roam extensively in the North Atlantic, south to about latitude 40°N, west

to the Grand Banks and Nova Scotia, and north to Greenland and the North Cape.

Fulmars are petrels—a group of birds which, together with their larger relatives the albatrosses, are among the best examples in Nature of perfect adaptation to a specialised way of life. On land they would starve to death, for they take all their food from the sea, riding out the howling gales which can sweep across the Atlantic. It is still not known whether or how they sleep at sea, for there must be many days on end when they can survive only on the wing.

Three other members of the petrel group breed on our rocky western coasts and spend the rest of the year wandering the ocean. Two of them, the storm petrel and Leach's petrel, are no bigger in body size than a blackbird, but with longer wings. It is not known how far westwards either of them roams; but the storm petrel occurs off West Africa and

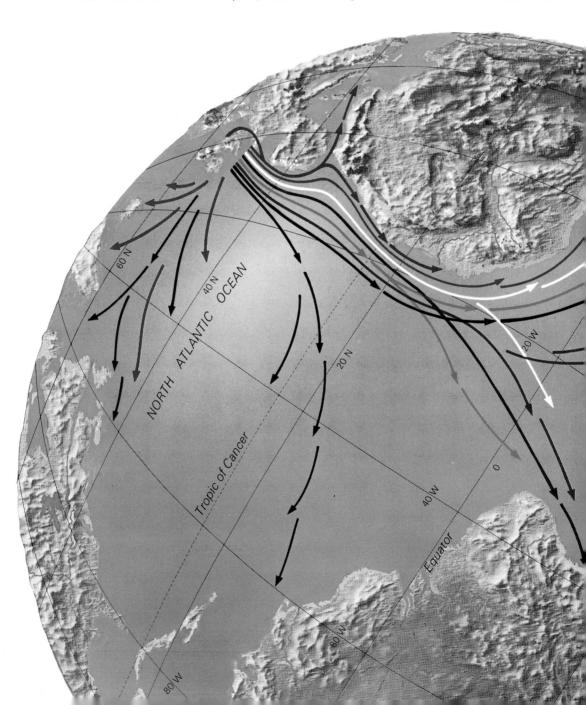

the Cape of Good Hope in winter; and Leach's petrel, which also reaches the Cape, is thought to be most abundant in equatorial waters between West Africa and Brazil.

Thanks to ringing, more is known about the movements of the remaining petrel, the Manx shearwater. From its island colonies along the west coast of Britain, it travels south-west to winter off the coasts of Brazil, Uruguay and northern Argentina.

Our two breeding species of skuas, the great skua and the Arctic skua, both head out into the Atlantic after the breeding season. It is probable that the great skua normally remains in the North Atlantic, though it has been reported off Durban and the coast of South America. The most southerly point reached by an Arctic skua ringed in Britain is Angola. Sandwich terns ringed in Britain have been recovered in winter in South African waters.

The off-shore birds feed over the continental shelf, an undersea plateau stretching up to 200 miles from the land. They include three

large gulls—great black-backed, lesser black-backed and herring gull; also the gannet and two auks—the razorbill and the guillemot. Of the British gulls, only the lesser black-back is a truly migratory species, travelling as far south as Senegal during the first few winters of its life; but thousands of north European gulls of all species migrate to spend the winter in British waters.

The movements of the gannet are similar to those of the lesser black-back, with immature birds making the longest journeys, and reaching a southern limit at about Senegal. The razorbill and guillemot—as well as the puffin, which is rather more oceanic and sometimes crosses the Atlantic—probably migrate as much by swimming as by flying; for this reason they suffer most in any big oiling disaster—such as the 1967 wreck of the *Torrey Canyon*.

Scottish auks regularly appear off the coast of Norway each autumn, while many from southern colonies move south to Spain, some penetrating to the Mediterranean.

Among the inshore feeders are the black-headed gull, common gull, cormorant and shag. The two gulls, particularly the black-headed, can also be classed as land-birds, because they can pick a good living all the year round on newly ploughed land or on refuse dumps. Some of those which are born inland possibly never see the sea.

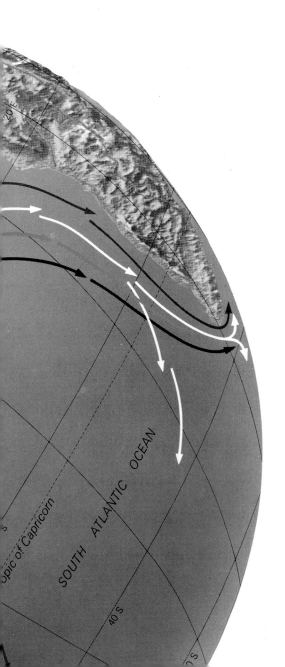

The arrows do not indicate precise routes; many of these birds disperse over wide areas, far from shipping routes.

KEY TO ROUTES

LEACH'S PETREL

GREAT SKUA

GANNET

ARCTIC SKUA

MANX SHEARWATER

KITTIWAKE

FULMAR

STORM PETREL

SANDWICH TERN

ARCTIC TERN

Theories of navigation

HOW BIRDS FIND THEIR WAY OVER UNKNOWN COUNTRY

By ringing migratory birds, scientists have finally discovered where many of them go to when they leave Britain. Ringing has also helped to establish some of the routes taken to get there—some birds cover the ground between their summer and winter quarters so fast that they must fly by an almost direct route. These discoveries concentrated attention on one of the most challenging riddles in the whole study of bird behaviour: how to explain the accuracy and apparent ease with which birds can find their way.

Almost all man's knowledge about how birds navigate has resulted from scientific experiments under carefully controlled conditions. Observing birds in the wild reveals what they can do; to find out how they do it, scientists create an artificial world in which they can dictate when the sun rises or sets, when clouds cover the sky, and when one pattern of stars gives way to another.

Starting off in the right direction

Late in the summer, adult cuckoos leave Britain on a journey which carries them across Europe, the Mediterranean and the Sahara to their winter quarters in central and southern Africa. A few weeks later, the young cuckoos leave the territories of their foster-parents and set out after their real parents. The young birds have never made the journey before, but they turn south and fly the right distance to arrive at a destination which is new to them, though traditional to the species as a whole.

Thousands of generations of cuckoos, following a route which is unvarying from one year to the next, have shuttled back and forth between these same nesting and wintering grounds. Once, for some ancestor in the dim past, the journey may have been one of exploration; but for young cuckoos today it appears to have become a matter of obeying an inborn drive to fly in a particular direction over a particular distance—no more a question of choice than is the colour of its plumage.

This instinct is not unique to cuckoos. The young of many other migratory birds leave before or after their parents on journeys they have never made before. Scientists who moved young hooded crows, white storks and starlings from the areas where they were born found that they migrated in a direction parallel to the traditional route and ended up as far from the species' winter quarters as they were from the summer ones at the start.

Knowing when to stop

It is known that captive birds become restless shortly before they set out on their migratory journeys. Some make short flights in the direction they are about to fly in, and even face that way when perched. In the wild, they presumably fly off to their summer or winter quarters when the restlessness becomes so great that they can no longer control it.

The urge to migrate also measures how far they should fly. The restlessness of a young cuckoo flying south to its winter quarters is so programmed that it abates when the bird has flown the right distance.

When the drive gives out, the bird settles down, in a habitat and a climate suited to its feeding habits.

A bird's stamina, too, is balanced against the

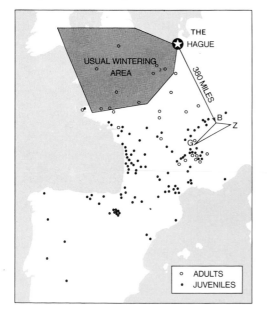

ADULTS
JUVENILES

TESTING THE BUILT-IN 'COMPASSES' OF OLD AND YOUNG STARLINGS

In 1958, the Dutch ornithologist Dr A. C. Perdeck carried out an experiment which involved catching more than 11,000 starlings at The Hague as they migrated south-west to winter along the coasts of Belgium and France and in southern Britain. He had them carried inland, ringed and set free at Basle (B), Zurich (Z) and Geneva (G). Later, 354 birds were recovered. The young starlings, which had never migrated before, had for the most part continued flying south-west on a course parallel to the 'right' one. Many of the older birds, which had visited the winter quarters at least twice before, corrected for their displacement inland by flying north-west.

The following spring, the young starlings returned to the areas where they were born. But in the autumn they flew to the place where they had wintered the year before.

The experiment showed that these young starlings were born with the instinct to fly in a particular direction. The older birds, which knew their destination because they had been there before, altered their direction of flight although the route they had to follow was completely new to them.

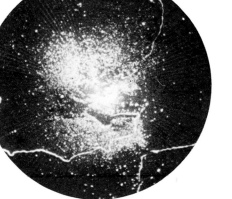

FOLLOWING BIRDS BY RADAR

Radar sets are powerful enough to pick up a single bird 50 miles away, flying at 21,000 ft. The screen on the left covers, a section of sky over south-east England on an August evening. Interpreted on the diagram, it shows birds, probably warblers, moving in huge numbers across the Channel from just south of East Anglia, pushing an 'advancing front' out to sea. Smaller numbers, probably of waders, were migrating across the North Sea, and along the coast of France.

distance it has to fly on migration; the energy-giving fat reserves put on in the weeks of feeding before it leaves are exhausted after a given amount of flying, and the bird must then settle.

Led home by the sun or the stars

In the past ten years or so, scientists have made remarkable progress towards a better understanding of a bird's sense of direction —the sense which can guide it over thousands of miles of unknown land and sea.

When fog or bad weather cast a gloom over the sky, migrating birds often scatter in all directions as if confused. Experiments have shown that this occurs because many of them are guided by the sun.

A German scientist, Dr Gustav Kramer, put starlings which were restless to migrate in a circular cage lit only by the sun. They fluttered to the side of the cage facing the direction in which they would have been flying in the wild. When he tricked them into thinking that the sun had moved across the sky—by deflecting its rays with mirrors—he found that they changed direction accordingly. They kept to a constant bearing in relation to the sun's apparent position—though not, of course, to the world outside.

Another German scientist, Dr Franz Sauer, played a major part in explaining how night-migrants set their course. He built a cage which allowed the birds placed inside it to see nothing outside except the sky. In it he put blackcaps, garden warblers and lesser white-throats—all night migrants. They found their bearings as soon as they could see the stars; and they seemed bewildered when the sky was overcast or the moon so bright that the stars were hardly visible.

To test his belief that the birds were steering by the stars, Sauer exposed them to an artificial night sky in a planetarium. In spring he shone a spring sky on the ceiling and the birds turned in the direction in which they would have been migrating. When he turned the image of the sky in different directions, the birds turned too, twisting like compass needles jerked out of true.

To move in any compass direction without a compass is not as baffling a problem as it sounds. Only two pieces of information are necessary: the position of the sun (or, by

night, the stars) and a knowledge of the time.

This can be tested by pointing the hour hand of a watch at the sun. For an observer in the northern hemisphere, a line bisecting the angle between the hour hand and 12 o'clock will always point due south; and the other compass directions follow from this.

A bird's 'clock'

The fact that birds can set and follow a course by using the sun and the stars implies that they have some kind of an internal clock and that they allow for the movement of the sun and the stars across the sky. A bird flying due south must keep the sun ahead of it at noon; and to stay on route it must allow the sun to move round to shine on its right shoulder —for by 3 p.m., the sun will have moved 45° to the west.

A bird does not have to puzzle this out: its ability to fly by the sun or the stars is inborn. It is not known how the ability was developed in the first place; but once developed, it must clearly have been reinforced by natural selection, with the better navigators standing a better chance of leaving offspring.

Even so, individual migrants are sometimes inefficient at navigation. Some of our rarest visitors, such as the Siberian thrush (which has been recorded in Britain only three times in the last 30 years), may be individuals with a poor sense of direction.

Resetting a bird's clock

The time-keeping ability of a bird seems to depend on the natural light/dark cycle of day changing to night, or night to day.

Two starlings were exposed for about two weeks to artificial days on which the sun rose and set six hours before it should have. At the end of this time, they were shown the natural sun when the real time was 3 p.m. and the artificial time 9 a.m. The birds turned at right angles to the direction in which they ought to have been migrating—a 'mistake' consistent with their clocks being six hours slow.

Experiments with homing pigeons have shown that their clocks, too, can be made fast or slow if the birds are exposed to a light/dark cycle behind or ahead of the real one, and that this upsets their ability to fly in the right direction.

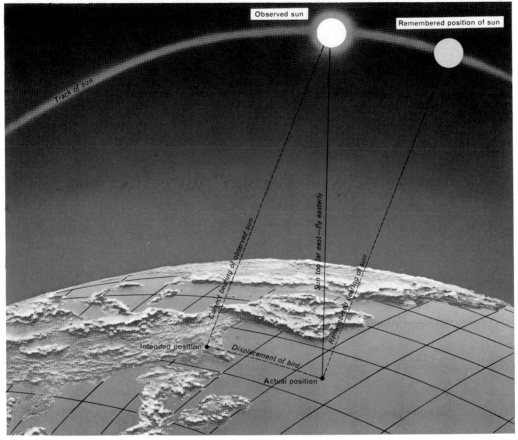

Observed sun

Remembered position of sun

Track of sun

Correct bearing of observed sun

Sun too far east—fly easterly

Remembered bearing of sun

Intended position

Displacement of bird

Actual position

THE HOMING INSTINCT: CORRECTING LONGITUDE

THE PROBLEM: a bird has been moved from its home, and is too far to the west.

THE THEORY: it remembers the position of the home sun at any given time and in some way realises that the sun has not moved far enough along its path through the sky for it to be in the 'correct' position.

ACTION: the bird flies eastwards, until the actual sun is at the same position along its path as the remembered sun; this brings the bird on to the correct line of longitude for home.

The last leg of the journey

The pin-point accuracy with which swallows return each spring to the nests which they occupied the previous year can only come about if the birds can recognise the places in which they built their nests. A bird, with its superb eyesight, certainly uses ordinary land-marks to guide it over the last few miles to its home; and many birds making short journeys overland probably have no better method of finding their way. Homing pigeons released up to 12 miles from their loft return by following landmarks which they have learnt as they fly around the area.

Many birds are capable of something even more remarkable than steering a fixed course. They can get home even when high winds or long journeys in search of food take them far from the places they know. To return, they must, in effect, work out exactly where they are in relation to home and calculate which course to steer.

The skill with which they do this has often been demonstrated by homing pigeons. But the longest journeys on record were made by ocean birds. A Manx shearwater, taken to Boston, Massachusetts, covered the 3050 miles back to its nest on Skokholm Island, off the Pembroke coast, in 12 days; and a Laysan albatross flew 4120 miles from the Philippines to its nest on Midway Island in the mid-Pacific in 32 days.

Many theories have been put forward to explain the homing ability of birds. One is that they scatter at random, so that some reach home by eventually coming across land-marks which they recognise; but this takes no account of the large proportion of birds which home successfully.

They might fly spirally, covering a wider area with each turn of the circle; but the speed with which they return discounts this. Or birds might remember every turn of their outward journey. Scientists tested this theory

THE SKY SEEN BY A

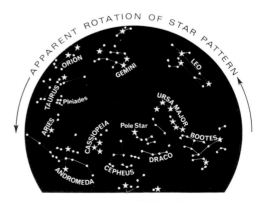

APPARENT ROTATION OF STAR PATTERN

ORION

GEMINI

LEO

TAURUS

Pleiades

ARIES

URSA MAJOR

CASSIOPEIA

Pole Star

BOOTES

DRACO

ANDROMEDA

CEPHEUS

NORTHERN SKY IN SPRING This is the star pattern which night-flying migrants on the way to Britain would see at 8 p.m. on a March evening.

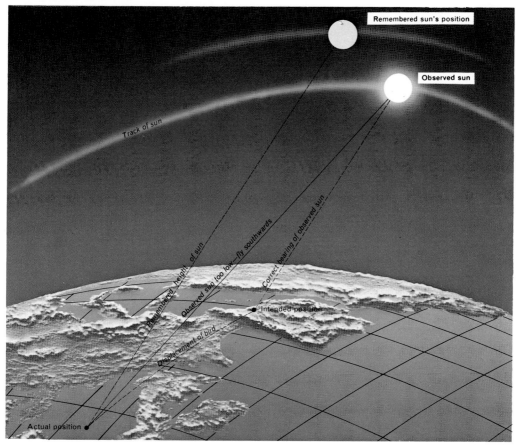

Remembered sun's position

Observed sun

Track of sun

Remembered height of sun

Observed sun too low—fly southwards

Correct bearing of observed sun

Intended position

Displacement of bird

Actual position

THE HOMING INSTINCT: CORRECTING LATITUDE

THE PROBLEM: a bird has been moved from its home and is too far to the north.

THE THEORY: it remembers the height of the home sun in the sky at noon, and somehow realises that the sun it sees is not climbing fast enough.

ACTION: the bird flies southwards, until the actual sun is climbing as fast as the home sun. It is now at the correct latitude. (Corrections for latitude and longitude are simultaneous, but they have been separated to show the principles involved.)

by putting birds in darkened cages on revolving turn-tables and then releasing them far from home; the birds still returned. More recent theories suggest that birds are sensitive to the earth's magnetic field; and experimental evidence is inclined to show that this may be true.

The most likely explanation seems to be that the birds are using the same aids as when steering a fixed course—the sun and the stars. To do this, they would have to remember the position of the sun or stars at any given time at home. The difference between what they remembered and what they saw would tell them in which direction to fly; and they would keep flying until, like a man using a range-finder on a camera, they had brought together the two different images.

This theory provides a working model, in human terms, of the principles involved in navigation. How a bird applies these principles remains one of the mysteries of bird behaviour, to solve which a man would have to be able to think like a bird.

NIGHT MIGRANT IN THE NORTHERN HEMISPHERE

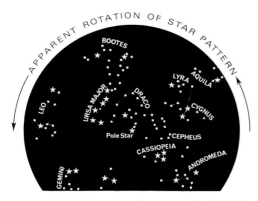

APPARENT ROTATION OF STAR PATTERN

BOOTES

LYRA

AQUILA

LEO

URSA MAJOR

DRACO

CYGNUS

Pole Star

CEPHEUS

CASSIOPEIA

ANDROMEDA

GEMINI

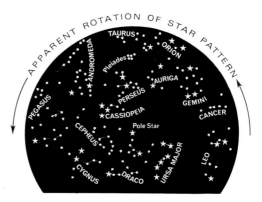

APPARENT ROTATION OF STAR PATTERN

TAURUS

ANDROMEDA

ORION

Pleiades

AURIGA

PERSEUS

GEMINI

PEGASUS

CASSIOPEIA

CANCER

CEPHEUS

Pole Star

LEO

CYGNUS

DRACO

URSA MAJOR

NORTHERN SKY IN SPRING By 4 a.m. the following morning, all the constellations seen the night before would have revolved around the pole star.

NORTHERN SKY IN AUTUMN At 4 a.m. on a September morning, a night-flying migrant on the way to its winter quarters would see this sky.

Moving on land and water

SPECIAL ADAPTATIONS OF LEGS, FEET AND WINGS

BIRDS are spectacularly successful in their ability to exploit the elements of air, land and sea, though few species are equally well adapted to all three. Swifts, among the most acrobatic of flyers, have such weak legs that they sometimes sleep on the wing; ducks and divers, with legs set well back for swimming, are notoriously awkward when walking; and some foreign species, such as ostriches, penguins or the kiwis of New Zealand, have lost the power of flight.

The reason why some birds hop, while others walk or run, has nothing to do with how 'advanced' they are in evolutionary terms. Differences in gait depend basically on differences in environment.

Hopping, walking and running

For a bird which spends much of its time in trees or bushes, the best way of moving from branch to branch is by hopping. But hopping is an inefficient, energy-consuming way of getting about on flat ground. Species such as larks, pipits and starlings, which spend a good deal of time on the ground, have therefore evolved a way of moving on land which is more economical—walking.

The 'standard' foot in birds has four toes, one pointing backwards and the other three forwards. In running birds, such as the partridge, the hind toe has been reduced to little more than a stub, so keeping to a minimum the area of the foot which is in contact with the ground. The same result is achieved by a sprinter, running on the balls of his feet in a 100 metre race.

Long legs are an obvious advantage for birds such as herons which wade into the shallows

THE GRIP OF A PERCHING BIRD

When a perching bird settles on its branch a mechanism comes into operation which locks its toes firmly around the branch. Tendons passing down the back of its leg to its toes are automatically pulled taut over its ankle bone, so that the toes curl in. As long as the bird is in the squatting position, its toes stay clamped around the perch. They unlock only when it stands upright, releasing the tension on its tendons.

to hunt their prey. Equally, short legs are an advantage for birds such as finches, and for tits which habitually hang upside-down to get at food.

Apart from walking, running, hopping and perching, the feet of birds may be adapted for a variety of other uses.

Special feet for special jobs

The toes of the pheasant are equipped with strong claws for scratching in the soil to get at roots, earthworms and other items of food; and this game-bird has special out-growths on its legs—sharp spurs which it uses in fighting. The fierce talons of birds such as the eagle, the peregrine or the osprey are used for killing and gripping prey.

Woodpeckers have feet adapted to climbing trees, with two toes pointing backwards for support; and swifts have all four toes pointing forwards, the better to cling to some small protuberance on a vertical surface. Webbed feet or paddle-shaped toes help to drive swimming birds through the water.

Greenshanks, redshanks and most other waders have long toes, spread wide apart, to increase the area of foot that comes in contact with the ground so that they will not sink too readily in soft mud. In winter, ptarmigan grow densely packed insulating feathers on their feet and develop long, wide claws and a row of flat scales along the sides of the toes— all adaptations which prevent them from sinking into snow.

Birds also use their feet for scratching and preening. Bitterns and nightjars have evolved what is known as a 'pectinated claw': the third toe is notched, providing a highly efficient preening comb.

Legs for swimming and diving

A bird's legs are more efficient as paddles if they are placed towards the rear of the body, like those of ducks and geese. But this makes the legs inefficient for movement on land, because they are too far from the bird's centre of gravity.

The structure of birds, with their light, thin bones, large air sacs and insulating layers of fat and feathers (which in turn trap a layer of air) makes them extremely buoyant. Gulls and gannets use the momentum of a sky dive to penetrate the water; but birds which dive from the surface must drive themselves down in some other way. This is why the rear positioning of the legs is so marked in grebes, divers and diving ducks; just as a ship's propeller is at the back of the ship, so the legs of these birds are at the ends of their bodies, providing power unimpeded by obstacles.

THE FEET OF LAND-BIRDS

A bird walks on its toes, not on the entire area of its foot; for what looks like a knee joint is in fact closer to being a heel. Most birds have four toes; three point forwards and one, known as the hallux, points to the rear. But there are many variations; the legs and feet of birds suit the kind of life they lead—where they live and even sometimes what they eat.

WALKING
The meadow pipit's hind claw is elongated to brace the bird and prevent it from falling backwards.

RUNNING
The partridge, which often runs, has a shortened hind toe, reducing the area of foot touching the ground.

PERCHING
The greenfinch's backward-pointing hind toe curls round to meet the other toes, clamping it to its perch.

CLIMBING
Strong claws and two backward-facing toes enable the great spotted woodpecker to climb by gripping bark.

CLINGING
The swift uses the claws on its four forward-facing toes as hooks and can cling to almost vertical surfaces.

HUNTING
The powerful talons of the eagle are used both for perching and for seizing and killing its prey.

THE FEET OF WATERSIDE BIRDS

WADING
The redshank has long, widely spaced toes adapted for walking on soft mud without sinking into it.

FISHING
Scales on the osprey's foot-pads are equipped with small spines, for grasping and carrying slippery fish.

The conditions underfoot beside stretches of water are extremely varied, and the adaptations of birds' feet reflect this. In one area the shore may be firm and dry, and in another soft and marshy. The feeding habits of water-side birds vary considerably, too. Redshanks wade into the shallows, looking for small water creatures; ospreys circle over the water, waiting to pounce on fish; and gulls scavenge along the tide-line.

Underwater swimmers have many other modifications which help to decrease buoyancy. They are usually heavier than land-birds of comparable size; and they can increase their specific gravity still further by compressing their feathers and air sacs, forcing out the air. The dabchick does this when it floats at different levels in the water; and the dipper is even able to walk along the bottom of a stream: it does this by facing against the current, tilting up its back, and allowing the force of the water to hold it down.

Birds which are not normally divers, but feed by dabbling on the surface, can stay down for brief periods when necessary. Mute swans, surface-feeding geese and such surface-feeding ducks as the mallard will dive on occasion, to escape their enemies.

Some birds—notably members of the auk family—use their wings instead of their feet for underwater propulsion. In the auks—puffins, guillemots and razorbills—the wings have become modified into strongly muscled paddle-shaped structures, with a consequent reduction in flying efficiency. The extinct great auk had lost the power of flight altogether. A few of the sea-going ducks, such as scoters, use legs and wings for underwater swimming.

Few diving birds regularly go below 20 ft; but within that depth, different species often keep to separate levels, so that each has its own underwater food-gathering niche.

Depth of diving

The shallowest divers are those which plunge from the sky; gulls and terns scoop fish from the top few inches of water, and gannets usually keep to the top 2 or 3 ft. Birds which dive from the surface go deeper. Pochards take food from about 3–8 ft; goosanders, golden-eyes and tufted ducks from 6–13 ft; common scoters at any depth up to 16 ft; scaup from 6–16 ft; and eider ducks from 10–20 ft.

Some go deeper still. Perhaps the 'champion' divers of all are long-tailed ducks, which take molluscs from the sea-bed, and have been recorded at depths up to 190 ft. Great northern divers normally fish between 20 and 65 ft; razorbills and guillemots have a niche between 30 and 40 ft; and cormorants have been caught in nets more than 130 ft deep.

Cormorants were used for centuries in China and Japan as trained fishing birds, with lines tied to their legs, and collars fastened round their throats to prevent them from swallowing their catch; in Japan the custom now lingers mainly as a tourist attraction.

THE FEET OF SWIMMING BIRDS

Birds which swim have either webbed feet or paddle-shaped toes to move them through the water. To work efficiently, both types of feet must move as much water as possible on the power stroke, and as little as possible on the recovery stroke. The amount of water that can be pushed back by the spread foot on the power stroke is a rough indication of how important swimming is in the life of each species.

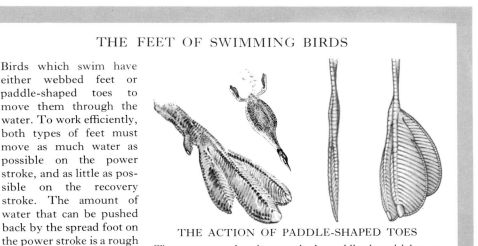

THE ACTION OF PADDLE-SHAPED TOES

The great crested grebe spreads the paddle-shaped lobes on its feet to give the power stroke maximum effect (left). Then the lobes are folded back (side view, right) to offer minimum resistance during the return stroke (seen from front, middle).

HALF-WEBBED

The phalarope is a wader which feeds in the water. It has evolved semi-webbed feet for swimming.

THREE WEBBED TOES

Webs between three toes increase the area of the mallard's foot, which is folded on the forward stroke.

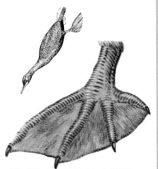

FOUR WEBBED TOES

The shag swims powerfully under water, propelled by feet which have webs between all four toes.

BIRD SOCIETY

Just as no man is an island, so no
bird can exist alone. Bird behaviour can be
studied in isolation in the laboratory, and much
has been learnt in this way; but laboratory theories
must be tested against patient observation in the field.
The emphasis in the following pages is on how
birds behave in their natural surroundings,
in the wild and among other birds.

CONTENTS

Instinct and learning

HOW BIRDS RESPOND TO THE CHALLENGES OF LIFE

FROM the moment a bird starts to break its way out of the egg, its behaviour is instinctive. Instinct tells the bird how to take food from its parents, how to fly, how to care for its feathers, how and when to migrate and how to navigate. A bird sings by instinct, pecks at food, threatens rivals and attracts a mate by instinct; it builds its nest by instinct; and, finally, it knows instinctively how to rear its own young.

Almost all these instincts can be improved by learning—the process of sifting experience and applying its lessons to modify behaviour or acquire new skills. But a bird's capacity for learning is limited compared with that of most mammals; and the limits are not simply those imposed by the size of the bird's brain.

How intelligent are birds?

Recent experiments suggest that the learning process in birds and mammals is controlled by different parts of the brain. In both, the cerebrum, or front part of the brain, consists of two main sections, known as the cortex and the corpus striatum. The more 'intelligent' the species of mammal (taking intelligence to mean the measure of performance in laboratory-devised intelligence tests) the thicker and more highly developed its cortex.

In man, at the top of the intelligence scale, the cortex is best developed of all, with a surface area greatly increased by intricate folds and convolutions.

In birds, the cortex is poorly developed—a mere smooth layer over the striatum, the control centre for instinctive behaviour. The striatum, on the other hand, is well developed in birds—a relatively huge pad, crammed with nerve cells. The traditional view was that the intelligence of birds was limited by poor development of the cortex. Early workers on bird behaviour, faced with a seemingly endless repertory of instinctive habits in the species they were studying, understandably stressed instinct and neglected the importance of learning in birds. The two forms of behaviour were considered to be distinct and largely uninfluenced by one another.

In fact the intelligence of birds (as measured by tests) is not as limited as was once supposed. Ravens have counted up to eight in laboratory experiments; and much of the behaviour of birds in the wild is an amalgam of instinct and learning.

It is now known that the brain of a bird and the brain of a mammal function in different ways, so that the poor development of a bird's cortex is not a factor limiting its learning ability. This ability appears to be related to the development of a part of the corpus striatum known as the hyperstriatum, and to a swelling on top of it, known as the wulst.

Instinctive behaviour is inborn, a part of the bird's genetic inheritance; and the bird has no choice but to follow the instincts which it shares with the rest of its species. A great crested grebe, for instance, threatens rivals by adopting a forward posture, with the head and neck low along the water; and it greets its mate by head-shaking, with the neck erect. There is no more a question of an individual grebe suddenly improvising a new movement —for example, scratching its head with its wing instead of its foot—than of its growing an extra wing.

In terms of modern communication, instinctive behaviour has been 'programmed' or

THE BRAIN OF A BIRD

In relation to their body size, birds have larger brains than any other class of backboned creatures except for mammals. The main parts of the brain, with their functions, are:

CEREBELLUM: large and well developed; it maintains balance and co-ordinates the complex movements of a bird in flight.

CORTEX: smooth and poorly developed in birds; it has been raised to show that it is a mere layer. In mammals, the cortex is thick and heavily convoluted, and it controls intelligence and learning ability.

CORPUS STRIATUM: lies beneath the cortex; a complex mass of nerve cells, controlling instinctive behaviour.

HYPERSTRIATUM: the part of the corpus striatum which appears to be linked with intelligence in birds.

WULST: a swelling on the hyperstriatum; it is connected with learning ability.

OPTIC LOBE: receives and 'translates' messages from the eyes.

(Illustration based on diagram from *The Brain of Birds* by Laurence Jay Stettner and Kenneth A. Matyniak. Copyright © 1968 by Scientific American, Inc. All rights reserved.)

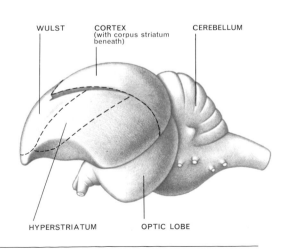

WULST   CORTEX (with corpus striatum beneath)   CEREBELLUM

HYPERSTRIATUM   OPTIC LOBE

'encoded' into the bird's central nervous system; it is a sort of species-memory, passed on from generation to generation in the genetic material of reproduction. Even if an individual bird has been reared in isolation from others of its species, it will behave instinctively; a wren, for instance, needs no lessons in singing.

'Trigger' situations

Most types of instinctive behaviour in birds are triggered off by some basically simple stimulus in the environment. When the stimulus comes from another bird of the same species it is called a *social releaser*.

The red breast of the robin is such a releaser, or 'trigger' mechanism; for the sight of red will induce aggressive behaviour in a robin which is defending its territory. Experiments have shown that a robin will even attack a bundle of red feathers on a wire.

The same colour releases a different set of instincts in the chick of the herring gull; it pecks at the red spot on the end of the parent's bill, stimulating it to regurgitate food. A herring gull chick can be induced to peck at various articles, including pencils, provided that there is a red spot on the end.

Both in the aggressive robin and in the hungry chick, the response to the stimulus is clearly instinctive, rather than logical and thought out. A robin, though, will eventually stop attacking red feathers, when the message finally gets through that they are no threat.

The shape of fear

The ability to recognise the stimulus is inborn, too—as it often is when the stimulus comes from a bird of a different species. Gamebirds and some other species, for instance, have an instinctive fear of certain shapes, such as the silhouettes of a flying hawk or a perching owl.

Young birds respond by instinct to the alarm calls of their parents. Many birds have evolved alarm calls which vary with the nature of the threat, and their young instinctively recognise each call. If a fox appears, a farmyard hen cries out with a call which indicates danger from a ground predator, and the chicks 'freeze' where they are, relying on stillness to escape detection. But if a sparrowhawk is about to pounce, the hen gives a different cry, a kind of air-raid warning; and the chicks react by scattering for cover.

Just as important as telling a bird what to do, instinct can warn it what not to do. The instinctive reluctance of birds to attack eyes, even those of another animal, is of obvious value when young are crowded together in one nest. This instinct may also explain the effectiveness of the protective eye-spot patterns on several species of insects.

Instinct plays a central part in display—the special postures, movements, songs and calls which birds use to defend their territory against rivals of the same species and to attract mates.

An element of learning may sometimes be involved; for the young of many seabirds, which wait some years before breeding, are able to observe the courtship and territorial displays of adults.

True display behaviour is stereotyped—as characteristic of a species as its plumage. It is also heavily ritualised. Many of the courtship displays of ducks contain elements derived from comfort movements, preening and drinking. In the process of evolution, actions such as these have become altered in form—through exaggeration, change of speed, rhythmic repetition, and so on—until they are so heavily ritualised that their origin is obscure.

Instincts that lead astray

Although instincts generally serve birds well —after all, they are products of natural selection—they do not always serve the best interests of an individual bird. This is because instincts are inflexible.

Instinct tells parent meadow pipits to push food into the wide, vivid gapes of their young; it tells them still more urgently to feed the wider gape of a young cuckoo, even when its own young have been pushed out of the nest and, if still alive, are begging unavailingly for food.

Instinct tells the rook to begin its nest by placing twigs across the forked branches of a tree; but it does not tell the bird to choose twigs which are longer than the gap they are to fill—with the result that it wastes energy by trying to build with sticks which fall through to the ground.

The best known instance of an instinct which hardly serves the bird's purposes is the egg-laying instinct of the farmyard hen. By instinct, it would stop laying as soon as it had laid a full clutch of eggs—enough to brood comfortably. If a hen is allowed to lay a clutch of about a dozen eggs, it will become broody, and try to hatch them; but if the eggs are taken away as they are laid, its instinct, heightened by centuries of selective breeding, will compel it to go on laying—a sheer waste of energy, from the bird's point of view.

Theories of learning

The learning ability of birds has been the subject of much modern research. However, this is mostly artificial and academic, concerned more with learning theory in general than with how learning may modify a bird's behaviour in the wild. The main preoccupation of researchers has been to classify learning into various categories—reflex conditioning, instrumental conditioning, trial-and-error learning, insight learning and so on.

The most valuable contribution made by learning theory to the understanding of the behaviour of birds in their natural surroundings is its insistence on the importance of conditioning. In this process, a 'blind' or undirected instinct is conditioned to respond to the correct stimulus.

A good example of the conditioning process in action is the way in which a bird learns the correct stimuli for the various actions it must perform to take care of its plumage (see Care of the plumage, p. 300). There is good evidence that these actions—bathing, sunning, dusting and anting—are instinctive, for they are performed by birds which have been raised in isolation from their own species. But while the inexperienced bird knows *how* to perform these instinctive activities, it does not at first recognise that water is the correct medium for bathing, sunshine is best for sunning, fine earth for dusting and worker ants for anting.

A young song thrush, bathing for the first time when drops of rain splash on its back, does not initially connect this experience with the puddle in front of it. The bird goes through all the bathing movements on dry land! The wetness of the rain is the stimulus which releases the behaviour pattern connected with bathing, but the bird must be conditioned by experience to realise that it can bathe in a puddle or a pool.

In the same way, the heat of the sun, the gritty texture of dust, and the effect of formic acid from ants on a bird's nasal organs, are stimuli which trigger off the first instinctive performances of these other methods of feather-care. These stimuli can be dispensed with later, when the bird learns to respond to the correct stimulus by sight.

Simple, positive conditioning is involved in the great majority of everyday behaviour patterns in the wild, including feeding and drinking; it continues in one form or another throughout the bird's life, increasingly adapting it to fit safely into its environment.

When conditioning goes wrong

In abnormal circumstances, conditioning can lead to a bird responding to an abnormal stimulus. A captive blue tit has been known to sun itself under the heat of an electric light bulb, and house sparrows to dust in bowls of sugar in a factory canteen.

But the most striking case of conditioning that has gone wrong concerns the hand-reared rook, Niger, belonging to the British naturalist Dr Maurice Burton. Rooks normally learn to ant by squatting in the middle of a swarm of ants that are discharging pungent formic acid. But in the absence of this stimulus, Niger learnt to wallow in lighted straw instead; the smoke of straw can have the same stimulating effect as the scent of formic acid.

Habituation, a negative form of conditioning, enables a bird to ignore a stimulus which experience shows to be irrelevant. A young bird is at first frightened by a host of unfamiliar objects, but gradually learns not to flee from those which prove to be harmless. This process is sometimes involved when wild birds become tame.

Another special form of conditioning is known as imprinting. In this process, the young of ducks and geese, and of other birds which can walk within hours of hatching, come to learn the characteristics of their own species only during a very limited period while they are growing.

Newly-hatched ducklings and goslings have no idea what their parents look like. If reared away from others of their species they either fail to establish any dependent relationships at all or come to regard other animals, or even inanimate objects, as their own species.

A human being can imprint himself or herself on a newly-hatched duckling by leading it, crawling on hands and knees, making quacking noises; and the quacking is only an optional extra, not absolutely necessary for the imprinting. There is even a case on record of ducklings waddling after a football.

Learning by imitation

As a general rule, young birds do not learn by imitating their parents; and the parents do not deliberately teach their young.

Birds fly by instinct as soon as they leave the nest, and need no teacher other than experience to improve their performance. Instinct does not provide the whole range of skills needed to make a successful landing, and young birds may misjudge distances and crash on their first few landings; but they soon discover how to avoid this. Stories of parent birds teaching their young to fly—or, in the case of some seabirds, to dive—may be discounted as a misinterpretation, based on the wishful thinking of the observer.

Much of what looks like imitation is, in fact, caused by the transference of mood from one bird to another so that it, too, starts to carry out the same activity. This process, known as social facilitation, may be observed in flocks of birds, when one bird, spotting a predator, flies up and the rest follow; or one starts feeding and the others do the same. The same kind of transference happens with humans when one person starts yawning or looking at his watch in company.

There are some ways, however, in which inexperienced birds do imitate adults. Feeding habits are learnt to the extent that young birds will watch where others feed, and what they feed on; but the actual technique of feeding—the way a thrush hammers open a snail or a nuthatch wedges nuts in the bark of trees before attacking them—is instinctive.

Imitation is probably responsible, too, for sporadic outbreaks of doorstep milk-stealing among blue tits and great tits. One or more birds in a district learn that pecking through the glinting foil of milk-bottle tops will bring a reward of cream, and others follow their example.

Learning to sing

An even more notable exception to the rule that birds do not learn by imitation is in the songs of some species. In most birds—the whitethroat, swallow, wren and bullfinch, for instance—the male's song is instinctive. If individual birds of these species are reared in isolation their songs develop normally, like their repertoire of call-notes. But some species, especially starlings, will mimic phrases from other birds' songs; the reason for this is not understood.

Yet other species need to learn their own songs. An isolated chaffinch will develop an incomplete version of the typical chaffinch song; in the wild, the young male listens to the songs of its adult neighbours and shapes its own primitive song to theirs by imitation.

Living together

THE UNITS OF BIRD SOCIETY

SOME birds begin to live socially while still inside the egg. About three days before hatching, the embryo chicks of grouse, for example, begin to cheep. There is evidence that this is a form of communication from egg to egg, with the function of synchronising hatching; for the species which cheep are always birds which leave the nest within a few hours of hatching, and those which cheep the loudest tend to be those which hatch more or less together.

Cheeping can also be a form of communication between adults and chick, as in the case of the guillemot. The chick cheeps as it begins to hatch and the parent birds answer back, so that it learns to recognise their calls even before it has hatched, and later responds only to these.

As a general rule, birds which are born naked, blind and helpless do not cheep inside the egg; but they begin to communicate with their own species soon after hatching— as soon as they sense the presence of their parents and open their bills to beg for food.

One mate or several?

More complicated forms of social behaviour follow later—courtship, song, threat and fighting all involve association, interaction and above all, communication with other birds. The main intercommunicating units of bird society are pairs, families, flocks and colonies; and for some species even sleeping is a social activity, with large numbers gathering in roosts.

The great majority of birds are monogamous —that is, the males have only one mate during the breeding season. There is often a simple biological reason for this: young birds usually need the full-time attention of both parents if they are to survive. But this reason does not

apply in every case. Cuckoos lay their eggs in other birds' nests, and neither sex has any responsibility for rearing the young: yet cuckoos are monogamous. So, too, are ducks, though the males usually have nothing to do with raising their young. In both these cases, monogamy can be explained by complicated factors involving the timing of breeding and the availability of mates.

Other forms of pair association are polygamy (in which one bird, usually the male, has several mates) and promiscuity (in which the birds meet only for mating, and no bond is formed).

The kind of pair bond is broadly related to the availability of food. Taking the world's birds as a whole, the relatively few species which are polygamous are mainly seed-eaters, producing young at a time of year when seeds are in plentiful supply. The few which are promiscuous live mainly on plants and fruit— again the kind of food which is readily available when the young hatch. Birds which feed their young on insects are rarely anything but monogamous, for the young are helpless for the first few days after hatching and are unable to catch the insects themselves. But among British birds, wrens and pied fly-catchers, both mainly insect-eaters, are sometimes polygamous.

Long-lived pair bonds

Most monogamous birds (the robin may be taken as typical) pair with a different mate each new breeding season. But some long-lived birds, especially seabirds, pair for life.

Studies of the kittiwake, which lives for an average of nearly 14 years, show that old-established pairs usually rear more young than those birds which change mates in successive seasons. Gannets, which live for an average

THE PECK ORDER AMONG ROOKS

In small flocks of rooks, every bird has its recognised position in a social hierarchy known as a peck order. Birds high in the order eat before those lower down; and in times of food shortage this ensures that at least the highest-ranked birds survive. There may be fighting from time to time, especially when the system is being established, but in the long run bickering over food—which wastes time and energy—is reduced.

Wood-pigeons, too, have a peck order; and the system is similar to the peck order of farmyard hens, in which the hens actually peck one another.

PIPING OF THE OYSTERCATCHERS

The exact meaning of the 'piping performance' of oystercatchers is not clear, but the ceremony occurs when the birds are excited—in courtship or territorial encounters. Small groups of oyster-catchers, often in pairs, run up and down with their bills pointing at the ground, at the same time uttering far-carrying piping calls which stimulate other birds to start parading and calling.

of 16 years, fulmars (14 years) and shags (nearly 16 years) benefit in much the same way by choosing the same mate for season after season.

Other examples of birds which pair for life are jackdaws and greylag geese. In both species, young birds pair up in the spring following the year of hatching, and stay together for a year before they begin breeding. If a jackdaw's mate dies, the survivor will look for a new partner; but a greylag goose in the same situation will remain single for the rest of its life.

Jackdaws are unusual, too, in that they are among the few British species which stay paired during the winter. Even when they join up with wandering feeding flocks, paired jackdaws will keep together.

Other species in which the pair bond lasts through winter are mistle thrushes, stonechats and marsh tits. Neither of the first two species joins flocks in winter, and marsh tits do so only if a flock of tits 'invades' their territory.

Most pair bonds, however, are disbanded outside the breeding season. The birds which formed them either become solitary—like the kingfisher, the robin and many birds of prey —or join winter feeding flocks.

The pheasant's harem

Among British birds, there are only a few species in which males mate with more than one female. An outstanding example is the cock pheasant, which runs a harem of up to half-a-dozen hens; another is the farmyard cockerel. In both cases, the hens disperse separately to nest after mating.

Male wrens and pied flycatchers may take one or a number of mates. Studies of the wren suggest that the reason for this variation within a single species is linked with the supply of food. Wrens tend to be polygamous in rich habitats, such as woodland, and mono-gamous in poorer habitats, such as moorland. Polygamy has also been reported in the case of the bittern and the corn bunting. No cases have been found in Britain of females taking

more than one mate. A minority of British birds have no sustained pair bond at all, but are promiscuous. They meet only for mating, each bird usually copulating with more than one member of the opposite sex.

Among our breeding species, only the capercaillie, black grouse and ruff are known to be promiscuous.

As with polygamy, promiscuity is possible only when the young can be reared by a single parent. Taking the world's birds as a whole, this situation is usually found in groups whose chicks are born covered with down, and able to run and feed themselves soon after hatching. When it occurs in species whose young are born helpless, the food supply is abundant and reliable, consisting mainly of seeds, fruit or green plants.

Breaking away from the family

Contrary to popular belief, family life is not well developed among the majority of British birds. The family is usually a temporary unit, staying together only until the young can fend for themselves, that is for a few days or weeks after they leave the nest.

In some cases, for instance among the gannets, Manx shearwaters and swifts, there is no family life at all once the young are able to fly. Young tawny owls, on the other hand, are fully dependent on their parents for food for up to three months after fledging.

In a few other species the family stays together after the young become able to support them-selves, and remains together for most or all of the time until the next breeding season. This situation is found mainly among swans and geese. Families of mute swans may be watched throughout the winter on lakes, rivers and streams in many parts of the country.

Even more strikingly, Bewick's swans migrate in family groups from their breeding areas abroad and travel to the British Isles, where they stay together all through the winter. Many British birds form integrated feeding flocks for at least part of the year, and

GROUPING OF THE AVOCETS

A little-understood social gathering is the 'grouping' of avocets, in which small numbers of birds, often paired, bow low, sometimes forming a circle with their long, upcurved bills facing inwards. The bowing is usually followed by fighting between the different pairs—mainly of a ritualistic nature—in which the male and female of the same pair keep close to one another.

a few, such as starlings and linnets, feed in flocks throughout the year.

Winter flocks, ranging over the countryside and the coastline, include birds which have migrated here from abroad as well as those which are resident in Britain all year.

The flocks may consist of a single species (as with starlings, wood-pigeons and many ducks) or be mixed. Rooks and jackdaws often forage together, and tit flocks may contain not only tits of more than one species but also other small woodland birds, such as goldcrests and treecreepers.

Lapwings, dunlin, knot and other waders sometimes form mixed flocks when flying or roosting, but usually separate when feeding. Much the same thing happens with finches; chaffinches, linnets, goldfinches, siskins and redpolls may mingle in flight, but normally feed separately.

A single flock may sometimes be composed of birds of one sex (as with tufted ducks and pochards), of juvenile birds only (as with starlings in late summer), of pairs (jackdaws) or of families (geese and swans).

The reason why some birds associate in flocks instead of feeding on their own has been much disputed. More research is needed before the complete facts are known, but three factors, often in combination, help to explain flocking in many species.

Benefits of flocking

The first is simply that there is safety in numbers. This is of particular benefit to birds which feed in open, exposed places, such as fields and estuaries. A predator, which would have little difficulty in taking a solitary bird, can be distracted and confused by sheer numbers when attacking a flock; and if a predator is sighted or makes an attack, one bird flying up or calling will warn the rest.

Secondly, if birds feel safer in flocks, it is highly probable that they feed more efficiently, because they can concentrate on what they are doing.

The third factor is the availability of food.

Some groups, such as the seed-eating finches and rooks, seek food which is abundant and easily taken in some areas, but scarce in others; flocking concentrates them quickly in the favourable areas.

Winter feeding flocks are not simply disorganised collections of birds; they are integrated through positive social behaviour.

In most flocks, cohesion is established by the individuals following one another, both while feeding and when in flight. Many species have conspicuous flashes or bars, usually of white, on the wings, tail or rump, which may act as 'flock markers'. These are particularly well developed in groups such as the waders, which carry out complicated flight manoeuvres, and in the finches. Visual markers are reinforced by special calls, especially flight-calls, by which the birds keep in touch with one another.

Keeping apart in flocks

In addition, many species organise their flocks through each bird maintaining its own individual distance, so that it does not come into bodily contact with other members of the flock. In this way a regular spacing is preserved, and each individual has room to move, feed, look about and take wing unhindered.

Relationships between the birds in these flocks are not based on individual recognition. The flock is essentially a collection of anonymous members—unlike the small flocks of rooks or wood-pigeons, in which individual recognition between birds is necessary to establish a peck order of precedence in feeding.

Many birds gather for group displays during courtship; but there are some cases in which the exact meaning of the display is far from clear, for the majority of the birds taking part are already paired.

Two of the oddest ceremonies involve groups of monogamous waders. Oystercatchers have a 'piping performance' in which small groups of birds, often in pairs, parade up and down uttering calls; and avocets have a 'grouping' ceremony in which a number of birds form an inward-facing circle, bowing to one another as a preliminary to ritualistic fighting. The screaming parties of the swifts are another example of group displays involving paired birds. On fine days, a number of birds fly quickly round together in the vicinity of the nesting colony, all uttering a high-pitched squealing.

Just as mysterious are the noisy winter gatherings of magpies; up to about 100 birds

spring and dash about, flirting wings and tails to exhibit the white parts of the plumage, as well as performing slow-motion flights. Jays have somewhat similar spring gatherings, but mainly in smaller numbers of about 3–30 birds. It is widely believed that these meetings are 'crow marriages', which enable unpaired birds to find mates.

However, this interpretation does not account for the presence of paired birds, which are always in the great majority.

Living in colonies

Only about 13 per cent of the world's birds nest in colonies, but in Britain the proportion is twice as high. This is because these islands attract so many seabirds, and seabirds as a group are the most colonial of birds, often returning year after year to traditional safe sites on cliffs and rocky islands.

Broadly speaking, there are two main types of colonial species: those such as gannets, rooks and herons, which form compact colonies; and those such as finches, reed warblers and avocets, which form loose colonies, with nests spaced further apart than the lie of the land seems to demand. For hole-nesters, including jackdaws, starlings, house and tree sparrows and swifts, the closeness of the nests depends largely on the distribution of suitable cavities.

Most colonial birds defend only as much territory as they need for a nesting space, but some hold much wider, well-defined territories within the colony. The Canada goose defends land on the lake island where its nest is situated and also on a stretch of mainland opposite, where the pair feed. The reed warbler defends a territory averaging about 300 sq. yds, but the pair feed largely outside this area.

Colonies of land-birds are usually fairly small; fewer than a dozen pairs may make up a colony of finches, for example. But there are exceptions: a colony of rooks may number

thousands of birds. The largest rookery (in fact the largest land-bird colony in Britain) is at Hatton Castle in Aberdeenshire, which has held as many as 9000 nests.

Waterside birds usually breed in small colonies. At a count taken in 1954, the number of nests in heronries in England ranged from four to 85, with an average of 21 to a colony.

Seabirds, especially those which nest compactly, often mass in staggering numbers at their breeding sites. The largest colony of fulmars in the British Isles is on St. Kilda in the Outer Hebrides, with a total of nearly 40,000 nests. The largest colony of gannets— up to 52,000 nests—is also on St. Kilda.

Skomer Island, off the Pembroke coast, holds a colony of 95,000 pairs of Manx shearwaters, and there are colonies of guillemots thousands strong on the Scottish islands. Black guillemots and shags, on the other hand, breed in relatively small colonies.

There are up to 16,000 breeding pairs of black-headed gulls at Ravenglass in Cumbria. Some 30,000 kittiwakes breed on Handa Island, Sutherland, and probably even more on Noss, in the Shetlands. The loose colonies of skuas vary from just a few pairs to more than 500 great skuas on Noss.

The most crowded seabird colonies are those of gannets and guillemots. In many gannetries, the birds leave no more than 3 ft between one nest and the next. Guillemots,

COLONY UNDER THE GROUND

Puffins dig nesting burrows up to 10 ft long, hacking at the ground with their powerful bills and scooping out earth with their large feet. They burrow even into hard, stony ground, though not so far as into cliff-top turf. A puffinry may number

thousands of pairs, and the ground can become so honeycombed that it will collapse in parts of the colony. Beyond a certain point, puffin colonies begin to decrease in size, because the birds literally dig themselves out of a home.

COLONY ON THE CLIFFS

Kittiwakes, like many other gulls, nest on cliff ledges. They build large nests mainly of seaweed to take two, three and sometimes four chicks. If the ledge is too narrow the birds still cling to the protection of the cliffs, building nests which jut out over a dizzy drop. The birds pair for life, and return year after year to the same ledge site, settling in compact colonies of 30,000 pairs and more.

which have no true nest, crowd closer still on their cliff-ledge sites—so close that their loomeries, or bazaars, have been referred to as bird 'slums'.

Hole-nesting seabirds, such as Manx shearwaters and puffins, which can excavate their own cavities, often nest so close together that the ground is honeycombed. The smaller storm petrels and Leach's petrels use ready-made holes and have to make do with what is available, so that their colonies can be compact or loose. But the colonies of skuas and most terns and gulls are deliberately loose.

Why nest in colonies?

The function of colonial nesting is much disputed among ornithologists and it is impossible to give clear-cut answers to questions such as:

Why are some species colonial rather than solitary nesters?

Why do some species form compact colonies and others loose ones?

Why do some species hold territories extending beyond the nest-site itself?

However, a comparison of colonial and solitary nesting species indicates where the answers lie.

Firstly, typically colonial species take food which though locally abundant is widely scattered—such as fish shoals, fruit or seeds. They would not be successful if they established separate nests and territories which might not correspond with their food supply.

Secondly, most colonial birds have young which stay in the nest for some time after hatching, and living in large groups gives them protection.

Another factor encouraging the development of colonial breeding could well be the shortage of suitable sites for nests. However, the significance of this factor has probably been exaggerated by some naturalists, especially when applied to seabirds.

The continuing existence of a colony at a traditional site indicates that the site is safe; and although nest-sites as such may not be scarce, traditional and safe sites are.

Colonies are safe places because they are often inaccessible to predators, because one alert bird can warn all the others if danger threatens, and because birds will sometimes join in a communal attack on an intruder.

The synchronisation of egg-laying is important, too; it means that there are fewer losses to predators than if eggs and birds were available over a longer period. This synchronisation is thought to arise from the close proximity of birds, with courtship displays by a few creating a mood which runs through the colony.

How it works

A closer look at some colony-dwelling birds will show how these various factors—feeding, safety and the availability of nest-sites—work out in practice.

Colony-dwelling finches feed on seeds in small flocks in the breeding season and form small colonies, often not far from good supplies of their food. Another finch, the chaffinch, includes a large proportion of insects in the diet of its young, and is territorial, not colonial.

The fish-eating heron is usually a solitary feeder and seems to be colonial so that it can use safe, traditional sites—and possibly so that it can gain information about the location of food, through watching other members of the colony.

Some species vary their social patterns to fit their surroundings. On many lakes where there is a narrow band of fringing vegetation, great crested grebes are territorial birds, with their nests spaced well apart; but on lakes where cover is scarce, or where there is one particularly safe area such as a reed-bed, these birds nest in loose colonies.

The sea-feeding, ground-nesting eider duck also forms colonies, mainly on islands free of ground predators. Eiders nesting on the mainland do so solitarily, relying on camouflage and the spacing out of the nests for protection.

It is only to be expected that birds feeding on shoals of fish will be colonial, for their food supply is abundant but scattered. Safety is an important factor for seabirds, too; and the relative safety of the breeding area has an influence on the structure of the colony.

Seabirds which nest in inaccessible places such as cliffs tend to form dense colonies like those of gannets and guillemots, making the most of the space available. Those nesting in less safe places such as marshes and sandbanks tend, like gulls and terns, to form loose colonies.

While most seabirds merely defend their own particular nests, gulls and terns go further and join forces against many predators, including carrion crows, foxes and stoats.

Sandwich terns have another anti-predator adaptation. They often nest within colonies of common terns or black-headed gulls, depending on the communal defence behaviour of these more aggressive species.

How birds sleep

Choosing the right place to sleep is a life-and-death matter for birds. In their efforts to outwit predators and survive the rigours of wintry nights, some birds creep into cracks and crevices; others fly miles across country, flocking together in hundreds of thousands; and some even 'cat-nap' in flight.

The sleeping site, whether occupied by one bird or by thousands, is called a roost. Rooks regularly travel anything from six to ten miles from the roost and back again in a day. Starlings range even further into the countryside—normally between 12 and 20 miles, and sometimes they will go as far as 30 miles.

As long as a roost proves safe and sheltered, birds are reluctant to forsake it, and usually move away only in response to severe disturbance or to fluctuations in their food supply.

Keeping out the cold

Loss of heat at night is a major problem for all creatures. A solitary bird roosting in an exposed place on a cold night may freeze to death. Its body can lose heat to the surrounding air faster than it can be replaced, sending the bird into a coma from which it may never recover.

All birds must maintain a constant body heat to survive, though in emergencies nestling swifts can live through a temporary drop in temperature by going into a state of torpidity in which their bodily processes are slowed down. For most birds, the daytime is one long meal, broken only by such necessary actions as searching for food, preening, courtship and defending territory. When night falls they must use the heat stored up by the food taken in during the day.

When they are sleeping and most likely to lose heat, birds fluff up their contour feathers to form an insulating layer of warm air. They reduce the area of their bodies exposed to the night air by hunching up (like pigeons), tucking their heads behind their wings (like robins) or pressing their bills into the side of the neck (like grebes).

Great tits and blue tits sleep in cavities in trees or buildings, to avoid draughts and to prevent the heat from escaping from their bodies. Long-tailed tits and goldcrests crowd into a small space, as many as ten at a time, and huddle together for warmth. As many as 80 swifts have been seen clinging to the side of a house—presumably for the same reason. Quails roost together in clusters with their heads pointing outwards, ready for a quick getaway if danger threatens.

In the Cairngorms in winter, the ptarmigan digs a hole in the snow in which to sleep. The warmth of this roost, like that of the Eskimo's igloo, depends on the fact that ice and snow are poor conductors of heat.

Birds are vulnerable to their natural enemies while they are asleep, and many species flock together for protection. Young birds and migrants unfamiliar with the countryside follow the lead of more experienced birds in seeking places relatively safe from predators. The fact that thousands of starlings or thrushes sleep in one location in the territory of a single tawny owl means that fewer individuals are likely to be taken by owls than if they were scattered, with a few pairs in the hunting grounds of individual owls.

It is in winter that flocks are at their biggest. Winter roosts of starlings, swollen by newly arrived juveniles and migrants from the Continent, commonly contain up to 500,000 birds, and one or two hold more than a million. One of the largest in Britain, at Denver, near King's Lynn in Norfolk, is thought to harbour several million birds.

Even these numbers are dwarfed by comparison with the flock of bramblings which filled two small pinewoods near the town of Thun in Switzerland in the winter of 1950–1. Their numbers were calculated at more than 70 million—nearly 12 times the entire human population of the country.

Counting the birds

Calculating the size of roosts is a specialised job, though the beginner can get some idea of the numbers in smaller flocks by positioning himself at a good vantage-point on the regular flight-lines into a roost, and counting the birds as they fly in. The reliability of an estimator's figures improves as his experience grows.

In the case of starlings, fairly accurate estimates can be made, for these birds fly into their roosts in a stream of relatively constant density—that is, a section taken from the beginning of the stream will contain roughly the same number of birds as a section of the same length towards the end. The experienced estimator may therefore photograph part of the stream to determine how many birds it contains, calculate the length of the stream and arrive at a fairly reliable figure for the total number of birds.

Roosts in towns
Starlings are the most numerous of Britain's flocking birds. Large numbers of them roost in the countryside, flying at dusk along familiar flight-lines to roost in trees, reeds or along sea cliffs, and returning the same way the next morning. But they are equally familiar in towns. On winter evenings, the roar of London traffic around Leicester Square is drowned by the chattering of thousands of starlings as they fly in from the country and circle to settle on the ledges of buildings. Greater London is the home of probably more than 3 million starlings.

The scene is repeated in towns all over Britain, mainly in the industrial north—in Bradford, Liverpool and Leeds, for example. Altogether there are some 70 urban roosting sites, on buildings, bridges and among trees in parks. Many of them are small, but the largest can contain more than 50,000 birds.

The rook is another well-known social roosting species. In spring and summer, rooks sleep in small rookeries; but in autumn and throughout the winter, birds from a number of colonies gather together, often accompanied by jackdaws, at a single 'super roost'. In eastern England, an average rook/jackdaw roost contains about 10,000 birds. Carrion crows and ravens sometimes establish roosts of their own (a recent raven flock in the Hebrides was 1200 strong), as well as sometimes sharing roosts with rooks and jackdaws.

The social roosting habits of various gulls have changed remarkably this century: the number of gulls roosting inland, mainly on lakes, reservoirs and flooded gravel-pits, has greatly increased.

Exchanging information
For most of these birds, sleeping flocks are a continuation of daytime feeding communities. But other birds which feed alone or in small groups during the daytime will sometimes flock together at night. The individual gains protection and possibly information about feeding-sites; for birds which return hungry after a less rewarding search for food may join the feeding party of more successful birds the next day.

Pied wagtails, for example, tend to feed alone by day, although there may be other individuals not too far away. But at night, they roost socially throughout the year, especially in winter, mainly in reed-beds.

Many roosts consist of at most a few hundred birds, but larger roosts of 1000 or more are known, some in towns. One famous roost of wagtails, in O'Connell Street, Dublin, holds well over 3000 birds at times.

Many birds, though, sleep singly, even when they feed in groups By choosing well-concealed roosts, spaced out in countryside which they know intimately, they make themselves less conspicuous to predators.

In summer, great tits sleep alone in thick foliage in the woods, though the females roost in the nest-hole while incubating and before the young grow so big that there is no space left. In winter, all great tits use holes in trees or buildings, which both protect them against enemies and help to keep them warm.

Woodpeckers roost singly, in holes of their own making, throughout the year. These are often old nests, but in winter the birds sometimes excavate special roost-holes. Tree-creepers used to sleep in cracks and crevices in trees and behind bark, or in shallow niches in rotting tree stumps which they excavated with their long, curved bills. In many parts of the country, however, this species has recently taken to roosting in hollows scooped in the soft, thick, spongy bark of the giant Wellingtonia, a redwood tree introduced to Britain halfway through the last century.

Sleeping on the wing
Ornithologists have often watched swifts taking off at dusk after a day of activity, and flying out to sea. Though it seemed highly improbable, they found that many birds appeared to stay on the wing all night. Some remarkable detective work has been done to show that this is, in fact, what happens.

The first step was to note how many birds took off in the evening, and confirm that not all of them returned before nightfall. Observation also showed that none of the birds came back to roost during darkness. An ornithologist finally clinched the argument by flying over the sea in a light aircraft. He found dozens of the birds still airborne.

Swifts seem able to sleep—or at least to 'cat-nap'—on the wing, probably as they glide high above the water between spells of flapping to gain height. Sooty terns must have a similar ability. These birds spend much of their life over the ocean, often miles from land, yet they can never settle on the sea because their plumage becomes waterlogged by salt water—they even have to snatch small fish from the surface, to avoid getting wet.

Most birds sleep during the night, when they are unable to feed, leaving the hours of daylight for foraging and nesting. The process is reversed in the case of night-hunting birds such as the owls, which need the cover of darkness to enable them to catch their prey, and therefore sleep during the day.

Waders, which feed along the seashore, regulate their lives not according to the light, but by the tide. Probing in mud-flats with their bills, they can locate food without the aid of light. So they eat when the tide is low and sleep when it is high, irrespective of the time of day.

Why birds sing

FROM DAWN CHORUS TO EVENSONG

NATURALISTS are not as quick as they were only a few years ago to dismiss the idea that birds may sing from sheer high spirits. But it is difficult to reconcile too sentimental an interpretation of bird-song with the basic utilitarianism of a bird's way of life. When a bird sings, it is using up time and energy which could equally well be spent in finding food. At the same time, it is advertising its presence to predators. Birds would have ceased singing long ago if the survival value of conspicuousness did not outweigh its dangers.

Song is only one element in the vocabulary of birds. Each bird has a number of calls, too—more than a dozen different sounds for many species, each with its own meaning.

The chaffinch has 13 different calls in addition to its song, and even its young have two different types of begging call, one before they fledge and one after. The collared dove has five calls—an alarm call, an aggressive call, two different notes used in courtship, and a call for showing a nest-site to its mate.

One important factor limiting how much a bird communicates vocally is the degree to which it can 'say' the same things visually—a display of plumage may be as effective as any call.

Songs and calls

It is often difficult to draw a precise line between a song and a call. But song is concerned primarily with defending a territory or attracting a mate, whereas the function of calls is to pass on other kinds of information, such as the fact that a predator is approaching. Songs tend to be complex arrangements of notes, uttered rhythmically and in most cases by the male; calls are generally short groups of up to four or five notes—aesthetically less pleasing, to human ears at least.

A bird can communicate many things by the sounds it makes. It can state its species, its sex, its individual identity, even its condition. It can trigger off sexual excitement, curiosity, alarm or fear in another bird. It can attract a mate or drive off a rival. It can pass on news—where food is to be found or where there is a possible nest-site. It can alert others to the presence of predators. But when it sings, the usual message is to broadcast its ownership of a territory.

At the beginning of the breeding season, two instincts shape the lives of a great number of birds—the instinct to lay claim to a territory and the instinct to find a mate. Song, functioning as language in the sense that it conveys information from one bird to another, makes both things possible.

Most species which sing can be distinguished from one another by their songs, and this, in fact, is a vital function of song—to state the bird's species. Just as distinctive plumage patterns and elaborate displays minimise the likelihood of cross-breeding between different species of ducks, so distinctive songs prevent cross-breeding between similar-looking songbirds such as the chiffchaff and willow warbler.

At the same time, a bird's song is a statement of its sex—in most cases male; in only a few species, such as the robin, in which both male and female hold territories in winter, does the female sing. The song is interpreted differently according to the sex of the hearer—the same sound attracts unmated females and repels intruding males.

A bird's song goes into even finer detail than this; by subtle variations in pitch, rhythm, or repertoire it may also state the bird's individual identity. The emphatic terminal flourish to each song-phrase makes the chaffinch's song one of the easiest to identify, and the basic rhythm of the songs of all cock chaffinches is recognisably the same. But each chaffinch has up to six minor variations on the theme. While singing, it will select one from its repertoire and, after repeating it several times, will change to another.

In addition to the variation in output of a single cock, chaffinch song also differs from district to district. One theme is replaced by another in a different area. As in human language, there is a pattern of regional dialects.

Territorial songs are long-range warnings from one bird to another. They must be loud and clear to be effective—certainly loud enough to be heard beyond the boundaries of the territory. A reed warbler's song can be heard about 300 yds away; its territory is usually about 300 sq. yds.

As a general rule, the less conspicuous a bird's plumage, the louder its song. Birds living and breeding in dense vegetation tend to sing more loudly than those in open habitats. The boom of the bittern, which nests among close-packed reeds, may be heard more than a mile away. Considering the size of the bird, the wren's song is incredibly penetrating; but the wren, which usually holds a territory of 2–3 acres, has to make itself heard in competition with the many songs of other birds living in dense woodland.

Driving home the message

The song also needs to be persistent to make its point, so birds repeat their song-phrases hundreds of times a day. The yellowhammer repeats its 'little-bit-of-bread-and-no-cheese' over and over again, from the beginning of the day to the end; by dusk it may have 'said' the same thing more than 1000 times. The sustained warbling of a skylark, delivered as the bird climbs into the sky or sinks gently earthwards from the apex of its flight, will go on for minutes on end, for 10–12 minutes in every hour of daylight; one bird was heard singing for 18 minutes without a pause, although 3–4 minutes is more usual.

Many species—the mistle thrush is one—choose commanding song-posts high in a tree, to ensure that their songs cover the widest possible area. Others add a visual effect to the advertisement by describing distinctive patterns in the sky. The whitethroat, a small warbler, performs what is almost a song-and-dance act when it accompanies its outburst of squeaky song by flying straight up from the hedge for a few feet before dropping back again. Song-flights are particularly characteristic of ground-living birds such as larks and pipits, which breed in open, treeless countryside.

A battle of nerves
Rival birds seldom resort to physical combat—the risk of real injury to both is too great to make this a practical way of settling an argument. Instead, they have evolved patterns of behaviour which achieve results without exposing them to danger. Their territorial songs, like their elaborate threat displays, are battles of nerves, each bird working out the tension built up by two conflicting impulses—the impulse to fight and the impulse to flee. A robin or wren intruding on another's territory usually keeps as quiet as possible. If spotted, it is likely to be sung at with particular intensity. It usually flees at once, back to its own territory; if it does not, the song is backed up by aggressive posturing. A chase may ensue; and only if that fails do the birds actually fight.

A bird singing in defence of its territory pays careful attention to the songs of other birds defending theirs. A robin or a wren, for instance, will pause after each phrase of its song, allowing rivals time to get in their 'answer'. By song 'duels' with its neighbours, a bird gets to know who and where its rivals are, and whether they are likely to cause trouble or can safely be ignored.

There is scientific truth in the belief that a cuckoo's call announces that spring has arrived. Bird-song is inextricably associated with the season in which it is delivered, and although some birds may sing at any time of the year, they are never more vociferous than in spring, when establishing a territory. As summer approaches, and paired birds turn their attention to building nests, laying eggs, incubating and raising their young, the songs of many species become more intermittent or subdued, or even cease altogether.

Some birds, such as crossbills, may sing softly as they prospect for nest-sites, and the male redstart sings as it displays before a nest-hole. Male wrens may sing snatches of song as they build nests, and other birds sing as they change places during incubation, or while they tend the young. The functions of many of these sounds are not precisely known, but often they serve to confirm and strengthen the bond between male and female.

Spring song erupts in response to hormone-induced changes in a bird's body—particularly the increase in size of its internal reproductive organs—caused by the extra hours of daylight. In autumn, too, physiological change seems to spur some birds into song. In winter, most birds fall silent, though the robin is a notable exception. Both male and female robins defend winter territories, and sing defiantly at one another until they start forming pairs, usually sometime in December.

Another name for the mistle thrush is 'storm cock'. It may have been given this name because it begins to sing in January, regardless of the weather. But rain and mist tend on the whole to inhibit bird-song.

The dawn chorus
In the daily cycle, as in the seasonal cycle, light is the key factor affecting bird-song—night changing to day has the same song-producing effect on birds as winter changing to summer. More birds sing for the 20–40 minutes around dawn than at any other time of day. It is hard to find a biological reason for this, although there is some advantage in so many birds singing at once, for each bird can find out what is going on around it. Birds do not generally sing as soon as they are awake.

WRITING IN THE SKY

In spring and summer, the sky becomes a stage on which the male tree pipit performs to attract a mate. With wings fluttering like those of a butterfly, it flies steeply up from its tree-top perch and begins to sing as it reaches the top of its climb—usually about 60 ft up. Still singing, it floats down with its wings raised and tail spread, finishing with a shrill 'seea-seea-seea' as it drops back on to the perch from which it started, or one near by.

They may first stretch, like other creatures, preen their feathers and fly off to a good song-perch. The blackbird is often the first to break into song, starting about 40 minutes before sunrise; it is closely followed by the song thrush, wood-pigeon, robin, mistle thrush, turtle dove, pheasant, willow warbler and wren, usually in that order.

Just as most birds sing less in the cold, dark months of the year, so the dawn chorus starts late if a heavy grey overcast dawn retards the lightening of the sky.

Night singers

Very few species sing continuously throughout the day. Most quieten down after the initial exuberance of the dawn chorus, and are subdued by about midday. There is a resurgence of song in the evening, and silence falls with the night for most species.

Birds which roost together frequently sing together before settling down for the night. Starlings flying to their roosts raise a great chorus of twittering and wheezing as they wheel through the sky. The reasons for their flight manoeuvres and choral effects are not clear to scientists, but one suggestion is that they are 'conferring' about the local food-supply; if food is due to run out, a large percentage of the birds will move on to a place where food is more abundant.

A bird which sings by night usually does so for the same reasons as a bird which sings by day; the call of a tawny owl is a statement of identity and a summons to its mate. The reason why nightingales sing by night is harder to establish. Like many other small song-birds, they migrate by night; and the males arrive from their winter quarters in April, some ten days ahead of the females. It seems likely that the males sing by night to compete for the females as they arrive. But two facts do not fit in with this theory: nightingales sing by day as well as at night, and other night migrants do not sing at night.

Many species of birds need all the hours of daylight to collect enough food, so when the time comes to migrate, they have to move at night. Those which travel in flocks have two problems: not to get lost, and not to collide with others in the flock. They cannot overcome these problems by sight alone, although they usually fly when the sky is clear enough for them to navigate by the stars. To keep together—and apart—they have evolved a special signal: a contact-note.

The 'see-ip' note of redwings, heard from the night sky in October and November when the annual influx of these handsome thrushes comes flooding across the North Sea, has just this function. It is used to maintain a flock 'structure', neither too loose nor too tight. Many day-flying flocks, such as geese and waders, probably use contact-notes in this way as well.

Sounds inherited and learnt

The whitethroat inherits from its parents a complete vocabulary of call-notes and songs. No learning is necessary; if a whitethroat lived its whole life without hearing another whitethroat sing, it would still develop all its calls and songs, and each one would be perfect in pitch, volume, rhythm and quality. This has been proved by experiments in which birds were reared from birth in sound-proof isolation.

Other birds are born with the innate ability to sing songs that are characteristic of the species in all but a few of the details. In such cases, learning completes the job which instinct started.

The chaffinch inherits the basic pattern of its song, but it learns the flourishes by imitating others of its species. When it first establishes a territory, its song is incomplete; but by imitating other males singing around it, it soon puts this right.

Learning by imitation is the starting-point for one of the great mysteries of bird behaviour —mimicry. Many wild birds incorporate in their songs the notes of other birds and even the sounds of inanimate objects. Some 30 British birds are reputed to be mimics. The most gifted of them all is the starling, though marsh warblers, reed warblers and blackcaps are sometimes very skilled. The starling may reproduce the sounds of such unlikely birds as tawny owls, partridges and domestic fowl; and there is a reliable account of one bird imitating the ringing of a telephone so effectively that it deceived the owner of the house on which it was perched.

Mimicry is so widely established as a factor of bird behaviour that scientists feel it must have some survival value. Many explanations have been put forward, but none of them can be fully substantiated. Perhaps it helps a bird to establish its individual identity. Or perhaps birds actually like playing with sounds and use mimicry as a 'self rewarding' veneer on their own songs.

A bird's 'early warning system'

Most birds live in constant danger of being struck down by predators. It is not surprising, therefore, that their language includes a highly effective anti-predator alarm system. The first

THE SNIPE'S DRUMMING

The snipe begins its territorial display by swooping down from the sky at an angle of about 45°, with its outer tail feathers—which are stiffer than the central ones—held at right angles to its line of descent. Air rushing past makes them vibrate and causes the drumming or 'bleating' sound by which the bird draws attention to itself.

The language of musicians, like that of birds, is one of notes, and many composers have written snatches of bird-song into their pieces. Beethoven put the nightingale (flute), quail (oboe), and cuckoo (clarinet) into his Pastoral Symphony, and the cuckoo, certainly, is instantly recognisable.

bird to spot potential danger raises an alarm which alerts all within hearing.

The danger may come from the air or from the ground, and many birds have evolved alarm calls which differentiate between the two kinds of menace. Alarms calling attention to aerial predators are usually brief and high-pitched—the kind of sound which is difficult to trace to a source. Birds hearing it scatter into cover. But the alarm summons to mob a ground predator, or one spotted in a tree, contains clues to the whereabouts both of the caller and the predator.

A few birds have an even more sophisticated alarm system. Jays have several different 'words' for danger, and sometimes give specific calls for specific predators. Often these resemble the cries of the predator itself. A 'chittering' call draws attention to squirrels; a popping noise—perhaps in imitation of a gun—to humans; and a shrill 'kik-kik-kik' to kestrels.

While the song of each species must be very different, so that no confusion can arise, their alarm calls are often very similar. The first bird to spot a hawk warns all local birds within hearing, not merely those of the same species as itself. The 'aerial predator' warnings given by the reed bunting, blackbird, great tit, blue tit and chaffinch are all very alike.

How sounds are produced

Most birds make sounds by means of the syrinx, a voice organ situated near the lungs. It consists of a resonating chamber and associated membranes. Air from the lungs is driven through these membranes, which can be relaxed or tightened and moved in relation to the resonating chamber, to change the character of the sound produced. Muscles change the shape of the syrinx, too, and the quality of the voice alters accordingly. The entire system is different from that of mammals, which produce sound in the larynx, situated in the throat, and use their lips and tongues to give form to the sound.

The most versatile singers are usually those with the most intricate syrinxes. But this does not always hold true; crows, which have highly developed syrinxes, are poor singers.

The smaller the bird, the higher-pitched its voice is likely to be. The firecrest, goldcrest and wren, all of them small, have some of the highest-pitched voices among British birds. The wren's voice vibrates at about 4000 cycles per second—the equivalent of the top note on a piano; and its delivery rate is too fast for a human ear to take in every note; in 5·2 seconds, it sings 56 notes, producing a 'tune' which only becomes intelligible to human ears if the song is slowed down on a tape recorder. At the other end of the scale, the bittern's boom is one of the lowest-pitched notes uttered by any British bird.

In addition to vocalising, birds can also use instrumental techniques. The flight-music of the mute swan comes from vibrations set up by its wing-beats. Probably the sound helps flocks of mute swans to keep together, as do the vocal flight-notes of the other European swans, the whooper and the Bewick's.

The 'bleating' or 'drumming' of the snipe—the humming sound created as the bird dives through the air—is also a mechanically produced sound.

But communicating mechanically has nowhere reached a higher degree of sophistication than among woodpeckers. Using the same technique as when they feed, they signal their presence and identity to one another with a sharp drumming, tapped out with an identifiable rhythm on trees.

Man imitates the birds

Attempts to imitate bird-song in human speech are probably as old as language itself. These attempts can never be satisfactory, for birds and humans produce sound in different ways. Birds, for instance, have neither lips nor teeth, and so cannot form consonants; yet the convention is accepted that birds can make most of the sounds in the alphabet. The yellowhammer is supposed to say 'little-bit-of-bread-and-no-cheese', and this phrase, though packed with sounds that no bird could make, is helpful in identifying the bird, because it repeats the rhythm of its song.

Many birds are named after the sounds they are traditionally supposed to make—and usually the name is as close an echo of the bird's song as human speech can give.

The chiffchaff, for instance, sounds as if it is saying something very near to 'chiff-chaff, chiff-chaff, chiff-chaff'. Other birds among the many whose names echo their songs are the peewit, the chough, the kittiwake and, of course, the cuckoo.

In other European languages, the cuckoo is called: kuckuck (German), cuco (Spanish), coucou (French), cuculo (Italian), kukuk (Hungarian), koekoek (Dutch), kukulka (Polish), and käki (Finnish).

The drive to establish territory

A SYSTEM OF LAND OWNERSHIP

A BLACKBIRD attacking its own reflection in a window or a car wing-mirror is following a behaviour pattern as deeply ingrained as the the urge to mate or to find food. For its aggression is connected with the defence of territory—and this is as important for the survival of the bird and its species as are eating and breeding.

By marking out an area of land and defending it against males of its own species a bird can gain monopoly access to food, nesting material and nest-sites, as well as a place where it can court its mate and rear its young unmolested by rivals.

There is usually no need to defend territory against birds of a different species, because they seldom take exactly the same food and they are not rivals for mates—although they may be for nest-sites.

The simplest definition of the word 'territory' is 'any defended area'—a definition which covers a treecreeper defending its winter roosting cavity at one extreme, and a golden eagle on its 'home range' at the other.

A home range is an area whose boundaries are not clearly defined, and in which birds keep apart from rivals of their own species by mutual avoidance rather than by disputes. A pair of golden eagles may hunt over a home range of up to 18,000 acres—more than 28 square miles. Partridges, too, are home-range birds.

By strict definition, many colony-dwelling birds are territorial even though, like gannets, they may defend only a few feet of space at the nest-site. So are black grouse when they are defending a patch of ground at their courtship arenas. But for the sake of convenience, the term 'territorial' is best confined to birds defending larger areas.

The size of the territory varies considerably from species to species. It can also vary within a single species according to local conditions, such as the richness of the food supply or the density of cover. Great crested grebes, for instance, defend anything from a few square yards round the nest to several acres, depending on the distribution of cover.

Defending territory

The means by which most birds advertise and enforce their territorial claims are song, special displays and—against persistent interlopers—threat or actual fighting. For a few species, including ravens and kestrels, mere physical presence on the territory is enough to stake a claim.

Most territorial species have a definite code of conduct, with the territory owner showing aggression only within its own defended area and fleeing when it is discovered trespassing in another bird's territory.

In an experiment to test the strength of this code, a robin was put in a cage within its own territory. It put a rival robin to flight by singing and displaying its red breast; but when the roles were reversed, and the caged robin was moved into the other bird's territory, it shrank back and would have fled if flight were possible.

A territory owner is usually secure in its own territory, though determined intruders can sometimes annex part or even all of an occupied territory by sustained hostility, especially in crowded habitats.

In many species the boundaries of territories are sharply defined by natural features, such as trees, bushes, clearings or woodland edges. This boundary is also defined by a bird's behaviour; it is the place where a bird's fear of its neighbour and its urge to attack the other bird are in balance.

Territory sizes can often be worked out by direct observation on colour-ringed or wing-tagged birds, or by counting the total of males or pairs and dividing it into the occupied

THE SIZE OF TERRITORY

GREAT CRESTED GREBE	A small area around the nest to several acres (Lakes)
RED GROUSE	5–15 acres (Moorland)
DABCHICK	¾ acre (Ponds)
PTARMIGAN	8 acres (Barren high ground)
LAPWING	2¼ acres and the air-space above (Farmland)
LITTLE RINGED PLOVER	Up to 1 acre and the air-space above (Gravel-pits)
TAWNY OWL	60–70 acres (Broad-leaved woodland)
REDSTART	Just over 1 acre (Broad-leaved woodland)
WHEATEAR	1–8 acres (Islands)
WILLOW WARBLER	⅙ acre to just over 1 acre (Commons)
REED WARBLER	About 300 sq. yds (Reed-beds)
MARSH TIT	1–16 acres (Broad-leaved woodland)
YELLOW-HAMMER	About ½ acre (Hedgerows)
CORN BUNTING	Just over 2 acres (Farmland)

These figures are based on studies of bird populations in restricted areas, and do not necessarily hold true for all birds throughout a species' range; the habitats in which they were studied are given in brackets.

SIX WAYS OF SHARING OUT AN AREA OF WOODLAND

The songs of a great variety of species ring through the broad-leaved woods in spring and summer; these are only some of the ways in which six acres might be divided up.

CHAFFINCHES Very common birds in this kind of wood; their territories include clearings and isolated trees from which to sing.

BLACKBIRDS The number of blackbirds and other thrushes is small; they need a better shrub layer to feed in, and their territories extend beyond the wood.

WREN Because there is no shrub layer this is a poor wood for wrens; the 6 acres might support only one bird, with a large amount of 'edge' territory.

BLUE TITS The lack of a shrub layer does not worry blue tits; they feed in the trees, and several pairs have territories in this wood.

GREAT TITS This is not a good wood for great tits; their territories are large because there is no good shrub layer to feed in.

ROBINS There is little dead ground between the territories of the highly aggressive robins; and a few areas are in dispute between pairs.

---

area. Another method, often useful with birds holding small territories, is chasing the bird and watching how far it goes before it encounters a neighbour or turns back. The borders of a robin's territory in a garden can be discovered by taking a large mirror into the garden and noting the places at which the bird attacks or retreats from its own reflection.

There are a few exceptions to the rule that territorial rivalry occurs only between birds of the same species. In areas where they breed close together, especially on the Continent, three species of plovers—ringed, little ringed and Kentish—defend territory against one another. Disputes have been recorded between reed and sedge warblers and between garden warblers and blackcaps. Within these pairs, the species are closely related, taking very much the same kind of food, and it is probably not a coincidence that their songs are similar. Often, however, these species hold overlapping territories.

Some birds which stay in Britain all year round, such as great tits, reed buntings, coots and ringed plovers, establish their territories in late winter and early spring after a winter spent as members of a flock. Other residents, such as blackbirds and wrens, which do not spend the winter in flocks but keep in touch with their territories throughout the year, start to defend them again more seriously at the same time.

Summer visitors, such as yellow wagtails, whitethroats, willow warblers and wheatears, set up territory later in the spring, after journeying from winter quarters abroad.

Choosing a territory

Generally speaking, the male bird is responsible for establishing the territory and defending it. The female joins him and usually accepts the boundaries of the territory as they are, though there are odd cases of a male having to adjust the boundaries to take in the wanderings of its mate (reported of the blackbird), or because she nested outside the original territory (reported of the snow bunting).

Red-necked phalaropes are exceptional in that the female chooses the territory and attracts a mate. In this species the female is more brightly coloured than the male, and many of the usual roles of the sexes are reversed.

In winter-flocking species, such as buntings, the males leave the flocks first and start to set up their territories by visiting them for increasing periods over a number of weeks. Finally a complete break is made and the bird stays in the territory, where it is later joined by a female.

Among summer visitors, such as nightingales and warblers, the males arrive from abroad first and almost immediately establish themselves; the females follow them and arrive ten days or so later.

In a few species, such as the great crested grebe, the birds first form pairs in open water and then seek and establish a territory together. Much the same thing happens with various ducks, such as the mallard, and with certain gulls, such as the herring gull, which pairs first in 'clubs' near the colony area and then establishes the real territory.

The black-headed gull, however, establishes a definite 'pairing territory' where a male stays until it has a mate; the pair later move into the real breeding territory. Similar pairing territories have been recorded in the greenshank.

Moving out for food

Many song-birds live more or less entirely within the boundaries of the breeding territory throughout the breeding season and find all or most of their food there, including food for their young. Some, however—reed warblers, for example—move outside the territory to find food. Ducks and many waders leave the breeding territory after the young have hatched, and take them away to a more suitable feeding area.

Most birds hold territory for the breeding season only, and only a few British species defend territory in winter. If they are resident

species, the winter territory is usually the same, at least in part, as the one held in summer.

The best-known example of a bird which is territorial in winter is the robin. The male and female birds hold separate plots, and both sexes sing to advertise their territories, which are only half the size, on average, of the summer ones. In effect, the male and female divide the joint summer territory between them—though in practice former mates need not necessarily be neighbours and they do not always pair up again in a combined territory the following year.

The male wren also maintains a winter territory, retiring to part of its former breeding territory from late summer onwards. Other species which hold individual territories in winter are the rock pipit, the great grey shrike (a rare winter visitor), and many birds of prey.

Very few species defend a joint winter territory. Marsh tits do so and will not tolerate neighbouring pairs, though they join passing tit flocks when these are within the territory.

Well-established blackbird pairs also tend to stay together in the former breeding territory throughout the winter, though they may leave the territory for much of the day to visit better feeding places elsewhere. Pairs of stonechats also occupy a common territory in winter—often the former breeding territory, though some pairs move right away from their summer haunts and settle in a new territory.

The value of territory

A system of territory-holding means that birds are dispersed more widely in suitable habitats than if the population crowded in without restraint. As a result, competition for such essentials as food, nest-sites and safe roosting places is much reduced.

Isolation from competitors is especially important for species such as owls and many insect-eaters, which specialise in catching hidden prey by skilled hunting techniques. Such birds often need to feed their young at frequent intervals, so it is important for them to be able to find food fairly near the nest; and familiarity with a restricted area probably enables the territory owner to find food more easily than if it had to forage more widely over a greater and largely unfamiliar area.

Another advantage is that once a female has entered a territory, pair formation—and later copulation—can proceed with the minimum interference from rivals.

Holding a territory is probably important, too, in maintaining the pair once it has been formed—by compelling the birds to remain together in a circumscribed area, rather than allowing them to wander at will.

In some species, joint defence of the territory together with mutual display afterwards probably helps to strengthen the pair-bond.

Finally, the spacing out of nests in a territorial system probably makes them harder for predators to find. In fact, concealment may well be a major function of territory in many ground-nesting birds, such as plovers.

Threat and fighting

HOW DISPUTES ARE RESOLVED IN THE COMPETITIVE WORLD OF BIRDS

COMPETITION between birds for territory, nest-sites, food and mates inevitably produces hostility. But natural selection ensures that only rarely does this hostility lead to full-blooded fighting: birds whose aggressive drive leads them to risk being killed or maimed usually do not live long enough to breed.

In many species, a single hostile encounter will be sufficient to decide which bird will have unquestioned priority in any future dispute.

When conflict threatens, all animals are torn between aggression and fear. Instead of fighting, most birds show their hostility by an elaborate system of bluff and threats—frightening calls or physical displays which stop short of violence.

Disputes over territory

Rivalry between birds of the same species is at its most intense and frequent during the breeding season, when the sex hormones make them more aggressive and they have to contend for territory, mates and nest-sites.

The establishment and defence of territory, in particular, is a major cause of threats and fighting. A bird is most aggressive near its nest, and is inclined to fight off all intruders. Further away, towards the edges of its territory, this aggression is balanced by fear of the rival from the neighbouring territory, and threat displays will usually take the place of violence.

A bird's urge to defend its own territory and respect that of its rival is deeply ingrained. A robin experimentally caged within its own territory has been known to drive off intruders by its song and threatening displays, even though it was in no position to back up threats with actual physical aggression.

Conflicts can break out when food is scarce, particularly among flocking birds such as finches, starlings, rooks and jackdaws. These disputes become serious only when the shortage is so severe as to reduce the birds' fear of one another.

When a great tit finds food, it threatens other members of the flock which come too close either by partly opening and raising its wings or by holding its head low and pointing it at the rival. One tit will rob another by flying at it and taking its place as it moves away from the food. The supplanted bird will occasionally retaliate, but usually it simply flies away and begins the search again.

Though the intensity of the struggle for food depends on how scarce it is, a time may come when there is no longer any point in fighting. A starving robin, for example, will not divert itself from the search for food by attacking another robin which encroaches on its territory in hard weather.

Warning off rivals

Apart from disputing for food and territory, birds will defend themselves if attacked by predators. They will also fight or threaten one another for a host of lesser causes, such as roosting perches, nest-sites, mates and—if they are flocking or colonial birds—to maintain a set distance between themselves and their neighbours.

Birds have many ways of avoiding conflict and the need to fight: they stake their claim to a piece of territory as ostentatiously as possible, and often treat intruders to spectacular displays of force. These displays are

MARKINGS THAT WARN

When threatening, a ringed plover bends its legs and displays its dramatic black and white markings.

THREAT IN A COLOUR

The yellow wagtail frightens rivals by stretching itself and showing off its brilliant yellow plumage.

aimed at showing that here is an aggressive bird of the same species, often of the same sex, which will attack if provoked. The effect is usually to make the intruder afraid, and force it to withdraw.

Noisy and dazzling flying displays are used by many species to advertise their choice of territory. The male little ringed plover flies round in wide circles, arcs or figures-of-eight, crying 'cree-a, cree-a, cree-a'. If it encounters a rival doing the same thing, its cry becomes a mechanical-sounding buzz, and it flies threateningly at the other bird, stalling before it with wings quivering in a V-shape.

Some birds do not even need to come face-to-face in order to compete for territory; robins have been observed to do it all by singing. The intruder enters alien country and sings; the occupant replies from a distance. The intruder comes deeper into the territory and sings again. At this, the occupant flies to within five yards of the newcomer, still hidden in the foliage, and replies more vigorously, staking its claim in forceful and direct fashion. This is often sufficient to put the intruder to flight.

Threats at close quarters

If song and flying displays fail to frighten off a rival, birds have a formidable repertoire of menaces to fall back on. At close quarters they make themselves look as big and fearsome as possible. They puff out their feathers, stiffen their crests or crown feathers, and show off any special plumage marks, colours or patterns. Then follows a series of menacing movements, many of them evolved from the first stages of jumping or flying up.

The robin stretches itself up, fluffs up the red feathers on its breast and displays them to its rival. In a similar way the great tit shows off its broad black chin, and breast-stripe bordered with yellow.

The ringed plover crouches forward on bent legs, showing off its black chest-patch, ruffling its back feathers and spreading its tail to show the white outer feathers.

Many birds enhance their basic postures by making the best display of their markings. The most striking feature of the yellow wagtail is the brilliant yellow of the feathers on its head, breast and belly; so the bird turns full-face towards its rival and stretches, to display its plumage to the full. The jay, on the other hand, can make itself look more daunting by standing sideways and ruffling and spreading its feathers to increase its size.

The shag adds movement to its armoury of threats. It erects its crest and the feathers on its neck and head, draws the head and neck slowly back, and then suddenly darts them forward at the rival, opening its bill wide and exposing its vivid yellow gape.

Frightened to death

Though all this threatening behaviour seldom leads to fighting in earnest, it is extremely successful in settling disputes. Most of the time it takes the form of stylised gestures, but is none the less frightening to the birds concerned; several cases have been reported of birds—including the blackbird—which died of ruptured hearts or blood vessels as a result of the emotional excitement of these mock battles.

Faced with an aggressor, birds are frequently uncertain what to do—whether to fight, submit, or bluff it out. As the struggle between aggression and fear goes on within them, they often adopt postures curiously irrelevant to the hostile situation. Many are drawn from other activities. Gulls will start preening themselves or feeding; waders such as the oystercatcher and the avocet adopt the sleeping position, with the head turned away sideways and the bill hidden.

Some birds also have a special 'quandary' posture; Sandwich terns and gulls, for instance, stand with heads bowed, as if staring at their feet. This posture may be a preliminary either to submission or to an attack.

Styles of fighting

Real battles are liable to break out in extreme circumstances, particularly when one bird threatens another's nest during the breeding season. Then it is usually the males which do the fighting, though their mates may occasionally join in, either tentatively trying to peck at the enemy, or attacking its mate. In a species such as the great crested grebe, where the sexes are difficult to tell apart, male may occasionally fight female, but most fights are between birds of the same sex; only rarely do they fully engage more than two birds.

MENACING PLUMAGE

The jay turns sideways to meet an enemy, ruffling and spreading its feathers to make itself look bigger.

TAKING REFUGE IN 'SLEEP'

Unsure whether to fight or flee, the oystercatcher hides its bill in its plumage, as if going to sleep.

ADMITTING DEFEAT

Some of the most spectacular battles of the bird world take place between male mute swans. When the fight is over, the losing bird submits to being pecked on the back of its head and neck.

Fights are usually brief and relatively bloodless. Among the exceptions are the spectacular battles between two mute swan cobs. The birds fight breast to breast in the water, necks intertwined, beating each other powerfully with their wings. These battles may last until both birds are exhausted, though their ultimate object is to seize the other's head and push it under the water.

Less protracted fights take place between the perching birds, which flutter breast to breast, grappling with their bills. Plovers fight like this, but they also use their feet. Game-birds, such as pheasants, have spurs on the backs of their legs with which they hack at each other, using vicious downward blows. Pigeons beat each other with their wings.

Grebes grapple in the water with bills interlocked, trying to drown the rival by forcing its head under the water. The great crested grebe has a long, pointed bill with which it tries to spear its enemies by coming at them under water. Coots lie back on the water, supporting themselves on wings held back, and strike out with the long, sharp claws on their toes.

Herring gulls and greater and lesser black-backed gulls seize each other by the bill and pull vigorously. Male gannets spread-eagle themselves, grip each other by the bill and push vigorously in the hope of toppling one another over the edge of the cliff.

Where a ledge is narrow, the dispute will be quickly decided, but in flatter parts of the colony the struggle can be prolonged and damaging—one gannet in every few hundred is blind in one eye as a result.

Birds usually direct their hostility at other birds, but many will attack any animal or human being which comes too near the nest. Seabirds can be particularly ferocious: skuas and some terns will fly straight at an intruder or dive at its head, striking out viciously with their feet; they have even been known to draw blood from a man's head. A breeding fulmar will shoot an oily, evil-smelling liquid from its mouth over anything which comes too near.

Submission and retreat

A game of bluff or an actual contest will usually end when one bird concedes defeat, most obviously by flying away. But when flight is impossible—for example, when a bird is cornered—a fresh set of stylised postures and movements comes into use, frequently the opposite of those which carried the threat. The bird stays motionless, head withdrawn, feathers fluffed up, and does its best to conceal the markings which at other times would be used to frighten enemies.

A submissive great tit ruffles its plumage and leans forward from the normal perching position to minimise the effect of its black frontal markings. A finch will do the same. But a mute swan which is beaten in combat lies prostrate in the water or on the bank with its neck stretched out, and submits to being pecked on the back of the head. Once the winner has established its victory in this way, however, it soon gives up the attack.

SKIRMISH ON A LEDGE

Two gannets, with their bills interlocked, battle to topple one another over the edge of a cliff.

BATTLE IN THE WATER

Long, sharp claws are used by these fighting coots to give vicious effect to each blow of their feet.

Finding and keeping a mate

THE BIZARRE WORLD OF BIRD COURTSHIP

BREEDING SEASON COLOURS

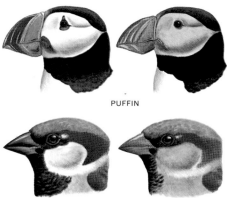

PUFFIN

HOUSE SPARROW

A puffin in the mating season (left), and the same bird at other times; the bright new colours help it to attract a mate. A male house sparrow in the breeding season (left) also shows distinctive markings.

BIRDS in the breeding season inhabit a strange and colourful world of ritual and response—a world where song, plumage and stereotyped display each have their part to play in attracting and courting a mate. These three elements are the 'language' of bird courtship, and a bird using them can spell out a number of messages: where it has established a territory; when it wishes to pair up; which sex and species it belongs to; where it has found a possible nest-site; and when it is ready to mate.

The distinctive displays of the males normally prove attractive only to females of the same species. By this means the chances of cross-breeding are reduced, and with them the danger of producing infertile eggs or sterile hybrids.

Plumage for the breeding season

Many birds have evolved special plumages and ornaments—crests, plumes and wattles— to emphasise their displays. The robin has its red breast, the jay its blue and black wing-patch, and the great tit a black, white and yellow head and breast. Herons have plumes, and grebes and ruffs use a variety of head ornaments in display.

Even the male house sparrow, unrelievedly drab for most of the year, has distinctive head-markings during the breeding season—a darker beak and bib, whiter cheeks and brighter colouring at the sides of the head.

The bill of the puffin flares into vivid reds, yellows and blues throughout the nesting season; and the plumage of many male ducks consists of an almost permanent multi-coloured display. Among most of the ducks which nest or winter in Britain there is, for much of the year, a striking difference between the plumages of males and females. The males are brightly coloured but the females are inconspicuous in drab browns and greys, more like one another than like their own mates.

The bright plumage of the male lasts through the winter and into summer, until the association between paired birds ends; then the female nests and rears the young unaided. From mid-summer to early autumn, the male moults into a dull, female-like 'eclipse' plumage, which makes it less conspicuous to predators during the vulnerable period when it is unable to fly.

In many species in which male and female plumages are alike, birds are often aggressive towards one another in the preliminary stages of courtship. The male discovers the sex of the bird to which it is displaying only by the other bird's reactions to the display; if an aggressive response is maintained it means that the other bird is a male, too.

Mutual displays

Courtship displays are often mutual between birds of similar plumage, particularly between large birds, such as many seabirds and fresh-water birds. Often male and female play identical roles simultaneously, as in the 'greeting' and nest-relief ceremonies of herons, when the birds meet after separations.

The so-called 'triumph ceremony' of the Canada goose is one of the most spectacular examples of mutual display: male and female run together and, with heads held low and necks extended, call loudly.

In the 'head flagging' ceremony of black-headed gulls, the birds threaten one another with heads low and the brown facial mask showing. Then suddenly they erect their necks and turn their heads, so as to present the white nape and hide the facial mask.

The great crested grebe has an intricate courtship dance in which both sexes take part. Not all birds with similar plumages display together, however; in starlings, wrens and various pigeons, display is left to the male alone.

Most courtship begins in the spring, before nesting gets under way. It is usually the male which takes the initiative. Exceptions are the red-necked phalarope and the dotterel—both birds in which the female is the larger, brighter sex, and in which the male has taken over the usual female duties of incubation and tending the young.

There are exceptions, too, to the rule that

HEAD FLAGGING

Both male and female black-headed gulls take part in courtship displays: here they start threatening one another, then suddenly turn their heads away.

TRIUMPH CEREMONY

A spectacular display of the breeding season is provided by Canada geese as they race together with necks outstretched, calling loudly.

birds start to pair up in the spring. A female robin will join a male during the winter, sometimes linking their territories together. Great crested grebes, too, begin forming pairs in winter, even before they have a territory. The male and female associate first in open water, and only then establish a territory.

Ducks also pair up in winter. Their early courtship is communal, though they are monogamous birds. Their displays are staged on water, and the chief role is played by the brightly coloured males. The display parties of some species—especially of the mallard, our most common duck—may consist wholly or largely of males at times; yet these displays are still part of courtship, for they are intended for the females.

Later in the season, the sexual energies of male mallards may lead them to pursue a duck with which they are not paired and attempt to mate by force. The drake flies after the duck until she is forced to land, then tries to copulate without going through the normal ritual. The 'raped' female mallard has a characteristic gesture of repulsion, coughing out single sharp calls, drawing back its head and ruffling its feathers.

Synchronising sexual rhythms

The reproductive cycles of birds which breed outside the Tropics are set in motion by changes in the length of the day. This response to variations in the amount of daylight is known as photoperiodism. Linked with alterations in the food supply, it leads to the

secretion of hormones which have a profound effect on bird activity.

Outside the breeding season, the internal sex organs of birds are small, as a weight-saving adaptation. But at breeding time there is a remarkable increase. The testes of house sparrows and starlings enlarge by between 300 and 500 times, and those of the brambling increase at least 360 times. In female starlings, the weight of the oviduct—the egg-laying passage—increases from about 20 mg. to 2500 mg.

Change of sex

In nearly all birds, only one of the female's two ovaries—the left one—plays a part in producing the egg; the right one remains small and undeveloped. If the working ovary becomes diseased or damaged, the right one can develop—but not as an ovary. It will become a testis, a male reproductive organ. It can even happen that a hen mothers chicks, loses the left ovary through disease, changes sex and becomes father to a further set of chicks.

The readiness of the normal female for mating, besides being affected by the amount of daylight, also depends on its mate; in many species, it is courtship that is largely responsible for inducing the necessary changes in its body and making it ready both to ovulate and to accept the male for copulation.

The amount of daylight required to trigger off the correct glandular response varies from species to species. Rooks, for instance, respond to the short days of February and

MUTUAL PREENING

Two jackdaws strengthen the link between them by preening feathers on each other's heads.

RITUAL OF THE CARESS

Mutual fear and aggression are reduced between these wood-pigeons by caressing one another.

COURTSHIP FEEDING

Like a parent with a nestling, a male robin brings food in its bill and passes it on to the female, so helping to strengthen the bond between them.

PRESENTING A FISH

A gift of food precedes copulation in kingfishers; the male presents a fish head-first to the female, so that she can swallow it without choking.

March: they lay their eggs in late March and April, which means that their young hatch in April and early May, to coincide with the peak availability of earthworms. But other species, such as summer-nesting whinchats, whose main food supply becomes available later in the year, respond to longer periods of daylight.

Courtship displays also help to establish a bond between male and female once they have started to associate as a pair. They do so by breaking down the aggressiveness and fear birds feel, even towards the opposite sex.

Such feelings arise out of the need to threaten and fight rivals for territory, food and mates; a bird cannot help feeling the same way towards its mate until they know one another better.

The presence of hostility in courtship sequences is well illustrated by the male grey heron, whose early display to a female includes postures identical to its threat behaviour towards rival males. When the female adopts the correct appeasing posture the male's feelings of aggression subside.

In general, though, true courtship displays are basically different in form from threat displays. They also help to promote individual and species recognition.

Individual recognition is especially important for colony-dwelling birds, with many birds of the same species living close together. Their courtship often begins after the male has taken up a nest-site, where it is joined by the female. The male's hostility towards rival males in defence of its site makes it, at least at first, also aggressive to any would-be mate. Later, however, the male and female often display together at the site.

The displays of the grey heron, gannet and shag may be taken as typical of the courtship of the larger colony-dwelling birds.

Strengthening the bond

Once birds have become paired, the bond between them—so important for most species if they are to be successful in raising young —is strengthened by special displays such as mutual preening, courtship feeding and showing a nest-site. The bond can be further strengthened by the joint defence of territory against rival birds.

Scientists prefer the term 'allopreening' (from the Greek word *allos,* meaning 'other') for what is usually called mutual preening, as it covers cases in which one sex preens the other, as with cormorants, as well as those in which the preening is truly mutual, as with shags and gannets.

Among native British birds, allopreening is characteristic of: gannets, cormorants, shags, grey herons, water rails, moorhens, coots, kittiwakes, guillemots and razorbills; all pigeons and doves (in which it is usually called 'caressing'); little owls (and probably other owls); swifts, house martins, bearded tits, ravens, rooks, jackdaws and choughs.

The preening is largely confined to the head and neck of the other bird, which may assume a special preening invitation posture.

The coot has a very well-developed invitation display, in which one of the birds ruffles out its black head feathers, arches its neck downwards and points its bill towards its feet. It 'freezes' in this posture, and when the display is performed on water, the entire head of the soliciting bird may disappear underwater for a few seconds. Sometimes both birds take up the invitation posture side by side, each waiting for the other to react.

An outlet for aggression

Since allopreening is confined largely to those areas of plumage which a bird cannot reach with its own bill, there is no reason to doubt that the behaviour is of some use in feather-care. In some groups, pigeons for example, the preening bird will detach dirt and parasites from the mate's plumage and eat or discard them.

However, it seems certain that the allopreening has more than this utilitarian function and is also an important form of bond strengthening behaviour. It is at times an outlet for aggressive tendencies: instead of pecking its mate, the other bird uses its bill for preening. Similarly, preening invitation displays are often submissive demonstrations of peacefulness.

Courtship. feeding between paired birds is more widespread than allopreening, though by no means universal. It is found chiefly in species in which the female carries out the duties of incubation. In some birds it occurs only during the early stages of the breeding cycle, but in the majority the male continues to bring food to the female during incubation.

Courtship feeding has been observed in many birds, and the form of the ritual varies greatly. In general, however, the female behaves like a begging chick and the male feeds it as a parent would. In fact, the habit may be of some value in preparing a bird to feed its young.

The food may be passed directly from one bill to the other, as with robins, kingfishers and terns; it may be regurgitated from bill to bill, as with crows, finches and pigeons; regurgitated on to the ground first, as with gulls; or picked up and then replaced on the ground, as with red-legged partridges.

In the day-hunting birds of prey, particularly the harriers, prey may be transferred from male to female in a spectacular aerial 'food-pass'. At the other extreme, no food may be passed at all in some cases, with the birds symbolically going through the motions of giving and receiving it.

When birds 'kiss'

The courtship feeding of finches is usually extremely stylised in the early stages, with male and female merely touching or 'scissoring' bills in a kind of kiss. As the breeding cycle progresses, the feeding tends to become more complete. In the bullfinch, for example, the male has frequently reached the stage of regurgitating food into its mate's bill by the time of nest-building; and this continues throughout incubation. Chaffinches are exceptional among the finches in that courtship feeding has not been observed among them.

Courtship feeding in pigeons, in which both sexes share the work of incubation—unlike finches—usually consists of formal 'billing' in which the male offers its open bill to the female which then inserts its own; sometimes this is followed by feeding by regurgitation. This billing, together with ritual preening behind the wing, is also part of the mating ceremony in pigeons.

Similarly, the male kingfisher brings a fish and gives it to the female before copulation.

THE FEEDING RITUAL
Bills meet, but no food passes; courtship feeding between hawfinches is at times completely formal.

However, in many other species, such as the robin, courtship feeding is independent of mating, though it often occurs at the same stage of the breeding cycle.

Most naturalists once regarded courtship feeding as a bond-forming display. Now, however, it is agreed that it is also of great value in some species in providing the female with extra nourishment to form its eggs. This is especially important for species which nest early, when suitable food may be scarce. In the majority of courtship-feeders, the female incubates the eggs on her own, and ritual feeding by the male makes a contribution to her nourishment right up to the time when the brooding of the young is over.

Showing a nest-site

In colony-dwelling birds, the male often attracts a female to its nest-site. In many other species, however, the male first attracts the female to its territory and then they choose a site together. Many such birds have special courtship displays, which serve to show the mate likely nest-sites.

These displays are especially well-developed in birds which nest on the ground or in holes in trees. In ground-nesting lapwings, for example, after mating or attempted mating (which may have been preceded by a display

DISPLAYING AND SHOWING A NEST-SITE
The male lapwing flies over its territory (left) to attract a female, and attempts to mate. Then it starts scraping out a hollow in the earth, as if showing the mate where they might build their nest.

CHASE AND DISPLAY IN THE COURTSHIP OF THE WREN

A series of vigorous chases (left), said to start when female entices male, accompanies the courtship of the wren. Later, male attracts female to the nest by singing loudly, with tail and wings quivering.

flight over the territory), the male runs off and starts scraping out a hollow in the earth. As it bends forwards to scratch, its tail is fanned and elevated to show off a black and white pattern which is accentuated by the chestnut undertail coverts.

Little ringed plovers have a scrape ceremony in which the male 'flags' its conspicuously patterned tail while turning in the hollow; then, as the female approaches, the male gets out on the rim and stands motionless with its tail fanned over the scrape. The female then initiates what has been called 'symbolic nest-relief', slipping under the male's tail into the hollow; and the male moves ceremonially away, picking up little stones and tossing them over its shoulder towards her.

Among woodland hole-nesting birds, nest-showing displays are often associated with bright and conspicuous patterns. The male redstart indicates its chosen hole by song and flight and also by displaying at the entrance. It either shows off its red breast and black and white forehead or, more usually, turns round and fans out its chestnut tail.

The great tit displays its black and white head pattern and the black and yellow of its breast conspicuously against the dark entrance of the nest cavity. Site-showing in the case of the highly camouflaged wren, on the other hand, is not linked with a bright display plumage. The male attracts a female to the domed nest it has built by a special nest-invitation display—singing loudly, with tail and wings outspread and quivering.

Many species have special displays which indicate their willingness to copulate and which stimulate the partner to respond. Male kingfishers and pigeons have what seems to human eyes a particularly charming habit of giving a 'present' of food to the female.

Mating displays

Mating displays are not always by male birds only: there are often soliciting displays by females. The female blackbird points its bill and tail up almost vertically, sleeking its feathers and running a little in front of the male, giving a soft, high-pitched call. The male, stimulated to follow, gives broken snatches of song, fans and trails its tail, raises the feathers of rump and crown and stretches its neck; copulation follows if the female permits.

The male redstart has a remarkable pre-mating display, in which it squats on a branch in front of the female with head low and neck stretched out, uttering a high-pitched hissing note. Its wide-open bill reveals its yellow gape. The bird fans out its tail and presses it down, opening its wings and quivering them, with their tips nearly touching above its back.

Redstarts also engage in vigorous sexual chases, flying rapidly in and out of the trees in their territory, especially after unsuccessful mating attempts. Sexual chases are characteristic of warblers, buntings, sparrows and many other song-birds. The pursuit of the female by the male is probably basically aggressive, though both sexes may well be sexually stimulated by it. In the wren, the female is thought to entice the male to pursue.

The male little ringed plover approaches the female with its body in the horizontal position,

THE MALE REDSTART COURTS A MATE

The male redstart begins its courtship by chasing the intended mate through the tree-tops. It displays at the nest-hole, tail fanned out, and crouches hissing before the female when ready for copulation.

THE 'LANGUAGE' OF DUCKS

SALUTING

The red-breasted merganser stretches its head and neck, calls and bows to the female and displays its red gape.

POUTING

The smew draws its head back between its shoulders and paddles along, moving its head backwards and forwards.

BURPING

The mandarin jerks out its throat and flicks its head quickly up and back again, giving a soft call.

VERTICAL CALLING

The shelduck straightens its neck, raises its head in salute, then whistles as it brings its head forward and down.

GRUNT-WHISTLING

The pintail rises up, keeping its bill close to the water, and sends up a shower of spray as it whistles and grunts.

HEAD-THROWING

A pochard circling round a female will suddenly throw back its head and neck, then jerk them forward quickly.

BUBBLING

The ruddy duck has air sacs under the feathers above its breast; it drums on these with its bill, forcing out bubbles.

HEAD-THROW KICKING

The goldeneye swims round the female, jerking its head back to touch its rump and kicking up a spurt of water.

HEAD-UP-TAIL-UPPING

The teal whistles, raises and draws back its head, lifts folded wings over its back, and cocks up its tail.

then gradually stretches up into an exaggerated upright posture with head high and chest pushed out. When close to the female, it 'marks time', often lifting its feet so high that they actually strike its own breast. If the female crouches, the male mounts; and after mating the birds run swiftly away from each other—probably as fear reasserts itself, though this behaviour may also be a useful safeguard against predators.

A female shag solicits by sitting in the nest with tail cocked while bending down and moving nest material. During mating, the male grips the female's neck in its bill and shakes gently. Mating in gannets is more vigorous, with the female meekly submitting to being bitten firmly on the back of the neck.

Among herons, mating often follows the presentation of a stick by the male, which also preens its mate's head; and the two birds engage in mutual billing.

Most birds have no external reproductive

LOVE-HATE DISPLAYS BY THE GREY HERON

Male's stretch display

Male's forward display

Male and female in greeting display

Male's upright display   Male's snap display

Grey herons breed early in the year, and the male guards and advertises its tree-top nest by repeating a loud and harsh 'frornk' and giving a 'stretch display'—a posture which seems basically hostile, though it is for the benefit of females as well as rival males.

The male first stretches its neck up, pointing the bill vertically and giving the first part of a special call, a short 'hoo'. Then it lowers itself down on the nest and 'curtsies' by arching its head over its back; during the curtsy, it gives the second half of the call, a gurgling 'ooo'.

If a female alights near the site, the male at first goes into the 'forward display', a posture used to frighten off rivals. With head and plumes erect, it coils back its neck and then stabs its head forward towards the female, opening its bill and giving the 'threat call', a loud 'gooo'. It may also assume the 'upright display' when the female is approaching, standing erect, with head and bill arched downwards, and often uttering a soft 'gog-gog-gog' call.

If the female stands her ground or returns repeatedly, the male becomes less aggressive, with fewer forward displays and more and more 'snap displays', indicating willingness to pair up. In this display, the male stretches its neck forward with the bill pointing down, lowers its head to the level of the nest—or below—by bending its legs, then opens its bill and snaps it shut.

Once the female is accepted at the site, the male starts flying out and returning with twigs. This leads to mutual 'greeting displays' as it alights, calling 'arre-arre-ar-ar' with neck erect and crest and plumes spread. The female repeatedly stretches erect then sinks down on the nest, eventually taking the twigs and adding them to the nest.

Other greeting ceremonies, involving the raising of the wings and plumes, also occur when the birds relieve one another at the site.

organs, though in a few species, including some ducks, geese and swans, the male has a penis. In the majority, the ducts leading from the testes of the male and the ovaries of the female end in their respective cloaca openings. In copulation, the male stands on the female's back, the cloacae are brought together, and sperm passes from male to female.

Mating often occurs several times a day over a period lasting from just before egg-laying begins until the last egg is laid. Great crested grebes, for instance, copulate eight, nine or ten times a day for 10–14 days. With other species, copulation can be far less frequent. Carrion crows and magpies mate once a day, early in the morning, in an act which takes 10–20 seconds.

Grebes and some other birds may also go through the mating ritual long before the female produces eggs, in which case the behaviour helps to maintain the pair bond. In other species, gannets for instance, copulation may start again at the end of the breeding season, although the female is not fertilised again.

The only mechanism preventing mating

COURTSHIP IN ACTION
HOW THE SHAG ATTRACTS A MATE

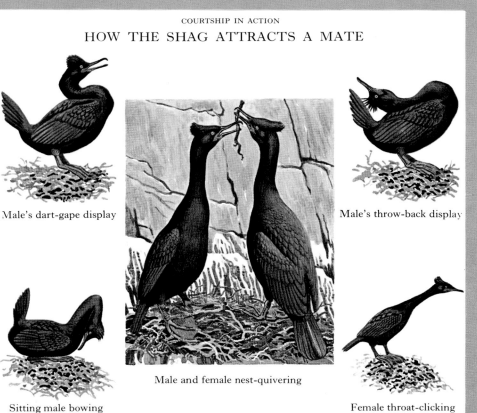

Male's dart-gape display

Male's throw-back display

Male and female nest-quivering

Sitting male bowing

Female throat-clicking

Shags are found at their nesting colonies mainly between March and August, and early in the season the male directs displays at both male and female birds. Only females respond, by approaching in the correct way.

The first display is the 'dart-gape', with tail fanned and cocked and chest pushed out; the bird arches its neck, draws back its head, then repeatedly darts it forwards and upwards, at the same time opening its bill and showing the vivid interior of its mouth.

This is followed by the 'throw-back' display, which the male performs mainly when the other bird looks at it or starts to approach. Arching its neck so that the back of the head rests on its back or is parallel to it, the male points its bill upwards or slightly backwards while vibrating its throat pouch.

When a female comes close, the male starts 'bowing', usually in a sitting position, pointing its bill towards its toes and cocking its tail sharply. The female usually stands over the male from the rear, 'throat-clicking'—stretching with neck out over the male's back, throat pouch lowered and vibrating to make a special clicking sound. Afterwards the female preens the male on the back of its head and neck.

In the early stages of pair formation, male and female often perform 'nest-quivering', both holding an item of nest material and quivering it, first with necks stretched up and then with heads lowered to the level of the nest.

With the exception of the 'dart-gape' and 'throw-back', which are exclusively male displays, all the other displays are performed at times by both sexes.

between birds from the same family is the 'scatter' of younger birds to find territories of their own. Such inbreeding is more likely to occur among colony-dwelling birds than among those which nest apart; but in any case it carries no threat to the species, for any genetic 'mistakes' would be quickly wiped out by natural selection.

Most bird species form monogamous pairs, at least for part of the breeding season, but in a few species, such as black grouse and ruff, the males take no part in any of the nesting duties, and meet the females only for mating.

In most of these promiscuous species there is intense competition between males for females, and this has resulted in the evolution of marked differences in size and appearance between the sexes. The males are usually larger and brighter and have evolved elaborate plumage characteristics matching their highly ritualised displays. The females are dull in plumage, mainly because they need to be camouflaged from predators when nesting.

The males establish communal display-grounds or arenas, usually called leks, to which the females are attracted in the early

COURTSHIP IN ACTION
THE NOISY ARENA OF THE BLACK GROUSE

Blackcocks in threat display

Female

The male black grouse, the blackcock, is strikingly different from the female, the greyhen. It has glossy black plumage, a lyre-shaped tail, white wing-bars, wrist-patches and undertail-coverts, and a red wattle above each eye.

In its advertising display, the male inflates its neck and chest, erects the wattles, droops its partly open wings and fans its tail over its back so that the undertail-coverts form a shield of white at the rear. Then it carries out formal encounters with its neighbours, some-times remaining stationary and at other times making little mincing runs or jumping up and down. Blackcocks fre-quently call, usually either crowing, a wheezy, tearing sound, or 'rookooing', a musical, dove-like bubbling sound.

There are occasional fights between males, and courts can change ownership, as males on the outskirts of the lek try to force their way to the centre. The mature and more vigorous males, occupying the central positions in the lek, secure by far the most matings—as many as 80 per cent in some leks.

When the greyhen appears and moves through the lek, it is courted by each male in turn. The blackcock parades round, often tilting its tail and body, though it may also sink down in front of the female. Mating follows if the female crouches.

days of the breeding season. In ground-living birds, leks are situated conspicuously in the open, often on a rise or hill. The site is traditional—used for generation after genera-tion—as long as it proves to be safe.

There may be more than one lekking ground in a district and many males usually collect at their own lek. This crowding increases the attractiveness of the lek to females, and so helps each male's chances of mating. It prob-ably also ensures greater safety against attacks by predators. Lekking usually begins early in the day—often before dawn—and may last all morning; but at least one species, the great snipe, gathers only at night.

Within the lek each male holds a fixed, small standing territory, or 'court', in which it dis-plays not only to females when they are present but also to other males. Highly ritualised threat displays are directed at males to emphasise the boundaries and ownership of the courts; they also serve to make the lek more conspicuous, and so it becomes more of a magnet to females.

A female entering the lek moves between the courts while all the males display. The female then selects one of them and they mate. It may go on to mate with other males; no cases have been recorded of a male rejecting the female. Females may also visit more than one lek for mating.

Because of the territory system within the lek, each established male is confined more or less to its own court; and, as the displays are basically static, there is relatively little inter-ference with mating once the female has stepped into any one court. The fighting and threat are for territory, not for females—though, of course, no lekking bird will attract a female unless it has first established a territory.

Among British breeding birds, only the black grouse and capercaillie, both game-birds, and the ruff, a wader, mate in leks. The habit is shared by one species which used to breed in this country, the great bustard, and two vagrant waders, the pectoral sandpiper and the great snipe.

COURTSHIP IN ACTION

THREAT AND INVITATION BY THE GANNET

Male advertises
for a female

Either sex may use
'pelican posture'

Male and female in mutual fencing

Male bites female's neck;
female faces away

Both sexes adopt
sky-pointing posture

Some gannets are present at their nesting colonies from January to November each year, but the peak period of occupation lies between March and September. Older, experienced males re-establish themselves at their former sites and threat and fighting between males over sites can be fierce and frequent. The male proclaims ownership of a site by the 'bowing' display, dipping its bill from side to side, with wings held out; and it gives a repeated threat call, a loud 'urrah-urrah'.

The bird's 'advertising-display' to prospecting females, which fly over repeatedly before landing, is like a low-intensity form of the bowing: it consists mainly of shaking the head from side to side, with wings closed.

When a female comes close, the male responds by 'neck biting', seizing her neck in its bill. Any female that is interested does not retreat or attack but behaves submissively, turning away the head and presenting the nape to the male in the 'facing away' posture. During such an encounter, the male also assumes the 'pelican posture' with its bill tucked down against its breast; this seems to be a gesture of appeasement.

The male eventually surrenders the site to the female, at first repeatedly flying out and landing back beside its new-found mate, and later also bringing nest material. When they are together at the site, male and female will both go into the pelican posture, and when they move about in this posture they will raise their closed wings in an 'elbows up' position.

This way of holding up the wings is even more characteristic of another display, 'sky pointing', a pose often taken up as a bird prepares to walk away from its mate or its nest. The bird stretches its neck with the bill usually pointing skywards but with the eyes focused forwards, and begins raising its feet slowly on the spot, showing the conspicuously coloured lines on the toes, before turning to fly or walk away. A special groaning call accompanies the display.

Throughout the breeding cycle, from the early stages of pair formation until after their single chick has fledged, gannets perform a special 'greeting ceremony' whenever a bird joins its mate at the site. The returning bird flies into the site calling, and its mate starts to shake its head rapidly.

Whether the male is returning to the nest, or is already on it, it almost invariably gives the female a neck bite and the female responds by facing away. Then they stand breast to breast and put on a display of 'mutual fencing', rapidly 'scissoring' their raised bills together. Calling goes on throughout the whole of this greeting display, and the bill actions are interspersed with downward movements of the head.

COURTSHIP IN ACTION

DISPLAY PARTIES OF THE MALLARD

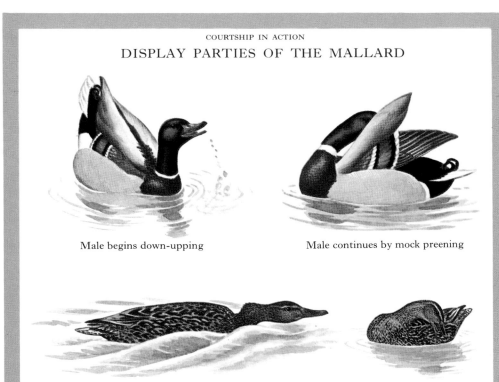

Male begins down-upping

Male continues by mock preening

Female takes to nod-swimming

Female replies by inciting

Mallard display bouts often start with 'preliminary shaking', in which one male in a group draws in its head, then repeatedly rises up in the water, thrusting and shaking its head. This activity is particularly infectious; once one bird starts, the others usually follow suit as the mood to court spreads through the group.

Shaking is commonly followed by 'grunt whistling', in which the bird first shakes its bill in the water, then rises up with its neck arched downwards and its bill close to the surface. In this position, the mallard draws its bill towards its breast and sends up a shower of water droplets. At the height of the movement it utters a sharp whistle followed by a grunt. Shaking may be followed by 'head-up-tail-upping', in which the male whistles and raises and draws back its head, lifts folded wings over its back and cocks its tail.

Another display is 'down-upping', in which the male dips its bill rapidly in the water, jerks up its head, raising a little spurt of water, and then whistles and quacks. There is also 'mock preening behind the wing', in which the bird partly lifts one wing on to its back to show its bright wing-patch, turns its head behind the wing and runs its bill along the quills near the wrist joint to produce a loud rattling noise.

When courting, the male mallard often points its head towards a particular female during grunt whistling or at the end of the head-up-tail-upping, then starts 'nod-swimming' round the intended mate, with head low and neck kinked. Then it raises its head again and attempts to lead the female by swimming away with head feathers compressed sideways, giving the head a high-peaked, shiny look.

The female mallard is mainly an onlooker at these courtship assemblies, but it will also swim in among the males, drawing their attention by nod swimming round as many of them as possible. Even more commonly, the female will perform 'inciting' movements to a particular male, swimming after it; at the same time the female may symbolically threaten another male, turning its head over its shoulder and uttering a special querulous call with open bill.

After a male and female have started to associate more definitely together, they will still attend winter courting parties during what is termed the 'engagement' stage of the pairing. But they direct their courtship mainly to each other. Later on in the cycle—at nesting time in February or March—they go off on their own to copulate.

Males of duck species related to the mallard, such as the teal and pintail, have similar displays, each with its own sequence and special features to aid species recognition.

COURTSHIP IN ACTION

THE COLOURFUL WORLD OF THE RUFF

Reeve

Resident ruff

Satellite ruff

In autumn and winter, the plumage of the ruff, or male bird, is as dull as that of the smaller reeve, or female; but the breeding season brings a dramatic transformation. The male develops an elaborate ruff, like a huge mane, round its head and neck, two long 'ear-tufts' on the top of its head and bare wattles on its face.

Two ruffs are seldom exactly alike, so that individual recognition is easy. The ruff and ear-tufts may be black, brown, red, yellow or white, and plain or patterned; the wattles may be different shades of red or yellow. The ruff and tufts may be of the same or contrasting colours in individual males.

Each male has the same pattern of plumage every breeding season, but as it gets older the display ornaments improve in size and brilliance; mature males have a larger wattled area and differently coloured legs and bill from younger ones.

There are three types of male at each ruff lek: resident birds, marginal birds and 'satellite' birds. The residents are the mature, established males, occupying 'courts' or 'residences' about a foot in diameter within the core of the lek. The marginal males, the young and perhaps the very old, are much less regular in attendance and wander from lek to lek. Satellite males do not possess residences of their own, but share the courts of resident birds. Marginal males may establish residences on the periphery of the lek and then, over the seasons, work their way deeper into it.

The third type of male, the 'satellite', is probably the most conspicuous of all during the mating season, because it has a large white ruff which it uses in displays. It does not own a residence, but visits different leks and makes use of the courts of resident birds there. Sometimes the satellite will be chased away by the resident, but more frequently—especially in small leks—it will be allowed to stay.

Evidently the satellite males are tolerated because their extreme conspicuousness attracts more females to the lek, so increasing the chances of matings for all.

Competition between males for residences can be acute. There is occasional serious fighting, though the birds remain in their own courts for most of the time.

When a female visits the lek, all the males display by squatting down and turning on the spot, each on its own court—though some courts are doubly occupied by a resident and a satellite. The female chooses a court and steps into it for copulation. Satellite males often mate with a female while their hosts are engaged in encounters with neighbours; the host mates after chasing off the satellite. Lekking takes place early in the day, often before dawn.

The dance of the great crested grebe

ADVERTISING

A single bird calls attention to itself—and to the fact that it is looking for a mate—with far-carrying croaking calls.

DISCOVERY CEREMONY

One bird approaches the other in a shallow underwater 'ripple dive', then rises up beyond it in the 'ghostly penguin display'. The second bird faces it in the 'cat display', and then they head-shake together.

STAGES IN THE HEAD-SHAKING CEREMONY

STAGE ONE Two birds meet; they approach one another with heads lowered threateningly, then raise them and spread their head ornaments while giving a 'ticking' call and shaking their down-pointed bills from side to side.

STAGE TWO They straighten up further, with tippets less fully spread, and both alternately waggle and sway their heads.

STAGE THREE One or both of the birds starts 'habit-preening'—dipping back its head to flick up one of its wing feathers.

INLAND lakes and reservoirs provide the setting for the courtship of the great crested grebe. Ceremonies begin in mid-winter, especially from January onwards, when the birds start forming pairs and taking up territories; they continue for weeks or even months, keeping the pairs together until nesting begins. Males and females play identical or interchangeable roles in this extravagant ritual of posture and display. 'Head-shaking' is the most common ceremony; it may be preceded by 'advertising' and the 'discovery ceremony', and followed by the 'penguin dance' or the 'retreat ceremony'. Other activities include 'fish offering' and 'inviting'.

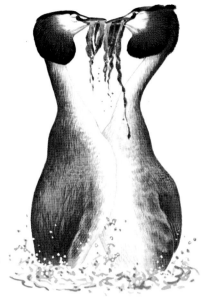

PENGUIN DANCE

After head-shaking, the birds dive to collect weed, then surface and swim towards one another; suddenly they rise breast to breast from the water, vigorously paddling their feet and swaying their bills, full of weed, from side to side.

STAGES IN THE RETREAT CEREMONY

STAGE ONE During the head-shaking ceremony one of the birds suddenly dashes away, 'patter-flying' across the water past its mate.

STAGE TWO The fleeing bird subsides into the 'cat display', pauses, then turns to face its mate, which has also assumed a partial 'cat display'.

FISH OFFERING

Sometimes the male gives its mate a courtship 'gift'—a small fish for her to eat.

INVITING

This display on the water is identical to the one performed later, on the nest, by birds soliciting copulation.

Nests and their builders

FROM SIMPLE HOLLOWS TO COMPLICATED FEATS OF CONSTRUCTION

BLACKBIRD'S CUP NEST
After establishing a foundation by lodging material in a bush, hedge or tree, the female blackbird builds a strong and secure nest of grass, roots, moss and twigs with a lining of mud and dried grass.

A NEST is a shelter in the battle for survival— a cradle in which eggs and helpless nestlings can be relatively safe from their enemies. But the origins of the instinct that leads a bird to build this cradle are obscure: reptiles, from which birds evolved, are not as a rule nest-builders. Nor, for that matter, is the building instinct found in all birds. Cuckoos manage well enough without it, and so do a handful of other species which have their own nest-sites but do no building. There are a bewildering variety of places chosen by British birds for their eggs, ranging from the nightjar's unadorned patch of clear ground to the intricate suspended nest of the goldcrest.

The origin of nests

This very variety provides a living laboratory of evolution, packed with clues which, if they do not solve the mystery of how nest-building originated, at least allow scope for intelligent guesswork.

The earliest birds, following the pattern of reptiles, probably laid their eggs in holes in the ground or in trees, covering them with earth or leaves. As competition for food and territory drove their descendants into more open country, the safest place for eggs would often be a depression or a simple scrape in the ground; and those which moved into marsh-land would look for a patch of firm ground sheltered by grass.

The first cup nests may have been formed as parent birds, turning on the eggs or going through courtship rituals, moulded the vegetation into primitive, cup-like shapes.

It is reasonable to suppose that, as birds extended the range of their habitats still further, the strength of associations imprinted on their nervous systems over millions of years made them instinctively seek to recreate platforms of grass and other materials—so making primitive nests.

Varying degrees of intricacy in the construction of nests are related to the different demands made on each species by the need to protect its eggs and young.

Types of nests

The simplest nest of all is, in fact, not a nest at all. The tawny owl, for instance, lays its eggs in a tree hole, and the stone curlew lays in a depression in the ground. The guillemot deposits its egg on a ledge, and the nightjar needs only a clear space on the ground. Though these were probably the earliest forms of nest, the birds themselves are not necessarily more primitive than others: the nest-building instinct can atrophy, return and wither away again as a species evolves.

Nests which call for some building fall broadly into two types: the simple nests made by nidifugous (nest-leaving) birds, whose chicks are able to quit the nest and run on the day of hatching; and the intricate nests of nidicolous (nest-attached) birds, whose nestlings are born naked and helpless. There are various intermediate stages between these two main types of nest.

SIMPLE NESTS The nests of ducks, geese, swans, waders, game-birds, grebes and divers—all of them nidifugous birds—are basically simple in design, and are sometimes little more than scrapes in the ground. But when they are built on water, like those of the moorhen or the coot, the nests may, for all their simplicity, be quite substantial.

MORE ELABORATE NESTS Between the nidifugous and the nidicolous birds come those whose young are able to leave the nest within a few days—among them many seabirds, such as gulls, terns and skuas.

INTRICATE NESTS Nests reach their greatest intricacy among the passerines, or perching birds. These birds are basically woodland dwellers, and the building instinct possibly evolved at a stage when they had even more enemies—rodents, snakes and so on—than they have now.

Blackbirds and song thrushes build cosy cup nests, and a few other woodlanders or former woodlanders gain added protection by building a dome over the cup. House sparrows, and very occasionally tree sparrows, do this when they nest in the open; dippers will build a dome unless the nest cup is in a deep cavity; and magpies protect the cup with a dome of sorts by giving it a canopy of twigs. Wrens, willow warblers, wood warblers and chiffchaffs build more intricate domes; but none can vie with the long-tailed tit's beauti-

SIMPLE NESTS ON THE GROUND AND ON WATER

Ground-nesting birds build simple nests, relying on camouflage for safety. The nightjar's nest is so simple, in fact, that it is a mere scrape in the ground. The lapwing's is only one stage more complicated—a rough lining of grass placed in a muddy hollow. Birds which nest on water may need substantial nests, but the nest construction is still basically simple—as with the great crested grebe's floating platform of water-weeds, reeds and rushes. When a grebe leaves the nest, it usually covers its eggs with weed, though there is not always time.

GREAT CRESTED GREBE

NIGHTJAR

LAPWING

fully made 'bottle' of lichen-covered moss, with the entrance hole placed near the top.

The part played by male and female in selecting a site varies from species to species. In some 75 of the most common British breeding birds, both sexes share in site-selection; in about 50 the female selects a site on her own; and in about 25 the male appears to play the leading role, although—as with the pied flycatcher, the redstart and the great tit—the female may make the final decision.

Which bird chooses the site?

The general rule is that when the plumage of the male and female differs dramatically, and when the cock bird expends a lot of energy in defending the territory by song, the female takes the major role in site-selection or nest-building.

'Female only' selection reaches its extreme in the black grouse; the sexes meet only for mating, and the blackcock may not even know where the greyhen has made the nest. When males play the major part in site-selection, they display from the nest-hole they have chosen. The pied flycatcher pops its head out to show a white frontal blaze, and the redstart, facing into the hole, fans out its bright orange tail.

In the case of many waders, the male makes several simple scrapes by turning its breast round on the ground, allowing the female to make the final choice. Occasionally, as with the pied wagtail, male and female may choose different sites—again with the female having the final say.

Each species has its preferred niche for nesting, though the sites favoured may vary in different regions. Tree-nesting ravens are common in Wales and western England but rare in Scotland, where they nest in high moorland or on cliffs; and on the Continent (though not in Britain) peregrines use the old nests of other birds. Some birds have their

favourite levels, too. If all the different species which might nest in a tall oak were there at the same time the tree would provide a vertical panorama of bird-life: there might be a crow nesting near the top; a wood-pigeon estab-lished lower in the tree; a mistle thrush in a fork or near the end of a bough; a blackbird in the shoots from the bark; a treecreeper behind the loose bark; an owl, jackdaw, stock dove or woodpecker in large holes; and a tit, nuthatch or redstart in small ones.

In Britain, it is rare to find small birds nesting high in trees. Only a few finches—in particular the goldfinch and, in conifers, the crossbill and the siskin—normally build their nests near the tree tops.

The sites waders choose are the result of balancing the need for cover against the need for a good view from which to see predators coming. Open sites are favoured by lapwings, avocets, ringed plovers, little ringed plovers, dotterels and oystercatchers. A tuft of grass, which acts as one side of the nest, is usually preferred by curlews, whimbrels and golden plovers. The greenshank usually chooses a site where there will be a stone or a dead branch on one side of its nest; and the wood-cock chooses a light cover of dead bracken. The black-tailed godwit, red-necked phala-rope, redshank, common sandpiper, dunlin and snipe generally keep their nests well hidden in grass. Several of these species may well nest in the same small area; snipe, red-shanks and lapwings occupy neighbouring niches in southern England.

Rivalry for sites

To protect their helpless young, wood-peckers, hoopoes, swifts and kingfishers nest in holes. Some doves, birds of prey and seabirds nest on ledges; and some birds use strongly built disused nests which others have built. There is often rivalry for sites among hole-nesters, and the same cavity may be used in successive years or even in the same season by different species.

Some birds build in more than one site. Male wrens may build as many as half a dozen nests, though the female lays in only one: she has a series of reserve nests, should anything happen to the main one.

A ladder hung on a wall will provide a series of identical sites which can confuse nest-builders. Song thrushes or blackbirds will build several nests between the rungs, sometimes not finishing any, sometimes laying in one and sometimes in two. This can also happen when two natural sites look alike. If the sequence of stimuli goes wrong, a bird may build several nests, yet not lay in any.

Attachment to sites

Many species show a strong attachment to particular sites. A grey wagtail will return year after year to the ledge of a bridge, an oystercatcher to a scrape on a rocky headland, or an eagle to its eyrie. Paired birds may ring the changes on two or three sites over the years. If one partner dies, the other will often find a new mate and use the same sites.

Some birds persist in returning to an un-suitable site. Terns have been known to build below the spring tide-line, so that their nests are washed away when the tide reaches its seasonal maximum—yet they go back for more of the same punishment.

Nests themselves are often used again, too. Blackbirds and house sparrows frequently use the same nest three times in one season, re-lining it each time. Herons' nests expand enormously through annual additions of material, and eagles' nests may be built up over the years.

Birds which nest in colonies—for protection and to be near their food supply—may use a site for hundreds of years; gannets, for example, have been established on the Bass Rock, at the mouth of the Firth of Forth, at least since the 15th century. But colony-dwelling birds may move their sites according to local conditions; tree-felling has driven herons and rooks from some areas, and terns are notorious for deserting their colonies.

Some birds try to find a nest-site similar to the one where they were hatched. A number of wheatears, for instance, used to make for some old tins on Dungeness beach where their parents nested, and mallards for the heads of pollard willows by the Thames. However, ringing shows that young song-birds seldom return exactly to their birth-places.

Adaptation to man-made sites seems complete in Britain in the case of swallows, almost complete with swifts, and predominant among house martins. House sparrows, starlings and jackdaws often nest on man-made sites; many birds will use nest-boxes, and robins, among other species, may even rear their broods in motor vehicles.

The nesting season

The timing of nest-building depends on how the female responds to the stimulus of court-ship. Weather is another factor, as rain softens the material and makes it easier to work into

Over the seasons, a big tree like this oak might provide sites for a wide variety of birds, each with its preferred niche for nesting. The little owl, great

the nest. The earliest nester among British birds is the golden eagle, which starts building in the autumn before it lays. The first to lay its eggs is the crossbill, which lays in January and feeds its young on seeds. The latest to start nesting is the hobby, which usually uses the old nest of some other bird, and lays in June or July.

The time taken to build a nest varies enormously. The start of the season may see a complete suspension of building activity if the weather becomes too cold; but a 'repeat' nest —a replacement for one that has been destroyed—may be built in a day at the height of the season. Starlings have been known to build nests in a few hours in the engine of an aircraft.

Birds whose young are nidifugous abandon their nests as soon as the chicks are dry from the eggs. The others stay until the young are fledged. After the nesting season, old nests may be used as roosts—sleeping places—by

F BIRD-LIFE IN AN OLD OAK TREE

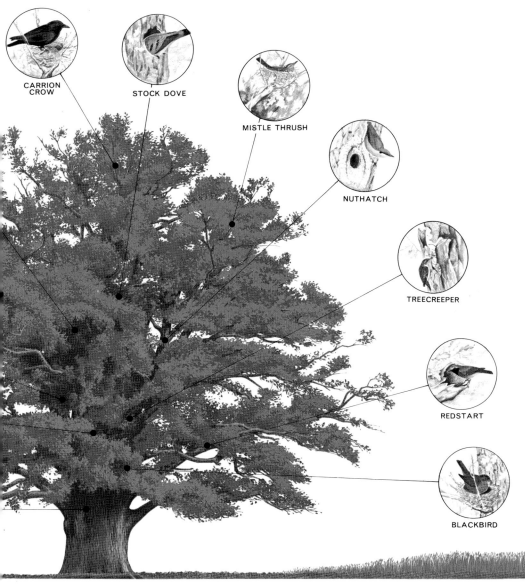

CARRION CROW

STOCK DOVE

MISTLE THRUSH

NUTHATCH

TREECREEPER

REDSTART

BLACKBIRD

spotted woodpecker, blue tit, jackdaw, stock dove, nuthatch and redstart look for or make cavities in the trunk and branches; the treecreeper finds a crack in the bark; the blackbird, mistle thrush and wood-pigeon nest in forks at different levels; and the carrion crow builds high up, out of reach of its enemies.

the original builder or by another species. Roost-sites, in their turn, may be chosen as nest-sites.

House sparrows build special winter nests, giving rise to the belief that they use the same nest all the year round. An exceptional swallow or martin may come near to nesting throughout the year by building a nest on its migration grounds.

Rooks start nest-building again in the autumn, but seldom lay eggs. In very mild autumns, blackbirds and starlings may lay again. The red-legged partridge is unique among British birds in that the hen may lay two clutches close together in time, brooding one in her own nest while the male broods the second in another nest.

The materials used in nest-building are mainly vegetable—sticks, heather, seaweed, grass, straw, lichen and moss, leaves, bark fibres, flower-heads, rotten wood, and so on. Animal materials include wool, hair, feathers,

down, cobwebs, bones, dung, droppings and, in the case of the song thrush and the swift, saliva; some birds use mineral materials such as mud and, in the lining of a ringed plover's scrape, pebbles.

Collecting materials

Many birds take their nesting material from the immediate vicinity. Grebes, for instance, build their floating platforms from what they can find conveniently near; and swifts snatch dry grass stems and feathers from the air, then work these materials with their saliva into a shallow cup under the eaves. Female ducks pluck the down from their own breasts; and there are records of a turtle dove's nest consisting entirely of small pieces of wire, and a crow's nest of sheep bones.

Some birds will even reach out for materials as they sit on the nest-site. At the other extreme, long-tailed tits, which may use up to 2000 feathers for a nest lining, often go

ONE HOME FOR
SEVEN BIRDS

Many species of birds nest in tree-holes, but not all do the hard work of hacking out the holes themselves. Woodpeckers are the best equipped birds of all to do this, and after a woodpecker has made the original cavity, other birds may use it as season follows season, enlarging it or blocking up part of the entrance if necessary. Some hole-nesters do little actual building—they simply cover the floor of the cavity with nesting material.

GREEN WOODPECKER   NUTHATCH   GREAT TIT

hundreds of yards in search of them. Some birds are pilferers. Tits take lining out of crows' nests; a sparrow will pluck feathers off a pigeon, and jackdaws will even pluck hairs from a donkey or wool from a sheep. Chaffinches, when they are disturbed, will dismantle their own nests and use the materials to rebuild elsewhere.

Construction methods

Each sex's share of the work varies as much in nest-building as it does in site-selection, incubation and care of the young. But the female always takes some part in the building; even in species such as the red-necked phalarope and the dotterel, where the task of incubation is left to the male, the female still helps with the simpler construction.

The male's share varies from none, as with the black grouse and most ducks, to building the main structure while the female adds the lining, as with the wren. Male finches accompany the females to the nest, but do not normally help to bring material.

The limitations of a bird's intellect are clearly revealed by the jackdaw, which drops sticks across a cavity and relies on their lodging securely in place. If the hole is too wide, the sticks simply fall through, piling up at the bottom—and the foundation is lost.

GOLDCREST'S HANGING NEST

This smallest of Britain's breeding birds weaves an intricate nest of moss and spiders' webs, suspends it from a conifer branch, and lines it with feathers. Both sexes take part in the building.

CUP NESTS The first stage in building complicated nests in tree- or bush-forks depends on the material lodging securely enough to make a foundation. In a typical case, the bird—a blackbird, for example—will crouch on the foundation and work the new material into shape by rotating round the site, pushing with its breast and beating its feet in short bursts, to press the material down. After about ten bursts, the bird will have rotated two or three times round the site.

The nest cup is built, therefore, by compacting the material, not by weaving it—though odd strands are pulled into the cup by the bird's beak. A very small young bird, if held in a cupped hand, will instinctively make the same movements, proving that this way of pressing with the breast is inherited. Simple as the process seems, it cannot be reproduced by comparatively clumsy human fingers.

Once the cup is the right height, the lining stage is reached. The lining usually consists of soft material; the song thrush is unique among British birds in preferring a hard lining. Blackbirds and several other birds specialise in mud linings, with a finer lining of dried grass on the inside. This is why blackbirds' nests sometimes support live mosses.

Cup nests in trees and hedges are usually built under the shelter of overhanging leaves, which keep them dry. In addition, the parent birds protect their nests and eggs by brooding during rain. But storms and high winds can still wreck a nest, leaving birds to rebuild.

HOLE NESTS Chief among specialised cavity nests are the burrows excavated by kingfishers and sand martins. A kingfisher will fly at a sandy bank time and again, pecking out sand until it has made a dent to which it can cling. It then excavates a tunnel about 2 ft long, rising slightly to a nest-hollow at the end. The achievement of the sand martin is even more remarkable, in that it is both small-billed and weak-footed, yet manages to dig a tunnel 2 ft long or more.

Other birds which excavate burrows are shelducks, Manx shearwaters, storm petrels and puffins. Most woodpeckers are superbly equipped to hack out tree holes for themselves; but some hole-nesters, such as ducks and owls, cannot excavate their own holes and

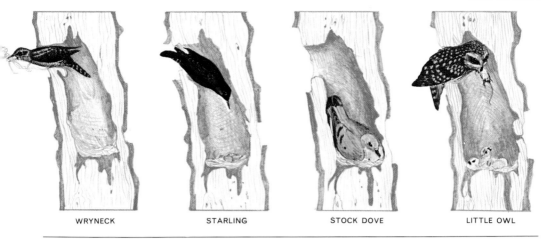

| WRYNECK | STARLING | STOCK DOVE | LITTLE OWL |

must look around for ready-made nest-site.

Generally, hole-nesters do little beyond covering the floor, once the hole is made or found. Those which, like the blue tit, build a fairly elaborate nest inside a hole, have probably taken to hole-nesting fairly recently in the history of their species.

BRACKET NESTS The mud nests of swallows are made up of pellets with small straws or grass stems running through them. A bump or a single nail can provide the initial purchase. The cup is then built up, with a first lining of grass and a second of feathers. The house martin builds in similar fashion, but under the eaves of buildings. Its nest is also deeper and has a small hole near the top.

HANGING NESTS To suspend their nests, gold-crests weave material round the tiny twigs at the end of a conifer bough; and the reed warbler weaves round reed stems.

'RAFT' NESTS Moorhens, grebes, coots and some ducks have to build fairly substantial nests because they build on water. Moorhens and coots may even build in the overhanging branches of a tree, and build up the sides of the nest if the water rises.

The size of the nest

Some birds appear to decorate their nests, bringing fresh greenery to the site after the eggs are laid—and in the case of eagles and buzzards, even after the young have been hatched. This may be either for decoration or for reasons of hygiene.

The size of the nest depends largely on the number of eggs in the clutch. A partridge needs a large nest because it can sit comfort-ably on up to 20 eggs, whereas the slender waders are in difficulties when their clutch exceeds their usual quota of four. Size also depends on whether the nest is built up year by year. Golden eagles, which start adding new material in the autumn, will eventually build up a nest 6 ft across and weighing more than a ton. At the other extreme, the whitethroat's nest weighs barely an ounce.

Rivalry between species breaks out both over sites—especially among hole-nesters—and over nests. A wren may try to build in a nest cup begun by swallows. Ducks of different species may try to oust one another from a site. Sometimes two species will lay in the same nest—blackbird and song thrush, great tit and blue tit, for instance. Usually the first-named of the pair wins.

Nest-sharing and 'take-overs'

Jackdaws, house and tree sparrows sometimes find a ready-made nest-site in rookeries or heronries. All they have to do to become 'lodgers' in a heron's nest is to find a hole in the side, and line it for their own use.

Nest 'take-overs' occur more frequently. Falcons and owls regularly nest in the old nests of ravens, crows or magpies. They never make a nest of their own, and occasionally they even oust less aggressive birds from a nest. Spotted flycatchers and, less often, redstarts, use the former nests of song thrushes and blackbirds; only the lining is their own. Gulls may nest in the down of an eider duck's nest, and house sparrows may use a blackbird's nest as a base for their own. Birds' nests may even be taken over by mice and bees.

SWALLOW'S BRACKET NEST

A nail on a barn wall can provide all the support a swallow needs for its snug cup nest. Both sexes share the building work, catching small straws and grass stems in the air and picking up mud with which to work them into pellets. The nest takes shape as pellets are placed on top of one another.

Eggs: the beginning of life

A COMPLETE WORLD INSIDE THE SHELL

To produce young by laying eggs is the equivalent of having a pregnancy outside the body; and for a flying creature this has many advantages. It means that a young bird, at the earliest stage of its development, is given a sheltered environment which supplies all its needs while the mother bird remains free and unencumbered to search for food or escape from predators.

Birds share this method of reproduction with spiders, fish, frogs and most reptiles, among other creatures; in mammals, further evolution has made it usual for the embryo to develop inside its mother's body.

The fact that birds, so highly evolved in many ways, have retained such a primitive way of giving birth to their young is an indication of the overriding importance of any factor that keeps down their weight.

Food for the developing chick

At the centre of the egg is the yolk, densely packed with nutrition for the developing embryo, which begins as a germ cell on its upper surface. About half of the yolk is made up of fats and proteins, and the rest is water. The amount of yolk in the egg varies from about 20 per cent in the case of birds which will be naked, blind and helpless on hatching, to around 35 per cent for those which will hatch with a covering of down and are strong enough to run about within a few hours.

When the egg is moved, the germ cell must remain on top of the yolk if it is to develop properly. This is achieved by a kind of tough skin, the vitelline membrane, which covers the yolk and continues on either side of it in a twisted strand called the chalaza; the ends of the two chalazae are attached to the shell membranes, and with the vitelline membrane they suspend the yolk and allow it to rotate, to compensate for any movement of the egg.

Surrounding the yolk is the albumen, or white. This is liquid, with a central gelatinous layer attached to the shell membranes at either end; the layer cushions the yolk if the egg is jarred.

Albumen is 90 per cent water and has great powers of water retention—a vital necessity, since the pores on the outer shell, through which oxygen is supplied to the embryo, could easily allow water vapour to escape. Albumen also contains an additional store of protein.

Two strong shell membranes surround the egg contents, and on these the shell is formed. The membranes prevent many harmful bacteria from entering the egg, and the albumen can prevent the growth of any which penetrate this first line of defence.

As the egg cools after being laid, it shrinks slightly and the two shell membranes pull apart at the larger end, leaving an air-space. The hatching chick breaks the inner membrane with its bill and takes its first breath of air from this space while still in the egg.

The shell consists of crystalline material, mostly calcium carbonate (lime), around a fine

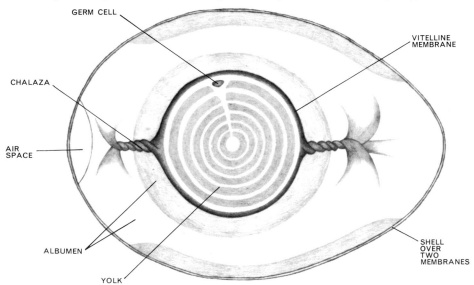

GERM CELL

VITELLINE MEMBRANE

CHALAZA

AIR SPACE

ALBUMEN

YOLK

SHELL OVER TWO MEMBRANES

INSIDE THE EGG

The egg is finely adapted for its purpose: its yolk supplies food for the developing embryo; its albumen cushions the yolk against shock, and together with the two shell membranes keeps out harmful bacteria; its shell lets in oxygen but is strong enough to protect the contents from damage; and the entire egg provides space in which the embryo can grow.

TAWNY OWL—spherical

SHOVELER
'normal' shape

GREAT CRESTED GREBE
long and thin

GREENSHANK—pear-shaped

THE SHAPES OF EGGS

The tawny owl's egg comes nearest to the ideal shape for maximum strength, but most birds lay eggs which, like the farmyard hen's egg, are rounded at one end and taper towards the other.

---

network of protein fibres. The calcium carbonate needed to form the shell normally comes from grit in the female's diet; but if the diet is deficient, it will be taken from the bird's own bones. If the female cannot provide enough calcium for the shells by one means or another, her eggs will not have the usual hard shells when they are laid, but will be soft-shelled, and soon damaged.

The strength of egg-shell

Egg-shell is an immensely strong substance —far stronger than it looks. It has been calculated that a hen's egg can withstand an even pressure equivalent to 10 tons per square inch. This is because of the arrangement of crystals in the shell; most have one end pointing towards the centre of the egg, and long edges which interlock with those of the surrounding crystals. Pressure from outside forces the crystals together, and they support one another like the stones of an arch; yet the relatively weak chick, when its time comes to hatch, easily breaks the shell from inside.

The inner surface of the shell is a mass of tiny knobs, which rest on the shell membranes and allow air to circulate round the egg inside the shell. The air enters through hundreds of holes between the shell crystals; these holes show to the naked eye as minute pits on the outer shell surface. The outer surface is glossy in the vast majority of eggs; but hen and goose eggs, with which people are most familiar, have a more matt finish (hence the term 'egg-shell finish'); and gannet and cormorant eggs have a soft white outer layer. The more usual glossy finish helps to shed water or dirt from the egg.

Why eggs are egg-shaped

The strongest possible egg, the one with its arrangement of shell crystals offering the most resistance to pressure from outside, would be as round as a table-tennis ball. But a perfectly spherical egg would be too small for adequate development of the embryo: the diameter of an egg is limited by the diameter of the oviduct down which it must pass when it is laid.

It has been suggested that the egg is spherical when it enters the oviduct but that its shape is modified as it is forced out. The pressure would be greatest at the leading end of the egg, and this would account for most eggs having one end more pointed than the other.

But some species lay eggs which are distinctive in shape. The eggs of waders and ledge-nesting auks are pear-shaped; those of grebes, shags and divers taper towards both ends; owls and many other birds of prey lay eggs which are almost round; and the eggs of swifts and swallows are long, with 'blunt' ends.

The reasons for these variations in shape are not always known, though in some cases the variation seems to serve a purpose. The pear shape of the guillemot's egg, for example, ensures that if the egg is moved, it rotates in a small arc round its tip instead of rolling away; and since guillemots lay on cliff ledges, with no nesting material to protect their eggs, this

CARRION CROW

GOLDCREST

MUTE SWAN

FROM THE LARGEST TO THE SMALLEST

The mute swan lays the largest egg among British birds, and the goldcrest lays the smallest. In general, the heavier the bird the larger the egg; but weight for weight, small birds produce relatively large eggs. Seven goldcrest eggs weigh as much as the bird itself, but a carrion crow would need to lay 15 eggs to balance its own weight, and a swan would have to lay about 25.

shape has definite survival value. In other cases the shape of the egg may be dictated by the shape of the parent bird's body. Diving birds, with their long, thin bodies, lay elongated eggs.

The size of eggs

Eggs are roughly related in size to the size of the birds which produce them. The mute swan, the largest British bird, lays the largest egg—about $4\frac{1}{2}$ in. × almost 3 in.; and the goldcrest, our smallest bird, produces the smallest egg—about $\frac{1}{2}$ in. × just under $\frac{2}{3}$ in.

But there are many complications within this general rule about size. One is that the smaller the bird, the larger the egg is in relation to it. The goldcrest's egg is a little over a seventh the total weight of the bird, and many other small song-birds lay eggs weighing a ninth as much as themselves. At the other end of the scale, the eggs of cormorants and shags are about a twenty-fifth the bird's weight. The reason why small birds lay disproportionately large eggs is probably that the smaller the egg, the greater is its surface area in relation to its volume—and the more heat and moisture it loses at the surface. As well as laying relatively heavy eggs, small birds also tend to lay more

BLACKBIRD

SNIPE

WATER RAIL

MISTLE THRUSH

SAME-SIZED BIRDS: DIFFERENT SIZED EGGS

The blackbird and the snipe weigh roughly the same, and so do the mistle thrush and the water rail. Yet there are differences in the sizes of their eggs— probably because the young of the two marsh birds are well developed on hatching, whereas the young of the two thrushes are born naked and helpless.

eggs than larger birds. The goldcrest may produce ten or more—a total weight nearly 1½ times its own body weight.

Birds of similar weight may produce eggs of very different sizes. Blackbirds and snipe weigh roughly the same, and so do mistle thrushes and water rails; but the two marsh birds—the snipe and the water rail—lay much larger eggs than the two song-birds. This is related to the fact that their chicks are precocial—that is, they hatch covered with down and so need a greater food supply in the egg for their extra development. However, quail and many other game-birds produce precocial chicks, but do not lay unduly large eggs. This in turn may be because game-birds lay large clutches and cannot provide enough material for larger eggs.

How many eggs?

A clutch is a group of eggs laid by a bird for incubation at one sitting. Most species normally produce one clutch each season, though for some species two and for others three are normal. Many birds which regularly have more than one brood are, like blackbirds, finches and sparrows, resident species which have a long breeding season because they are not involved in migration.

Time, the weather and the availability of food determine whether an extra brood is reared. In fine weather blackbirds, for example, breed from March until late summer, and will raise three broods, each taking 13 or 14 days to incubate and 13 or 14 days to fledge.

Many birds which are normally single-brooded will replace a clutch that is lost in the early stages of incubation; but some, such as petrels and divers, often do not—probably because they run out of time or energy. Most of the two- and three-brood species will lay one or two extra clutches if necessary.

A clutch may be lost through the bird deserting it when disturbed by a predator; but the longer the bird has sat on the eggs, the more reluctant it is to leave them—possibly because for many species it would be too late to start laying again.

Various ideas of what controls the size of the clutch have been put forward: the amount of food likely to be available when the young are in the nest; the amount of food the female can obtain when she is laying; and the number

THE SIZE OF A PARTRIDGE'S CLUTCH
The number of eggs a bird can cover probably sets the limit on the size of its clutch. But the bird does not always lay the maximum number; this partridge has 12 eggs, but partridge clutches containing as many as 18 eggs are not uncommon, and there is a case of 23 eggs probably laid by one hen.

of eggs the bird can comfortably sit on to incubate.

The size of the clutch is related to the number of young which can successfully be raised; but it does not always follow that the larger the clutch, the larger the number raised. If the parents have difficulty in finding food, some of their young may starve, so that the final number raised may be less than if the clutch had been smaller to start with. This has been well demonstrated in a study of swifts, undertaken in Oxford; it was found that in poor summers the birds raised fewer young from broods of three than from broods of two.

Whether this mechanism applies to all birds, in all climates, has been disputed. It has been shown that owls and other birds of prey lay larger clutches in years when their food is abundant. The number laid, however, is not always the maximum possible, because a replacement clutch can usually be laid if the first meets with disaster. Probably for birds with fixed clutch sizes the feel of the 'correct' size of clutch against the abdomen causes incubation to commence.

Most true seabirds—that is, birds which stay at sea except during the nesting period—have only one egg in a clutch. It is not known for certain why, but it may be that they cannot store enough reserves to produce more than one egg—either because food is scarce or because they cannot carry excess weight.

WHAT HAPPENS WHEN AN EGG IS LAID

A female bird has two ovaries, or egg-chambers, but in nearly all species only the left one is functional. Except in some birds of prey and some parrots, the right ovary and the right oviduct, or egg-laying passage, remain undeveloped—presumably as a weight-saving adaptation. When the bird is ready to breed, the ova—microscopic eggs clustered in the ovary—increase in size, one at a time, to form the yolks of the eggs. A ripe ovum passes into the funnel-shaped top of the oviduct, where fertilisation takes place. The progress of the fertilised ovum through the oviduct, and its final development into the egg, takes from 24 hours to a week, depending on the species. Albumen, chalazae and shell membranes are all added before the egg reaches the uterus; and there the albumen absorbs water and swells until the membranes are stretched tight, making a firm surface on which the shell layers and colouring are built up. Finally, the glossy outside surface is added, with other pigment markings, before the egg is expelled through the cloaca.

WHY COLOURS CHANGE

RAZORBILL

PUFFIN

CHIFFCHAFF   GARDEN WARBLER

When species whose ancestors nested in the open take to nesting in better-concealed places, their eggs become whiter and the markings are reduced. Such differences can be seen by comparing an egg of the ledge-nesting razorbill with that of the burrow-nesting puffin; or by comparing an egg from a chiffchaff's domed nest with one from the more open cup nest of a garden warbler.

TREE PIPIT EGGS

These differences in colour and in the amount of patterning may be adaptations to suit the variety of surroundings in which the tree pipit nests.

Some birds will carry on laying if eggs are removed from the clutch. By continually removing eggs so that a clutch is never completed, experimenters have tricked a wryneck, which normally lays eight or nine eggs, into laying 48 eggs in succession; and a house sparrow, normally with a clutch of three to five, has been tricked into laying a succession of 51 eggs.

The most extreme example of such additional laying is, of course, the domestic hen, which has laid a record of 361 eggs in 365 days. Its ancestor, the wild jungle fowl, lays about six eggs, and a hen left to itself will lay about a dozen eggs and then go broody and start to incubate them.

The trick does not necessarily work in reverse: the more common song-birds lay their usual number even if eggs are added to the nest; but pigeons, which lay two eggs, will lay only one more if an egg is put into the nest when they are about to begin laying.

Egg-collectors used to excuse their taking all but one of the eggs from a nest on the grounds that birds cannot count. In fact, experiments have shown that birds can count —a raven can count up to eight—but they probably do not count how many eggs they have laid.

The stimulus that prepares a female for laying is the presence of its mate, and most birds will not produce eggs unless they have a mate and a nest-site. The domestic hen, after centuries of selective breeding, is now an exception and regularly lays infertile eggs without having a mate. Some solitary females of species such as ducks, budgerigars and pigeons in captivity have been known to lay infertile eggs; but this may be because they have come to regard their owner or keeper as a substitute mate.

How eggs get their colour

The colouring and marking of birds' eggs is given by only two basic pigments—a blue and a buff-brown. The blue, when it is present, pervades the whole shell and without it the shell is white. Brownish colouring may be present on or just under the surface. On white shells this produces the yellow-buff-brown range of colours, and on blue shells it produces the green-olive range.

Markings on the shells are made by a single chemical substance which may appear as black, brown or red-brown. Spots of it are incorporated at various levels as the layers of shell build up during laying, through thin layers of blue or white shell. These spots, which may appear as pale grey, mauve or blue patches on the surface of the shell, do not dry until some time after the egg is laid; and they may be smeared into streaks as the egg is laid.

The function of colour and marking in eggs seems to be one of camouflage, but a surprising number of birds—and not only large birds with little to fear from enemies—lay white eggs. Most hole-nesting birds—owls, swifts, woodpeckers, kingfishers and martins, for example—lay white or pale blue eggs. This may be because their eggs are too well concealed to need camouflage; but it also has the positive advantage for the bird that its eggs show up well inside the dark nest.

Other birds—pigeons are among them—may have no need for camouflaged eggs because they begin incubation as soon as the first egg is laid and the eggs are seldom exposed.

White eggs with red-brown spots are typical of many small birds, such as tits and tree-creepers, which nest in holes or domed nests. The spots appear to have no function, and it has been suggested that they represent an intermediate stage in the evolution of a white egg from a patterned one.

Camouflaged eggs of similar colouring tend to occur in the same type of surroundings. Blue eggs are found in shaded places such as hedgerows or holes, and buff-brown eggs on open ground. The amount of patterning depends on whether a species usually lays in an exposed place or has a well-concealed nest.

Some species lay eggs which vary considerably in colour and pattern. The tree pipit is

PATTERNS THAT GIVE PROTECTION

NESTERS IN UNDERGROWTH The pheasant's eggs are covered for most of the time by the sitting bird; the bittern's egg is hidden among reeds; and the red-legged partridge's is usually placed among less dense undergrowth.

PHEASANT   BITTERN   RED-LEGGED PARTRIDGE

HEDGE AND TREE NESTERS In covered sites, eggs are white, blue or greenish-blue. The song thrush nests in fairly dense woodland and has only sparsely marked eggs. In crows, the pigment is so variable that even eggs in the same clutch may be different shades of blue and green.

CARRION CROW   JAY   SONG THRUSH

SHORE NESTERS Sand and shingle beaches or freshwater margins are the likely sites for these eggs. Their pale colours and finely speckled patterns give them ideal camouflage as they lie in bare scrapes in the ground. On shingle, it is scarcely possible to spot the eggs from more than a few feet away.

LITTLE TERN   COMMON SANDPIPER   RINGED PLOVER

MARSH, HEATH AND MOORLAND NESTERS Dark chocolate blotches camouflage the eggs of these birds, whose nests are seldom very substantial, often little more than a scrape in the ground, possibly with a lining of local vegetation.

LAPWING   STONE CURLEW   BLACK-HEADED GULL

NESTERS IN THE OPEN Eggs laid in open places on the ground are usually heavily marked and dull in colour. These three birds make little or no attempt to collect nesting material, but use what is at the site. The nest may therefore be scanty and the eggs are exposed until incubation begins.

RED GROUSE   GOLDEN PLOVER   MERLIN

one of these. Another is the guillemot; with the birds in huddled masses on cliff-sides, there is little need for camouflage, and it is the variations that help each bird to identify its single egg among the many on the bare ledge.

Apart from these two exceptional examples, minor differences between the eggs of individual birds are normal. In some birds, crows for example, there may also be variations between eggs in one clutch. The golden eagle lays two eggs, one of which is often distinctly patterned, the other almost free of patterning. A robin's clutch of six or seven eggs often contains an odd one out; and the last egg in a common tern's clutch of three normally differs from the other two. There are no known advantages in these variations, and they may arise simply because the pigment which gives eggs their colour runs out.

From egg to chick

THE DAYS BEFORE HATCHING

Aɴ egg begins to develop before it is laid, but once it is outside the parent's body this development will cease unless the egg is maintained at a temperature near to the blood-heat of the parent. Birds maintain this temperature by sitting on the eggs; and this process, known as incubation, usually begins just before the last egg of the clutch is laid.

Most small birds lay their eggs at the rate of one a day, and delaying the start of incubation ensures that the young hatch more or less simultaneously. This allows parent birds to give their full attention to looking after nestlings, at the time when food is most abundant. In the case of chicks, which are able to fend for themselves soon after hatching, it limits the period during which young birds, leaving the nest for the first time, are most vulnerable to predators.

But the hatching of species such as hawks, owls, herons, swifts, crows, grebes and divers, which have less reliable food supplies, is spaced out. Their nestlings usually hatch at the rate of one a day or one every two days, and there is a marked size-gradation within the family. This system of staggered hatching gives an advantage, during times of food shortage, to the older and stronger nestlings, which survive at the expense of the younger ones. Young birds of prey may even eat their weaker nest-mates.

The requirements of the embryo

A bird's egg must be kept at or near the blood heat of the parent bird, and this is helped in many species by the development of brood-patches—areas of bare skin on the underparts of the body which are swollen and richly supplied with blood.

Ducks, geese, cormorants and gannets have no brood patches; but the down plucked from their breasts by ducks and geese to line their nests conserves heat in the eggs. Gannets and cormorants incubate with their feet.

All species achieve even heating by periodically turning the eggs. Some chilling can be tolerated, and the occasional absence of the incubating parent for feeding, therefore, does no harm to the eggs.

In most species, both sexes take part in incubating, with the major share of the work falling to the female. Dotterels and red-necked phalaropes are exceptional in that incubation is by the male only. Among water-birds, such as grebes and shags, the work is divided equally, giving both parents a fair share of feeding time.

Change-overs are sometimes accompanied by a nest-relief ceremony; a returning gannet, for instance, will often bring a piece of sea-weed, and the two birds pass it to and fro, bowing and crossing bills.

When incubation is left to the female, the male often takes an active part in feeding and guarding its mate—as with falcons, eagles and many other birds of prey.

Sometimes, though, the male neither helps with incubation nor feeds its mate. This is especially so in birds which mate with more than one female. They are usually plant-eaters, and because this kind of food is easy to obtain during the nesting season, a single parent can adequately perform all the duties of incubation and rearing the young.

There is often a marked difference between the plumage of male and female if incubation is by one parent only; the female needs to be dull, to avoid making the nest conspicuous, but the male has less need for concealment and has often evolved showy display-plumes.

INCUBATION:

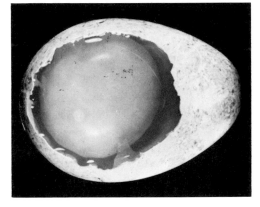

NEW-LAID TURKEY'S EGG The germ cell from which the embryo will grow is visible only as a pale spot (lower left) on the surface of the yolk.

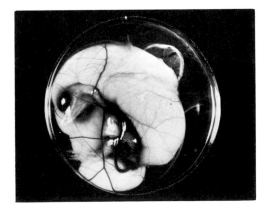

DAY 15 An eye (top left) shows clearly; main flight feathers (dark patches, lower centre) have developed; toes have claws (not seen).

The length of the incubation period is related to that of the period between hatching and fledging, for both reflect the growth-rate of the bird. A slow growth-rate—and therefore a long incubation period—is characteristic of birds such as the golden eagle, feeding on relatively scarce food. Other factors affecting the length of incubation are the size of the bird and the type of nest. Many birds which nest in holes have longer incubation periods than those nesting in more open places, because rapid growth is less urgently needed.

Among British birds, the fulmar has the longest incubation period, with both parents taking it in turn to incubate their single egg over a period of 52–53 days. At the other end of the scale, small warblers such as the whitethroat, garden warbler and blackcap bring their eggs to the point of hatching in only 11 days. The nests of these species are open, and the young are extremely vulnerable to predators while in the nest. Wrens and long-tailed tits, both of which have soundly constructed domed nests, have incubation periods of 14–15 days and 14–18 days.

Most birds in which incubation is by one sex only spend 60–80 per cent of the day on the nest. But female carrion crows may spend 95 per cent of the day or more on their eggs. Swallows, which incubate for about 70 per cent of the day, are constantly leaving their eggs and returning, so that in one study it was found that they averaged 79 incubating sessions a day. An incubating fulmar may put in a 'shift' of five days on the egg while its mate is feeding at sea.

Hatching

The embryo develops two structures which help it to break out of its shell—a strong 'hatching muscle' at the back of its neck, and a blunt, horny spike, the 'egg-tooth', on the top side of its upper bill at the tip; both disappear in the first few days after hatching.

Most song-birds hatch within a few hours, but larger birds usually take longer; the curlew, for instance, takes three days to hatch. Young grebes, however, hatch within a few hours—an adaptation against drowning in the waterlogged, floating nest.

The hatching bird starts to call before finally emerging from the egg (in the case of grouse, as much as three days before), thus establishing its first social contact with its parent. The parent usually does not help its offspring to hatch—though this has been recorded in a few species, including the water rail and stone curlew. In most species, however, the parent removes the broken egg-shells after the young have hatched. This is especially important for ground-nesting birds, for the conspicuous inside of the shell might attract predators.

FOUR WEEKS OF GROWTH INSIDE THE EGG

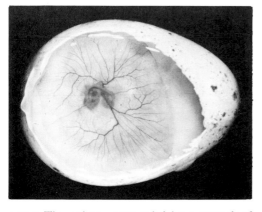

DAY 5 The embryo, surrounded by a network of blood vessels bringing nourishment from the yolk, begins to take shape; the head is on the right.

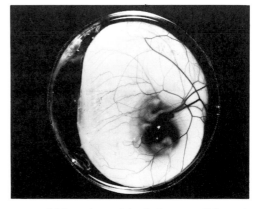

DAY 12 Main regions of the limbs are well formed; the beak takes shape; the leg has five toes (not seen), one of which will disappear.

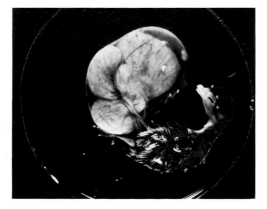

DAY 23 The embryo is fully formed, with its egg-tooth (white bump on beak); growth of features already present is the main change in the last week.

DAY 29 The chick has chipped through the shell with its egg-tooth and struggled free; it soon dries, and the egg-tooth disappears in a few days.

(Photographs by courtesy of Time-Life International.)

FEMALE RED GROUSE with its young; there may be a few more chicks under the adult's feathers.

The first few days of life

BIRDS WHICH LEAVE THE NEST WITHIN HOURS OF HATCHING

THE easiest way of identifying chicks— young birds which are able to run about almost as soon as they leave the egg—is by identifying the parent birds, which are usually close by. For to human eyes many groups of chicks look alike—mere fluffy bundles of feathers on what seem oversized, stilt-like legs.

Closer inspection will show that there are marked differences between the chicks of different species, with the plumage of the adult bird often foreshadowed in the down of the young one.

Not surprisingly, most birds whose young leave the nest soon after hatching have their nests on the ground; and many have evolved distraction displays when danger threatens, feigning a broken wing or some other injury to draw predators away from their young.

But not all are ground-nesters: goosanders and goldeneye usually nest in trees and mallards, the familiar brown ducks of park lakes, sometimes do so. This habit raises the question: how do their chicks, which leave the nest before they can fly, get safely to the ground? Since mallard chicks have been seen clinging to their mother's feathers in the water or climbing on to her back in moments of danger, it has been suggested that they may ride to the ground in much the same way. Attractive as the idea is, it is not borne out by observation. The correct explanation is that the chicks of such tree-nesting birds, when they scramble out of the nest and drop, fluttering, to the ground, are saved from injury by their extreme lightness.

THE CHICKS OF GAME-BIRDS

PHEASANT   PARTRIDGE   RED-LEGGED PARTRIDGE   QUAIL

CAPERCAILLIE   BLACK GROUSE   RED GROUSE   PTARMIGAN

RINGED PLOVER, tending its chicks as they feed, gives the alarm call; the chicks scatter.

RAIL CHICKS

| COOT | MOORHEN | WATER RAIL | SPOTTED CRAKE | CORNCRAKE |

WADER CHICKS

WOOD SANDPIPER   GREENSHANK   REDSHANK   DUNLIN   COMMON SANDPIPER

BLACK-TAILED GODWIT   RUFF   WOODCOCK   SNIPE

CURLEW   STONE CURLEW   OYSTERCATCHER   AVOCET

LAPWING   DOTTEREL   GOLDEN PLOVER   LITTLE RINGED PLOVER   RINGED PLOVER

375

FEMALE LITTLE TERN broods its young; the male comes back from the sea with a small fish.

GREBE AND DIVER CHICKS

SLAVONIAN GREBE   GREAT CRESTED GREBE   BLACK-NECKED GREBE   DABCHICK   RED-THROATED DIVER

GULL AND SKUA CHICKS

HERRING GULL   GREAT BLACK-BACKED GULL   COMMON GULL   BLACK-HEADED GULL

LESSER BLACK-BACKED GULL   KITTIWAKE   ARCTIC SKUA

TERN CHICKS

ROSEATE TERN   SANDWICH TERN   ARCTIC TERN   COMMON TERN   LITTLE TERN

CHICKS OF THE AUK FAMILY

PUFFIN   RAZORBILL   GUILLEMOT

YOUNG TUFTED DUCKS start diving for small insects and waterweed very soon after hatching.

DUCKLINGS

RED-BREASTED MERGANSER   GOOSANDER   PINTAIL   SHOVELER   MANDARIN

MALLARD   GADWALL   TEAL   GARGANEY   WIGEON

EIDER   TUFTED DUCK   COMMON SCOTER   POCHARD   SHELDUCK

CYGNETS AND GOSLINGS

MUTE SWAN   CANADA GOOSE   GREYLAG GOOSE

377

The race to maturity

HOW BIRDS SURVIVE THE DANGEROUS WEEKS FROM HATCHING TO ADULTHOOD

THREE weeks of prodigious growth lie ahead of the young cuckoo when it emerges from its newly broken shell. At this stage it is blind, naked and almost completely helpless, weighing—at $\frac{1}{14}$ oz.—less than a sixpenny piece. In three weeks it will be 50 times that weight—an adult-sized bird ready to leave the nest, capable of flying, and well on the way towards independence.

Young cuckoos belong to the large group of birds which ornithologists call 'altricial'. They are born incapable of fending for themselves —but they develop rapidly, conquering difficult habitats, building complex nests and competing against aggressive rivals for food and mates.

Two types of young

At hatching, an altricial bird has the one instinct necessary to ensure its growth and survival—it opens wide its mouth, stimulating the parents to provide an almost constant flow of food. During the first few weeks of its life it lives in the warmth and shelter of the nest (giving rise to the description 'nidicolous'— nest-attached).

Another large group of birds—known as 'precocial'—are born at a more advanced stage of their development. Like the domestic chick, they hatch with their eyes open, are covered with a coat of protective down and are able to run about almost at once. They leave the nest soon after the last of the brood has dried. This makes them 'nidifugous' (nest-leaving), though many may stay with the parents near the nest-site for some time afterwards.

Since birds evolved from reptiles, whose young are also precocial, it seems that the precocial state is the original or 'primitive' one for birds, and that the altricial state is the more 'advanced' one.

Though the young of many species combine features which are both altricial and precocial,

these two types of development represent basically different adaptations to the problem of keeping the young alive in the dangerous period after hatching, when they are most vulnerable to predators.

In general, precocial young (also known as chicks) have a longer incubation period, are born in more exposed nests on or near the ground, but move away quickly from the nest and are less dependent (if at all) on an abundant supply of food provided by the parents.

Altricial young, on the other hand (also known as nestlings while in the nest) often have a shorter incubation period, are born in less accessible nests in trees, but have a comparatively long period in the nest during which they cannot survive without constant feeding by the parents.

These two methods of surviving infancy are reflected in the different ways chicks and nestlings feed and grow.

The nestling emerges from its shell poorly developed in almost every respect except one— its digestive system. The nestling is a machine for growth—and grow it does: the robin from $\frac{1}{14}$ oz. to $\frac{7}{10}$ oz. in less than 12 days; the cuckoo from $\frac{1}{14}$ oz. to $3\frac{1}{2}$ oz. in three weeks; and the gannet from about $2\frac{1}{2}$ oz. to more than $9\frac{1}{2}$ lb. in ten weeks.

Frequency of feeding

To make this growth possible, one or both of the parents must work hard at finding food and bringing it back to the nest. Frequent small feeds prove the most efficient for increasing the size of nestlings, and a bird such as the great tit has been known to bring insects to the nest 900 times a day, or 60 times an hour—though a high rate like this is possible only if the food supply is abundant and near to the nest. Birds of prey tend to bring fewer, but larger, feeds.

Birds which have to travel far from the nest in search of food cannot make frequent feeding

ALERT AND HELPLESS YOUNG

THREE-DAY OLD
LAPWING CHICK

THREE-DAY OLD BLACKBIRD NESTLING

Alert and covered with down, the lapwing chick runs and feeds itself three days after hatching. But the blackbird nestling is blind and naked, totally dependent on its parents for food.

trips. Instead, they often bring back large feeds stored in throat pouches or in a sac in the throat, called the crop, and regurgitated for the young. Parent gannets average three feeding sessions a day between them for their single nestling, which puts its head inside the parent's mouth as the food is regurgitated. Swifts are fed by regurgitation every two hours on average, though they are capable of living for a day or longer without food in a state of torpor—almost suspended animation —when bad weather drives away the insects which their parents normally catch for them.

Many parent birds show a remarkable ability to vary the amount of food they collect according to the needs of their brood. They will frequently increase the amount of food brought back to the nest as the young get bigger and hungrier; and the female pied flycatcher will even react to the death of the male by collecting as much food herself as both did before.

The larger the brood, the more frequently the parents will visit the nest with food; but individual nestlings in a large brood seldom get as much food as those in a smaller one, and are often smaller and presumably weaker as a result when they leave the nest.

Enriching the diet

To achieve maximum growth, nestlings often need richer food than the usual diet of their parents would provide. The mainly seed diet of the house sparrow, for example, lacks the amount of protein needed for rapid development, so the bird turns to catching insects to feed its young.

A study has shown that animal matter makes up less than 5 per cent of the diet of an adult bird, but nearly 70 per cent of the diet of its young.

Pigeons have become better adapted to a seed diet. They are unique in producing a milk, similar in composition to that of mammals. This milk, which appears as a cheesy mass in the crop, is rich in protein and is given to the young about twice a day, and the nestlings themselves store it in the crop.

Among the great majority of British birds, both parents feed the nestlings; and in species such as the blackbird, in which only the female broods, the male often takes on the larger part in feeding at first. But among those song-birds which are sometimes polygamous (the wren and pied flycatcher for example), the female often has to rear the brood alone. In some of the day-flying birds of prey, such as the sparrowhawk, and in many of the crow family, the female and young are entirely dependent on the male for food for much of the time that the young are in the nest.

The method of feeding the young varies between different groups of birds. Most song-birds, and many other species, simply bring items such as insects in the bill and push them more or less intact into the wide-open gapes of the nestlings.

Birds of prey such as hawks and owls tear up the prey when the young are small and feed them on tiny morsels. Shrikes dismember prey for their nestlings in the same way. The

CRYING OUT FOR FOOD

Nestlings like these blackcaps prompt their parents to feed them by opening wide their bills. The bright pink interior of the bill—the gape—stimulates the parents to feed them.

male kestrel catches the prey and brings it to the female, who tears it up in small pieces and feeds it to the young. If the female dies, the male goes on providing prey for the young, but often does not take over the female's task of tearing it into small pieces; so if the young are too small to tear the prey apart themselves, they may die in the nest, surrounded by an abundant supply of uneaten food.

The young of petrels, shearwaters, gannets, cormorants, shags, pigeons, swifts, some woodpeckers and some song-birds are fed by regurgitation.

The feeding of precocial young, which leave the nest shortly after hatching, is far less complicated. They come from eggs containing a higher proportion of yolk (up to 35 per cent) and any remaining from the growth of the embryo is taken into the stomach and rapidly absorbed before hatching. The fat from the yolk is stored, partly in the liver and partly under the skin, and it provides a reserve for the bird to fall back on, enabling it to survive without food for several days after hatching if necessary.

Chicks, being better developed than nestlings when they are born, develop less quickly, and so need less food. Many of them play a part in foraging for their own food, and some are led to it by the parents. Those which nest on or near the ground or near water feed on small creatures such as insects and spiders, or on vegetable matter that can easily be picked up. Young game-birds will instinctively peck at green objects, and this helps them to find their first food items (such as aphids) without previous experience.

Learning to catch food

Not all chicks can feed themselves from birth, however, for sometimes it takes considerable skill to catch the kind of food they need. The precocial young of grebes, terns and auks, for instance, eat fish, and those of nightjars eat insects taken in flight; the chicks of all these species need to be fed by the parent birds.

A pair of great crested grebes with four chicks will bring on average about 20 small fish an hour throughout the day for the whole of the 12 week rearing period, reaching a peak of some 40 feeds an hour on some days and in all providing well over 20,000 fish.

Some chicks—those of skuas and gulls, for example—leave the nest but cannot find the

BEGGING FOR FOOD

The hungry young herring gull begs for food by pecking at the red spot on its parent's bill. This prompts the parent to regurgitate the food it has collected on to the ground, and pick out pieces to feed to the young. When it gets older, the chick takes food for itself from the parent's bill.

food they need near by. So they, too, have to be fed by their parents. They stay near the nest while the parents travel considerable distances in search of food.

Birds which feed their young seem to do so partly in response to an instinct which asserts itself in the breeding season, and partly because they are stimulated by the begging of the young. On rare occasions this instinct can produce odd results. It has been known to make adult starlings bring food to the nest and deposit it there as much as a week before the eggs hatch; or to subside in swallows and martins at the end of the season, to the point where they desert the young and begin migrating.

In any case, the feeding instinct is powerfully supplemented by the begging of the young—gaping with mouths wide open, calling and even moving in the nest. At first, nestlings will gape blindly upwards whenever the nest is jarred as if the parent had just landed, though not when it is shaken by the wind. They also have sensitive yellow flanges at the sides of the bill, and will beg for food when these are touched by the parent. Later, when they can see, nestlings gape and call whenever the parent is in sight.

Calling for food

Gaping is made more effective by markings on the inside of many birds' mouths. These markings attract the parents' attention and provide a target at which they can aim food. The crows have bright pink interiors to their mouths; woodlarks and skylarks have three black spots; and bearded tits have rows of white, peg-like projections which stand out against the black background and red surround of the mouth.

Most nestlings give calls to encourage the parents to feed them, some relying on calls alone; young pigeons are known as 'squeakers', from the high-pitched hunger-call they give.

The young gannet pesters the parent by pointing its bill upwards, swaying its head

and making lunges at the adult's bill; when older, it also utters a 'yipping' begging-call.

Among chicks which are fed by their parents, young great crested grebes swim towards a parent which is carrying a fish, 'peeping' vociferously and splashing up the water behind them with their feet. This begging behaviour of older chicks also serves to prevent the adults from attacking them, by showing that the chicks are submissive.

Parents make no attempt to share out food, but feed the nearest or highest begging head, which is usually that of the strongest hungry youngster. When a nestling has received enough food, it tends to subside, and another can take the best position.

If any nestling gapes unnecessarily and receives food it does not need, the adult will sometimes withdraw any it has not promptly swallowed. As long as the parents can maintain a sufficiently rapid rate of feeding, all the young will get a more or less equal share of food.

But as soon as there is a food shortage, the shares become unequal. Among chicks which hatch out at different times, the first-hatched and the biggest and strongest will usually be able to get the biggest share of available food, while the others will often starve. When all the young hatch out at the same time, the whole brood is likely to weaken and die. A cuckoo which fails to oust nestlings of the host bird from the nest is usually strong enough to win any battle for food. Among predatory species, the weakest nestling will sometimes be eaten by its parent or another nestling when food is short.

How the young are reared

It takes birds some time after hatching before they are able to control their own temperature. Until then they are dependent on their parents for heat, though the degree of brooding (warming) needed differs in chicks and nestlings.

At first, nestlings will take on the temperature of their surroundings, and until they can maintain a constant temperature (when they are between one and three weeks) they need the almost constant warmth of their parents; a drastic drop in the temperature of the surrounding air will kill them.

Chicks are less liable than nestlings to lose warmth, for their temperature control starts while they are still in the egg. But the complete insulation of the adult state is acquired more slowly, often at between two and three weeks, and chicks need to be brooded—at least intermittently.

Most species brood their young by crouching over them—a particularly effective method in cup-shaped nests. But other methods have been evolved where conditions require them. Parent cormorants brood their young with their feet, in the same way as they incubate eggs. Grebes shelter their chicks among the feathers of the back, because of the wetness of the nest. Most chicks, however, are brooded on the ground.

Brooding and sheltering are especially important at extremes of temperature and on wet days, to prevent either chilling or over-heating. Species such as hawks, herons and many song-birds with open nests often shield their young from the hot sun by spreading their wings over them.

The parents of nidifugous chicks lead them away from the nest-site after hatching. In some species, such as lapwings, the family remains in the parents' breeding territory; but in many others, such as oystercatchers and many ducks, the chicks are led right away from the nesting area to a more suitable feeding ground. This may mean a long and dangerous overland journey, during which the chick's yolk supply will tide it over until food is available. In large towns, mallard broods sometimes attract attention when they cross roads and hold up the traffic while on their way to water.

If they come across walls, ditches, fences or other obstacles, adult waders will sometimes pick up their young and carry them over. The parent woodcock or redshank flies with one chick at a time, holding it tightly between its legs and, in the case of the woodcock at least, keeping it in position with the bill. Adult great crested grebes carry their chicks on their backs for up to three weeks after hatching, their bodies providing a sort of floating nest, dry and safe from predators. In an emergency, they will even submerge with the young still aboard, deliberately imprisoning them under the wings to stop them rising to the surface again. The mute swan also carries its young on its back at times during the first weeks after hatching.

Keeping the nest clean

Many birds with young which stay in the nest after hatching have a strong instinct to keep the nest clean. The accumulated droppings of a brood reared in the nest for two or three weeks would be a serious hazard to health, and any droppings close to the nest can give away its position to predators.

Droppings from the young of many song-birds, particularly those in less well-hidden nests, are enclosed in gelatinous capsules. When the nestlings are young these are eaten by the parent, and later they are taken and deposited some way from the nest. The parents will also clear the nest of uneaten food and even dead nestlings.

Species less vulnerable to predators are not so careful; some, such as hawks and king-fishers, have young which defecate out of the nest, either over the side or into the entrance tunnel; many seabirds make no attempt to clear the nest at all.

Young birds grow to adult body size remarkably quickly compared with reptiles or mammals—in as little as two weeks in the case of some of the smaller, open-nesting song-birds, such as whitethroats.

But it is difficult to say when they are fully grown, for there is seldom any clear indication. Even when a bird has reached adult body weight, it is often not fully developed in other ways—it cannot fly, perhaps, or has not yet got its body feathers. In addition, the young of some birds which gather food far away

BIGGER THAN THE PARENT

Some birds increase their body weight so much after hatching that they become heavier than the parent. This Leach's petrel, at seven weeks old, weighs $2\frac{1}{2}$ oz., its parents $1\frac{1}{2}$ oz. The extra weight may be needed when the fledgling begins to fend for itself and may go without food for days.

from the nest go on gaining weight even after they reach the adult weight—the gannet becomes 50 per cent heavier, for example. This excess weight consists of stored fat, which tides the fledgling over when it leaves on its own for the sea, until it can feed itself.

The problem is further complicated by the fact that birds do not develop symmetrically; instead, one feature which is important to a species grows more quickly than others. Cover-haunting species, such as moorhens, have only rudimentary wings for many weeks, though the body and legs grow quickly. But grouse chicks, which need to flutter or fly at a much earlier stage to avoid capture by predators, have wings that are capable of some flight before the rest of the feathering is complete.

How much of this development goes on in the nest depends mainly on how safe the nest is. Precocial young may leave in a matter of hours; but altricial nestlings stay for anything from a mere 13 or 14 days, in the case of the blackbird, to as long as eight weeks in the swift, which is reared in a much safer nest in a hole or crevice. Seabirds tend to have longer nesting periods, with gannets staying in the nest for up to 14 weeks.

When families break up

Even altricial birds are still dependent on their parents after they leave the nest; and the fledglings are fed and protected until they complete feather-growth and can forage for themselves. How long this takes depends mainly on the availability of food. Blackbirds spend about 13 days in the nest, and can find the insects and worms they need after another 20 days. Tawny owls, on the other hand, have to be fed by their parents for up to three months after leaving the nest before they catch prey for themselves.

It is even harder to determine the total length of time that chicks spend with their parents, though some, such as swans and geese, are known to stay together as a family unit throughout the whole of the winter after they are born. In the majority of species, however, the chicks probably become independent shortly after they are able to fly.

The struggle for food

FEEDING TECHNIQUES OF SPECIALISTS AND ALL-ROUNDERS

BIRDS live at what, for humans, would be fever heat—at a normal temperature when awake of about 41°C (106°F), rising as high as 43·5°C (110°F) during exercise. To maintain this temperature, and to provide the energy which it burns at a furious rate, a small bird may take about one-third of its body weight in food every day; a larger bird, which loses heat less quickly, needs about one-seventh.

The reason for this difference in the rate of heat loss is that heat is lost through the surface, and large creatures have less surface area in relation to their volume than small ones. Doubling the size of a bird halves the rate at which it loses heat.

Food taken by an insect-eating or flesh-eating bird is broken down by acid secretions and crushed by the muscular walls of the gizzard. In some species, further digestion takes place in one or two long, thin sacs, which open low down in the gut.

Birds which live mainly on vegetable food have a more elaborate digestive tract. The elastic walls of the lower gullet expand into a crop where food can be stored for later digestion. The crop of the wood-pigeon in winter may hold 3–4 oz. of grain or clover leaves. The gizzard of a seed-eater or a leaf-eater is exceedingly muscular. In the folds of its rough, horny lining it grinds food against the grit which must be regularly swallowed to provide additional crushing machinery. Vegetarian birds always have two large intestinal sacs, and these are essential for adequate nutrition; a red grouse with its sacs obstructed by disease or parasites will starve to death in the midst of plenty.

Feeding techniques

Though birds' bills vary greatly with feeding habits, even an unspecialised bill—like that of the song thrush—can be used to pick a minute gall-wasp from a leaf; to dig a 2 in. hole to reach a beetle pupa; to tug an earthworm from the ground; to swing a snail-shell against a stone; or to gulp down a ripe cherry.

Surprisingly little use is made of the feet in feeding: only hawks and owls actually seize their prey with their feet; but tits, shrikes, ravens, crows, jays, magpies and crossbills hold morsels with their feet when breaking them up. Game-birds regularly dig with their feet in litter and soft earth, and thrushes do so occasionally.

Nuthatches and great spotted woodpeckers wedge nuts in cracks of trees before splitting open the shells. Herring gulls have developed an even more sophisticated method of getting at food: they pick up mussels then drop them from the air to shatter them on the shore.

Grey herons stalk through the shadows, seeking prey which they stab with their long bills. Kingfishers catch their prey with a shallow dive from a perch. Ospreys and gannets hurtle down from the sky. Grebes and divers propel themselves underwater with their feet, searching for food; and auks (razorbills, guillemots and puffins) 'fly' underwater, using their wings for propulsion.

Killing the prey

Owls and falcons use sheer speed to fly their prey down. Peregrines, which strike with the claws, in full flight, will kill birds heavier than themselves. But most species which kill on the ground take relatively small prey: in a rough-and-tumble with large prey, their feathers might get broken. A *coup de grâce* is given with a bite at the base of the skull.

Kingfishers batter the heads of the fish they catch on the perch; this not only kills the fish but probably makes it easier to swallow.

Song thrushes are well known for their habit of carrying snails to be broken open upon anvil stones. Apparently this species does not tell whether shells are empty or full by their weight, but by the sound made when they strike upon the anvil; for dry and empty shells are often found unbroken beside favourite stones.

Birds' meal times vary with their size and with the season. In winter, a small bird has to feed right through the day to secure enough fuel to maintain warmth during the night; but most species are subject to less urgent demands and a midday break, sometimes with a sleep, is a frequent part of the day's routine for many larger birds. Some birds of prey can secure a day's food in one or two kills, and will hunt at the same hours, along the same tracks, day after day.

Herring gulls observed feeding inland in Cornwall in late September had three feeding periods—at dawn, midday and late afternoon —separated by two rests.

During the East Anglian herring season, great black-backed gulls, which follow the fishing fleets, fed only once in 48 hours. During incubation, Manx shearwaters fast for several days at a stretch; but this is insignificant compared with the months-long fasts of incubating male emperor penguins during the Antarctic winter.

Day and night control the feeding routines of most birds, but surface-feeding ducks and many waders follow the ebb and flow of the tide. Woodcock, snipe and dabbling ducks living inland may feed at any time of the day, but prefer the night. Among owls, the short-eared owl is unusual in being largely a daylight hunter, though there is no truth in the belief that other owls are dazzled by strong light and therefore cannot hunt by day.

Blackbirds in autumn and starlings in spring take earthworms in the early morning hours, and other kinds of food later in the day.

Many foods are, of course, available only seasonally, but that is not the only factor determining when they are eaten. Song-thrushes have two periods of snail-eating—mid-winter and high summer—but this reflects not so much the availability of snails as the lack of other, preferred foods. Summer drought locks worms and insect larvae below the baked surface of the soil; and in the winter hard frost causes a dearth of other food. In a mild winter thrushes will not eat snails, and in a rainy summer they will eat very few.

During the first day after a snowfall, ground-feeding birds are often scarce. This is possibly because the heat-loss while seeking food is greater than the loss while at rest, and it is not worth losing the extra heat on the off-chance of finding food. Only when their reserves of fat have been used up are birds driven to seek food—or perish.

The urge to forage

Feeding activities are stimulated by actual appetite and by a drive to hunt for food. At times, hunger is completely satisfied before the urge to forage is exhausted, and then the bird will abandon the prey it secures. A song thrush will leave a large earthworm to burrow back into the soil; a peregrine will knock down a moorhen and fly on with never a backward glance. Jays and tits, which store nuts and acorns, may be discharging an unsatisfied foraging drive; but for the nutcracker the storage of food is essential for survival through the winter. Tits have been known to fly into houses and tear paper; and this may also be attributed to an unsatisfied urge to hunt in a particular manner—presumably for prey which shelters under thin bark.

Co-operation in hunting by birds of a single species is rare. At times, a score or more cormorants will fish strung out in a line,

diving more or less simultaneously; presumably each bird turns some fish towards its neighbours. Grey herons hunt alone, but before the number of frogs decreased in the Norfolk Broads, their emergence on the grazing marshes was the signal for herons to walk in line, snapping up their prey in hundreds.

It has been suggested that in the mixed flocks of tits, warblers and treecreepers which roam through the woods in late summer, each bird unconsciously acts as a 'beater' for the others; but it may be that the main advantage of this social feeding is the warning of attack provided by so many pairs of eyes.

Some birds take advantage of the feeding habits of others without offering anything in return. Chaffinches will pick the pips from the cores of crab-apples hacked open by fieldfares; and greenfinches will nibble the actual fruit.

'Pirate' birds

In hard weather, dabchicks accompany mute swans and coots, presumably gleaning small organisms driven from the weeds which the bigger birds root up. Blackbirds and robins will follow the track of a mole; and in continental forests, robins follow the rootings of wild boars.

A few species of birds are piratical, living at the expense of other species. Great skuas steal fish from other seabirds. When a fish-carrying gannet is sighted, one or two skuas close in to hustle and mob it until it regurgitates its load of fish. In recent years, the black-headed gull has also become parasitic, stealing earthworms from lapwings. Blackbirds sometimes snatch earthworms from song thrushes. In one spring, it was calculated that the song thrushes lost nearly one-tenth of their catch to blackbirds.

Birds which hunt for themselves from the first begin by pecking at any small object that contrasts with its background, and so learn to distinguish the edible from the inedible.

Some birds which are fed by their parents may learn to recognise food by the appearance of what is brought to the nest; but a swift, which is fed in the dark with regurgitated

DIFFERENCES IN DIET BETWEEN TWO RELATED BIRDS

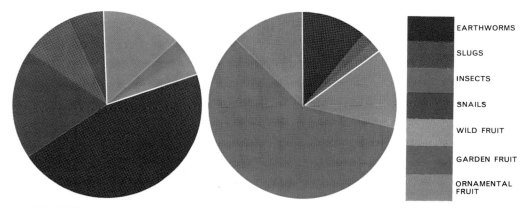

EARTHWORMS

SLUGS

INSECTS

SNAILS

WILD FRUIT

GARDEN FRUIT

ORNAMENTAL FRUIT

SONG THRUSH—mainly a flesh-eater

BLACKBIRD—mainly vegetarian

Song thrushes and blackbirds, both members of the thrush family, have a diet which includes similar items, but in strikingly different proportions. White lines dividing animal foods (various shades of brown) from fruit (different shades of green) show that animal foods make up more than three-quarters of the song thrush's diet, but less than a quarter of the blackbird's.

insects, must either learn by experience when it takes the wing or have an inborn tendency to pursue flying insects.

Avoiding competition

When food is short, birds may face competition not only from members of their own species, but also from birds of other species. One method of avoiding competition is for each species to have its own special habitat. Shags, for example, tend to work rocky and open shores, while the closely allied cormorants fish in estuaries and along sandy beaches. But even when the two species do meet, they show different preferences; shags pursue the smaller species of fish and cormorants the larger.

In English woodland, five species of tits may share one habitat, often working in mixed flocks; yet in a winter feeding party there are often different levels for food-gathering. Great tits hunt largely on the ground; marsh tits in the shrub layer up to about 20 ft; blue tits and coal tits at all heights from just above the ground to the tree tops; and long-tailed tits at higher levels than the marsh tits.

When the great tits do leave the ground, they hunt much in sycamores; blue tits spend a lot of time foraging in oaks, coal tits in conifers and marsh tits in hazels and elders. Even on the same tree, different species have their feeding niches—blue tits, for example, probing among buds and along slender twigs, while marsh tits feed more on larger limbs and branches.

All distinctions of feeding habits between different tits break down when there is a temporary superabundance of food—when, for instance, a woodland area suffers a plague of the defoliating caterpillars of the winter moth. During such a plague, a 60 ft oak may harbour 200,000–400,000 caterpillars—and all kinds of species make the most of this abundance, deserting their usual niches.

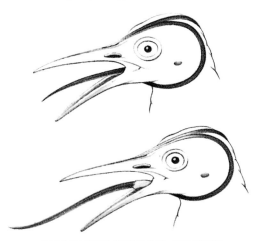

THE WOODPECKER'S TONGUE

Thanks to an ability to extend its tongue four times the length of its upper beak, the green woodpecker can winkle out an insect about 5 in. behind the bark of a tree. After the bird has chiselled through the bark, its tongue licks into holes made by woodborers and hooks the insects out on backward-pointing barbs. The tongue itself is the end portion of a flexible system of bones and tissue—known as the hyoid—that wraps up and around the woodpecker's head and is anchored near its right nostril.

Even when two closely allied birds take the same foods, their diets may be very different. For example: worms, slugs, insects and fruit appear in the diets of two members of the thrush family—the song thrush and the blackbird; yet animal foods occur nearly five times more frequently in the song thrush's diet than in the other bird's. Snails figure prominently in the diet of the song thrush, but not in the blackbird's diet. Blackbirds cannot crack out large snails, though this could never be guessed from an anatomical comparison of the two birds. Other differences in diet are equally strange: song thrushes eat great numbers of yew berries, while blackbirds eat very few; song thrushes prefer large beetles such as cockchafers, while blackbirds prefer ants.

Most birds drink when they have the opportunity, though some species survive on 'metabolic' water—water released in the digestion of food. Seabirds can, and do, drink sea-water and get rid of superfluous salt by secretion of highly concentrated brine from glands situated at the base of the beak. Crows and sand-grouse bring water to their young, transporting it in the throat or by soaking their breast plumage.

All birds conserve water by producing a very highly concentrated urine, almost a paste of uric acid crystals; and in very dry weather by reducing song and, with it, evaporation of moisture from the lungs.

All-purpose and specialist bills

Gulls and crows, Nature's scavengers, take a relatively wide range of both animal and vegetable foods with their all-purpose bills. But other birds, seeking to avoid competition within their preferred habitat, have become increasingly specialised feeders and depend on a fairly narrow selection of foods.

If their methods of feeding differ, species which are otherwise alike in size and general structure may show striking differences in the design of their bills. Conversely, species which are unlike in other ways may have similar bills if they share roughly the same feeding habits; this is because of the process known as convergent evolution, which produces similarities of design between unrelated species if they face similar challenges. The kingfisher and the heron, for example, feed by spearing fish, and both have evolved dagger-shaped bills.

The rook, a specialised feeder on insects and earthworms, has a longer bill than that of its nearest relative, the carrion crow, which takes worms much less often. Other soil feeders have taken this development even further—the snipe, woodcock, curlew, black-tailed godwit and dunlin, which probe for food in soft mud, have extremely long bills; and each species avoids competition with the others by probing at a different depth.

All the finches have the hard, conical bills typical of seed-eaters; but the bill of each species is slightly different from the rest. The most powerful, that of the hawfinch, can crack a cherry stone. At the other extreme, the thinner-billed goldfinch extracts the seeds of teasels by boring for them.

THE MANY SHAPES OF BILLS

SHEARING

Wigeon uses short, wide bill to crop grass and plants

PRISING

Oystercatcher strikes into shell of prey and levers it open

FILTERING

Avocet skims insects from the surface of mud or shallow water

TEARING

Golden eagle's strong, hooked bill is designed to tear flesh apart

PROBING

Woodcock uses long, thin bill to probe for worms in soft earth

HAMMERING

Green woodpecker chisels into bark for hidden insects

GRASPING

Red-breasted merganser grips slippery fish in serrated bill

SPEARING

Grey heron's long, dagger-like bill is well suited to spearing fish

SIFTING

Spoonbill sifts animal organisms from shallows with spatulate bill

INSECT-EATERS

Whitethroat has forceps-like bill

Treecreeper probes tree bark

Swift gapes to catch insects

SEED-EATERS

Hawfinch cracks cherry stones

Redpoll eats small birch seeds

Crossbill picks seeds from cones

The hunters and the hunted

THE BATTLE OF WITS BETWEEN PREDATORS AND THEIR PREY

MILLIONS of years of evolution have produced groups of unrelated predatory birds with remarkably similar features—the long talons, hooked bills and large, forward-facing eyes of owls, falcons, eagles and hawks. These are the birds of prey, the swift and powerful killers of the air which search out prey with their keen eyes, pounce on victims with vicious talons and devour them with strong, curved bills.

The birds of prey, along with scavengers, egg-thieves and predatory mammals, make inroads into bird populations, taking their toll of the adult members of a species and often having a devastating effect on eggs and young.

Conspicuous eggs are particularly vulnerable. Studies show that as many as six out of every ten eggs laid by wood-pigeons may be pillaged before they can hatch out. Most of the eggs are taken by jays, but they may also be eaten by magpies and other crows, squirrels, and even stoats and weasels. The white eggs, which are easy to detect in their flimsy nest of twigs, are taken in large numbers only when food scarcity forces the parent birds to leave the nest unattended.

Even adult birds, alert as they are against enemies, can fall victim in significant numbers when the need for rapid food-finding during the breeding season makes them take risks. In a single month, sparrowhawks killed 8 in every 100 house sparrows in one continental area under study—four times the number dying from all other causes. During the same month, 8 per cent of the tree sparrows in the same study area, and 7 per cent of the tree pipits, were killed by sparrowhawks. The redstart, great tit and jay all lost 6 per cent, and the turtle dove 5 per cent.

Weeding out the weaklings

Despite this slaughter, it is the scarcity of food rather than the ravages of predators that determines the size of bird populations.

Predators tend to kill weak birds rather than fit and active ones, because they make easier targets. So when food is short, there are more weak birds for the hunters to catch; they are always on the lookout for a trailing wing or a bird walking awkwardly — anything that gives away the victim's weakness.

Much of the persecution of predatory birds and other animals, past and present, stems from the belief that the numbers of the prey species are controlled by predation—that the fewer predators the more game-birds. In fact it is a fallacy to believe that under natural conditions any predator seriously depletes the overall stock of its prey; if it did so, it would risk harming its own chances of survival.

The wood-pigeon provides a good illustration of how predators, by singling out weaklings, may actually help the survival of a species. A cartridge subsidy used to be granted to anyone shooting this agricultural pest, until it was demonstrated by the Ministry of Agriculture that shooting was not, in fact, reducing the population. In the long run, it was merely removing birds which would have died of winter starvation anyway—and probably increasing the survival chances of the rest by killing off their competitors at an earlier stage. A similar waste of effort seems to be involved when farmers shoot young rooks in late spring, since most of the birds would in any case die later because of summer food shortage.

In the long run, the predator helps the prey species by killing sick, diseased, unwary and otherwise abnormal birds and increasing the overall fitness of the population.

Hunters by day and night

Relatively few birds of prey rely on killing full-grown birds for the major items of their diet; in the British Isles, these few include the three falcons—the hobby, the merlin and the peregrine—the sparrowhawk and the large goshawk, a rare bird here, though it is widespread on the Continent.

All take their food mainly in flight, and hunt by day, though the hobby and sparrowhawk are also active at dusk. In some districts these two regularly harass roosting birds, such as swallows and starlings, especially when the latter are arriving at or leaving their roosting sites.

In all these birds of prey, and in eagles, the female is larger than the male—an adaptation most marked in specialist bird-hunters. It has the effect of reducing competition for food between the sexes. The female preys on larger birds, and the smaller and more agile male catches enough small birds to feed itself, the female and the young in the breeding season.

Another bird that lives entirely by predation is the great grey shrike, a song-bird with a hawk-like bill, which winters in Britain and takes many birds in the wintering area—though mammals (mainly voles) and insects figure largely in its summer diet elsewhere.

But the majority of the predatory birds in Britain have a mixed diet. These predators include the golden eagle, three harriers (marsh harrier, Montagu's harrier and hen-harrier) some of the owls, and the great black-backed gull.

Other predators taking fewer birds include the buzzard (in some parts of the country now the commonest bird of prey), kestrel, various skuas and gulls, several of the crows and the red-backed shrike.

There remains a varied list of predatory British birds which either kill adult birds occasionally or prey only on eggs and young; birds such as the heron, specialised hawk-like birds such as the honey buzzard (which eats wasps and bees), the fish-eating osprey, some of the rails, a few gulls, the largely innocuous little owl and some of the crows.

No British mammals live entirely off birds, but birds feature prominently in the diet of foxes, pine martens, wildcats and, probably, introduced mink. Hedgehogs, grey and red squirrels, polecats and otters all rob nests of eggs and young.

Finally, man himself is an important 'predator' on bird-life because of the damage he does with firearms, pesticides and, largely illegally, with traps and prisons.

Ironically, perhaps, the birds to suffer most from man's activities have been birds of prey such as the osprey and the white-tailed eagle. Until a short time ago, they had both disappeared from Britain, their nests robbed by egg-collectors and their adults shot by gamekeepers.

The osprey, now a protected bird, returned to Britain in the mid-1950's, while a few white-tailed eagles now nest again in western Scotland following a recent re-introduction programme.

Peril from pesticides

In modern times, the greatest threat to our birds of prey came in the period 1955–64. Since the Second World War synthetic chemicals have been used increasingly to control agricultural pests. One particular new kind of insecticide, dieldrin, was introduced as a cereal

INTIMIDATING THE ENEMY

A young tawny owl is far from being a helpless victim when faced by a marauding squirrel or pine marten. In an attempt to frighten off the enemy it will fluff up its plumage, spread wide its wings and stare back defiantly with large, shining eyes.

seed-dressing, with disastrous, unforeseen results for birds.

Small mammals and birds feeding on the dressed seed accumulated the poison in their body fat. In turn, high doses built up in the predators that fed on them. Thousands died. Many that survived suffered infertility or laid thin-shelled eggs, due to their ingestion of another insecticide, DDT. Peregrines and sparrowhawks were wiped out over wide areas of Britain. Many golden eagles failed to breed—dead sheep are part of their diet, and dieldrin was used as a sheep-dip.

The most hazardous uses of dieldrin were phased out through the 1960's, and our birds of prey were saved from extinction in the nick of time. Dieldrin was finally banned in 1981 and DDT in 1982. But it will be many more years before their residues in the environment disappear altogether.

Escape from predators

The constant battle of wits between birds and their natural enemies is a struggle in which the weapons are camouflage, bluff and, above all, vigilance.

Adult birds, especially of the smaller species, are constantly on the alert for danger, particularly when they are moving from cover into the open, feeding in exposed places and roosting. Blackbirds will often dip sharply when they leave cover, and travel near the ground, especially across roads. This gives them a better chance of evading sparrowhawks.

While feeding in open ground or other exposed places, birds will look up and around them frequently, cocking their heads to one side to examine any suspicious-looking bird flying over. Even when preening and resting in relatively safe places, they still glance up periodically in case predators are approaching.

Many species crouch and 'freeze' when they see a bird of prey, lowering their bodies close to the ground or perch and keeping still until the danger has passed. This happens with garden birds such as robins, as well as with birds which live on the ground, such as partridges and waders. Crouching helps to conceal the bird by eliminating tell-tale shadow and movement. When alarmed in the

open, cover-loving birds such as wrens will dive into the nearest shelter and 'freeze' there.

Types of camouflage

Many birds escape their enemies by being camouflaged in their natural habitat. In species such as the nightjar, both sexes have specially coloured or patterned plumage; but in others it is only the more vulnerable sex which is camouflaged. When the male takes no share in incubation—as with the black grouse, for example—it is usually the female which has what is called cryptic plumage.

Ducks, which take sole charge of sitting on the eggs, are camouflaged all year round; but drakes acquire an inconspicuous body plumage only when they are unable to fly because they have moulted their flight feathers and so are far less likely to escape from a predator once spotted.

One of the simplest types of camouflage disrupts the normal effects of light and shade. When light falls on an object it emphasises that object's shape by causing highlights on the upper surface and shadow on the lower. The plumage of many birds reverses this effect by having the upper parts dark and the underside pale. This sort of camouflage is found particularly among birds of bare, open

Bittern
Grey heron
Osprey
Kite
Sparrowhawk
Buzzard
Golden eagle
Marsh harrier
Peregrine
Hobby
Kestrel
Coot
Great skua

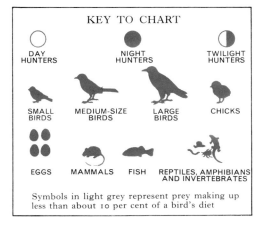

KEY TO CHART

DAY HUNTERS   NIGHT HUNTERS   TWILIGHT HUNTERS

SMALL BIRDS   MEDIUM-SIZE BIRDS   LARGE BIRDS   CHICKS

EGGS   MAMMALS   FISH   REPTILES, AMPHIBIANS AND INVERTEBRATES

Symbols in light grey represent prey making up less than about 10 per cent of a bird's diet

terrain such as seashores and estuaries; and it is very common in waders, such as dunlin, in their winter plumage.

In another kind of camouflage, a bird's plumage matches its most usual background in tone, colour and pattern. The most striking examples are those birds whose winter plumage is white to match the snow, for example ptarmigan in winter. Ptarmigan look quite different in summer, with their brown, mottled plumage resembling the rocks and open ground of their highland breeding grounds. Similarly, the plumage of pheasants (especially the hen) blends well with the shadowed leaf-mould of the woodland floor.

There are many more examples, among British birds, of plumage which matches the surroundings. Nightjars look like pieces of fallen log when they sit on the ground in their wood-edge habitat; and bitterns merge with the reeds of the marshes where they live.

The plumage of other birds is marked with special patterns which break up the outline. Ringed plovers and little ringed plovers, for example, have black markings on the face and breast which make them difficult to distinguish among pebbles on a beach, especially since the rest of the body is shaded to eliminate highlights and shadows.

ND THEIR VICTIMS

Black-headed gull									
Herring gull									
Barn owl									
Long-eared owl									
Little owl									
Tawny owl									
Red-backed shrike									
Jay									
Magpie									
Jackdaw									
Rook									
Carrion crow									
Raven									

Protective plumages reduce the chances of birds being detected by a predator, especially when the birds crouch motionless near the ground. Golden plovers and ptarmigan will lie prone in this way, and the chicks of ground-nesting species such as waders and gulls 'freeze' when they are warned of danger by their parents' calls.

More striking still is the 'pole attitude' of the bittern, when the bird stretches up its neck, bill vertical, so that, aided by the long, dark stripes on the neck, its whole body blends with the surrounding reeds. As with many birds which are both hunter and hunted, this camouflage also helps the bittern to be inconspicuous when it is searching for prey.

The coloration of most birds is a compromise between the need to hide from predators and the need to advertise their presence to other birds of the same species during courtship, defence of territory and so on. The prominent black 'moustache' and pink bill of male bearded tits, for example, are used to draw attention to them in encounters with other members of the species, though the conspicuousness of these features must increase the danger of the birds being spotted by predators.

A small number of vulnerable but unpalatable species, such as kingfishers, survive by being brightly coloured and very conspicuous, even when young. Predators find them distasteful and learn not to hunt them.

Birds have evolved ways of concealing their nests, eggs and young, as these are particularly vulnerable to predators. Nests may be built in places which enemies have difficulty in reaching, particularly holes in trees, cliffs and buildings.

Just over 30 British breeding birds are hole-nesters, most of them (such as jackdaws, tits, sparrows, redstarts, swifts, wrynecks, and some owls, ducks and pigeons) using existing holes. A few other birds, including sand martins, kingfishers and various woodpeckers, excavate their own. Nuthatches are unique

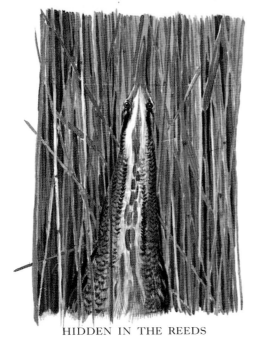

HIDDEN IN THE REEDS

The bittern's plumage matches the reeds among which it lives. When alarmed, it stretches up to show the long, dark stripes on its neck, which are patterned like reeds, and holds its bill vertical. In this position it freezes motionless; or if there is a breeze it sways with the reeds.

among British birds in that they use existing holes but restrict access by cementing up part of the entrance with mud.

The main reason why more birds do not nest in holes seems to be the shortage of suitable sites. Small cavities or niches—like those used by robins or spotted flycatchers, by swallows nesting inside buildings or by rock doves in caves—are probably the next safest places. Domed nests which are difficult for a predator to enter are built by house martins and magpies, and the mud nest of the martin is particularly safe. House sparrows usually nest in a hole; but in areas where holes are scarce, they often build domed nests in vegetation.

Species which build open nests in vegetation screen them as best they can. Some also site them in well-protected places; linnets, for example, build their nests well hidden in bushes, and goldcrests sling theirs under a leafy branch of a tree. Birds which nest on the ground either have camouflaged eggs, as plovers do, or conceal the eggs. Game-birds and ducks conceal theirs in vegetation, and ducks also cover the eggs with down.

Leaving the nest early

Open nests in vegetation and on the ground are the most vulnerable of all to predators—especially when they contain young. Studies have shown that fewer young survive from such nests than from those in holes or other more sheltered sites. To minimise this danger, the young of birds which nest in the open have often become adapted to leaving the nest as soon as possible, so that they are not killed before they can fly. Chicks of these species often leave within a few hours, or at most a day or two, and are camouflaged, crouching when danger threatens.

Birds which are blind and helpless on hatching tend to develop at a rapid rate if they are in vulnerable, open nests, and often fly within a relatively short time—13 days in the case of the blackbird. This extremely fast growth is made possible by their parents feeding them prodigious quantities of food—often the nestlings will eat their own weight of food every day. At the nestling stage these birds remain quietly in the nest and crouch down when alarmed.

Because it is so vital for these young to leave the nest as rapidly as possible, feather-growth takes precedence even over the need to increase body weight, and birds which fail to get their fair share of food in the nest will still leave fully feathered, though seriously underweight.

As hole-nesting birds are much less at risk, their young can grow more slowly and the adults can afford to bring them food less frequently. This in turn enables the adults to rear a larger family than open-nesting birds; hole-nesting great tits, for example, raise over twice as many young as chaffinches, which nest in the open.

Safety in numbers

Camouflage is frequently the best defence for birds which nest and feed individually or in small numbers. But for those which normally flock together, sheer numbers will provide the best protection against the hunter.

Bird flocks show group responses in the presence of a predator. Flocks of starlings and

MERGING WITH FERNS AND LEAVES

Foraging for weeds and insects on the woodland floor, the female pheasant is camouflaged from its natural enemies, mainly foxes and stoats. Its dark upper plumage remains sombre even in bright light, and its markings blend with the ferns and dead leaves among which it moves. Its paler underside reduces the effect of tell-tale shadow. When surprised, the bird runs for shelter and crouches down until the danger has passed.

waders become compact in flight, making it difficult for birds of prey, such as sparrow-hawks or peregrines, to pick on an isolated bird as a victim—and these predators very seldom fly into the midst of a bunched flock. Flocks will also perform manoeuvres in tight formation, making the predator's task of catching one of the birds harder still. The sudden, unanimous swervings and dippings of a mass flock of dunlin or knot, or the 'falling leaf' descent towards the ground of a lapwing flock, frequently serve to outwit predators.

Placid birds, such as Sandwich terns, take advantage of the aggressiveness of such species as common terns and black-headed gulls. Sandwich terns form a colony within the colony, relying on the bolder birds to drive away predators such as crows and foxes. Colonial nesting black-necked and Slavonian grebes both rely on the protection of black-headed gulls, often building their usual float-ing nest near gull colonies and concealing their eggs with nest material when danger causes them to leave. Eider ducks, red-breasted mergansers, tufted ducks and other birds will also cling to the protection of gull colonies.

Raising the alarm

Birds have a variety of calls to warn one another of the approach of a predator; some-times an alarm call will tell whether an attack is coming from the ground or from the air. The 'hawk alarm', usually a short note, will warn of danger from a flying bird of prey, and is often given when the bird is either crouch-ing close to the ground or is 'frozen' in an upright position. This call is similar in many different species of song-bird, and the call is often made in such a way that the bird giving the warning does not give away its position.

Another kind of alarm call indicates that predators are in the vicinity, but that there is no immediate danger. These calls may tell where the calling bird is and where the predator is, and may summon other birds to mob it. Birds such as jays even give specific calls for different sorts of predators, often with a note that seems to imitate the noise made by the predator—a 'chittering' call for squirrels and a shrill 'kik-kik-kik' for kestrels.

Flocks of starlings will often mob a flying predator by moving towards and round it. A few larger species, especially ravens and carrion crows, will do the same singly or in pairs, flying repeatedly at a passing peregrine or swooping over a heron on the ground, cawing loudly.

The mobbing of a stationary predator or one moving over the ground is more common. A perched sparrowhawk or tawny owl may be mobbed by small birds, especially tits, finches and thrushes. They fly towards it and away again, repeatedly giving loud excited 'scolding' calls and flicking it with wings and tail—almost as if daring it to attack them.

Unlike the hawk-alarms given to warn of the presence of flying birds of prey, these mobbing-calls are easy to locate, consisting of notes which are short and have a wide range of pitch. The well-known 'chink' and 'chook-chook' notes of the blackbird are mobbing-calls. Such calls attract other birds in the neighbourhood, and these join in mobbing the predator. Foxes, stoats and cats may all be mobbed in the same way. Indeed, mobbing is such a powerful instinct that birds will even mob a stuffed owl set up in a suitable place.

The value of mobbing

Ornithologists argue about why birds mob predators at all. This behaviour certainly warns other birds of the presence of the predator and reduces its hunting efficiency by removing the element of surprise. But surely it would be safer for the bird giving the alarm to move off and keep out of the way instead? After all, a second predator may be attracted by the commotion. Why does a mobbing bird do something which seems to be for the benefit, not of the individual itself, but of the population as a whole?

Perhaps there is at work here some kind of 'kin selection', for by its warning the bird may save the lives of closely related adult birds in its local population, all of which carry its type of genes. Alternatively, the individual may still benefit in the long run if the predator leaves the area because of the mobbing, and in future hunts there less frequently or less efficiently.

The mobbing of predators by breeding birds when their eggs and young are threatened is much easier to understand. Such mobbing is well developed in large waders which nest in open habitats such as fields, and it is essentially aerial and vocal. Lapwings will call

CAMOUFLAGED ON THE BEACH

The ringed plover, as it sits on its nest on an open beach, has no cover to protect it from attack by ground predators such as foxes, or to shelter it from egg-thieving crows. For this bird, concealment is the only defence. The black markings on its face and breast break up its outline; and when it stands, the light colouring of its underparts eliminates shape-re-vealing shadow. The bird will stay motionless when it senses danger.

FEIGNING INJURY

Dogs, foxes or hedgehogs on the lookout for eggs or chicks are likely to be distracted from their search if they get too near to the nest of a little ringed plover. For the · parent bird will attempt to draw off the predator by running away from the nest, then squatting on the ground, flapping a wing awkwardly as though it were broken. The hunting animal, sensing an easy kill, is drawn to follow, leaving eggs or young unharmed. Once it has drawn the attacker away, the plover makes its escape without difficulty.

and fly after carrion crows which pass over the nesting territory, while species such as black-tailed godwits and redshanks will fly round human intruders on the breeding grounds, calling noisily.

When camouflage fails to hide a bird, and mobbing does not intimidate the attacker, the victim may still escape—particularly if it is strong and swift, with quick reflexes. To fight would usually be to undertake an unequal battle, for it is for just this sort of situation that the predator has been adapted by thousands of years of evolution. But the selected victim may still have a chance of making its escape.

Outflying the hunter

Individual birds, when chased, will take evasive action by twisting and turning in the air and diving for cover as soon as possible. A few species, such as swifts, are so fast that they can outfly most predators. More frequently, a bird will try to get out of the way. Water-birds dive underwater. Ducks scuttle along the surface, diving suddenly and emerging to move off in a new, unexpected direction. Waders such as the common sandpiper will also dive to escape attacks from the air and by man—especially when wounded.

Finally, blackbirds and other thrushes may sometimes escape even from the jaws of a predator—by having a 'fright moult'. These birds have dense, loose plumage on their backs, and can struggle free, leaving the predator with nothing more than a mouthful of feathers.

Distracting the enemy

Many birds have most to fear from attacks on their eggs or young. Those which nest on the ground, especially plovers and other waders, will try to draw off dogs and foxes that are menacing the nest by acting as if injured, so making the predator hunt them instead.

These 'distraction displays' often show off the bird's conspicuous (usually white) markings on the wings and tail. The bird may fan and drag its tail along the ground, flap its wings 'helplessly', and generally give the impression that it has broken a wing, and will make an easy victim.

Waders such as the dunlin make themselves look like small rodents, creeping along the ground or running with a weaving motion, sometimes with the closed wings twitching up and down, and always uttering high-pitched squeaks.

Other displays to distract predators are merely eye-catching and unusual, without involving obvious imitation.

Distraction displays take advantage of the instinctive behaviour of the predator, playing

IMITATING
THE SURROUNDINGS

At dusk the nightjar is on the wing, hunting for insects which it catches in flight. But during the hours of daylight it is usually resting on the ground, in heathland or on the edge of a wood, often with little natural cover to hide it and its nest from enemies. However, the bird can remain inconspicuous even in these surroundings, camouflaged by plumage markings which make it look like the fallen logs among which it often settles.

MOBBING THE ATTACKER

A small group of lapwings nesting together will often choose attack as their best method of defence. When one of them spots a carrion crow flying overhead on the look-out for unattended nests from which to steal eggs or young, it gives the 'mobbing' call. The lapwings set off in angry pursuit, calling loudly and flying around and at the predator. The commotion they set up often alerts other birds which join in and help repel the intruder. Mobbing may serve to teach their young to recognise a natural enemy.

on the almost irresistible temptation felt by hunting creatures to run after and try to catch any impeded, fluttering object. These displays are effective against dogs and foxes.

Frightening off an attacker

When confronted at close quarters by a predator, some birds threaten the intruder by increasing their size and conspicuousness, by performing sudden movements or by making loud or 'sinister' noises. Such threats are made by larger species when defending their nest or young.

A stone curlew has been known to spread out its wings, showing the conspicuous white markings that are normally hidden, erect all its feathers and jump upwards to strike at a swooping falcon, which made off. Similarly, when a man approached, a particularly bold avocet stood over its eggs calling, with its wings extended over the nest.

Mute swans are renowned for protecting their nests, hissing vehemently and often striking out with their powerful wings. Even a young owl which has not yet learnt to fly will fluff up its plumage and spread out its wings, staring back at the attacker with large eyes in a big round face and clicking its bill aggressively.

A unique and very effective display is made by tits such as the great tit when they are disturbed while incubating or brooding inside the nest-hole. Whenever they hear scratching at the entrance of the hole, they hiss loudly and make a booming sound by beating their wings. The noise they make strongly suggests the presence of an unseen snake or a bees' nest within the hole, and may frighten off the predator.

Going into the attack

All these reactions to predators have so far stopped short of physical contact—even mobbing is an inhibited form of attack. Birds usually attack only the less dangerous predators, which they have a good chance of frightening away. But there are a few species which are particularly bold when predators threaten their nests or young.

One song-bird, the mistle thrush, will fly at and attack marauding birds and mammals, and even occasionally human beings. Colony-dwelling seabirds, such as black-headed gulls, common terns and great and Arctic skuas, will 'dive-bomb' ground predators such as dogs, foxes and human beings, aiming at the head and often drawing blood.

Waders do not normally attack predators, though several of the larger species, such as the oystercatcher, avocet and curlew, will perform menacing attacking-flights, swooping in but flying up at the last minute.

PROTECTING THE NEST

The avocet defends its nest on sandy flats or mud-flats against raids by crows and black-headed gulls in search of eggs. When confronted at close quarters, it will resort to intimidation—rising up over the nest, cocking its tail, spreading its wings to show their striking black and white markings and calling out defiantly. Avocets have been known to display like this in the face of human intruders —and even to 'warn off' cows and horses, which might accidentally step on the nest.

The survival of the fittest

FACTORS LIMITING BIRD POPULATION

For birds in the wild, life is a continuous struggle for survival. Starvation and violent death, from predators or in accidents, threaten them throughout their lives. Only the fittest —and luckiest—survive into anything approaching old age. Without these dangers to keep it in check, the bird population would be immense; for apart from expanding species, such as the fulmar and the collared dove, which have found new habitats to exploit in the present century, birds produce many more young than can survive.

Struggle for food

A pair of great tits, for example, usually produce between eight and ten eggs in a clutch. If they consistently produced ten eggs, and they and all their offspring survived and went on breeding at the same rate, then at the end of ten years there would be many millions of great tits.

The main reason why this does not happen is that there is not enough food to support all the birds.

After the breeding season, the newly fledged young bring the population of a species to a peak. This increased number of birds has to compete more fiercely for a share of the food available; and those individuals which fail in the struggle for food must weaken and fall easy victims to predators.

In this way the number of each species of bird stays more or less the same from one year to the next—for as long, in fact, as the amount of food available remains at a constant level and there are no other environmental changes, such as the loss of a habitat or the discovery of new habitats.

Seasons of lean . . . and plenty

The fundamental importance of food and habitat as population-controlling factors can best be shown by a close examination of the life histories of various species.

In Britain and other northern countries, the long days of spring and summer bring an abundance of insects and seeds, and the breeding seasons of most birds are timed to take advantage of this fact. Rooks, starlings and lapwings nest in March, April and May, when the soil-dwelling creatures on which they feed—such as earthworms and insect larvae—are in good supply.

Leaf-eating caterpillars reach the peak of their numbers in late May and June; and birds such as the tits lay their eggs in late April or early May, so that their young hatch at a time when there is a good supply of caterpillars for them to eat.

The whinchat and the spotted flycatcher breed later—in mid-summer, when most flying insects emerge to provide food for them and their young. About the same time, the seeds of weeds are ripening and they are freely available until autumn for the seed-eating birds, which therefore tend to breed later still and to have longer breeding seasons than the insect-eating species.

Perhaps the most striking example of the way in which birds' breeding seasons are adapted to their sources of food is found in the crossbill, which feeds on pine seeds when they are ripe, but before they have fallen to the ground in April; it breeds in winter, from January to April.

Even in the breeding season, when food is generally plentiful, there may be quite large variations in the amount available. If bad weather has spoilt the birds' harvest and there is not enough to eat, young birds may starve —either in the nest because their parents cannot find food for them, or when they start fending for themselves because they cannot compete successfully for the food available.

On the other hand, a summer with more than the usual abundance of food will encourage many birds to produce more broods of young than usual. Blackbirds and song thrushes, for example, may produce four broods or even five, instead of their normal two or three.

The parched earth

The breeding season, with its plentiful supply of food, brings the bird population to a peak as juvenile birds join the surviving adults. But now the food supply begins to decline. The heat of mid-summer can bring droughts, baking the ground hard and driving earthworms down from the solid surface into more moist regions where they are out of reach of a bird's probing bill.

Blackbirds and other species which normally take worms compete for alternative foods, such as fruit or seeds. These birds go back to their normal diet in about September, when rains bring worms back to the surface again; and they usually have enough to eat in the winter, unless the ground is frozen.

Seed-eaters, such as greenfinches, face different problems. Their usual food is abundant in summer, when the seeds ripen, and into early autumn, when they are shed by the plants. Until early winter there are still seeds lying on the ground to be picked up by birds; but they become scarce in the depths of winter, so this is the worst time for the seed-eaters.

As the amount of food available declines, there comes a point at which the number of

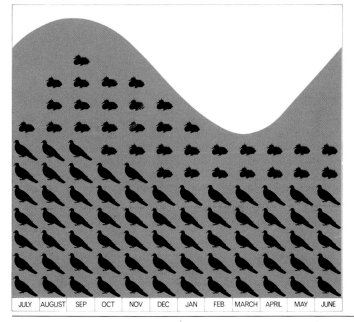

THE PATTERN OF POPULATION CHANGE

For a bird population to remain fairly constant from year to year, the number of young which survive must be roughly equal to the number of adults which die. This is well demonstrated in studies of the wood-pigeon (left), a species which breeds mainly in autumn, when grain is ripe and there is enough food for both adults and young. Most birds face a food crisis at some time of the year; and for wood-pigeons this comes in February and March, when grain is scarce. Many of them starve in these months. The greatest inroads are made into the numbers of young birds; in the struggle for survival, they have not the experience to compete with adults for the limited food available.

ADULT   YOUNG BIRD   FOOD SUPPLY

birds—increased in the breeding season—is too great for the food supply. Individual birds must now compete for the food available —and the competition grows fiercer as the stock of food goes down.

In this struggle for survival, adult birds have considerable advantages. They have already gone through at least one season of shortage, so they have learnt how to cope with it.

Experience has taught them the best places to search for food; and they tend to be bigger and stronger than the juvenile birds, so that if they have to fight for food, they usually win. This means that the majority of the birds which die in the time of famine are juveniles.

From the high point at the end of the breeding season, the population declines until there are just enough birds to eat all the available food. The proportion of juvenile birds in this reduced population depends on the gap left by adult birds which died earlier in the year.

The breeding season, although it presents no problems of food shortage, can be a time of danger for adult birds; the death-rate of adult starlings, for example, increases when they have young to tend. They must feed their hungry nestlings as quickly as possible, and therefore take greater risks as they search for food, often falling victim to predators.

Seabirds, too, are more at risk to predators when they come to breed on the unfamiliar land; they show their fears by nesting on remote islands or inaccessible cliffs; and the 'sitting duck' is proverbially an easy target for the hunter, human or animal.

Many birds by-pass the lean season by migrating when food resources run out in one area. Regular migrant birds—such as swifts, swallows and house martins, insect-eating species which breed in Britain and winter in the Tropics—are exploiting food stocks which are available at different times of the year in different parts of the world. They are forced out of their summer haunts by food shortage, and they cannot breed in the areas where they winter because the food stocks there cannot supply the increased demands of

a breeding season both for the migrants and for the established resident birds.

Partial migration is often a way in which juvenile birds can move on to another stock of food in order to escape from unsuccessful competition with adults. A proportion of Britain's wood-pigeons, for example, go to Portugal, Spain and the neighbouring districts of France in winter; those which stay are faced with a food shortage during February and early March, when frost holds up the growth of green clover and weed leaves, and the seeds of weeds and cereals are not ready for eating.

Life-expectancy

The first year of life is the most hazardous for birds; the number of young birds produced is usually much too great for all of them to survive through times of food shortage. But once a bird reaches maturity, the risks it faces become more or less constant in each year; it has already crossed the great barrier of surviving its first famine and can compete with other adults on equal terms.

For adult birds, the annual mortality rate and the expectation of further life remain constant. The death rate is still high and few wild birds can reach the maximum age to which they have been known to live in captivity or when protected.

Large birds, such as the heron, face fewer dangers from predators than do small birds such as the robin, and therefore usually live longer. High adult death rates are usually found in species which produce a great many offspring; for the young birds must eat, before they die, some food which would otherwise have been available for adults.

Blue tits in Britain, producing an average of 11·6 eggs in each clutch, have an adult mortality rate of 73 per cent; but in the Canary Islands, where the average clutch-size is 4·3 eggs, the death rate among adult blue tits is only 36 per cent.

For two British species of pigeon—the wood-pigeon and the stock dove—the adult death

HOW LONG THEY LIVE

Species	Annual adult mortality rate (per cent of population)	Adult's average life-expectancy (years)	Maximum ages recorded in the wild (years)
Swift	18	5·6	17
Herring gull	30	2·8	28
Heron	31	2·7	20
Wood-pigeon	36	2·3	21
Woodcock	37	2·2	12
Blackbird	42	1·9	9
Starling	52	1·4	16
Robin	62	1·1	11
Mallard	65	1·2	16

rates are similar, although the stock dove produces almost twice as many young as the wood-pigeon. This higher birth rate is balanced by a higher death rate among juvenile stock doves.

Many migrating birds suffer higher mortality rates than closely related species which stay in one place throughout the year. Apart from the risks of accidental death on long migration flights across oceans, mountains and deserts, migrants have to contend with a move to un-familiar surroundings where some birds, particularly young ones, may be killed because they are unaware of the dangers.

It is always advantageous for a bird to spend its life in one small area where it can learn the best places to look for food and the best places to take cover if danger comes suddenly; only when these advantages are outweighed by such considerations as the scarcity of suitable food does it migrate.

Disease, predators and accidents
Ultimately, starvation is the main factor controlling bird populations, but there are other factors which can operate powerfully. One is disease, which can rage rapidly through a crowded population. Surprisingly, for creatures which are plagued with feather parasites, epidemics are rare among birds; one of the most spectacular recent cases was in the 1950's, when the population of common terns wintering in South Africa was deci-mated by an epidemic disease.

But disease affecting a bird's food can be a major threat. The spread of myxomatosis, which killed millions of rabbits in the mid-1950's, had a devastating effect, too, on the numbers of buzzards, which depended on rabbits as their main item of prey. In much the same way, an epidemic disease which destroyed beds of eel-grass in the North Sea early this century led to a catastrophic decline in the numbers of Brent geese, which then relied almost exclusively on this plant for their winter diet.

Hawks, owls and bird-eating mammals such as foxes tend to move in where a growing population makes for easier hunting. But losses by disease and predation are both in the end dependent on the birds' food supply; for the weaker members of the population are the first to die or be taken by predators.

Accidents, too, take their toll. Hundreds of birds in migrating flocks may be wiped out by storms at sea or by colliding in darkness with man-made obstacles such as lighthouses.

Yet these disasters rarely reduce the number of birds which survive into the next breeding season. The birds which die accidental deaths leave a gap in the population, and the food which they would have eaten goes to feed other members of their species which might otherwise have starved.

Birds on the advance
The numbers of birds can increase dramati-cally, because of reduced mortality when a species finds a new niche to exploit. The collared dove, for instance, first reached Britain in 1952, after a headlong advance which took it across Europe in 40 years. By 1992, there were more than 100,000 pairs of them in these islands.

The numbers of some seabirds are increasing, too. This is partly because they are recovering from reductions at the turn of the century, when they were hunted as a source of food and feathers, but mainly because the expand-ing fishing industry is providing them with easily found food, in the form of offal thrown overboard from boats. The most dynamic range-expansion among seabirds has been that of the fulmar. Early in the last century, the only place where fulmars nested in Britain was on remote St. Kilda, in the Outer Hebrides; but today there are some 500,000 pairs of fulmars nesting on cliffs all round Britain except in the south-east.

Several species have been helped, too, by Britain's post-war building boom. Gravel-pits had to be dug to satisfy a growing demand for building materials, and they provided a new, man-made habitat for little ringed plovers and for great crested grebes. The plovers moved into Britain for the first time and have increased to several hundred pairs; the great crested grebe population has risen from a few dozen to several thousand pairs.

Only when these expanding species have exploited their new-found food supplies and living space to the limit will the factors which keep a bird population at a stable level come into full and vigorous operation.

BIRDS
AND MAN

The attitude of man to birds has undergone
a significant change in the past 150 years. For
centuries birds were exploited by man, either as food
or for sport; and when not regarded with callous indifference
as victims, they were held in superstitious awe because of
their mysterious power of flight. But in the 19th century
the conservation movement began to gather impetus,
and today in the British Isles it is widely accepted
that birds are worth studying—and worth
preserving—for their own sake.

CONTENTS

Attracting birds to your garden

AN ALL-YEAR-ROUND SOURCE OF INTEREST AND PLEASURE

You can increase the number and variety of birds in your garden by providing them with food, nest-boxes, roosting cover and water for bathing. But the first decision to be taken is whether it is in the interest of the birds that you should; birds will settle in a garden even if you have a cat, but most cats are bound, sooner or later, to cause casualties.

Most birds soon become comparatively indifferent to the presence of humans in a garden. Some, such as robins and chaffinches, even appear to enjoy human companionship, even though the enjoyment has a practical basis in the grubs and worms turned up by the gardener's fork. There is nothing so effective for attracting robins as the regular digging over of the soil.

Flowers to plant

If you can strike a balance between your pride as a gardener and your love of birds, you will also be rewarded by visits from the shyer and less common species. Many birds prefer the seeds of weeds to those of garden flowers; but apart from the fact that weeds are unsightly, it is not advisable to encourage them into your garden. The Ministry of Agriculture, Fisheries and Food, or your local council, can order you to destroy 'injurious' weeds such as spear thistles, field thistles, curled dock, broad-leaved dock and ragwort.

If the presence of other weeds is too much for you as a gardener, you can compromise by planting seed-bearing flowers, particularly sunflowers and Michaelmas daisies, and by

WHEN SUMMER IS OVER
Dead sunflowers and Michaelmas daisies should not be cut down at once, for their seeds attract birds.

not being in too much of a hurry to cut down and clear away their dead stems.

Water, both for drinking and bathing, is as great an all-the-year-round attraction for birds as food—especially in built-up areas which lack surface water in dry weather. Ideally, the water should be in a small pond with shallow edges so that the birds can walk into it; but a shelving bird-bath or even a small bowl with a couple of inches of water, is always attractive. Birds bathe in summer and winter alike, no matter how cold it is; starlings especially are always eager to bathe even when it has been necessary to break thick ice.

If you have a small bird-bath in the garden, a night-light in a tin or in an inverted flower-pot beneath the bowl will prevent the water from freezing, unless temperatures fall very low; but glycerine should never be added to the water: it clings to the birds' beaks and prevents them from preening properly.

If you have attracted birds into your garden with food and water during summer, when ample natural supplies of both are normally available, there is a moral obligation to maintain these supplies during winter when they are scarce.

Hard weather is, in fact, the time when you may expect to attract the largest number of birds into your garden, particularly if you have planted berry-bearing shrubs. The list of suitable berries is almost endless, but birds are especially fond of the berries of cotoneaster and japonica, berberis, holly, rowan, cherry hawthorn, pyracantha, stranvaesia (also known as photinia) and viburnum. Thrushes and blackbirds especially will be attracted into gardens with berries; and in 'waxwing winters', the years when these strikingly crested birds invade the British Isles from the Continent, a good supply of berries could bring unusual and exotic visitors to even a suburban garden.

Food to put out

Berries are a natural food, but are acceptable to only a limited number of birds. For the remainder, artificial food will have to be provided, in the form of either table scraps or specially prepared food placed in special containers. Remember that, unless some care is given to the scattering of the food, the bulk of it will be hogged by the larger or more aggressive species, such as black-headed gulls, starlings and sparrows.

The first-choice food of almost all birds is fat meat or bone marrow. Bacon or ham rinds and shredded suet come into this category; but bones and meat should be cooked, or there is the danger of birds carrying off lumps

BERRIES, THE WINTER STAND-BY FOR BIRDS

COTONEASTER

STRANVAESIA

HOLLY

HAWTHORN

VIBURNUM (OPULUS)

BERBERIS

Berries in your garden guarantee that it will attract birds, even in the depths of winter. In fact, the harder the weather, the more birds will come, for they are forced to rely on berries when their normal food supply is locked in the ground by frost.

of meat which could spread disease. The second favourite is bread and cheese—preferably wholemeal bread—though to avoid attracting mice and rats, no more of these foods should be put out than the birds can dispose of before nightfall. The third choice is nuts—cob-nuts, peanuts or coconuts.

Tits are not the only birds which like nuts; chaffinches and jays will carry away an endless succession of peanuts; and great spotted woodpeckers, not particularly common birds, can often be attracted by whole-shelled nuts. But dried, shredded coconut should *never* be fed to birds, because they cannot digest it, and may even die from eating it. Take care, too, not to hang a coconut in your garden during the nesting season, because nestlings cannot digest it.

Finally, rotten apples appeal to blackbirds and thrushes, and grain and cage-bird seeds will keep finches and sparrows occupied for hours; but grain is likely to produce some unusual weeds in the flower-garden.

All birds are partial to specially prepared foods—either those sold commercially, or those mixed in the kitchen. One good, easy-to-make mix is boiled rice or oatmeal, congealed with melted fat; or you might tempt birds with a mixture of pressure-cooked bones and fish scraps; or again with a pudding of stale bread or cake crumbs and currants, cemented with fat. If you wedge small portions into crevices in trees, smaller birds will have a share before the food is carried away by jackdaws, starlings, jays or magpies.

Many bird-lovers may be repelled by the idea of feeding birds on live mealworms. But these beetle larvae are irresistibly attractive to all insect-eating birds, and naturalists have been studying the habits of robins for many years by attracting them with mealworms. A robin fed on mealworms can quickly be hand-tamed, provided that each robin is fed in its own part of the garden, since they are extremely aggressive territorially.

If you are not too squeamish, a stock of mealworms can be raised in a large tin, with holes punched in its top and the bottom lined with sawdust or rags, beneath a supply of bran or wholemeal bread; if some of the larvae are allowed to pupate and change into beetles, your stock of mealworms will go on replenishing itself.

Food for small birds

One of the problems of feeding birds in a garden is that of preventing aggressive species, such as sparrows and starlings, from eating food intended for such birds as tits and siskins. These smaller birds obtain much of their food by hanging upside-down from branches, so the solution is to let coconuts and bones hang free, and to thread nuts in strings or place them in wire baskets made from two 6 in. squares of small-mesh wire-netting clasped together. Sparrows and chaffinches will still sometimes get at the food by hovering in front of it and pulling through the mesh, but this cannot be prevented.

If you plan to attract more birds to your garden by putting out food regularly, it is best to have a bird-table. A simple one, like that illustrated on the next page, can be made easily and cheaply. The table should be sited at least three yards from bushes or trees, which might give cover to lurking cats.

HOW TO MAKE A BIRD-TABLE

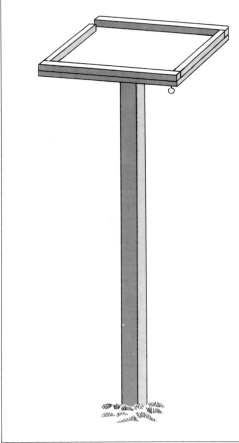

MATERIALS NEEDED: 18 × 12 × ½ in. exterior-quality plywood for top; 5 ft of 1 × 1 in. wood for 'lip'; 5 ft 6 in. of 2 × 2 in. wood for post; twelve 1¼ in. brass screws or galvanised nails; four 4 in. metal angle-brackets, with ½ in. screws for fixing to post and top; hooks as required.

CONSTRUCTION: 1. Cut the 1 in. square rod and fix to the plywood on all four sides, leaving a 2 in. gap at one corner for drainage and cleaning. 2. Join the post to the top with the angle-brackets. 3. Paint wood with a low-toxic preservative, and angle-brackets with gloss paint. 4. Sink post 18in. into the ground. 5. Screw in hooks from which to hang strings of nuts and other food.

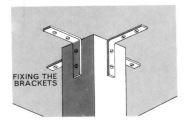

FIXING THE BRACKETS

KEEPING OFF CATS: do not erect the table closer than, say, 3 yards to bushes or other cover where cats might lurk. Cats can be prevented from climbing the post by fixing a 'collar' of wire-netting 9 in. from the top of the post. The netting should be about 9 in. wide, with its top edge nailed to the post and the bottom edge spread out, forming a funnel.

You can learn a great deal about how birds build their nests and care for their young by making a garden nest-box. Again, a simple version can be made cheaply and easily; suitably adapted, it may attract some of the 30 or so species which use next-boxes in Britain—including such garden favourites as tits and robins. When the breeding season is over, it may be used again—as a roosting-site.

The type of bird likely to use a nest-box depends on the size of the entrance hole, as the table shows.

If nuthatches nest in your box, they may well plaster mud over the entrance hole, reducing its size so as to keep out larger birds. For large birds, such as jackdaws, kestrels, stock doves and tawny owls, you will need to make a box at least double the size of the basic one shown here, and the design may have to be modified (see p. 401).

Birds begin looking for nest-sites some time before actually beginning to build, so you must put up the nest-box in good time—about the middle of March for most birds. Make sure that it is fixed firmly to its support, and that the lid is securely fastened so that it will not be blown off or vibrate in a strong wind.

The box should face away from the midday sun, and if you are fixing it to a tree, watch out for a tell-tale green line on the trunk. This indicates a runnel of water, and makes it a bad site for the box. If the box is inclined forward, this will keep out sun and driving rain.

Lining the box with nest material is a waste of time, because the prospective occupants invariably collect their own material, and will build on top of your lining.

If you take great care, you can follow the progress of nesting birds, but too much disturbance of the box may make them desert their eggs or may frighten the young away before they are able to fly, making them easy victims for cats. The golden rules are:

1. Never touch eggs, young or sitting parents.

2. Spend as little time as possible at the nest-box, and replace the lid gently.

3. Try not to visit the nest during incubation. If a visit reveals less than the bird's usual clutch, laying is probably still in progress. Allow at least one day for each egg still to be laid before looking again.

4. Never visit the nest when the young are more than half-grown. (If in doubt, check the fledging period in the section of this book on individual birds.)

5. Clean out the nest-box at the end of the nesting season. The lining may be infested with parasites.

You can often increase the number of birds nesting in a large garden by improving the 'natural' conditions—putting up ledges under the beams of outhouses for swallows to nest on, or enlarging crevices in the bark of trees or among ivy stems for treecreepers.

Nest-boxes provide pleasure and instruction when sited in gardens, but they are also

HOW TO MAKE A NEST-BOX

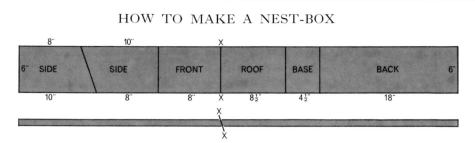

MATERIALS NEEDED: one piece of unplaned softwood board (either cedar, which lasts well, or deal, which is cheaper) 6 in. wide, ¾ in. thick and 4 ft 9 in. long; a 6 × 2 in. piece of rubber (old car tyre inner tube is ideal), waterproof canvas or leather; two dozen 1½ in. nails; one dozen copper tacks; a pair of catches and screws for the lid.

CONSTRUCTION: cut the board to the lengths shown in the diagram; the cut between front and roof is best made by holding the saw at an angle, so giving one sloping edge for the front and another for the roof. This cut should make the upper side of the roof ¼ in. longer than the lower side.

Draw the entrance hole on the front with a pair of compasses (see table below for size) and cut it out with an electric drill or a brace and bit. Alternative methods are to make a small initial hole with a gimlet, hand drill or bradawl, then enlarge it with a chisel or cut round the circle with a coping saw.

ASSEMBLY: 1. Nail one side to back. 2. Nail base to back and side. 3. Nail other side to back and base. 4. Place front and roof in position, to check that the front does not project too high. 5. Nail front in position. 6. Tack rubber hinge to roof as shown, then place the roof in position and tack the hinge to the back. 7. Fit a catch at each side, to hold roof firm. 8. If you have used deal, paint the outside of the box with a low-toxic wood preservative, such as Cuprinol.

This nest-box is ideal for the birds listed in the table, but its design and dimensions do not make it suitable for swifts, house martins and larger birds, such as starlings, jackdaws, kestrels or tawny owls. The British Trust for Ornithology (address: The Nunnery, Thetford, Norfolk IP24 2PU) publishes an inexpensive booklet, *Nest-boxes*, giving full information on how to make nest-boxes for these and many other species.

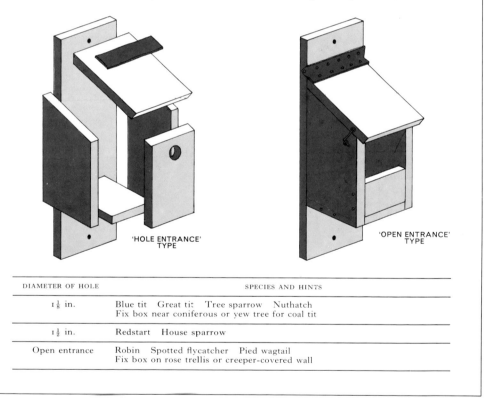

'HOLE ENTRANCE' TYPE   'OPEN ENTRANCE' TYPE

DIAMETER OF HOLE	SPECIES AND HINTS
1⅛ in.	Blue tit Great tit Tree sparrow Nuthatch Fix box near coniferous or yew tree for coal tit
1½ in.	Redstart House sparrow
Open entrance	Robin Spotted flycatcher Pied wagtail Fix box on rose trellis or creeper-covered wall

established in bird reserves, to increase the number of breeding birds. In a few woods in England and Wales, colonies of pied fly-catchers, which usually nest in holes in trees, are being helped in this way. In Sweden, goldeneye ducks, which also nest in tree holes, have been 'boxed' successfully for many years. These ducks have recently been persuaded to nest in the Scottish Highlands by the provision by the RSPB of boxes beside those lochs where the ducks are in the habit of staying late in the spring. Similarly, flask-shaped baskets made of osiers or straw are being used successfully in Holland to attract mallard.

The depleted population of barn owls in Britain may depend for its survival on artificial nest-boxes in the form of barrels; for their supply of natural nesting places in barns and hollow trees is being reduced year by year as modern agricultural methods bring a new look to the countryside.

How to watch birds

A BEGINNER'S GUIDE TO A FASCINATING HOBBY

ANYONE can study birds, simply by taking a stroll through the park; for a city park often supports a bigger and more varied bird population than an equal area of countryside.

The starting point for a bird-watcher is often simply an interest in identifying the birds seen in a park, in a garden or on a country drive. The 'breakthrough' comes when you learn not only to identify birds from their plumage, but also how to interpret their behaviour: to tell the difference between an alarm call and a contact call; to recognise one apparently haphazard posture as part of a bird's threat display, and another, just as purposeless to untrained eyes, as a bird's way of showing submission.

Putting birds at ease

On the day you see a green-headed drake mallard 'aimlessly' shaking its head at a duck on a park lake, and realise that what you are looking at is really part of a precise and highly ritualised courtship display, you have become a real bird-watcher. And on the day you spot your first rarity—an avocet, perhaps, probing in the tidal shallows with its slender, up-curving bill, or a hoopoe, exotic with its huge, black-tipped fan of a crest—you could be 'hooked' for life on birds.

If you have an inquiring mind, a receptive and musical ear and a retentive visual and aural memory, you are off to a good start as a bird-watcher. You will also need to learn (or to re-discover, for everybody as a child has played games of hide-and-seek) how to move silently and unobtrusively through woods and fields.

You will find, though, that most birds are not unduly concerned by your activities; they may stop feeding and study you for a while, but if you make no conspicuous movements they will usually resume feeding. The important thing is to avoid any action that might alarm them. Walk slowly and deliberately, making use of whatever cover is available, but taking care not to appear in their field of view or disappear from it suddenly. Raise and lower binoculars gently.

How close you can get to a particular bird depends on what bird it is, and where it lives. In a city park, wood-pigeons will feed on grain at your feet; in the country, where they are shot, it may be difficult to get within 100 yds of them.

Similarly, moorhens, though tame in a park, tend to be wary birds in the country, scuttling into cover as you approach. The degree of tameness usually depends on how familiar the birds are with human beings, though some dotterels and ptarmigan, which nest on the summit of Highland hills and rarely encounter man, are so tame that they will allow themselves to be stroked while sitting on their eggs.

The more you know about birds, the more productive and enjoyable your bird-watching will be. So study the sections of this book dealing with identification, feather-care, flight, feeding, roosting, territory, threat and fighting, courtship, nesting and all the other activities which make up the life of birds.

If you are prepared to begin watching birds without the help of binoculars, or cannot afford a pair at first, so much the better; for you will end up by being a more proficient naturalist. Without binoculars, you may not be able to determine the colouring of birds in flight; but this simply means that you will have

THE VALUE OF BINOCULARS

Seen with the naked eye, an Arctic tern in the middle of a flock is little more than a white speck.

A magnification of ×7 makes identification marks visible. *Photograph: Eric S. Hosking.*

to learn to recognise them by their silhouettes and their manner of flight. Once you have seen the distinctive flickering wings of a flock of lapwings, for example, you will never need binoculars to identify them. Similarly, you do not need binoculars to tell you that a very small brown garden bird with tail cocked over its back must always be a wren; and a large, dazzling white bird, plunging into the sea from a height of 100 or 200 ft, can only be a gannet. Above all, without binoculars, you will learn to identify birds from their songs and call-notes.

While there are some species whose plumage is virtually indistinguishable in the field, no two—mimicry apart—have identical songs. Once heard, you could never in a lifetime for-

get the difference between the monotonous, two- or three-note reiteration of the chiffchaff and the diminuendo of the willow warbler— the sweetest song in the woods. Yet even ornithologists have difficulty in telling these two birds apart by sight.

One way of learning birds' songs is by listening to recordings; another is by going into the countryside with an experienced bird-watcher; but there is a special satisfaction in mastering them by yourself.

The problem, for the beginner, is that all the birds seem to sing at once, making it difficult to isolate a particular song. In fact, many species have their favourite times for singing. With the help of the chart on this page, you can build up a 'memory bank' of favourite

THE SOUND OF BIRDS

BIRD	BEST SONG MONTHS	VOICE	OTHER HINTS
Blackbird	Late February–early July	SONG A rich, sweet succession of whistling phrases with piping notes CALLS Alarm call is the familiar metallic chatter, often reduced to intermittent 'pink-pink' notes; also a high 'seee'	Musical song, usually given from tree or building, often leads the dawn and evening choruses
Chaffinch	February–early July	SONG A rollicking cadence, ending with a flourish CALLS A sharp 'pink-pink' and a 'tsup' flight-note	Song given in short bursts; 'pink' call resembles one of the great tit calls
Dunnock	Mid-October–late July	SONG High, piping 'weeso, sissi-weeso, sissi-weeso, sissi-weeso', lasting 4 or 5 seconds CALLS Shrill 'tseep', sometimes repeated rapidly	Sings in bursts of 4–5 seconds usually from hedge or bush; sometimes from tree or in flight
Great tit	January–mid-June	SONG Variable, but usually a repeated 'tea-cher, tea-cher', a high and a low metallic note CALLS Many and variable, a soft 'tsee-tsee-tsee' and a sharp 'chwink' are common	Monotonous two-note song often lasts for minutes
Greenfinch	March–July	SONG A repetition of the nasal 'tsweee' call and a rattling twitter and 'cheu-cheu-cheu' note CALLS A long drawn out nasal 'tsweee' is most common	Song, often given from tree tops or in flight, tends to continue for long spells
Mistle thrush	Late December–early June	SONG Loud, whistling phrases, with notes like a blackbird's CALLS A sharp 'chich' and a continuous grating 'churr' of alarm	Song lacks fullness and variety of song thrush's; often given in bad weather
Nightingale	Mid-April–early June	SONG Rich, varied and rapid succession of liquid phrases, with jarring 'croak' notes interspersed; loud 'chooc-chooc-chooc-chooc' notes give way to slow crescendo of repeated 'pioo' sounds CALLS Soft 'hweet' and 'tucc-tucc'; hard 'tacc-tacc' and harsh 'krrrr' and 'tchaaaa' of alarm	Sings freely by day as well as by night, but is often hidden in tangle of under-growth, and is therefore difficult to locate
Robin	August–mid-June	SONG Short, liquid, warbling phrases of 1–3 seconds CALLS 'Tic-tic' when excited; also high-pitched 'tsweee' and soft 'tsit'	Pauses between phrases to allow rivals to answer; female robins also sing
Skylark	February–June; and October	SONG Spirited, shrill warbling, usually sustained without a break for about 3 minutes, sometimes 5 CALLS Loud, liquid 'chirrup'; sometimes a whistle	Sings most spectacularly in flight display; also on rare occasions from ground or low bush
Song thrush	Mid-November–June	SONG Succession of musical phrases with much repetition, lasting 5 minutes and more; phrases popularly given as 'Did you do it?-Did you do it?' and 'I saw you-I saw you' CALLS Thin 'sipp' or 'tic'; 'tchook-tchook' of alarm	Sometimes mimics other birds; song almost invariably delivered from perch
Wren	February–July; and December	SONG A rapid succession of penetrating and jubilant trills CALLS A rather loud scolding 'churr-r-r', or a sharp 'tic-tic-tic'	Very loud for so small a bird; given in bursts
Yellowhammer	Late February–August	SONG A monotonous 'tit-tit-tit-tit-tit-tit-tit-teee', the last note higher than the rest CALLS A sharp 'twink' or 'twit'; sibilant 'twit-up'	Song usually given from a prominent perch

songsters by choosing your time of year to listen to them. Whenever you can pick out an individual song, always look for the bird making it.

Choosing binoculars

Sooner or later you will want a pair of binoculars. If you are not technically minded, choose an 8 x 40 glass, which is ideal for every-day watching; but there are three factors to take into account when making a considered choice of binoculars: magnification, clarity and precision of the lenses, and weight.

Binoculars are classified by two numbers. On the 8 x 40 mentioned above, 8 is the number of times the picture is magnified, 40 the diameter of the object-lens in millimetres. If you go for stronger magnification, say 10 times, you will see a bigger picture of your subject from farther away, but it may be more fuzzy and you will have to focus more often if the subject moves. For the same degree of magnification, a large object lens will gather more light than a small one, and this is useful in dense woodland or during dark winter afternoons; but it will make your binoculars heavier. Weight is important: the proper place for binoculars when bird-watching is round the neck, ready for immediate use; and a large pair will quickly cause fatigue.

The binoculars most frequently used by bird-watchers are:

7 x 40: ideal where light conditions are bad; requiring less frequent focusing.

8 x 40: better magnification, good light-gathering power.

10 x 40: high magnification, but a shallow depth of focus.

Today, most binoculars come from Germany or Japan. They are available in a great range of prices, the most expensive (those favoured by professionals) being the roof prism models of Carl Zeiss, Leica and Bausch & Lomb. Most modern binoculars offer good value, so long as they suit your needs. When possible, buy from a specialist dealer and try various kinds first.

The more expensive pairs have the advantage of being lighter and more compact, and giving a brighter image and more detail. They are also less likely to be seriously damaged if they accidentally get wet. Whatever you pay, make sure you buy binoculars which are suitable for bird-watching, for there are many on the market which are not.

Be sure to get a pair which are focused by means of a centre wheel, and can be adjusted by a slight movement of the fingertips—not one in which both eye-pieces have to be focused separately.

The fact that you wear spectacles does not debar you from using binoculars. Either wear spectacles which can be pushed up quickly, or use binoculars with shallow eye-cups. Better still, you can buy binoculars designed to be used with spectacles.

Other equipment

Some ornithologists include a telescope and tripod in their equipment when watching wading birds on estuary mud-banks, or sea-birds on their nesting cliffs. But telescopes are expensive and, despite their greater powers of magnification, they are not of great value to beginners, who need to be able to focus quickly on birds which are fairly close.

The hide is one simple piece of equipment used by bird-photographers which can be of great value to bird-watchers, and it is to be found in superior form on many bird reserves and wildfowl sanctuaries. For anyone who wants to watch birds at close quarters for long periods, it is invaluable.

Page 407 carries instructions on how to make a hide which will meet all the requirements of a bird-watcher or photographer; a rough-and-ready version can be adapted from the basic plan. If you use a hide on a mud-bank, for watching wading birds or gulls, make sure you read the tide-tables correctly or you may be caught by the incoming tide.

Using a hide

Care has to be taken when setting up a hide to avoid disturbing the birds you intend to watch. Apart from sabotaging your expedition, you run the risk of causing the bird to desert the nest. So set up the hide at the first instance at some distance from the nest, and move it nearer day by day.

How quickly you can get as close as you need will depend on the tameness of the bird in question: but never impose a hide on a bird if it shows signs of nervousness.

Taking care not to disturb birds is regarded as so important that the bird protection laws were strengthened in 1967, and disturbance became an offence in certain circumstances, along with killing birds and raiding nests.

It is now illegal to disturb any bird on Schedule 1 of the Wildlife and Countryside Act 1981 while it is on or near a nest, if that nest contains eggs or when the parents have dependent young. Exceptions are made for ornithologists and scientists engaged in valuable work where some disturbance is unavoidable; and for photographers who sometimes run the risk of disturbing birds.

But such ornithologists and bird photographers still need a licence, and application for that must be made to English Nature, the Countryside Council for Wales, or Scottish Natural Heritage (see pages 416–17), where all applications are closely scrutinised. Similar licences are needed by anyone who wants to ring or mark birds.

Making notes

Precise, detailed notes, jotted down on the spot and written up later in more permanent form are an invaluable aid to bird-watching.

A technique used by many experienced bird-watchers is to make a rapid sketch of the bird and jot down notes about its plumage, bill shape and so on, round the drawing. You do not need any artistic skill to do this: a circle will do for the head, a rough oval for the body, and another rough outline will give the shape of the wings. It is always a good idea to indicate the length of the legs and to draw one wing raised, showing any special markings.

PAGE FROM A BIRD-WATCHER'S NOTEBOOK

DRAWING Make a rough sketch and note any special marks and features—for example eye-stripes, wing-bars, shoulder-flashes, crest, long legs, forked tail—as well as general appearance.

SIZE Compare with common bird, such as house sparrow, blackbird or rook.

HABITAT Say whether seen on land or water, or in flight.

NUMBER AND ACTION Say whether in flock or alone; note hopping or running action, straight or bounding flight, any special characteristics such as strutting or hovering.

CALLS AND SONG Very difficult to set down; best compared with calls or song of a bird you know.

CONCLUSION These birds breed July–August; the nest may be hidden in the hedgerow near by.

Notes should be as precise and informative as possible. From the kind of information given above, a bird can usually be identified by using the keys on pp. 18–37. Rare birds are illustrated on pp. 267–80. With experience, the form of note-taking can be adapted to suit personal styles; most bird-watchers, for instance, will soon be able to drop the 'reminder' headings on the left.

Black cap
Thick, dull-coloured bill
Pink underparts
White wing-bar
White rump
Dark tail, slightly forked

DATE, TIME, PLACE: July 12th 1969, 2 p.m., near Chagford, Devon
SIZE: Large sparrow
HABITAT: Farmland (hedgerow)
WEATHER, LIGHT, RANGE: Cloudy and dull, 30 yds
BINOCULARS OR NAKED EYE: 7 x 50 binoculars
NUMBER AND ACTION: Two, in intermittent, slightly bounding flight
CALLS AND SONG: Short, soft whistle — no comparison
CONCLUSION: Bullfinch

Thorough notes on a bird which you cannot recognise in the field may enable you to identify it when you have time to consult this book, or talk to an experienced ornithologist. They may also enable you to be credited with sighting an unusual bird. If you think that you have spotted a rarity, send a copy of your notes to your local bird-watching society. They will vet them before passing them on, if approved, to the national bird-watching journal, British Birds.

Records of rare birds are examined by the Rarities Committee of the journal, and are likely to be rejected when submitted by only one individual, unless he is recognised as a specialist, or unless the bird bears certain unmistakable characteristics.

The most helpful aid to identifying birds is still an experienced companion in the field, and there are today innumerable regional bird-watching societies which you can join. If you are interested, you can then take part in their field meetings. But if you prefer to be alone, the age-old method of trial and error works out in the end, and has the advantage of allowing you to concentrate fully on the subject, without either you or the bird being distracted.

Starting a project
One of the charms of bird-watching is that there is always something new to see or hear. If your taste is for detailed study, you can start a research project on some subject which, up to now, has been neglected by ornithologists.

Not much is known, for example, about how long individual birds sing at different times of the year. This is something that can be studied in a garden, if you can find a bird with distinguishing marks that make it recognisable from day to day—a blackbird with a white feather on one wing, perhaps, or a chaffinch with a white tail.

Alternatively, you might take a census of the number of birds in your garden, noting the proportion of males to females or of adults to juveniles.

Changes are going on all the time in the type and number of birds in any district; and these changes are accelerated by new building or the adoption of different farming methods. So keeping track of bird distribution in your garden or locality can be a fascinating and rewarding pastime.

Visiting observatories
Once you have become adept at recognising the birds of your immediate locality, you may wish to go further afield. Many observatories can provide simple accommodation for experienced bird-watchers who wish to take part in the work of the observatory. Entry is not automatic; observatories admit only those people they consider to be sufficiently experienced. Visitors may spend a part of each day helping to count or ring birds; the rest of the time they pursue their own interests. They pay a small charge to cover the accommodation provided.

A full list of observatories and how to apply to visit them will be sent, on receipt of a stamped, addressed envelope, by the British Trust for Ornithology, The Nunnery, Thetford, Norfolk IP24 2PU.

Observatories accepting visitors include Dungeness in Kent, Spurn Head at the mouth of the Humber, and some on more remote islands, such as Fair Isle, between the Orkneys and Shetlands.

Photographing birds

HOW TO TAKE BETTER PICTURES

IN bird photography, an obvious and dominant problem is to get close enough to the subject. Except for large, tame birds like mute swans, a telephoto lens is almost essential.

At one time, virtually all bird photographs were taken at the nest from hides. Hide photography still has its place, but with advances in the quality, weight and relatively low cost of telephoto lenses, many successful pictures can now be obtained by stalking or from a car window.

However the photograph is taken, there is one golden rule: the welfare of the subject must come first. Don't disturb the bird unnecessarily, especially at the nest. If you are trying to stalk a rarity, remember that others may be watching it too, and will be extremely displeased if *you* are the one who causes it to fly off!

In Britain you must, by law, have a licence to photograph certain birds at or near the nest (see p. 404). The Royal Society for the Protection of Birds produces a leaflet, *Wild Birds and the Law*, which lists them. Licences are normally granted only to experienced bird photographers.

Cameras and equipment

Most bird photographers today, including professionals, use 35 mm single-lens reflex (SLR) cameras. These have many advantages—relatively cheap film, light weight, interchangeable lenses, and a through-the-lens viewfinder which shows exactly what is being photographed.

Many incorporate automatic metering and focusing systems, and so allow the photographer more time to concentrate on composition. The newly introduced digital cameras—which, instead of using film, record images for scanning into computers—are as yet unsuitable for bird photography.

The range and cost of telephoto lenses vary a great deal. The amateur, wanting slides of birds for record purposes or to illustrate a lecture, can usefully start out with two: a 70-210 mm zoom, the variable magnifications of which are especially useful when framing and composing pictures of birds at the nest; and a 500 mm mirror lens (equivalent to 10 x magnification) for longer distance work. A tripod or other support should be used; as well as magnifying the subject, long telephotos also magnify camera shake.

Many fine 35 mm SLR camera systems are available. Most come from Japan, and even the least expensive will produce excellent results in the right hands.

Birds are colourful, and most photographers prefer to use colour film rather than black-and-white. Two types are available: negative film, from which prints have to be made; and reversal film, producing transparencies or slides, which are normally viewed by projecting them onto a screen. The latter is recommended—the results are sharper and more permanent. Prints can made if necessary.

The sharpest images and best colour results are achieved with slower films, of 25-100 ISO—the film speed ratings marked on the box. Especially if you hope to sell your photographs to colour magazines, use the Kodachrome or Fujichrome versions of these films.

In the poor light conditions encountered all too frequently in Britain, faster colour films (200 or even 400 ISO) may have to be used, especially for birds in flight where a fast shutter speed is vital. The results will be perfectly acceptable for most purposes.

In close-up work, electronic flash may be used to augment poor light or to 'freeze' action, for example of a bird bathing or of tits squabbling on a peanut string. Birds are not disturbed by the flash.

Choosing a subject

As good a place as any to start bird photography is in the garden. Baiting with different foods will attract a variety of species, but ensure that neither the bait nor the place it is put are so obtrusive that they dominate and detract from the picture. Many small birds will come to garden ponds to bathe and drink, and so provide photographic opportunities. So do birds feeding on rowan, cotoneaster or other colourful berries.

Seabird colonies on cliffs are excellent places at which to photograph birds in flight (but do take care near the edge). A keen eye and quick reflexes are called for. Do not expect perfect results every time the shutter is clicked. One successful picture in ten is a good average.

Birds have been photographed at the nest so often that it is rare to see a fresh picture. A hide will almost always be necessary but must be erected or moved into place extremely carefully to avoid distress to the birds.

Hides can also be used in many other situations—notably where birds congregate to feed, drink or roost. High tide wader roosts on estuaries are especially profitable and exciting. Good pictures can also be taken from permanent viewing hides on nature reserves.

Many bird-watchers take photographs as an aid to identification or as a record of what has been seen, especially on trips abroad. To make the best use of the results, always note the date and location of each picture. Label slides the moment they come back from the processors, before you forget.

Movies demand different techniques, as well

HOW TO MAKE A HIDE

MATERIALS NEEDED: 21 ft of $\frac{7}{8}$ in. dowel; 3 ft of 1 in. 16 swg aluminium tube; 12 ft 10 in. of $\frac{1}{4}$ in. mild steel rod; two pieces 8 oz. canvas, 14 ft × 36 in. wide; one piece 8 oz. canvas, 4 ft × 17 in.; 3 ft of cloth tape; 1 ft of elastic tape.

CONSTRUCTION—LEGS: 1. Mark the aluminium tube in four 6 in. lengths and four 3 in. lengths, and cut with a hacksaw. 2. Cut four pieces of dowel 33 in. long and insert one end of each piece into a 6 in. piece of aluminium tube to a depth of 3 in., securing with glue or pins; sharpen the other ends to a point. 3. Cut four pieces of dowel 30 in. long and insert one end of each into a 3 in. piece of tube until ends are flush, securing with glue or pins. 4. Drill $\frac{1}{2}$ in. dia. hole 2 in. deep in the centre of the tube-sheathed ends of these pieces; the prongs of the roof supports will be inserted into these four holes.

ROOF FRAME: 1. Cut two pieces of mild steel 38 in. long and bend into 2 in. prongs at ends of each, to peg into holes drilled in legs. 2. Cut two pieces 39 in. long, bend 2 in. prongs at ends, and bend slightly in centre so that roof will shed rain. 3. Assemble frame by socketing legs together and driving prongs into holes drilled.

COVER: 1. Take two pieces of 14 ft canvas, turn up all four short sides 6 in. and sew down to make ballast pockets, leaving gaps to fill with stones. 2. Lay one piece across the other to form an equal cross, and sew together. 3. Lay cross over roof, sew three sets of meeting edges completely to ground level and fourth 12 in. down from roof. 4. Sew 6 in. lengths of cloth tape to each side

of unstitched edge at 12 in. intervals, to make flap fastenings. 5. Cut 18 × 18 in. hole in one face of tent, 4 ft from ground. 6. Cut four equilateral triangles with 19 in. sides from remaining piece of canvas and sew them together to form pyramid-shaped funnel. 7. Cut point from pyramid to give hole just large enough to take camera lens. 8. Sew elastic draw-string round opening (this is for a single-lens reflex camera). 9. Sew funnel to opening in tent. 10. Cut 1 in. peepholes at eye level in other three sides and sew canvas flaps over them from inside.

In normal conditions this hide will be stable, but if guy-ropes are needed, sew tape to the four top corners of the canvas, as attachment points.

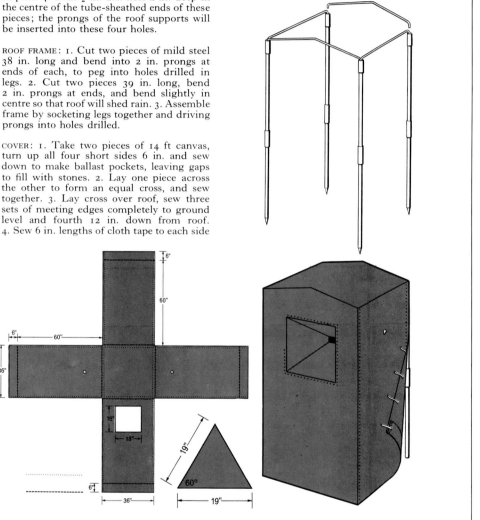

as equipment. Professional wildlife film-makers use 16 mm cameras. But these are bulky and the film expensive. Most amateurs making home 'movies' will use the convenient 8 mm camcorders (video cameras) which have now superseded Super 8 cine.

Whereas a still photograph stands on its own, movies need careful research and a script before shooting begins. Without them much time will be wasted and the result will be a string of unrelated shots of birds, of little interest to the viewer.

The subject does not need to be exotic to hold attention but there must be a good story line.

Many recent successful bird films have been of familiar species—the house sparrow, blue tit, robin and mute swan all come to mind.

When scripting and shooting, remember to build a sequence. Pan or zoom sparingly. Instead, use the zoom at successive fixed focal lengths to produce different shots of the same bird, in the sequence: long-shot, medium-shot, close-up.

Most amateur films tend to be too long, so be drastic when editing. Avoid repetition and for both movies and stills do not forget to include pictures of the habitat in which the birds are found.

Recording bird-song

SCOPE FOR THE AMATEUR TO BREAK NEW GROUND

IN 1900, a crude wax cylinder crackled out a few distinct notes of the song thrush. The first recording of a wild bird's song had been painstakingly produced by Cherry Kearton, the British naturalist, in Surrey. It was the beginning of a new way of studying birds.

He was followed by other pioneers, using primitive disc-cutting equipment. Ludwig Koch, the German violinist and singer, began the study of bird-songs which was to make him famous. The horizons of Kearton's new world had widened.

A library of songs

Today the recording of bird-songs is still one of the most rewarding of nature studies; and it still offers the ornithologist the hope of new discoveries. Relatively few of the 200 commonest British birds have had their complete vocabularies recorded. The rook, for example, produces sounds which are not yet on tape. So, too, do the grasshopper warbler, the green woodpecker and even the house sparrow.

Before switching on your sound recorder, prepare the ground thoroughly by watching the habits of the birds you wish to record. Map out a programme of study, for if you have something to aim at, the results will be more satisfying. For example, you might decide to record the sounds of one particular bird, such as the house sparrow. Alternatively, you may want to build up a small tape library of bird-song from a particular habitat such as a woodland or estuary.

As well as the songs and calls of the birds themselves, sensitive microphones can also pick up and exaggerate other sounds—from aircraft, traffic and machinery. Small wonder then that keen recordists are most active in remote places and at dawn, when bird-song is often at its best and extraneous, background sound is minimal.

There is infinite scope for the recording of bird dialects—those of the chaffinches, for instance—although this involves a lot of travelling. There is scope, too, for the taping of sounds vital to the identification of birds in the field. The chiffchaff and the willow warbler are just two of the birds which are extremely difficult to distinguish from each other except when they sing.

One of the most amusing experiments is to play back the recorded sound of a bird in its own territory. It will assume the sound to be that of an intruder. An aggressive bird, such as a robin, may even attack the tape recorder. Most birds will sing back excitedly in an attempt to frighten away the invader and a flick from 'play back' to 'record' can provide some first-rate tapes. Discretion is needed when carrying out such experiments as they can disrupt an individual bird's normal activity. Especial care should be taken with scarce and rare breeding birds.

Much can be learned, too, from replaying recorded bird-songs at reduced speeds. The song of the swift is a high-pitched screech to the human ear; but slowed down, the sound will reproduce as a melodious warble with distinct notes. Similarly, when a wren's song is slowed down, it becomes much more meaningful to human ears and, in a sense, it becomes nearer to what birds themselves actually hear, for it has been proved that they can distinguish individual notes in a phrase so rapid that the notes merge in human ears.

Sonograms

An alternative way of analysing recordings of bird-songs is by means of audio-spectography or 'sonograms'. Produced by specialist equipment, these are graphs which provide visual representations of sound patterns—in both pitch (vertical scale) and duration (horizontal scale). Amplitude may be indicated by the

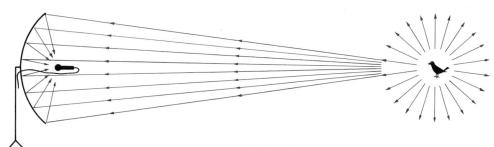

THE PARABOLIC REFLECTOR

This is a device which operates like a mechanical ear. It collects sounds at up to 40 times the distance of an open microphone, and is invaluable for recording bird-songs in mountainous regions or extensive marshes.

Note that the microphone is set up facing the reflector, not the singing bird. The device has been largely superseded by the directional or gun microphone, which is much easier to use.

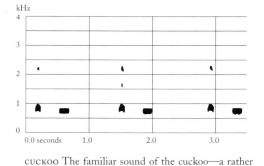

CUCKOO The familiar sound of the cuckoo—a rather low-frequency song, repeated at 1½ second intervals.

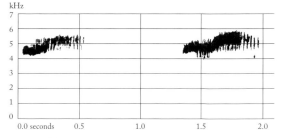

SWIFT To the human ear, a loud, high-pitched scream, but actually composed of distinct notes.

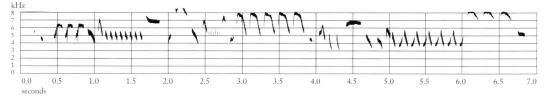

WREN Complex, rapid song (here lasting for 7 seconds) quite clearly comprising individual phrases and notes.

SONOGRAMS — REPRESENTING BIRD-SONGS VISUALLY

One way of studying recordings of bird-songs is by audio-spectrography. The 'sonograms' produced provide a visual representation of the song—pitch is shown in the vertical scale (in kilocycles or kiloherz) and duration is shown in the horizontal scale (in seconds). The sonograms shown above are based on information taken from *Birds of the Western Palearctic*, edited by Stanley Cramp, by permission of Oxford University Press.

depth of shading—the darker the shade, the louder the sound.

The three sonograms above show the slowed-down songs of the cuckoo, swift and wren.

Sound spectography can even be used to identify and separate the voice-patterns of individual birds of the same species. Analysis of the booming songs of bitterns in a recent year showed that there were only 16 individual males in the whole of Britain—fewer than was originally thought as it could be shown that the singing birds wandered widely within the large reed-beds which form their habitat.

Equipment

Modern recording equipment allows an enormous variety of experiments to be carried out. Portable machines enable the naturalist to record birds which live in remote places such as the upper reaches of mountains or deep forest, or which are heard only in extensive marshes. They can also, of course, be taken on overseas holidays to capture the sounds and atmosphere of exotic wildlife locations.

Only four decades ago, many tape recorders needed a mains electricity supply or at best a car battery to operate them. Even as recently as 20 years ago the serious bird-song recordist carried a large, heavy, reel-to-reel tape recorder, a microphone and an umbrella-sized cone known as a parabolic reflector. This last device, which still has its uses, can be beamed towards an area of sound and operates like a huge, mechanical ear, collecting sound and concentrating it into a microphone. It enables a bird's song to be recorded at up to 40 times the distance allowed by the older type of open microphone.

Today, parabolic reflectors have been largely replaced by increasingly efficient lightweight and small directional microphones. Used like a gun, they have an operational angle of only a few degrees, and collect sound in much the same way as the cumbersome reflectors. The more sophisticated the design, the less difficulty there will be with wind interference.

Most sound recordists have now abandoned their reel-to-reel machines and use much smaller cassette or digital recorders. There are many types to choose from. Technology is advancing rapidly and advice from your dealer or from the manufacturers will help you to choose the equipment most suitable for recording birds.

At least to start with, the beginner will probably be content with an inexpensive model with which to learn and experiment. A possible option is to combine a directional microphone with a camcorder—to obtain 'three dimensional' images.

Be warned, though, the hobby—once it takes a hold—can be addictive. Many dedicated amateurs now produce recordings of commercial quality. A 'mystery call' may be recorded which defies identification even by experts. One American ornithologist taped a bird-song which was later found to be that of a type of nightjar thought to have been extinct for many years.

Organisations concerned with recordings of bird-songs include the Wildlife Sound Recording Society, which circulates tapes made by its members, and the British Library of Wildlife Sounds (BLOWS), a member of the National Sound Archive that is building up a collection of tapes.

Birds in domestication

5000 YEARS OF BREEDING IN FARMYARD, CAGE AND AVIARY

THE domestication of birds in the service of man is as old as history. By the time of the first written records, about 3000 BC, pigeons were established in Egypt both as food and as message carriers; and the Egyptian goose was domesticated soon afterwards. By 1400 BC, the domestic hen was part of the everyday scene in China and Egypt; and in Greek and Roman times the artificial breeding of new types was well advanced.

It is probable that the Romans brought this knowledge to Britain; for although domestic fowl were recorded at Glastonbury as early as 250 BC, Julius Caesar claimed, some 200 years later, that the Ancient Britons used them not as food but for entertainment as fighting cocks.

But birds are not only kept to be eaten. The Romans themselves regarded the sacred geese of the Capitol as watchdogs, and were great lovers of ornamental fowl. Today many species of birds are domesticated purely for their decorative value, and for the pleasure they give as pets.

Birds are also still kept, though not as much as they once were, to provide feathers for bedding, arrows and darts; for fashion ornaments; and, in the case of hawks and cormorants, to catch food for their masters.

Today, domesticated birds can be broadly divided into those kept for food, and those in cage, aviary and sanctuary, which are kept for human enjoyment or to be studied.

THE ANCESTOR OF THEM ALL

Centuries of domestication have produced 70 different breeds of chicken from the wild red jungle fowl (top). These include: (1) the old English game-bird; (2) the black Minorca; (3) the Sebright bantam; (4) the Rhode Island red; (5) the white Wyandotte; and (6) the game-bird bantam.

SOUTH AMERICAN WILD DUCK

One of the ducks specially bred and reared for eating in Britain is the Muscovy, descended from this wild species of South and Central America.

TABLE BIRD FROM AMERICA

Turkish merchants brought the turkey to this country in the 16th century from North America, where it is still a wild species in some areas.

In Britain today there are some 70 different breeds of domestic chicken, most of them kept to provide meat, eggs or both. All can be traced back to the same ancestral species—the red jungle fowl, *Gallus gallus*, which is still wild in parts of Asia.

This omnivorous scrub- and jungle-dwelling bird has sired what has become, through domestication, the world's most numerous species; for there is little doubt that there are more domestic fowl in existence than any other bird.

Breeding for the table

Two predominant types of fowl have evolved in Europe. From the Mediterranean countries came the ancestors of breeds such as the Andalusian, Leghorn, Minorca and Spanish—active little birds which laid many white eggs and were reluctant to go broody.

From the chilly, damp countries of northern Europe came larger, more placid hens which laid light brown or cream-coloured eggs and gave rise to the 'heavy' breeds such as the Sussex, Orpington, Marennes and Dorking.

All these types have their 'bantamised' equivalents—tiny birds, often half the size of the original, though they lay relatively large eggs. These birds are kept as pets or as show birds.

The nine British types of domestic goose, all descended from the wild greylag (except the Chinese, which is derived from Siberia's swan goose), are by no means as common as they were even 50 years ago. The Emden and Toulouse breeds, introduced from Germany and France respectively about 100 years ago, are probably the most popular; they are self-sufficient if allowed to forage for grass and greenery, and they do not lend themselves to modern factory farming.

Another domestic bird which resists these methods is the duck, once a resident on every farmyard and on almost every village pond. The farmyard duck is alone among Britain's domesticated birds in that it is the only one whose wild ancestor, the mallard, is prolific throughout the country.

The Indian runner, introduced to Britain in 1835, is known to go back 2000 years, to the time when it was domesticated in Java. But today's most popular food breeds, the

Aylesbury (for meat) and the Khaki Campbell (for eggs) have both become established within the past 200 years.

The pigeon, developed from the rock dove, and possibly the first domesticated bird, is nowadays not used for food as much as it used to be; but in the Middle Ages, and up to a century ago, the dovecote provided a valuable supplement to the Briton's winter larder.

The turkey comes to Europe

Of the major edible birds, the turkey is becoming increasingly important as breeders learn how to overcome its juvenile diseases, how to produce more and cheaper birds, and how to breed them smaller.

But despite these advances, today's turkey bears a close resemblance to the North American bird, which was brought to England by Turkish traders (possibly giving rise to its name) in 1521. The newcomer quickly replaced the peacock and mute swan—and later the goose—as a table bird.

Another bird which has changed little under domestication is the guineafowl, which was bred in Greece in the 4th century BC, although not introduced to England until 1550. Two hundred years later it was a common domestic bird, but since then it has declined rapidly, though its eggs and meat are still counted as delicacies.

The quail, on the other hand, is prized

AFRICAN GUINEAFOWL

In more than 2000 years, the domestic guineafowl (behind) has hardly changed, except in colour, from the wild variety, which is still found in Africa.

A CAGEFUL OF COLOUR, MUSIC AND MIMICRY

Birds from many parts of the world, popular for their plumage, song or powers of mimicry, are caged in Britain. They include (1) zebra finch; (2) African grey parrot; (3) cockatiel; (4) budgerigar; (5) peach-faced lovebird; (6) Java sparrow; (7) Norwich canary (a show bird); and (8) roller (song) canary.

among epicures mainly for its eggs; and the Japanese form of the common quail is now bred and kept in increasing numbers.

Enter the budgerigar

In 1840, the artist and author John Gould brought from Australia a bird which was to become the most popular cage-bird the world has ever known. He described the species: 'As cage-birds they are as interesting as can possibly be imagined; for independently of their highly ornamental appearance, they are constantly coquetting, squabbling and assuming every variety of graceful posture.' Gould's bird was the budgerigar–a small, seed-eating, predominantly green parakeet.

The descendants of Gould's wild budgerigars and others have been bred and inter-bred in their hundreds of thousands, until today there are anything up to 5 million of these cheerful, companionable birds in homes throughout the country, and the importing of wild strains has become rare.

Most budgie owners keep birds as household pets; but there are three other categories of live-bird keepers—the aviculturist, who keeps his birds for study and enjoyment; the fancier, who breeds birds to meet set 'show' standards which often differ greatly from those of the wild form; and the scientist, who keeps birds in cages to study them under carefully controlled conditions in a laboratory.

No firm figures are available for a 'popularity chart' of British cage-birds, but the list of the top half-dozen probably reads something like this: (1) budgerigar; (2) canary; (3) zebra finch; (4) Bengalese finch; (5) Java sparrow; (6) Indian hill mynah. Parrots and lovebirds are also well-established favourites.

The canary, which was overtaken by the budgerigar in the early 1930's, came originally from the Canary Islands. It was for centuries bred in and exported from Germany, where it was first domesticated in the early 16th century.

Now that they are no longer a general household pet, canaries are kept by aviculturists, or fanciers who breed them either to produce vividly coloured plumages ranging from shades of yellow to deep orange-red or, in the case of roller canaries, for that soft, sweet, musical song which has always been their main attraction.

The highly sociable zebra finch, another Australian bird which inhabits the same type of country as the budgerigar, is now bred in domestication virtually throughout the world. The Bengalese finch, a small dull-coloured bird, is the same size as the zebra finch, though it is less hostile, breeds more easily, and is readier to tolerate humans.

The Bengalese, an oriental bird descended

from the sharp-tailed finch, gets its name from dealers who at one time termed all Oriental or African finches 'Bengali'. It was first domesticated in China, then introduced to Japan, where most of today's breeding stock originated.

It has much the same history as the large, vividly coloured Java sparrow, which is a common cage-bird in the East. In Britain and Europe, Java sparrows are not as numerous as Bengalese and zebra finches, mainly because they are not easy to breed—and also because it is virtually impossible to distinguish the sexes, which raises obvious breeding problems.

All these 'top birds' are easy-to-keep seed-eaters, with one exception. This is the Indian hill mynah, which demands a mixed diet including fruit and insects and yet has made a remarkable advance in popularity in the last few years almost solely because of its astonishing powers of mimicry.

Though it is now illegal to capture and cage wild British birds, there is also a strong and reviving interest in breeding such British finches as the linnet, bullfinch and goldfinch, which are among the most handsome of birds; and even highly specialised birds as difficult to breed as woodpeckers, humming birds and birds of paradise, are kept and bred by enthusiasts.

Apart from these cage-birds, there are an enormous number of pigeons and doves, of at least 150 distinct strains. These are kept for a variety of reasons including food, sport, laboratory experiments, and as show birds.

Mis-shapen show birds
Show birds have been so highly developed by fanciers to meet purely arbitrary standards that many species are now a caricature of the original wild form. Breeds such as the short-faced tumbler and the owl pigeon have bills so mis-shapen that they cannot feed their own young. Show fantails are so in-bred that their heads are thrown back to rest on their multi-feathered tails and they can barely walk; while fairy swallows have such large feathers on their legs and feet that they have difficulty in taking a step without tripping.

All these are a long way removed from the domestic pigeon's common ancestor, the rock dove. This trim, lively bird is still numerous around parts of the coasts of Scotland and Ireland, though in most other regions it has become inter-bred with feral or domesticated pigeons.

The popular barbary dove bears a much closer resemblance to its ancestor, the African collared dove. Despite this affinity, the pale, buff-coloured barbary dove is unique in that no domesticated bird ever has the much darker colour of the wild form. The barbary dove is also possibly the tamest of domesticated birds, for its instinctive fear of humans seems to have been entirely bred out, while it still retains an innate fear of predatory birds. On the other hand, its homing instinct is much weaker than that of pigeons. Escaped birds have been known to breed in the wild in Lancashire and elsewhere.

Of the 24 species of fowl regularly bred in Europe purely for ornament and decoration, the peacock is undoubtedly the most striking. The astounding beauty of the Indian blue peacock, or the Javan green, has made them objects of veneration, of superstition, and even—to the Hindus—of worship. Alexander the Great first saw them when he invaded India, and promptly passed a law that they must not be killed.

The Romans, however, had no such scruples and made them the centre-pieces at their feasts, beginning a custom that lasted well into the Middle Ages. Today, peacocks are prized exhibits at sanctuaries, stately homes and parks, standing up to our climate without apparent discomfort; they provide an unparalleled sight when, in courtship, they display their 'eyed' trains—which are actually enlarged upper tail-coverts supported by the bristly feathers of the true tail.

The peacock, like the domestic fowl, is really a type of pheasant, and along with many members of this family has taken readily to domestication. The ring-necked pheasant is a well-known game-bird, but several other species—such as the golden, silver, argus and Lady Amherst's pheasants—are kept solely for their striking plumage.

Ornamental waterfowl
Even more popular as ornamental birds are the various species of waterfowl, kept in numerous parks and zoos. The best-known and most comprehensive selection is at the Wildfowl Trust at Slimbridge, Gloucestershire, where most of the world's 147 species of ducks, geese and swans are either residents or visitors, along with a few exotic relatives such as flamingoes. Strictly speaking, not all of these birds are domestic, since some of them do not breed readily in captivity; but many species are bred in private collections as well as public ones.

An encouraging trend in the world-wide domestication of birds is the emphasis on preservation rather than exploitation. At least one species, the Hawaiian goose, has been saved from probable extinction by having bred since 1949 at Slimbridge. Attempts are being made in other parts of the world to save other species by similar methods.

THE STATELY PEACOCK

Many members of the pheasant family take readily to domestication; the peacock, fanning the 'eye' feathers of its train, is the most striking.

Threats to bird life

WHY CONSERVATION IS NEEDED ... AND HOW IT WORKS

WITH some 58 million people living in the British Isles, it is not surprising that there have been, and will continue to be, many clashes between what is good for human beings and what is good for birds.

Our tampering with the countryside has benefited dynamic species such as the wood-pigeon and the black-headed gull, which are able to exploit new sources of food. But others are less lucky; evolution has programmed them to fit into a particular niche in a particular habitat, and when deprived of it in the interests of human progress, they either move elsewhere or die out altogether.

The changing face of Britain

No one who regularly visits the countryside can fail to notice how quickly it is changing. Where once there were open fields there are now housing estates; coniferous woods stand where oak and ash were once dominant; and the booming holidays industry is making inroads into once-lonely stretches of coastline.

Large birds are the first to suffer when humans move into an area—for they need large areas in which to live and breed. The great bustard has been lost to Britain—except as a very rare vagrant—since before 1850.

The draining of marshlands and the reclamation of mud-flats has deprived many ducks, geese, waders and other birds of valuable feeding and breeding grounds. The black tern, which used to breed in the fens of Cambridgeshire and Lincolnshire, has been lost to Britain since the middle of the 19th century; and the bittern, marsh harrier and avocet, wiped out in the marshes in the 19th century, have returned there only because of a new public attitude towards conservation.

Some seabirds, such as terns and ringed plovers, depend on undisturbed shingle banks and sandy shores for their nest-sites, and cannot survive when these places are overrun by holidaymakers. They nest on the ground, and their eggs—though safe from predators because they blend with their surroundings—may be trodden on by humans.

Wild rough ground and heaths are nesting places for species such as the stone curlew, which are disappearing as housing developments swallow up the land. Plantations of coniferous trees, advancing up the slopes of hill country, are suitable mainly for a small number of highly specialised birds; the rough mixed woodland and copses they often replace were the homes of nightingales—which are lost for ever—and redstarts, woodpeckers and warblers, which return as the plantations age. The great estates, with their mixed woods and wide variety of habitats,

provided natural sanctuaries for birds—which are lost when these areas are divided up and built on.

Until about 50 years ago, Britain was richer than any other country in Europe in the number and variety of its small birds. Unlike the agricultural land of France and Germany, with large open fields, Britain's farmland was divided into small fields bounded by hedges and copses. These provided cover, nest-sites and feeding places for yellowhammers, hedge sparrows, linnets, chaffinches and blackbirds, among others.

With the advent of prairie-type farming—large fields divided by wire fences—this great reservoir of small song-birds is lost. It has been estimated that over 150,000 miles of hedgerow have been eliminated since the end of the Second World War, although the rate of destruction has slowed down over recent years.

Other advances in farming techniques have also had an adverse effect on birds. The corncrake, which is shy and needs plentiful cover for its nest, could not stand up to the introduction of modern agricultural machinery; forage harvesters crush eggs, young, and sometimes the sitting adults themselves. The lapwing, which often lays on ploughed land, was frequently saved by the ploughman turning his horse aside to avoid the eggs—consideration it cannot expect from a man driving a tractor.

As modernity comes to the farms, the barn owl is losing its favourite nest-site in the old-fashioned wooden barn; and all hole-nesting birds suffer when old trees are cut down.

Man the destroyer

It is when man alters the environment that birds are most seriously threatened with extinction; but there are less universal threats, just as important for the individual birds. Every year thousands of seabirds die a lingering death on the beaches, coated in oil and unable to help themselves.

An estimated $2\frac{1}{2}$ million birds are killed on Britain's roads annually; and others are fatally wounded after flying into pylons, buildings or overhead wires.

In the Middle Ages, birds of prey were protected by game laws. Then came a time when they were killed as a threat to game. More recently, the threat came to them from another quarter—pesticides which poisoned their prey.

The use of chemicals to get rid of insects, rodents and weeds revolutionised agriculture, but it also had disastrous consequences for birds. In the spring of the years 1956-61,

WHEN A HEDGE IS CUT DOWN

BLACKBIRD YELLOW-HAMMER LINNET HEDGE SPARROW

ROBIN LESSER WHITETHROAT WREN CHAFFINCH

Small fields bounded by hedges, once the hallmark of British farmland, provide an ideal niche for many song-birds, with plenty of food and cover for nests.	But modern machinery has made larger fields more economical, and farmers cut down their hedges to make them . . . leaving the birds homeless.

thousands of pigeons, finches, pheasants and other birds died after eating seeds treated with the insecticides aldrin and dieldrin.

Aldrin, dieldrin and the other persistent organochlorine insecticides were withdrawn as seed-dressings—and from agriculture generally—more than 30 years ago, and the mass mortality incidents involving farmland birds came to an end. At the top of the 'food-chain', sparrowhawks and peregrines, whose numbers had declined alarmingly through eating contaminated prey, began their recovery which has continued to the present day.

While they rarely cause the direct deaths of large numbers of birds, modern agricultural pesticides continue to have widespread adverse effects on farmland birds by reducing their food supply of insects and weed seeds.

During the past 60 years a new menace has arisen for seabirds—waste oil, discharged by tankers and other ships. Birds coated with oil cannot fly or swim; they are buffeted by the waves or struggle ashore only to die of starvation, exposure or poisoning. Post-mortems on birds with only a small patch of oil on their plumage have revealed lungs full of oil, and intestines which have entirely disintegrated.

When the 61,263 ton tanker *Torrey Canyon* was wrecked off Land's End in March 1967, some 100,000 tons of crude oil poured out of its holds. About 100,000 birds died; and of the 7849 birds collected for treatment, less than 1 per cent finally survived.

The *Torrey Canyon* disaster was an accident. But some of the oil-slicks floating on the sea are put there deliberately. An international convention has been adopted to limit the discharge of waste oil into the sea by shipping, but the only solution is complete prohibition coupled with enforcement.

The bird-strike menace

While man has been responsible for many threats to bird-life, birds in turn have caused the loss of human life. They are a potential danger at airports. The largest human death-toll directly attributable to birds so far was the loss of 62 lives when a Lockheed Electra airliner crashed after hitting a flock of starlings over Boston in 1960.

Accidents to military planes on low-level flights over our coasts are numerous and costly—the RAF alone spends nearly £20 million a year on bird-strike repairs; and civil airlines are worried by the the Ministry of Defence's refusal to publish details of these incidents. Only once has bird-strike been officially blamed as the cause of a civil air-crash in Britain.

Scientists have tried many bird-deterrent devices at airports, none of them wholly successful. Amplified recordings of bird distress calls have been found useful in making birds scatter for cover when a plane is on the runway, and the RAF use this system at some airfields. They also use bangs and flashes to disperse the birds, but the use of falcons had to be discontinued because of the scarcity and

415

expense of trained handlers. One civilian airport tried using amplified Elvis Presley records, but with little success.

Currently, the most promising research into in-flight bird deterrents is being carried out by Canadian experts who are devising a microwave transmitter which projects a high-intensity radio beam a mile ahead of the aircraft, disorientates birds, and causes them to fall out of the plane's path.

Protecting birds and saving their habitats

The protection of birds dates back at least to the harsh forest laws of Norman times; but then, and for centuries to come, the object was to preserve falcons, hawks and their prey for the hunting pleasure of aristocrats.

Birds were regarded as the personal property of those on whose land they were found, and even as late as the early part of the 19th century the penalties for poaching were savage. In these circumstances, game-birds, and for a time birds of prey, enjoyed a fair measure of effective protection, though not for any humane reasons.

The Game Act of 1831, which has some provisions still in force today, provided for the protection of game-birds by establishing a period during which they were not allowed to be shot. Black grouse, bustards, red grouse, partridges and pheasants were designated as 'game', and only people in possession of a game certificate were allowed to shoot them. Some of the provisions of later acts also applied to woodcock, snipe, quail and corn-crakes, though these species have never legally been 'game'.

The attitude that birds were merely a source of food or an object of sport changed slowly. During the 17th and 18th centuries the interest in birds developed along various lines: killing birds and taking their eggs for study; collecting stuffed specimens in glass cases; collecting eggs in cabinets; and the approach pioneered by the naturalist Gilbert White (1720-93), author of *The Natural History of Selborne*, of watching birds to find out more about their habits.

In 1822 the first Bill for the protection of animals was introduced by the humanitarian Richard Martin, and in 1824 the Society (later Royal) for the Prevention of Cruelty to Animals was founded. But wild birds were not considered worth protecting until 1869 when an Act for the preservation of seabirds was passed. Before this it was a common Victorian sport to go out in a boat and shoot seabirds.

This was followed in 1872 by an Act for the 'protection of certain birds during the breeding season', which covered 79 species, including all the birds mentioned in the previous Act and adding a list of waders, ducks and song-birds. Eight years later an Act was passed which included provisions for the protection of all wild birds.

In 1885 a Plumage League was formed as a protest against the use of birds' feathers and stuffed bodies for the decoration of hats and dresses. This was merged into the Society (later Royal) for the Protection of Birds, founded in 1889.

In 1922 a small group of ornithologists from the U.S.A., England, France and Holland met in London, and the International Committee (later Council) for Bird Preservation was founded. This was the first international organisation to be concerned with the preservation of wildlife; it has grown into a world-wide organisation, with branches in 60 different countries. In the 1990s it was renamed Birdlife International. A large and expanding headquarters staff is based in Cambridge.

The conservation movement

The only way to stop many birds from being driven out of Britain is to set aside areas which provide for their basic needs. The first bird sanctuary was established by Charles Waterton at Walton Hall in Yorkshire in 1843. He amazed his gamekeeper by forbidding him to shoot owls, and was one of the first people to put up nest-boxes.

In the early days, a sanctuary was considered inviolate—a place where no species could be killed or vegetation controlled. This proved to be a mistake; colonies of terns were taken over by gulls, and woodland sanctuaries became impenetrable tangles of undergrowth.

Bird preservation has become a more positive concept today, and entails careful management of the land.

The conservation movement received an important boost in 1949 by the foundation of the Nature Conservancy, which became

A BIRD BEYOND PROTECTION

The great auk stood about 30 in. high and had adapted so completely to an aquatic life that it could no longer fly. Its range once extended over the North Atlantic, from the coasts of America to Europe. In the British Isles it bred on St. Kilda and was also recorded in the Orkneys and on the coast of Waterford, Ireland. But great auks were mercilessly slaughtered by fishermen for food and bait; and this continued persecution, along with what a writer of the day described as 'the ruthless trade in its eggs and skin', led to their extermination in 1844.

THE LAW PROTECTING BIRDS

The Protection of Birds Acts 1954–67 were superseded in 1981 by the Wildlife and Countryside Act.

This Act protects wild birds, their nests and their eggs at all times, with certain exceptions. It is now an offence for any person to kill, injure or take, or attempt to kill, injure or take any wild bird; to take, damage or destroy the nest of any wild bird while it is in use; to take or destroy an egg of any wild bird; or to disturb a rare bird while it is on or near a nest containing eggs or has dependent young.

Licences may be issued to take or kill birds for scientific, educational and other purposes, such as preventing serious damage to crops.

Certain harmful birds can be killed at any time and their eggs may be taken or destroyed by 'authorised persons', including owners and occupiers acting on land in their occupation.

The list of birds regarded as harmful includes carrion crows, hooded crows, a number of gulls, house-sparrows, jays, magpies, rooks, wood-pigeons and collared doves.

A few other birds—mainly various ducks and geese—may be killed at certain times of the year; the close season, when they cannot be killed, usually extends from February 1 to August 31.

Taking the eggs of any wild bird other than those birds listed as harmful is an offence for which there may be a fine of up to £1000 per egg.

If the eggs are those of a rare species—such as the chough, peregrine or Dartford warbler—the penalty *for each egg*, is a fine of up to £2000.

In general, it is an offence to possess or sell wild birds' eggs, even blown ones, except under licence. It is now an offence to have captive birds of prey, unless they have been registered; and to exhibit competitively many species of cage birds.

Certain methods of killing, capturing or frightening off birds are prohibited—traps of most sorts, poisoned or drugged bait, explosives, birdlime, nets, live bird decoys, certain large-bore shotguns, gas or electrical devices to frighten birds.

Full details concerning the law and its protection of birds are available in a booklet entitled *Wild Birds and the Law*, obtainable from the RSPB (see below).

---

responsible for some 400,000 acres of nature reserves all over the country. These cover a selection of all the natural habitats of Great Britain. In 1991-2 the Conservancy was split into three: ENGLISH NATURE, Northminster House, Peterborough PE1 1UA; COUNTRYSIDE COUNCIL FOR WALES, Plas Penrhos, Fford Penrhos, Bangor, Gwynedd LL57 2LQ; and SCOTTISH NATURAL HERITAGE, 12 Hope Terrace, Edinburgh EH9 2AS.

About 4000 'sites of special scientific interest', mostly in private ownership, are afforded some protection by these three bodies.

COUNTY TRUSTS FOR NATURE CONSERVATION These now cover every county in England and Wales. In Scotland they are represented by a central Wildlife Trust, and in N. Ireland by the Ulster Trust for Nature Conservation. The trusts own or lease reserves, managing them jointly with local authorities or private landowners. They also organise nature trails and information centres, lectures, film-shows and exhibitions.

THE ROYAL SOCIETY FOR NATURE CONSERVATION (The Green, Witham Park, Waterside South, Lincoln LN5 7JR) This society, in addition to owning, leasing and managing reserves itself, is now chiefly concerned with the support and encouragement of the County Trusts for Nature Conservation. It has wide powers, under a Royal Charter, to promote nature conservation at home and abroad.

THE BRITISH TRUST FOR CONSERVATION VOLUNTEERS (1 Waterworks Cottages, Sandford Mill Road, Chelmsford, Essex CM2 6NY) This trust provides opportunities for volunteers to take an active part in conservation during weekends and holidays. It works largely with the statutory agencies and has affiliation with local conservation bodies country-wide.

THE BRITISH TRUST FOR ORNITHOLOGY (The Nunnery, Thetford, Norfolk IP24 2PU) This body studies Britain's birds and their habitats, and conducts nationwide surveys of bird populations in a unique partnership with scientists and volunteers. (See pages 460-1.)

THE NATIONAL TRUST (42 Queen Anne's Gate, London SW1H 9AS) The first function of the National Trust is to preserve places of historic interest or natural beauty; but it also preserves the plant and animal life on its land. The trust owns a number of important bird reserves on the Farne Islands off the coast of Northumberland, the Calf of Man, Wicken Fen in Cambridgeshire, Blakeney Point and Scolt Head Island in Norfolk, and other places.

THE ROYAL SOCIETY FOR THE PROTECTION OF BIRDS (The Lodge, Sandy, Beds. SG19 2DL) Some of the most important of the nature reserves in Britain belong to this society. Havergate Island, off the Suffolk coast— where the avocet returned to breed after being lost to Britain for more than 100 years—is one of theirs; so is Minsmere, one of the few places where the marsh harrier still breeds. An East Anglian breeding place of the blacktailed godwit and ruff—a reserve on the Ouse Washes along the Cambridgeshire-Norfolk border—was taken off the society's 'secret list' in May, 1969; and the ospreys on the society's Scottish reserve at Loch Garten have now been seen by about a million people.

The RSPB manages 140 reserves with a total area of 240,000 acres, and these reserves give shelter to such rare birds as the bearded tit; bittern and Dartford warbler. The society has an adult membership of 1 million and its own club for young people, the Young Ornithologists' Club, which has 120,000 members. THE WILDFOWL AND WETLANDS TRUST (Slimbridge, near Gloucester GL2 7BT) In the late 1920s a slump in the numbers of migratory wildfowl—in particular wild geese and ducks—was causing concern. In 1935 the British Section of the International Committee for Bird Preservation began to study the reasons for the decline, and the two reports it published led to the Wild Birds (Ducks and Geese) Protection Act of 1939. In 1954 the British Section handed over the work of its wildfowl sub-committee to the Severn Wildfowl Trust, which had existed since 1947.

The scientific study and conservation of wildfowl are now the special province of the Wildfowl and Wetlands Trust—and a greater variety of wild ducks, geese and swans can be seen in its various collections at Slimbridge in Gloucestershire, and in Carmarthenshire, Co. Down, Co. Durham, Lancashire and Sussex, than anywhere else in Britain.

THE ROYAL SOCIETY FOR THE PREVENTION OF CRUELTY TO ANIMALS (Manor House, Causeway, Horsham RH12 1HG) This society is today as much concerned about birds as about animals. The society issues leaflets and posters on bird protection, its inspectors tour schools to give children a better understanding of bird-life, and as a society it has helped to reform the laws on the protection of birds.

But laws can be broken; and an important part of the duty of an RSPCA inspector is to bring prosecutions, not only in cases of cruelty but also against people who illegally cage, sell or take the eggs of wild birds. THE SCOTTISH WILDLIFE TRUST (Cramond House, Kirk Cramond, Cramond Glebe Road, Edinburgh EH4 6NS) Formed in 1964, the Trust manages 83 reserves, including Loch of Lowes, one of the osprey nesting sites; the total area under its control is over 44,000 acres. THE WORLD WIDE FUND FOR NATURE (WWF) (Panda House, Weyside Park, Godalming, Surrey GU7 1XR) This is the British arm of the international organisation which set up in 1961 and has its headquarters in Switzerland. It has raised and distributed many millions of pounds for nature conservation projects throughout the world.

First aid for birds

A bird which allows itself to be captured easily is already weak and may be near its end. Often the kindest treatment for a sick or injured bird is to put it out of its misery. This happens in nature, because these birds are the ones most likely to fall victim to predators.

When a small bird has to be destroyed, a sharp twist and tug of the neck is quick and painless. A heavy blow to the base of the skull is the best way of killing a larger bird. But many people either have no experience of this

kind or cannot bring themselves to do it, and for them the best solution is to call the local branch of the RSPCA.

An injured bird needs protection from predators, as well as warmth, correct food, and the minimum of disturbance. Given these, it can sometimes be nursed back to full health. This chart gives a guide to the treatment for various ailments and injuries, though it is always best to consult a vet or the RSPCA before starting any treatment.

Symptoms	Cause	Treatment
Plumage clogged with oil	Self evident	If heavily oiled, the bird is best put out of its misery. If only lightly oiled, treatment is possible; but the bird will need tending until the next annual moult, as waterproofing of the feathers is destroyed. Do not use hay bales to confine the birds, or hay as bedding; birds can contract a disease from it. Give sea water to seabirds, and avoid handling any bird roughly. Best to contact the RSPCA about treatment
Broken wing or leg	Road accidents, collision with overhead wires, gunshot wounds	If the break is high on the wing or leg, the bird is best destroyed. If near the wing-tip, the bird can be cured by cutting the primary feathers off short, so that the wing cannot be used until the next moult. Breaks below the 'knee-joint' can be splinted
Multiple injuries, internal injuries (broken legs and wings, bleeding from beak, gashes in body)	Road accidents, collision with overhead wires, gunshot wounds	The most merciful treatment is to have the bird destroyed
Laceration or loss of feathers	Attack by cat, gunshot wounds	If the bird's condition is serious, it is best to destroy it. If the wound is minor, any visible shot should be extracted and the wound washed with clean, warm water and then dried carefully. The bird will need to be looked after until its feathers grow again
Young bird found away from nest on ground	Fall from nest	Destroy nestling if it is tiny and naked. If the bird is well grown and feathered it is probably still being fed by its parents, so leave well alone
General exhaustion	Harsh weather, disease or starvation	If ill, the bird may be breathing badly, drastically underweight, and possibly suffering from diarrhoea. Unless you can get it to a vet it is best to destroy it. Birds that are merely exhausted and hungry need food, rest and shelter for a few days or possibly weeks

Birds in folklore and religion

ENDURING TRADITIONS . . . AND FORGOTTEN ONES

BELIEFS which go back deep into time lie behind many of our present-day attitudes to birds. People have often regarded birds as having close affinities with man because, like humans, birds go on two legs, sing, dance, show off and construct homes. Dances from many different cultures are copied from the displays of birds; in the Outer Hebrides there are dances called 'The waddling of the ducks' and 'Cocks' combat'.

Man's first attempts at weaving were possibly inspired by watching birds build their nests; and paintings in the rock caverns of France and the rock shelters of Spain suggest that, as far back as the Old Stone Age, ceremonies were performed in which birds were imitated.

Birds have often been regarded as evil omens. Miners working at Llanbradach Colliery near Caerphilly in Mid Glamorgan were alarmed one day in September 1901 to find that a robin had built its nest in the underground pump-room. There was a widespread belief in the South Wales coalfield that seeing a wild bird at the colliery could be a warning of disaster. Shortly after the discovery there was an explosion, and eight men were killed.

Only the previous May, 81 people had been killed in an explosion at the nearby Senghenydd Colliery after a robin had been found underground. Another bird was reported to have been seen underground at Morfa Colliery, near Port Talbot, West Glamorgan in March 1890. The local community, terrified by the news, held midnight meetings to discuss what to do. On March 10 there was an explosion, and 87 miners died.

The guardian ravens

Beliefs connecting birds with forthcoming death or disaster are the modern versions of ancient traditions. The owl has long been regarded as a bird of death and doom over most of Europe and Asia. The Romans believed that if a barn owl perched on a house, it meant that someone inside was going to die; and this belief persisted in parts of Britain until well into the present century.

Beliefs about ravens have a similarly long history. During the last war, for example, people took a lively interest in the tame ravens which are kept at the Tower of London; according to legend, Britain will be invaded if the ravens are lost. This belief in the raven as a protector goes back at least as far as the 13th century, when a raven's head was supposed to have been buried on Tower Hill, in order to guard the people of the capital against their enemies.

Listening for the cuckoo

Some birds were thought to warn of disaster or foretell good fortune, according to the circumstances in which they were sighted.

In parts of Scotland, it is still lucky to hear the cuckoo while you are out walking, but not before you have eaten breakfast. The Welsh used to believe that you would flourish if you were standing on grass or green leaves when the bird sang, but if you were on barren ground you would not live to hear its call another year. Children in many parts of Britain still believe that it is unlucky to see a single crow or magpie, but lucky to see two, and they recite a version of this rhyme: 'One for sorrow, two for mirth, three for a wedding, four for a birth.'

The Greeks and Romans believed that their gods used natural signs such as birds to give warnings and advice. The Romans had a college of augurs, at which young men were trained in the complicated business of interpreting the behaviour of birds. The augur would divide the sky into four parts with a ceremonial staff, and predict from the type of birds he could see, and their positions, whether the gods favoured the course of action being considered.

Legend says that when the Greek forces were on their way to attack Troy in 1194 BC, they saw a serpent seize nine sparrows from a tree. The augur travelling with the expedition said this meant that they would have to fight for nine years before they captured Troy—and that is what happened.

The marriage oracle

Similar beliefs in birds as oracles can be found all over the world, and the present-day saying 'a little bird told me' is probably a relic of this. In the Faroe Islands, an unmarried girl would go out on a February morning and throw three objects at a hooded crow—a stone, a bone and a piece of turf. If the bird flew out to sea, that is where she would expect her future husband to come from. If it settled on a house she would marry a man from that family, and if it stayed where it was she would know she was going to remain a spinster.

Though many such ideas seem fanciful to us, some of the oldest examples embodied good common sense. When the Viking Floki Vilgerdsson set out in AD 846 on a voyage of discovery, he took ravens with him and set them loose in mid-ocean. The birds flew high to spy out the nearest land, and Vilgerdsson followed in the direction they eventually took. With them as his guides he discovered an island which he called Iceland.

It is doubtful whether there is as much good sense in the belief that the weather can be forecast by watching how birds behave, but it remains one of the most enduring ideas in folklore.

Until 100 years ago the colour of a goose's breast-bone was said to foretell the severity of the coming winter. If it was dark, the weather would be harsh; if lighter, it would be mild. Though the exact connection has become lost, the modern custom of breaking the 'wishbone' of a domestic fowl and making a wish is probably a remnant of this ancient belief.

Some methods of forecasting seem to have survived unscathed. Even today, people in some parts of Scotland confidently expect bad weather if the red-throated diver (they call it the 'rain-goose') is particularly noisy; and throughout Europe the singing of robins, the drumming of woodpeckers and snipe, and the presence of ravens, skuas, gulls and fulmars were all taken, at one time or another, as signs of an impending storm.

The woodpecker punished

A number of stories surround birds of the woodpecker family. In France and Germany it is said that the green woodpecker refused to join the other birds in hollowing out rivers, seas and pools at the time of the Creation, and was condemned by God to drink only rainwater. So its song became a cry for rain.

In Sweden, the black woodpecker, a species not found in Britain, is nicknamed 'Gertrude's fowl'. A story is told about Christ and St. Peter being refused a cake by a woman called Gertrude when they stopped at her house during a long journey. As a punishment, Gertrude was turned into a black woodpecker and made to hack away at the bark of trees in search of food and to sing for rain when she was thirsty.

Ancient peoples also used birds to tell them when one season was ending and another beginning. When the kite returned from its winter migration the Greeks knew they could safely start sheep-shearing; when the swallow followed, it was time to leave off winter clothing; and when the crane started on its way to the warmer climate of Africa, it meant that boats should be beached for the winter.

A cuckoo rhyme, based on a similar idea, survives in parts of Wales and Shropshire:

'When the cuckoo comes to the bare thorn,
Sell your cow and buy your corn;
But when she comes to the full bit,
Sell your corn and buy your sheep.'

The reasoning is that if plants have shown little sign of life by the time the cuckoo arrives, the harvest will be late and therefore poor—a good reason to stock up with fodder and reduce the number of animals to be fed through the next winter. If, on the other hand, vegetation has started to grow, it is safe to sell corn and build up flocks, for the harvest should be good and fodder plentiful.

Birds and magic

Reminders of cuckoo lore are still with us today in names such as Cuckoo Bush Mound and Cuckoo Bush Hill at Gotham in Nottinghamshire, and in more than a dozen other places in England and Wales. These names may commemorate the time when, according to legend, local inhabitants captured a cuckoo and tried to imprison it in a bush or hedge, so as to hold on to the fine weather it was supposed to bring.

Until about 200 years ago, remedies for sickness usually involved some form of magic. Most of Europe followed the ancient Greeks and Romans in believing that the way to cure blindness, for example, was to eat the heart of a raven or owl, or the gall of an eagle—all birds well known for their keen eyesight. Similarly, the mild and placid temperament of a dove could be used to draw out fever; the bird was cut in half and applied to the soles of the patient's feet.

The custom still found in parts of Yorkshire of giving owl broth as a cure for whooping cough may be a survival of this idea: if the owl hoots and whoops without becoming ill, broth made from the bird should help to conquer whooping cough.

Many birds were thought to have special stones with magical powers. The Greeks and Romans believed that the eagle found it difficult to lay its eggs, and kept a stone in the nest to induce the right mood. Any woman who could get hold of such a stone was assured of an easy childbirth. In the same way, a stone from a swallow's nest would restore sight, and one from a crane's would turn ordinary metal to gold. The raven had three stones: one for childbirth, one to make the owner invisible and one to lengthen life or revive the dead or dying. Stones, in fact, are seldom found in the nests of these birds.

Birds and witchcraft

More complicated cures might involve finding a scapegoat—such as a bird or animal—to which the illness could be transferred by the use of witchcraft.

One ceremony in Wales, which survived until a century ago, had become curiously interwoven with Christian beliefs. People suffering from epilepsy bathed in the sacred well at Llandegla in Clwyd and walked three times round it, throwing in money and repeating the Lord's Prayer. Then a cock (or, in the case of a woman patient, a hen) was carried round the well, and patient and bird spent the night under the altar of the local church. When the patient left the following morning, the disease was supposed to have been transferred to the bird.

The yellowhammer used to be associated with witchcraft in places as far apart as

Scotland and the area around Prague. In both places, young boys would kill its young and rob its nests because they believed it to be an agent of the devil. They called it 'Devil's Bird', and believed that it had three drops of the devil's blood in its veins.

Probably the most widespread of witchcraft ceremonies was the 'wren hunt', which still happens in Southern Ireland and possibly the Isle of Man. It was once performed in France, southern England and Wales, and takes place on Boxing Day. It used to involve the capture and killing of a wren—at all other times of the year a sacred bird—followed by a procession through the village and burial in the churchyard. Few, if any, birds are caught these days. Although the ceremony's origins are obscure, it seems to have been aimed at banishing evil influences which often appear to be taking over in the depths of winter.

Birds and fertility

When spring came, primitive people would celebrate the triumph of the powers that had brought the earth back to life, and would hold rituals and ceremonies aimed at increasing the fertility of the creatures they hunted or the crops they grew.

Man the hunter would decorate his cave with pictures of the birds and animals he hunted, hoping thereby to make them plentiful. Later, man the crop-grower believed the cuckoo to have special powers over the fertility of plants, and worshipped it accordingly throughout Europe and Asia.

The swallow, the cock and the goose were at one time believed to have similar powers over fertility. The custom of eating a goose at the feast of St. Michael (September 29) or St. Martin (November 11), which still survives in parts of England, probably has its roots in pre-Christian rituals, when a goose was sacrificed to increase the fertility of crops and stock. Traces of such ceremonies have been found in many parts of Britain and the Continent.

Incidentally, there is no such symbolism attached to eating a turkey at Christmas. The bird was introduced to Britain from North America only in the 16th century, probably too late to play a part in folklore.

In central Europe, the cock was regarded as the spirit of the corn; and in Germany, Hungary and Poland until a century ago, a cock was ceremonially killed at harvest time and buried in the fields to make sure that the next year's crop would be abundant.

Birds were thought to influence human as well as animal and plant fertility. In north and west Wales, the custom of carrying a cuckoo at weddings, to ensure that the couple's marriage was blessed with children, survived into the 20th century; and in China, around Moscow, and in parts of France a couple getting engaged or married used to receive—and sometimes still do—a goose as a gift.

This supposed influence over so many aspects of man's life—food, weather, seasons, predicting the future—meant that birds have been playing a major part in religious beliefs and customs from the earliest times.

Birds and religion

Birds have often been regarded as having supernatural qualities—mainly because of their mysterious powers of flight. In the Christian and Hebrew traditions, birds have a favoured part to play in God's design. The raven and the dove were chosen by Noah to look for land when the flood-waters began to go down; and the farmyard cock became the symbol of repentance when it crowed to remind St Peter that he had betrayed Christ three times.

On to these Biblical stories, tradition has grafted a number of others concerning birds. In the Hebrides they say that the sign of the cross on the oystercatcher's breast was the bird's reward for covering Christ with seaweed and hiding Him from His enemies beside the Sea of Galilee. Similarly the raven, thought to have been originally a white bird, was turned black by Christ, according to a legend from the Tyrol, as a punishment for muddying the water of a stream from which He wanted to drink.

Expelled from the ark

At the Crucifixion the birds played conflicting roles. In England it was said that the robin, trying to remove the thorns from Christ's head, pricked its hitherto grey breast, which has stayed red ever since in honour of the event. The same thing happened in Spanish legend to the swallow's throat as it tried to remove the nails. But the sparrow which brought them back was punished, according to a Russian story, by having its legs fastened together, forcing it to hop awkwardly from place to place instead of running.

A similar story, found in England during the Middle Ages and echoed in many other parts of the world, explains the colouring of the kingfisher or halcyon. The bird was thought to have been grey when Noah released it from the ark to search for land; but it flew so high that it took on the blue colour of the sky, and scorched its breast-feathers by flying too near the sun.

Noah was angry at this escapade, and refused to let the kingfisher back into the ark, forcing it to perch on the roof and search for food in the water—as it does today.

Throughout Christian history, birds have been associated with saints. The eider ducks which are numerous on the Farne Islands, off the coast of Northumberland, are still called St Cuthbert's ducks, after the saint who protected them when he had his hermitage there in the seventh century.

In pre-Christian times, birds themselves were sometimes regarded as gods. The goose was a supernatural creature to primitive agricultural peoples, and was sacrificed in many parts of the world in festivals of the sun.

Two birds figured among the deities of ancient Egypt—the ibis-headed Thoth, god of wisdom; and the falcon-headed Horus, a sky-god whose eyes were the sun and the moon. Some 2500 years before Christ, the cult of a new god, Osiris, spread over Egypt, and Horus was adopted as the son of Osiris and his wife Isis. The legend grew up that when Osiris was murdered by a rival god, Setekh, Horus avenged his father's death. In the process, Horus damaged his left eye—the moon—and this provided an explanation of the moon's phases.

The ancient Greeks also worshipped a god who sometimes took the form of a bird. She was Pallas Athene, patroness of Athens and goddess of war, who was said to appear as an owl. This probably gave rise to the modern expression 'wise as an owl', for she was also goddess of wisdom.

Traces of more recent bird worship have been found in the New World. The Aztecs of Mexico, whose civilisation dates from the 12th century, revered a bird-god called Huitzilopochtli, or humming-bird of the south. The god, who wore a humming-bird's feathers fastened to his left leg, was protector and guide to the Aztecs during their journeys, and human sacrifices were made in his temples.

Guide for the spirit

As well as being gods, birds were widely believed to be the spirits of the dead. The Romans used to set free an eagle over a funeral pyre, so that the spirit of the deceased could enter the bird and be conducted to heaven. Similar rites are still observed among primitive people in parts of Africa and among North American Indians.

In Britain today, fishermen can occasionally be heard talking of gulls as the spirits of dead seamen. The belief has been recorded on the east coast of England, in Cornwall, Ireland, and Sutherland in the north of Scotland. Across the channel in Brittany, sailors believe that skippers who deal harshly with their crews during their lifetime become storm petrels when they die.

Beliefs like these show how birds once played an important part in colouring people's outlooks, and sometimes still do. They also help to explain why we still use birds to symbolise many abstract ideas.

The cartoonist who draws a statesman going to a peace conference as a dove with an olive-branch in its mouth is harking back thousands of years to the Old Testament story of the flood, when the dove sent out by Noah brought back news that land had been sighted, and that there was to be peace again between God and man. The dove, and the olive branch which it carried from the Mount of Olives, have stood for peace ever since.

Threat of the raven

But the history behind many other widely accepted symbols is often obscure. We talk of being ravenous, without perhaps realising that it is a reference to the proverbial appetite of the raven. We say someone is cock-sure, without thinking of the proud stance of the cock; and cock-a-hoop again refers to the bird with its hoop or crest erect.

The word cuckold, once commonly used to describe the deceived husband, comes from the cuckoo, which at one time was believed to get its young into the nests of other birds by adultery with the occupant.

As recently as 1855, mothers in West Yorkshire are said to have kept their children in order by threatening, 'The black raven will come'—a long-forgotten reference to the raven on the standard of the Vikings, whose approach was dreaded in that part of the country 1000 years before.

In heraldry, the martin (or martlet as it is called) is still used on the coat of arms of a fourth son. Because of the thick plumage on its legs, the bird was at one time believed to have no feet—an ingenious analogy with the fourth son who, unlike his older brothers, can never hope to inherit any land on which to settle.

Other symbols involving birds are met less frequently today, despite their picturesque origins in folklore. Medieval literature took from the Romans the idea that the crane was the most vigilant of creatures. It was supposed to stand guard on one leg, holding a stone; if it nodded off, it would drop the stone and wake itself up.

Greek mythology was the source of the story of Halcyon, the most faithful of wives, who waited loyally for her husband Ceyx when he was lost on a sea journey. As a reward, the couple were turned into kingfishers—symbols of marital fidelity—so that they would always be together. The gods also then calmed the seas, where kingfisher courtship was thought to take place, so that mating should be undisturbed. Hence our term 'halcyon days', applied to times of peace and happiness.

The strangest symbol of all was probably the owl in ancient Egypt. The Egyptians, like other early peoples, feared owls and believed that they brought evil and death. But they had one use for the bird—or at least for its image: the king used to send an owl to a minister as a sign that his services were no longer required. Almost invariably the unhappy recipient would take his own life.

Birds in sport

PARTNERS OF MAN ... OR HIS VICTIMS

USING or killing birds for sport dates back to the time when 'man the hunter' became 'man the farmer'; when his once-wild prey had become caged or domesticated meat; and when falconry and other methods of hunting could be enjoyed for their own sake rather than as an essential part of survival.

The origin of sports such as cock fighting and pigeon racing can also be traced to the days when wildfowl and pigeons were caged and reared for human consumption. Once cocks had been observed fighting, it did not seem out of place—in an age marked by barbarity—to enjoy watching these combats and to breed special strains of bird for this brutal sport. Pigeon racing, it is not hard to visualise, was born soon after the discovery that these birds could be trained to return over long distances to their home roost. At least as long ago as 1204 BC, the Egyptians were using them to send military messages.

But generally speaking, the role of the bird in sport is that of the victim; and almost as old as the history of birds as victims in sport are the laws which ensure that the bird stays alive long enough to be killed at the 'right' time. Today's game laws and seasons are the successors of the harsh Forest Laws imposed by William the Conqueror to protect his own hunting enjoyment.

Falconry

The origins of falconry are not clearly defined. It may have started as a means of procuring food about 2000 BC in China or Korea, although some authorities give it an Arabian development. By AD 500 it had reached most parts of Europe, including Britain, and had become a sport as well as a method of providing food.

For centuries, falconry was unchallenged as the king of hunting sports in every European court. Then came the enclosing of fields; and although hawks can be flown in any type of country, wide open spaces are essential for the flying of falcons. The development of effective guns in the 17th century furthered the decline of the sport, but falconry has never become extinct in Britain.

Today there are several falconers' clubs as well as a number of enthusiasts who prefer to work independently.

Falconry has undergone a great change since the beginning of the 20th century. At one time a trainer stayed with the bird, night and day, for up to a week; but today a falcon can be given no more than an hour's handling each day and be reasonably tame and flying loose within 8-10 days.

A bird will work for another falconer just as well as for its original trainer, but it may take a few days for man and bird to become accustomed to each other. Most falconers prefer to train their birds themselves, so a trained bird is unlikely to fetch as high a price as an untrained one.

All birds of prey are now protected in Britain, and a licence is necessary to take or import one. By law, most birds of prey in captivity must be registered with the Department of the Environment, and must be ringed. Extra controls on taking, importing, and keeping birds of prey have led to increasing attempts to breed them in captivity, with degrees of success varying with the species.

Cock fighting

Matching two fighting cocks against one another is possibly the oldest of all bird pursuits. It emerged from Asia in the 5th century BC, spread to the ancient Greeks and later to the Romans, who in turn introduced it to Britain.

Here the sport flourished until it was made illegal in 1849.

Illegal cock fighting still survives in Britain and secret 'mains', or tournaments, are held, mainly in the north of England. Abroad, 'cocking' is still supported in central Europe, the south-east of the United States and in Latin America.

Cock fighting was always a pastime in which the betting provided more attraction than the actual event. Nevertheless, every effort was made to ensure a full spectacle. The spurs of the cock—natural outgrowths on the legs—were equipped with much more lethal metal spurs, intended to inflict death or serious injury; and the cocks' wing-tips were cut to so sharp a point that the birds could blind one another as they flapped their wings.

Numerous stories were passed round from one owner to another about methods of training a cock to be a still more savage fighter. Among other fads, owners licked the faces of their birds, or gave them human urine.

Shooting

The shooting of game-birds for sport was traditionally the prerogative of a small and wealthy landed minority—if only because it demands the expensive services of game-keepers to manage large tracts of country.

Today, however, this expense has become more than most landed gentry can shoulder alone, and shooting has become a sport for a much wider cross-section of the population, each of whom bears part of the cost as a member of a shooting syndicate.

Even so, as the cost of managing grouse moors has soared, many owners have sold out to forestry interests; and forests and red grouse do not go together. The numbers shot in Britain each year have fallen from about $2\frac{1}{2}$ million in the early part of the 20th century to around half a million by the end of it.

Pheasant shooting relies mainly on the release of birds bred in captivity. Its artificial nature means that it can be carried out on almost any kind of lowland farmland. Already popular, more and more farmers are turning to the sport to diversify their business interests.

The principal birds shot for sport, and their shooting seasons, are:

PARTRIDGE (Season: September 1–February 1; breeds late April and early May). Of the two species, the native partridge, rather than the introduced red-legged, is considered the élite by sportsmen. But during the 20th century, probably because of changing farming practices and bad weather during breeding seasons, partridge stocks have steadily declined and most estates no longer shoot them.

PHEASANT (Season: October 1–February 1; breeds early May). Introduced in the 11th century, the pheasant was hunted with cross-bows and hawks by the Normans, then stalked with muskets or pursued with nets until the development of effective guns allowed the birds to be shot in flight after being driven from the ground by beaters.

Today the sport is so popular that pheasants on estates are generally reared in captivity; and although every effort is made by game-keepers to make them reasonably wild by the start of the season, beaters often have to work hard to get them up in the air and over the line of waiting guns.

RED GROUSE (Season: August 12–December 10; breeds late April). The shooting of this bird for sport did not start until the mid-19th century, when breech-loading shotguns became available. Since then, Parliament has traditionally started its summer vacation in time for the start of the grouse season on the 'Glorious Twelfth'.

The birds are driven over butts on a moor. Stocks of grouse are variable, depending on a variety of different factors, and many more die of natural causes than over the guns. The record grouse slaughter was at Lord Sefton's Lancashire moor in 1915 when, on a single day, 2929 birds were shot by only eight guns.

WOOD-PIGEON This is not considered a game-bird, though it provides the everyday sport of thousands of people.

The wood-pigeon is a crop-eating pest, and from the farmer's point of view 4 million should be shot every year, as against the $2\frac{1}{2}$ million currently killed.

WILDFOWL The shooting of ducks and geese has long been the sport of a hardy, skilled minority who brave often bitter weather in boats or hides on icy marshes to shoot fast-moving and elusive prey. However, it is now becoming increasingly popular as the cost of other forms of game-bird shooting rises.

Pigeon racing

In 1810, London pigeon fanciers were sending their birds by boat to Southampton, Margate and Southend—the earliest instances in this country of organised long-distance pigeon races. Since then—and especially since the spread of the railway network allowed birds to be taken even farther from their lofts—pigeon racing has grown into a sport pursued by some 500,000 fanciers, owning an estimated 10 million racing birds.

The vast majority of pigeon fanciers live in the industrial north, where betting and prize money are added attractions.

The birds are trained by being released at increasing distances from their home lofts: some fanciers even introduce female birds before a race, to encourage the racing bird to return faster. Selective breeding has given present-day pigeons far greater speeds than their wild ancestors. Homing speeds of 60 mph over distances of 600 miles or so are common, but the 'absolute' record is claimed for an Ulster bird which in 1961 covered 186 miles at an average 97 mph.

The Queen has her own racing pigeons, that are kept in new lofts, which were built in 1992, at Sandringham, in Norfolk.

Birds frequently change hands for large sums of money, and in 1994 a stock pigeon named 'Invincible Spirit' was bought by a British fancier for £110,800.

WHERE TO SEE BIRDS

Because Britain stands at a migratory
cross-roads on the edge of the world's
largest land-mass, it is a staging post where
huge numbers of migrants swell our resident
population before flying on to their summer or winter
quarters. More species have found a home, either
permanent or temporary, within these shores
than in any country on the Continent.

CONTENTS

Access to some of the places in this region-by-region guide to
bird-watching is by permit only. In all cases it is best to check whether you
need permission to visit the spot of your choice; it is rarely refused.

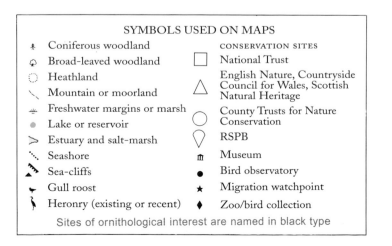

SYMBOLS USED ON MAPS

⚲ Coniferous woodland	CONSERVATION SITES
♀ Broad-leaved woodland	☐ National Trust
⬭ Heathland	△ English Nature, Countryside Council for Wales, Scottish Natural Heritage
⟍ Mountain or moorland	
⚓ Freshwater margins or marsh	○ County Trusts for Nature Conservation
● Lake or reservoir	
⟩ Estuary and salt-marsh	⬯ RSPB
⋰ Seashore	⬟ Museum
⟩ Sea-cliffs	● Bird observatory
⌐ Gull roost	★ Migration watchpoint
⟨ Heronry (existing or recent)	◆ Zoo/bird collection

Sites of ornithological interest are named in black type

THE rugged coast-line of the south-west has been sculpted through thousands of years of battering by the sea. The tall cliffs of Cornwall's north coast, which take the full impact of waves whipped up by Atlantic gales, are impressive, simply as pieces of natural architecture. They are doubly impressive for the bird-watcher.

Nearly every species of seabird to be found in southern England breeds on these coasts. The off-shore islands to the north and south-west are particularly rich in bird-life. There are established colonies of gulls, terns, guillemots, razorbills and puffins in the Scilly Isles. Another island, Lundy, actually takes its name from an old Norse word for puffin. Some of the largest colonies are on the uninhabited islands, and these islands attract rare breeding birds, too. The Isles of Scilly, notably Annet, with their breeding Manx shearwaters and storm petrels have birds which breed nowhere else in England.

The south coast of this region is more gentle, with its hundreds of small harbours, coves and inlets, and stretches of gleaming mud-flats left when the tide ebbs. A mild climate makes this coast a favourite wintering ground for a variety of waders and waterfowl. Rarities such as spoonbills and little egrets may be seen on the Exe Estuary; and avocets—including some of those that breed on the Suffolk coast—winter regularly on both the Exe and Tamar.

The Loe Pool and Slapton Ley, where birds are plentiful at any time of year, are particularly notable for rare passage migrants in spring and autumn. Apart from these sites, though, there are few stretches of fresh water and consequently fewer freshwater birds than in other coastal regions. The estuaries are also comparatively small, again limiting the number of birds which can feed on them. Most of the estuaries of the south coast are really drowned valleys formed by a rise in sea level at the end of the last Ice Age.

The most striking features of the peninsula's interior landscape are the steep-sided combes, often densely wooded, and the moors—Exmoor, Bodmin Moor, and the bleak granite uplands of Dartmoor. Ravens and buzzards are common both in the combes and along the coast. The conditions on Dartmoor and Exmoor have encouraged some of our more northern species, such as the red grouse, ring ouzel and merlin, to remain farther south than anywhere else in the British Isles; but black grouse have recently disappeared completely.

At the same time, the damp climate has discouraged other birds—the nightingale is found only in eastern parts of Devon and the lesser whitethroat breeds in Devon and Somerset, but only rarely in Cornwall. The chough, too, is now extinct in its former stronghold on the north coast of Cornwall; and peregrines, once a common sight as they beat along the coast looking for prey, are now scarcer, largely because of the after-effects of pesticides.

The South-West Peninsula

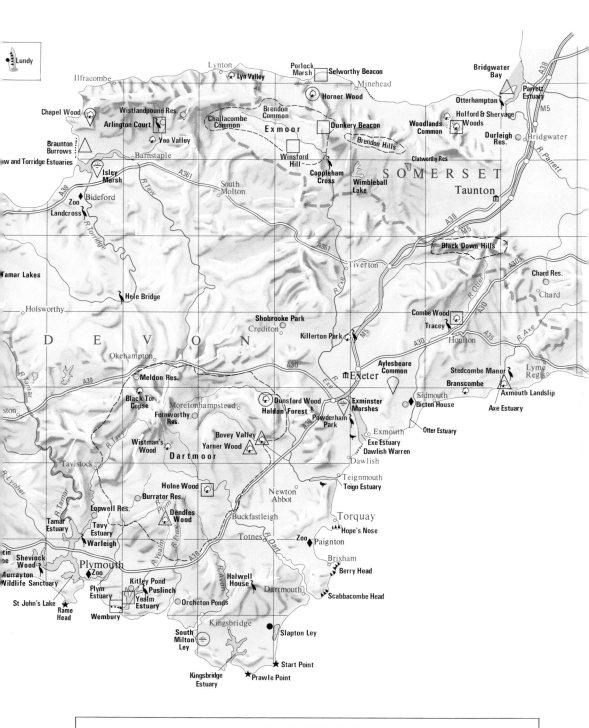

PICK OF THE YEAR

JANUARY: Brent geese on the Exe Estuary

FEBRUARY: ravens start to nest on cliffs and rocky ledges and occasionally in trees near the coastline

MARCH: herons begin to nest in their tree-top colonies

APRIL: pied flycatchers arrive in Devon hill woodlands from tropical Africa

MAY: guillemots jostle for position at their coastal breeding colonies

JUNE: ring ouzels are rearing young on Dartmoor

JULY: young buzzards begin to fly

AUGUST: coveys, or family parties, of red grouse on Exmoor; shooting begins on the 12th

SEPTEMBER: waders on the estuaries; passage of seabirds at St. Ives

OCTOBER: Asian rarities and American vagrants may be seen on Isles of Scilly

NOVEMBER: small numbers of avocets arrive to winter on the Tamar Estuary

DECEMBER: wintering chiffchaffs in sheltered south coast valleys

Wessex and

WESSEX is the name Thomas Hardy rescued from oblivion to describe the part of England which has the high downlands of Salisbury Plain as its geographical centre, with ranges of chalk which reach out into Dorset, Hampshire and the Berkshire Downs. Along the southern margin of this chalk country lies the other outstanding feature of Wessex—the heath and forest country which stretches almost without a break from Dorchester to Southampton.

The heathland is the last stronghold of one of the shyest and rarest of English breeding birds, the Dartford warbler. The best way to find it is to listen for its harsh, 'churring' call. Here, the luckiest and most determined bird-watcher might also catch a distant glimpse of the very rare honey buzzard, which raids wasps' nests for its food; the scythe-winged hobby, which resembles a giant swift; and the Montagu's harrier; but the once widespread red-backed shrike has gone.

The yellow-eyed stone curlew, largely nocturnal in its habits, is still found in the open downs of Wessex, once one of the last refuges of the great bustard, which vanished from Britain in the early 19th century. Another prize 'catch' for the keen bird-watcher is the quail, which is like a small partridge. This bird is seldom seen, for it keeps to thick crops and reveals its presence only by its monotonous 'wet-my-lips' call.

Chalk country is not all bare open downland; it is famous, too, for its sheltered parklands and valleys lined with broad-leaved woods. In such a valley lies Selborne, a place of pilgrimage for naturalists; for it was here that the Reverend Gilbert White studied local wildlife 200 years ago and wrote the *Natural History* which made him one of the founders of modern ornithology. Selborne Hanger, a beechwood near the village, is still reached by a zigzag path which White helped to make.

PICK OF THE YEAR

JANUARY: an abundance of grebes, ducks and waders at Poole Harbour, Dorset
FEBRUARY: flocks of redwings and fieldfares fly to communal roosts in woodland
MARCH: wheatears arrive on the south coast
APRIL: nightingales and other vagrants arrive in the Thames valley
MAY: hundreds of swans are nesting at Abbotsbury swannery
JUNE: nightjars in the New Forest heathland
JULY: hobbies' eggs start hatching; this rare falcon breeds mainly in Hampshire
AUGUST: shelducks assemble in Bridgwater Bay to moult
SEPTEMBER: stone culews at Quarley Hill; migrants at Portland Bill Observatory
OCTOBER: Brent geese at Langstone Harbour
NOVEMBER: black-tailed godwits on Hampshire estuaries
DECEMBER: white-fronted geese at Slimbridge and on marshes on the Hampshire Avon

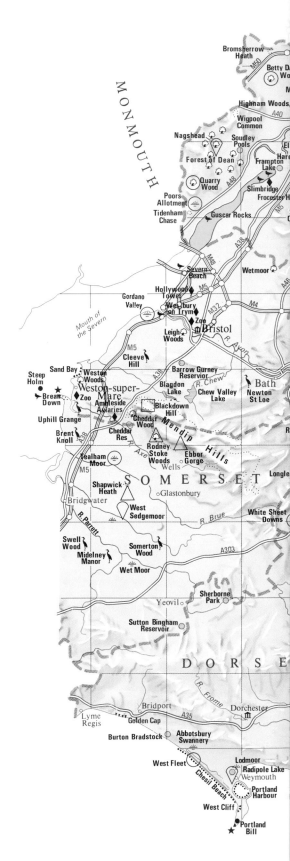

the Thames Valley

NORTHAMPTON

WARWICK

RCESTER

WORCESTER

Salcey Forest
Weston Underwood ◆ Emberton
◆ Tyringham Park
Great Linford ◆ Newport Pagnell
Willen Lake
A5

Grimsbury Res.
Banbury

Tadmarton & Wiggington Heaths
Foxcote
Buckingham

Rammamere Heath

Great Tew
Ardley Wood
BUCKS   BEDFORD

Chipping Norton
Weston Fen
Bicester
Calvert Jubilee
Aylesbury
College Lake

Hewletts Res.
Dowdeswell Res.
Bourton-on-the-Water ◆
Cheltenham
A40

Wychwood Forest
Blenheim Palace
OXON
Witney
Otmoor
Boarstall Decoy
Menmarsh
Stone
Weston Turville

Coombe and Bacombe Hills
Little Hampden Common

Buckbolt Wood
Wood and Woods
rwick Woods

Cirencester
A419

Fairford Gravel Pit
Lechlade Gravel Pit
Wytham Woods
Farmoor
Oxford
Stanton Wd.
Waterperry Wood
Shotover Hill

Chinnor Hill
Hampden Common

Bagley Wood
Radley
Stanton Harcourt
Nuneham Courtenay
Beacon Hill
Aston Wood
Hambleden

Hodgemoor Woods
Long Grove Wood
Church Wood
Hedgerley
Stoke Common
Black Park

Shellingford Pond
Buscot
Watchfield Common Wood
Sutton Courtenay
Watlington Hill & Park
Mongewell Woods
High Wycombe

Leigh ◆
North Meadow, Cricklade
Wantage
Marlow
Gravel Pits
Cookham Marsh
Burnham Beeches
Tapiow

Braydon Pond
Swindon
Coate Water
Lambourn Downs
The Ridgeway
Ashbury Wood
Unhill Bottom
Maidenhead
Chilterns
Slough Sewage Farm
Windsor
Eton
Wraysbury

Cotswold Water Park
Wood

Avon
Tockenham Res.
Marlborough Downs
Eyford Down
Marlborough
R. Kennet
Snelsmore Common
Englefield Park
Reading
Theale
Dinton Pastures
Windsor Forest
Winkfield Zoo
Windsor Great Park
Ham Island
Great Meadow Pond
Virginia Water

Chippenham
A4

Bowood Park
Savernake Forest
Hamstead Marshall
Benham Park
Newbury
Thatcham
Bucklebury Common
Greenham and Crookham Commons
Burghfield Common
Silchester Common
Stratfield Saye
Englemere Pond

Devizes
Martinsell Downs
Pewsey Vale
Wilton Water
The Chase
Highclere
Walbury Hill
Woolton Hill
Kingsclere
A339

WILTSHIRE
Everleigh Ashes
Fleet Pond
Aldershot

Salisbury Plain
Weyhill Zoo
Andover
A303
Quarley Hill
Chilbolton Common
Leckford
Stockbridge Down
Basingstoke
Alton
Alice Holt Forest
SURREY

Hurdcott Park
Clarendon Park
Avington
Winchester
Woolmer Pond
Selborne Hanger
Woolmer Forest

Fonthill Lake
Salisbury
Petersfinger Pits
HAMPSHIRE
Petersfield
Oxenbourne Down
WEST SUSSEX

Garston Wood
Martin Down
Godshill
Bramshaw Gravel Pit
Zoo
Curdridge Wood
Catherington Down
South Downs

Cranborne Chase
Cranborne Common
Blashford Gravel Pit
Southampton
NEW FOREST
North Solent
Wickham
Fareham
Farlington Marshes
Havant
Chichester Harbour

Wimborne
Minster
A31
Hatchet Pond
Needs Ore Point
Southampton Water
Titchfield Haven
Langstone Hr.
Hayling Island

Christchurch
Bournemouth
Hinton Admiral
Sowley Pond
Cowes
Portsmouth
Gilkicker Point
Ryde

Brownsea Island
Poole
Poole Harbour
Little Sea
Studland Bay
Studland Heath
Swanage
Durlston Head

Stanpit Marsh
Christchurch Harbour
Hurst Castle Spit
Hengistbury Head
The Needles
Keyhaven
Newtown Marsh
Town Copse
Parkhurst Forest
Firestone Copse
Borthwood Copse
Main Bench
ISLE OF WIGHT
Brading Marsh
Zoo
Sandown
St Catherines Point

Arne Heath
Cliffs

0 Miles   5   10   20
Scale

English Channel

THE south-east, dominated and almost overwhelmed by the ever-spreading conurbation of London, is still one of Britain's better areas for watching birds, thanks mainly to the birds' adaptation to a constantly changing environment. The casualties of the urban sprawl are inevitably numerous, for there are now no really large areas of wild country left in the region, though it is peppered with woods and heaths.

But as scrub and ground-nesting birds, such as warblers, whinchats and yellow wagtails, retreat in the face of man's invasion, so swans, gulls, sparrows and pigeons advance to scavenge in the detritus of our civilisation; and the reservoirs, gravel-pits and sewage farms which fringe the metropolis now offer homes for a wealth of wildfowl and waders which were only occasional visitors to the region even 80 years ago.

But for 20 miles around London, most of the countryside is trodden by humans; all the woodland either planted or managed; and all the water polluted or used by man. Only those species that have been able to adapt to new circumstances, or that are able to live in close proximity to man have been able to survive as breeding birds.

Species like the blue and great tits, blackbirds and robins have increased as a result of man's benevolence; others, such as song thrushes and spotted flycatchers, are able to co-exist with man in the ideal habitat created in the form of suburban gardens. Species that can readily change their habitat and food do well; those that are less adaptable decline and eventually disappear altogether.

In fact, the wintering roosts of starlings which descend on Leicester Square in their thousands at dusk, heedless of the traffic grinding beneath them, provide one of Britain's major bird-watching spectacles. On winter evenings, too, long lines of gulls wing their way both east, to the Thames Estuary, and west to the London reservoirs. At least

(continued on p. 432)

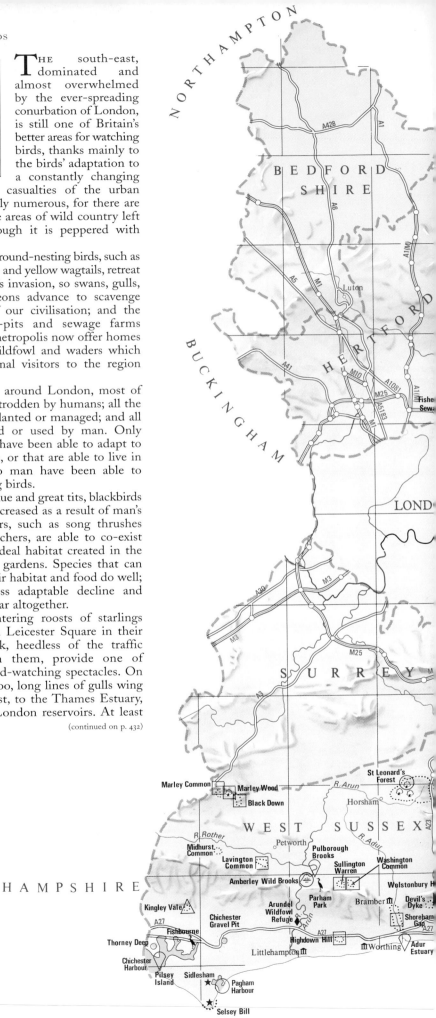

The South-East

The South-East (continued)

three times as many gulls now spend their winters inland as in 1959. These reservoirs, along with sewage farms and gravel pits, play a major role in swelling the region's bird list; for without them it is certain that many migrants would not stop anywhere near the city. Winter-visiting ducks include goosanders and goldeneyes. Some species are as common on these stretches of water as anywhere in the country.

The reservoirs, which covered just over 500 acres in 1900, now occupy almost 5000 acres; and at peak periods in winter they harbour nearly 10,000 ducks and 150,000 gulls, which spend their nights on the waters.

Gravel-pits have played an important part in the spread of a recent breeding species, the little ringed plover, and are also a favourite site of great crested grebes. They are one of the chief habitats of reed warblers, yellow wagtails and other marsh species.

Like the reservoirs, sewage farms are another by-product of London's growth whose ornithological importance went relatively unnoticed for many years. At one farm, Perry Oaks, more than 30 different waders have been seen since the Second World War— only a few hundred yards from London's Heathrow Airport.

But now these artificial marshes are being closed down and amalgamated into a few modern works, which are far less attractive places for birds.

The geese of Foulness

Farther away from the city, the Thames Estuary in both Kent and Essex, and the Essex estuaries as far north as Harwich, are important wintering grounds for large numbers of waders, ducks and geese. The area from Foulness to the River Blackwater, with its mud-flats, is probably the most important single area in Europe for the dark-breasted Brent goose.

Most of the region's unspoilt coastline is around the east coast, for the Sussex coast has been highly developed along almost its entire length. Dungeness, the extreme south-eastern tip of England, is far and away the most valuable site on the Channel coast; and its vast expanse of shingle provides the only breeding colony of common gulls in the south. Some breeding terns are still present; but the Kentish plover, for which this was once renowned, last nested in 1956 and the stone curlew last bred in 1965.

In winter, large flocks of common scoters may be seen on the inshore waters; hen-harriers and rough-legged buzzards swoop over the shingle; and the Mediterranean gull has become more frequent and begun to nest in recent years.

Where suburbia ends

Another factor of enormous importance in helping to preserve the bird-life of the area is the Green Belt, that cordon of land around London which was established in 1938 to provide a barrier against the city's ever-increasing sprawl. Although parts of it have been sacrificed—and more will undoubtedly follow—the Belt offers a home for a variety of birds which would otherwise surely have been submerged in suburbia.

Despite the inroads of civilisation, the south-east has many rarities of its own. The nightingale is still more numerous in the wooded wealds of Surrey, Sussex and Kent than anywhere else in Britain. The black redstart—a newcomer of only 50-60 years' standing—nests in small numbers in the London area and the Kent coastal towns. Kent was also the last regular home of the fast-declining wryneck, which now breeds only occasionally in Britain.

Other notable sights of the region include the very large flock of non-breeding mute swans on the Stour Estuary in Essex; the roof-nesting colonies of herring gulls at Hastings and Dover; and the long-eared owls' roost at Northward Hill RSPB Reserve in Kent.

Established 'foreigners' in the region include the red-legged partridge, which has become more numerous than the native grey partridge in parts of Essex; and Lady Amherst's pheasant, which escaped from Woburn Park in Bedfordshire to establish itself firmly in many neighbouring woods.

PICK OF THE YEAR

JANUARY: Brent geese on Essex estuaries

FEBRUARY: white-fronted geese on the Thames estuary

MARCH: early migrants at Dungeness and Sandwich Bay

APRIL: nightingales arrive and start to sing in the Kent woods

MAY: spotted flycatchers establish territories in some London parks and open spaces

JUNE: little ringed plovers breed at many gravel-pits

JULY: green sandpipers and wood sandpipers on marshy gravel-pits

AUGUST: black terns at Staines Reservoirs; rarities can be seen on the 'patch' at Dungeness

SEPTEMBER: little stints and curlew sandpipers arrive on coastal lagoons

OCTOBER: thousands of starlings roost in London—especially in Leicester Square and on the buildings along Piccadilly

NOVEMBER: goosanders and goldeneyes arrive on the reservoirs around London

DECEMBER: Mediterranean gulls flock together with black-headed gulls at Copt Point, Folkestone

WHERE TO SEE BIRDS

South Wales

THE upper reaches of the mountains dominating this region belong to the birds of prey. Buzzards patrol on the wing, hunting rabbits and other victims; and ravens perform spectacular aerobatics. The high hill country is a refuge, too, for two birds of prey which have undergone a remarkable expansion in recent years—the peregrine and the kite.

Although kites were once reduced to fewer than ten pairs in the steep-sided woods of central Wales, up to as many as 100 pairs are breeding there now. The best chance of seeing them would be to watch from the road on the eastern side of Tregaron Bog.

Lower down the hillsides, pied flycatchers breed in oakwoods, together with wood warblers and common redstarts; and where young conifer plantations have begun to grow on the slopes, they provide the black grouse with its favourite habitat—the edge of woodland and moorland.

The moorlands themselves are home to most of the typical northern breeding birds—among them the golden plover, dunlin, red grouse and common sandpiper.

The chough, which is found mainly in Ireland, also breeds on the west coast of Wales, particularly in Pembrokeshire, and on Skomer and Ramsay islands.

Two birds of prey—the peregrine and buzzard—and also the raven range over these windswept outposts, which are also home to teeming colonies of seabirds. The gannetry on Grassholm is the largest and most southerly in England and Wales; and Skomer and Skokholm in particular provide breeding grounds for Manx shearwaters, storm petrels, razorbills, guillemots, puffins, kittiwakes and shags.

SHROPSHIRE

Gilfach
Elan Valley Reservoirs
Dyffryn Wood
Knighton
E. Teme Floods
Wigmore Rolls
Wigmore Moor
Radnor Forest
Byton Moor
Combe Moor
Shobdon Decoy Pool
Berrington Pool
Llandrindod Wells
Leominster
Llanwefr Pool
P O W Y S
H E R E F O R D
R. Arrow
R. Lugg
Pen-y-Wern
Builth Wells
Newchurch
Gwenffrwd
Llanbedr Hill
Rhosgoch Common
Dinas
Llan-Bwch-llyn
R. Wye
Hereford
Malvern Hills
Mynydd Eppynt
Oderw Pool
River Lugg Floods
Haugh Wood
Midsummer Hill
Ledbury
Llandovery
R. Usk
R. Dore
R. Wye
R. Lugg
B. Frome
R E
Black Mountains
A465
Ross-on-Wye
Llyn-y-Fan Fawr
Brecon
Llangorse Lake
M50
ountain
Brecon Beacons
Llyn Cwm-llwch
Llanthony Valley Woods
R. Wye
Fforest Fawr
Talybont Res.
Sugar Loaf
G L O U C E S T E R
R. Neath
Craig-y-Cilau
Cwm Clydach
Ty-mawr Pond
Abergavenny
Monmouth
Llwyn-on Res.
A465
Vale of Neath Woodlands
A465
Pontiscill Res.
G W E N T
Wye Valley Woodlands
Merthyr Tydfil
R. Taf
Llyns Fach and Fawr
R. Rhondda
Pontypool
Llandegfedd Res.
Piercefield Park
Neath
ynlyn Bog
M4
Wentwood Res.
Chepstow
Caerphilly Cefn Onn
A4042
A48
M4
M4
Caldicot Level Floods
glwys ynnid Res.
Kenfig Pool
Garth Wood
Newport
Severn Estuary
Kenfig Burrows
Ewenny Moors
M4
Llanishen and Lisvane Res.
Bridgend
Hensol
R. Taf
Usk Estuary
Peterstone Wentlooge
Pysgodlyn Mawr
R. Ely
Roath Park
Ewenny and Ogmore Downs
Mynydd-y-Glew
Rhymney Outlet
Cardiff
SOUTH GLAMORGAN
Sully Wood
Penarth Flats and Taff Estuary
A48
Nash Point
Barry
Lavernock Point
Flat Holm

0   Miles   5   10   15   20
Scale

PICK OF THE YEAR

JANUARY: ravens flock to communal tree-roosts in Pembrokeshire and Powys

FEBRUARY: buzzards and ravens roam the hills, often competing for the carcases of dead sheep

MARCH: buzzards begin to build their large stick nests in trees or on ledges

APRIL: gannets on Grassholm

MAY: wood warblers in the hill woods

JUNE: pied flycatchers and young buzzards make their first, unsteady flights

JULY: young choughs leave their island breeding grounds and visit the Pembrokeshire coasts in family parties

AUGUST: Manx shearwaters tend their chicks in nest burrows on the islands of Skokholm and Skomer

SEPTEMBER: migrant warblers and chats are numerous on the coast and islands of Pembrokeshire

OCTOBER: flocks of migrant thrushes and larks, bound for wintering grounds in southern Ireland, can be seen on Skokholm and Skomer

NOVEMBER: winter roosts of rooks and jackdaws in farming areas

DECEMBER: vast flocks of oystercatchers winter near Whitford Burrows

North Wales

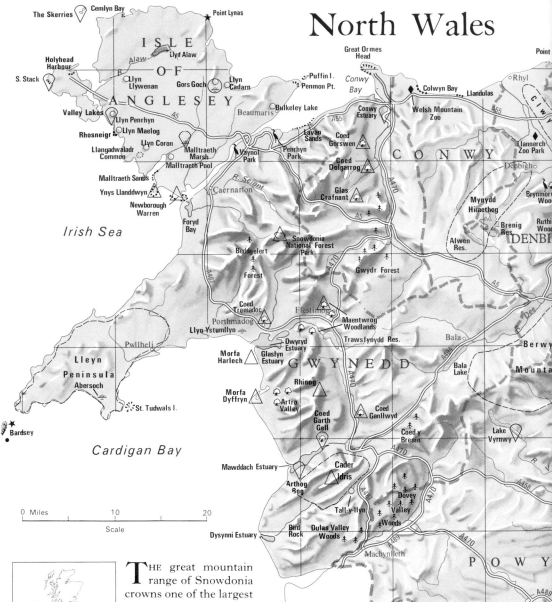

THE great mountain range of Snowdonia crowns one of the largest tracts of untamed landscape and unspoilt sea coast in Britain.

The crags and high moorlands are good places to observe ravens, which nest at nearly 3000 ft and lay their eggs while there is still snow on the ground. This is excellent country, too, in which to see the rare peregrine, largest of our breeding falcons.

The streams which rise in the mountains and moors make their way to the sea through sheltered valleys of oakwoods. In spring and summer these rich woodlands teem with bird-life. Common here are two small hole-nesting birds, the redstart and the pied flycatcher, and two which nest on the ground, the wood warbler and the tree pipit. These remote woodlands are also the refuge of that splendid bird of prey, the buzzard.

The chough, the main rarity of the region, breeds along the coastal cliffs of the Lleyn Peninsula, on the offshore island of Bardsey,

and in inland slate quarries. The spread of conifer plantations, while threatening open-country birds, has brought new riches to the bird-life of the region. The siskin, once confined to .Scotland and Ireland, has now colonised North and mid-Wales; and goldcrests and coal tits breed in surprisingly large numbers in these woodlands. Bustling seabird colonies at South Stack, Anglesey, the Lleyn Peninsula and the Ormes give an even greater sense of abundance and activity.

The region also includes the meres of Shropshire, an important breeding centre for the Canada goose and a good place in which to watch the intriguing courtship displays of the great crested grebe.

Map labels:

Hoylake
Wirral Country Park
Dee Estuary
Gayton Sands
Shotton Pools
Connah's Quay
Flint
FLINTSHIRE
Padeswood Pool
Eaton Hall
Mersey Estuary
Frodsham Lagoons
Delamere Forest
Chester
Zoo
Oak Mere
Huxley
Pettypool Wood
Gt. Budworth Mere
Marbury Reed Beds
Tabley Mere
Tatton Mere
Knutsford Mere
Altrincham Sewage Farm
Stockport
Rostherne Mere
Bollin Valley Woods
Macclesfield
Macclesfield Forest
Langley Res.
N. Rode Pool
Dane Valley
Sandbach Flashes
Crewe
CHESHIRE
DERBY
Wrexham
WREXHAM
Berwyn Moors
Llangollen
Cholmondeley Meres
Baddiley Mere Res.
Bar Mere
Comber Mere
Combermere Abbey
Doddington Pool
Marbury Meres
Hanmer Mere
Fenn's Moss
Whixall Moss
Ellesmere Meres
Oswestry
Halston
Hawk Lake
Sambrook Pool
STAFFORD
SHROPSHIRE
Allscot Sugar Refinery
Trench Pool
Telford
Shrewsbury
Shrewsbury Sewage Farm
Atcham Bridge
Severn Valley
Bomere Pool
Berrington Pool
Venus Pool
Leighton Park
Marton Pool
Stiperstones
Chirbury
Long Mynd
Hope Bowdler Hill
Benthall Edge
Bridgnorth
Walcot Park
Wenlock Edge
R. Clun
Ludlow
Wyre Forest
HEREFORD

PICK OF THE YEAR

JANUARY: divers, grebes and scoters off Ynys Llanddwyn, Anglesey

FEBRUARY: many species of duck on the Shropshire and Cheshire meres

MARCH: ring ouzels arrive in hills

APRIL: cormorants at inland colony at Bird Rock

MAY: pied flycatchers in hillside oakwoods

JUNE: house martins busy at their colonies in towns and on bridges

JULY: nightjars give their 'churring' call in Merionethshire countryside

AUGUST: terns leave their colonies on the coast of Anglesey

SEPTEMBER: autumn migrants, including chats and warblers, at Bardsey Island Observatory

OCTOBER: Huge flocks of waders—including many oystercatchers and knots—at Hilbre Island and Gayton Sands

NOVEMBER: late autumn gales blow rarities into the Mersey and Dee estuaries

DECEMBER: pintail and other wild fowl concentrate to feed on the Dee Estuary

The Midlands

SOUTH YORKSHIRE

Longdendale Reservoirs
Glossop
Derwent Res.
Ladybower Res.

Toddbrook Res.
Upper Goyt Valley
Combs Res.
Buxton
Chee Tor
Wye Valley Dales
Miller's Dale
Cressbrook Dale
Monsal Dale
Taddington Dale
Barbrook Res.
Chatsworth Park
Welbeck Park
Thoresby Park
Worksop
Chesterfield

CHESHIRE

Upper Dane Valley Woods
Haddon Hall
Lathkill Dale
Derbyshire Dales
Stanton Moor Edge
Pan's Garden
Sherwood Forest
Matlock
Oyston Res.
Mansfield
Mansfield Res.
Newstead Abbey

Rudyard Res.
Leek
Tittesworth Res.
Riber Castle
DERBYSHIRE
Ripley
NOTTI
SH

Combes Valley
Churnet Valley Woods
Star Wood
Weaver Hills
Hinkley Wood
Ashbourne
Dovedale

Stoke-on-Trent
Westport Lake
Hawksmoor Wood
Trentham Park
Osmaston Park
Kedleston Park
Wollaton Park
Nether
Notting

Cop Mere
Chartley Moss
Uttoxeter
Sudbury Park
Radbourne Park
Derby
Attenborough

STAFFORDSHIRE
Trent Floods
R. Trent

Doxey Marshes
Stafford
Blithfield Res.
Branston
Calke Park
Staunton Harold Res.
Burton-upon-Trent
Oakley Wood
Hemington

Cannock Chase
Catton Hall
Blackbrook Res.
Piper Wood
Charnwood Forest
Swithland Res.
Ratcliff

SHROPSHIRE
Gailey Pool
Lichfield
Whittington Sewage Farm
Charnwood Lodge
Bradgate Pk.
Ulverscroft
Cronston Res.

Belvide Res.
Chasewater
Alvecote Pools
Twycross
Groby Pool
Soar Val
LEICES
Lei

M54
Sutton Park
Kingsbury Water Park
Aston Fir Wood

Wolverhampton
Sandwell Valley
Shustoke Res.
Nuneaton
Burbage Wood
Saddingto

Wren's Nest
Zoo Dudley
Edgbaston Park
Birmingham
Coventry
Combe Abbey
Stanfo Res.
Naseb

Kinver Edge
Bartley Res.
Brandon Marsh
Rugby
N

Kidderminster
Wyre Forest
Chaddesley Woods
Bittell Res.
Clowes Wood
Earlswood Lakes
Bubbenhall Wood
Ryton Wood
Draycote Water
Ravens

Bromsgrove
Waverley Wood
Wappenbury Wood
M45

Upton Warren
WARWICKSHIRE
Daventry Res.

Kyre Pool
Kyre Park
Westwood Park
Wootton Pool
Warwick
Warwick Park
Napton Res.

WORCESTER
Worcester
Chesterton Pool

Stratford-upon-Avon
Wormleighton Res.
Boddington Res.

Temple Grafton

Malvern Hills
Croome Park
Evesham

Bredon Hill

M50

GLOUCESTER   OXFORD

Thousands of acres of wild moorland stretch across the face of Derbyshire and Staffordshire. Untamed sanctuaries in what was once a land of factory chimneys and grimy industrial towns, they turn the green of spring into myriad shades of purple and brown.

The red grouse can be seen rising up over Cannock Chase, while the dipper breeds on the Dove and many other streams in northern Staffordshire and Derbyshire, as well as on streams in the central parts of Worcestershire.

The moors near Leek in Staffordshire also hold one of the few remaining natural stocks of black grouse in England.

The very rare marsh warbler, which slings its nest between the stems of tall water-plants, can occasionally be seen in the valleys of the River Avon in Worcestershire. Nightingale and reed warbler nest throughout the region, but the cirl bunting has unfortunately long since disappeared.

Two introduced species of waterfowl breed wild on some of the many man-made stretches of water in the Midlands: the Canada goose throughout the region, and the North American ruddy duck, which is spreading rapidly.

Reservoirs also provide roosts for a large number of gulls—particularly Rutland Water and the Eye Brook Reservoir in Leicestershire; Belvide and Blithfield reservoirs in Staffordshire; and Hollowell and Pitsford reservoirs in Northamptonshire.

The Trent valley also holds many interesting breeding species, including black-headed gulls and common terns, which have established colonies on a few flooded gravel-pits.

PICK OF THE YEAR

JANUARY: many wildfowl on Rutland Water and on Staffordshire reservoirs

FEBRUARY: occasional Bewick's swans among the many wildfowl on Eye Brook Reservoir

MARCH: wheatears can often be seen on many reservoirs in the region

APRIL: pied flycatchers arrive in north Derbyshire; black grouse at their lek in north Staffordshire

MAY: blackcaps, chiffchaffs and other warblers singing in woodland territories

JUNE: great crested grebes carrying chicks on their backs on lakes and reservoirs

JULY: common and green sandpipers arrive on the margins of many reservoirs and lakes

AUGUST: herds of mute swans on Blithfield Reservoir, Rutland Water and Chasewater

SEPTEMBER: waders on autumn migration in Trent valley; north-east of Nottingham is a good place to see them

OCTOBER: small flocks, or 'wisps', of snipe appear by lakes and reservoirs

NOVEMBER: flocks of ducks and geese on Eye Brook, Blithfield and Pitsford reservoirs and Rutland Water

DECEMBER: winter flocks of Canada geese in Kedleston and Osmaston parks

East Angli

North Sea

Humber

Humber Wildfowl Refuge
Barton-upon-Humber gravel pit
Goxhill gravel pit
Killingholme gravel pit
Estuary
Grimsby Docks
Cleethorpes

Scunthorpe
M181
M180
Epworth
Twigmoor Gull Ponds
Twigmoor Warren
Tetney Haven
Tetney Marshes

Scotton Common
Laughton
Donna Nock
Covenham Res.
A18
A15

Wharton Wood
Corringham
Thonock
Gainsborough
Market Rasen
Louth
Legbourne Wood
Muckton Wood
Saltfleet Haven
Saltfleetby-Theddlethorpe Dunes

R. Trent
Old R. Ancholme
A16
Great Eau
Huttoft Bank
Sea Bank Clay Pits
Chapel Point

A57
A158
Doddington
Lincoln
Newball
Willoughby Wood
A46
Lincoln gravel pit
Bardney gravel pit
R. Bain
Spilsby
A158

Revesby Res.
Skegness

Stapleford Moor
LINCOLNSHIRE
Troy Wood
Friskney Decoy Woods
Gibraltar Point

A17
Evedon Wood
R. Witham
Friskney Flats
Sc
Brancaster
Thornham Harbour
Wrangle Flats
Holme-next-the-Sea
Tit
M

Sleaford gravel pit
A16
Boston
Freiston Delphs
Hunstanton
The Wash

A1
Frampton Marsh
Heacham Harbour
Snettisha
Snettisham
Denton Res.
Harlaxton
Dersing
Hea

A17
Terrington Marsh
Roy
Com

Spalding
R. Welland
R. Nene
Kings Lynn
N
Norfol

A16
Islington
A10

LEICESTER
Stamford
Borough Fen Duck Decoy
Guyhirn
Downham Market

Ailsworth Heath
Peakirk
A47
Denver Sluice
R. Ouse
Hilgay

Castor Hanglands
Nene Washes
Welney Washes
B

Milton Park
Peterborough
Eldernell
Weeting H

Ferry Meadows
Fletton gravel pit
Pymore Bridge
Lakenheath Fen
Little Ouse R

Holme Fen
Fortrey
Chettisham
Lakenheath Warren

Woodwalton Fen
Pingle Wood
Mepal gravel pit
Ely
Ely Beet Factory
Weather

Aversley Wood
Monks Wood
Earith Washes
R. Ouse
Wicken Fen
Hall Yard Woods
Tuddenham Fen
Tuddenham Heath
Cavenham
Chippenham

NORTHAMPTON
CAMBRIDGESHIRE
Hemingford Grey gravel pit
Huntingdon
St. Ives gravel pit
Landbeach gravel pit
Milton Country Park
Newmarket

Grafham Water
Kimbolton
A14
A14
A14

Little Paxton
A1
A1198
Battisham

St. Neot's
Cambridge
Wilbraham Fen
Fulbourn Fen
M11

BEDFORD
R. Cam
Gog Magog Hills
Wandlebury

A10
Fowlmere

0 Miles 5 10 20 30
Scale

ESSEX

440

and Lincolnshire

THE low-lying counties of East Anglia make up what is almost unarguably Britain's best bird-watching region.

Richest of all in bird-life are the Fens and the Broads. Wicken Fen, a wilderness of sedge and reed maintained by the National Trust, is alive with warblers. Long-eared owls, marsh harriers and bearded tits also occur. Cley Marshes and Blakeney Point are among the best places in England to see passage waders, along with all kinds of vagrants and migrants.

The Norfolk Broads attract bearded tits and many water birds. Hickling Broad has Bewick's swans, goldeneyes, ruffs, black-tailed godwits, garganeys, sedge warblers,

terns and herons. Suffolk has large colonies of avocets at Minsmere and Havergate Island.

The heaths in south-western Norfolk and north-western Suffolk include, among their breeding birds, crossbills, gadwalls, and ringed plovers; golden pheasants breed wild in the Breckland; and the Ouse Washes have masses of waterfowl, especially in winter.

PICK OF THE YEAR

JANUARY: tens of thousands of knot winter at Snettisham and elsewhere on the Wash

FEBRUARY: purple sandpipers can be seen on rocks below Hunstanton cliffs

MARCH: booming of bitterns can be heard on Norfolk Broads and at Minsmere and Cley

APRIL: avocets nest at Havergate Island, Minsmere, Titchwell and Cley

MAY: bearded tits at Minsmere and Cley

JUNE: stone curlews breed in Breckland

JULY: chicks hatch in terneries at Blakeney Point, Scolt Head Island and Minsmere

AUGUST: migrating wood sandpipers, ruffs and other waders at Ouse Washes

SEPTEMBER: wrynecks, bluethroats and barred warblers occasionally on Norfolk coast

OCTOBER: thrushes, skylarks and starlings begin to arrive for the winter

NOVEMBER: Bewick's swans and other wild-fowl on Ouse and Nene Washes

DECEMBER: snow buntings, Lapland buntings and twite on Wash salt-marshes

---

North Sea

The North-West

DUMFRIES AND
GALLOWAY

Campfield Marsh
Bowness Common
Moricambe Bay
Grune Point
Glasson
Moss
Wampool
Estuary
Newton Marsh

Esk Estuary
Rockcliffe Marsh
Eden Estuary
Burgh Marsh
Monkhill Lough

Thurstonfield
Lough
Carlisle

Talkin
Tarn
Tindale
Tarn

Geltsdale

Waver Estuary
Oulton Gravel Pit

C U M B R I A

Siddick
Pond
R. Derwent
Cockermouth
Penrith
Whins Pond

Workington
Bassenthwaite
A66
A66

Holme Wood
Keswick
Barrow Wood
Derwent
Water

Glencoyne
Wood

Whitehaven
Scale Wood
Naddle Low Forest

St Bees Head
Burtness
Wood
Ennerdale
Water
Watendlath Fell
Hawes
Water

Woodend Pool
Lake District
Sunbig
Tarn

Ambleside

Hardknott
Nat. For. Park
Windermere

Drigg Point and
Ravenglass Sanctuary
Muncaster
Cas.
Coniston
Water
Brantwood
Kendal
Killington
Res.

Wyndhammere

Roudsea
Wood

Duddon
Estuary
Dallam Tower

Hodbarrow
Pennington
Res.
Eaves and
Waterslack Woods

Barrow-in-Furness
Leighton
Moss
Farleton
Knott

Walney
Island
Morecambe Bay

Foulney I.
Morecambe

Heysham
Harbour
Lancaster
Forest
of
Bowland

Lune
Estuary

Cockerham and
Pilling Marshes

Fleetwood
Wyre-Lune
Estuaries

Wyre Estuary
Saltmarshes
L A N C A S H I R

R. Wyre

Stanley Park
M55
R. Ribble

Blackpool
A583
Preston
Blackburn

Clifton Marsh
Freckleton Flashes
Freckleton
Sewage Farm
Ribble Estuary
Guide Res.

Southport
Wildfowl Reserve
Dar

Marshside
Rivington
Res.

Southport
Hesketh Park
Chorley

Ainsdale
Freshfield
& Formby
Dunes
Martin Mere

Formby
Wigan

Alt Estuary
Pennington
Flash
Leig

Seaforth
A580
Bootle
St Helens
Risley Me
Eccleston Mere

Irish Sea

Liverpool
Bay
Liverpool
Warrington
M62

Mersey Estuary

Isle of Man inset

Point of Ayre

Ballaugh
Curraghs
Ramsey Mooragh
Ramsey

Ballaugh
Maughold Head

Peel
Isle
of Man

Greeba Gap
Eairy &
Kionslieu Dams
Douglas

Castletown
Aldrick
Black
Head
Calf of Man
Spanish Head
Langness

ERUPTING volcanoes, Ice Age glaciers and centuries of ravaging by tempest and flood have all served to shape the peaks and luxuriant valleys of Cumbria and Lancashire.

The mountains of the Lake District, scarred by steep slopes of loose, jagged stone, rise gently from expanses of shining water. Here, among the woods and rolling moorland, nearly a dozen varieties of hill bird make their home—most of the northern and western hill birds, in fact, which breed south of the Scottish Highlands. They are the raven, buzzard, peregrine, merlin, ring ouzel, twite, common sandpiper, dipper, grey wagtail and golden plover.

Hanging oakwoods

The Lake District's oakwoods, hanging on steep valley sides, also provide nesting places for the pied flycatcher. When winter storm clouds mask the tops of the Lakeland mountains, the lakes themselves provide a home for wild ducks such as the goosander and the goldeneye, as well as whooper swans.

High among the more remote and stony peaks of the Pennines, rarer visitors to the region may occasionally be seen—the dunlin, for example, a member of the sandpiper family which nests in a grass tussock. Even the golden eagle, not usually found south of the mountains of Scotland, has recently spread back again into the area and nested again since 1969 after an absence of 200 years.

In contrast with its hinterland, the coastline of the north-west is low and flat, with estuaries and salt-marshes stretching almost all the way from the Solway to the wide expanse of Liverpool Bay. Large flocks of geese can be seen on the three main groups of estuaries along this coast, honking and cackling as they make their way from the roosting area to feed in the fields.

On the Ribble Estuary below Preston the geese are mainly pink-footed; but where the rivers of the Solway Firth meet the sea, there are flocks of pink-feet, greylags and—at their only regular location in England—barnacle geese.

There are geese, too, in Morecambe Bay; but here they are outnumbered by huge and noisy flocks of oystercatchers. These birds anger local fishermen who claim that they make serious inroads on the cockle harvest—a claim strenuously denied by ornithologists. Some of the oystercatchers stay to breed, and they will mob any intruder setting foot in their breeding grounds.

Two species of the duck family have become common along this coast. The red-breasted merganser has been breeding here and spreading south in recent years; and on Walney Island, a low, sandy spit which lies just outside the busy industrial town of Barrow-in-Furness, a huge breeding colony of eiders has established itself.

Seabirds breed in many places along the Cumbria and Lancashire seaboard. Several of the low, sandy islets in the Morecambe Bay area are the sites of terneries, closely guarded by wardens appointed by local naturalists' trusts.

At St. Bees Head, just south of Whitehaven, there are large colonies of guillemots, razorbills, kittiwakes and other seabirds—and even a few black guillemots. Drigg dunes are a breeding ground for terns and black-headed gulls.

Birds of the lagoons

When it comes to watching birds at close quarters, no site in Lancashire can rival the Leighton Moss bird sanctuary. It is an extensive reed marsh set among limestone hills, with several large, shallow lagoons where flocks of waterfowl congregate. Visitors can watch, from tall wooden hides on stilts, birds such as the bittern and the reed warbler—without disturbing them.

Also on view at the sanctuary are the teal, shoveler, garganey, water rail, grasshopper warbler, marsh harrier and a wide variety of migrant waders.

PICK OF THE YEAR

JANUARY: flocks of oystercatchers winter in Morecambe Bay

FEBRUARY: chaffinches and greenfinches flock to communal roosts on farmland

MARCH: ravens incubate their eggs in the Lake District

APRIL: herons lay in their tree-top colonies; the eggs are often plundered by crows when people disturb sitting birds

MAY: cock pied flycatchers carry food to their incubating mates in the oak-woods of the Lake District

JUNE: young dippers and grey wagtails feed along the hill streams of the Pennines

JULY: on the high Pennine moors young twites begin to flock among the heather

AUGUST: coveys of red grouse on the high moors; the shooting season starts on the 12th

SEPTEMBER: migrant willow warblers and other small birds at Grune Point, Cumbria

OCTOBER: huge flocks of waders arrive on the Lancashire coastline

NOVEMBER: greylag and pink-footed geese arrive to winter on the English side of the Solway

DECEMBER: flocks of whooper swans winter in family parties throughout the Lake District

From Humber to Tyne

NORTHUMBERLAND

Newcastle
upon Tyne
Shibdon Pond
Gateshead

Jarrow
Slake
South Shields
Marsden Bay

R. Tyne

R. Derwent

Washington
Wildfowl Refuge
Sunderland

Derwent Res.

Stanley
Zoo

A19

R. Wear

Hisehope Res.
Smiddy Shaw
Res.
Waskerly Res.
Tunstall Res.

Durham

Hawthorn Dene

Castle Eden Denes
Black Hall Rocks

D U R H A M

R. Wear

A167

Hurworth
Burn Res.

West
Hartlepool

Heugh Battery
Hartlepool Bay
Teesmouth Estuary

Redcar

North
Sea

Upper
Teesdale

R. Tees

Adder Wood
Witton-le-Wear

Cowpen
Marsh

CUMBRIA

Barnard Castle

A1(M)

A66

Darlington

A135

Middlesbrough

R. Tees

A66

A1

Scaling Res.

Richmond

Northallerton

North York Moors

Hambleton
Hills

Kingtho
Woo

Leyburn

R. Swale

N O R T H

Thirsk

Gormire
Lake

Rye Dale Woods

Pickering

R. Rye

Kirb
Mis

R. Ure

Leighton
Res.

Y O R K S H I R E

Ripon

A19

Scamps

Colt Park
Hesleden
Gill
Craven
Pennines
Oxenber Wood
Malham
Tarn

Roundhill
Res.

Woo Gill
Tarns
Gouthwaite
Res.

Pateley
Bridge

Studley Park

Fountains
Abbey
Woods

R. Nidd

R. Ouse

Castle
Howard

A64

M

A65

R. Wharfe

Grass
Wood
Glasshouses
Dam

Austwick
Moss

Settle

Stocks Res.
Gargrave

R. Ribble

Skipton

Barden Moor Res.

Bolton Abbey
Wood
Chelker Res.
Ilkley

Fewston Res.
Swinsty Res.

Harrogate

Lindley Wood
Res.

Linton
Common

Wetherby

A1(M)

A1237 A64

York

A1079

A64

White Moor
Res.

Keighley

Rombalds
Moor

R. Wharfe

Harewood
Park
Eccup Res.

A58

A1

Healaugh

A64

Moreby
Park

R. Derwent

Wheldrake
Floods

Skipwith
Common

Hardcastle
Crags
Bradford

W E S T

Halifax

A646

R. Calder

A58

A650

Leeds

Y O R K S H I R E

M62

Swillington
Ings

Fairburn
Res.

Ardsley
Res.

Nostell Dam

A63

Fairburn Ings

Pontefract

M62

Selby

A63

A1041

R. Ouse

A63

Goole

Blackto
Sands

A62

Huddersfield

Wakefield

A638

Wintersett
Res.

Shirley
Pool

R. Don

Marsden Moor

Southern

A628

A616

Worsborough
Res.
Stainborough
Woods

Barnsley

R. Dearne

A61

A1(M)

Doncaster

Potteric Carr

A18

A630

A614

Pennines

S O U T H

Y O R K S H I R E

A61

Rotherham

M18

Sheffield

M1

A57

D E R B Y

T HE pounding of the ocean against lime-stone rocks has produced the architecture of the Yorkshire, Cleveland and Durham coast—stretches of curiously shaped cliffs with sculptured caverns and caves, and tall rocks which stand alone on the seashore, cut off from the cliffs to which they once belonged.

Many rocks along this seaboard are populated by turbulent colonies of birds. The largest—the 3 ft long gannet—can be seen off the Yorkshire coast, gliding, flapping and plummeting into the sea when it spies one of the small fish on which it preys.

The bird established its first mainland colony in Britain on the Bempton Cliffs north of Bridlington—an area which it shares with guillemots, razorbills, puffins, kittiwakes, rock doves and feral pigeons.

In winter, many gulls desert the cliffs and make their way to stretches of water inland. There are roosts, mainly of black-headed gulls, at Hornsea Mere, a few miles north of Hull, and on five of the Yorkshire reservoirs —Ardsley, Barden Moor, Eccup, Stocks and Wintersett. Farther west, in the Yorkshire Pennines, there are two dozen or so colonies of black-headed gulls, the largest of them at Woo Gill Tarns, near Pateley Bridge, in Nidderdale.

Inland tracts of water also provide a winter home for flocks of waterfowl, more numerous in low-lying country, but still to be found on many of the small reservoirs among the hills of west Yorkshire. The Humber has a fine flock of pink-footed geese which feed on the Yorkshire wolds and roost on the estuary at the National Wildfowl Refuge on Whitton Sands. The Canada goose, which was originally introduced to this country as an ornamental species from North America, now breeds wild in many parts of Yorkshire, and flocks in winter at Nostell Dam reservoir.

A multitude of swallows

One of the greatest spectacles which the region provides for the bird-watcher is the sight of thousands of swallows and sand martins arching and soaring in effortless display over their autumn roost at Fairburn Ings, about 12 miles to the south-east of Leeds. A huge sheet of water now covers land which flooded as mineworkings beneath it caused it to subside. Numbers have now sadly declined, but until recently the sky was filled at dawn and dusk with a quarter of a million birds gathering for the long journey to Africa.

Hill and moorland birds, including the pied flycatcher, raven, buzzard, peregrine and merlin, may be seen on the eastern flank of the Pennines; but they are less frequent here than in the west.

To study birds at close quarters there is nowhere better in the region than the observatory at Spurn Head—a narrow ridge of shingle several miles long, on the north side of the Humber mouth. The site, where many rare birds and huge numbers of more common migrants can be seen, belongs to the Yorkshire Naturalists' Trust.

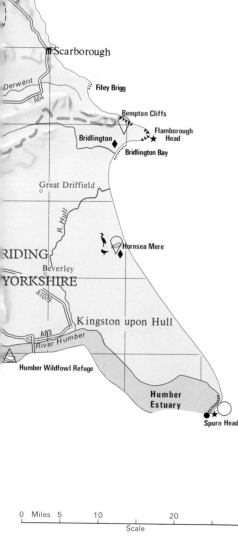

PICK OF THE YEAR

JANUARY: divers, scaup and scoter winter off Flamborough Head

FEBRUARY: bramblings from northern Europe feed alongside sparrows and chaffinches on the stubble-fields

MARCH: garden-nesting robins and song thrushes start laying; in woods and on farmland, they usually start later

APRIL: black-headed gulls arrive at moorland gulleries

MAY: pied flycatchers breed in dale woodlands

JUNE: gannets, razorbills, guillemots and other seabirds crowd together on the cliff ledges at Bempton

JULY: kittiwakes and cormorants flock to Marsden Rock in South Tyneside

AUGUST: in one day four British species of skua may be seen off Flamborough Head

SEPTEMBER: thousands of swallows and sand martins roost at Fairburn Ings

OCTOBER: purple sandpipers arrive to winter in Hartlepool Bay

NOVEMBER: large flocks of pink-footed geese feed on wolds and roost in Humber wildfowl refuge on Whitton Sands

DECEMBER: thousands of gulls roost in Teesmouth

The area immediately north of the Solway Firth is famous for its geese; and along the Solway, the best place for seeing geese is the nature reserve at Caerlaverock. This wide salt-marsh, with mud-flats and mountains beyond, makes a spectacular setting for noisy flocks of pink-footed geese and greylags from Iceland and barnacle geese from Spitsbergen in the Arctic.

A late winter's day at Caerlaverock can also be made memorable by the sight of whooper swans, ducks—including wigeon, pintail and teal—and by the large flocks of redwings and fieldfares in the fields beyond.

The cliffs at Burrow Head and at the tip of the Mull of Galloway have large colonies of razorbills, kittiwakes, guillemots and shags. These seabirds can also be seen—together with puffins, great and lesser black-backed gulls and a pair of peregrines—on the remote, rocky island of Ailsa Craig. But they are all overshadowed by the birds which have made this small, cone-shaped island famous for centuries—the spear-billed, dazzling white gannets.

The islands of the Inner Hebrides, with their bleak mountains and steep cliffs, are also rich in bird-life. Among the more rewarding of them for the ornithologist is Islay, where choughs find their only home in Scotland.

Two other members of the crow family provide interest for bird-watching in this region, for it is here that the ranges of the carrion crow and the hooded crow merge. The south-west corner of Dumfries and Galloway is the farthest south that the grey-backed hoodie breeds, and in a strip from there to Stirling can be seen the full range of intermediate varieties formed when it breeds with the all-black southern carrion crow. This zone of overlap is only 15-20 miles wide, and from this it would appear that the hybrids are at some still unexplained disadvantage in relation to their pure-bred parents.

Two other birds of the north which have now moved south into this region are the capercaillie and the very rare golden eagle. A few pairs of eagles now breed on the remoter mountain crags of these counties.

Atlantic Ocean

Lismore

Kerr

HEBRIDES

Lui

Scarba

Colonsay

A R G Y L L

N

Oronsay

Jura

Tayvallich
Taynish
Woods

INNER

Loch
Gruinart

Inver

Loch Gorm
Loch Indaal

Bridgend

Islay

Gigha

Mull of Oa

Torri
C

Campb

S

PICK OF THE YEAR

JANUARY: geese—white-fronted, greylag and at times the rare bean— at Threave wildfowl refuge

FEBRUARY: large flocks of oystercatchers on the Solway

MARCH: cormorants return to their large inland breeding colony, at Castle Loch, near Mochrum

APRIL: northern waders pause at the Solway on their way to their breeding grounds

MAY: gannets incubate their eggs on Ailsa Craig and Scar Rocks

JUNE: tern chicks hatch at colonies on sand or shingle beaches of the southern coast of west Scotland

JULY: nightjars, a declining species, can still

be heard 'churring' at dusk on some of the moors in Galloway

AUGUST: fulmars on Ailsa Craig, and on the cliffs of the mainland coast, brood their single chicks

SEPTEMBER: thousands of starlings at winter roosts on the ledges of buildings in Glasgow

OCTOBER: barnacle geese at Caerlaverock and on Islay

NOVEMBER: flocks of purple sandpipers on the Ayr coast

DECEMBER: black-tailed godwits of the Icelandic sub-species winter in flocks on the Nith Estuary; they are most easily seen when they are feeding on the estuary mud-flats at low tide

The Western Lowlands

HIGHLAND

Glasdrum
Wood

Rannoch Moor
Loch Ba

Ben Lui

Inversnaid

Queen Elizabeth
Nat. Forest Park

Argyll National
Forest
Park

Ross
Wood

Loch
Ard
Forest

Flanders
Moss

R. Forth

Stirling

Loch Eck

Loch Lomond

Buchanan
Castle

Carron
Valley Res.

R. Carron

Falkirk

Garadbhan
Forest

BUTE

Ardmore
Point

Dumbarton

Clyde

Milngavie Res.
Bardowie
Loch

Forth & Clyde Canal

Loch
Thom

Greenock

Possil
Marsh

Gadloch

Bute

L. Dhu

Loch Fad

Rothesay

Gt
Cumbrae I.

Paisley

Castle
Semple Loch

Zoo

Glasgow

Hogganfield
Loch

Airdrie

Inchmarnock

Loch
Quien

Lochwinnoch

Kelburn
Castle

Camphill
Res.

Barr
Loch

Stanley
Dam

L. Libo

Barrhead
Dams

Carmunnock &
Rogerton Resr.

Hamilton
Low Parks

Bothwell
Bridge

Motherwell

Barons Haugh

Crane
Loch

Little
Cumbrae

Hunterston
Sands

High Dam
Dunwan Dam

Lochgoin

R. Avon

Falls of Clyde

Lanark

R. Clyde

Carnwath
Moss

Glen
Diomhan

Horse I.

Kilmarnock

Corehouse

Brodick
Wood

Arran

Holy Is.

Enterkine
Wood

Glenbuck
Loch

BORDERS

Ayr

Loch
Martnaham

Loch o' the
Lowes

Sanquhar

Moffat

Culzean
Castle & Pond

Maybole

R. Nith

Bargany

Ailsa
Craig

Loch
Doon

Nithsdale
Woodlands

Ae
Forest

Loch
Macaterick

DUMFRIES

Loch
Moan

The
Merrick

Rhinns
of
Kells

W. Skelston

AND

Knowetop
Lochs

Fountainbleau
and Ladyport

Lochmaben
Lochs

Corsewall
Point

Glen Trool
Nat. Forest
Park

Caldons
Wood

Clatteringshaws
Loch

New
Galloway

Whitcairn

Loch Ken

Dumfries

Craigs Moss

Wood
of Cree

Clatteringshaws

GALLOWAY

Auchenreoch
Loch

Racks

Loch Ryan

Newton
Stewart

Machermore

Cairnsmore
of Fleet

Ken-Dee
Marshes

Milton
Loch

Lochrutton
Loch

Nith
Estuary

Lochar
Estuary

Kirkconnell
Flow

Caerlaverock

Cree

Greenlaw Dam

Townhead of
Threave

Carlingwark
Loch

Southerness
Point

Solway Firth

Lochinch
Castle Lochs

Stranraer

Portpatrick

Castle L.

Mochrum
Loch

Wigtown
Bay

Kirkcudbright
Bay

Auchencairn
Bay

Luce
Bay

Scar
Rocks

Burrow
Head

Mull of
Galloway

0 Miles 5   10   20   30   40

Scale

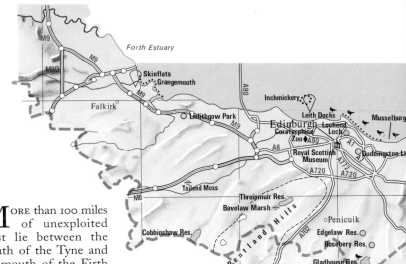

More than 100 miles of unexploited coast lie between the mouth of the Tyne and the mouth of the Firth of Forth; and from autumn to spring, grebes, divers and seagoing ducks abound along the whole length of it. Particularly good places to see them are: the shore between Bamburgh and Seahouses, overlooking the Farne Islands; Cresswell Dunes; St. Mary's Island; and the Lindisfarne National Nature Reserve, which extends from Cheswick Sands to Budle Bay. The reserve is also notable in winter for the presence of Brent geese—usually from 500 to 2000 of them—and for large numbers of wigeon and whooper swans.

Spring on this coast brings a host of small migrants. The first chiffchaffs and wheatears arrive in late March and early April; willow warblers, swallows, whitethroats and spotted flycatchers follow later.

Summer is the season to explore the inland hills; the grass and heather uplands of the Cheviots, the Lammermuirs and the Pentlands are ideal country for black and red grouse, golden plovers, dunlin, merlins, ring ouzels, woodcock, redpolls and siskins.

Cresswell Ponds are a good place to watch waders on migration. In late June, wood sandpipers and green sandpipers can be seen on the muddy edges of the ponds; and they are soon joined by ruffs, ringed plovers and common sandpipers. In September curlew sandpipers arrive from the Siberian Arctic *en route* for their winter quarters in Africa.

Large numbers of seabirds breed on the high cliffs at St. Abb's Head and Dunstanburgh; and Dunstanburgh also has a colony of cliff-breeding house martins. Terns and a great variety of other seabirds breed on the islands of the Forth: Inchmickery, Fidra, Eyebroughy and Lamb. Lamb also has a colony of cormorants, and in late summer as many as 2000 eiders go to Eyebroughy, the smallest of the islands, to moult. Gulls, terns and other seabirds also breed in great profusion on the Farnes, which for many years have been a centre for ornithologists from all over Britain.

One small, isolated island at the entrance to the Forth provides one of the greatest ornithological experiences of the region; this is the Bass Rock, with eiders and thousands of breeding pairs of gannets.

DUMFRIES

AND GALLOWAY

PICK OF THE YEAR

JANUARY: grebes, sometimes including scarce red-necked, in Aberlady Bay

FEBRUARY: purple sandpipers on rocky parts of the Northumberland coast

MARCH: shags and other seabirds return to breed on the Farne Islands

APRIL: black grouse at their display grounds in the Border Forest Park

MAY: gannets are incubating on the Bass Rock

JUNE: terns, including the Sandwich tern, are breeding on islands in the Firth of Forth

JULY: kittiwakes feed chicks on cliff nests at Craigleith and at St. Abb's Head

AUGUST: large flocks of eider ducks gather off Holy Island and the Farnes to stay on the sea during their flightless moult period

SEPTEMBER: four species of skua migrate across the Firth of Forth near Grangemouth

OCTOBER: large numbers of dunlin, redshanks and other waders in Aberlady Bay

NOVEMBER: pale-breasted Brent geese are present on sand-flats at Holy Island

DECEMBER: snow buntings and twites feed in flocks on salt-marshes at Aberlady Bay

The Eastern Lowlands and Border Country

Craigleith Bass Rock
Lamb
Fidra
Craigleith
North Berwick

Aberlady Bay

Tyninghame Tyninghame Estuary
Dunbar
Barns Ness

St. Abbs Head

North Sea

Whiteadder Water

Lammermuir

Watch Water Res.

Primrosehill Pond

Duns Castle

Berwick upon Tweed
Tweed Estuary

Hule Moss

Cheswick Sands
Goswick Sands
Holy I.

Gordon Moss

Fenham Flats
Ross Links

The Hirsel

Budle Bay
Bamburgh
Farne Is.
Seahouses

Galashiels

Bemersyde Moss

Junction Water

Kelso
Hoselaw Loch

D E R S

Whitlaw Mosses

Hoselaw Moss

Yetholm Loch

Chillingham Park

Newton Pool

Hare Moss
Dunhog Moss

Dunstanburgh
Cullernose Point

Jedburgh

wick

Alnwick

The Cheviots

Northumberland

Wauchope Forest

Coquet I.

Hauxley

Catcleugh Res.

N O R T H U M B E R L A N D

National

Otterburn

Font Res.

Rothley Lakes

Creswell Dunes
Cresswell Ponds

Border

Kielder Water

Comb Rigg Moss

Morpeth

Forest Park

Park

Lee Hall

Bolam

Capheaton

Seaton Sluice
Colt Crag Res.

A19 Holywell Ponds
St Mary's I.

Seaton Burn Ponds

Greenlee Lough
Broomlee Lough
Grindon Lough
Muckle Moss

Whittledene Res.

Gosforth Park
Tynemouth

Newton Pool

Hancock Museum

Swallow Ponds

Haltwhistle

Hexham

Newcastle upon Tyne

C U M B R I A

D U R H A M

0 Miles   5   10   20   30

Scale

The North-West Highlands and Scottish Islands

Atlantic Ocean

Kyle of Durness
Faraid Head
Cape Wrath ★
Clo Mor
Durne

Butt of Lewis
Loch Stiapavat

Loch Eriboll

Borve

Gualinn
Eilean Ard
Loch Laxford
Strath Beag

▼ ⸙ Flannan Is.

Handa
L. More

Glen Valtos

Little Loch Roag

Stornoway Castle
Loch Branahuie

North Minch

Loch Assynt

Inchnadamph

Inverpolly Forest

Loch Sionascaig
Inverpolly
Loch Lurgainn

Summer Isles

St Kilda

Priest Island

Ben Mór Coigach
Rhidorroch

Glen Ei

Harris

Shiant Is.

Little Ullapool
Loch Broom
Loch Broom

Amat Forest

R. Car

Loch Ewe

Loch Gairloch

Fionn Loch

A835

Black W

Newton Estate

Loch Maree
Loch Maree

Loch Fannich
Loch

Balranald

Loch Scadavay

North Uist

Island of Rona

Beinn Eighe

R. Bran
Loch Luichart

Monach Is.

Coulin

R. Orrin

Loch Torridon

Achnashellach

Loch Bee

Neist Point
Orbost

Isle of Skye

Coille Dhubh
Rassal Ashwood

R. Farrar
R

Stoneybridge Lochs
Loch Druidibeg

Raasay

Loch Carron

Loch Monar
Strathglass

Corrir

Loch an Duin

South Uist

Kyle of Lochalsh

Guisachan

Kylerhea

R. Affric
Loch Affric

Glen Moriston

A887
Glen Loyne

Barra

Canna
Sanday

Northbay
Castlebay

Rhum

Loch Quoich

R. Garry
Glengarry Forest

Loch Lochy

Mallaig

Loch Arkaig

Eigg

Loch Morar

A830

Glen Loy Forest

Mingulay
Berneray

Muck

Doire Donn
Loch Shiel

Fort William

Loch a' Mhill Aird

Glenborrodale
Loch Sunart

Ardgour
Oakwood

Coll

Tobermory

Calgary
Burg

Tiree

Treshnish Isles
Ulva
Island of Mull

ARGYLL AND BUTE

Loch Spelve

Iona

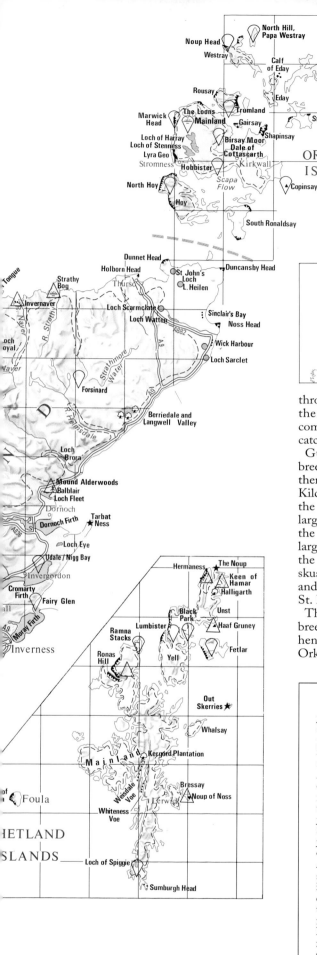

THE bleak north-west of the Scottish mainland is largely given over to 'deer forest'—wild, damp, open country with little vegetation to provide birds with food and cover. Yet the golden eagle, ptarmigan, greenshank and the red-throated and black-throated divers all breed in the region. Red-breasted mergansers are common breeders on sea lochs, and oyster-catchers and curlews are numerous on the coast.

Gulls and auks are the most numerous breeding birds on the islands off the coast, and there are waders in plenty on the Hebrides. St. Kilda, 40 miles to the west of North Uist, is the home of the rare St. Kilda wren—slightly larger than the mainland form. The islands of the St. Kilda group also have the world's largest gannetry. Storm petrels breed widely on the Inner and Outer Hebrides. The Arctic skua breeds on Coll, North Uist and Lewis; and the great skua breeds on both Lewis and St. Kilda.

The Orkneys and Shetlands have most of the breeding seabirds of the Hebrides, as well as hen-harriers and short-eared owls on the Orkneys, and whimbrels on the Shetlands.

PICK OF THE YEAR

JANUARY: glaucous and Iceland gulls, waders and waterfowl in Stornoway Harbour

FEBRUARY: golden eagles return to their eyries in the mountains

MARCH: herons are nesting on Lewis

APRIL: native, wild greylag geese are nesting on Loch Druidibeg, South Uist

MAY: black-throated divers are nesting on the islands in the larger Highland lochs

JUNE: red-necked phalaropes are breeding in Shetland

JULY: tens of thousands of kittiwakes nest on one cliff face on Handa Island

AUGUST: fulmar chicks hatch on the cliffs

SEPTEMBER: small numbers of shearwaters in Hebridean seas

OCTOBER: whooper swans begin to arrive in the Hebrides and on west coast lochs

NOVEMBER: greylag geese in the Sound of Harris

DECEMBER: hundreds of barnacle geese on some Hebridean islands

The North-East Highlands

THE mountains, moors, pinewoods and seashores of Scotland's eastern Highlands provide homes for a rich variety of birds, some of which breed nowhere else in Britain. The high moors are the domain of red grouse, the high summits the haunts of ptarmigan. The golden eagle also has its stronghold in the high country. Greenshanks and dotterel—extremely rare as breeding birds outside the Highlands—nest on these moors; and among the peaks of the Cairngorms, above the 3000 ft level, nest snow buntings.

The pine forests in the Spey valley provide a home for the crested tit and the Scottish crossbill. Capercaillies and siskins also live in the coniferous woods, and black grouse breed in the scrubland on their borders.

The eastern Highlands have meadow pipits, twites, ring ouzels, cuckoos, dippers, common sandpipers, golden plovers and dunlin; and redwings have begun to breed regularly in the Highlands.

The region's lochs and rivers have a similarly wide variety of breeding birds, including the Slavonian grebe, red-throated and black-throated divers, common scoter, goosander, wigeon, pintail and gadwall. The whooper swan is a winter visitor, although it no longer stays to breed. Loch Leven in Kinross, just south of the Highland line, is one of Britain's outstanding breeding sites for waterfowl.

Other remarkable sites for birds are Hatton Castle, north of Aberdeen, once the largest rookery in Britain with 9000 nests; the Ythan Estuary in the same region, with its big colony of eider ducks; and the Isle of May in the Firth of Forth, famous for its breeding seabirds.

But the region's best bird-watching centre is probably the Spey valley resort of Aviemore, within easy reach of the famous osprey eyrie at Loch Garten.

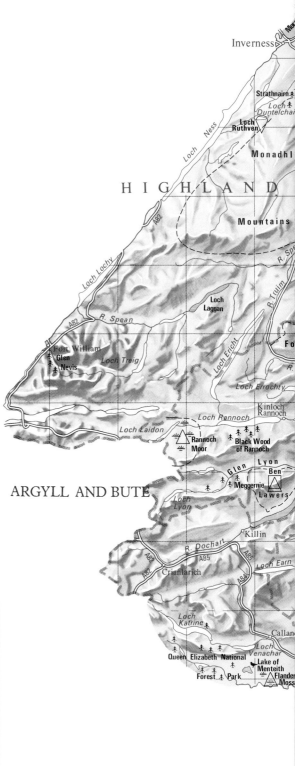

PICK OF THE YEAR

JANUARY: large flocks of snow buntings winter on farmland along the Spey valley

FEBRUARY: Scottish crossbills start nesting in Spey valley; these birds have heavier bills than common crossbills

MARCH: rooks nesting in large rookeries on coastal plain

APRIL: ospreys return to Loch Garten

MAY: golden eagles in the Cairngorms are feeding their newly hatched young by the end of the month

JUNE: ptarmigan chicks hatch towards the end of the month, in nests more than 3000 ft up in the Cairngorms

JULY: guillemot chicks leave the colonies on the Isle of May and at Fowlsheugh

AUGUST: little gulls visit Kilconquhar Loch

SEPTEMBER: Arctic skuas in the Firth of Forth

OCTOBER: grey geese arrive on Loch Leven and Carsebreck

NOVEMBER: gulls roost on Lake of Menteith

DECEMBER: flocks of whooper swans, wintering geese, and many species of duck on Loch Leven

Moray Firth

Lossiemouth
Oakenhead
Loch Spynie
Speymouth
Banff
Troup Head
Pennan Head
Kinnaird Head
Fraserburgh

Buckie Loch
Findhorn Bay
Culbin Sands
Culbin Forest
Forres
Elgin
A96
Fochabers
A98
R. Deveron
Loch of Strathbeg

Nairn
Darnaway Forest Pools
Darnaway Forest
A96
Peterhead
Peterhead Bay
Buchan Ness

Loch Flemington

M O R A Y
R. Spey
Huntly
R. Ythan
Bullers of Buchan

Ballindalloch
Clashindarroch Forest
Ellon
Whinnyfold
Meikle Loch
Cotehill Loch
Sand Loch
Sands of Forvie
Ythan Estuary

Grantown-on-Spey
R. Avon
Benachie
Inverurie

R. Dulnain
Tornashean Forest
Pitfichie
R. Don
Kemnay Floods
Parkhill
Blackdog

Loch Garten
Abernethy Forest
Loch Vaa
L. Pityoulish
Aviemore
Glenmore
Loch Morlich
A B E R D E E N S H I R E
Loch of Skene
Aberdeen
Don Estuary
Girdle Ness

An Ellan
Rothiemurchus
Cairngorm
Upper Glen Avon
Hazlehead Park Zoo
Kingcausie

Insh Marshes
Loch Einich
Mountains
Morrone Wood
Dinnet Oakwood
R. Dee
Banchory

Glen Fleshie
Mar Forest
Braemar
R. Dee
Ballater
Glentanar
Fetteresso Forest

Ballochbuie
R. Muick
Lochnagar
Stonehaven
Fowlsheugh

R. North Esk
Drumtochty Forest

Caenlochan
Glen Clova
A N G U S
R. South Esk
Johnshaven
St Cyrus
North Din Wood
Montrose

Blair Atholl
Glen Isla
Dun's Dish
Montrose Basin

Ben Vrackie
Loch of Lintrathen
Kirriemuir
Rescobie Loch
Balgavies Loch
Lunan Bay

Loch Tummel
Loch of Forfar
North Sea

PERTHSHIRE
Aberfeldy
Marlee Loch
Loch Clunie
Dunkeld
Stormont Loch
Crombie Mill
Craigton Res.
Arbroath

AND
Loch of Lowes
R. Isla
Coupar Angus
A92

KINROSS
R. Tay
Dundee
Buddon Ness

Dupplin Loch
Perth
Firth of Tay
Morton Lochs
Tentsmuir
Cairnie Pier
Eden Estuary

A91
Cupar
Cameron Res.
Fife Ness

A915
Largo Bay
Kilconquhar Loch
Elie Ness
Isle of May

Kinross
Loch Leven
Vane Farm
Buckhaven

Alloa
Gartmorn Dam
Loch Fitty
Forth
Peppermill Dam
Tulliallan Castle
Loch Gelly
Kincardine
Town Loch
Dunfermline
Firth
of
Inchkeith
Forth

0 Miles 5   10   20   30   40
Scale

Uplands flaming with yellow gorse or mauve autumn heather run nearly to the sea along much of the coast of Ireland. The cliff barriers of the south-west look out across narrow fjords, pointing fingers of land towards the horizon. But in the east, rocky headlands give way to marshes and pastures as the low-lying central plain pushes through to the sea.

Tiny islands are sprinkled prolifically off this coast, echoing with the cries of seabirds which seek their refuge there. Dazzling white gannets flying overhead keep a watch on three of the islands where they have established colonies—Great Saltee, Co. Wexford; Bull Rock, Co. Cork; and Little Skellig, Co. Kerry. Ornithologists at the observatory on Clear Island, Co. Cork, occasionally sight rare species of shearwaters and petrels among the regular visitors.

Choughs, ravens and peregrines can all be seen along the south-west coast, together with the more usual seabirds. There are many important seabird colonies: on the Cliffs of Moher, and the cliffs from Kilkee to Loop Head, Co. Clare; on the Blasket Islands off Co. Kerry; and on the east coast, in many places in Co. Dublin, including Howth Head and Lambay Island.

Terns, including the roseate tern, seek out the low-lying shores of the Irish Sea for their breeding grounds—particularly around the coast of Co. Wexford; and black guillemots nest on Bray and Wicklow Heads, Co. Wicklow.

Large flocks of geese spend the winter in southern Ireland. The marshes around Wexford Harbour are one of their favourite haunts. Geese found here include white-fronts of the orange-billed Greenland race, greylags, barnacles and occasionally snow geese from Arctic America.

Brent geese can be seen further out in the estuary, as well as at Bannow Bay and Tacumshin Lake in Co. Wexford; Baldoyle Bay, Dublin Bay, and the Rogerstown and Swords Estuaries, Co. Dublin.

The region is less rich in land-birds, though hundreds of pied wagtails can be seen roosting in O'Connell Street in Dublin City every winter; and there are garden warblers in the Shannon Valley and blackcaps in the Powerscourt area of Co. Wicklow.

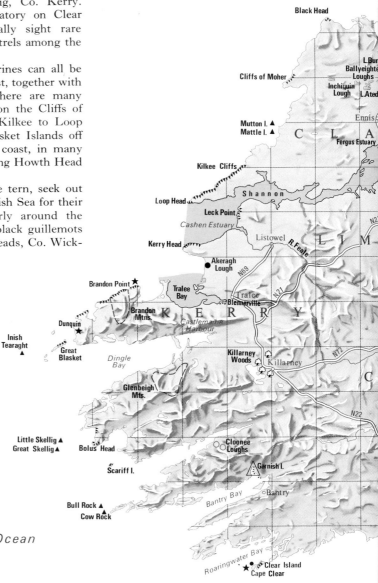

The South of Ireland

PICK OF THE YEAR

JANUARY: barnacle geese on the west coast

FEBRUARY: Brent and greylag geese on Dublin and Wicklow coasts

MARCH: tree-nesting cormorants return to Lough Bunny, Co. Clare

APRIL: crows and magpies, breeding earlier in Ireland's warm, wet climate than in England, may already have young in the nest

MAY: choughs, more common in Ireland than anywhere in the British Isles, feed their young in cliff-nests or crag-nests

JUNE: colonies of gannets are breeding on Great Saltee, Bull Rock and Little Skellig

JULY: terns at Malahide and elsewhere on the east coast

AUGUST: pectoral sandpipers and other vagrant waders from North America often appear near lakes on west coast

SEPTEMBER: seabirds, including occasional rarities such as albatrosses and great shearwaters, feed or migrate on west coast; Cape Clear is a good place to see them

OCTOBER: black-tailed godwits in Cork Harbour and on Shannon Estuary

NOVEMBER: geese of many different kinds gather near Wexford Harbour

DECEMBER: pied wagtails roost in O'Connell Street, Dublin

Forbidding cliffs and headlands, wind-swept peninsulas and wide, sweeping bays fringed by breakers—this is the seaboard of the north and west of Ireland, the safe and unspoilt breeding ground of great colonies of seabirds. The elegant roseate tern is still found on the east coast of the region, but as in the rest of the British Isles, it is declining. Here, too, are the storm petrel and black guillemot.

Off Co. Mayo in the west, where cliffs guard Achill Island's pastures and dark bogland, stands the Bills of Achill; these rocks are almost inaccessible to man, and a refuge for breeding seabirds—guillemots, razorbills, puffins, shags, fulmars, kittiwakes and the larger gulls.

Farther north, auks and fulmars breed on the Stacks of Broad Haven off the north coast of Mayo, and at Horn Head in Donegal, which is said to have the largest seabird colony in Ireland. Black guillemots also nest on the east coast, around Bangor harbour and Ballywalter pier in Co. Down.

Several distinctive subspecies of birds, subtly different from their close relatives across the Irish Sea, are found inland—the jay, dipper, coal tit and red grouse. In coastal districts the chough, now somewhat a rarity in the rest of the British Isles, can be seen frequently.

Some of the birds typical of the Scottish Highlands can be seen in this region, although they are extremely rare—the red-throated diver in parts of Donegal and the red-necked phalarope in Mayo.

Waterfowl in the region include the eider duck and the common scoter. Eiders breed as far south as Innishmurray Island, off Co. Sligo, and eastwards into Co. Down. Flocks of many kinds of geese—including greylags, white-fronts, Brents and barnacles—winter on the loughs. Good places to see them are: Blacksod Bay and Achill Sound, Co. Mayo; Strangford Lough and Downpatrick Marshes, Co. Down; and Lough Foyle, Co. Londonderry.

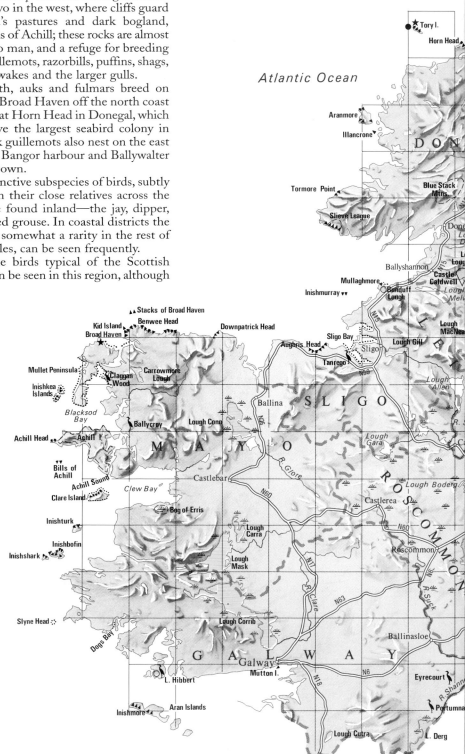

The North of Ireland

Inishtrahull

Malin Head

Rathlin
Cliffs   Rathlin I.

Sheep I.

Fair Head

White Head

Bann
Estuary
Coleraine

Trawbeaga
Bay

Lough
Swilly

Lough
Foyle   Binevenagh

North Channel

Londonderry

LONDONDERRY

Ballymena

Larne

Swan
Island   Larne Lough

Lough Beg

Ballymacormick Point

Copeland Is.

Bangor

Strabane

R. Owenkillew

Jordanstown

Belfast Lough

A N T R I M

Cookstown

Bellevue
Zoo   Craigavad   Newtownards

Omagh

R. Mourne

T Y R O N E

Lough
Neagh

Belfast

Stormont Castle

Portmore
Lough

Duncrue St
Marsh

Castle
Espie   Ballywalter

Parkanaur Dungannon

Lisburn

Strangford
Lough

Tullydowey
L. Brantry

Portadown
L. Castledillon

Hillsborough

Clea Lakes

Portaferry

Caledon
Decoy   Armagh

Quintin
Castle

wer Lough
le Woodlands
Enniskillen

Caledon
Ulster
Canal

D O W N

Downpatrick
Marshes

Strangford
Bay

ARMAGH

Monaghan

Newry Canal

R. Bann

Tollymore
Forest Park

Dundrum
Bay   St John's Point

Upper Lough
Erne

Ballyward
Lake

Drombanagher

Newry

Mourne
Mtns.

Newcastle

M O N A G H A N

R. Annalee

Mourne Park

handra

Farnham

Cavan

Carlingford
Lough   Green Island

Irish Sea

L O U T H

0 Miles   10   20   30   40
Scale

M E A T H

North Channel

PICK OF THE YEAR

JANUARY: barnacle geese feed in flocks on the mud-flats and marshes of many islands off the west coast; Sligo Bay is a good mainland site.

FEBRUARY: herons begin building their nests in the tree tops

MARCH: first of the summer migrants, including the ring ouzel and wheatear, arrive

APRIL: towards the end of the month, cormorants begin laying in the inland tree colony at Lough Cutra, Galway

MAY: a few pairs of garden warblers, rare in Ireland, begin laying around Lower Lough Erne and Lough Ree

JUNE: choughs, most common on the west coast, feed their young in cliff nests

JULY: colonies of roseate terns, often mingling with other species of terns, on the coast of Co. Down

AUGUST: young fulmars are still in the nest on many of the west coast cliffs; they leave about seven weeks after hatching

SEPTEMBER: Ireland is off the main migration routes, but this is a good month for spotting migrants on Copeland and Tory Islands

OCTOBER: starlings begin to fly in masses to their roosts on trees and buildings in the centre of Belfast

NOVEMBER: white-fronted geese from Greenland winter in Shannon Valley

DECEMBER: Slavonian grebes dive and swim after small fish in Lough Swilly

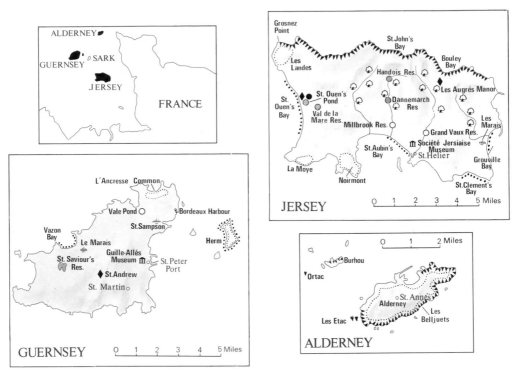

The Channel Islands

THE granite outcrops of the Channel Islands, washed by the Gulf Stream and caressed by warm, westerly winds, have more in common with the Continent than with mainland Britain. Indeed, their birds are usually excluded from zoogeographical studies of the British Isles.

Perhaps surprisingly, in view of their climatic advantages, the islands have only one species which does not breed in Britain. This is the European short-toed treecreeper, indistinguishable in the field from our own species apart from its voice. The Kentish plover, which ceased breeding in south-east England in 1956, clung on in the Channel Islands rather longer, but now nests only occasionally.

With these exceptions, the birds of the Channel Islands cover a remarkably similar range to those in England. The sandy coves of the inhabited isles and the steep cliffs of the uninhabited ones provide much the same kind of habitat as England's south-west coastline, and the bird lists are virtually identical.

Seabirds find the scattered, uninhabited islands and rocks off Alderney particularly attractive; guillemots, razorbills, kittiwakes, shags and the larger gulls are abundant there. Puffins and storm petrels breed on Burhou and neighbouring islets.

Most of the land of the two largest islands, Jersey and Guernsey, has been cultivated or developed; but around parts of their coastline and over most of the smaller islands, the country has sparse woodland, with much of the undeveloped land well covered with bracken or scrub.

If Britain were to suffer a succession of severe winters, it is possible that the Channel Islands would have a third species that could not breed in mainland Britain—the Dartford warbler. After every harsh winter, it is very difficult to find Dartford warblers in Britain; but they have long been established in Jersey and have occasionally bred in the dense scrub on the south side of Guernsey.

PICK OF THE YEAR

JANUARY: short-toed treecreeper can be seen in the woods

FEBRUARY: cormorants—a common sight as they feed off-shore—start to acquire the white thigh-patch characteristic of their breeding plumage

MARCH: razorbills and guillemots begin to return to their breeding colonies on the islets off Alderney

APRIL: cirl buntings, rare now in mainland Britain, but still found on Jersey, begin their courtship

MAY: Dartford warblers are raising their young

JUNE: gannets are feeding fish to their young in the colonies on the rocks off the coast of Alderney

JULY: ringed plovers tend their young on the shores

AUGUST: storm petrel chicks are still in the burrows on Burhou and other islets

SEPTEMBER: migrating warblers and chats rest on Jersey and other islands

OCTOBER: chaffinches from northern Europe join the migrants resting on the islands

NOVEMBER: small numbers of redwings and fieldfares arrive for the winter

DECEMBER: small flocks of Brent geese gather on the coastal mud-flats of several islands

COUNTING
AND LISTING
THE BIRDS

Every newcomer to the study of birds begins by
making a list—if only a mental one—of birds seen and
recognised. But without guidance, list-making can be a barren
exercise, leading only to a long and unmanageable collection of
names. If a list is to have any use it should give some insight
into how birds relate to one another or to their environments;
and this is what ornithologists, confirmed list-makers,
seek to do when they count and classify birds.

CONTENTS

The Census of British Birds

KEEPING TRACK OF THE CHANGING FORTUNES OF BRITISH BIRDS

KNOWING how and why bird populations are changing is essential for effective bird conservation in Britain. The British Trust for Ornithology (BTO) has an international reputation for its monitoring programmes, ranging from the Common Birds Census (CBC), which was unique when it was introduced in 1962, to its newest, the Breeding Bird Survey (BBS), which began in 1994. The BBS is supported by a partnership of BTO, the Joint Nature Conservation Committee and the Royal Society for the Protection of Birds. These studies focus on the numbers of commoner British land birds and rely on the help of thousands of skilled voluntary birdwatchers across the country to measure population change. Keeping track of bird numbers from year to year has the added advantage that birds act as a useful barometer to the health of the wider countryside.

The surveys cannot count all the individuals of common species year after year, but sample surveys are carried out in representative areas. Combining data from sample plots reveals a comprehensive picture of how national populations are faring.

Common Birds Census

The CBC is probably the best-known survey of its kind in the world, and has operated for more than three decades. It is based on what is called a 'territory-mapping' method, in which birdwatchers select plots and carry out about ten well-spaced visits, each breeding season, to record the activities and positions of all the birds they see or hear. These records are translated by trained BTO staff to maps of territory boundaries for each species. Currently, about 230 plots are surveyed each year, mainly in the south and east of Britain. Changes in the number of territories recorded from year to year, when combined across plots, provide a national index of population trend for more than 50 of the most abundant birds.

The CBC has documented much new information about British birds. For example, wrens and other small resident birds are hit hard by freezing weather, but their populations soon bounce back, given mild winters; whereas summer migrants, such as the whitethroat, whose numbers have been reduced by drought in their winter quarters in Africa, have taken many years to recover. Each species is different in the way it reacts to environmental change and in its resilience to new conditions.

Perhaps the most striking finding from the CBC to date is the dramatic decline in the numbers of many seed-eating farmland birds since the 1970s; for example, between 1969 and 1994, tree sparrow numbers decreased on farmland by 89 per cent, grey partridge by 82 per cent, corn bunting by 80 per cent, turtle dove by 77 per cent and reed bunting and skylark by around 60 per cent. These changes have been caused by sophisticated farming practices which have made farmland less supportive of breeding birds. Traditional crop rotations and winter stubbles have been lost, depriving birds of the varied seeds and weeds they need. Spring-sown cereals have been replaced by autumn sowings, which means that, by the time spring comes, the crops are too high for ground-nesting birds. Grassland management has intensified—the regular cutting of silage grass physically damages birds, eggs and nests—and there has been an increase in the use of pesticides and fertilisers, reducing the numbers of insects, weeds and seeds the birds eat. The effects of these changes are indirect—unlike the direct effect of poisonous chemicals used in the 1950s—in that they reduce food supplies and nesting areas for the birds and, consequently, their ability to maintain or increase their numbers.

The plight of familiar, sometimes abundant birds that are in population decline is reflected in the Red Data Birds List. Species of high conservation concern—red-listed birds—now include grey partridge, turtle dove, skylark, song thrush, spotted flycatcher, tree sparrow, linnet, bullfinch, reed bunting and corn bunting, alongside rarer species such as bittern, red kite and corncrake. If the steep declines among common birds continue unabated, they will soon be rare themselves.

Not all species are in decline, and some have increased greatly. Birds on the increase include collared dove, stock dove, wood-pigeon, carrion crow, magpie, sparrowhawk, great spotted woodpecker, nuthatch and blackcap.

The colonisation of western Europe by the collared dove is remarkable. Since the 1930s this now familiar garden species has expanded its range from the Near East to reach most parts of Europe, breeding in Britain for the first time in Norfolk in 1955. The CBC charts the spectacular increase in British collared dove numbers up to the 1980s and the subsequent population stability.

Both carrion crow and magpie seem to have adapted to the loss of wild space by scavenging in urbanised areas, and have benefited from less persecution by gamekeepers.

The recovery of the sparrowhawk is a direct result of the removal of organochlorine pesticides that took such a heavy toll of their population in the 1950s and 1960s; numbers in most places are back to their pre-decline levels.

The reasons for increases among other species

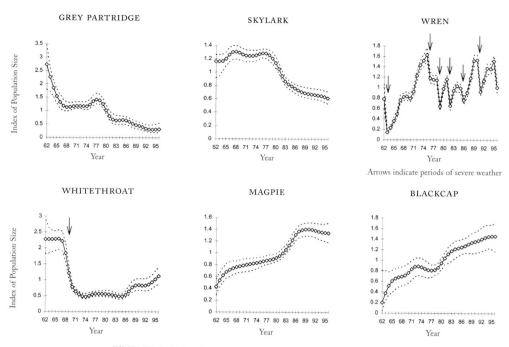

THE FLUCTUATING NUMBERS OF SIX SPECIES

These figures show the changing fortunes of some of the common British birds. This information comes from the British Trust for Ornithology's Common Birds Census. An index of population size is plotted against time in years; a doubling or halving of the index indicates a doubling or halving of population size. The dotted lines indicate the extremes from which the averages are drawn.

The indices for all but the wren show the averaged trend; the wren graph shows year-by-year changes. Grey partridge and skylark numbers have declined dramatically in recent years due to intensification of agriculture. Wren and whitethroat numbers reflect the response to cold winter weather in Britain and to drought in winter grounds in trans-Saharan Africa, respectively.

The reduction in gamekeeping, along with increasing urbanisation, has allowed magpies to flourish, especially during the 1980s, but the reasons for the major increase in blackcap numbers remain unclear.

are more obscure; but some will have benefited from practices such as set-aside and leaving margins of uncultivated land at the edges of fields.

Breeding Bird Survey

Despite the undoubted achievements of the CBC, its uses have been limited by the geographical and habitat limitations of its plots and by the time required for mapping field-work and territory analysis. The BBS was developed with the aim of replacing the CBC's population monitoring role after a period of overlap. The BBS has a better geographical scope of monitoring and covers all habitats, consequently monitoring more bird species. The keys to achieving these improvements were to use a simplified survey method and a formal random sampling design.

BBS is based on 1 km² squares of the National Grid, chosen by computer, on a random basis, to ensure they are representative of the country-side as a whole. Two survey lines are set up across each square, and three site visits are made, one to set up the survey route and two to count birds. Already, more than 2000 BBS squares are surveyed by skilled volunteers each year across the whole country. This means it is possible to monitor around 100 different species from year to year—the best coverage of birds and their habitats ever available here.

The BBS is still relatively new and many years of repeat surveys will be needed to pick up long-term trends in breeding bird numbers, but already it has shown that more than half of British skylarks, dunnocks, goldfinches, linnets and reed buntings breed on farmland, and half of our starlings and house sparrows breed in built-up areas, alongside about a quarter of our song thrushes and blackbirds. This proves that the same species of bird may rely on different habitats in the countryside and means that it is possible to put figures to how bird populations are divided among habitats and, as a result, rate the conservation value of each habitat.

About the BTO

The BTO is the leading research organisation studying Britain's birds and their habitats. Since 1933, tens of thousands of BTO members and other volunteers have monitored bird populations throughout Britain in a unique partnership with the survey organisers and scientists based at the Trust's headquarters in Thetford, Norfolk. The research is impartial and often has an important role to play in shaping conservation measures.

The BTO conducts many nationwide surveys in addition to the CBC and BBS, including Garden Birdwatch—an ongoing survey of garden birds—and the Nest Records Scheme—a survey of nesting among Britain's birds. The BTO also administers the National Bird-ringing Scheme, which provides valuable insights into the survival rates and movements of birds, and also organises initiatives such as National Nest-box Week. Any birdwatcher can get involved: the keen beginner is as welcome as the seasoned expert. Contact the Membership Secretary, British Trust for Ornithology, at the address given on page 417.

The rarest on record

Almost every year some lucky bird-watcher is still able to find a new species to add to the list of birds seen in the British Isles. These lists include records up to 1997.

BIRDS FROM OCEANIC ISLANDS

Black-browed albatross *Diomedea melanophris;* about 30 records

Fea's petrel *Pterodroma feae;* 20 records, all 1974-97

Capped petrel *Pterodroma hasitata;* 2 records, in Nov-Dec 1850, Dec 1984

Bulwer's petrel *Bulweria bulwerii;* 4 records, in 1837, 1908, 1975, 1990

Little shearwater *Puffinus assimilis;* 90 records, the majority since 1957

Wilson's petrel *Oceanites oceanicus;* 22 coastal records, plus others at sea

White-faced petrel *Pelagodroma marina;* 1 record, in Jan 1897

Swinhoe's petrel *Oceanodroma monorhis;* several, 1989-94

Madeiran petrel *Oceanodroma castro;* 2 records, in Nov 1911 and Oct 1931

Magnificent frigatebird *Fregata magnificens;* 1 record, summer 1953

Bridled tern *Sterna anaethetus;* 21 records (some birds found dead), 1931-94

Sooty tern *Sterna fuscata;* 26 records, but only 10 since 1955

Ancient murrelet *Synthliboramphus antiquus;* 1 record, in 1990-1

BIRDS FROM AFRICA

Allen's gallinule *Porphyrula alleni;* 1 record, in Jan 1902

Lesser crested tern *Sterna bengalensis;* 6 records, all 1982-97, including one breeding with Sandwich tern as mate

House swift *Apus affinis;* 12 records, all between 1967 and 1997

White-crowned black wheatear *Oenanthe leucopyga;* 1 record, June 1982

Trumpeter finch *Rhodopechys githaginea;* 7 records, in 1971 (2), 1981, 1984, 1985, 1987, 1992

BIRDS FROM NORTH AMERICA

Pied-billed grebe *Podilymbus podiceps;* 20 records, all since 1963

Black duck *Anas rubripes;* 22 records, all 1954-97

Lesser scaup *Aythya affinis;* 20 records, all since 1987

Bufflehead *Bucephala albeola;* 9 records, 1830-1994

Hooded merganser *Mergus cucullatus;* 5 records, most in 19th century

Sora *Porzana carolina;* 12 records, 1864-1991

Killdeer *Charadrius vociferus;* 54 records, the majority since 1957

American golden plover *Pluvialis dominica;* 200 records, now annual

Semipalmated sandpiper *Calidris pusilla;* 85 records, all since 1953

Western sandpiper *Calidris mauri;* 8 records, all since 1953

Least sandpiper *Calidris minutilla;* 35 records, 29 since 1962

White-rumped sandpiper *Calidris fuscicollis;* 400 records, now annual

Baird's sandpiper *Calidris bairdii;* 190 records, now noted annually

Stilt sandpiper *Micropalama himantopus;* 27 records, 1 in 1954, rest since 1962

Eskimo curlew *Numenius borealis;* 7 records, last in 1887

Upland sandpiper *Bartramia longicauda;* 48 records, the majority since 1960

Greater yellowlegs *Tringa melanoleuca;* 32 records, all 20th century

Solitary sandpiper *Tringa solitaria;* 29 records, majority since 1962

Spotted sandpiper *Actitis macularia;* 120 records, the majority since 1957; pair bred in Scotland in 1975

Wilson's phalarope *Phalaropus tricolor;* 270 records, all since 1954

Laughing gull *Larus atricilla;* 80 records, the majority since 1957

Franklin's gull *Larus pipixcan;* 33 records, 1970-96

Bonaparte's gull *Larus philadelphia;* 100 records, most of them since 1961

Forster's tern *Sterna forsteri;* 26 records, all since 1954

Black-billed cuckoo *Coccyzus erythropthalmus;* 13 records, latest 1990

Common nighthawk *Chordeiles minor;* 14 records, 1927-89

Chimney swift *Chaetura pelagica;* 5 records, 1982 (2), 1986, 1987, 1991

Belted kingfisher *Ceryle alcyon;* 5 records, 1908 and 1978-85

Cliff swallow *Hirundo pyrrhonota;* 6 records, all 1983-97

American pipit *Anthus rubescens;* 6 records, latest 1996

Hermit thrush *Catharus guttatus;* 6 records, all 1975-95

Grey-cheeked thrush *Catharus minimus;* 43 records, all since 1953

Swainson's thrush *Catharus ustulatus;* 21 records, all since 1956

American robin *Turdus migratorius;* 31 records, all since 1952

Red-eyed vireo *Vireo olivaceus;* 110 records, all since 1951

Black-and-white warbler *Mniotilta varia;* 15 records, in 1936 and 1975-96

Northern parula *Parula americana;* 16 records, 1966-8 (3), 1983-95 (13)

Yellow warbler *Dendroica petechia;* 5 records, 1964-95

Yellow-rumped warbler *Dendroica coronata;* 22 records, in 1955, 1960, 1968-95

Blackpoll warbler *Dendroica striata;* 35 records, all since 1968

American redstart *Setophaga ruticilla;* 7 records, 1967, 1968, 1982 (2), 1983, 1985 (2)

Northern waterthrush *Seiurus noveboracensis;* 7 records, 1958-96

Yellowthroat *Geothlypis trichas;* 6 records, 1954, 1984 (2), 1989, 1996, 1997

Scarlet tanager *Piranga olivacea;* 7 records, all in autumn, since 1973

Song sparrow *Melospiza melodia;* 7 records, all 1959-94

White-throated sparrow *Zonotrichia albicollis;* 21 records, 1 in 1909 and the rest 1961-96

Dark-eyed junco *Junco hyemalis;* 20 records, in 1905 and 1960-96

Rose-breasted grosbeak *Pheucticus ludovicianus;* 24 records, all 1957-95

Bobolink *Dolichonyx oryzivorous;* 20 records, 1962-96

Baltimore oriole *Icterus galbula;* 19 records, all since 1958

The following North American birds have been noted just 1-4 times: **Double-crested cormorant** *Phalacrocorax auritus* (1988-9, 1995-6); **Green heron** *Butorides striatus* (1889, 1982, 1987); **Redhead** *Aythya americana* (1996-7); **Bald eagle** *Haliaeetus leucocephalus* (1973, 1987); **American kestrel** *Falco sparverius* (2 in 1976); **American purple gallinule** *Porphyrula martinica* (Nov 1958); **American coot** *Fulica americana* (1981, 1996); **Sandhill crane** *Grus canadensis* (1905, 1981, 1991); **Semipalmated plover** *Charadrius semipalmatus* (1978, 1997); **Short-billed dowitcher** *Limnodromus griseus* (1985); **Hudsonian godwit** *Limosa haemastica* (1982-3, 1988); **Royal tern** *Sterna maxima* (1954, 1965, 1971, 1979); **Elegant tern** *Sterna elegans* (July 1982); **Least tern** *Sterna antillarum* (1990-1); **Mourning dove** *Zenaida macroura* (Oct 1989); **Yellow-bellied sapsucker** *Sphyrapicus varius* (1975, 1988); **Eastern phoebe** *Sayornis phoebe* (April 1987); **Tree swallow** *Tachycineta bicolor* (June 1990); **Cedar waxwing** *Bombycilla cedrorum* (Feb-March 1996); **Northern mockingbird** *Mimus polyglottus* (1982, 1988); **Brown thrasher** *Toxostoma rufum* (1966-7); **Grey catbird** *Dumetella carolinensis* (April 1987); **Varied thrush** *Zoothera naevia* (Nov 1982); **Wood thrush** *Hylocichla mustelina* (Oct 1987); **Veery** *C. fuscescens* (1970, 1987, 1995); **Red-breasted nuthatch** *Sitta canadensis* (1989-90); **Yellow-throated vireo** *Vireo flavifrons* (Sept 1990); **Philadelphia vireo** *Vireo philadelphicus* (1985, 1987); **Evening grosbeak** *Hesperiphona vespertina* (1969, 1980); **Golden-winged warbler** *Vermivora chrysoptera* (Jan-April 1989); **Tennessee warbler** *Vermivora. peregrina* (2 in 1975, 1982, 1995); **Chestnut-sided warbler** *Dendroica pensylvanica* (1985, 1995); **Blackburnian warbler** *Dendroica fusca* (1961, 1988); **Cape May warbler** *Dendroica tigrina* (June 1977); **Magnolia warbler** *Dendroica magnolia* (Sept 1981); **Bay-breasted warbler** *Dendroica castanea* (Oct 1995); **Ovenbird** *Seiurus aurocapillus* (1969, 1973, 1977, 1985); **Hooded warbler** *Wilsonia citrina* (Sept 1970); **Wilson's warbler** *W. pusilla* (Oct 1985); **Summer tanager** *Piranga rubra* (Sept 1957); **Eastern towhee** *Pipilo erythrophthalmus* (June 1967); **Lark sparrow** *Chondestes grammacus* (1981, 1991); **Savannah sparrow** *Passerculus sandwichensis* (1982, 1987); **Fox sparrow** *Zonotrichia iliaca* (June 1961); **White-crowned sparrow** *Zonotrichia leucophrys* (2 in 1977, 1 in 1995); **Indigo bunting** *Passerina cyanea* (1985, 1996); **Brown-headed cowbird** *Molothrus ater* (April 1988).

BIRDS FROM EUROPE

White-billed diver *Gavia adamsii;* 190 records, nearly all since 1957

Cattle egret *Bubulcus ibis;* 75 records, including 20 individuals in 1992

Great white egret *Egretta alba;* 90 records, most since 1958

Harlequin duck *Histrionicus histrionicus;* 14 records, most recent in 1996

Black kite *Milvus migrans;* 250 records, now annual

Egyptian vulture *Neophron percnopterus;* 2 records, October 1825 and September 1868

Griffon vulture *Gyps fulvus;* 3 records, 1 in spring 1843, 2 in June 1927

Pallid harrier *Circus macrourus;* 6 records, 1931-96

Spotted eagle *Aquila clanga;* 14 records, all before 1915

Lesser kestrel *Falco naumanni;* 17 records, 11 before 1926, rest 1968-92

Eleonora's falcon *Falco eleonorae;* 3 records, 1977, 1981, 1985

Sociable plover *Vanellus gregarius;* 38 records, since 1860

White-tailed plover *Vanellus leucurus;* 4 records, 1975, 1979, 1984 (2)

Marsh sandpiper *Tringa stagnatilis;* 100 records, most since 1963

Terek sandpiper *Xenus cinereus;* 46 records, all since 1951

Slender-billed gull *Larus genei;* 6 records, 1960, 1963, 1971 (2), 1987 (2)

Great black-headed gull *Larus ichthyaetus;* 5 records, all 1859-1932

Brünnich's guillemot *Uria lomvia;* 35 records, majority since 1968

Great spotted cuckoo *Clamator glandarius;* 39 records, all but 6 since 1958

Hawk owl *Surnia ulula;* 11 records, 1830-1983

Red-necked nightjar *Caprimulgus ruficollis;* 1 record, in Oct 1856

Pallid swift *Apus pallidus;* 11 records, 1978-96

Calandra lark *Melanocorypha calandra;* 6 records, all since 1961

White-winged lark *Melanocorypha leucoptera;* 2 records, 1869, 1981

Lesser short-toed lark *Calandrella rufescens;* 5 records (43 birds) 1956-92

Crested lark *Galerida cristata;* 20 records: 10 in 19th century, 10 from 1947 to 1996

Crag martin *Ptyonoprogne rupestris;* 4 records, all 1988-95

Red-rumped swallow *Hirundo daurica;* more than 300 records, all but 3 since 1949

Citrine wagtail *Motacilla citreola;* 100 records, all since 1954

Rufous bushchat *Cercotrichas galactotes;* 11 records, 4 in 19th century, rest 1951-80

Thrush nightingale *Luscinia luscinia;* 125 records, 1 in 1911, the rest since 1957

Red-flanked bluetail *Tarsiger cyanurus;* 16 records, 1903, 1947, 1956, 1960, 1971-95

Moussier's redstart *Phoenicurus moussieri;* 1 record, April 1988

Isabelline wheatear *Oenanthe isabellina;* 12 records, in 1887 and 1977 onwards

Pied wheatear *Oenanthe pleschanka;* 35 records, latest 1996

Rock thrush *Monticola saxatilis;* 28 records, most recent Oct 1996

Blue rock thrush *Monticola solitarius;* 2 records, 1985, 1987

Fan-tailed warbler *Cisticola juncidis;* 4 records, 1962, 1976, 1977, 1985

River warbler *Locustella fluviatilis;* 28 records, from 1961 onwards

Moustached warbler *Acrocephalus melanopogon;* pair bred in 1956; 5 other records, 1951 (2), 1952, 1965, 1979

Blyth's reed warbler *Acrocephalus dumetorum;* 40 records, most since 1957

Olivaceous warbler *Hippolais pallida;* 17 records, all since 1951

Booted warbler *Hippolais caligata;* 70 records, 1936 and 1959 onwards

Marmora's warbler *Sylvia sarda;* 3 records, 1982, 1992, 1993

Spectacled warbler *Sylvia conspicillata;* 2 records, 1992, 1997

Sardinian warbler *Sylvia melanocephala;* 53 records, all since 1953

Rüppell's warbler *Sylvia rueppelli;* 5 records, 1977, 1979, 1990, 1992, 1995

Desert warbler *Sylvia nana;* 10 records, all between 1970 and 1993

Orphean warbler *Sylvia hortensis;* 6 records, 1948, 1955, 1967, 1981, 1982, 1991

Bonelli's warbler *Phylloscopus bonelli;* 140 records, now annual in autumn

Collared flycatcher *Ficedula albicollis;* 20 records, all 1947-97

Wallcreeper *Tichodroma muraria;* 10 records: 6 before 1938, 4 since 1969

Short-toed treecreeper *Certhia brachydactyla;* 18 records, all since 1979

Penduline tit *Remiz pendulinus;* 120 records, all 1966-97

Spanish sparrow *Passer hispaniolensis;* 6 records, all 1966-97

Rock sparrow *Petronia petronia;* 1 record, in 1981

Two-barred crossbill *Loxia leucoptera;* 120 records, most since 1957

Pine grosbeak *Pinicola enucleator;* 9 records, but only 3 since 1957

Rock bunting *Emberiza cia;* 6 records, 1902-67

Cretzschmar's bunting *Emberiza caesia;* 2 records, June 1967 and June 1979

Yellow-breasted bunting *Emberiza aureola;* 200 records, majority since 1966

Black-headed bunting *Emberiza melanocephala;* 130 records, most since 1958

Spotless starling *Sturnus unicolor;* first in 1998

BIRDS FROM ASIA

Steller's eider *Polysticta stelleri;* 14 records, 1830-1996

Houbara bustard *Chlamydotis undulata;* 5 records, 4 in 1847-98 and 1 in 1962

Oriental pratincole *Glareola maldivarum;* 5 records, 1981-93

Black-winged pratincole *Glareola nordmanni;* 32 records, most since 1955

Lesser sandplover *Charadrius mongolus;* 1 in 1997

Greater sandplover *Charadrius leschenaultii;* 12 records, all since 1978

Caspian plover *Charadrius asiaticus;* 4 records, 1890, 1988 (2), 1996

Pacific golden plover *Pluvialis fulva;* 40 records, 1976-96

Great knot *Calidris tenuirostris;* 2 records, Sept 1989, Oct 1995

Red-necked stint *Calidris ruficollis;* 4 records, 1986, 1992, 1994, 1995

Long-toed stint *Calidris subminuta;* 2 records, 1970, 1982

Sharp-tailed sandpiper *Calidris acuminata;* 24 records, most since 1956

Little whimbrel *Numenius minutus;* 2 records, both Aug-Sept, in 1982 and 1985

Grey-tailed tattler *Heteroscelus brevipes;* 2 records, 1981, 1994

Ross's gull *Rhodostethia rosea;* 75 records, all but 2 since 1960

Aleutian tern *Sterna aleutica;* 1 record, in 1979

Pallas's sandgrouse *Syrrhaptes paradoxus;* major irruptions till 1908, bred 1888-9; only 7 records since, all 1964-90

Rufous turtle dove *Streptopelia orientalis;* 5 records, latest 1975

Egyptian nightjar *Caprimulgus aegyptius;* 2 records, June 1883 and June 1984

Needle-tailed swift *Hirundapus caudacutus;* 8 records, most recent 1991

Pacific swift *Apus pacificus;* 3 records, 1981, 1993, 1995

Blue-cheeked bee-eater *Merops superciliosus;* 8 records, 1921-97

Bimaculated lark *Melanocorypha bimaculata;* 3 records, 1962, 1975, 1976

Blyth's pipit *Anthus godlewskii;* 8 records, 1882, 1990-6

Olive-backed pipit *Anthus hodgsoni;* 200 records, 1 in 1948, remainder since 1964

Pechora pipit *Anthus gustavi;* 62 records, most since 1967

Siberian rubythroat *Luscinia calliope;* 2 records, 1975, 1997

White-throated robin *Irania gutturalis;* 2 records, June 1983, May 1990

Desert wheatear *Oenanthe deserti;* 54 records, all but 8 since 1949

Siberian thrush *Zoothera sibirica;* 6 records, in 1954 and 1977-94

Eyebrowed thrush *Turdus obscurus;* 16 records, all since 1964

Dusky thrush *Turdus naumanni;* 10 records, in 1905 and 1959-91

Black-throated thrush *Turdus ruficollis;* 40 records, all but 2 since 1957

Pallas's grasshopper warbler *Locustella certhiola;* 20 records, latest 1997

Lanceolated warbler *Locustella lanceolata;* 70 records, 1908-96

Paddyfield warbler *Acrocephalus agricola;* 40 records, most since 1969

Thick-billed warbler *Acrocephalus aedon;* 2 records, Oct 1955 and Sept 1971

Pallas's warbler *Phylloscopus proregulus;* 1000 records, now autumn annual

Radde's warbler *Phylloscopus schwarzi;* 170 records, 1 in 1898, remainder since 1961

Dusky warbler *Phylloscopus fuscatus;* 180 records, 1 in 1913, the rest since 1961

Eastern Bonelli's warbler *Phylloscopus orientalis;* 3 records, 1987, 1995, 1997

Brown shrike *Lanius cristatus;* 1 record, in 1985

Isabelline shrike *Lanius isabellinus;* 50 records, 1 in 1950, remainder 1959-97

Steppe grey shrike *Lanius pallidirostris;* 14 records, 1956-97

Black-faced bunting *Emberiza spodocephala;* 1 record, in March 1994

Pine bunting *Emberiza leucocephala;* 36 records, latest in 1996

Yellow-browed bunting *Emberiza chrysophrys;* 3 records, 1975, 1980, 1992

Pallas's reed bunting *Emberiza pallasi;* 3 records, 1975, 1981, 1990

Red-headed bunting *Emberiza bruniceps;* 200 records, but mainly cage-bird escapes

The birds of the world

A GUIDE TO SCIENTIFIC CLASSIFICATION

THE number of different kinds of birds surviving throughout the world used to be put as high as 25,000. All were obviously birds, because they all had toothless bills, two wings (or the remains of them), two legs, feathers and warm blood; and all laid eggs.

But many ornithologists suspected that this number was inflated because what was basically the same species was being given different names wherever it showed a regional variation.

In addition, confusion was caused by the fact that a single species had different names in different countries, or parts of countries.

The modern system of names and groups stems from the work of the Swedish naturalist Carl von Linné (usually known by the Latin version of his name, Linnaeus) and especially from the 1758 edition of his book *Systema Naturae*. His system draws on Latin as an international language.

How the system works

The modern system of classifying birds is like a pyramid, with the base formed by some 8600 different species. A convenient definition of the word species is: 'an interbreeding group of birds which do not normally mate with other such groups'.

The next division above the species is the genus—a group of species showing strong similarities. The scientific name of a bird gives the genus first, then the species. Thus, the scientific name of the golden eagle is *Aquila chrysaëtos* (eagle, golden). When a bird is identified by three names in this book, the third one shows that it belongs to a sub-species or separate race. The hooded crow, for example, is *Corvus corone cornix*; the third name distinguishes it from the carrion crow, *Corvus corone corone*, with which it can interbreed.

When there are strong points of similarity between one genus and another the birds in them are said to belong to the same family. The golden eagle, for instance, is one of the *Accipitridae* (literally swift-winged birds). Families with broadly similar characteristics are grouped together into 27 Orders; and the golden eagle falls into the Order of *Falconiformes* (falcon-like birds). Finally, all of the Orders make up the Class *Aves* (birds).

The golden eagle can be classified as follows:

CLASS	*Aves*	(Birds)
ORDER	*Falconiformes*	(Falcon-like birds)
FAMILY	*Accipitridae*	(Hawks and eagles)
GENUS	*Aquila*	(Eagles)
SPECIES	*Aquila chrysaëtos*	(Golden eagle)

This elaborate system is of great value to scientists. It has enabled them to reduce the 25,000 kinds of bird at one time recognised to some 8600 genuinely different species. But it is only a framework made for their convenience, and a fallible one at that. Many birds are difficult to group, and ornithologists have often differed over which group a particular bird belongs to.

Placing a bird in the right Order depends primarily on subtle features of its anatomy—especially of the palate, bill, legs, feet and breastbone. Such features are a more trustworthy guide to how closely birds are related than, for instance, the shape of the wings.

Britain's share of the world's birds

In Britain there is a fair cross-section of the birds of the world. Many absentees are birds such as the toucan and the hornbill, which rely largely on fruit throughout the year, or the hummingbird and sunbird, which are equally dependent on nectar. A climate as highly seasonal as ours seldom allows a constant supply of any one type of food.

Generally speaking, specialised feeders on fruit, leaves, nectar and large insects are absent. Some of the game-birds provide exceptions—particularly the grouse, which feeds on the virtually evergreen heather; and the red-backed shrike, which takes many large insects but is a migrant. Migration allows birds to live in Britain for just as long as their type of food is available. The availability of small insects in summer, for instance, attracts swifts, swallows and martins, warblers and flycatchers.

Other species are absent because the conditions which produced them in other parts of the world did not apply in Britain.

Still other absentees are due to the actions of man, in destroying the habitats or in shooting birds and spraying crops with poisonous chemicals. These absentees include the great bustard and the black tern.

Geographical divisions

As well as classifying birds into Orders, families and so on, zoologists have also split them up geographically, dividing the world into six major regions and one minor one. The vast majority of species breed in one region without the breeding range overlapping far into another, though the boundaries between regions are often transitional zones rather than precise lines.

The regions are:

PALAEARCTIC Europe; Near and Middle East; Africa north of the Sahara; islands of north Atlantic; Asia north of the Himalayas;

ETHIOPIAN Africa south of the Sahara;

MALAGASY (SUB-REGION) Madagascar; islands in the western Indian Ocean;

ORIENTAL Rest of Asia south of the Himalayas; Borneo; Malaysia; Sumatra;

AUSTRALASIAN Australia; New Zealand; New Guinea; Flores and Celebes;

NEARCTIC North America;

NEOTROPICAL South and Central America; Caribbean.

Other oceanic islands and Antarctica are not included in any region.

Most of the birds in the British list breed only in the Palaearctic region, but a few are found in other regions as well, including the Neotropical (roseate tern), Australasian (common tern) and Malagasy (peregrine).

THE NATURAL ORDERS OF BIRDS

Struthioniformes
OSTRICH: 1

Rheiformes
RHEAS: 2

Casuariiformes
CASSOWARIES: 3
EMUS: 2

Apterygiformes
KIWIS: 3

All of the birds in the four groups above, sometimes known collectively as Ratites, are flightless, and most are large

Tinamiformes
Very like game-birds, but not related
TINAMOUS: 32

Sphenisciformes
The great auk, which became extinct in 1844, came nearest to being a replacement in northern seas
PENGUINS: 17

Gaviiformes
Web-footed, fish-eating birds; usually breed on lakes and ponds and live on sea in winter; known as 'loons' in N. America
DIVERS: 4 (3)

Podicipediformes
Fish-eaters, with lobed toes
GREBES: 20 (4)

Procellariiformes
Mainly large birds, with long, narrow wings
ALBATROSSES: 14
PETRELS and SHEARWATERS: 56 (2)
STORM PETRELS: 18 (2)
DIVING PETRELS: 18

Pelecaniformes
Fish-eating birds; expert divers
TROPIC BIRDS: 3
PELICANS: 6
GANNETS: 9 (1)
CORMORANTS: 30 (2)
DARTER: 1
FRIGATE BIRDS: 5

Ciconiiformes
Many of these are large, long-legged birds, living in marshes
HERONS: 59 (2)
SHOEBILL: 1
HAMMERHEAD: 1
STORKS: 16
IBISES and SPOONBILLS: 28 (1)
FLAMINGOES (though some ornithologists put them in a separate Order): 6

Anseriformes
SCREAMERS: 3
DUCKS, GEESE and SWANS: 145 (30)

Falconiformes
Day-hunting birds of prey
NEW WORLD VULTURES: 6
HAWKS and OLD WORLD VULTURES: 207 (8)
FALCONS and CARACARAS: 58 (4)
SECRETARY BIRD: 1

Galliformes
Game-birds; mainly ground-dwelling grain-eaters, capable only of short bursts of flight
MEGAPODES: 10
CURASSOWS: 38
GROUSE: 18 (4)
PHEASANTS and QUAIL: 165 (4)
GUINEAFOWL: 7
TURKEYS: 2
HOATZIN (often put in a separate Order; they have claws on their wings): 2

Gruiformes
A mixed group, including coots which are poor flyers but are at home on water, and cranes, which fly over vast distances on migration
MESITES: 3
BUTTON-QUAILS: 15
CRANES: 14
LIMPKIN: 1
TRUMPETERS: 3
RAILS and COOTS: 132 (5)
FINFOOT: 3
KAGU: 1
SUNBITTERN: 1
SERIEMA: 2
BUSTARDS: 23

Charadriiformes
This Order includes the wading birds and those which have evolved from them—the gulls, terns and auks
JACANAS: 7
PAINTED SNIPE: 2
OYSTERCATCHERS: 6 (1)
PLOVERS and SURF BIRDS: 63
SNIPE and SANDPIPERS: 77 (22)
AVOCETS: 7 (1)
PHALAROPES: 3 (1)
CRAB-PLOVER: 1
STONE CURLEWS: 9 (1)
PRATINCOLES and COURSERS: 16
SEED-SNIPE: 4
SHEATH-BILLS: 2
SKUAS: 4 (2)
GULLS and TERNS: 82 (12)
SKIMMERS: 3
AUKS and AUKLETS: 22 (4)

Columbiformes
Good flyers; grain- or fruit-eaters; the extinct dodo was an outsized flightless pigeon
SANDGROUSE: 16
PIGEONS: 289 (6)

Psittaciformes
Vegetarian birds, found in the Tropics
PARROTS: 315

Cuculiformes
Some build nests, but most lay their eggs in the nests of other birds
TURACOS: 19
CUCKOOS and ANIS: 127 (1)

Strigiformes
Most are night hunters; their large, frontally placed eyes have high light-gathering power
BARN-OWLS: 11 (1)
OWLS: 123 (4)

Caprimulgiformes
Twilight hunters, living off insects which are taken on the wing
OILBIRD: 1
FROGMOUTHS: 12
POTOOS: 5
OWLET-FROGMOUTHS: 7
NIGHTJARS: 67 (1)

Apodiformes
The most aerial of birds; swifts even sleep on the wing
SWIFTS: 76 (1)
CRESTED SWIFTS: 3
HUMMINGBIRDS: 319

Coliiformes
These are small, long-tailed birds found only in Africa; their diet consists mainly of fruit and insects
MOUSEBIRDS: 6

Trogoniformes
Small to medium-sized birds of tropical forests in Africa and South America; mainly tree-living, varied diets of insects and seeds
TROGONS: 34

Coraciiformes
These birds are often brightly coloured
KINGFISHERS: 87 (1)
TODIES: 5
MOTMOTS: 8
BEE-EATERS: 24
CUCKOO ROLLERS: 1
GROUND ROLLERS: 16
HOOPOE: 1 (1)
WOOD-HOOPOES: 6
HORNBILLS: 45

Piciformes
Woodpeckers, the largest family in the group, are highly specialised at boring into wood for insects
JACAMARS: 15
PUFF-BIRDS: 30
BARBETS: 72
HONEY-GUIDES: 11
TOUCANS: 37
WOODPECKERS: 224 (4)

Passeriformes
Perching birds; all have their toes so arranged that they can grip a perch; all are known as song-birds, though a few, such as shrikes, do not have complex songs
BROADBILLS: 14
WOODCREEPERS: 63
OVENBIRDS: 209
ANTBIRDS: 238
ANTPIPITS: 12
TAPACULOS: 28
PITTAS: 23
ASITYS: 2
NEW ZEALAND WRENS: 4
TYRANT FLYCATCHERS: 365
MANAKINS: 59
COTINGAS: 90
PLANTCUTTERS: 3
LYREBIRDS: 2
SCRUB-BIRDS: 2
LARKS: 74 (2)
SWALLOWS: 75 (3)
PIPITS and WAGTAILS: 48 (6)
CUCKOO-SHRIKES: 58
BULBULS: 109
LEAFBIRDS: 10
SHRIKES: 72 (1)
VANGAS: 11
WAXWINGS and SILKY FLYCATCHERS: 7 (1)
PALCHAT: 1
DIPPERS: 5 (1)
WRENS: 63 (1)
MOCKINGBIRDS: 30
ACCENTORS: 12 (1)
THRUSHES, WARBLERS and FLYCATCHERS: 1361 (29)
(Including, for convenience, the babblers)
TITS: 64 (7)
NUTHATCHES: 23 (1)
TREECREEPERS: 11 (1)
AUSTRALIAN TREECREEPERS: 6
FLOWERPECKERS: 54
SUNBIRDS: 106
WHITE-EYES: 80
HONEYEATERS: 160
BUNTINGS and TANAGERS: 383 (5)
NEW WORLD WARBLERS: 109
HAWAIIAN HONEYCREEPERS: 22
VIREOS: 41
NEW WORLD ORIOLES: 88
FINCHES: 176 (11)
WEAVER-FINCHES and WHYDAHS: 108
SPARROWS: 155 (2)
STARLINGS and OXPECKERS: 103 (1)
ORIOLES: 32
DRONGOS: 20
WATTLEBIRDS: 3
MAGPIE-LARKS: 2
WOODSWALLOWS: 10
BELL-MAGPIES: 13
BOWERBIRDS: 17
BIRDS OF PARADISE: 43
CROWS: 100 (8)

Total: 8514 (217)

The generally accepted method of classification is followed here, starting with the most primitive birds and, as far as is possible in the present state of knowledge, working through to the most advanced—the crows. Orders are listed in bold type, and families in capitals. The first figure after a family name gives the number of species belonging to it throughout the world; the figure in brackets gives the number of species commonly seen in Britain, and illustrated on pp. 38–266.

BRITISH BIRDS IN THEIR FAMILIES

Diver family
Black-throated diver
Great northern diver
Red-throated diver
Grebe family
Slavonian grebe
Great crested grebe
Red-necked grebe
Black-necked grebe
Dabchick
Petrel family
Fulmar
Cory's shearwater
Great shearwater
Sooty shearwater
Balearic shearwater
Manx shearwater
Storm petrel family
Storm petrel
Leach's petrel
Gannet family
Gannet
Cormorant family
Shag
Cormorant
Heron family
American bittern
Bittern
Little bittern
Night heron
Squacco heron
Little egret
Heron
Purple heron
Ibis family
Spoonbill
Glossy ibis
Stork family
White stork
Black stork
Flamingo family
Flamingo
Duck family
Greylag goose
Brent goose
Canada goose
Barnacle goose
Red-breasted goose
White-fronted goose
Pink-footed goose
Snow goose
Lesser white-fronted goose
Bean goose
Bewick's swan
Whooper swan
Mute swan
Ruddy shelduck
Shelduck
Egyptian goose
American wigeon
Pintail
Shoveler
Teal
Blue-winged teal
Wigeon
Mallard
Garganey
Gadwall
Red-crested pochard
Pochard
Tufted duck
Scaup
Ferruginous duck
Mandarin duck
Eider
King eider
Velvet scoter
Common scoter
Surf scoter
Long-tailed duck
Goldeneye
Smew
Goosander
Red-breasted merganser
Ruddy duck
Hawk family
Osprey
Honey buzzard
Kite
Sea eagle
Goshawk
Sparrowhawk
Buzzard
Rough-legged buzzard
Golden eagle
Marsh harrier
Hen-harrier
Montagu's harrier
Falcon family
Merlin
Peregrine

Gyr falcon
Hobby
Kestrel
Red-footed falcon
Grouse family
Red grouse
Ptarmigan
Black grouse
Capercaillie
Pheasant family
Partridge
Red-legged partridge
Quail
Bobwhite quail
Pheasant
Reeves's pheasant
Lady Amherst's pheasant
Golden pheasant
Crane family
Crane
Bustard family
Great bustard
Little bustard
Rail family
Water rail
Little crake
Spotted crake
Baillon's crake
Corncrake
Moorhen
Coot
Oystercatcher family
Oystercatcher
Sandpiper family
Kentish plover
Little ringed plover
Ringed plover
Dotterel
Golden plover
Grey plover
Lapwing
Turnstone
Sanderling
Dunlin
Knot
Curlew sandpiper
Purple sandpiper
Pectoral sandpiper
Little stint
Temminck's stint
Ruff
Buff-breasted sandpiper
Broad-billed sandpiper
Long-billed dowitcher
Spotted redshank
Lesser yellowlegs
Wood sandpiper
Common sandpiper
Greenshank
Green sandpiper
Redshank
Black-tailed godwit
Bar-tailed godwit
Curlew
Whimbrel
Woodcock
Snipe
Great snipe
Jack snipe
Avocet family
Black-winged stilt
Avocet
Phalarope family
Grey phalarope
Red-necked phalarope
Stone curlew family
Stone curlew
Pratincole family
Cream-coloured courser
Pratincole
Skua family
Long-tailed skua
Arctic skua
Pomarine skua
Great skua
Gull family
Herring gull
Yellow-legged gull
Common gull
Lesser black-backed gull
Iceland gull
Glaucous gull
Great black-backed gull
Mediterranean gull
Little gull
Black-headed gull
Sabine's gull
Kittiwake
Ivory gull
Whiskered tern

White-winged black tern
Black tern
Gull-billed tern
Caspian tern
Little tern
Roseate tern
Common tern
Arctic tern
Sandwich tern
Auk family
Little auk
Razorbill
Guillemot
Black guillemot
Puffin
Pigeon family
Rock dove
Feral pigeon
Stock dove
Wood-pigeon
Collared dove
Barbary dove
Turtle dove
Parrot family
Ring-necked parakeet
Cuckoo family
Cuckoo
Yellow-billed cuckoo
Barn owl family
Barn owl
Owl family
Snowy owl
Short-eared owl
Long-eared owl
Scops owl
Tengmalm's owl
Little owl
Tawny owl
Nightjar family
Nightjar
Swift family
Swift
Alpine swift
Kingfisher family
Kingfisher
Bee-eater family
Bee-eater
Roller family
Roller
Hoopoe family
Hoopoe
Woodpecker family
Wryneck
Green woodpecker
Black woodpecker
Great spotted woodpecker
Lesser spotted woodpecker
Lark family
Short-toed lark
Shore lark
Woodlark
Skylark
Swallow family
Sand martin
Swallow
House martin
Pipit family
Tawny pipit
Red-throated pipit
Pechora pipit
Richard's pipit
Meadow pipit
Rock pipit
Tree pipit
Pied wagtail
Grey wagtail
Yellow wagtail
Shrike family
Red-backed shrike
Great grey shrike
Lesser grey shrike
Woodchat shrike
Waxwing family
Waxwing
Dipper family
Dipper
Wren family
Wren
Accentor family
Alpine accentor
Dunnock
Flycatcher family
Savi's warbler
Grasshopper warbler
Great reed warbler
Aquatic warbler
Marsh warbler

Sedge warbler
Reed warbler
Icterine warbler
Melodious warbler
Blackcap
Garden warbler
Subalpine warbler
Whitethroat
Lesser whitethroat
Barred warbler
Dartford warbler
Arctic warbler
Greenish warbler
Chiffchaff
Yellow-browed warbler
Wood warbler
Willow warbler
Firecrest
Goldcrest
Pied flycatcher
Red-breasted flycatcher
Spotted flycatcher
Thrush family
Whinchat
Stonechat
Black-eared wheatear
Wheatear
Black redstart
Redstart
Robin
Nightingale
Bluethroat
Redwing
Blackbird
Song thrush
Fieldfare
Ring ouzel
Mistle thrush
White's thrush
Bearded tit
Tit family
Long-tailed tit
Coal tit
Blue tit
Crested tit
Great tit
Willow tit
Marsh tit
Nuthatch family
Nuthatch
Treecreeper family
Treecreeper
Bunting family
Corn bunting
Cirl bunting
Yellowhammer
Ortolan bunting
Little bunting
Rustic bunting
Reed bunting
Lapland bunting
Snow bunting
Finch family
Chaffinch
Brambling
Serin
Goldfinch
Greenfinch
Siskin
Linnet
Redpoll
Twite
Arctic redpoll
Scarlet rosefinch
Pine grosbeak
Crossbill
Scottish crossbill
Two-barred crossbill
Bullfinch
Hawfinch
Sparrow family
House sparrow
Tree sparrow
Starling family
Rose-coloured starling
Starling
Oriole family
Golden oriole
Crow family
Jay
Magpie
Nutcracker
Chough
Raven
Hooded crow
Carrion crow
Rook
Jackdaw

All the birds of the British Isles are given above, apart from the extreme rarities listed on pp. 462–3. Italic type means that a species is illustrated in the guide to rarer birds on pp. 267–80. Profiles and illustrations of the more common birds are given on pp. 38–266.

INDEX

Figures in the bolder type refer to full-page illustrated entries, giving profiles of the birds and distribution maps. Figures in italics are for references which include other illustrations.

Y

ACKNOWLEDGMENTS

Many people and organisations assisted in the preparation of this book. The publishers wish to thank all of them, particularly:

David Bradbury; the staff at the British Museum (Natural History); the British Trust for Ornithology, especially for their permission to adapt an illustration on handling ringed birds; Broadway Arts Ltd; Dr A. J. Charig; the City of Leicester Museum for their invaluable assistance to Raymond Harris Ching; William Condry; John Ebdon (Director of the London Planetarium); Eric Evans; Michael Evans; Christopher Harrigan; Tom Hey; the Home Office; Eric J. Hosking (Vice-President, the Royal Society for the Protection of Birds); the Inter-Governmental Maritime Consultative Organisation; Dr G. V. T. Matthews (Director of Research, the Wildfowl Trust, Slimbridge); John Meek; Dr Kenneth Mellanby (Director of the Nature Conservancy's Monks Wood Experimental Station); Raymond Mills; Brian Norman Associates Ltd; the *Radio Times* Hulton Picture Library; R. O. Richards; the Royal Society for the Protection of Birds, especially for permission to adapt illustrations and instructions on building a bird-table and a nest-box; John Stevens; Judith Taylor; Professor C. Tyler (Head of the Department of Physiology and Biochemistry at Reading University); Giles Wordsworth; the Worshipful Company of Dyers; and the Worshipful Company of Vintners.

The publishers also acknowledge their indebtedness to the following books and journals which were consulted for reference or as sources of illustrations:
Books: *Adaptive Coloration in Animals* by Hugh B. Cott (Methuen); *Animal Dispersion in Relation to Social Behaviour* by V. C. Wynne-Edwards (Oliver and Boyd); *Animal Navigation* by J. D. Carthy (Allen & Unwin); *Animal Societies* by Remy Chauvin (Gollancz); *The Biological Significance of Climatic Changes in Britain* edited by C. G. Johnson and L. P. Smith (Institute of Biology); *Biology and Comparative Physiology of Birds* by A. J. Marshall (2 volumes, Academic Press); *Bird* by Lois and Louis Darling (Methuen); *The Bird Faunas of Africa and its Islands* by R. E. Moreau (Academic Press); *Bird Navigation* by G. V. T. Matthews (Cambridge); *Bird Photography as a Hobby* by Eric Hosking and Cyril Newberry (Stanley Paul); *Bird Recognition* by James Fisher (Penguin Books); *Bird Watching as a Hobby* by W. D. Campbell (Stanley Paul); *The Birds* by O. and K. Heinroth (Faber); *The Birds* by Roger Tory Peterson (Time-Life International); *Birds in Action* by Eric Hosking and Cyril Newberry (Collins); *Birds in Britain* by Kenneth Richmond (Odhams); *Birds in the Balance* by Philip Brown (Deutsch); *The Birds of the British Isles* by David Armitage Bannerman (12 volumes, Oliver and Boyd); *Birds of the British Isles* by Eric Fitch Daglish (Dent); *The Birds of the British Isles and Their Eggs* by T. A. Coward (3 volumes, Warne); *Birds of the London Area*, London Natural History Society (Hart-Davis); *Birds of the North Kent Marshes* by E. H. Gillham and R. C. Holmes (Collins); *The Birds of the Palaearctic Fauna* by Charles Vaury (Witherby); *Birds of the Soviet Union* by G. P. Dement'ev and others (Israel Programme for Scientific Translations); *Birds of the World* by James L. Peters and others (12 volumes, 3 more projected, Museum of Comparative Zoology, Cambridge, Mass.); *British Birds of Prey* by Philip Brown (Deutsch); *British Birds* by F. B. Kirkman and F. C. R. Jourdain (Nelson); *The British Islands and Their Vegetation* by A. G. Tansley (Cambridge); *The British Isles—A Systematic Geography* edited by J. W. Watson and J. B. Sissons (Nelson); *Changes in Status of British Breeding Birds* by J. L. F. Parslow (Witherby, in preparation); *Collins Guide to Bird Watching, Collins Pocket Guide to British Birds, Collins Pocket Guide to Nests and Eggs* all by R. S. R. Fitter (Collins); *Comparative Studies on the Behaviour of the Anatinae* by K. Z. Lorenz (Avicultural Society); *Die Vögel Mitteleuropas* by J. Bauer and others; *Development of Behaviour in Precocial Birds* by M. M. Nice (Linnaean Society, New York); *Ecological Adaptations for Breeding in Birds* by David Lack (Methuen); *The Effects of the Recent Climatic Changes on the Bird Life of Iceland* by F. Gudmundsson (International Ornithological Congress); *English Social History* by G. M. Trevelyan (Longmans); *Fair Isle and Its Birds* by Kenneth Williamson (Oliver and Boyd); *The Field Guide to the Birds of Britain and Europe* by Roger Peterson, Guy Mountfort and P. A. D. Hollom (Collins); *Finding Nests* by Bruce Campbell (Collins); *Folklore and Folk Stories of Wales* by Marie Trevelyan (Elliot Stock); *The Folklore of Birds* by Edward A. Armstrong

(Collins); *Fossil Birds* by W. E. Swinton (British Museum); *Fugler-Sangen* by Poul Bondesen (Rhodos, Copenhagen); *The Fulmar* by James Fisher (Collins); *Functional Anatomy of Birds* by Alastair N. Worden (Cage Birds); *Fundamentals of Ornithology* by Josselyn van Tyne and Andrew J. Berger (Chapman and Hall); *The Gods had Wings* by W. J. Brown (Constable); *The Greenshank* by Desmond Nethersole-Thompson (Collins); *The Handbook of British Birds* edited by H. F. Witherby (5 volumes, Witherby); *The Handbook of North American Birds* by Ralph S. Palmer and others (American Ornithologists' Union); *Handbook of Waterfowl Behaviour* by P. A. Johnsgard (Constable); *Haunts of British Birds* by Niall Rankin (Collins); *The Hawfinch* by Guy Mountfort (Collins); *The Heron* by F. A. Lowe (Collins); *The Herring Gull's World* by Niko Tinbergen (Collins); *A History of British Birds* by the Rev. F. O. Morris (Bell); *The House Sparrow* by J. D. Summers-Smith (Collins); *How to Study Birds* by Stuart Smith (Collins); *Instructions to Young Ornithologists*: (1) *Bird Biology* by J. D. Macdonald, (2) *Bird Behaviour* by Derek Goodwin, (3) *Bird Migration* by Robert Spencer, (4) *Sea Birds* by Mary E. Gillham, (5) *Birds' Nests and Eggs* by C. J. O. Harrison, (6) *Domestic Birds* by Derek Goodwin, (7) *Ducks, Geese and Swans* by John Welman (Museum Press); *The Kingfisher* by Rosemary Eastman (Collins); *The Language and Lore of Schoolchildren* by Iona and Peter Opie (Oxford); *The Lapwing* by E. A. R. Ennion (Methuen); *The Lapwing in Britain* by K. G. Spencer (Brown); *The Life of Birds* by Joel Carl Welty (Constable); *The Life of the Robin* by David Lack (Witherby); *The Life of Vertebrates* by J. Z. Young (Oxford); *London's Natural History* by R. S. R. Fitter (Collins); *The Migration of Birds* by Jean Dorst (Heinemann); *A Mosaic of Islands* by Kenneth Williamson and James Morton Boyd (Oliver and Boyd); *Mysterious Senses* by V. B. Droscher (Hodder & Stoughton); *The Myth of the Pent Cuckoo* by J. E. Field (Elliot Stock); *The Native Pinewoods of Scotland* by H. M. Steven and A. Carlisle (Oliver and Boyd); *Natural History in the Highlands and Islands* by F. Fraser Darling (Collins); *The Natural Regulation of Animal Numbers* by David Lack (Oxford); *Nesting Birds, Eggs and Fledglings* by Winwood Reade and Eric Hosking (Blandford Press); *A New Dictionary of Birds* edited by Sir A. Landsborough Thomson (Nelson); *On Aggression* by Konrad Lorenz (Methuen); *The Oxford Book of British Birds* by Bruce Campbell (Oxford); *Phoenix Reborn* by Maurice Burton (Hutchinson); *Pigeons and Doves of the World* by Derek Goodwin (British Museum); *The Popular Handbook of British Birds* by P. A. D. Hollom (Witherby); *Population Studies of Birds* by David Lack (Oxford); *Provincial Names and Folklore of British Birds* by C. Swainson (Folklore Society); *Puffins* by R. M. Lockley (Collins); *Radar Ornithology* by Eric Eastwood (Methuen); *The Reader's Digest Complete Atlas of the British Isles* and *The Reader's Digest Great World Atlas* (The Reader's Digest Association); *The Redstart* by John Buxton (Collins); *Reed Warblers* by P. E. Brown and M. G. Davies (A. & C. Black); *Sea Birds* by James Fisher and R. M. Lockley (Collins); *Sea Birds* by Charles Vaucher (Oliver & Boyd); *The Shell Bird Book* by James Fisher (Ebury Press and Michael Joseph); *A Study of Bird Song* by Edward A. Armstrong (Oxford); *A Study of Blackbirds* by D. W. Snow (Allen & Unwin); *Studies on Great Crested Grebes* by K. E. L. Simmons (Avicultural Society); *Swifts in a Tower* by David Lack (Methuen); *The Succession of Life Through Geological Time* by K. P. Oakley and H. M. M. Wood (British Museum); *The Territorial Imperative* by Robert Ardrey (Atheneum Publications, New York); *Where to Watch Birds* by John Gooders (Deutsch); *Wildlife in Britain* by Richard Fitter (Penguin Books); *Wings of Light* compiled by Garth Christian (Newnes); *The Wood-pigeon* by R. K. Murton (Collins); *The World in the Past* by B. Webster Smith (Warne); *The World of Birds* by James Fisher and Roger Tory Peterson (Macdonald); *The Wren* by Edward A. Armstrong (Collins); *The Yellow Wagtail* by Stuart Smith (Collins).

Journals: *Alauda* (Société d'Etudes Ornithologiques); *Animals; Ardea* (Nederlands Ornithologische Union); *The Auk* (American Ornithologists' Union); *Avicultural Magazine* (Avicultural Society); *Behaviour*; *Bird Banding*; *Bird Study* (British Trust for Ornithology); *Birds* (Royal Society for the Protection of Birds); *British Birds*; *British Journal of Animal Behaviour*; British Trust for Ornithology's *Field Guides*; *Bulletins* of the International Council for Bird Preservation; *Condor* (Cooper Ornithological Club); *Ibis* (British Ornithologists' Union); *Journal für Ornithologie* (Deutsche Ornithologen Gesellschaft); *L'Oiseau* (Société Ornithologique de la France); *Philosophical Transactions of the Royal Society*; *Reports* of the British Association for the Advancement of Science; *The Wilson Bulletin* (Wilson Ornithological Society).